Middle School 3-2
학교시험 완벽대비

KB087724

2학기 전과정

적중100plus

영어 기출문제집

중3

동아 | 윤정미

Best Collection

구성과 특징

교과서의 주요 학습 내용을 중심으로 학습 영역별 특성에 맞춰 단계별로 다양한 학습 기회를 제공하여
단원별 학습능력 평가는 물론 중간 및 기말고사 시험 등에 완벽하게 대비할 수 있도록 내용을 구성

Words & Expressions

Step1   Key Words 단원별 핵심 단어 설명 및 풀이
Key Expression 단원별 핵심 숙어 및 관용어 설명
Word Power 반대 또는 비슷한 뜻 단어 배우기
English Dictionary 영어로 배우는 영어 단어

Step2   실력평가 단원별 수시평가 대비 주관식, 객관식 문제풀이

Step3   서술형 대비 학업성취도 및 수행능력평가 대비 서술형 문제풀이

Conversation

Step1   핵심 의사소통 소통에 필요한 주요 표현 방법 요약
핵심 Check 기본적인 표현 방법 및 활용능력 확인

Step2   대화문 익히기 교과서 대화문 심층 분석 및 확인

Step3   교과서 확인학습 빈칸 채우기를 통한 문장 완성 능력 확인

Step4   기본평가 시험대비 기초 학습 능력 평가

Step5   실력평가 단원별 수시평가 대비 주관식, 객관식 문제풀이

Step6   서술형 대비 학업성취도 및 수행능력평가 대비 서술형 문제풀이

Grammar

Step1   주요 문법 단원별 주요 문법 사항과 예문을 알기 쉽게 설명
핵심 Check 기본 문법사항에 대한 이해 여부 확인

Step2   기본평가 시험대비 기초 학습 능력 평가

Step3   실력평가 단원벌 수시평가 내비 주관식, 객관식 문제풀이

Step4   서술형 대비 학업성취도 및 수행능력평가 대비 서술형 문제풀이

Reading

Step1   구문 분석 단원별로 제시된 문장에 대한 구문별 분석과 내용 설명
확인문제 문장에 대한 기본적인 이해와 인지능력 확인

Step2   확인학습A 빈칸 채우기를 통한 문장 완성 능력 확인

Step3   확인학습B 제시된 우리말을 영어로 완성하여 작문 능력 키우기

Step4   실력평가 단원별 수시평가 대비 주관식, 객관식 문제풀이

Step5   서술형 대비 학업성취도 및 수행능력평가 대비 서술형 문제풀이
교과서 구석구석 교과서에 나오는 기타 문장까지 완벽 학습

Composition

|영역별 핵심문제|

단어 및 어휘, 대화문, 문법, 독해 등 각 영역별 기출문제의 출제 유형을 분석하여 실전에 대비하고 연습할 수 있도록 문제를 배열

|단원별 예상문제|

기출문제를 분석한 후 새로운 시험 출제 경향을 더하여 새롭게 출제될 수 있는 문제를 포함하여 시험에 완벽하게 대비할 수 있도록 준비

|서술형 실전 및 창의사고력 문제|

학교 시험에서 점차 늘어나는 서술형 시험에 집중 대비하고 고득점을 취득하는데 만전을 기하기 위한 학습 코너

|단원별 모의고사|

영역별, 단계별 학습을 모두 마친 후 실전 연습을 위한 모의고사

교과서 파헤치기

- **단어Test1~3** 영어 단어 우리말 쓰기, 우리말을 영어 단어로 쓰기, 영영풀이에 해당하는 단어와 우리말 쓰기
- **대화문Test1~2** 대화문 빈칸 완성 및 전체 대화문 쓰기
- **본문Test1~5** 빈칸 완성, 우리말 쓰기, 문장 배열연습, 영어 작문하기 복습 등 단계별 반복 학습을 통해 교과서 지문에 대한 완벽한 습득
- **구석구석지문Test1~2** 지문 빈칸 완성 및 전문 영어로 쓰기

Contents

Lesson	5	**The Team Behind the Team**	5
Lesson	6	**Stories for All Time**	59
Lesson	7	**Technology in Our Lives**	119
Lesson	8	**The Joseon Dynasty Through Paintings**	173
Special Lesson		**Finding the Good in Your Friends**	227

〈Insight on the textbook〉 교과서 파헤치기   01~107

〈책 속의 책〉 정답 및 해설   01~69

이책의 차례

Lesson 5

The Team Behind the Team

의사소통 기능

- 빈도 묻고 말하기
  A: How often do you exercise?
  B: I exercise once a week.

- 제안이나 권유하기
  I suggest you exercise more often.

언어 형식

- 현재분사
  Pacers usually have flags or balloons **showing** their finish time.

- as ~ as
  They are **as** important **as** the players.

Words & Expressions

Key Words

- **achieve** [ətʃíːv] 동 달성하다, 성취하다
- **activity** [æktívəti] 명 활동
- **allow** [əláu] 동 허용하다
- **already** [ɔːlrédi] 부 이미
- **assistant** [əsístənt] 명 보조자
- **attention** [əténʃən] 명 주의, 주목
- **breathe** [briːð] 동 숨쉬다
- **carry** [kæri] 동 운반하다
- **check** [tʃek] 동 점검하다
- **cheer** [tʃiər] 동 응원하다
- **cheerleader** [tʃíərliːdər] 명 응원단
- **choose** [tʃuːz] 동 선택하다
- **crew** [kruː] 명 팀, 조
- **direction** [dirékʃən] 명 방향
- **especially** [ispéʃəli] 부 특히
- **expensive** [ikspénsiv] 형 값비싼
- **experienced** [ikspíəriənst] 형 경험 있는
- **flag** [flæg] 명 깃발
- **full** [ful] 형 가득 찬
- **harmony** [háːrməni] 명 조화, 화합
- **hidden** [hídn] 형 숨겨진
- **hire** [haiər] 동 고용하다
- **hurt** [həːrt] 동 다치다
- **invisible** [invízəbl] 형 (눈에) 보이지 않는, 볼 수 없는
- **join** [dʒɔin] 동 가입하다
- **lead** [liːd] 동 이끌다
- **limit** [límit] 명 한계
- **main** [mein] 형 주된
- **manage** [mǽnidʒ] 동 관리하다
- **pacer** [péisər] 명 페이서, 보조를 맞춰 걷는 사람
- **particular** [pərtíkjulər] 형 특정한
- **perfect** [pəːrfikt] 형 완벽한
- **pit** [pit] 명 (자동차 경주의) 피트
- **pole** [poul] 명 막대기
- **promote** [prəmóut] 동 홍보하다
- **recommendation** [rèkəməndéiʃən] 명 추천
- **register** [rédʒistər] 동 등록하다
- **several** [sévərəl] 형 몇몇의
- **Sherpa** [ʃə́ːrpə] 명 셀파
- **shoot** [ʃuːt] 동 쏘다
- **suggest** [səgdʒést] 동 제안하다
- **suit** [suːt] 명 정장, 옷 한 벌
- **support** [səpɔ́ːrt] 동 돕다, 지원하다
- **tapper** [tǽpər] 명 두드리는 사람
- **target** [táːrgit] 명 목표
- **therefore** [ðɛ́ərfɔ̀ːr] 부 그러므로
- **tribe** [traib] 명 부족, 종족
- **trophy** [tróufi] 명 트로피
- **wear** [wɛər] 동 입다, 신다, 쓰다
- **windy** [wíndi] 형 바람이 심한

Key Expressions

- **be good at** ~을 잘하다
- **be good for** ~에 좋다
- **be over** 끝나다
- **depending on** ~에 따라
- **do stretching** 스트레칭을 하다
- **get attention** 주목을 받다
- **give a speech** 연설하다
- **guide runner** 가이드 러너(시각 장애인의 눈 역할을 해주는 선수)
- **have difficulty -ing** ~에 어려움을 겪다
- **How about ~?** ~은 어때?
- **in many ways** 여러 가지 면에서
- **in short** 간단히 말해서
- **keep track of** ~을 파악하다
- **look for** ~을 찾다
- **most of all** 무엇보다도
- **not ~ at all** 결코 ~ 아닌
- **on one's own** 혼자서
- **once a week** 일주일에 한 번
- **play an important role** 중요한 역할을 하다
- **put up** (텐트 등을) 치다, 세우다
- **sign up for** 등록하다, 신청하다
- **stay on the track** 트랙에 머무르다
- **take bowling lessons** 볼링 수업을 받다
- **take care of** ~을 돌보다
- **wear out** (낡아서) 떨어지다, 헤지다
- **would like to** ~하고 싶다

Word Power

※ 서로 비슷한 뜻을 가진 어휘

- ☐ **achieve** 달성하다 : **accomplish** 성취하다
- ☐ **cheer** 응원하다 : **encourage** 용기를 불어 넣다
- ☐ **hire** 고용하다 : **employ** 고용하다
- ☐ **register** 등록하다 : **enroll** 등록하다

- ☐ **allow** 허용하다 : **permit** 허가하다
- ☐ **main** 주된 : **major** 주된
- ☐ **suggest** 제안하다 : **propose** 제안하다
- ☐ **tribe** 부족 : **clan** 부족

※ 서로 반대의 뜻을 가진 어휘

- ☐ **allow** 허용하다 ↔ **forbid** 금지하다
- ☐ **experienced** 경험 있는 ↔ **inexperienced** 경험 없는
- ☐ **hire** 고용하다 ↔ **fire** 해고하다

- ☐ **expensive** 값비싼 ↔ **cheap** 값싼
- ☐ **full** 가득 찬 ↔ **empty** 비어 있는
- ☐ **visible** 눈에 보이는 ↔ **invisible** 보이지 않는

※ 동사 – 명사

- ☐ **achieve** 달성하다 – **achievement** 성취
- ☐ **allow** 허용하다 – **allowance** 허용, 용돈
- ☐ **promote** 홍보하다 – **promotion** 홍보

- ☐ **act** 행동하다 – **activity** 활동, **action** 활동, 행동
- ☐ **breathe** 숨쉬다 – **breath** 호흡
- ☐ **suggest** 제안하다 – **suggestion** 제안

※ in+형용사, im+형용사

- ☐ **impatient** 초조해 하는
- ☐ **impolite** 무례한
- ☐ **incomplete** 불완전한
- ☐ **independent** 독립적인
- ☐ **inexperienced** 경험이 없는

- ☐ **imperfect** 불완전한
- ☐ **impossible** 불가능한
- ☐ **indirect** 간접적인
- ☐ **ineffective** 효과가 없는
- ☐ **informal** 격식을 차리지 않는

English Dictionary

- ☐ **achieve** 달성하다, 성취하다
  → to succeed in doing or getting something you want
  원하는 것을 하거나 얻는 것에 성공하다

- ☐ **breathe** 숨쉬다
  → to take air into your body and let it out again
  공기를 체내로 빨아들이고 다시 내보내다

- ☐ **crew** 팀, 조
  → a group of people with a particular skill who work together 함께 일하는 특정한 기술을 가진 한 무리의 사람들

- ☐ **hire** 고용하다
  → to pay someone to work for you
  당신을 위해 일을 하도록 누군가에게 돈을 지불하다

- ☐ **invisible** (눈에) 보이지 않는, 볼 수 없는
  → not able to be seen 볼 수 없는

- ☐ **pit** (자동차 경주의) 피트
  → the area beside a race track where cars are repaired or get more gas during a race 경주를 하는 동안 차들이 수리되거나 기름을 넣는 경주 트랙 옆에 있는 구역

- ☐ **register** 등록하다
  → to put someone's or something's name on an official list 공식적인 명단에 이름을 올리다

- ☐ **support** 돕다, 지원하다
  → to say that you agree with a person, group, or idea
  어떤 사람, 그룹 또는 생각에 동의한다고 말하다

- ☐ **tribe** 부족, 종족
  → a group of people who have their own language and ways of living
  자신들의 언어와 생활 방식을 가지고 있는 사람들의 집단

- ☐ **trophy** 트로피
  → a metal cup or other objects that someone gets for winning a game or race
  경기 또는 경주에서 이겨서 얻는 금속 컵 또는 다른 물체들

- ☐ **wear out** (낡아서) 떨어지다, 헤지다
  → to use something a lot so that it no longer works, or can no longer be used 어떤 것을 많이 사용하여 더 이상 작동하지 않거나 더 이상 사용될 수 없다

01 다음 짝지어진 단어의 관계가 같도록 빈칸에 알맞은 말은?

> impolite – rude : achieve – _____

① accomplish
② register
③ join
④ suggest
⑤ accompany

02 주어진 영어 설명에 맞게 문장의 빈칸에 알맞은 말을 쓰시오.

> Many stars are _____ to the eye.

> <영어 설명> not able to be seen

➡ _____

03 밑줄 친 부분의 의미로 알맞지 <u>않은</u> 것은?

① It <u>is</u> probably <u>good for</u> you to get some criticism now and then. (~에 좋다)
② It's hard to <u>keep track of</u> the children's comings and goings. (~을 쫓다)
③ <u>In short</u>, there is a lot of disagreement about the best way to punish children. (간단히 말해서)
④ When you do something unusual, you <u>get attention</u> and artists want attention. (주목을 받다)
⑤ Does the rent vary <u>depending on</u> the model of car? (~에 따라)

04 다음 빈칸에 들어갈 가장 알맞은 말을 고르시오.

> How many students _____ for the English class?

① supported
② wore
③ kept
④ registered
⑤ achieved

05 다음 <보기>의 단어를 사용하여 자연스러운 문장을 만들 수 <u>없는</u> 것은?

> ┤ 보기 ├
> give   tribe   cheer   target

① I can't understand why they wanted him to _____ a speech.
② I always _____ for my home team.
③ There is a _____ to my patience.
④ Who is the _____ market?
⑤ They began as a _____ in the 12th century.

06 다음 빈칸에 알맞은 말이 바르게 짝지어진 것을 고르시오.

> • Many students _____ the plans to change school uniforms.
> • The band has gone on tour to _____ their new album.

① depend – promote
② depend – need
③ register – take
④ support – need
⑤ support – promote

01 다음 영영풀이에 알맞은 어휘를 〈보기〉에서 찾아 쓰시오.

┌─── 보기 ───┐
  hire register achieve support
└────────────┘

(1) to say that you agree with a person, group, or idea
(2) to succeed in doing or getting something you want
(3) to pay someone to work for you
(4) to put someone's or something's name on an official list

➡ (1) _____ (2) _____ (3) _____
   (4) _____

02 다음 짝지어진 두 단어의 관계가 같도록 빈칸에 알맞은 말을 쓰시오.

(1) possible : impossible
   = dependent : _____
(2) achieve : achievement
   = breathe : _____

03 다음 우리말에 맞도록 빈칸에 알맞은 말을 쓰시오. (철자가 주어진 경우 그 철자로 시작할 것.)

(1) 물건이란 오래 쓰면 닳기 마련이다.
   → It's normal for things to _____ out with long use.
(2) 미나는 그 영화를 몇 번 봤다.
   → Mina has seen the movie s_____ times.

(3) 나는 목표를 이루기 위해 최선을 다해야 한다.
   → I should try my best to a_____ my goal.
(4) 그는 삼촌의 추천으로 그 소년을 고용했다.
   → He hired the boy on the r_____ of his uncle.

04 우리말에 맞게 한 단어를 추가하여 주어진 단어를 알맞게 배열하시오.

(1) 나는 우리의 위치를 파악하면서 지도를 따라갔다. (I, position, map, our, followed, keeping, the, of)
   ➡ _____
      _____

(2) 내 성격은 사람에 따라 바뀐다. (personality, person, changes, depending, the, my)
   ➡ _____

(3) 그 집은 몇 그루의 나무 뒤로 시야에서 가려져 있었다. (the house, trees, sight, some, hidden, behind, from)
   ➡ _____
      _____

(4) 그는 그 문제를 혼자서 해결했다. (he, his, the problem, fix, managed, on, to)
   ➡ _____
      _____

Conversation

1 빈도 묻고 말하기

A How often do you exercise? 너는 얼마나 자주 운동을 하니?
B I exercise once a week. 나는 일주일에 한 번 운동을 해.

- 어떤 일이나 현상이 반복될 때, 상대방에게 어떤 활동을 하는 횟수, 즉 빈도를 물어 볼 때는 often(자주)을 사용하여 'How often do you ~?(얼마나 자주 ~하니?)'라고 표현한다. 숫자가 포함된 구체적인 횟수를 물어볼 때는 'How many times do you ~?(몇 번 ~하니?)'라고 좀 더 구체적으로 물어볼 수 있다.

- 대략적인 빈도를 말할 때는 always, usually, often, sometimes, never 등과 같은 빈도부사를 사용하고, 구체적인 빈도를 나타낼 때는 '횟수+a day/week/month/year'로 특정 기간 동안의 횟수를 표현한다. 횟수를 나타내는 표현은 once(한 번), twice(두 번), 그리고 세 번 이상부터는 'three times'처럼 '기수+times'로 나타낸다. 자주하는 것을 강조해서 'every day/week/month/year(매 ~마다)'라고 하기도 한다. 빈도부사는 주로 조동사나 be동사 뒤에, 그리고 일반동사 앞에 쓰고, 구체적인 횟수를 나타내는 말은 대부분 문장의 끝 부분에 쓴다.

빈도 묻기

- How often do you ~?   얼마나 자주 ~하니?
- How many times do you ~?   몇 번 ~하니?

빈도 말하기

- always(항상), usually(보통), often(자주), sometimes(가끔), never(결코 ~ 아닌)
- (주어+동사+) ~ times a day/week/month/year. 하루/일주일/한 달/일 년에 ~번 …한다.

핵심 Check

1. 다음 대화의 빈칸 (A)에 들어가기에 적절한 것은?

B: _____ (A) _____ do you play basketball?
G: I play once a week, but I want to play more often.
B: I suggest you join my basketball club. We play three times a week.
G: That sounds good! It'll be fun to play with you.

① How much   ② How often
③ How many   ④ What time
⑤ How often times

② 제안이나 권유하기

> • I suggest you exercise more often. 나는 네가 더 자주 운동해야 한다고 제안해.

■ 상대방에게 어떤 일이나 행동을 제안하거나 권유할 때는 동사 'suggest(제안하다)'를 사용하여 'I suggest (that)+주어+(should+)동사원형 ~'의 구문으로 나타낸다. 이때 that과 should는 생략하여 말할 수 있다.

■ 'suggest'를 이용한 표현은 'suggest + that ~ (should) 절' 이외에도 'suggest+-ing', 'suggest+wh-절', 'suggest+wh- to do' 등으로 나타내기도 한다. 한편 'suggest'는 '제안하다'는 뜻 이외에도 '암시하다, 시사하다, 말하다' 등의 의미를 가지는데 제안하는 의미 이외의 경우에는 that절에 should를 사용하지 않는다.

■ 제안, 권유를 나타내는 유사한 표현으로 'Let's ~.(~하자)', 'had better ~(~하는 편이 낫다)', 'Why don't you/we ~?(~하는 것이 어때?)', 'May I suggest that ~?(~하는 것이 어떠세요?)' 등이 있다.

■ 'How about'과 'What about'은 'How/What about 명사/~ing?(~는 어때?)'의 형태로 쓰며 상대에게 제안, 권유하는 의미와 함께 상대의 의견을 물어보는 의미로도 사용한다.

■ 상대방의 제안이나 조언에 답할 때 'That's a good/great idea!', 'I'll give it a try.' 또는 'OK, I'll ~'이라고 답할 수 있다.

제안이나 권유

• I suggest (that) 주어+(should)+동사원형 ~	~하라고 제안한다.
• suggest+-ing/wh-절/wh- to do	~을 제안하다
• Let's ~	(같이) ~하자.
• had better ~	~하는 편이 낫다
• Why don't you/we ~?	~하는 것이 어때?
• May I suggest that ~?	~하는 것이 어떠세요?
• How[What] about ~ing?	~하는 것이 어떠니?

핵심 Check

2. 다음 대화의 밑줄 친 우리말을 주어진 어휘를 이용하여 영작하시오.

A: Minsu, how often do you exercise?

B: I exercise once a week.

A: <u>나는 네가 더 자주 운동하기를 제안해.</u> (suggest, exercise, often)

B: OK. I'll try.

➡ _____

Listen and Talk A 1

B: ❶How often do you play basketball?

G: I play ❷once a week, but I want to play more often.

B: ❸I suggest you join my basketball club. We play three times a week.

G: That sounds good! ❹It'll be fun to play with you.

B: 얼마나 자주 농구를 하니?
G: 일주일에 한 번 해. 그런데 더 자주 하고 싶어.
B: 네가 우리 농구 동아리에 들어오기를 제안해. 우리는 일주일에 세 번 농구를 해.
G: 좋은 생각이야! 같이 하면 재미있을 거야.

❶ '얼마나 자주 ~하니?'라는 의미로 상대방에게 어떤 활동을 하는 횟수나 빈도를 물어 볼 때 쓰는 표현이다.
❷ 'once a week'은 '일주일에 한 번'이라는 의미로 횟수를 나타내는 표현이다.
❸ suggest 다음에 that이 생략되어 있으며 join 앞에는 should가 생략되어 있다.
❹ It은 가주어이고 'to play with you'가 진주어이다.

Check(√) True or False

(1) The boy wants to know how often the girl plays basketball.　　T ☐　F ☐

(2) The girl won't join the boy's club.　　T ☐　F ☐

Listen and Talk C

W: Hello. Welcome to Sports World. May I help you?

B: Yes, I came to register for a swimming class.

W: Is this your first time ❶taking swimming lessons?

B: Yes, it is. I don't know ❷how to swim at all.

W: I see. How often do you want to take classes?

B: I want to take classes twice a week. I'd like to take classes on weekdays and not on weekends.

W: Then, ❸I suggest that you take the Beginner 2 class. This class meets on Tuesdays and Thursdays.

B: ❹That sounds good. I'd like to sign up for that class. How big is the class?

W: The class has a limit of 10 people.

B: ❺That's perfect.

W: 안녕하세요. Sports World에 오신 것을 환영합니다. 무엇을 도와드릴까요?
B: 네, 수영 수업을 등록하려고 왔어요.
W: 수영 수업을 받는 것이 이번이 처음인가요?
B: 네. 저는 수영하는 법을 전혀 알지 못해요.
W: 알겠어요. 얼마나 자주 수업을 받고 싶으신가요?
B: 일주일에 두 번 수업을 듣길 원해요. 주말이 아니라 주중에 수업을 듣고 싶어요.
W: 그럼, 초급 2반을 들을 것을 권합니다. 이 수업은 화요일과 목요일에 있어요.
B: 좋아요. 그 수업에 등록할게요. 그 수업은 몇 명이 듣나요?
W: 그 수업은 제한 인원이 열 명입니다.
B: 좋아요.

❶ taking은 앞에 나온 time을 수식하는 현재분사이다.
❷ know의 목적어로 '의문사+to부정사'가 쓰이고 있다. 'not ~ at all'은 '전혀 ~ 아니다'라는 뜻이다.
❸ 상대방에게 어떤 일이나 행동을 제안하거나 권유할 때 쓰는 표현이다.
❹ That은 'This class meets on Tuesdays and Thursdays.'를 가리킨다.
❺ That은 'The class has a limit of 10 people.'을 가리킨다.

Check(√) True or False

(3) The boy wants to take swimming lessons.　　T ☐　F ☐

(4) The Beginner 2 class has a limit of 10 people.　　T ☐　F ☐

Listen and Talk A 2

B: I don't swim often. How about you, Kate? How often do you swim?

G: I swim four times a week.

B: ❶ That often? Anyway, ❷it'll be fun swimming together today.

G: Yes, but before we swim, I suggest we do stretching exercises.

B: ❸That's a good idea.

❶ That은 지시부사로 쓰여 '그렇게, 그 정도로'의 의미이다.
❷ it은 가주어이며 진주어는 'swimming together today'이다.
❸ 상대방의 제안이나 조언에 답하는 표현이다.

Listen and Talk A 3

B: Suji, how often do you take bowling lessons?

G: Twice a week. I'm just a beginner. I heard you're very good.

B: Well, I love bowling. Hmm. Your bowling ball ❶looks heavy for you. I suggest you use a lighter ball.

G: OK. I'll look for a lighter ❷one, then.

❶ 'look+형용사'로 '~하게 보이다'라는 의미이다.
❷ one은 'bowling ball'을 대신하는 부정대명사이다.

Listen and Talk A 4

B: Mina, how often do you come here ❶to run?

G: Every day.

B: Can I run with you today?

G: Sure, but I suggest you wear running shoes. Your shoes ❷aren't good for running.

❶ to부정사의 목적을 나타내는 부사적 용법이다.
❷ be good for: ~에 좋다

Listen and Talk B

A: Minsu, how often do you exercise?

B: I exercise once ❶a week.

A: I suggest you exercise more often.

B: ❷OK. I'll try.

❶ a는 'per(~마다)'의 의미이다.
❷ 상대방의 제안이나 조언에 답하는 표현이다.

Talk and Play

A: Jiho, ❶how often do you exercise?

B: I exercise ❷three times a week.

A: That's good.

❶ 'how many times do you exercise a week?'이라고 좀 더 구체적으로 물어 볼 수도 있다.
❷ 3번 이상의 경우 '기수+times'로 나타낸다. 요즘에는 twice 대신에 'two times'라고 하기도 한다.

Review 1

B: Mina, how often do you swim?

G: I swim every day.

B: Can I ❶go swimming with you this afternoon?

G: Sure, but ❷I suggest you bring a swimming cap. Without a swimming cap, you ❸aren't allowed in the pool.

❶ 'go -ing'는 '~하러 가다'라는 의미이며 주로 오락을 나타낼 때 쓰인다. (go studying: X)
❷ 'you'd better bring a swimming cap.'으로 바꿔 쓸 수 있다.
❸ '허락되는' 것이므로 수동태로 써야 한다.

Review 2

B: Somi, ❶is your piano practice over?

G: Yes, it is.

B: How often do you practice?

G: I practice twice a week.

❶ 'be over'는 '끝나다'라는 의미이다.

Review 3

W: Hello. May I help you?

B: Yes, I came to register for a soccer class.

W: I see. How often do you want to ❶take classes?

B: I want to take classes twice a week. I'd like to take classes ❷on weekends.

W: Then, I suggest that you take the Beginner 1 class. This class meets on Saturdays and Sundays.

B: ❸That sounds good.

❶ take classes: 수업을 듣다
❷ on weekends: 주말에
❸ That은 'This class meets on Saturdays and Sundays.'를 가리킨다.

● 다음 우리말과 일치하도록 빈칸에 알맞은 말을 쓰시오.

Listen and Talk A 1

B: How _____ do you play basketball?

G: I play _____ a week, but I want to play _____ often.

B: I _____ you join my basketball club. We play _____ _____ a week.

G: That sounds _____! It'll be fun _____ _____ with you.

Listen and Talk A 2

B: I don't swim often. How _____ you, Kate? _____ _____ do you swim?

G: I swim _____ _____ a week.

B: _____ often? Anyway, _____ 'll be fun _____ together today.

G: Yes, but before we swim, I _____ we _____ _____ exercises.

B: That's a good idea.

Listen and Talk A 3

B: Suji, _____ _____ do you _____ bowling lessons?

G: _____ a week. I'm just a _____. I heard you're very good.

B: Well, I love bowling. Hmm. Your bowling ball looks _____ for you. I _____ you _____ a lighter ball.

G: OK. I'll look _____ a lighter _____, then.

Listen and Talk A 4

B: Mina, _____ _____ do you come here _____ _____?

G: Every day.

B: Can I run with you today?

G: Sure, but I _____ you _____ running shoes. Your shoes aren't _____ _____ running.

Listen and Talk B

A: Minsu, _____ _____ do you exercise?

B: I exercise once _____ week.

A: I _____ you exercise more often.

B: OK. I'll _____.

B: 얼마나 자주 농구를 하니?
G: 일주일에 한 번 해. 그런데 더 자주 하고 싶어.
B: 네가 우리 농구 동아리에 들어오기를 제안해. 우리는 일주일에 세 번 농구를 해.
G: 좋은 생각이야! 같이 하면 재미있을 거야.

B: 난 수영을 자주 하지 않아. 넌 어떠니, Kate? 얼마나 자주 수영을 하러 가니?
G: 일주일에 네 번 수영을 해.
B: 그렇게 자주? 어쨌든 오늘 같이 수영을 하면 재미있을 거야.
G: 응, 그런데 우리가 수영하기 전에 스트레칭을 하는 것을 제안해.
B: 좋은 생각이다.

B: 수지야, 너는 얼마나 자주 볼링 수업을 받니?
G: 일주일에 두 번 받아. 나는 초보야. 난 네가 볼링을 잘한다고 들었어.
B: 음, 난 볼링을 좋아해. 흠. 네 볼링공이 무거워 보인다. 더 가벼운 공을 쓰는 것을 제안해.
G: 알겠어. 그럼 더 가벼운 공을 찾아봐야겠다.

B: 미나야, 넌 달리기를 하러 이곳에 얼마나 자주 오니?
G: 매일 와.
B: 오늘 너와 함께 달리기를 해도 될까?
G: 물론이야, 하지만 네가 운동화를 신는 것을 제안해. 네 신발은 달리기에 적합하지 않아.

A: 민수야, 너는 얼마나 자주 운동을 하니?
B: 나는 일주일에 한 번 운동을 해.
A: 더 자주 운동하기를 제안해.
B: 알겠어. 시도해 볼게.

Listen and Talk C

W: Hello. Welcome to Sports World. May I help you?
B: Yes, I came _____ _____ _____ a swimming class.
W: Is this your first time _____ swimming lessons?
B: Yes, it is. I don't know _____ _____ _____ _____
_____.
W: I see. _____ do you want to _____ classes?
B: I want to _____ classes _____ _____ _____. I'd like to
_____ classes _____ weekdays and not _____ weekends.
W: Then, I suggest _____ you _____ the Beginner 2 class. This
class meets _____ Tuesdays and Thursdays.
B: That _____ _____. I'd like to _____ _____ _____ that
class. How big is the class?
W: The class has _____ _____ _____ 10 people.
B: That's perfect.

Talk and Play

A: Jiho, _____ _____ do you exercise?
B: I exercise _____ _____ _____ _____.
A: That's good.

Review 1

B: Mina, _____ _____ do you swim?
G: I swim every day.
B: Can I _____ _____ with you this afternoon?
G: Sure, but I _____ you _____ a swimming cap. _____ a
swimming cap, you _____ _____ in the pool.

Review 2

B: Somi, is your piano practice _____?
G: Yes, it is.
B: _____ _____ do you practice?
G: I practice _____ _____ _____.

Review 3

W: Hello. May I help you?
B: Yes, I came to _____ _____ a soccer class.
W: I see. _____ _____ do you want to _____ classes?
B: I want to _____ classes _____ _____ _____. I'd like to
_____ classes _____ weekends.
W: Then, I _____ that you _____ the Beginner 1 class. This class
meets _____ Saturdays and Sundays.
B: That sounds _____.

해석

W: 안녕하세요. Sports World에 오신 것을 환영합니다. 무엇을 도와드릴 까요?
B: 네, 수영 수업을 등록하려고 왔어요.
W: 수영 수업을 받는 것이 이번이 처음 인가요?
B: 네. 저는 수영하는 법을 전혀 알지 못해요.
W: 알겠어요. 얼마나 자주 수업을 받고 싶으신가요?
B: 일주일에 두 번 수업을 듣길 원해요. 주말이 아니라 주중에 수업을 듣고 싶어요.
W: 그럼, 초급 2반을 들을 것을 권합니 다. 이 수업은 화요일과 목요일에 있 어요.
B: 좋아요. 그 수업으로 등록할게요. 그 수업은 몇 명이 듣나요?
W: 그 수업은 제한 인원이 열 명입니다.
B: 좋아요.

A: 지호야, 너는 얼마나 자주 운동을 하 니?
B: 나는 일주일에 세 번 운동을 해.
A: 좋다.

B: 미나야, 너는 얼마나 자주 수영을 하 니?
G: 나는 매일 수영을 해.
B: 오늘 오후에 너와 수영하러 가도 될 까?
G: 물론이지, 하지만 수영 모자를 챙기 는 것을 제안해. 수영 모자 없이 수 영장에 들어가는 것은 허락되지 않 아.

B: 소미야, 피아노 연습은 끝났니?
G: 응, 그래.
B: 얼마나 자주 연습을 하니?
G: 나는 일주일에 두 번 연습을 해.

W: 안녕하세요. 무엇을 도와드릴까요?
B: 네, 축구 수업을 등록하러 왔어요.
W: 알겠습니다. 얼마나 자주 수업을 수 강하기를 원하나요?
B: 일주일에 두 번 수강하고 싶어요. 주 말에 수업을 수강하는 게 좋아요.
W: 그럼, 초급 1반을 수강하기를 제안 드려요. 이 수업은 토요일과 일요일 에 있어요.
B: 좋아요.

01 다음 빈칸 (A)에 알맞은 문장은?

> B: _____ (A) _____
>
> G: I play once a week, but I want to play more often.

① I would like to play basketball.

② Would you like to play basketball?

③ How often do you play basketball?

④ Do you play basketball?

⑤ Can you play basketball?

02 주어진 어휘를 이용하여 밑줄 친 우리말을 영작하시오.

> B: I don't swim often. How about you, Kate? How often do you swim?
>
> G: I swim four times a week.
>
> B: That often? Anyway, it'll be fun swimming together today.
>
> G: Yes, but before we swim, 스트레칭을 하는 것을 제안해. (suggest, stretching exercises) (6 words)
>
> B: That's a good idea.

➡ _____

[03~04] 다음 대화를 읽고 물음에 답하시오.

> B: Suji, how often do you take bowling lessons?
>
> G: (A)일주일에 두 번. I'm just a beginner. I heard you're very good.
>
> B: Well, I love bowling. Hmm. Your bowling ball looks heavy for you. I __(a)__ you use a lighter ball.
>
> G: OK. I'll look for a lighter one, then.

03 다음 영영풀이를 참고하여 대화의 빈칸 (a)에 알맞은 말은?

> to make a proposal

① register ② support ③ suggest ④ guess ⑤ pursue

04 밑줄 친 (A)의 우리말을 3 단어로 쓰시오.

➡ _____

01 다음 중 짝지어진 대화가 어색한 것은?

① A: How often do you exercise?
  B: I exercised a lot.
② A: How did you win the race?
  B: I kept track of the time very well.
③ A: I have breakfast every day.
  B: That's good.
④ A: Somi, is your piano practice over?
  B: Yes, it is.
⑤ A: I think I have a cold.
  B: I suggest you go see a doctor.

[02~05] 다음 대화를 읽고 물음에 답하시오.

W: Hello. Welcome to Sports World. May I help you?
B: Yes, I came to register for a swimming class.
W: Is this your first time taking swimming lessons?
B: Yes, it is. (a)저는 수영하는 법을 전혀 알지 못해요.
W: I see. How often do you want to take classes?
B: I want to take classes twice a week. I'd like to take classes __(A)__ weekdays and not __(A)__ weekends.
W: Then, _____(B)_____ the Beginner 2 class. This class meets on Tuesdays and Thursdays.
B: That sounds good. I'd like to sign up for that class. How big is the class?
W: The class has a limit of 10 people.
B: That's perfect.

02 빈칸 (A)에 공통으로 들어갈 말을 고르시오.

① about ② on ③ for
④ at ⑤ in

03 위 대화의 빈칸 (B)에 들어갈 알맞은 말을 주어진 어휘를 배열하여 쓰시오.

>
> I, you, that, take, suggest

➡ _____

04 밑줄 친 (a)의 우리말에 맞게 주어진 어휘를 이용하여 영작하시오. (how, all)

➡ _____

05 위 대화의 내용과 일치하지 않는 것은?

① The boy visited Sports World.
② The boy wants to register for a swimming class.
③ The boy wants to take classes twice a week.
④ The Beginner 2 class meets on Tuesdays and Thursdays.
⑤ The boy already signed up for the Beginner 2 class.

06 다음 대화가 자연스럽게 연결되도록 (A)~(D)를 순서대로 가장 적절하게 배열한 것은?

(A) I suggest you play computer games less often.
(B) Seonmi, how often do you play computer games?
(C) I play computer games every day.
(D) OK. I'll try.

① (B) – (A) – (C) – (D)
② (B) – (C) – (A) – (D)
③ (B) – (C) – (D) – (A)
④ (C) – (B) – (D) – (A)
⑤ (C) – (D) – (B) – (A)

[07~08] 다음 대화를 읽고 물음에 답하시오.

> **A:** Hojun, how (a)[often / much] do you read a book?
>
> **B:** I read a book twice (b)[a / the] week.
>
> **A:** I suggest you (c)[read / will read] more books.
>
> **B:** _____ (A) _____

07 위 대화의 빈칸 (A)에 들어갈 말로 알맞은 것을 <u>모두</u> 고르시오.

① Will you try?

② OK. I'll try.

③ Excuse me, but will you read more?

④ I'll give it a try.

⑤ Enjoy your reading.

08 위 대화의 괄호 (a)~(c)에서 알맞은 것을 골라 바르게 짝지은 것은?

	(a)	(b)	(c)
①	often	a	read
②	often	the	read
③	often	a	will read
④	much	the	will read
⑤	much	a	will read

[09~10] 다음 대화를 읽고 물음에 답하시오.

> **B:** Somi, is your piano practice ___(A)___ ?
>
> **G:** Yes, it is.
>
> **B:** How often do you practice?
>
> **G:** _____ (B) _____

09 '피아노 연습이 끝났는지' 묻는 질문이 되도록 위 대화의 빈칸 (A)에 알맞은 말을 고르시오.

① up ② down ③ for

④ over ⑤ on

10 위 대화의 빈칸 (B)에 들어갈 말로 가장 적절한 것은?

① I play a lot.

② I practice very much.

③ I practice twice a week.

④ I practice playing the piano.

⑤ I practice playing computer games.

11 다음 대화의 밑줄 친 부분의 의도로 가장 적절한 것은?

> **A:** Hajun, <u>how often do you eat late at night?</u>
>
> **B:** I eat late at night five times a week.
>
> **A:** I suggest that you eat late at night less.

① 궁금증 표현하기 ② 제안하기

③ 설명 요청하기 ④ 반복 요청하기

⑤ 빈도 묻기

[12~13] 다음 대화를 읽고 물음에 답하시오.

> **W:** Hello. (①) May I help you?
>
> **B:** Yes, I came to register for a soccer class.
>
> **W:** I see. (②) How often do you want to take classes?
>
> **B:** (③) I want to take classes twice a week. (④) I'd like to take classes on weekends.
>
> **W:** (⑤) This class meets on Saturdays and Sundays.
>
> **B:** That sounds good.

12 위 대화의 (①)~(⑤) 중 주어진 문장이 들어갈 곳은?

> Then, I suggest that you take the Beginner 1 class.

① ② ③ ④ ⑤

13 How often will the boy take the soccer class?

➡ _____

[01~03] 다음 대화를 읽고 물음에 답하시오.

W: Hello. Welcome to Sports World. May I help you?

B: Yes, I came to register for a swimming class.

W: Is this your first time taking swimming lessons?

B: Yes, it is. I don't know how to swim at all.

W: I see. How often do you want to take classes?

B: I want to take classes twice a week. (a)주말이 아니라 주중에 수업을 듣고 싶어요.

(A) The class has a limit of 10 people.

(B) That's perfect.

(C) That sounds good. I'd like to sign up for that class. How big is the class?

(D) Then, I suggest that you take the Beginner 2 class. This class meets on Tuesdays and Thursdays.

01 위 대화의 (A)~(D)를 알맞은 순서로 배열하시오.

➡ _____

02 괄호 안에 주어진 어휘를 이용하여 밑줄 친 (a)를 11 단어로 쓰시오.

➡ _____
_____ (like, take classes, weekdays, not)

03 How many people can the Beginner 2 class have? Use the words "up to."

➡ _____

[04~05] 다음 글을 읽고 물음에 답하시오.

Do you like riding a bike? Then, I suggest you join our club, Fun Wheels. We ride bikes once a week, on Saturdays. We ride along the river or in parks. (a)함께 자전거를 타는 것은 즐거워. (fun, bikes, to)

04 What does the writer suggest?

➡ _____

05 괄호 안에 주어진 어휘를 이용하여 밑줄 친 우리말 (a)에 맞게 6 단어로 쓰시오.

➡ _____

[06~07] 다음 대화를 읽고 물음에 답하시오.

B: Mina, how often do you swim?

G: I swim every day.

B: Can I go swimming with you this afternoon?

G: ___(A)___, but (a)수영 모자를 챙기는 것을 제안해. (suggest, bring, a swimming cap) Without a swimming cap, you aren't allowed in the pool.

06 위 대화의 빈칸 (A)에 알맞은 말을 (1) 1 단어로, (2) 2 단어로 쓰시오.

➡ (1) _____ (2) _____

07 괄호 안에 주어진 어휘를 이용하여 밑줄 친 우리말 (a)에 맞게 7 단어로 쓰시오.

➡ _____

Grammar

① 분사

> • Pacers usually have flags or balloons **showing** their finish time.
> 페이서들은 보통 자신들의 완주 시간을 나타내는 깃발이나 풍선을 가지고 있다.
>
> • The girl **waiting** at the bus stop is my sister.
> 버스 정류장에서 기다리고 있는 소녀는 내 여동생이다.

■ 현재분사는 '동사원형+-ing' 형태로 형용사처럼 명사를 앞 또는 뒤에서 꾸며준다. 일반적으로는 명사 앞에서, 다른 어구와 함께 구(phrase)를 이룰 때는 명사 뒤에서 꾸민다.

 • The **singing** bird is very big. 노래를 하고 있는 새는 매우 크다.

 • The bird **singing in the tree** is very big. 나무에서 노래를 하고 있는 새는 매우 크다.

■ 현재분사(-ing)는 능동/진행, 과거분사(p.p.)는 수동/완료의 의미를 갖는다.

 • Jack is **sleeping** on the floor. Jack은 바닥에서 자고 있다.

 • My hobby is to collect the **fallen** leaves. 내 취미는 낙엽을 모으는 것이다.

■ 명사를 뒤에서 꾸미는 분사구는 '주격 관계대명사+be동사'가 생략된 것으로 볼 수 있다.

 • The men (**who are**) **climbing** the mountain are Africans. 그 산을 등반하는 사람들은 아프리카인들이다.

 • Tom watched the movie (**which was**) **made** by the director.
 Tom은 그 감독에 의해 만들어진 영화를 보았다.

■ 분사는 명사를 꾸며주는 역할 외에도, 주어나 목적어를 보충 설명하는 서술 용법이 있다. 이 경우, 주격 보어 또는 목적격 보어가 된다.

 • The idol star was standing **surrounded** by her fans. 그 아이돌 스타는 그녀의 팬들에게 둘러싸인 채 서 있었다.

 • She kept them **raising their hands**. 그녀는 그들이 계속해서 손을 들고 있도록 했다.

 • Matilda felt her shoulder **pushed** by someone. Matilda는 누군가에 의해 그녀의 어깨가 밀리는 것을 느꼈다.

■ 분사와 동명사의 구분은 수식받는 명사의 능동성이나 용도 여부를 통해 판단한다.

 • Look at a **singing** bird. 노래를 부르는 새를 보아라. (능동-현재분사)

 • This is a **singing** room. 이것은 노래방이다. (용도-동명사)

핵심 Check

1. 다음 괄호 안에서 알맞은 단어를 고르시오.

 (1) The woman (wearing / wore) glasses is my teacher.

 (2) The actor had his arms (breaking / broken) in the accident.

② as 형용사/부사 as

• They are **as important as** the players. 그들은 선수들만큼이나 중요하다.
• Jason can run **as fast as** Mike. Jason은 Mike만큼 빠르게 달릴 수 있다.

■ 'as 형용사/부사 as …' 구문은 '…만큼 어떠한[어떻게]'라는 뜻이다.

• I am **as hungry as** you. 나는 너만큼 배가 고프다.
• Canada is **as large as** the USA. 캐나다는 미국만큼 크기가 크다.

■ 'as ~ as' 사이에는 형용사/부사의 '원급'만 들어갈 수 있다.

• Peter was as ~~happier~~ as his brother. (×) Peter는 그의 형만큼 행복했다. (→ happy)
• Jim walks as ~~fastest~~ as his friends. (×) Jim은 그의 친구들만큼 빨리 걷는다. (→ fast)

■ 'as ~ as'의 부정은 not을 앞에 쓰며, 앞의 as 대신 so를 쓸 수 있다.
'not as[so] 형용사/부사 as …' 구문은 '비교급' 의미가 된다.

• Sujin is **not so[as] tall as** Eric. Sujin은 Eric만큼 키가 크지는 않다. (Eric이 Sujin보다 크다.)
  = Sujin is **less tall than** Eric. = Eric is **taller than** Sujin.
• Turtles are **not as[so] slow as** snails. 거북이들은 달팽이만큼 느리지는 않다.
  = Snails are **slower than** turtles.

■ 원칙적으로 'as 형용사/부사 as …'에서 대명사의 격을 구분해서 써야 한다.

• Susan loves him **as much as** I. Susan은 나만큼 그를 사랑해. (내가 그를 사랑하는 것만큼)
• Susan loves him **as much as** me. Susan은 나만큼 그를 사랑해. (Susan이 나를 사랑하는 것만큼)

  cf. 그러나, 의미의 혼동이 없을 경우 격을 구분하지 않고 사용하기도 한다.
  • Simpson is **as lazy as I**.   (○) (as lazy as I am)
  • Simpson is **as lazy as me**. (○) 관용적으로 사용

■ 'as ~ as' 사이에 들어가는 말이 명사를 수식하면 형용사, 동사를 수식하면 부사를 쓴다.

• Minju drives as [~~good~~ / **well**] as Sein (does). Minju는 Sein만큼이나 운전을 잘한다.
• The cake that Mary baked for me was as [~~softly~~ / **soft**] as the sponge.
  Mary가 내게 구워 준 케이크는 스폰지처럼 부드러웠다.

핵심 Check

2. 다음 우리말과 같은 뜻이 되도록 주어진 단어를 알맞은 순서로 배열하시오.

(1) 오늘은 어제만큼이나 바람이 분다. (as, is, today, yesterday, windy, as)

➡ _____

(2) 그 램프는 의자만큼 크지 않다. (as, the stool, is, the lamp, tall, so, not)

➡ _____

01 다음 as ~ as 문장에서 어법상 <u>어색한</u> 부분을 바르게 고쳐 쓰시오.

(1) The clock is as more expensive as the furniture.

_____ ➡ _____

(2) They arrived at the airport as earliest as we did.

_____ ➡ _____

(3) Frank is not as honest than Jerome.

_____ ➡ _____

(4) The villagers were as diligent as them in other towns.

_____ ➡ _____

02 다음 중 어법상 바르지 <u>않은</u> 것은?

① The man <u>using</u> the photocopier is Saunders.
② The kids <u>singing</u> downstairs are my students.
③ The people <u>watching</u> the fight were shocked.
④ The girl <u>digging</u> the hole in the garden is my daughter.
⑤ The room <u>crowding</u> with insects is already reserved.

03 다음 대화의 밑줄 친 부분 중에서 어법상 <u>잘못된</u> 곳을 고르시오.

A: ①<u>Is</u> Australia ②<u>bigger</u> ③<u>than</u> Brazil?
B: No. It is not so ④<u>bigger</u> ⑤<u>as</u> Brazil.

04 다음 우리말에 맞게 주어진 어구를 바르게 배열하시오. (필요하면 어형을 바꿀 것.)

(1) 길 건너편에서 손을 흔들고 있는 소녀는 Sarah이다. (is, the street, the girl, Sarah, wave, across)

➡ _____

(2) 우리나라를 향해 접근 중인 폭풍은 강한 위력을 갖고 있다. (our country, a strong force, the storm, has, approach)

➡ _____

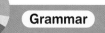

01 다음 우리말을 바르게 영작한 것은?

> 호박은 오이만큼 맛있지 않다.

① A pumpkin is not also yummy but as a cucumber.
② A pumpkin is no less yummy as a cucumber.
③ A pumpkin is very not yummy as a cucumber.
④ A pumpkin is not so yummy as a cucumber.
⑤ A pumpkin is as not yummy as a cucumber.

02 다음 문장에서 어법상 틀린 부분을 찾아 바르게 고쳐 쓰시오.

> I saw her pictures taking in London.

➡ _____ ➡ _____

03 다음 표의 내용과 일치하지 않는 것은?

	Sam	John
Age	6	6
Weight	22kg	23kg
Height	135cm	129cm

① Sam is as old as John.
② John is not so tall as Sam.
③ John is not as heavy as Sam.
④ Sam is not as short as John.
⑤ John is not so light as Sam.

04 다음 괄호 안의 단어의 알맞은 형태가 순서대로 바르게 짝 지어진 것은?

> • The audience (attend) the lecture can be given the free coupons.
> • The time (spend) playing computer games by the kids is too much.
> • The concert was (excite).

① attending – spending – exciting
② attending – spent – excited
③ attending – spent – exciting
④ attended – spending – excited
⑤ attended – spent – exciting

05 다음 중 어법상 옳은 것은?

① Those rocks are as harder as steel.
② The walking stick is as long as the snake.
③ The mouse is as faster as the cat.
④ Jinhee is as tallest as her mother.
⑤ The boxer is as heavier as the other.

06 다음 중 밑줄 친 부분의 쓰임이 다른 하나는?

① There is a <u>singing</u> elephant in Bangkok.
② The officer <u>standing</u> next to the police car is Corbie.
③ The <u>sleeping</u> baby is Jane's son.
④ The kids forgot <u>opening</u> the door.
⑤ The girl <u>looking</u> at him was happy.

07 다음 우리말을 영어로 옳게 옮긴 것은?

> 내 배낭은 수진이의 배낭만큼 크다.

① My backpack is big as Sujin's backpack.
② Sujin's backpack is so big as mine.
③ My backpack is as big as Sujin.
④ My backpack is as big as Sujin's.
⑤ My backpack is big enough as Sujin.

08 다음 중 짝지어진 두 문장의 의미가 서로 다른 것은?

① My team played better than his.

→ His team didn't play as well as mine.

② Susan is slimmer than Yujin.

→ Yujin isn't as slim as Susan.

③ Julie arrived earlier than Thomas.

→ Thomas didn't arrive as early as Julie.

④ I've lived here longer than Peter.

→ Peter haven't lived here as long as I.

⑤ Ron picked more berries than Sean.

→ Sean picked as many berries as Ron.

09 다음 중 밑줄 친 부분의 쓰임이 어색한 것을 모두 고르면?

① People thought the movie was <u>touched</u>.

② The story by the comedian is so <u>boring</u> that everyone wants to get out.

③ The football game was the most <u>excited</u> in my life.

④ How many <u>developing</u> countries are there in the world?

⑤ The thief tried to climb over the wall <u>covered</u> with snow.

서답형

10 다음 각 문장에서 어법상 어색한 부분을 하나씩 찾아서 알맞게 고치시오.

(1) Have you met the girl sung the song in the hall?

_____ ➡ _____

(2) Bentley found the seashells using by the people in ancient times.

_____ ➡ _____

(3) There were a lot of players ran in the playground.

_____ ➡ _____

 11 다음 중 어법상 어색한 것을 모두 고르면?

① The girl pointing at me was Jenny.

② The people I meeting here were so good.

③ The pictures got stolen by the thief were found in a different country.

④ The boy in a wide pool swims fast is Domus.

⑤ The girls walking their dogs talked to the strangers.

12 다음 문장의 빈칸에 들어갈 말로 가장 알맞은 것은?

> Five baby penguins eat as _____ as two adults.

① most   ② more

③ better   ④ good

⑤ much

서답형

13 다음 예시와 같이 두 문장을 한 문장으로 연결할 때, 빈칸에 알맞은 말을 넣으시오.

> • The old lady is watching the film.
> • She is my grandma.
> → The old lady watching the film is my grandma.

(1) • The table is very old.

• It was made by my ancestors.

→ The table _____ _____ _____

_____ _____ very old.

(2) • There were some flies.

• They were buzzing around the jam.

→ There _____ _____ _____

_____ _____ the jam.

서답형

14 Translate the following Korean into English as directed below.

> 검은 선글라스를 끼고 있는 남자들이 버스를 탔다.

<Directions>
- Use the words: sunglasses, on, wear, get, men, black (Change the form if necessary.)
- Complete it with 9 words in total.

➡ The _____
the bus.

15 다음 중 밑줄 친 부분의 쓰임이 같은 것끼리 짝지어진 것은?

ⓐ Participants are expected to be in the <u>waiting</u> room.
ⓑ There were no more trains <u>leaving</u> after 11 p.m.
ⓒ The girls <u>dancing</u> in the middle of the square are my granddaughters.
ⓓ My aunt <u>living</u> in Paris spent most of her money collecting the luxury bags.
ⓔ Choose an appropriate <u>sleeping</u> bag for your camping.

① ⓐ, ⓑ   ② ⓐ, ⓒ
③ ⓐ, ⓑ, ⓔ   ④ ⓑ, ⓒ, ⓓ
⑤ ⓓ, ⓔ

16 다음 문장의 밑줄 친 부분이 어색한 것은?

① Shane decided to get up as <u>early</u> as possible.
② It would be good for your health to drink as <u>many</u> water as possible.
③ The medical staff examined the patient as <u>quickly</u> as possible.

④ After the car accident, Sarah walks as <u>often</u> as possible.
⑤ Remember to call your mom as <u>soon</u> as possible.

17 다음 중 어법상 어색한 문장들의 개수는 모두 몇 개인지 고르시오.

보기
ⓐ The clocks producing in Switzerland are among the best ones in the world.
ⓑ The basketball player calling the Black Mamba was Kobe Bryant.
ⓒ The baby ducks walked zigzag made the noisy sounds.
ⓓ The song composed by the singer became popular.
ⓔ There are many tourists taken photos in the forbidden areas.

① 1개   ② 2개   ③ 3개   ④ 4개   ⑤ 5개

18 다음 중 주어진 문장과 가장 가까운 뜻을 가진 문장을 고르시오.

> Alicia is the strongest student in her class.

① Alicia is stronger than most of the students in her class.
② No other student in her class is as strong as Alicia.
③ No one in her class is the strongest for Alicia.
④ Alicia is as strong as any other student in her class.
⑤ Alicia isn't as strong as any other student in her class.

01 다음 표를 보고 괄호 안에 주어진 단어를 이용하여, 표의 내용과 일치하도록 영작하시오. (단어 변형 불가능)

	Dave	Sean	Key
Age	16	15	16
Weight	65kg	67kg	62kg
Height	175cm	175cm	178cm

(1) Dave _____.
(old, as, Key)
(2) Sean _____.
(old, so, Key)
(3) Sean _____.
(tall, as, Dave)
(4) Dave _____.
(tall, so, not)
(5) No one _____.
(heavy, so)
(6) No one _____. (tall, so)

02 다음 그림을 보고, 우리말에 맞게 괄호 안의 어휘를 이용하여 빈칸을 채우시오.

Unlike his friends (A)_____(hold) their arms high, Yunho was standing at the court (B)_____(look) at them.
(팔을 높이 들고 있는 그의 친구들과는 달리, Yunho는 코트에서 그들을 바라보며 서 있었다.)

03 다음 우리말을 괄호 안에 주어진 단어를 이용하여 영작하시오. (어형 변화 가능)

(1) Minju는 그녀의 선생님만큼 영어를 자유롭게 말할 수 있다. (speak, free, can)
→ Minju _____
_____.

(2) Sein은 그 가수처럼 노래를 잘 불렀다. (sing, well)
→ Sein _____.

(3) 내 남동생은 엄마만큼 자주 설거지를 한다. (do, often, my mom)
→ My brother _____
_____.

(4) 그 영화는 원작 소설만큼 재미있지는 않았다. (novel, so, interest, original)
→ The movie _____
_____.

04 다음 괄호 안의 단어들을 바르게 배열하여 문장을 완성하시오. (단, 동사를 어법상 알맞은 형태로 변형할 것.)

(1) Daisy was watching _____
_____. (the, in, garden, flowers, plant, my)

(2) The _____
are waiting for their teacher. (the, stand, girls, office, near, post)

(3) The book _____.
(by, write, is, Mark Twain, excite)

(4) Who are the _____
_____? (the, dance, music, gentlemen, disco, to)

05 다음 그림을 보고, 우리말에 맞게 괄호 안의 어휘를 이용하여 빈칸을 채우시오.

(1)

• 석봉은 엄마가 떡을 자른 것만큼 반듯하게 글씨를 쓰지 못했다.

Seokbong _____

_____ the rice cake.

(could, cut, neatly, as, write, as, not)

(2)

• 그는 생각한 것만큼 살이 빠지지 않아서 실망했다.

He was disappointed because he _____

_____.

(lose, weight, not, thought, much, as, as)

06 다음 〈보기〉에 주어진 동사를 한 번씩만 사용하여 어법에 맞게 바꿔 빈칸을 완성하시오.

┌─── 보기 ───┐

appear   make   write   cover   know

Parasite is the film (A)_____ by director Bong, who is well (B)_____ for the movie *Host*. Its poster shows the black band (C)_____ the eyes of the characters, (D)_____ the movie more mysterious. There are many stairs (E)_____ in the movie, which symbolizes the status of the characters.

07 다음 각각의 두 문장을 분사를 활용하여, 괄호 안의 조건에 맞게 한 문장으로 고치시오.

(1) I met a lady. She was wearing a colorful skirt. (명사를 뒤에서 수식)

→ I met _____.

(2) Those are the books. The books were copied illegally. (명사를 앞에서 수식)

→ Those _____.

(3) My kids saw an airplane. The airplane is flying between the clouds. (명사를 뒤에서 수식)

→ My kids saw _____

_____.

(4) The violin is so expensive. It is made by the master craftsman. (명사를 뒤에서 수식)

→ The violin _____

_____.

(5) Be careful not to wake up the baby. She is sleeping. (명사를 앞에서 수식)

→ Be _____

_____.

08 다음 그림을 보고, 괄호 안의 단어를 적절한 분사로 활용하여 빈칸에 알맞게 채우시오.

➡ Minho found his father _____(sleep) in the sofa, _____(wear) his suit as soon as he came home from work.

Reading

교과서

Hidden People in Sports

In sports, only the players get a trophy or medal, but they don't win on their own. There are people who help the players. These people are often hidden and don't get attention. However, they are as important as the players. Here are some examples.

Pacers in a Marathon

Pacers run with other runners and lead them in a marathon. Pacers are experienced runners, and their job is to help other runners manage their race better. There can be several pacers in a race. Each pacer runs at different speeds and finishes the race in different times. Pacers usually have flags or balloons showing their finish time.

Runners can choose a pacer depending on their target finish time. For example, if a runner wants to finish the race in four hours, the runner will follow the four-hour pacer. Since the pacer keeps track of the time, the runner can achieve his or her goal of finishing the marathon in a particular time more easily. In short, pacers run but they don't run to win. They run for others.

---

hidden 숨겨진, 숨은

trophy 트로피

on one's own 혼자서, 혼자 힘으로(= alone, by oneself)

attention 주목, 관심

experienced 경험이 풍부한, 능숙한

several 몇몇의

depending on ~에 따라

target 목표, 목표로 하는 대상

keep track of (계속해서) ~을 파악하다, ~에 주의를 기울이다

achieve 달성하다, 성취하다

particular 특정한

in short 요컨대, 요약하면

 확인문제

● 다음 문장이 본문의 내용과 일치하면 T, 일치하지 <u>않으면</u> F를 쓰시오.

1 Pacers are experienced runners and help other runners to manage their race better. ☐

2 Each pacer runs at the same speed. ☐

3 Runners can choose a pacer depending on their target finish time. ☐

4 Runners keep track of the time. ☐

5 The runner can achieve his or her goal of finishing the marathon in a particular time more easily by following a pacer. ☐

6 Pacers run to win. ☐

Pit Crews in Car Racing

You may only see the car and the driver during most car races, but there is a team behind the driver. This team is called a pit crew. A pit
수동태(be동사+과거분사): ~으로 불린다
is a place on the side of the race track, and drivers stop there several
형용사구
times during a race. The main job of the pit crew is to check the car
to부정사의 명사적 용법(보어)
and change the tires. Changing the tires is especially important because
= to change(to check와 병렬 구조) 동명사 주어 동명사 주어는 단수 취급
the tires wear out easily in a high speed race.

A pit stop can be as short as 2 seconds, and there are as many as 20
동등 비교
members on a crew. Therefore, the pit crew has to work in perfect
그러므로(결과를 말할 때 쓰이는 연결어)
harmony. The driver may get all the attention, but as people say, "Races
~일지도 모른다(약한 추측) get attention: 주목을 받다
are won in the pits."

Sherpas in Mountain Climbing

The word *Sherpa* comes from the Sherpa tribe, which lives in
계속적 용법의 관계대명사
the eastern part of Nepal. Sherpas have good climbing skills and
know their way around the mountains well. They also have little
= Sherpas
difficulty breathing high up in the mountains. Therefore, mountain
have difficulty/trouble/a hard time –ing: ~하는 데 어려움이 있다
climbers started to hire Sherpas to help them climb Mount Everest.
= hiring help+목적어+(to+)동사원형, them = mountain climbers

Sherpas lead mountain climbers to the top of the mountain. They
lead A to B: A를 B로 이끌다 = Sherpas
support climbers in many ways. For example, they put up tents and
여러 방면에서 = Sherpas V1
carry climbers' bags. Sherpas are often called the invisible people of
V2 ↔ visible
Mount Everest because people often see a picture of only the climbers
at the top of the mountain.

---

pit 피트(자동차 경주 도중에 급유, 타이어 교체나 수리를 하는 곳)

crew (같은 일에 종사하는) 팀, 조

especially 특히

wear out (낡아서) 떨어지다, 못 쓰게 되다, 닳아 버리다

second 초

therefore 그러므로

harmony 조화, 화합

tribe 종족, 부족

eastern 동쪽의, 동쪽에 위치한

skill 기량, 기술

breathe 숨을 쉬다

hire 고용하다

support 지원하다, 지지하다

put up (텐트, 벽 등을) 치다, 세우다

invisible 보이지 않는, 볼 수 없는

확인문제

● 다음 문장이 본문의 내용과 일치하면 T, 일치하지 <u>않으면</u> F를 쓰시오.

1 A pit is a place on the side of the race track, where drivers stop several times during a race. ☐

2 The main job of the pit crew is to check the condition of the driver. ☐

3 The pit crew has to work in perfect harmony. ☐

4 The Sherpa tribe lives in the northern part of Nepal. ☐

5 Sherpas have little trouble breathing high up in the mountains. ☐

6 Sherpas are often called the visible people of Mount Everest. ☐

• 우리말을 참고하여 빈칸에 알맞은 말을 쓰시오.

1 _____ People in Sports

2 In sports, only the players get a trophy or medal, but they don't win _____ _____ _____ .

3 There are people _____ help the players.

4 These people are often _____ and don't _____ _____ .

5 However, they are _____ _____ _____ the players.

6 _____ _____ some examples.

7 _____ in a Marathon

8 Pacers _____ _____ other runners and _____ them in a marathon.

9 Pacers are _____ runners, and their job is to help other runners _____ _____ _____ _____ _____ .

10 _____ _____ _____ several pacers in a race.

11 Each pacer runs _____ _____ _____ and finishes the race _____ _____ _____ .

12 Pacers usually have flags or balloons _____ their finish time.

13 Runners can choose a pacer _____ _____ their target finish time.

14 For example, if a runner wants to finish the race _____ _____ _____ , the runner will follow the _____-hour pacer.

15 Since the pacer _____ _____ _____ the time, the runner can achieve his or her goal of finishing the marathon in a particular time more _____ .

16 In short, pacers run but they don't run _____ _____ .

17 They run _____ _____ .

18 Pit Crews in _____ _____

19 You may only see the car and the driver _____ most car races, but there is a team _____ _____ _____ .

1 스포츠 속 숨은 조력자들

2 스포츠에서 선수들만 트로피나 메달을 받지만, 그들은 혼자 힘으로 이긴 것이 아니다.

3 그 선수들을 돕는 사람들이 있다.

4 이 사람들은 종종 숨겨져 있고 주목을 받지 못한다.

5 하지만 그들은 선수들만큼 중요하다.

6 여기 몇 가지 예가 있다.

7 마라톤의 페이서들

8 페이서들은 마라톤에서 다른 선수들과 함께 달리며 그들을 이끈다.

9 페이서들은 경험이 많은 선수들이며 그들의 역할은 다른 선수들이 경기를 더 잘 운영하도록 돕는 것이다.

10 한 경기에는 여러 명의 페이서들이 있을 수 있다.

11 각각의 페이서는 다른 속도로 달리고 다른 시간대에 경기를 마친다.

12 페이서들은 주로 자신들의 완주 시간을 나타내는 깃발이나 풍선들을 가지고 있다.

13 선수들은 자신들의 목표 완주 시간에 따라 페이서를 선택할 수 있다.

14 예를 들어, 한 선수가 4시간 안에 경기를 마치고 싶다면, 그 선수는 4시간 페이서를 따라갈 것이다.

15 페이서가 시간을 계속해서 파악하기 때문에, 선수는 특정 시간에 마라톤을 완주하려는 자신의 목표를 더 쉽게 달성할 수 있다.

16 요컨대, 페이서들은 달리지만 우승을 하기 위해 달리는 것은 아니다.

17 그들은 다른 선수들을 위해 달린다.

18 자동차 경주의 피트 크루

19 여러분은 대부분의 자동차 경주에서 자동차와 레이서만 보겠지만 그 레이서 뒤에는 팀이 있다.

20 This team _____ _____ a pit crew.

21 A pit is a place _____ _____ _____ _____ _____ _____, and drivers stop there several times during a race.

22 The main job of the pit crew is _____ _____ the car and change the tires.

23 _____ the tires _____ especially important because the tires _____ _____ easily in a high speed race.

24 A pit stop can be _____ _____ _____ 2 seconds, and there are _____ _____ _____ 20 members on a crew.

25 Therefore, the pit crew has to work _____ _____ _____.

26 The driver may _____ _____ _____ _____, but as people say, "Races are won _____ _____ _____."

27 Sherpas in Mountain Climbing

28 The word *Sherpa* _____ _____ the Sherpa tribe, which lives in the eastern part of Nepal.

29 Sherpas have _____ _____ _____ and know their way around the mountains well.

30 They also _____ _____ _____ _____ high up in the mountains.

31 Therefore, mountain climbers started to hire Sherpas _____ _____ _____ Mount Everest.

32 Sherpas _____ mountain climbers _____ the top of the mountain.

33 They support climbers _____ _____ _____.

34 For example, they _____ _____ tents and carry climbers' bags.

35 Sherpas are often called the _____ people of Mount Everest because people often see a picture of only the climbers _____ _____ _____ _____ the mountain.

20 이 팀은 피트 크루라고 불린다.

21 피트는 경주 트랙의 한쪽에 있는 공간으로 레이서들은 경주 도중에 그곳에서 여러 번 정지한다.

22 피트 크루가 하는 주요 역할은 자동차를 점검하고 타이어를 교체하는 것이다.

23 빠른 속도의 경주에서는 타이어가 쉽게 마모되기 때문에 타이어를 교체하는 것이 특히 중요하다.

24 피트에서의 정지는 짧게는 2초 정도이고 한 팀에는 많게는 20명에 이르는 구성원이 있다.

25 그러므로 피트 크루는 완벽한 조화를 이루며 일해야 한다.

26 레이서만 주목을 받을지 모르지만 사람들이 말하는 것처럼, "경주의 우승은 피트에서 이루어진다."

27 등반에서의 셰르파

28 'Sherpa'라는 단어는 셰르파족에서 유래되었는데, 셰르파족은 네팔의 동쪽 지역에 산다.

29 셰르파는 훌륭한 등반 기량을 갖고 있으며 산 지리를 잘 안다.

30 그들은 또한 산의 높은 곳에서 호흡하는 데 어려움이 거의 없다.

31 그래서 등산가들은 자신들이 에베레스트산을 등반하는 것을 돕는 셰르파를 고용하기 시작했다.

32 셰르파는 등산가들을 산 정상까지 이끈다.

33 그들은 여러 방면에서 등산가들을 지원한다.

34 예를 들면, 그들은 텐트를 치고 등산가들의 가방을 운반한다.

35 셰르파는 종종 에베레스트산의 보이지 않는 사람들로 불리는데, 왜냐하면 사람들이 산 정상에서 등산가들만 찍힌 사진을 자주 보기 때문이다.

● 우리말을 참고하여 본문을 영작하시오.

1 스포츠 속 숨은 조력자들
➡ _____

2 스포츠에서 선수들만 트로피나 메달을 받지만, 그들은 혼자 힘으로 이긴 것이 아니다.
➡ _____

3 그 선수들을 돕는 사람들이 있다.
➡ _____

4 이 사람들은 종종 숨겨져 있고 주목을 받지 못한다.
➡ _____

5 하지만 그들은 선수들만큼 중요하다.
➡ _____

6 여기 몇 가지 예가 있다.
➡ _____

7 마라톤의 페이서들
➡ _____

8 페이서들은 마라톤에서 다른 선수들과 함께 달리며 그들을 이끈다.
➡ _____

9 페이서들은 경험이 많은 선수들이며 그들의 역할은 다른 선수들이 경기를 더 잘 운영하도록 돕는 것이다.
➡ _____

10 한 경기에는 여러 명의 페이서들이 있을 수 있다.
➡ _____

11 각각의 페이서는 다른 속도로 달리고 다른 시간대에 경기를 마친다.
➡ _____

12 페이서들은 주로 자신들의 완주 시간을 나타내는 깃발이나 풍선들을 가지고 있다.
➡ _____

13 선수들은 자신들의 목표 완주 시간에 따라 페이서를 선택할 수 있다.
➡ _____

14 예를 들어, 한 선수가 4시간 안에 경기를 마치고 싶다면, 그 선수는 4시간 페이서를 따라갈 것이다.
➡ _____

15 페이서가 시간을 계속해서 파악하기 때문에, 선수는 특정 시간에 마라톤을 완주하려는 자신의 목표를 더 쉽게 달성할 수 있다.
➡ _____
_____

16 요컨대, 페이서들은 달리지만 우승을 하기 위해 달리는 것은 아니다.
➡ _____

17 그들은 다른 선수들을 위해 달린다.
➡ _____

18 자동차 경주의 피트 크루

➡ _____

19 여러분은 대부분의 자동차 경주에서 자동차와 레이서만 보겠지만 그 레이서 뒤에는 팀이 있다.

➡ _____

20 이 팀은 피트 크루라고 불린다.

➡ _____

21 피트는 경주 트랙의 한쪽에 있는 공간으로 레이서들은 경주 도중에 그곳에서 여러 번 정지한다.

➡ _____

22 피트 크루가 하는 주요 역할은 자동차를 점검하고 타이어를 교체하는 것이다.

➡ _____

23 빠른 속도의 경주에서는 타이어가 쉽게 마모되기 때문에 타이어를 교체하는 것이 특히 중요하다.

➡ _____

24 피트에서의 정지는 짧게는 2초 정도이고 한 팀에는 많게는 20명에 이르는 구성원이 있다.

➡ _____

25 그러므로 피트 크루는 완벽한 조화를 이루며 일해야 한다.

➡ _____

26 레이서만 주목을 받을지 모르지만 사람들이 말하는 것처럼, "경주의 우승은 피트에서 이루어진다."

➡ _____

27 등반에서의 셰르파

➡ _____

28 'Sherpa'라는 단어는 셰르파족에서 유래되었는데, 셰르파족은 네팔의 동쪽 지역에 산다.

➡ _____

29 셰르파는 훌륭한 등반 기량을 갖고 있으며 산 지리를 잘 안다.

➡ _____

30 그들은 또한 산의 높은 곳에서 호흡하는 데 어려움이 거의 없다.

➡ _____

31 그래서 등산가들은 자신들이 에베레스트산을 등반하는 것을 돕는 셰르파를 고용하기 시작했다.

➡ _____

32 셰르파는 등산가들을 산 정상까지 이끈다.

➡ _____

33 그들은 여러 방면에서 등산가들을 지원한다.

➡ _____

34 예를 들면, 그들은 텐트를 치고 등산가들의 가방을 운반한다.

➡ _____

35 셰르파는 종종 에베레스트산의 보이지 않는 사람들로 불리는데, 왜냐하면 사람들이 산 정상에서 등산가들만 찍힌 사진을 자주 보기 때문이다.

➡ _____

_____

[01~03] 다음 글을 읽고 물음에 답하시오.

Pacers in a Marathon

Pacers run with other runners and lead them in a marathon. Pacers are experienced runners, and their job is (A)to help other runners manage their race better. There can be several pacers in a race. Each pacer runs ⓐ＿＿ different speeds and finishes the race ⓑ＿＿ different times. Pacers usually have flags or balloons showing their finish time.

01 위 글의 빈칸 ⓐ와 ⓑ에 들어갈 전치사가 바르게 짝지어진 것은?

	ⓐ	ⓑ		ⓐ	ⓑ
①	at	in	②	on	for
③	on	from	④	for	in
⑤	at	for			

02 위 글의 밑줄 친 (A)to help와 to부정사의 용법이 같은 것을 모두 고르시오.

① He was happy to help other runners.
② It's good to help other runners.
③ I decided to help other runners.
④ It's time to help other runners.
⑤ She is too weak to help other runners.

03 According to the passage, which is NOT true?

① Pacers follow other runners in a marathon.
② Pacers help other runners manage their race better.
③ The speed of each pacer is different.
④ In a race, there can be several pacers.
⑤ Pacers' flags or balloons show their finish time.

[04~06] 다음 글을 읽고 물음에 답하시오.

In sports, only the players get a trophy or medal, but they don't win (A)on their own. There are people who help the players. These people are often hidden and don't get attention. ＿ⓐ＿, they are as important as the players. Here are some examples.

04 위 글의 빈칸 ⓐ에 들어갈 알맞은 말을 고르시오.

① That is   ② However
③ Similarly   ④ As a result
⑤ In addition

05 위 글의 밑줄 친 (A)on their own과 바꿔 쓸 수 있는 말을 모두 고르시오.

① lonely   ② beside themselves
③ alone   ④ on behalf of them
⑤ by themselves

06 위 글의 뒤에 올 내용으로 가장 알맞은 것을 고르시오.

① the players who get a trophy or medal
② how to achieve one's goal
③ players who work in perfect harmony
④ hidden people in sports
⑤ the noticeable people in sports

[07~10] 다음 글을 읽고 물음에 답하시오.

Pit Crews in Car Racing

You may only see the car and the driver during most car races, but there is a team behind the driver. This team is called a pit crew. A pit is a place on the side of the race track, and drivers stop there several times during a race. The main job of the pit crew is to check the car and change the tires. (A) Changing the tires is especially important because the tires wear out easily in a high speed race.

(B)피트에서의 정지는 짧게는 2초 정도이고 한 팀에는 많게는 20명에 이르는 구성원이 있다. Therefore, the pit crew has to work in perfect harmony. The driver may get all the attention, but as people say, "Races are won in the ___ⓐ___."

07 위 글의 빈칸 ⓐ에 들어갈 알맞은 말을 고르시오.

① tracks ② pits
③ fields ④ stadiums
⑤ cheering sections

08 Why do drivers stop at a pit several times during a race? Fill in the blanks (A) and (B) with suitable words.

They stop there to (A)_____ the car and (B)_____ the tires.

09 아래 〈보기〉에서 위 글의 밑줄 친 (A)Changing과 문법적 쓰임이 같은 것의 개수를 고르시오.

보기
① He is changing the tires.
② She gave up changing the tires.
③ I saw my dad changing the tires.
④ Changing the tires, he sang a song.
⑤ He is good at changing the tires.

① 1개 ② 2개 ③ 3개 ④ 4개 ⑤ 5개

10 위 글의 밑줄 친 (B)의 우리말에 맞게 주어진 어휘를 이용하여 영작하시오.

as short as, as many as

➡ _____

_____

[11~13] 다음 글을 읽고 물음에 답하시오.

(①) Each pacer runs at different speeds and finishes the race in different times. (②) Pacers usually have flags or balloons showing their finish time. (③) For example, if a runner wants to finish the race in four hours, the runner will follow the four-hour pacer. (④) Since the pacer keeps track of the time, the runner can achieve his or her goal of finishing the marathon in a particular time more easily. (⑤) ___ⓐ___, pacers run but they don't run to win. They run for others.

11 위 글의 빈칸 ⓐ에 들어갈 알맞은 말을 고르시오.

① For example ② Additionally
③ However ④ In short
⑤ On the other hand

12 위 글의 흐름으로 보아, 주어진 문장이 들어가기에 가장 적절한 곳은?

Runners can choose a pacer depending on their target finish time.

① ② ③ ④ ⑤

13 위 글의 주제로 알맞은 것을 고르시오.

① the speed of each pacer
② the flags or balloons showing pacers' finish time
③ runners' target finish time
④ the pacer's secret of keeping track of the time
⑤ the role of pacers in a marathon

[14~16] 다음 글을 읽고 물음에 답하시오.

Sherpas in Mountain Climbing

The word *Sherpa* comes from the Sherpa tribe, which lives in the eastern part of Nepal. Sherpas have good climbing skills and know their way around the mountains well. They also have little ⓐdifficulty breathing high up in the mountains. Therefore, mountain climbers started to hire Sherpas to help them climb Mount Everest.

Sherpas lead mountain climbers to the top of the mountain. They support climbers in many ways. For example, they put ____ⓑ____ tents and carry climbers' bags. Sherpas are often called the invisible people of Mount Everest because people often see a picture of only the climbers at the top of the mountain.

14 위 글의 밑줄 친 ⓐdifficulty와 바꿔 쓸 수 있는 말을 고르시오.

① trouble   ② question
③ difference   ④ solution
⑤ conflict

15 위 글의 빈칸 ⓑ에 들어갈 알맞은 말을 고르시오.

① in   ② up   ③ on
④ for   ⑤ with

16 서답형 Why are Sherpas often called the invisible people of Mount Everest? Fill in the blank with a suitable word.

> Because it is a picture of only the (A)_____ at the top of the mountain that people often see.

[17~19] 다음 글을 읽고 물음에 답하시오.

(A)In sports, only the players get a trophy or medal, but they win on their own. There are people who help the players. These people are often ____ⓐ____ and don't get attention. However, (B)they are as important as the players. Here are some examples.

17 서답형 위 글의 빈칸 ⓐ에 hide를 알맞은 형태로 쓰시오.

➡ _____

18 서답형 위 글의 밑줄 친 (A)에서 흐름상 어색한 부분을 찾아 고치시오.

_____ ➡ _____

19 서답형 위 글의 밑줄 친 (B)they가 가리키는 것을 본문에서 찾아 쓰시오.

➡ _____

[20~22] 다음 글을 읽고 물음에 답하시오.

Pit Crews in Car Racing

You may only see the car and the driver during most car races, but there is a team behind the driver. This team is called a pit crew. A pit is a place on the side of the race track, and drivers stop there several times during a race. (A)The main job of the pit crew is to check the car and change the tires. Changing the tires is especially important because the tires wear out easily in a high speed race.

(B)A pit stop can be as shorter as 2 seconds, and there are as much as 20 members on a crew. Therefore, the pit crew has to work ___ⓐ___ . The driver may get all the attention, but as people say, "Races are won in the pits."

20 위 글의 빈칸 ⓐ에 들어갈 알맞은 말을 고르시오.

① without stopping
② one after another
③ in perfect harmony
④ from time to time
⑤ little by little

21 위 글의 밑줄 친 (A)를 다음과 같이 바꿔 쓸 때 빈칸 (a)와 (b)에 들어갈 알맞은 단어를 쓰시오.

> The main job of the pit crew is (a)_____ the car and (b)_____ the tires.

22 위 글의 밑줄 친 (B)에서 어법상 **틀린** 부분을 찾아 고치시오. (두 군데)

_____ ➡ _____, _____ ➡ _____

[23~25] 다음 글을 읽고 물음에 답하시오.

Sherpas in Mountain Climbing

The word *Sherpa* comes from the Sherpa tribe, which lives in the (A)[east / eastern] part of Nepal. Sherpas have good climbing skills and know their way around the mountains well. They also have (B)[little / much] difficulty breathing high up in the

mountains. Therefore, ⓐ등산가들은 자신들이 에베레스트산을 등반하는 것을 돕는 세르파를 고용하기 시작했다.

Sherpas lead mountain climbers to the top of the mountain. They support climbers in many ways. For example, they put up tents and carry climbers' bags. Sherpas are often called the (C)[visible / invisible] people of Mount Everest because people often see a picture of only the climbers at the top of the mountain.

23 위 글의 괄호 (A)~(C)에서 문맥이나 어법상 알맞은 낱말을 골라 쓰시오.

➡ (A) _____ (B) _____ (C) _____

24 위 글의 밑줄 친 ⓐ의 우리말에 맞게 주어진 어휘를 알맞게 배열하시오.

> climb / started / to help / Sherpas / them / Mount Everest / mountain climbers / to hire

➡ _____
_____

 25 위 글을 읽고 대답할 수 **없는** 것을 고르시오.

① Is the word *Sherpa* named after the place?
② Where does the Sherpa tribe live?
③ What skill do Sherpas have?
④ How do Sherpas have little difficulty breathing high up in the mountains?
⑤ Do people often see the picture of Sherpas at the top of Mount Everest?

[01~02] 다음 글을 읽고 물음에 답하시오.

In sports, only the players get a trophy or medal, but they don't win on their own. There are people who help the players. These people are often hidden and don't get attention. However, (A)they are ⓐ important ⓑ the players. Here are some examples.

01 위 글의 빈칸 ⓐ와 ⓑ에 공통으로 들어갈 알맞은 말을 쓰시오.

➡ _____

02 다음 빈칸 (a)와 (b)에 알맞은 단어를 넣어 (A)they에 대한 소개를 완성하시오.

They help the players win in sports, but they are often (a)_____ without getting (b)_____.

[03~06] 다음 글을 읽고 물음에 답하시오.

Pacers in a Marathon

Pacers run with other runners and lead them in a marathon. Pacers are experienced runners, and their job is to help other runners manage their race better. There can be several pacers in a race. Each pacer runs at different speeds and finishes the race in different times. ⓐPacers usually have flags or balloons showing their finish time.

Runners can choose a pacer depending on their target finish time. For example, if a runner wants to finish the race in four hours, the runner will follow the four-hour pacer. Since the pacer keeps track of the time, the runner can achieve his or her goal of finishing

the marathon in a particular time more easily. In short, ⓑ페이서들은 달리지만 우승을 하기 위해 달리는 것은 아니다. They run for others.

03 다음 문장에서 위 글의 내용과 <u>다른</u> 부분을 찾아서 고치시오.

The speed of each pacer is the same.

_____ ➡ _____

04 위 글의 밑줄 친 ⓐ를 다음과 같이 바꿔 쓸 때 빈칸에 들어갈 알맞은 말을 두 단어로 쓰시오.

➡ Pacers usually have flags or balloons _____ _____ their finish time.

05 위 글의 밑줄 친 ⓑ의 우리말에 맞게 주어진 어휘를 이용하여 8 단어로 영작하시오.

to win

➡ _____

06 본문의 내용과 일치하도록 다음 빈칸 (A)와 (B)에 알맞은 단어를 쓰시오.

Runners can achieve their goal of finishing the marathon in (A)_____ _____ _____ more easily by choosing a pacer depending on their target finish time because the pacer (B)_____ _____ _____ the time.

[07~09] 다음 글을 읽고 물음에 답하시오.

Pit Crews in Car Racing

You may only see the car and the driver (A)[during / while] most car races, but there is a

38 Lesson 5. The Team Behind the Team

team behind the driver. This team is called a pit crew. A pit is a place on the side of the race track, and drivers stop there several times during a race. The main job of the pit crew is to check the car and (B)[change / changing] the tires. Changing the tires is especially important because the tires wear out easily in a high speed race.

A pit stop can be as (C)[short / shortly] as 2 seconds, and there are as many as 20 members on a crew. Therefore, the pit crew has to work in perfect harmony. The driver may get all the attention, but as people say, "@Races are won in the pits."

07 위 글의 괄호 (A)~(C)에서 문맥이나 어법상 알맞은 낱말을 골라 쓰시오.

➡ (A) _____ (B) _____ (C) _____

08 다음 문장에서 위 글의 내용과 다른 부분을 찾아서 고치시오.

> Drivers stop at a pit several times after a race.

_____ ➡ _____

09 다음 빈칸 (A)와 (B)에 공통으로 들어갈 두 단어를 넣어 위 글의 밑줄 친 @가 의미하는 것을 완성하시오.

> When drivers stop at a pit to check the car and change the tires, the (A)_____ _____ has to work in perfect harmony in a very short time, and so the skillful work of the (B)_____ _____ plays a very important role in winning the race.

[10~13] 다음 글을 읽고 물음에 답하시오.

Sherpas in Mountain Climbing

The word *Sherpa* comes from the Sherpa tribe, (A)which lives in the eastern part of Nepal. Sherpas have good climbing skills and know their way around the mountains well. They also have little difficulty ___@___ high up in the mountains. Therefore, mountain climbers started to hire Sherpas to help them climb Mount Everest.

Sherpas lead mountain climbers to the top of the mountain. They support climbers in many ways. For example, they put up tents and carry climbers' bags. (B)Sherpas are often called the invisible people of Mount Everest because people often see a picture of only the sherpas at the top of the mountain.

10 위 글의 빈칸 @에 breathe를 알맞은 형태로 쓰시오.

➡ _____

11 위 글의 밑줄 친 (A)which를 두 단어로 쓰시오.

➡ _____

12 위 글의 밑줄 친 (B)에서 흐름상 어색한 부분을 찾아 고치시오.

_____ ➡ _____

13 다음 빈칸 (A)와 (B)에 알맞은 단어를 넣어 Sherpas에 대한 소개를 완성하시오.

> The Sherpa tribe lives in the eastern part of Nepal, and Sherpas (A)_____ mountain climbers to the top of the mountain because they have (B)_____ _____ and know their way around the mountains well.

교과서

구석구석

After You Read B

Host: Is there anything interesting about your job?
_{-thing으로 끝나는 부정대명사는 형용사가 뒤에서 수식한다.}

Pacer: Pacers have flags or balloons showing their finish time.
_{능동이나 진행의 의미를 나타내는 '동사원형+-ing' 형태의 현재분사로, 앞의 명사 수식}

Pit Crew: A pit stop can be as short as 2 seconds. So the pit crew has to work
_{as+형용사/부사+as: ~만큼 ···한/하게}
in perfect harmony.

Sherpa: Sherpas like me have little difficulty breathing high up in the
_{have difficulty -ing: '~하는 데 어려움이 있다'}
mountains.

구문해설 • **pit**: 피트(자동차 경주 도중에 급유, 타이어 교체나 수리를 하는 곳)
• **crew**: (같은 일에 종사하는) 팀, 조 • **harmony**: 조화, 화합 • **breathe**: 숨을 쉬다

Think and Write

Cheerleaders in Football Games

Although people usually don't think that cheerleaders are a part of a football
_{'양보'의 부사절을 이끄는 접속사: ~할지라도}
team, they play an important role in a football game. By cheering at a game,
_{by V-ing: ~함으로써(방법, 수단)}
they create team spirit. They also encourage their team and fans. To do their
_{to부정사의 부사적 용법 '목적'}
job well, cheerleaders need to be good
_{to부정사의 명사적 용법 'need의 목적어'}
at jumping and dancing. Most of all, they need to work as hard as players.
_{전치사+동명사   병렬(and)+동명사   ~만큼 ···한(as 원급 as)}

구문해설 • **usually**: 보통, 대개 • **play a role in ~**: ~에서 역할을 하다 • **cheering**: 응원
• **team spirit**: 공동체 정신 • **fit**: 건강한 • **be good at**: ~를 잘하다
• **most of all**: 무엇보다도

Around the World

1. In swimming, a tapper uses a long pole to help a blind swimmer swim.
_{to부정사의 부사적 용법(목적) help의 목적격보어로 동사원형(= to swim)}

2. In a race, a guide runner runs with a blind runner and helps him or her
_{runs와 병렬 관계}
stay on the track.
_{help의 목적격보어로 동사원형(= to stay)}

3. In blind football, a shooting assistant tells his or her team players
which direction to shoot.
_{'의문사+to부정사'로 tells의 직접목적어(which는 direction을 수식하는 의문형용사임)}

구문해설 • **tapper**: 두드리는 사람 • **guide runner**: 가이드 러너(시각장애인의 눈 역할을 해주는 선수)
• **assistant**: 보조자 • **direction**: 방향

해석

사회자: 여러분의 직업에 관해 어떤 흥미로운 것이 있나요?

페이서: 페이서는 자신들의 완주 시간을 나타내는 깃발이나 풍선들을 가지고 있어요.

피트 크루: 피트에서의 정지는 짧게는 2초 정도입니다. 그래서 피트 크루는 완벽한 조화를 이루며 일해야 해요.

셰르파: 저와 같은 셰르파는 산의 높은 곳에서 호흡하는 데 어려움이 거의 없어요.

미식축구 경기에서의 치어리더

사람들이 보통 치어리더는 미식축구팀의 일원이라고 생각하지 않을지라도 그들은 축구 경기에서 중요한 역할을 한다. 경기에서 응원을 함으로써 그들은 공동체 정신을 만들어낸다. 그들은 또한 팀과 팬들을 격려한다. 자신의 역할을 잘하기 위해, 치어리더들은 몸을 건강하게 관리하고 강해야 한다. 그들은 또한 점프하는 것과 춤추는 것을 잘해야 한다. 무엇보다도, 그들은 선수들만큼이나 열심히 일해야 한다.

1. 수영에서, tapper는 시각 장애인 수영 선수가 수영하는 것을 돕기 위해 장대를 사용한다.

2. 달리기에서, guide runner는 시각 장애인 선수와 함께 달리며 그들이 트랙에서 벗어나지 않도록 돕는다.

3. 시각 장애인 축구에서, shooting assistant는 자신의 팀 선수들에게 슛하는 방향을 말해 준다.

01 〈보기〉의 밑줄 친 join과 같은 의미로 쓰인 것을 고르시오.

┤ 보기 ├

For reasons of his own, he refused to join the club.

① What do you think of that new gym that you joined?

② He joined one section of pipe to the next.

③ Are you free on Thursday to join us for dinner?

④ In 1189, Richard joined forces with Philip II of France against his father.

⑤ It was glued tightly so the join could not be seen.

02 다음 영영풀이에 해당하는 단어를 주어진 철자로 시작하여 빈칸에 쓰고, 알맞은 것을 골라 문장을 완성하시오.

• c_____ : a group of people with a particular skill who work together

• p_____ : special, or more than usual

• d_____ : the way something or someone moves or faces

(1) Is there a _____ type of book he enjoys?

(2) The film _____ entered the sea to shoot the scene.

(3) I lost all sense of _____.

03 다음 문장의 빈칸에 〈영영풀이〉에 해당하는 단어를 쓰시오.

It's normal for things to _____ _____ with long use.

〈영영풀이〉 to use something a lot so that it no longer works, or can no longer be used

➡ _____

04 다음 빈칸 (A)~(C)에 알맞은 말을 쓰시오. (주어진 철자로 시작하여 쓸 것.)

• They lived in (A)h_____ with each other.

• Teenagers often have (B)d_____ expressing themselves.

• Tourism is expected to play an important (C)r_____ in the development of the nation's economy.

05 다음 괄호 안에 주어진 어휘를 이용하여 빈칸에 알맞게 쓰시오.

(1) Good will is an _____ asset. (visible)

(2) She was _____ and needed a guiding hand. (experience)

(3) As time went on, he grew more and more _____. (patient)

Conversation

[06~07] 다음 대화를 읽고 물음에 답하시오.

(A) (a)<u>That</u> often? Anyway, it'll be fun swimming together today.

(B) I swim four times a week.

(C) Yes, but before we swim, I suggest we do stretching exercises.

(D) I don't swim often. How about you, Kate? How often do you swim?

That's a good idea.

06 주어진 문장 앞에 나올 대화의 순서로 알맞은 것은?

① (B) – (A) – (C) – (D)

② (C) – (B) – (A) – (D)

③ (D) – (A) – (C) – (B)

④ (D) – (B) – (A) – (C)

⑤ (D) – (B) – (C) – (A)

07 위 대화의 밑줄 친 (a)That과 같은 용법으로 쓰인 것은?

① Look at <u>that</u> man over there.

② She was so tired <u>that</u> she couldn't think straight.

③ Are you sure she's <u>that</u> young?

④ He is the greatest novelist <u>that</u> has ever lived.

⑤ There was no hope <u>that</u> she would recover her health.

08 다음 중 짝지어진 대화가 <u>어색한</u> 것은?

① A: I clean my room once a week.

   B: I suggest that you clean your room more often.

② A: How much do you eat fast food?

   B: I eat fast food three times a week.

③ A: I have breakfast every day.

   B: That's good.

④ A: This class meets on Saturdays and Sundays.

   B: That sounds good.

⑤ A: May I help you?

   B: Yes, I came to register for a swimming class.

[09~10] 다음 대화를 읽고 물음에 답하시오.

W: Hello. Welcome to Sports World. May I help you?

B: Yes, I came to register for a swimming class.

W: Is this your first time taking swimming lessons?

B: Yes, it is. I don't know how to swim at all.

W: I see. How often do you want to take classes?

B: I want to take classes twice a week. I'd like to take classes on weekdays and not on weekends.

W: Then, I suggest that you take the Beginner 2 class. This class meets on Tuesdays and Thursdays.

B: That sounds good. I'd like to (a)<u>sign up</u> for that class. How big is the class?

W: The class has a ___(A)___ of 10 people.

B: That's perfect.

09 주어진 〈영영풀이〉를 참고하여 위 대화의 빈칸 (A)에 알맞은 말을 쓰시오.

〈영영풀이〉

the largest or smallest amount of something such as time or money that is allowed because of a rule, law, etc.

➡ _____

10 밑줄 친 (a)sign up과 같은 뜻의 어휘를 대화에서 찾아 쓰시오.

➡ _____

Grammar

11 다음 중 어법상 올바른 문장은?

① The movie directing by Bong won the four Oscars this year.
② He showed me the car which invented by the scientist.
③ She has a pet dog naming "Bow".
④ These are the books printed in the city of Paju last year.
⑤ Some politicians inviting to the meeting didn't come.

[12~13] 다음 빈칸 (A)~(C)에 들어갈 말이 바르게 짝지어진 것은?

12
> • Vicky received a letter ___(A)___ in French.
> • The man ___(B)___ the guitar in the band looked happy.
> • The boy ___(C)___ his bicycle is Charlie.

	(A)	(B)	(C)
①	written	playing	fixing
②	writing	playing	fixing
③	writing	played	fixed
④	written	playing	fixed
⑤	written	played	fixing

13
> • Mina runs as ___(A)___ as her brother.
> • The volleyball players jump as ___(B)___ as deer.
> • The steak is as ___(C)___ as a pizza.

	(A)	(B)	(C)
①	fast	high	big
②	fast	highly	big
③	faster	high	bigger
④	faster	higher	bigger
⑤	fastest	higher	biggest

14 다음 우리말을 영어로 옮긴 문장들 중 어법상 어색한 것을 고르시오.

① Peter는 TV를 켜 둔 채로 잠이 들었다.
　→ Peter fell asleep with the TV on.
② Amy는 다리를 꼰 채로 책을 읽었다.
　→ Amy read a book with her legs crossing.
③ 선생님은 팔짱을 낀 채로 학생들이 그림 그리는 모습을 쳐다보았다.
　→ The teacher saw his students drawing pictures with his arms folded.
④ 그 가수는 눈을 감은 채로 피아노를 연주하며 부드럽게 노래를 불렀다.
　→ The singer sang softly while playing the piano with her eyes closed.
⑤ Bill의 친구들은 옷이 땀으로 젖은 채로 교실로 뛰어 들어왔다.
　→ Bill's friends ran into the classroom with their clothes wet with sweat.

15 다음 두 문장을 분사를 이용하여 한 문장으로 만들 때, 빈칸에 적절한 단어를 써 넣으시오.

> • The card is for Mike.
> • Susan wrote the card.

➡ The card _____ _____ _____ _____ _____ Mike.

16 다음 밑줄 친 부분의 쓰임이 나머지와 다른 것은?

① The actor was <u>playing</u> an evil character in the movie.

② The family <u>eating</u> fast food every day have difficulty running.

③ The students <u>studying</u> together for the final exam will get good grades.

④ The dogs <u>protecting</u> their puppies were not moving at all.

⑤ My uncle was busy <u>finishing</u> his project through the summer.

17 다음 중 어법상 <u>어색한</u> 것을 고르시오.

① Mary's nose is as long as Kevin's.

② The toy train his mom bought for David wasn't so strong as the toy doll.

③ Sally is as tall and slim as the tree near the playground.

④ The light is much faster than any other thing in the world.

⑤ The books written by Shakespeare are not so more valuable as his plays.

18 다음 중 밑줄 친 단어의 바로 앞에 '주격 관계대명사+be동사'가 생략되어 있다고 볼 수 <u>없는</u> 것을 <u>모두</u> 고르면?

① Don't feed the animals <u>approaching</u> the visitors in the zoo.

② There weren't any brave mice to wake up the <u>sleeping</u> cat.

③ What is the language <u>spoken</u> in Ivory Coast?

④ The toys <u>made</u> in China are quite dangerous to play with.

⑤ Bob was so <u>interested</u> in the ancient architecture that he majored in history.

⑥ The trucks <u>parked</u> in the parking lot should be moved away.

⑦ The professor's lecture was <u>boring</u> rather than interesting.

[19~20] 다음 글을 읽고 물음에 답하시오.

Runners can choose a pacer depending on their target finish time. For example, if a runner wants to finish the race in four hours, the runner will follow the four-hour pacer. Since the pacer keeps track of the time, the runner can achieve his or her goal ⓐ<u>of</u> finishing the marathon in a particular time more easily. In short, pacers run but they don't run to win. ⓑ<u>They run for themselves.</u>

19 위 글의 밑줄 친 ⓐof와 문법적 쓰임이 같은 것을 고르시오.

① He lives in the north <u>of</u> Seoul.

② Look at the plate made <u>of</u> wood.

③ There is no possibility <u>of</u> my winning the game.

④ His poem expresses his love <u>of</u> nature.

⑤ He is a man <u>of</u> ability.

20 위 글의 밑줄 친 ⓑ에서 흐름상 <u>어색한</u> 부분을 찾아 고치시오.

_____ ➡ _____ 또는 _____

[21~23] 다음 글을 읽고 물음에 답하시오.

Pit Crews in Car Racing

You may only see the car and the driver during most car races, but there is a team behind the driver. This team is called a pit crew. A pit is a place on the side of the race track, and drivers stop there several times during a race. The main job of the pit crew is to check the car and change the tires.

Changing the tires is especially important because the tires wear out easily in a high speed race.

A pit stop can be as short as 2 seconds, and there are as many as 20 members on a crew. ___ⓐ___, the pit crew has to work in perfect harmony. The driver may get all the attention, but ⓑas people say, "Races are won in the pits."

21 위 글의 빈칸 ⓐ에 들어갈 알맞은 말을 고르시오.

① However   ② Nonetheless

③ That is   ④ Alternatively

⑤ Therefore

22 위 글의 밑줄 친 ⓑas와 같은 의미로 쓰인 것을 고르시오.

① As we go up higher, the air grows colder.

② As rust eats iron, so care eats the heart.

③ This box can be used as a table.

④ As it was getting dark, we soon turned back.

⑤ This is twice as large as that.

23 According to the passage, which is NOT true?

① A pit crew is a team behind the driver.

② A place on the side of the race track is called a pit.

③ The main job of the pit crew is checking the car and changing the tires.

④ A pit stop can be as short as 2 minutes, and there are as many as 20 members on a crew.

⑤ The pit crew has to work perfectly harmoniously.

[24~25] 다음 글을 읽고 물음에 답하시오.

Sherpas in Mountain Climbing

The word *Sherpa* comes from the Sherpa tribe, which lives in the eastern part of Nepal. Sherpas have good climbing skills and know ①their way around the mountains well. ② They also have little difficulty breathing high up in the mountains. Therefore, mountain climbers started to hire Sherpas to help ③them climb Mount Everest.

Sherpas lead mountain climbers to the top of the mountain. ④They support climbers in many ways. For example, ⑤they put up tents and carry climbers' bags. Sherpas are often called the invisible people of Mount Everest because people often see a picture of only the climbers at the top of the mountain.

24 밑줄 친 ①~⑤ 중에서 가리키는 대상이 나머지 넷과 다른 것은?

①   ②   ③   ④   ⑤

25 위 글의 주제로 알맞은 것을 고르시오.

① the origin of the word *Sherpa*

② the role of Sherpas in mountain climbing

③ the reason Sherpas have good climbing skills

④ the visible people of Mount Everest

⑤ the climbers at the top of the mountain

01 출제율 95%

다음 중 짝지어진 단어의 관계가 나머지와 <u>다른</u> 것은?

① perfect – imperfect
② allow – permit
③ complete – incomplete
④ hire – fire
⑤ full – empty

02 출제율 100%

밑줄 친 부분의 의미로 알맞지 <u>않은</u> 것은?

① In a race, a guide runner runs with a blind runner and helps him or her <u>stay on the track</u>. (트랙에 머무르다)
② How do I <u>sign up for</u> your milage program? (~에 등록하다)
③ It's <u>not at all</u> easy to deal with customers. (결코 ~ 아닌)
④ It was what she wanted <u>most of all</u>. (대부분)
⑤ She'd rather die than <u>give a speech</u>. (연설하다)

03 출제율 95%

다음 주어진 우리말에 맞게 빈칸을 채우시오. (주어진 철자로 시작할 것)

(1) Tom은 사서로 고용되었다.
➡ Tom was h_____ as a librarian.
(2) 그것이 끝나자 우리는 모두 안도의 한숨을 내쉬었다.
➡ We all breathed a sigh of relief when it was o_____.
(3) 우리는 그의 연설에 집중해야 한다.
➡ We have to pay a_____ to his speech.

04 출제율 90%

다음 빈칸에 공통으로 들어갈 알맞은 말을 쓰시오.

- He's able to take care _____ himself.
- Bank statements help you keep track _____ where your money is going.

[05~06] 다음 대화를 읽고 물음에 답하시오.

W: Hello. May I help you?
B: Yes, I came to register for a soccer class.
W: I see. How often do you want to take classes?
B: I want to take classes twice a week. I'd like to take classes on weekends.
W: Then, I suggest that you take the Beginner 1 class. This class meets on Saturdays and Sundays.
B: (A)That sounds good.

05 출제율 100%

위 대화를 읽고 대답할 수 <u>없는</u> 질문을 고르시오.

① When did the boy make a visit to the place?
② How often does the boy want to take a soccer class?
③ When does the boy want to take a soccer class?
④ When does the Beginner 1 class meet?
⑤ What class does the woman suggest that the boy take?

06 출제율 90%

위 대화의 밑줄 친 (A)That이 가리키는 것을 25자 내외의 우리말로 쓰시오.

➡ _____

[07~09] 다음 대화를 읽고 물음에 답하시오.

> B: Suji, how often do you take bowling lessons?
> G: Twice a week. (①) I'm just a beginner. (②) I heard you're very good.
> B: Well, I love bowling. (③) Hmm. Your bowling ball looks heavy for you. (④)
> G: OK. (⑤) I'll look for a lighter (a)one, then.

출제율 100%

07 (①)~(⑤) 중 주어진 문장이 들어갈 곳은?

> I suggest you use a lighter ball.

①   ②   ③   ④   ⑤

출제율 90%

08 Why does the boy suggest that Suji use a lighter ball? Answer in English with a full sentence.

➡ _____

출제율 95%

09 위 대화의 밑줄 친 (a)one이 가리키는 것을 찾아 쓰시오.

➡ _____

출제율 100%

10 다음 그림을 보고, 괄호 안의 단어를 적절한 분사로 바꿔 빈칸을 채우시오.

➡ Jeffrey was _____(embarrass) with the _____(break) bicycle as he didn't know how to fix it.

출제율 100%

11 다음 밑줄 친 부분 중 어법상 어색한 것을 고르시오.

① My friend's husband is <u>as busy as</u> a honeybee.
② The comedian could speak Japanese <u>as fluently</u> as a native.
③ The Spanish language spoken in most of Latin America is not <u>as hardly as</u> Korean.
④ All the students in class H act <u>as nicely as</u> the nobles.
⑤ The dress that my daughter wore tonight looked <u>as lovely as</u> the queen's.

출제율 100%

12 다음 중 밑줄 친 부분의 성격이 나머지 넷과 <u>다른</u> 것은?

① Volunteers are picking up the trashes <u>fallen</u> on the beach.
② Do you know the girl <u>smiling</u> at me?
③ A lot of visitors come to see Monet's pictures <u>displayed</u> in the museum.
④ She couldn't help <u>being</u> scared of the news that the war broke out.
⑤ I received a huge box <u>filled</u> with the lego bricks from my uncle.

출제율 95%

13 다음 표에 대해 설명하는 각 문장들 중 옳지 <u>않은</u> 것은?

	Mary	Paul	Jim	Steve	Yuna
Age	16	14	16	16	15

① Mary is as old as Steve.
② Paul is not as old as Yuna.
③ Jim isn't as old as Paul.
④ Steve is not older than Mary.
⑤ Yuna isn't as old as Steve.

[14~16] 다음 글을 읽고 물음에 답하시오.

Pacers in a Marathon

Pacers run with other runners and lead them in a marathon. ⓐPacers are experiencing runners, and their job is to help other runners manage their race better. There can be several pacers in a race. Each pacer runs at different speeds and finishes the race in different times. Pacers usually have flags or balloons showing their finish time.

Runners can choose a pacer depending on their target finish time. For example, if a runner wants to finish the race in four hours, the runner will follow the four-hour pacer. Since the pacer keeps track of the time, the runner can achieve his or her goal of finishing the marathon in a particular time more easily. ⓑIn short, pacers run but they don't run to win. They run for others.

출제율 95%

14 위 글의 밑줄 친 ⓐ에서 어법상 틀린 부분을 찾아 고치시오.

_____ ➡ _____

출제율 90%

15 위 글의 밑줄 친 ⓑIn short와 바꿔 쓸 수 없는 말을 고르시오. (2개)

① In brief
② In addition
③ To put it shortly
④ In a word
⑤ In other words

출제율 100%

16 위 글을 읽고 알 수 없는 것을 고르시오.

① What do pacers do?
② At first, how do pacers decide their running speed?
③ What do pacers usually have?
④ How can runners choose a pacer?
⑤ How can the runner achieve his or her goal of finishing the marathon in a particular time more easily?

[17~19] 다음 글을 읽고 물음에 답하시오.

Pit Crews in Car Racing

You may only see the car and the driver during most car races, but there is a team behind the driver. This team is called a pit crew. A pit is a place on the side of the race track, and drivers stop there several times during a race. The main job of the pit crew is to check the car and change the tires. Changing the tires is especially important because the tires wear out easily in a high speed race.

A pit stop can be as short as 2 seconds, and there are as many as 20 members ___ⓐ___ a crew. Therefore, the pit crew has to work ___ⓑ___ perfect harmony. The driver may get all the attention, but as people say, "Races are won in the pits."

출제율 90%

17 위 글의 빈칸 ⓐ와 ⓑ에 들어갈 전치사가 바르게 짝지어진 것은?

	ⓐ	ⓑ			ⓐ	ⓑ
①	on	to		②	at	with
③	in	to		④	on	in
⑤	at	in				

출제율 95%

18 다음 중 위 글의 pit crew에 대한 설명을 바르게 하지 못한 사람을 고르시오.

① 수희: 우리는 그들을 대부분의 자동차 경주에서 흔히 볼 수 있어.
② 혜민: 그들은 경주 트랙의 한쪽에 있는 공간인 피트에서 일해.

③ 영재: 그들은 주로 자동차를 점검하고 타이어를 교체해.

④ 진규: 한 팀에 많게는 20명에 이르는 구성원이 있어.

⑤ 민성: 그들은 완벽한 조화를 이루며 일해야 해.

19 위 글의 제목으로 알맞은 것을 고르시오.

① What Do You Need to Be a Pit Crew?
② Where Is a Pit?
③ What Does a Pit Crew Mainly Do?
④ Why Do Drivers Stop at a Pit during a Race?
⑤ How Many Members Are There in a Pit Crew?

[20~21] 다음 글을 읽고 물음에 답하시오.

Sherpas in Mountain Climbing

The word *Sherpa* comes from the Sherpa tribe, which lives in the eastern part of Nepal. (①) They also have little difficulty breathing high up in the mountains. (②) Therefore, mountain climbers started to hire Sherpas to help them climb Mount Everest. (③)

Sherpas lead mountain climbers to the top of the mountain. (④) They support climbers in many ways. (⑤) For example, they put up tents and carry climbers' bags. Sherpas are often called the invisible people of Mount Everest because people often see a picture of only the climbers at the top of the mountain.

20 주어진 영영풀이에 해당하는 단어를 본문에서 찾아 쓰시오.

a group of people of the same race, language, and customs

➡ _____

21 위 글의 흐름으로 보아, 주어진 문장이 들어가기에 가장 적절한 곳은?

Sherpas have good climbing skills and know their way around the mountains well.

①　　②　　③　　④　　⑤

[22~24] 다음 글을 읽고 물음에 답하시오.

1. In swimming, a tapper uses a long pole to help a blind swimmer swim.
2. In a race, a guide runner runs with a blind runner and helps ⓐhim or her stay on the track.
3. In blind football, a shooting assistant tells ⓑhis or her team players ⓒwhich direction to shoot.

22 위 글의 밑줄 친 ⓐhim or her와 ⓑhis or her가 가리키는 것을 각각 본문에서 찾아 쓰시오.

➡ ⓐ _____ ⓑ _____

23 위 글의 밑줄 친 ⓒ를 다음과 같이 바꿔 쓸 때 빈칸에 들어갈 알맞은 말을 두 단어로 쓰시오.

➡ which direction _____ _____ shoot

24 본문의 내용을 참조하여 다음 빈칸 (A)~(C)에 알맞은 단어를 쓰시오.

(A) _____ _____ , (B) _____ _____ _____ , and (C) _____ _____ _____ are the assistants in the Paralympic Games.

[01~03] 다음 대화를 읽고 물음에 답하시오.

W: Hello. Welcome to Sports World. May I help you?

B: Yes, I came to register for a swimming class.

W: Is this your first time taking swimming lessons?

B: Yes, it is. I don't know how to swim at all.

W: I see. How often do you want to take classes?

B: I want to take classes twice a week. I'd like to take classes on weekdays and not on weekends.

W: Then, I suggest that you take the Beginner 2 class. This class meets on Tuesdays and Thursdays.

B: That sounds good. I'd like to sign up for that class. How big is the class?

W: The class has a limit of 10 people.

B: That's perfect.

01 How come the woman suggests the boy take the Beginner 2 class? Use the word, 'because'. (11 words)

➡ _____

_____

02 How often does the boy want to take the swimming lessons?

➡ _____

03 On which days will the boy take the swimming classes?

➡ _____

_____

04 다음 우리말과 같은 뜻이 되도록 주어진 단어들을 알맞게 배열하시오.

(1) 인도의 인구 성장률은 중국의 그것만큼 빠르다. (as, China, rate, population, as, is, of, fast, growth, that, India's)

➡ _____

_____

(2) 중국 정부는 일본 정치 지도자들만큼이나 부끄러움을 모른다. (the Japanese, as, is, the Chinese, political, unashamed, government, as, leaders)

➡ _____

_____

05 다음 중 밑줄 친 부분을 어법에 맞게 고치고, 고친 단어의 종류, 즉 품사가 다른 하나를 찾아 그 이유를 설명하시오.

ⓐ Suji burned her finger with boil water.

ⓑ I read aloud some poems write by Yun Dongju.

ⓒ The train leave for New York is cancelled because of the disease.

ⓓ Sandra drew a beautiful mountain cover with snow.

ⓔ The baby cry on the bed was certainly feeling hungry.

ⓕ You need to buy a sleep bag for camping with us.

ⓖ Please listen to the fantastic music compose by Ludwig Beethoven.

➡ ⓐ _____ ⓑ _____ ⓒ _____

ⓓ _____ ⓔ _____ ⓕ _____

ⓖ _____

이유: _____

[06~08] 다음 글을 읽고 물음에 답하시오.

Pacers in a Marathon

Each (A)[pacer runs / pacers run] at different speeds and finishes the race in different times. Pacers usually have flags or balloons showing their finish time.

Runners can choose a pacer depending on their target finish time. For example, if a runner wants to finish the race in (B)[four hours / four-hour], the runner will follow the (C)[four hours / four-hour] pacer. Since the pacer keeps track of the time, ⓐ선수는 특정 시간에 마라톤을 완주하려는 자신의 목표를 더 쉽게 달성할 수 있다. In short, pacers run but they don't run to win. They run for others.

06 위 글의 괄호 (A)~(C)에서 어법상 알맞은 낱말을 골라 쓰시오.

➡ (A) _____ (B) _____
(C) _____

07 위 글의 밑줄 친 ⓐ의 우리말에 맞게 한 단어를 보충하여, 주어진 어휘를 알맞게 배열하시오.

> finishing the marathon / more easily / the runner / his or her goal / in a particular time / can achieve

➡ _____
_____

08 What is a pacer's role in a marathon? Answer in English with a full sentence. (10 words)

➡ _____
_____

[09~11] 다음 글을 읽고 물음에 답하시오.

Pit Crews in Car Racing

You may only see the car and the driver during most car races, but there is a team behind the driver. This team ___ⓐ___ a pit crew. A pit is a place on the side of the race track, and drivers stop there several times during a race. The main job of the pit crew is to check the car and change the tires. ⓑ Changing the tires are especially important because the tires wear out easily in a high speed race.

A pit stop can be as short as 2 seconds, and there are as many as 20 members on a crew. Therefore, the pit crew has to work in perfect harmony. The driver may get all the attention, but as people say, "Races are won in the pits."

09 위 글의 빈칸 ⓐ에 call을 알맞은 형태로 쓰시오.

➡ _____

10 위 글의 밑줄 친 ⓑ에서 어법상 틀린 부분을 찾아 고치시오.

_____ ➡ _____

11 다음 빈칸 (A)와 (B)에 알맞은 단어를 넣어 'pit'에 대한 소개를 완성하시오.

> A pit is a place on (A)_____ _____ of the race track where drivers stop several times during (B)_____ _____ to check the car and change the tires.

01 주어진 표현을 이용하여 〈보기〉와 같이 다음 대화의 빈칸에 알맞은 말을 쓰시오.

> A: How _____? 　　B: I _____.

> ┤ 보기 ├
> A: How often do you have breakfast? 　　B: I have breakfast every day.

> have breakfast / play computer games / eat late at night / take swimming classes
> every day / three times a week / five times a week / twice a week

02 다음 학생들의 체력 측정 기록표를 보고, as ~ as를 사용하여, 내용에 맞게 자유롭게 영작하시오.

	Sein	Minju	Seohyun	Bona	Ahrin
100m record (seconds)	18	19	21	18	20
standing jump (cm)	44	36	34	36	42
ball throwing (m)	19	21	27	16	27

(1) _____

(2) _____

03 다음 내용을 바탕으로 스포츠 분야의 숨은 조력자인 치어리더에 관한 설명문을 쓰시오.

> **Who:** cheerleaders in football games
> **What they do:**
> • cheer at a game
> • create team spirit
>
> **What they need to be or do:**
> • be fit and strong
> • be good at jumping and dancing
> • encourage their team and fans

> **Cheerleaders in Football Games**
> Although people usually don't think that cheerleaders are a part of a football team, they play an important role in a football game. By (A)_____ at a game, they create (B)_____. They also encourage (C)_____. To do their job well, cheerleaders need to be (D)_____. They also need to be good at (E)_____.

단원별 모의고사

01 다음 짝지어진 단어의 관계가 같도록 빈칸에 알맞은 말을 쓰시오. (주어진 철자로 시작할 것)

> suggest – propose : employ – _____

[02~03] 주어진 영어 설명에 알맞은 어휘를 빈칸에 쓰시오.

02
> I can hardly _____ in this cave.

> <영어 설명> to take air into your body and let it out again

➡ _____

03
> We can learn the culture of the Masai _____ in this class.

> <영어 설명> a group of people who have their own language and ways of living

➡ _____

04 다음 빈칸에 알맞은 말로 짝지어진 것을 고르시오.

> • We do not _____ smoking in the hall.
> • I _____ that we go out to eat.

① register – promote
② register – suggest
③ allow – promote
④ allow – suggest
⑤ permit – manage

05 다음 우리말을 주어진 어휘를 이용하여 영작하시오.

(1) 내 부츠가 닳기 시작한다. (boots, wear, beginning)

➡ _____

(2) 교통 체증이 있어서 우리는 지하철을 타야 한다. (heavy traffic, there, therefore, should, take)

➡ _____
_____

(3) 특별히 생각해 둔 식당이 있나요? (have, particular, in mind)

➡ _____

[06~07] 다음 대화를 읽고 물음에 답하시오.

B: Mina, how ⓐoften do you swim?
G: I swim every day.
B: Can I go ⓑto swim with you this afternoon?
G: Sure, but (a)수영 모자를 챙기는 것을 제안해.(bring, a swimming cap) ⓒWithout a ⓓ swimming cap, you ⓔaren't allowed in the pool.

06 위 대화의 밑줄 친 우리말 (a)에 맞게 주어진 어휘를 이용하여 영작하시오. (7 words)

➡ _____

07 밑줄 친 ⓐ~ⓔ 중 어색한 것은?

① ⓐ   ② ⓑ   ③ ⓒ   ④ ⓓ   ⑤ ⓔ

[08~09] 다음 대화를 읽고 물음에 답하시오.

B: Mina, how often do you come here to run?
G: Every day.
B: Can I run with you today?
G: Sure, but _____(A)_____. (wear, running, should, shoes) Your shoes aren't good for running.

08 위 대화의 빈칸 (A)에 알맞은 말을 주어진 어휘를 이용하여 8 단어로 쓰시오.

➡ _____

09 Why does Mina come here every day?

➡ _____

[10~12] 다음 대화를 읽고 물음에 답하시오.

W: Hello. Welcome to Sports World. May I help you?
B: Yes, I came to register for a swimming class.
W: Is this your first time taking swimming lessons?
B: Yes, it is. I don't know _____(A)_____ at all.
W: I see. How often do you want to take classes?
B: I want to take classes twice a week. I'd like to take classes on weekdays and not on weekends.
W: Then, I suggest that you take the Beginner 2 class. This class meets on Tuesdays and Thursdays.
B: That sounds good. I'd like to sign up for that class. How big is the class?
W: The class has a ___(B)___ of 10 people.
B: That's perfect.

10 위 대화의 빈칸 (A)에 'how I should swim'과 같은 뜻의 말을 3 단어로 쓰시오.

➡ _____

11 위 대화의 빈칸 (B)에 알맞은 것을 고르시오.

① limit   ② harmony
③ circumstance   ④ boundary
⑤ member

12 위 대화의 내용과 일치하지 <u>않는</u> 것은?

① 소년은 수영 수업을 등록하려고 왔다.
② 소년은 수영 수업을 받는 것이 이번이 처음이다.
③ 소년은 수영하는 법을 전혀 알지 못한다.
④ 소년은 주말에 수업을 듣고 싶어 한다.
⑤ 초급 2반의 제한 인원은 열 명이다.

13 다음 그림을 보고, 괄호 안에 주어진 단어를 활용하여 글자 수 조건에 맞게 영작하시오.

• Reporter: Is there anything interesting about your job?
• Pacer: (A) Pacers _____
_____. (페이서들은 자신들의 출발 시간을 나타내는 깃발이나 풍선을 가지고 있어요.) (flags, show, start, balloons, or, 8 단어)
• Pit Crew: (B) The pit crew has to work in perfect harmony _____
_____. (피트에서의 정지는 짧게는 2분 정도이기 때문에, 피트 크루는 완벽한 조화를 이루며 일해야 합니다.) (can, short, as, since, a pit stop, 11 단어)

14 다음 밑줄 친 부분 중 어법상 <u>어색한</u> 것을 고르시오.

① Susan was <u>interested</u> in Egypt.
② I know the great baseball player <u>called</u> Lion King.
③ My mom likes to listen to the sound of rain <u>falling</u> onto the roof.
④ I bought much stationery <u>included</u> paper, pencils, erasers, and so on.
⑤ There were <u>broken</u> pieces of the glass.

15 다음 우리말과 일치하도록 괄호 안의 단어를 바르게 배열하시오.

(1) 내 필통은 Mina의 것만큼 가볍다. (case, light, as, pencil, is, Mina's, as, my).

➡ _____

(2) Isabelle은 John만큼 키가 크지만, 그녀의 몸무게는 그만큼 되지 않는다. (John, Isabelle, as, is, isn't, as, so, tall, heavy, but, he, she, as).

➡ _____

16 다음 문장의 빈칸을 괄호 안의 단어를 사용하여 어법에 맞게 쓸 때, 〈보기〉의 빈칸에 들어갈 말과 쓰임이 <u>다른</u> 것을 <u>모두</u> 고르면?

┌─ 보기 ┐

My grandfather has a scar _____ (make) at the war field on his forehead.

① Look at the statue _____ (place) in front of the building.
② Mom cleared the pieces of the dishes _____ (break) by my mistake.
③ Joshua wants to buy some ice boxes _____ (design) to keep beer bottles cold.
④ The CEO of the company cancelled the meeting _____ (schedule) tomorrow.
⑤ A lot of volunteers gathered to help the elderly _____ (live) alone.

17 다음 우리말을 괄호 안에 주어진 단어를 알맞게 배열하여 영작하시오. (동사는 어법에 맞게 형태 변화 가능)

엄마는 '백주부'라고 불리는 남자만큼 맛있는 요리를 만드신다.
(as, make, call, as, dishes, a man, mom, delicious, 'Housewife Baek')

➡ _____

18 다음 중 밑줄 친 단어의 쓰임이 어법상 <u>어색한</u> 것은?

① Who is that girl <u>wearing</u> a colorful evening dress?
② Jane can recite the whole poem <u>written</u> by Yoon Dongju.
③ You can see laundries <u>hanging</u> on the washing lines on sunny days.
④ My father has collected many old coins <u>making</u> in ancient days.
⑤ Please remember the legendary singer <u>called</u> 'Mawang, the Devil King'.

[19~20] 다음 글을 읽고 물음에 답하시오.

Pacers in a Marathon

Runners can choose a pacer depending on their target finish time. For example, if a runner wants to finish the race in four hours, the runner will follow the four-hour pacer. Since the pacer ⓐ _____ the time, the runner can achieve his or her goal of finishing the marathon in a particular time more easily. In short, pacers run but they don't run ⓑto win. They run for others.

19 위 글의 빈칸 ⓐ에 들어갈 알맞은 말을 고르시오.

① catches up with
② puts up with
③ comes up with
④ keeps track of
⑤ makes up for

20
아래 〈보기〉에서 위 글의 밑줄 친 ⓑto win과 to부정사의 용법이 <u>다른</u> 것의 개수를 고르시오.

┌─ 보기 ─────────────────────┐
① My dream is <u>to win</u> a marathon.

② She practiced hard every day <u>to win</u> a marathon.

③ The best way <u>to win</u> a marathon is to practice running every day.

④ I really want <u>to win</u> a marathon.

⑤ She is strong enough <u>to win</u> a marathon.
└────────────────────────────┘

① 1개　② 2개　③ 3개　④ 4개　⑤ 5개

[21~23] 다음 글을 읽고 물음에 답하시오.

Pit Crews in Car Racing

You may only see the car and the driver during most car races, but there is a team behind the driver. (①) This team is called a pit crew. (②) A pit is a place on the side of the race track, and drivers stop there several times during a race. (③) Changing the tires is especially important because the tires wear out easily in a high speed race. (④)

A pit stop can be as short as 2 seconds, and there are as many as 20 members on a crew. (⑤) Therefore, the pit crew has to work in perfect harmony. ⓐThe driver may get all the attention, but as people say, "Races win in the pits."

21
위 글의 흐름으로 보아, 주어진 문장이 들어가기에 가장 적절한 곳은?

┌────────────────────────────┐
The main job of the pit crew is to check the car and change the tires.
└────────────────────────────┘

①　　②　　③　　④　　⑤

22
위 글의 밑줄 친 ⓐ에서 어법상 틀린 부분을 찾아 고치시오.

_____ ➡ _____

23
본문의 내용과 일치하도록 다음 빈칸 (A)와 (B)에 알맞은 단어를 쓰시오.

┌────────────────────────────┐
During most car races, the driver may get all (A)_____ _____, but a team called a (B)_____ _____ plays an important role helping the driver win the race behind the driver.
└────────────────────────────┘

[24~26] 다음 글을 읽고 물음에 답하시오.

Sherpas in Mountain Climbing

The word *Sherpa* comes from the Sherpa tribe, which lives in the eastern part of Nepal. Sherpas have good climbing skills and know their way around the mountains well. They also have little difficulty breathing high up in the mountains. ⓐ , mountain climbers started to hire Sherpas to help them climb Mount Everest.

Sherpas lead mountain climbers to the top of the mountain. They support climbers in many ways. ⓑ , they put up tents and carry climbers' bags. Sherpas are often called the invisible people of Mount Everest ⓒ왜냐하면 사람들이 산 정상에서 등산가들만 찍힌 사진을 자주 보기 때문이다.

24
위 글의 빈칸 ⓐ와 ⓑ에 들어갈 알맞은 말을 고르시오.

① Therefore – For example

② In other words – By contrast

③ In addition – Thus

④ Whereas – Moreover

⑤ For example – Likewise

25 위 글의 밑줄 친 ⓒ의 우리말에 맞게 주어진 어휘를 이용하여 16 단어로 영작하시오.

because, often, of, at the top of

➡ _____

_____

26 According to the passage, which is NOT true?

① The word *Sherpa* is named after the Sherpa tribe.

② The Sherpa tribe lives in the eastern part of Nepal.

③ Sherpas know their way around the mountains well.

④ It's not easy for Sherpas to breathe high up in the mountains.

⑤ Sherpas put up tents and carry climbers' bags.

[27~29] 다음 글을 읽고 물음에 답하시오.

Cheerleaders in Football Games

(A)[Although / As] people usually don't think that cheerleaders are a part of a football team, they play an important role in a football game. By cheering at a game, they create team spirit. They also encourage their team and fans. To do their job well, cheerleaders need to be fit and strong. They also need to be good (B) [at / for] jumping and dancing. ⓐMost of all, they need to work as (C)[hard / hardly] as the players.

27 위 글의 괄호 (A)~(C)에서 문맥상 알맞은 낱말을 골라 쓰시오.

➡ (A) _____ (B) _____ (C) _____

28 위 글의 밑줄 친 ⓐMost of all과 바꿔 쓸 수 있는 말을 모두 고르시오.

① At first   ② First of all

③ After all   ④ Above all

⑤ More than anything else

29 다음 중 '미식축구 경기에서의 치어리더'에 대한 설명으로 옳지 않은 것을 고르시오.

① 공동체 정신을 만들어낸다.

② 팀과 팬들을 격려한다.

③ 몸을 건강하게 관리하고 강해야 한다.

④ 점프하는 것과 노래 부르는 것을 잘해야 한다.

⑤ 선수들만큼이나 열심히 일해야 한다.

MEMO

Lesson

6

Stories for All Time

의사소통 기능

- 축하 · 유감 표현하기
  Congratulations on winning the gold medal. /
  I'm sorry to hear that.

- 감정 표현하기
  A: What's up?
  B: My smartphone is broken. I'm very upset.

언어 형식

- 과거완료
  People asked him where he **had got** the
  furniture.

- 관계대명사 what
  The table was **what** every dealer dreamed of.

Key Words

- **accept**[əksépt] 동 받아들이다
- **add**[æd] 동 더하다
- **announcement**[ənáunsmənt] 명 발표
- **antique**[æntíːk] 명 골동품
- **attach**[ətǽtʃ] 동 붙이다, 첨부하다
- **bored**[bɔːrd] 형 지루한
- **bring**[briŋ] 동 가지고 오다
- **broken**[bróukən] 형 고장 난
- **charge**[tʃɑːrdʒ] 동 (금액을) 청구하다
- **cheaply**[tʃíːpli] 부 싸게
- **class president** 반장
- **collection**[kəlékʃən] 명 수집
- **dealer**[díːlər] 명 판매상, 중개인
- **disappointed**[dìsəpɔ́intid] 형 실망한
- **eighteenth-century** 명 18세기 형 18세기의
- **elect**[ilékt] 동 선출하다
- **endless**[éndlis] 형 끝없는
- **exactly**[igzǽktli] 부 정확하게
- **excited**[iksáitid] 형 흥분한
- **favor**[féivər] 명 호의
- **favorite**[féivərit] 형 좋아하는
- **flu**[fluː] 명 독감
- **furniture**[fə́ːrnitʃər] 명 가구
- **hug**[hʌg] 동 끌어안다, 포옹하다
- **luckily**[lʌ́kili] 부 다행스럽게

- **offer**[ɔ́ːfər] 명 제의, 제안
- **order**[ɔ́ːrdər] 동 주문하다, 지시하다, 명령하다
- **owner**[óunər] 명 주인
- **pay**[pei] 동 지불하다
- **play**[plei] 명 연극
- **pound**[paund] 명 파운드 (영국의 화폐 단위)
- **practice**[prǽktis] 명 연습
- **price**[prais] 명 가격
- **priceless**[práislis] 형 값을 매길 수 없는, 대단히 귀중한
- **prize**[praiz] 명 상
- **receive**[risíːv] 동 받다
- **recycle**[riːsáikl] 동 재활용하다
- **reproduction**[riprədʌ́kʃən] 명 복제품
- **role**[roul] 명 역할, 배역
- **saw**[sɔː] 명 톱
- **shocked**[ʃɑkt] 형 충격 받은
- **sorry**[sɑ́ri] 형 유감스러운
- **speech contest** 말하기 대회
- **tightly**[táitli] 부 단단하게, 꽉
- **unfortunately**[ʌnfɔ́ːrtʃənətli] 부 불행하게도
- **upset**[ʌ́pset] 형 속이 상한, 불쾌한
- **while**[hwail] 접 ～하는 동안
- **worth**[wəːrθ] 명 가치 형 ～의 가치가 있는
- **yet**[jet] 부 아직

Key Expressions

- **be known for ～** ～로 유명하다
- **be proud of ～** ～을 자랑스러워하다
- **cannot help -ing** ～하지 않을 수 없다
- **congratulations on ～** ～에 대하여 축하하다
- **cut off ～** ～을 잘라내다
- **do one's best** 최선을 다하다
- **dream of ～** ～에 대하여 꿈꾸다
- **fall over** 넘어지다

- **look for ～** ～을 찾다
- **on one's way** ～로 가는 길에
- **remember -ing** ～한 것을 기억하다
- **so ～ that ...** 너무 ～해서 …하다
- **take a look** 살펴보다
- **take advantage of ～** ～을 이용하다
- **take out** 꺼내다
- **with a straight face** 정색하며, 무표정한 얼굴로

Word Power

※ 서로 비슷한 뜻을 가진 어휘

- □ **broken** 고장 난 : **damaged** 손상된
- □ **dealer** 판매상, 중개인 : **trader** 거래자
- □ **endless** 끝없는 : **infinite** 무한한
- □ **offer** 제안 : **proposal** 제안
- □ **priceless** 값을 매길 수 없는 : **invaluable** 매우 귀중한

- □ **cheaply** 싸게 : **inexpensively** 싸게
- □ **disappointed** 실망한 : **dissatisfied** 불만스러운
- □ **exactly** 정확하게 : **precisely** 정확하게
- □ **play** 연극 : **drama** 드라마
- □ **role** 역할, 배역 : **part** 역할

※ 서로 반대의 뜻을 가진 어휘

- □ **accept** 받아들이다 ↔ **reject** 거절하다
- □ **attach** 덧붙이다 ↔ **detach** 떼어내다
- □ **cheaply** 싸게 ↔ **expensively** 비싸게
- □ **favorite** 좋아하는 ↔ **hated** 싫어하는
- □ **priceless** 값을 매길 수 없는 ↔ **valueless** 가치 없는

- □ **add** 더하다 ↔ **subtract** 빼다
- □ **bored** 지루한 ↔ **excited** 흥미진진한
- □ **disappointed** 실망한 ↔ **satisfied** 만족한
- □ **luckily** 다행스럽게 ↔ **unluckily** 불행하게
- □ **tightly** 단단하게, 꽉 ↔ **loosely** 느슨하게

※ 접두사 re — re+동사

- □ **re + produce → reproduce** 복제하다, 번식하다
- □ **re + cycle → recycle** 재활용하다
- □ **re + use → reuse** 다시 이용하다, 재생하다

- □ **re + play → replay** 다시 하다, 재생[재연]하다
- □ **re + view → review** 재검토하다, 회고하다
- □ **re + act → react** 반응하다

※ 접미사 less — 명사+less

- □ **price + less → priceless** 값을 매길 수 없는
- □ **end + less → endless** 끝없는
- □ **harm + less → harmless** 해가 없는
- □ **sleep + less → sleepless** 잠 못 이루는

- □ **count + less → countless** 셀 수 없이 많은
- □ **care + less → careless** 부주의한
- □ **hope + less → hopeless** 절망적인
- □ **speech + less → speechless** 말을 못 하는

English Dictionary

- □ **antique** 골동품
  - → an old object such as a piece of furniture or jewelry that has a high value
  - 높은 가치가 있는 가구나 보석 같은 오래된 물품
- □ **attach** 붙이다
  - → to fasten or join to one thing to another
  - 무엇인가를 다른 것에 고정하거나 결합하다
- □ **charge** (요금을) 청구하다
  - → to ask people to pay a particular amount of money for something
  - 사람들에게 무엇인가에 대한 특정 금액의 돈을 지불하라고 요구하다
- □ **dealer** 판매상
  - → someone who buys and sells a particular product
  - 특정한 상품을 사고파는 사람

- □ **knock** 두드리다
  - → to hit a door with your hand so that someone inside knows you are there 안에 있는 사람이 밖에 누군가가 있다는 것을 알도록 손으로 문을 두드리다
- □ **priceless** 값을 매길 수 없는
  - → extremely valuable 매우 가치가 있는
- □ **reproduction** 복제품
  - → a copy of something such as a picture
  - 그림과 같은 어떤 것을 모사한 것
- □ **saw** 톱
  - → a tool for cutting wood or materials, typically with a long, thin steel blade 전형적으로 길고 얇은 강철 날이 있는 나무나 재료를 자르는 도구

01 다음 짝지어진 단어의 관계가 같도록 빈칸에 알맞은 말은?

broken – damaged : precisely – _____

① exactly   ② cheaply
③ tightly   ④ luckily
⑤ endlessly

서답형

02 주어진 영어 설명에 맞게 문장의 빈칸에 알맞은 말을 쓰시오.

_____ makes perfect, you know.

<영어 설명> doing something regularly in order to be able to do it better

➡ _____

03 밑줄 친 부분의 의미로 알맞지 <u>않은</u> 것은?

① I cannot help falling in love with her. (~하지 않을 수 없다)
② I definitely remember sending the letter. (~할 것을 기억하다)
③ She tried to turn her dream of running her own business into reality. (~에 대한 꿈)
④ Pope Francis was on his way to Mexico for a five-day visit. (~로 가는 길이었다)
⑤ He then said with a straight face, "This table is a reproduction. It's worth only a few pounds." (정색하며)

04 다음 빈칸에 들어갈 가장 알맞은 말을 고르시오.

This picture is a _____ of *Sunflowers* by Van Gogh.

① charge   ② worth
③ product   ④ reproduction
⑤ furniture

05 다음 <보기>의 단어를 사용하여 자연스러운 문장을 만들 수 없는 것은?

┤ 보기 ├
offer   saw   charge   dealer

① You need a powerful _____ to cut through metal.
② The _____ closes at the end of the week.
③ Don't forget to _____ the files.
④ They _____ $100 for the membership.
⑤ Her father bought a truck from a car _____.

06 다음 빈칸에 알맞은 말이 바르게 짝지어진 것을 고르시오.

• She is known _____ her patience.
• Don't forget to take _____ the garbage.

① as – from
② to – on
③ to – out
④ for – on
⑤ for – out

01 다음 영영풀이에 알맞은 어휘를 〈보기〉에서 찾아 쓰시오.

┌── 보기 ──
antique knock attach saw

(1) a tool for cutting wood or materials, typically with a long, thin steel blade
(2) to fasten or join to one thing to another
(3) to hit a door with your hand so that someone inside knows you are there
(4) an old object such as a piece of furniture or jewelry that has a high value

➡ (1) _____ (2) _____ (3) _____

   (4) _____

02 다음 짝지어진 두 단어의 관계가 같도록 빈칸에 알맞은 말을 쓰시오.

(1) add – subtract :
   accept – _____
(2) hopeful – hopeless :
   valueless – _____

03 다음 우리말에 맞도록 빈칸에 알맞은 말을 쓰시오. (철자가 주어진 경우 그 철자로 시작할 것.)

(1) 그 미술관에서 대단히 귀한 미술품 몇 점이 도난당했다.
   → A number of p_____ works of art were stolen from the gallery.
(2) 저는 항상 제 곰 인형을 안고 자요.
   → I always h_____ my teddy bear when I'm in bed.

(3) 사진을 어떻게 스캔해서 이메일에 첨부하나요?
   → How do I scan a photo and _____ it to an email?
(4) 새로 가구를 사는 것은 너무 비용이 많이 드는 것으로 드러날 수도 있다.
   → Buying new _____ may prove too costly.

04 우리말에 맞게 한 단어를 추가하여 주어진 단어를 알맞게 배열하시오.

(1) 잃어버린 개에 대해 미안한 감정을 느끼지 않을 수 없다. (I, dog, can't, lost, sorry, feeling, the, for)
  ➡ _____
    _____

(2) 그 여자는 나의 긴 금발 머리를 자르기 시작했다. (the woman, my, hair, long, cut, began, blond, to)
  ➡ _____
    _____

(3) 꿈이 실현된 것을 축하합니다. (dream, congratulations, true, come, making, a)
  ➡ _____
    _____

(4) 이것은 균형 문제를 야기시킬 수 있으며 사람이 자주 넘어질 수 있습니다. (balance problems, the person, this, cause, fall, may, may, frequently, and)
  ➡ _____
    _____

Conversation

① 축하 · 유감 표현하기

- **Congratulations on winning the gold medal.** 금메달을 딴 것을 축하해.
- **I'm sorry to hear that.** 그 말을 들으니 유감이야.

■ 'Congratulations on ~.'은 '~을 축하합니다.'의 뜻으로 이 경우에는 항상 복수형인 'congratulations'를 쓴다. 'Congratulations.(축하합니다.)'만 가지고도 축하의 의미를 전달하지만 보통 뒤에 전치사 on을 써서 무엇에 대하여 축하하는지 구체적으로 덧붙이는 경우가 많다. 격식을 갖추어 표현할 때는 'Please accept my congratulations on ~.(~에 대하여 축하합니다.)'라고 할 수 있다.

■ '잘했다.'는 의미로 축하하거나 상대를 칭찬하는 경우에는 'You did a good job.', 'You are pretty good.', 'You are doing well.', 'You did a fine job.', 'Great!', 'Well done!', 'Bravo!'와 같은 표현을 사용한다.

■ 'I am sorry.'는 상대에게 사과하는 말로 '미안합니다.'에 해당하지만 'I'm sorry to hear ~.'라고 할 때는 '~을 듣고 유감스럽게 느낀다.'는 의미로 유감이나 안타까움을 나타내는 표현이 된다. 'Sorry. I'm afraid I can't ~/ you can't ~.(미안하지만 ~는 안 됩니다.)'도 역시 유감을 나타내는 표현이다. '너무 안됐다.'라는 뜻으로 유감을 표현할 때는 'That's too bad.', 'That's terrible.', 'That's really sad.' 등의 표현을 사용한다.

축하 · 유감 표현하기

- Congratulations on ~.   ~을 축하합니다.
- Please accept my congratulations on ~.   ~에 대하여 축하합니다.
- You did a good job. / You are doing well. / Great!   잘했다.
- I'm sorry to hear ~.   ~을 들으니 유감입니다.
- Sorry. I'm afraid I can't ~ / you can't ~.   미안하지만 ~는 안 됩니다.
- That's too bad. / That's terrible. / That's really sad.   너무 안됐다.

핵심 Check

1. 다음 대화의 순서를 자연스럽게 배열한 것은?

(A) That's wonderful. Congratulations!

(B) Sue, you look excited. What's up?

(C) Thanks. I'm really happy to have a chance to work for my class.

(D) I was elected as class president. I'm so excited.

① (A) – (D) – (B) – (C)   ② (B) – (A) – (C) – (D)
③ (B) – (D) – (A) – (C)   ④ (C) – (A) – (D) – (B)
⑤ (D) – (A) – (B) – (C)

② 감정 표현하기

A What's up? 무슨 일이니?

B My smartphone is broken. I'm very upset. 내 스마트폰이 고장 났어. 아주 기분이 좋지 않아.

■ 'I'm upset.(나는 속이 상한다.)'는 불쾌하거나 불만스러운 감정을 나타내는 표현이다. 감정을 나타낼 때는 'I'm+감정형용사.(나는 ~하다.)' 또는 'I feel+감정형용사.(나는 ~하다고 느낀다.)'에 해당하는 표현을 사용한다.

감정을 나타내는 형용사는 다음과 같다.

- upset 속상한, 화난
- excited 흥분한, 신난
- disappointed 실망한
- happy 행복한
- pleased 기쁜
- thankful 감사하는
- proud 자랑스러운
- satisfied 만족한
- delighted 기쁜
- nervous 불안한
- worried 걱정하는
- depressed 우울한
- scared 겁먹은
- bored 지루한
- embarrassed 당황한

■ 'I'm proud of ~.(나는 ~가 자랑스럽다.)'는 긍정적인 감정을 나타내며, 감정을 표현할 때 'I'm glad 감정형용사 ~.' 또는 'I feel 감정형용사 ~.'에서 사용하는 감정형용사 뒤에는 접속사 that과 함께 '주어+동사 ~'가 이어져서 감정의 원인을 나타낸다. 이때 접속사 that은 대부분 생략한다.

감정 표현하기

- I'm upset. / I feel upset. (나는 기분이 나쁘다.)
- I'm glad ~. (~하게 되어 기뻐.) = I feel glad ~.
- I'm worried ~. (~하게 되어 걱정이야.) = I feel worried ~.
- I'm pleased ~. (~하게 되어 기뻐.) = I feel pleased ~.
- I'm delighted ~. (~하게 되어 기뻐.) = I feel delighted ~.

핵심 Check

2. 다음 우리말을 주어진 단어를 이용하여 영작하시오.

G: You don't look so good, Inho. What's the matter?

B: I have the flu.

G: 안됐다. (that / bad) Did you see the doctor?

B: Yes. I'm taking medicine.

G: Well, I hope you feel better soon.

B: Thanks.

➡ _____

Listen and Talk A 1

B: Sue, you ❶look excited. ❷What's up?

G: I was elected as class president. ❸I'm so excited.

B: That's wonderful. ❹Congratulations!

G: Thanks. I'm really happy ❺to have a chance ❻to work for my class.

B: Sue, 신나 보인다. 무슨 일이니?
G: 나 학급 회장으로 당선되었어. 정말 신나.
B: 멋지다. 축하해!
G: 고마워. 우리 반을 위해서 일할 기회가 생겨서 정말 기뻐.

❶ look+형용사: ~해 보이다   ❷ What's up?: 무슨 일이야?   ❸ 'I'm+감정형용사'로 감정을 나타내는 표현이다.
❹ 'Congratulations'는 '축하합니다.'의 뜻으로 항상 복수형인 'congratulations'를 쓴다. 'Congratulations.'만 가지고도 축하의 의미를 전달하지만 보통 뒤에 전치사 on을 써서 무엇에 대하여 축하하는지 구체적으로 덧붙이는 경우가 많다.
❺ to have는 부사적 용법(원인)으로 쓰였다.   ❻ to work는 형용사적 용법으로 쓰였다.

Check(√) True or False

(1) Sue was elected as class president.　　　　　　　　T ☐ F ☐

(2) The boy envies Sue.　　　　　　　　T ☐ F ☐

Listen and Talk C

B: Excuse me, Ms. Carter. Can I ask you a question? Did I get the main role in the play?

W: Yes, you ❶did. Congratulations, Jiho! You're going to be Romeo in ❷our school play, *Romeo and Juliet*.

B: Really? ❸I'm so excited. Thank you so much, Ms. Carter.

W: I know ❹how much you wanted the role. ❺I'm so happy for you.

B: Thank you. What about Sumi? Did she get ❻the role she wanted, too?

W: Unfortunately, no. She's very disappointed.

B: Oh, ❼I'm sorry to hear that. Anyway, when is the first practice?

W: It's at 2 p.m. on September 20th, in the acting club room. You'll get a text message about ❽it soon.

B: OK. I'll be ❾there.

B: 실례합니다. Carter 선생님. 질문 하나 해도 될까요? 제가 연극에서 주인공 역할을 맡게 됐나요?
W: 응, 그래. 축하해, 지호야! 너는 우리 학교 연극 "로미오와 줄리엣"에서 로미오를 하게 될 거야.
B: 정말요? 너무 신나요. 감사합니다, Carter 선생님.
W: 네가 얼마나 그 역할을 원했는지 내가 알지. 나도 정말 기쁘구나.
B: 감사합니다. 수미는 어떻게 됐어요? 수미도 원했던 역할을 맡게 됐나요?
W: 유감스럽게도 아니란다. 수미가 무척 실망했어.
B: 아, 정말 유감이네요. 그런데 첫 연습은 언제인가요?
W: 9월 20일 2시에 연극 동아리 방에서 할 거야. 그것에 관해서 문자 메시지를 곧 받게 될 거야.
B: 네. 연습 때 갈게요.

❶ did는 'got the main role in the play'를 대신하는 대동사이다.   ❷ our school play와 *Romeo and Juliet*은 동격이다.
❸ 'I'm+감정형용사'로 감정을 나타내는 표현이다.   ❹ '의문사+주어+동사'로 이루어진 간접의문문이다.
❺ 'I'm+감정형용사'로 감정을 나타내는 표현이다.   ❻ the role과 she 사이에 목적격 관계대명사 that이나 which가 생략되어 있다.
❼ '정말 유감이네요.'라는 뜻으로 유감을 나타내는 표현이다.   ❽ it은 the first practice를 가리킨다.   ❾ there는 the acting club room을 가리킨다.

Check(√) True or False

(3) Jiho will act as Romeo in his school play, *Romeo and Juliet*.　　　　T ☐ F ☐

(4) Sumi will act as Juliet in her school play, *Romeo and Juliet*.　　　　T ☐ F ☐

Listen and Talk A 2

G: Tim, congratulations on ❶winning the gold medal in the school marathon.
B: Thanks, Suji. I'm very happy.
G: You ❷must be very proud of yourself.
B: Yes, I am. I did my best.

❶ on 뒤에서 축하의 구체적인 내용을 밝히고 있다.
❷ must: ~임에 틀림없다

 Listen and Talk A 3

B: Mina, is ❶anything wrong?
G: Well, I lost my smartphone. ❷I'm upset.
B: Oh, ❸I'm so sorry to hear that. Do you remember ❹when you used it last?
G: Well, I ❺remember taking it out of my bag at the snack shop.
B: Then, let's go back to the snack shop ❻to look for it.

❶ -thing으로 끝나는 부정대명사를 wrong이 뒤에서 수식하고 있다.
❷ 'I'm+감정형용사'로 감정을 나타내는 표현이다.
❸ 유감을 나타내는 표현이다.
❹ '의문사+주어+동사'로 이루어진 간접의문문이다.
❺ remember+ing: 과거에 ~한 것을 기억하다
❻ 부정사의 부사적 용법(목적)이다.

 Listen and Talk A 4

G: You don't look so good, Inho. ❶What's the matter?
B: I have the flu.
G: ❷That's too bad. Did you see the doctor?
B: Yes. I'm ❸taking medicine.
G: Well, I hope you feel better soon.
B: Thanks.

❶ What's the matter? = What's wrong?
❷ 유감을 나타내는 표현이다.
❸ take medicine: 약을 먹다

 Listen and Talk B

A: What's up?
B: I won first prize in the English speech contest. ❶I'm so excited.
A: That's wonderful. ❷Congratulations!

❶ 'I'm+감정형용사'로 감정을 나타내는 표현이다.
❷ '축하합니다.'라는 뜻으로 항상 복수형인 'congratulations'를 쓴다.

 Listen and Talk D

Last summer, I lost my dog, Bomi. She disappeared ❶while I was drinking water in the park. Luckily, I was able to find her two days later. ❷I was so happy that I hugged her tightly.

❶ while+절(주어+동사), during+명사(구)
❷ so ~ that ...: 너무 ~해서 …하다

 Talk and Play

A: What's up?
B: I was ❶chosen as the leader of the school band. ❷I'm so excited.
A: That's wonderful. Congratulations!

A: What's up?
B: My bike is broken. ❷I'm very upset.
A: That's too bad. I'm sorry to hear that.

❶ chosen = elected
❷ 'I'm+감정형용사'로 감정을 나타내는 표현이다.

 Review 1

B: You look excited, Sally. What's up?
G: I'm going to go to the Dream Concert.
B: Congratulations! I know ❶how much you wanted to go.
G: Thanks. I'm so happy to get a chance ❷to see my favorite singer.

❶ '의문사+주어+동사'로 이루어진 간접의문문이다.
❷ 형용사적 용법으로 쓰인 to부정사이다.

 Review 2

B: You don't look good, Sumi. What's the matter?
G: Well, I didn't get a role in the school play. ❶ I'm very disappointed.
B: Oh, ❷I'm so sorry to hear ❸that. But I'm sure you can ❹get a role next time.
G: Thanks. I'll try harder next time.

❶ 'I'm+감정형용사'로 감정을 나타내는 표현이다.
❷ 유감을 나타내는 표현이다.
❸ that은 앞 문장의 'didn't get a role in the school play'를 가리킨다.
❹ get a role: 역할을 맡다

● 다음 우리말과 일치하도록 빈칸에 알맞은 말을 쓰시오.

Listen and Talk A 1

B: Sue, you look _____. What's _____?
G: I was _____ as class president. I'm so _____.
B: That's wonderful. Congratulations!
G: Thanks. I'm really happy _____ _____ a chance _____ _____ for my class.

B: Sue, 신나 보인다. 무슨 일이니?
G: 나 학급 회장으로 당선되었어. 정말 신나.
B: 멋지다. 축하해!
G: 고마워. 우리 반을 위해서 일할 기회가 생겨서 정말 기뻐.

Listen and Talk A 2

G: Tim, congratulations _____ winning the gold medal in the school marathon.
B: Thanks, Suji. I'm very happy.
G: You _____ be very _____ _____ _____.
B: Yes, I _____. I did my _____.

G: Tim, 학교 마라톤에서 금메달을 딴 것을 축하해.
B: 고마워, 수지야. 정말 행복해.
G: 너 자신이 정말 자랑스럽겠다.
B: 응, 맞아. 난 최선을 다했어.

Listen and Talk A 3

B: Mina, is _____ _____?
G: Well, I lost my smartphone. I'm _____.
B: Oh, I'm so _____ _____ _____ that. Do you remember _____ _____ _____ _____ _____ last?
G: Well, I remember _____ it _____ of my bag at the snack shop.
B: Then, let's go back to the snack shop _____ _____ for it.

B: 미나야, 무슨 안 좋은 일 있니?
G: 스마트폰을 잃어버렸어. 기분이 안 좋아.
B: 오, 정말 유감이야. 마지막으로 그것을 언제 사용했는지 기억하니?
G: 음, 매점에서 그것을 가방에서 꺼냈던 것은 기억나.
B: 그러면, 그것을 찾으러 매점에 돌아가자.

Listen and Talk A 4

G: You don't look so _____, Inho. What's _____ _____?
B: I have _____ _____.
G: That's too _____. Did you see the doctor?
B: Yes. I'm _____ _____.
G: Well, I hope you _____ _____ soon.
B: Thanks.

G: 인호야, 너 몸이 안 좋아 보인다. 무슨 문제 있니?
B: 나 독감에 걸렸어.
G: 참 안됐구나, 병원은 가 봤니?
B: 응, 약을 먹고 있어.
G: 얼른 나았으면 좋겠다.
B: 고마워.

Listen and Talk B

A: What's _____?
B: I won _____ _____ in the English speech contest. I'm so _____.
A: That's wonderful. _____!

A: What's _____?
B: My smartphone is _____. I'm very _____.
A: That's too _____. I'm _____ _____ _____ that.

A: 무슨 일이니?
B: 영어 말하기 대회에서 1등 상을 받았어. 정말 신이 나.
A: 멋지다. 축하해!

A: 무슨 일이니?
B: 내 스마트폰이 고장 났어. 아주 기분이 좋지 않아.
A: 참 안됐구나. 유감이야.

Listen and Talk C

B: Excuse me, Ms. Carter. Can I ask you a question? Did I _____ the _____ _____ in the play?

W: Yes, you did. Congratulations, Jiho! You're going to be Romeo in our school play, *Romeo and Juliet*.

B: Really? I'm so _____. Thank you so much, Ms. Carter.

W: I know _____ _____ _____ _____ the role. I'm so _____ _____ you.

B: Thank you. What _____ Sumi? Did she _____ the _____ she wanted, too?

W: Unfortunately, no. She's very _____.

B: Oh, I'm _____ _____ _____ that. _____, when is the first practice?

W: It's _____ 2 p.m. _____ September 20th, _____ the acting club room. You'll _____ a text message _____ it soon.

B: OK. I'll be there.

Listen and Talk D

Last summer, I lost my dog, Bomi. She disappeared _____ I was drinking water in the park. Luckily, I _____ _____ _____ find her two days later. I was _____ _____ _____ I hugged her tightly.

Talk and Play

A: What's up?

B: I was _____ as the leader of the school band. I'm so _____.

A: That's wonderful. Congratulations!

A: What's up?

B: My bike is _____. I'm very _____.

A: That's _____ _____. I'm _____ _____ _____ _____.

Review 1

B: You look _____, Sally. What's _____?

G: I'm going to go to the Dream Concert.

B: Congratulations! I know _____ _____ _____ _____ to go.

G: Thanks. I'm so happy _____ _____ a chance _____ _____ my favorite singer.

Review 2

B: You don't look _____, Sumi. What's _____ _____?

G: Well, I didn't get a role in the school play. I'm very _____.

B: Oh, I'm so _____ _____ _____ _____. But I'm sure you can get a role next time.

G: Thanks. I'll _____ _____ next time.

해석

B: 실례합니다. Carter 선생님. 질문 하나 해도 될까요? 제가 연극에서 주인공 역할을 맡게 됐나요?

W: 응, 그래. 축하해, 지호야! 너는 우리 학교 연극 "로미오와 줄리엣"에서 로미오를 하게 될 거야.

B: 정말요? 너무 신나요. 감사합니다, Carter 선생님.

W: 네가 얼마나 그 역할을 원했는지 내가 알지. 나도 정말 기쁘구나.

B: 감사합니다. 수미는 어떻게 됐어요? 수미도 원했던 역할을 맡게 됐나요?

W: 유감스럽게도 아니란다. 수미가 무척 실망했어.

B: 아, 정말 유감이네요. 그런데 첫 연습은 언제인가요?

W: 9월 20일 2시에 연극 동아리 방에서 할 거야. 그것에 관해서 문자 메시지를 곧 받게 될 거야.

B: 네. 연습 때 갈게요.

지난 여름에 나는 내 개 보미를 잃어버렸어. 보미는 내가 공원에서 물을 마시고 있는 동안 사라졌어. 다행히도, 나는 이틀 후에 그녀를 찾을 수 있었어. 나는 너무 행복해서 그녀를 품에 꼭 안았어.

A: 무슨 일이니?

B: 나는 학교 밴드의 리더로 뽑혔어. 정말 신이 나.

A: 멋지다. 축하해!

A: 무슨 일이니?

B: 내 자전거가 고장 났어. 아주 기분이 좋지 않아.

A: 참 안됐구나. 유감이야.

B: Sally, 너 신나 보인다. 무슨 일이니?

G: 나 Dream 콘서트에 가.

B: 축하해! 네가 얼마나 가고 싶어 했는지 알아.

G: 고마워. 나는 내가 가장 좋아하는 가수를 볼 기회를 얻어서 정말 기뻐.

B: 수미야, 너 기분 안 좋아 보인다. 무슨 일 있니?

G: 학교 연극에서 역할을 맡지 못 했어. 난 정말 실망했어.

B: 오, 정말 유감이야. 그렇지만 넌 분명 다음 기회에 역할을 맡을 수 있을 거야.

G: 고마워. 다음에는 더 많이 노력할 거야.

01 다음 대화의 빈칸 (A)에 알맞은 것은?

> B: Sue, you look excited. What's ___(A)___ ?
> G: I was elected as class president. I'm so excited.
> B: That's wonderful. Congratulations!
> G: Thanks. I'm really happy to have a chance to work for my class.

① on   ② over   ③ up   ④ from   ⑤ along

02 주어진 어휘를 이용하여 밑줄 친 우리말을 영작하시오.

> G: Tim, 금메달을 딴 것을 축하해 in the school marathon.
>   (congratulations, win, the gold medal)
> B: Thanks, Suji. I'm very happy.
> G: You must be very proud of yourself.
> B: Yes, I am. I did my best.

➡ _____

[03~04] 다음 대화를 읽고 물음에 답하시오.

> G: You don't look so good, Inho. What's the matter?
> B: I have the flu.
> G: (a)That's too bad. Did you see the doctor?
> B: Yes. I'm taking ___(A)___ .
> G: Well, I hope you feel better soon.
> B: Thanks.

03 다음 영영풀이를 참고하여 대화의 빈칸 (A)에 알맞은 말을 쓰시오.

> a substance that you drink or swallow in order to cure an illness

➡ _____

04 밑줄 친 (a)를 sorry와 that을 이용하여 바꿔 쓰시오.

➡ _____

01 다음 중 짝지어진 대화가 <u>어색한</u> 것은?

① A: She's very disappointed.

   B: That's wonderful. Congratulations!

② A: My bike is broken. I'm very upset.

   B: That's too bad.

③ A: Well, I didn't get a role in the school play. I'm very disappointed.

   B: Oh, I'm so sorry to hear that. But I'm sure you can get a role next time.

④ A: I'm going to go to the concert.

   B: Congratulations! I know how much you wanted to go.

⑤ A: What's up?

   B: I was chosen as the leader of the school band. I'm so excited.

[02~05] 다음 대화를 읽고 물음에 답하시오.

B: Excuse me, Ms. Carter. Can I ask you a question? Did I get the main role in the play?

W: Yes, you did. Congratulations, Jiho! You're going to be Romeo in our school play, *Romeo and Juliet*.

B: Really? I'm so excited. Thank you so much, Ms. Carter.

W: (a)네가 얼마나 그 역할을 원했는지 내가 알지. (much, the role) I'm so happy for you.

B: Thank you. What   (A)   Sumi? Did she get the role she wanted, too?

W: Unfortunately, no. She's very disappointed.

B: Oh,   (B)   . Anyway, when is the first practice?

W: It's at 2 p.m. on September 20th, in the acting club room. You'll get a text message   (A)   it soon.

B: OK. I'll be there.

---

02 빈칸 (A)에 공통으로 들어갈 말을 고르시오.

① on   ② about   ③ in

④ at   ⑤ for

서답형

03 위 대화의 빈칸 (B)에 들어갈 알맞은 말을 주어진 어휘를 배열하여 쓰시오.

> sorry, I'm, that, hear, to

➡ _____

서답형

04 밑줄 친 (a)의 우리말에 맞게 주어진 어휘를 이용하여 영작하시오.

➡ _____

05 Jiho와 Sumi에 관한 위 대화의 내용과 일치하지 <u>않는</u> 것은?

① Jiho got the main role in the play.

② Jiho is going to be Romeo in his school play.

③ Jiho thanked Ms. Carter very much.

④ Sumi didn't get the role she wanted in the play.

⑤ Jiho already knew when the first practice was.

서답형

06 대화가 자연스럽게 연결되도록 (A)~(C)를 순서대로 가장 적절하게 배열하시오.

> (A) I won first prize in the English speech contest. I'm so excited.
>
> (B) What's up?
>
> (C) That's wonderful. Congratulations!

➡ _____

[07~08] 다음 대화를 읽고 물음에 답하시오.

B: Mina, is anything wrong?

G: Well, I lost my smartphone. I'm upset.

B: Oh, _____(A)_____ Do you remember when you used it last?

G: Well, I remember ____(B)____ it out of my bag at the snack shop.

B: Then, let's go back to the snack shop to look for it.

07 위 대화의 빈칸 (A)에 들어갈 말로 적절한 것은?

① congratulations!

② please accept my congratulations.

③ I'm so sorry to hear that.

④ I'm glad to hear that.

⑤ you did a good job.

서답형

08 위 대화의 빈칸 (B)에 take를 알맞은 형태로 쓰시오.

➡ _____

[09~10] 다음 대화를 읽고 물음에 답하시오.

B: You look (a)[exciting / excited], Sally. What's up?

G: I'm going to go to the Dream Concert.

B: _____(A)_____ I know how much (b)[did you want / you wanted] to go.

G: Thanks. I'm so happy (c)[to get / getting] a chance to see my favorite singer.

09 위 대화의 빈칸 (A)에 들어갈 말로 알맞지 <u>않은</u> 것을 <u>모두</u> 고르시오.

① Congratulations!   ② Great!

③ That's terrible.   ④ Bravo!

⑤ I'm sorry to hear that.

중요

10 위 대화의 괄호 (a)~(c)에서 알맞은 것으로 짝지은 것은?

	(a)	(b)	(c)
①	excited	you wanted	to get
②	excited	you wanted	getting
③	excited	did you want	to get
④	exciting	you wanted	getting
⑤	exciting	did you want	getting

11 다음 대화의 밑줄 친 부분의 의도로 가장 적절한 것은?

A: What's up?

B: My smartphone is broken. I'm very upset.

A: That's too bad. <u>I'm sorry to hear that.</u>

① 감정 표현하기   ② 희망 표현하기

③ 빈도 말하기   ④ 축하 표현하기

⑤ 유감 표현하기

[12~13] 다음 대화를 읽고 물음에 답하시오.

G: You don't look so good, Inho. What's the matter? (①)

B: I have the flu.

G: (②) Did you see the doctor?

B: Yes. I'm taking medicine. (③)

G: Well, I hope you feel better soon. (④)

B: (⑤) Thanks.

중요

12 위 대화의 (①)~(⑤) 중 주어진 문장이 들어갈 곳은?

That's too bad.

①   ②   ③   ④   ⑤

서답형

13 Why doesn't Inho look so good? Answer by beginning with 'Because'.

➡ _____

[01~03] 다음 대화를 읽고 물음에 답하시오.

B: Excuse me, Ms. Carter. Can I ask you a question? Did I get the main role in the play?

W: Yes, you did. Congratulations, Jiho! You're going to be Romeo in our school play, *Romeo and Juliet*.

B: Really? I'm so excited. Thank you so much, Ms. Carter.

W: I know how much you wanted the role. (a) 나도 너 때문에 정말 기쁘구나. (happy, so, for)

B: Thank you. What about Sumi? Did she get the role she wanted, too?

(A) It's at 2 p.m. on September 20th, in the acting club room. You'll get a text message about it soon.

(B) OK. I'll be there.

(C) Oh, I'm sorry to hear that. Anyway, when is the first practice?

(D) Unfortunately, no. She's very disappointed.

01 위 대화의 (A)~(D)를 알맞은 순서로 배열하시오.

➡ _____

02 괄호 안에 주어진 어휘를 이용하여 밑줄 친 (a)의 우리말을 5 단어로 쓰시오.

➡ _____

03 When will Jiho visit the club acting room? Use the words "at" and "on".

➡ _____
_____

[04~05] 다음 글을 읽고 물음에 답하시오.

Last summer, I lost my dog, Bomi. She disappeared while I was drinking water in the park. Luckily, I was able to find her two days later. (a)나는 너무 행복해서 그녀를 품에 꼭 안았어. (her, happy, that, tightly, hug)

04 What happened to the writer last summer?

➡ _____

05 괄호 안에 주어진 어휘를 이용하여 밑줄 친 우리말 (a)에 맞게 9 단어로 쓰시오.

➡ _____

[06~07] 다음 대화를 읽고 물음에 답하시오.

B: You don't look good, Sumi. What's the matter?

G: Well, I didn't get a role in the school play. I'm very disappointed.

B: Oh, I'm so sorry to hear (a)that. But I'm sure you can get a role next time.

G: Thanks. I'll try harder next time.

06 위 대화에서 주어진 영영풀이에 해당하는 말을 찾아 쓰시오.

> one of the characters that an actor or singer can play in a film, play, or opera

➡ _____

07 위 대화의 밑줄 친 (a)that이 가리키는 것을 본문에서 찾아 쓰시오.

➡ _____

Grammar

1 '과거완료' had+과거분사

> • People asked him where he **had got** the furniture.
> 사람들은 그에게 가구를 어디서 구했는지 물었다.
>
> • When Mr. Boggis came back, the legs **had been cut** off.
> Mr. Boggis가 돌아왔을 때, 다리들은 이미 잘려 있었다.

■ 과거완료시제는 'had+과거분사' 형태로 표현하며, 과거의 어느 시점을 기준으로, 그 이전에 일어난 동작이나 상태를 나타낸다.

　• My son liked the pen that I **had bought** for him. 내 아들은 내가 사 준 펜을 좋아했다.

■ 과거의 특정 시점을 기준으로 그 이전에 일어난 동작의 완료, 경험, 계속, 결과를 나타낸다.

　(1) 완료: '막 ~했었다'는 의미로 과거 이전에 시작된 동작이 과거의 어느 시점에 완료된 일을 나타낸다. 보통 already, yet 등의 부사와 함께 쓰인다.

　　• Lucy **had just finished** talking with her mom on the phone. Lucy는 엄마와의 전화 통화를 방금 막 끝냈다.

　(2) 경험: '~한 적이 있었다'는 의미로 과거 이전부터 과거의 어느 시점까지의 경험을 나타낸다. 보통 never, ever, once, twice, before 등의 부사(구)와 함께 쓰인다.

　　• We **had never heard** of the rock band before. 우리는 전에 그 록밴드에 대해 들어 본 적이 없었다.

　(3) 결과: '(과거 이전에) ~해서, 그 결과 …했다'는 의미로 과거 이전의 동작이 과거의 어느 시점의 결과에 영향을 미치는 것을 나타낸다.

　　• Sam **had lost** the letter from his wife when he got cancer. Sam이 암에 걸렸을 때, 그는 아내에게서 온 편지를 잃어버렸다.

　(4) 계속: '계속 ~하고 있었다'는 의미로 과거 이전부터 과거의 어느 시점까지 계속되는 동작이나 상태를 나타낸다. 보통 since ~, for ~ 등과 함께 쓰인다.

　　• Robert **had lived** in Seoul for 11 years when he moved to Jeju. Robert가 제주도로 이사갔을 때, 그는 서울에서 11년간 살았었다.

■ 부정문은 'had not+과거분사', 의문문은 'Had+주어+과거분사 ~?', 과거 어느 시점을 기준으로 전부터 진행 중인 동작을 강조할 때 과거완료진행형 'had+been+V-ing'을 쓴다.

　• I was very tired as I **had not slept** well for several days. 며칠 동안 잠을 잘 못 자서 나는 매우 피곤했다.

　• **Had** the singers **seen** each other before? 그 가수들이 전에 서로 만난 적 있나요?

　• Mom **had been cleaning** my room when I called home. 내가 집에 전화했을 때, 엄마는 내 방을 청소 중이셨다.

핵심 Check

1. 다음 괄호 안에서 알맞은 말을 고르시오.

　(1) They wondered how the dealer (has / had) got the chair.

　(2) My dog had never seen a cat until she (meets / met) Molly.

2 '관계대명사' what

> • The table was **what** every dealer dreamed of. 그 탁자는 모든 판매상이 꿈꾸는 것이었다.
> • We ate **what** Mom had cooked for us. 우리는 엄마가 우리를 위해 요리해 주신 것을 먹었다.

■ what은 선행사를 포함하는 관계대명사이다.

  • We ate **what** Mom gave us. 우리는 엄마가 우리에게 주신 것을 먹었다.
    = We ate **the thing(s) that** Mom gave us.
  • **What** I wanted to buy yesterday was the car. 내가 어제 사고 싶었던 것은 그 차였다.
    = **The thing that** I wanted to buy yesterday was the car.

■ 관계대명사 what은 명사절을 이끈다.

  • **What** you said to me was unbelievable. 네가 나에게 말하는 것은 믿을 수가 없었다. (주어)
  • I saw **what** you did on the stage. 나는 무대 위에서 네가 한 것을 보았다. (목적어)
  • Sandra is aware of **what** James was interested in. Sandra는 James가 관심을 가지고 있었던 것을 알고 있다. (전치사의 목적어)
  • These are **what** he bought in Paris. 이것들은 그가 파리에서 산 것이다. (보어)

■ 관계대명사 what과 의문대명사 what이 이끄는 문장의 구조는 동일하며, 구분은 해석으로 한다. 관계대명사 what은 '~하는 것'으로, 의문대명사 what은 '무엇(을/이) ~지'로 해석한다.

  • They wondered **what** I made with the wood. 그들은 내가 그 나무로 무엇을 만들었는지 궁금해 했다. (의문대명사)
  • **What** I made with the wood was a spoon. 내가 그 나무로 만든 것은 숟가락이었다. (관계대명사)

■ 관계대명사 what의 관용적인 표현들

  • A man's worth lies not so much in **what he has** as in **what he is**. 사람의 가치는 그의 재산보다는 그의 인격에 있다.
  • He is **what is called** a gentleman. 그는 말하자면 신사이다.
  • **What's better[worse]** is that we don't know what happened to you. 더욱 좋은[나쁜] 것은 우리가 너에게 무슨 일이 생겼는지 모른다는 것이다.

핵심 Check

2. 다음 우리말에 맞게 괄호 안의 단어를 바르게 배열하시오.

  (1) 이 사탕은 내가 먹고 싶었던 것이다. (eat, candy, I, this, wanted, is, what, to)

    ➡ _____

  (2) 그녀는 그녀의 남편이 집에 가져온 것을 좋아했다. (home, what, husband, her, she, brought, liked)

    ➡ _____

01 다음 빈칸에 들어갈 말로 알맞은 것은?

> When I came home, my sister ＿＿＿＿＿＿ to bed.

① goes　　　② to go　　　③ has gone

④ going　　　⑤ had gone

02 다음 문장에서 어법상 어색한 단어를 한 개씩만 찾아 고치시오.

(1) The guests were surprised at which the queen showed them.

　＿＿＿＿＿＿ ➡ ＿＿＿＿＿＿

(2) All what Louise told us was a lie.

　＿＿＿＿＿＿ ➡ ＿＿＿＿＿＿, ＿＿＿＿＿＿ ➡ ＿＿＿＿＿＿

(3) That the students liked best was baseball.

　＿＿＿＿＿＿ ➡ ＿＿＿＿＿＿

03 다음 밑줄 친 부분 중 어법상 옳은 것을 고르시오.

① My grandparents <u>had lived</u> in Suwon for 10 years until now.

② The police <u>had found</u> the file that the spy had hidden.

③ Andy opened the tuna can that his mom <u>had bought</u> the day before.

④ When <u>had</u> the girl <u>married</u> the nobel prize winner?

⑤ Smith <u>has left</u> for Singapore before his parents arrived.

04 다음 문장의 밑줄 친 부분을 한 단어로 바꾸시오.

> Mr. Boggis bought <u>the things that</u> Rummins had at a low price.

➡ ＿＿＿＿＿＿＿＿＿＿

01 다음 밑줄 친 부분이 어법상 어색한 것은?

① After all the passengers had escaped, the captain jumped off the ship.

② Susan had broken her leg, so she couldn't play basektball yesterday.

③ He had already left the house when his friend came.

④ I lost the key that my uncle from London had given to me.

⑤ Brenda asked her friend to repair the drone which has broken down.

02 다음 빈칸에 알맞은 것은?

| Is that _____ Bush wanted to wear? |

① which   ② those
③ when   ④ what
⑤ how

[03~04] 다음 중 밑줄 친 부분이 어법상 옳은 것을 고르시오.

03 ① The baby girls liked the doll what their uncles had bought for them.

② Is this hat what he is looking for?

③ All of them knew what the professor would give them a special lecture.

④ Laura bought a new car what her daughter could drive.

⑤ What the girl told him a lie was not surprising.

04 ① My math teacher required that I had finished the test.

② Ann and Kate had lived in the city before they had moved there.

③ For the past three years, Sam had read the books regarding the future.

④ The treasures had been taken to France, but he brought them to Korea.

⑤ David is hungry because he had not eaten anything so far.

서답형

05 다음 문장에서 어법상 어색한 단어 한 개를 찾아서 고치시오.

| The woman reached the station after the train has left. |

➡ _____

06 다음 빈칸에 알맞은 말이 순서대로 바르게 짝지어진 것은?

| • Since _____ Mr. Boggis wanted was only the legs of the table, Bert cut them off.
• Mr. Boggis was very shocked to see the table _____ had been cut off. |

① which – which   ② what – what
③ what – that   ④ which – that
⑤ that – which

[07~08] 다음 중 어법상 어색한 문장은?

07 ① His family knew what he was doing.
② Mary bought what her friend wanted.
③ Tom showed her what Sean had invented.
④ What Julie liked to read is the book.
⑤ Elizabeth sang the song what her daughter was interested in.

① These are not what I wanted to read.
② All my friends loved the game that the producer had made.
③ A lot of people liked what the idol band showed on the Internet.
④ Which the director told them on the stage kept them motivated.
⑤ That is not the thing which the boss was talking about.

09 다음 중 밑줄 친 부분의 쓰임이 〈보기〉와 같은 것은?

┌─── 보기 ───┐

The student <u>had</u> already <u>solved</u> the problem when the teacher told them to start the quiz.

└──────────┘

① When Mr. Boggis came back, they <u>had cut</u> off the legs of the table.
② Michael <u>had played</u> volleyball in Spain before he moved to Brazil.
③ The Browns <u>had lived</u> in London for two years when I visited them.
④ My cousin <u>had been</u> sick in bed for a week when I visited him.
⑤ Durant <u>had</u> never <u>been</u> sick until last week after the car accident.

[10~11] 다음 밑줄 친 what 중에서 같은 용법으로 쓰이지 않은 것은?

10 ① They will receive <u>what</u> Chris sent five months ago.
② <u>What</u> the director said at the awards inspired the audience.
③ The reporter asked the actor <u>what</u> she was planning to do.
④ My kids liked <u>what</u> the magician showed them on the stage.
⑤ These are <u>what</u> Mr. Boggis suggested.

① All of my friends wondered <u>what</u> Tiffany had given to me for the present.
② That's not <u>what</u> Aaron meant to say.
③ Sophie accepted <u>what</u> they offered.
④ The player got <u>what</u> he threw at him.
⑤ Volunteering for the orphans was <u>what</u> Helen wanted to do.

[12~13] 다음 중 어법상 옳은 문장은?

12 ① Amy noticed the way which her boyfriend gained much weight.
② We don't know the reason which it's so cold and dry nowadays.
③ Mom took us to what Daddy first met her when she was only 15.
④ Brian forgot the thing what Sam asked him to do.
⑤ The athletes did what they could do best at the game.

13 ① The audience has been sitting for half an hour before the musical started.

② When Bob met Anna, she had already finished the meal.

③ We can't see the spider now as our neighbor's boy had killed it.

④ Jessy found the pencil that Sumin had been given to her.

⑤ Rena has never eaten rice noodles until she visited Vietnam.

서답형

14 다음 우리말을 주어진 단어들을 배열하여 영작할 때, what 과 is는 각각 몇 번째로 나오는가?

선생님이 보여주는 것에 집중하세요.
(to, is, pay, the, showing, attention, teacher, what)

➡ what: _____ is: _____

서답형

15 다음 두 문장을 한 문장으로 표현할 때, 빈칸에 들어갈 알맞은 말을 쓰시오.

• Henry started to play the violin six years ago.

• He was still playing the violin when I visited him two years ago.

➡ Henry _____ _____ _____ the violin for _____ years when I visited him two years ago.

서답형

16 다음 우리말을 영작할 때, 빈칸에 들어갈 알맞은 말을 쓰시오.

이제 Laura는 과거의 그녀가 아니다.
= Now, Laura is not _____ she _____.

서답형

17 어법상 어색한 문장을 모두 고르시오.

ⓐ The thing cannot be cured must be endured.

ⓑ To take some light exercise every day is a good habit what makes you energetic.

ⓒ The participants are expected to do which the researchers ask them to do.

ⓓ It would make us think about what we could or couldn't do.

ⓔ That she teaches can differ from those she knows.

ⓕ I think what he says is not improtant.

ⓖ You may not believe that I've just heard.

➡ _____

서답형

18 우리말과 일치하도록 괄호 안에 주어진 단어들을 바르게 배열하시오.

선생님이 나에게 최근에 일어났던 좋은 일 하나를 적으라고 말했다.
→ The teacher (to, one, had, recently, write down, told, good, that, happened, me, thing).

➡ _____
_____

Grammar 서술형 시험대비

01 주어진 두 문장을 관계대명사 what을 이용하여, 하나의 문장으로 만드시오.

(1) • Irene believed the thing.
 • The professor explained it.
 ➡ _____
 _____

(2) • The thing was boring.
 • It was discussed in the meeting.
 ➡ _____
 _____

(3) • Mom bought the things.
 • They were much cheaper than I thought.
 ➡ _____
 _____

★중요
02 다음 우리말과 일치하도록 괄호 안에 주어진 단어들을 바르게 배열하여 문장을 완성하시오.

(1) 도둑이 집에 침입했다는 것을 가족들 중의 누구도 몰랐다.
 ➡ None of the family knew that _____
 _____. (into, the thief, broken, the house, had)

(2) Mr. Boggis는 사람들이 그것의 가치를 몰랐던 가구를 구입했다.
 ➡ Mr. Boggis bought _____
 _____. (people, value, realized, whose, not, had, the furniture)

(3) 사람들은 그에게 어디서 그 가구를 구했는지 물어보았다.
 ➡ People asked _____
 _____. (had, the furniture, him, where, got, he)

(4) 아빠가 집에 돌아왔을 때, 그는 Sunny가 고양이에게 먹이를 준 것을 발견했다.
 ➡ When Daddy came back home, he _____. (the cat, Sunny, had, found, fed)

03 다음 주어진 〈조건〉과 우리말에 맞게 영작하여, 빈칸을 채우시오.

┤ 조건 ├
1. 총 10 단어를 쓸 것.
2. 과거완료시제를 반드시 사용할 것.
3. the table, its value, sell, know 등을 활용할 것.

Mr. Boggis가 테이블을 팔라고 할 때까지 Rummins는 그것의 가치를 알지 못했다.
→ Until Mr. Boggis told him _____
_____.

★중요
04 다음 그림을 보고, 우리말과 일치하도록 괄호 안에 주어진 어휘를 알맞게 배열하시오.

(1)

Minho가 미술관에서 본 것들은 세계적인 예술 작품들이었다. (saw, the museum, paintings, world-famous, Minho, were, what, at)

➡ _____
_____

(2)

Jisu는 엄마가 생일 선물로 사준 것에 깜짝 놀랐다. (surprised, had bought, her birthday, her mother, Jisu, for, at, was, what)

➡ _____

_____

(3)

할머니가 돌아오셨을 때, 우리는 벌써 모든 과자를 먹었다. (Grandma, all, when, had, the cookies, came, already, back, we, eaten)

➡ _____

_____

(4)

Rachel은 Harry가 벌써 설거지를 해놓고, 그의 식사를 끝낸 것을 발견했다. (already, his meal, the dishes, found, finished, washed, and, had, had, Rachel, Harry)

➡ _____

_____

05 다음 문장에서 어법상 어색한 부분을 찾아 바르게 고쳐 쓰시오.

(1) Sean had not recognized Janet as he didn't meet her before.

➡ _____

(2) Please show us that you put in your bag.

➡ _____

(3) What the doctor asked me to help the patient was not surprising.

➡ _____

_____

(4) I don't believe that you told me.

➡ _____

(5) Sue was shocked that somebody has stolen her laptop during the lunchtime.

➡ _____

_____

06 다음 문장에서 어법상 어색한 한 단어만을 찾아 바르게 고쳐 문장 전체를 다시 쓰시오.

(1) That people believed in the past is not believed today.

➡ _____

_____

(2) That is far different from which Brian has been expecting.

➡ _____

_____

(3) What she met Chris yesterday is true.

➡ _____

(4) Martin succeeded in business, and that was better, he was engaged to his girl friend.

➡ _____

_____

Grammar **81**

Reading

One Lucky Sunday

Cyril Boggis was an antique furniture dealer in London. He was known for buying good things at a low price and then selling them at a high price. People asked him where he had got the furniture, but he just said, "It's a secret."

Mr. Boggis' secret was simple. He went to small towns every Sunday and knocked on doors. He told people that he was a furniture dealer. People didn't know how valuable their things were, so Mr. Boggis took advantage of them. He was able to buy things very cheaply.

Now it was another Sunday, and Mr. Boggis was in a small town again. At a house he visited, he met two men. One was Rummins, the owner, and the other was his son Bert.

"I buy old furniture. Do you have any?" asked Mr. Boggis.

"No, I don't," said Rummins.

"Can I just take a look?" asked Mr. Boggis.

"Sure. Please come in," said Rummins.

---

antique 골동품의; (귀중한) 골동품
furniture 가구
dealer (특정 상품을) 사고파는 상인
be known for ~로 알려지다, ~로 유명하다
price 값, 가격, 물가
knock 두드리다
take advantage of ~을 이용하다
owner 주인, 소유자

---

be known for: ~로 알려져 있다　*전치사 for 다음에 동명사 buying과 selling이 연결*
good things　*과거완료시제, 사람들이 물어본 시점보다 가구를 산 시점이 더 앞서 있다.*
where ~ furniture
간접의문문
take advantage of: ~을 이용하다　*them = people*
두 개 중 먼저 언급된 것: one, 나머지 것: the other

확인문제

● 다음 문장이 본문의 내용과 일치하면 T, 일치하지 <u>않으면</u> F를 쓰시오.

1　Cyril Boggis was an antique furniture dealer in London. ☐

2　Cyril Boggis informed people of where he had got the furniture. ☐

3　Mr. Boggis went to small towns every Sunday and knocked on doors. ☐

4　People knew how valuable their things were. ☐

5　Mr. Boggis was able to buy things very cheaply by taking advantage of people. ☐

6　Rummins didn't allow Mr. Boggis to take a look. ☐

Mr. Boggis first went to the kitchen, and there was nothing. He then moved to the living room. And there it was! A table which was a priceless piece of eighteenth-century English furniture. He was so excited that he almost fell over.

a table which was a priceless piece of eighteenth-century English furniture

which 이하는 관계대명사절, 선행사인 a table을 수식. furniture: 셀 수 없는 명사이므로 앞에 수량을 나타내는 표현인 a piece of 사용

so+형용사+that+주어+동사: 매우 ~해서 …하다

"What's wrong?" Bert asked.

= What's the matter?

"Oh, nothing. Nothing at all," Mr. Boggis lied. He then said with a straight face, "This table is a reproduction. It's worth only a few pounds."

lie–lied–lied: 거짓말하다

be worth: ~의 가치가 있다. worth 뒤에 명사나 동명사 사용

He then added, "Hmm, I think I may buy it. The legs of my table at home are broken. I can cut off the legs of your table and attach them to mine."

the table

The legs of my table at home: 문장의 주어. legs가 복수여서 동사 are가 쓰임.

the legs of your table

mine = my table

"How much?" Rummins asked.

"Not much, I'm afraid. This is just a reproduction," said Mr. Boggis.

Rummins의 탁자

"So how much?"

"Ten pounds."

"Ten? It's worth more than that."

Rummins의 탁자   10파운드

priceless 값을 매길 수 없는, 대단히 귀중한

fall over 넘어지다

with a straight face 정색하며, 무표정한 얼굴로

reproduction (예술 작품의) 복제품, 복제화

worth (금전 등의 면에서) ~의 가치가 있는

cut off ~을 잘라내다

attach 붙이다, 첨부하다

offer 제의, 제안

📎 **확인문제**

● 다음 문장이 본문의 내용과 일치하면 T, 일치하지 <u>않으면</u> F를 쓰시오.

1 Mr. Boggis first went to the kitchen. ☐

2 A table which was a priceless piece of eighteenth-century English furniture was in the kitchen. ☐

3 Mr. Boggis was so excited that he almost fell over. ☐

4 The table Mr. Boggis found in the living room was a reproduction. ☐

5 Mr. Boggis said that the legs of his table at home were broken. ☐

6 Mr. Boggis said that the table was worth more than ten pounds. ☐

"How about fifteen?"

"Make it fifty."

"Well, thirty. This is my final offer."

"OK, it's yours, but how are you going to take it? This thing will not
_{Rummins의 탁자}   _{Rummins의 탁자}
go in a car!"

"We'll see," Mr. Boggis said and went out to bring his car.
_{to부정사의 부사적 용법으로 목적}

On his way to the car, Mr. Boggis couldn't help smiling. The table
_{couldn't help ~ing: ~하지 않을 수 없었다}
was what every dealer dreamed of. He couldn't believe his luck.
_{선행사가 포함된 관계대명사: ~인 것, ~하는 것. the thing that과 같은 의미}

"Dad, what if this thing doesn't go in his car? He might not pay you,"
_{what if ~?: ~하면 어쩌지, ~라면   this thing = Rummins의 탁자}
_{어떻게 될까?}
said Bert.

Rummins then had an idea. "What he wants is only the legs. Let's cut
_{선행사가 포함된 관계대명사: ~인 것, ~하는 것. the thing that과 같은 의미}
the legs off for him," said Rummins. "Great idea!" said Bert. Bert then

took out a saw and began to cut off the legs.

When Mr. Boggis came back, the legs had been cut off. "Don't
_{과거완료 수동태: 탁자 다리를 자른 것이 Boggis 씨가 돌아온 시점보다 앞서 일어난 일이기 때문에}
_{과거완료 시제 사용, 탁자 다리는 Rummins와 Bert에 의해 잘려진 것이기 때문에 수동태로 쓰임.}
worry, this was a favor. I won't charge you for this," said Rummins.
_{Bert가 탁자 다리를 자른 일}   _{Bert가 탁자 다리를 자른 일}
Mr. Boggis was so shocked that he couldn't say anything.
_{so+형용사+that ~ 구문, 너무 충격을 받아서 아무 말도 할 수 없었다}

on one's way to ~로 가는 길에
cannot help ~ing ~하지 않을 수 없다
believe 믿다
pay (값·비용·대가 등을) 지불하다
take out 꺼내다
saw 톱
favor 호의, 친절
charge (요금·값을) 청구하다
shock 충격을 주다, 깜짝 놀라게 하다

📎 **확인문제**

● 다음 문장이 본문의 내용과 일치하면 T, 일치하지 <u>않으면</u> F를 쓰시오.

1   Rummins agreed to sell his table for thirty pounds. ☐

2   On his way to the car, Mr. Boggis couldn't smile. ☐

3   Rummins' table was what every dealer dreamed of. ☐

4   Mr. Boggis didn't pay Rummins because the table didn't go in his car. ☐

5   Bert took out a saw and began to cut off the legs of the table. ☐

6   Rummins charged Mr. Boggis for cutting off the legs of the table. ☐

우리말을 참고하여 빈칸에 알맞은 말을 쓰시오.

1 One _____ Sunday

2 Cyril Boggis was _____ _____ _____ _____ in London.

3 He was known for buying good things _____ _____ _____ _____ and then selling them _____ _____ _____ _____.

4 People asked him _____ _____ _____ _____ the furniture, but he just said, "It's a secret."

5 Mr. Boggis' secret was _____.

6 He went to small towns _____ _____ and knocked on doors.

7 He told people that he was _____ _____ _____.

8 People didn't know _____ _____ _____ _____ _____, so Mr. Boggis _____ _____ _____ them.

9 He was able to buy things _____ _____.

10 Now it was _____ _____, and Mr. Boggis was in a small town again.

11 _____ _____ _____ he visited, he met two men.

12 _____ was Rummins, the owner, and _____ _____ was his son Bert.

13 "I buy _____ _____.

14 Do you have _____?" asked Mr. Boggis.

15 "No, I _____," said Rummins.

16 "Can I just _____ _____ _____?" asked Mr. Boggis.

1 어느 운수 좋은 일요일

2 Cyril Boggis는 런던의 골동품 가구 판매상이었다.

3 그는 좋은 물건을 낮은 가격에 사서 높은 가격에 파는 것으로 유명했다.

4 사람들은 그에게 어디서 가구를 구했는지 물어봤지만, 그는 "그건 비밀이에요."라고만 말했다.

5 Boggis 씨의 비밀은 단순했다.

6 그는 매주 일요일 작은 마을들을 방문해서 문을 두드렸다.

7 그는 사람들에게 자신이 가구 판매상이라고 말했다.

8 사람들은 자신들의 물건들이 얼마나 값진 것인지 몰랐으므로 Boggis 씨는 그들을 이용했다.

9 그는 물건들을 매우 싸게 살 수 있었다.

10 일요일이 또 찾아왔고 그날 Boggis 씨는 다시 어느 작은 마을에 있었다.

11 그는 방문한 집에서 두 남자를 만났다.

12 한 명은 주인인 Rummins였고, 다른 한 명은 그의 아들인 Bert였다.

13 "저는 고가구를 삽니다.

14 고가구가 있으신가요?" Boggis 씨가 물었다.

15 "아니요." Rummins가 말했다.

16 "한번 둘러봐도 될까요?" Boggis 씨가 물었다.

17 "_____. Please come in," said Rummins.

18 Mr. Boggis first went to the kitchen, and _____ _____ _____.

19 He then _____ _____ the living room.

20 And _____ _____ _____!

21 A table which was _____ _____ _____ _____ eighteenth-century English furniture.

22 He was _____ excited _____ he almost fell over.

23 "What's _____?" Bert asked.

24 "Oh, _____. Nothing at all," Mr. Boggis lied.

25 He then said _____ _____ _____ _____, "This table is a reproduction.

26 _____ _____ only a few pounds."

27 He then added, "Hmm, I think I _____ _____ it.

28 The legs of my table at home _____ _____.

29 I can cut off the legs of your table and _____ _____ _____ _____."

30 "_____ _____?" Rummins asked.

31 "Not much, I'm _____.

32 This is just _____ _____," said Mr. Boggis.

33 "_____ how much?"

34 "Ten _____."

35 "Ten? _____ _____ more than that."

18 Boggis 씨는 먼저 부엌에 갔는데 아무것도 없었다.

19 그런 다음 그는 거실로 옮겼다.

20 그리고 그곳에 그것이 있었다!

21 18세기 영국 가구인 매우 귀중한 탁자가.

22 그는 몹시 흥분해서 거의 넘어질 뻔했다.

23 "무슨 일이세요?" Bert가 물었다.

24 "오, 아무것도 아니에요. 전혀 아무 일도 아닙니다." Boggis 씨는 거짓말을 했다.

25 그리고 나서 그는 정색하며 말했다 "이 탁자는 복제품입니다.

26 몇 파운드의 가치밖에 안 돼요."

27 그리고 그는 덧붙였다. "흠, 제 생각에 제가 살 수도 있을 것 같아요.

28 우리 집에 있는 탁자 다리가 부러졌거든요.

29 당신의 탁자 다리를 잘라서 제 탁자에 붙일 수 있겠어요."

30 "얼마 줄 거예요?" Rummins가 물었다.

31 "유감이지만 많이 줄 수는 없어요.

32 이것은 복제품일 뿐이니까요." Boggis 씨가 말했다.

33 "그래서 얼마 줄 수 있는데요?"

34 "10파운드요."

35 "10이요? 그것보다는 가치가 더 나가요."

36 "_____ _____ fifteen?"

37 "_____ _____ fifty."

38 "Well, thirty. This is my _____ _____."

39 "OK, it's _____, but how are you going to take it?

40 This thing will not _____ _____ a car!"

41 "We'll see," Mr. Boggis said and went out _____ _____ his car.

42 _____ _____ _____ to the car, Mr. Boggis _____ _____ _____.

43 The table was _____ every dealer dreamed _____.

44 He _____ _____ his luck.

45 "Dad, _____ _____ this thing doesn't go in his car?

46 He might not _____ _____," said Bert.

47 Rummins then _____ _____ _____.

48 "_____ _____ _____ is only the legs.

49 Let's _____ _____ _____ _____ for him," said Rummins.

50 "_____ _____!" said Bert.

51 Bert then _____ _____ a saw and began to cut off the legs.

52 When Mr. Boggis came back, the legs _____ _____ _____ _____.

53 "Don't worry, this was _____ _____.

54 I won't _____ you _____ this," said Rummins.

55 Mr. Boggis was _____ shocked _____ he couldn't say anything.

36 "15는 어때요?"

37 "50으로 하지요."

38 "음, 30이요. 이게 제 마지막 제안입니다."

39 "그러죠, 이제 당신 겁니다. 그런데 이걸 어떻게 가져갈 건가요?

40 이게 차에 들어가지 않을 거예요!"

41 "한번 보죠." Boggis 씨가 말하고는 자신의 차를 가지러 밖으로 나갔다.

42 차로 가는 길에 Boggis 씨는 싱글벙글하지 않을 수 없었다.

43 그 탁자는 모든 판매상이 꿈꾸는 것이었다.

44 그는 자신의 운을 믿을 수 없었다.

45 "아버지, 만약 이게 차에 안 들어가면 어떻게 하죠?

46 그가 값을 지불하지 않을 수도 있어요." Bert가 말했다.

47 Rummins는 그때 생각이 떠올랐다.

48 "그가 원하는 건 오직 다리뿐이야.

49 그를 위해서 다리를 자르자." Rummins가 말했다.

50 "좋은 생각이에요!" Bert가 말했다.

51 그런 다음 Bert는 톱을 꺼내서 다리를 자르기 시작했다.

52 Boggis 씨가 돌아왔을 때, 다리는 잘려 있었다.

53 "걱정하지 마세요. 호의로 한 거예요.

54 이것에 대해 비용을 청구하지는 않을게요." Rummins가 말했다.

55 Boggis 씨는 너무 충격을 받아서 아무 말도 할 수 없었다.

● 우리말을 참고하여 본문을 영작하시오.

1 어느 운수 좋은 일요일

➡ _____

2 Cyril Boggis는 런던의 골동품 가구 판매상이었다.

➡ _____

3 그는 좋은 물건을 낮은 가격에 사서 높은 가격에 파는 것으로 유명했다.

➡ _____

4 사람들은 그에게 어디서 가구를 구했는지 물어봤지만, 그는 "그건 비밀이에요."라고만 말했다.

➡ _____

5 Boggis 씨의 비밀은 단순했다.

➡ _____

6 그는 매주 일요일 작은 마을들을 방문해서 문을 두드렸다.

➡ _____

7 그는 사람들에게 자신이 가구 판매상이라고 말했다.

➡ _____

8 사람들은 자신들의 물건들이 얼마나 값진 것인지 몰랐으므로 Boggis 씨는 그들을 이용했다.

➡ _____

9 그는 물건들을 매우 싸게 살 수 있었다.

➡ _____

10 일요일이 또 찾아왔고 그날 Boggis 씨는 다시 어느 작은 마을에 있었다.

➡ _____

11 그는 방문한 집에서 두 남자를 만났다.

➡ _____

12 한 명은 주인인 Rummins였고, 다른 한 명은 그의 아들인 Bert였다.

➡ _____

13 "저는 고가구를 삽니다.

➡ _____

14 고가구가 있으신가요?" Boggis 씨가 물었다.

➡ _____

15 "아니요." Rummins가 말했다.

➡ _____

16 "한번 둘러봐도 될까요?" Boggis 씨가 물었다.

➡ _____

17 "그럼요. 들어오세요." Rummins가 말했다.

➡ _____

18 Boggis 씨는 먼저 부엌에 갔는데 아무것도 없었다.

➡ _____

19 그런 다음 그는 거실로 옮겼다.

➡ _____

20 그리고 그곳에 그것이 있었다!

➡ _____

21 18세기 영국 가구인 매우 귀중한 탁자가.

➡ _____

22 그는 몹시 흥분해서 거의 넘어질 뻔했다.

➡ _____

23 "무슨 일이세요?" Bert가 물었다.

➡ _____

24 "오, 아무것도 아니에요. 전혀 아무 일도 아닙니다." Boggis 씨는 거짓말을 했다.

➡ _____

25 그러고 나서 그는 정색하며 말했다. "이 탁자는 복제품입니다.

➡ _____

26 몇 파운드의 가치밖에 안 돼요."

➡ _____

27 그리고 그는 덧붙였다. "흠, 제 생각에 제가 살 수도 있을 것 같아요.

➡ _____

28 우리 집에 있는 탁자 다리가 부러졌거든요.

➡ _____

29 당신의 탁자 다리를 잘라서 제 탁자에 붙일 수 있겠어요."

➡ _____

30 "얼마 줄 거예요?" Rummins가 물었다.

➡ _____

31 "유감이지만 많이 줄 수는 없어요.

➡ _____

32 이것은 복제품일 뿐이니까요." Boggis 씨가 말했다.

➡ _____

33 "그래서 얼마 줄 수 있는데요?"

➡ _____

34 "10파운드요."

➡ _____

35 "10이요? 그것보다는 가치가 더 나가요."

➡ _____

36 "15는 어때요?"

➡ _____

37 "50으로 하지요."
➡ _____

38 "음, 30이요. 이게 제 마지막 제안입니다."
➡ _____

39 "그러죠, 이제 당신 겁니다. 그런데 이걸 어떻게 가져갈 건가요?
➡ _____

40 이게 차에 들어가지 않을 거예요!"
➡ _____

41 "한번 보죠." Boggis 씨가 말하고는 자신의 차를 가지러 밖으로 나갔다.
➡ _____

42 차로 가는 길에 Boggis 씨는 싱글벙글하지 않을 수 없었다.
➡ _____

43 그 탁자는 모든 판매상이 꿈꾸는 것이었다.
➡ _____

44 그는 자신의 운을 믿을 수 없었다.
➡ _____

45 "아버지, 만약 이게 차에 안 들어가면 어떻게 하죠?
➡ _____

46 그가 값을 지불하지 않을 수도 있어요." Bert가 말했다.
➡ _____

47 Rummins는 그때 생각이 떠올랐다.
➡ _____

48 "그가 원하는 건 오직 다리뿐이야.
➡ _____

49 그를 위해서 다리를 자르자." Rummins가 말했다.
➡ _____

50 "좋은 생각이에요!" Bert가 말했다.
➡ _____

51 그런 다음 Bert는 톱을 꺼내서 다리를 자르기 시작했다.
➡ _____

52 Boggis 씨가 돌아왔을 때, 다리는 잘려 있었다.
➡ _____

53 "걱정하지 마세요. 호의로 한 거예요.
➡ _____

54 이것에 대해 비용을 청구하지는 않을게요." Rummins가 말했다.
➡ _____

55 Boggis 씨는 너무 충격을 받아서 아무 말도 할 수 없었다.
➡ _____

[01~03] 다음 글을 읽고 물음에 답하시오.

Now it was another Sunday, and Mr. Boggis was in a small town again. At a house he visited, he met two men. One was Rummins, the owner, and the other was his son Bert.

"I buy old furniture. Do you have any?" asked Mr. Boggis.

"No, I don't," said Rummins.

"Can I just take a look?" asked Mr. Boggis.

"Sure. Please come in," said Rummins.

Mr. Boggis first went to the kitchen, and there was nothing. He then moved to the living room. And there it was! A table which was a(n) _____ⓐ_____ piece of eighteenth-century English furniture. He was so excited that he almost fell over.

"What's wrong?" Bert asked.

"Oh, nothing. Nothing at all," Mr. Boggis lied. He then said with a straight face, "This table is a reproduction. It's worth only a few pounds."

01 위 글의 빈칸 ⓐ에 들어갈 알맞은 말을 모두 고르시오.

① invaluable
② priceless
③ valueless
④ precious
⑤ worthless

02 위 글의 주제로 알맞은 것을 고르시오.

① the pleasure of finding valuable furniture
② how to spend Sundays in a small town
③ the effective way to collect old furniture
④ a lie of a furniture dealer to get greater profits

⑤ how to distinguish an imitation from an original

03 위 글의 마지막 부분에서 알 수 있는 'Mr. Boggis'의 성격으로 알맞은 것을 모두 고르시오.

① sincere
② cunning
③ straightforward
④ frank
⑤ dishonest

[04~06] 다음 글을 읽고 물음에 답하시오.

Cyril Boggis was an antique furniture dealer in London. (①) He was known for buying good things at a low price and then selling ⓐ them at a high price. (②) People asked him where he had got the furniture, but he just said, "It's a secret."

(③) He went to small towns every Sunday and knocked on doors. (④) He told people that he was a furniture dealer. (⑤) People didn't know how valuable their things were, so Mr. Boggis took advantage of them. He was able to buy things very cheaply.

04 위 글의 흐름으로 보아, 주어진 문장이 들어가기에 가장 적절한 곳은?

Mr. Boggis' secret was simple.

①　　②　　③　　④　　⑤

05 다음 빈칸 (A)와 (B)에 알맞은 단어를 넣어, 위 글의 밑줄 친 ⓐthem이 가리키는 것을 완성하시오.

> It refers to the (A)_____ _____ that Cyril Boggis bought at (B)_____ _____ _____.

06 According to the passage, which is NOT true?

① Mr. Boggis dealt in antique furniture.

② Mr. Boggis told people where he had got the furniture.

③ Mr. Boggis went to small towns on Sundays.

④ People didn't know the true value of their things.

⑤ Mr. Boggis was able to buy things very cheaply by taking advantage of people.

[07~09] 다음 글을 읽고 물음에 답하시오.

He then added, "Hmm, I think I may buy it. The legs of my table at home are broken. I can cut off the legs of your table and attach them to mine."

"How much?" Rummins asked.

"Not much, I'm afraid. This is just a reproduction," said Mr. Boggis.

"So how much?"

"Ten pounds."

"Ten? It's worth more than that."

"How about fifteen?"

"Make it fifty."

"Well, thirty. This is ①my final offer."

"OK, it's yours, but how are ②you going to take it? This thing will not go in a car!"

"We'll see," Mr. Boggis said and went out ⓐto bring his car.

On his way to the car, Mr. Boggis couldn't help smiling. The table was what every

dealer dreamed of. ③He couldn't believe his luck.

"Dad, ⓑ만약 이게 차에 안 들어가면 어떻게 하죠? He might not pay ④you," said Bert.

Rummins then had an idea. "What ⑤he wants is only the legs. Let's cut the legs off for him," said Rummins. "Great idea!" said Bert. Bert then took out a saw and began to cut off the legs.

07 밑줄 친 ①~⑤ 중에서 가리키는 대상이 나머지 넷과 다른 것은?

①　　　②　　　③　　　④　　　⑤

08 아래 〈보기〉에서 위 글의 밑줄 친 ⓐto bring과 to부정사의 용법이 같은 것의 개수를 고르시오.

> ┤ 보기 ├
> ① What a fool she is to believe such a thing!
> ② It is dangerous for children to play with matches.
> ③ I have some assignment to do today.
> ④ He didn't live to see the work finished.
> ⑤ His fault is to talk too much.

① 1개　② 2개　③ 3개　④ 4개　⑤ 5개

09 위 글의 밑줄 친 ⓑ의 우리말에 맞게 9 단어로 영작하시오.

➡ _____

[10~12] 다음 글을 읽고 물음에 답하시오.

Cyril Boggis was an antique furniture dealer in London. He was known for buying good things at a low price and then selling them at a high price. ⓐ사람들은 그에게 어디서 가구를 구했는지 물었다, but he just said, "It's a secret."

Mr. Boggis' secret was simple. He went to small towns every Sunday and knocked on doors. He told people that he was a furniture dealer. People didn't know how valuable their things were, so Mr. Boggis took advantage of them. ⓑHe was able to buy things very expensively.

서답형

10 위 글의 밑줄 친 ⓐ의 우리말에 맞게 주어진 어휘를 알맞게 배열하시오.

where / him / asked / the furniture / got / people / he / had

➡ _____

서답형

11 위 글의 밑줄 친 ⓑ에서 흐름상 어색한 부분을 찾아 고치시오.

_____ ➡ _____

12 Which question CANNOT be answered after reading the passage?

① What kind of job did Mr. Boggis have?
② Was Mr. Boggis's job profitable?
③ Did Mr. Boggis tell people the place he bought his items?
④ How long did Mr. Boggis do his work?
⑤ Did people in small towns know how valuable their things were?

[13~15] 다음 글을 읽고 물음에 답하시오.

He then added, "Hmm, I think I may buy it. The legs of my table at home (A)[is / are] broken. I can cut off the legs of your table and attach ①them to ②mine."

"How much?" Rummins asked.

"Not much, I'm afraid. This is just a reproduction," said Mr. Boggis.

"So how much?"

"Ten pounds."

"Ten? It's worth more than that."

"③How about fifteen?"

"Make it fifty."

"Well, thirty. This is my final offer."

"OK, it's (B)[mine / yours], but how are you going to take it? ④This thing will not go in a car!"

"We'll see," Mr. Boggis said and went out to bring his car.

On his way to the car, Mr. Boggis couldn't help smiling. The table was (C)[that / what] every dealer dreamed of. He couldn't believe ⑤his luck.

"Dad, what if this thing doesn't go in his car? He might not pay you," said Bert.

Rummins then had an idea. "What he wants is only the legs. Let's cut the legs off for him," said Rummins. "Great idea!" said Bert. Bert then took out a saw and began to cut off the legs.

서답형

13 위 글의 괄호 (A)~(C)에서 문맥이나 어법상 알맞은 낱말을 골라 쓰시오.

➡ (A) _____ (B) _____ (C) _____

14 다음 중 위 글의 밑줄 친 ①~⑤에 대한 설명이 옳지 않은 것을 고르시오.

① them은 the legs of your table을 가리킨다.
② mine은 the legs of my table을 의미한다.
③ "What about fifteen?"으로 바꿀 수 있다.
④ This thing은 Rummins의 탁자를 가리킨다.
⑤ '30파운드에 모든 판매상이 꿈꾸는 탁자를 사게 된 것'을 가리킨다.

15 위 글의 제목으로 알맞은 것을 고르시오.

① Hmm, I Think I May Buy It!

② Not Much, I'm Afraid

③ Unbelievable! I'm the Luckiest Man in the World!

④ A Man Who Has Something Undone by His Own Trick

⑤ What If This Thing Doesn't Go in My Car?

[16~18] 다음 글을 읽고 물음에 답하시오.

Cyril Boggis was an antique furniture dealer in London. He was known for buying good things ____ⓐ____ a low price and then (A)selling them ____ⓐ____ a high price. People asked him where he had got the furniture, but he just said, "It's a secret."

Mr. Boggis' secret was simple. He went to small towns every Sunday and knocked ____ⓑ____ doors. He told people that he was a furniture dealer. People didn't know how valuable their things were, so Mr. Boggis took advantage of them. He was able to buy things very cheaply.

16 위 글의 빈칸 ⓐ와 ⓑ에 들어갈 전치사가 바르게 짝지어진 것은?

	ⓐ ⓑ		ⓐ ⓑ
①	in – to	②	at – on
③	for – at	④	at – to
⑤	in – on		

17 위 글의 밑줄 친 (A)selling과 문법적 쓰임이 같은 것을 모두 고르시오.

① I saw him selling things.

② My job is making shoes.

③ It's no use crying over spilt milk.

④ What was he carrying in his hand?

⑤ She finished doing her homework.

18 위 글의 제목으로 알맞은 것을 고르시오.

① How to Be an Antique Furniture Dealer

② Do You Want to Sell Things Expensively?

③ Where Did Mr. Boggis Get the Furniture?

④ The Secret of Mr. Boggis' Profitable Business

⑤ The Way to Buy Good Things Cheaply

[19~21] 다음 글을 읽고 물음에 답하시오.

Now it was another Sunday, and Mr. Boggis was in a small town again. At a house he visited, he met two men. One was Rummins, the owner, and the other was his son Bert.

"I buy old furniture. Do you have any?" asked Mr. Boggis.

"No, I don't," said Rummins.

"Can I just ____ⓐ____ a look?" asked Mr. Boggis.

"Sure. Please come in," said Rummins.

Mr. Boggis first went to the kitchen, and there was nothing. He then moved to the living room. And there ⓑit was! A table which was a priceless piece of eighteenth-century English furniture. He was so excited that he almost fell over.

"What's wrong?" Bert asked.

ⓒ"Oh, nothing. Nothing at all," Mr. Boggis lay. He then said with a straight face, "This table is a reproduction. It's worth only a few pounds."

19 위 글의 빈칸 ⓐ에 들어갈 알맞은 말을 <u>모두</u> 고르시오.

① have   ② make

③ keep   ④ let

⑤ take

서답형

20 위 글의 밑줄 친 ⓑit이 가리키는 것을 본문에서 찾아 쓰시오.

➡ _____

_____

서답형

21 위 글의 밑줄 친 ⓒ에서 어법상 틀린 부분을 찾아 고치시오.

_____ ➡ _____

[22~25] 다음 글을 읽고 물음에 답하시오.

On his way to the car, Mr. Boggis couldn't help smiling. ⓐ그 탁자는 모든 판매상이 꿈꾸는 것이었다. He couldn't believe his luck.

"Dad, what if this thing doesn't go in his car? He might not pay you," said Bert.

Rummins then had an idea. "What he wants is only the legs. Let's cut the legs off for him," said Rummins. "Great idea!" said Bert. Bert then took out a saw and began to cut off the legs.

When Mr. Boggis came back, the legs had been cut off. "Don't worry, this was a favor. I won't ⓑcharge you for this," said Rummins. Mr. Boggis was so shocked that he couldn't say anything.

서답형

22 위 글의 밑줄 친 ⓐ의 우리말에 맞게 주어진 어휘를 알맞게 배열하시오.

> what / dealer / was / of / every / the table / dreamed

➡ _____

중요

23 위 글의 밑줄 친 ⓑcharge와 같은 의미로 쓰인 것을 고르시오.

① I charge a gun with powder.

② What did they charge for the repairs?

③ He took charge of the farm after his father's death.

④ You charge yourself with a heavy task.

⑤ The charge for admission is free.

24 위 글에 어울리는 속담으로 가장 알맞은 것을 고르시오.

① Look before you leap.

② A penny saved is a penny earned.

③ Grasp all, lose all.

④ Nothing ventured, nothing gained.

⑤ Like father, like son.

중요

25 위 글에서 알 수 있는 Mr. Boggis의 심경 변화로 가장 알맞은 것을 고르시오.

① upset → frustrated

② nervous → shocked

③ satisfied → bored

④ hopeful → nervous

⑤ delighted → disappointed

[01~03] 다음 글을 읽고 물음에 답하시오.

Cyril Boggis was an antique furniture dealer in London. He was known (A)[by / for] buying good things at a (B)[high / low] price and then selling them at a (C)[cheap / high] price. People asked him where he had got the furniture, but he just said, "It's a secret."

Mr. Boggis' secret was simple. He went to small towns every Sunday and knocked on doors. He told people that he was a furniture dealer. People didn't know how valuable their things were, so Mr. Boggis took advantage of ⓐthem. He was able to buy things very cheaply.

01 위 글의 괄호 (A)~(C)에서 문맥이나 어법상 알맞은 낱말을 골라 쓰시오.

➡ (A) _____ (B) _____ (C) _____

02 위 글의 밑줄 친 ⓐthem이 가리키는 것을 본문에서 찾아 쓰시오.

➡ _____

03 다음 빈칸 (A)와 (B)에 알맞은 단어를 본문에서 찾아 넣어, Boggis 씨가 가구를 구입하는 방식을 완성하시오.

Mr. Boggis bought good things very (A)_____ in a way that was dishonest by making use of people who didn't know how (B)_____ their things were.

[04~06] 다음 글을 읽고 물음에 답하시오.

Now it was another Sunday, and Mr. Boggis was in a small town again. At a house he visited, he met two men. One was Rummins, the owner, and the other was his son Bert.

"I buy old furniture. Do you have any?" asked Mr. Boggis.

"No, I don't," said Rummins.

"Can I just take a look?" asked Mr. Boggis.

"Sure. Please come in," said Rummins.

Mr. Boggis first went to the kitchen, and there was nothing. He then moved to the living room. And there it was! A table which was a priceless piece of eighteenth-century English furniture. ⓐ그는 몹시 흥분해서 거의 넘어질 뻔했다.

"What's wrong?" Bert asked.

"Oh, nothing. Nothing at all," Mr. Boggis lied. He then said with a straight face, "This table is a reproduction. It's worth only a few pounds."

04 위 글의 밑줄 친 ⓐ의 우리말에 맞게 주어진 어휘를 알맞게 배열하시오.

fell / excited / he / almost / that / he / so / over / was

➡ _____

05 주어진 영영풀이에 해당하는 단어를 본문에서 찾아 쓰시오.

a copy of something such as a piece of furniture or a work of art

➡ _____

06 다음 빈칸 (A)와 (B)에 알맞은 단어를 넣어, 위 글에서 Boggis 씨가 말한 거짓말의 내용을 완성하시오.

> Mr. Boggis said that the table was a replica and it was worth (A)_____ _____ _____ pounds though he realized its real (B)_____.
>
> *replica: (실물을 모방하여 만든) 복제품

[07~09] 다음 글을 읽고 물음에 답하시오.

He then added, "Hmm, I think I may buy it. The legs of my table at home are broken. I can cut off the legs of your table and attach them to mine."

"How much?" Rummins asked.

"Not much, I'm afraid. This is just a reproduction," said Mr. Boggis.

"So how much?"

"Ten pounds."

"Ten? ⓐIt's worth more than that."

"How about fifteen?"

"Make it fifty."

"Well, thirty. This is my final offer."

"OK, it's yours, but how are you going to take it? This thing will not go in a car!"

"We'll see," Mr. Boggis said and went out to bring his car.

On his way to the car, ⓑMr. Boggis couldn't help smiling. The table was what every dealer dreamed of. He couldn't believe his luck.

"Dad, ⓒwhat if this thing doesn't go in his car? He might not pay you," said Bert.

Rummins then had an idea. "What he wants is only the legs. Let's cut the legs off for him," said Rummins. "Great idea!" said Bert. Bert then took out a saw and began to cut off the legs.

07 위 글의 밑줄 친 ⓐ과 바꿔 쓸 수 있는 말을 두 단어로 쓰시오.

➡ _____

08 위 글의 밑줄 친 ⓑ를 (1) 원형부정사를 사용하여, (2) to부정사를 사용하여 고칠 때, 빈칸에 들어갈 알맞은 말을 쓰시오.

➡ (1) Mr. Boggis _____ _____ smile.
　(2) Mr. Boggis _____ _____ _____ _____ to smile.

09 위 글의 밑줄 친 ⓒ를 다음과 같이 바꿔 쓸 때 빈칸에 들어갈 알맞은 말을 쓰시오.

➡ (1) what will _____ if this thing doesn't go in his car?
　(2) what should we _____ if this thing doesn't go in his car?

[10~12] 다음 글을 읽고 물음에 답하시오.

When Mr. Boggis came back, the legs ⓐ_____. "Don't worry, this was a favor. I won't charge you for this," said Rummins. ⓑMr. Boggis was so shocked that he couldn't say anything.

10 위 글의 빈칸 ⓐ에 cut off를 알맞은 형태로 쓰시오.

➡ _____

11 위 글의 밑줄 친 ⓑ를 다음과 같이 바꿔 쓸 때 빈칸에 들어갈 알맞은 단어를 쓰시오.

➡ Mr. Boggis was _____ shocked _____ say anything.

12 Why was Mr. Boggis so shocked when he came back? Answer in English beginning with "Because".

➡ _____

After You Read A Read and Complete

① One Sunday, Mr. Boggis, an antique furniture dealer, went to a small town
to buy furniture.
to부정사의 부사적 용법(목적)

② At Rummins and Bert's house, Mr. Boggis found a table, a priceless piece
= invaluable
of eighteenth-century English furniture.

③ Mr. Boggis lied to Rummins and Bert that the table was just a reproduction.
lie–lied–lied: 거짓말하다
His final offer for the table was thirty pounds and Rummins accepted it.
his final offer for the table

④ Since what Mr. Boggis wanted was only the legs of the table, Bert cut them
선행사를 포함하는 관계대명사   cut off them(×)
off. Mr. Boggis was very shocked to see the table.
to부정사의 부사적 용법(원인)

구문해설 • antique 골동품의; (귀중한) 골동품 • furniture 가구 • dealer (특정 상품을) 사고파는 상인
• priceless 값을 매길 수 없는, 대단히 귀중한 • reproduction (예술 작품의) 복제품, 복제화
• offer 제의, 제안 • cut off ~을 잘라 내다 • shock 충격을 주다, 깜짝 놀라게 하다

Around the World

Fantastic Mr. Fox: A fox protects his family from three mean farmers.
protect A from B: A를 B로부터 지키다
Matilda: A girl uses her special powers to help her friends.
to부정사의 부사적 용법(목적)
Charlie and the Chocolate Factory: A boy visits the best chocolate factory
최상급
in the world.
'in+장소(보통 단수)'로 최상급 수식

구문해설 • protect: 보호하다, 지키다 • mean: 비열한, 심술궂은

Think and Write

Review of the story, *One Lucky Sunday*

This story was written by Roald Dahl. It is about Mr. Boggis, who was an
관계대명사(계속적 용법)
antique furniture dealer. In the story, he lied to Rummins that his table was
보통은 자동사이나 that절을 취하는 타동사로 쓰임   접속사
a reproduction and offered 30 pounds to buy it. Mr. Boggis said he only
부사적 용법(목적)
wanted the legs of the table, so Bert cut them off for him. This surprised Mr.
접속사   '타동사+대명사 목적어+부사' cut off them(×)
Boggis who really wanted the whole table. I think Mr. Boggis was not a good
주격 관계대명사
man because he lied to people. What I like the most about this story is the
관계대명사   단수
surprising ending. I think this story is very interesting.
능동(현재분사)   능동(현재분사)

구문해설 • antique furniture: 골동품 가구 • dealer: 판매상, 딜러 • reproduction: 복제품
• cut off: 잘라내다

01 〈보기〉의 밑줄 친 charge와 같은 의미로 쓰인 것을 고르시오.

┤ 보기 ├

He charged a relatively modest fee.

① What do you charge for work of this type?

② His charge was to obtain specific information.

③ She forgot to charge the battery, she said.

④ I am charged to give you this letter.

⑤ A service charge of 15% was added on to the bill.

02 다음 영영풀이에 해당하는 단어를 주어진 철자로 시작하여 빈칸에 쓰고, 알맞은 것을 골라 문장을 완성하시오.

• v_____ : worth a lot of money

• o_____ : a statement that you are willing to do something for someone or give someone something

• f_____ : things such as chairs, beds, tables, and cupboards

(1) We got rid of all the old _____.

(2) The job _____ was simply too good to refuse.

(3) The book provides _____ information on recent trends.

03 다음 대화의 빈칸에 〈영영풀이〉를 참고하여 알맞은 어휘를 쓰시오.

A: It's a great chance.

B: Yes. I'd like to take _____ of this opportunity.

<영영풀이> to make good use of something or an opportunity

04 다음 빈칸 (A)~(C)에 알맞은 말을 쓰시오. (주어진 철자로 시작하여 쓸 것.)

• Come here now and (A)t_____ a look out the window.

• The weather became so bad (B)t_____ they had to turn back.

• They were (C)p_____ of their children's achievements.

05 괄호 안에 주어진 어휘를 이용하여 빈칸에 알맞게 쓰시오.

(1) Photocopy machines can _____ documents. (produce)

(2) We should _____ used things. (cycle)

(3) There are _____ stars in the night sky. (count)

Conversation

[06~07] 다음 대화를 읽고 물음에 답하시오.

G: You don't look so good, Inho. What's the matter?
(A) Yes. I'm taking medicine.
(B) That's too bad. Did you see the doctor?
(C) Well, _____(a)_____ .
(D) I have the flu.
B: Thanks.

06 주어진 문장 사이에 나올 대화의 순서로 알맞은 것은?

① (B) – (A) – (C) – (D)
② (C) – (B) – (A) – (D)
③ (D) – (A) – (C) – (B)
④ (D) – (B) – (A) – (C)
⑤ (D) – (B) – (C) – (A)

07 위 대화의 빈칸 (a)에 알맞지 않은 것을 고르시오.

① I hope you feel better soon.
② I hope you get well soon.
③ I doubt you feel better soon.
④ I want you to feel better soon.
⑤ I wish you could get well soon.

08 다음 중 짝지어진 대화가 어색한 것은?

① A: What's up?
   B: My smartphone is broken. I'm very upset.
② A: I passed the final test. I'm so excited.
   B: That's a shame.
③ A: That's wonderful. Congratulations!
   B: Thanks.
④ A: You must be very proud of yourself.
   B: Yes, I am. I did my best.

⑤ A: I remember taking it out of my bag at the snack shop.
   B: Then, let's go back to the snack shop to look for it.

[09~10] 다음 대화를 읽고 물음에 답하시오.

B: Excuse me, Ms. Carter. Can I ask you a question? Did I get the main role in the play?
W: Yes, you did. Congratulations, Jiho! You're going to be Romeo in our school play, *Romeo and Juliet*.
B: Really? I'm so excited. Thank you so much, Ms. Carter. (①)
W: I know how much you wanted the role. I'm so happy for you. (②)
B: Thank you. What about Sumi? Did she get the role she wanted, too? (③)
W: Unfortunately, no. She's very disappointed. (④)
B: Oh, I'm sorry to hear that. (⑤)
W: It's at 2 p.m. on September 20th, in the acting club room. You'll get a text message about it soon.
B: OK. I'll be there.

09 위 대화의 (①)~(⑤) 중 주어진 문장이 들어갈 곳은?

> Anyway, when is the first practice?

①   ②   ③   ④   ⑤

10 위 대화를 읽고 답할 수 없는 질문을 고르시오.

① Did Jiho get a role in his school play?
② What is Jiho's role in his school play?
③ Why is Jiho so excited?
④ Why didn't Sumi get the role she wanted?
⑤ Will Jiho get a text message?

Grammar

[11~12] 다음 대화를 참고하여 아래 주어진 빈칸에 적절한 단어를 쓰시오.

11

Tom: Lisa, what did the boss offer to you?
Lisa: To go to New York.
Tom: Wow, that was a dramatic promotion. How did you feel about it?
Lisa: I was so happy to hear that.

➡ Lisa felt happy about _____ her boss had offered.

12

Frank: Miles, did you meet James?
Miles: Yes, I did.
Frank: You didn't know him before, did you?
Miles: Yeah.

➡ Miles _____ _____ _____ James before he met him.

13 다음 각 문장의 밑줄 친 부분이 과거완료시제의 용법 중 어떤 것에 해당하는지 〈보기〉에서 찾아 기호를 쓰시오.

┌ 보기 ┐
ⓐ 완료 ⓑ 경험 ⓒ 결과 ⓓ 계속

(1) Mr. Boggis <u>had</u> already <u>left</u> the town when Bert came to see him. (_____)
(2) Belinda <u>had</u> never <u>seen</u> the snow until she came to Hokkaido. (_____)
(3) By the time Mr. Boggis arrived at the house, they <u>had cut</u> the legs of the chair off. (_____)

(4) Sam <u>had lived</u> in Daegu for 10 years by last month. (_____)
(5) I found somebody <u>had broken</u> the door of my car. (_____)
(6) April didn't recognize the businessman because she <u>had</u> never <u>met</u> him before. (_____)
(7) When the princess woke up, seven little guys <u>had prepared</u> food. (_____)
(8) I <u>had waited</u> for the actor for almost a day before the preview started. (_____)

[14~15] 다음 중 어법상 <u>어색한</u> 문장을 고르시오.

14 ① I don't believe what cannot be seen.
② What is important to you is also important to me.
③ Rice and water are what you need to make *Juk*, the Korean porridge.
④ Simpson got up so early what he could catch the train.
⑤ Aiden gave the people what he thought was the best for them.

15 ① My wife lost the necklace that I had bought for her for our anniversary.
② Susan couldn't recognize the director of the movie, because she has never seen him before.
③ All of my classmates were really full because we had had so much pizza.
④ When the dancers arrived at the concert, the singer had just finished her first song.
⑤ Janet had read the fairy tale book before she went to bed.

16 다음 두 문장의 의미가 같도록 빈칸에 들어갈 알맞은 말을 쓰시오.

> Anna didn't notice the thing that Elsa had done for her birthday.
> = Anna didn't notice _____ Elsa had done for her birthday.

17 다음 빈칸에 알맞은 말이 바르게 짝지어진 것은?

> • The tourists showed me the photos _____ they had taken in front of the pyramids in Egypt.
> • Cathy didn't have lunch as she _____ a lot for breakfast.

① what – had eaten
② that – has been eating
③ which – had eaten
④ what – ate
⑤ that – has eaten

18 다음 두 문장을 관계대명사를 이용하여, 하나의 문장으로 만드시오.

(1) • Her neighbors know the thing.
   • Sarah did it five years ago.

➡ _____

(2) • These are not the things.
   • Jinwoo has always wanted them.

➡ _____

(3) • Tell your teacher the things.
   • They have bothered you.

➡ _____

19 다음 괄호 안에서 어법상 알맞은 것을 고르시오.

(1) Mr. Boggis felt guilty after Rummins (had cut / has cut) the legs of the table.

(2) Charlotte learned that Roald Dahl (had written / wrote) the famous book *Charlie and the Chocolate Factory*.

(3) Matilda (has gone / had gone) to Venice before the director of the film visited to see her.

(4) A lot of BTS's fans in America and Europe said they (have been / had been) learning Korean.

(5) My daughter found and ate the chocolate cookies that her mother (had hidden / has hidden) in the kitchen.

(6) They wonder when Mr. Boggis (had gotten / got / has gotten) the precious old furniture.

Reading

[20~22] 다음 글을 읽고 물음에 답하시오.

Cyril Boggis was an antique furniture dealer in London. He was known for buying good things at a low price and then ⓐ them at a high price. People asked him where he had got the furniture, but he just said, "It's a secret."

Mr. Boggis' secret was simple. He went to small towns every Sunday and knocked on doors. He told people that he was a furniture dealer. ⓑPeople didn't know how valuable their things were, so Mr. Boggis took advantage of them. He was able to buy things very cheaply.

20 위 글의 빈칸 ⓐ에 sell을 알맞은 형태로 쓰시오.

➡ _____

21 위 글의 밑줄 친 ⓑ를 다음과 같이 바꿔 쓸 때 빈칸에 들어갈 알맞은 단어를 쓰시오.

➡ _____ people didn't know how valuable their things were, Mr. Boggis took advantage of them.

22 위 글을 읽고 Cyril Boggis에 대해 알 수 <u>없는</u> 것을 고르시오.

① What was his occupation?
② Where did he live?
③ How much money did he earn from his work?
④ What was his secret of making money?
⑤ Where did he go every Sunday?

[23~24] 다음 글을 읽고 물음에 답하시오.

Now it was another Sunday, and Mr. Boggis was in a small town again. At a house he visited, he met two men. One was Rummins, the owner, and the other was his son Bert.

"I buy old furniture. Do you have any?" asked Mr. Boggis.

"No, I don't," said Rummins.

"Can I just take a look?" asked Mr. Boggis.

"Sure. Please come in," said Rummins.

Mr. Boggis first went to the kitchen, and there was nothing. He then moved to the living room. And there it was! A table which was a priceless piece of eighteenth-century English furniture. He was so excited that he almost fell over.

"What's wrong?" Bert asked.

"Oh, nothing. Nothing at all," Mr. Boggis lied. He then said with a straight face, "This table is a reproduction. It's worth only a few pounds."

23 위 글의 제목으로 알맞은 것을 고르시오.

① A Busy Day of an Antique Furniture Dealer
② There Was No Furniture in Rummins' Kitchen
③ Mr. Rummins Wants to Sell a Priceless Piece of Furniture
④ A Cunning Lie to Get More Profits
⑤ Oops! It's a Reproduction.

24 According to the passage, which is NOT true?

① On another Sunday, Mr. Boggis was in a small town again.
② At a house he visited, he met Rummins and his son Bert.
③ Mr. Boggis first went to the kitchen, and there he found a priceless piece of eighteenth-century English table.
④ Mr. Boggis said the table was a reproduction.
⑤ Mr. Boggis said the table was worth only a few pounds.

[25~27] 다음 글을 읽고 물음에 답하시오.

He then added, "Hmm, I think I may buy it. The legs of my table at home are broken. I can cut off the legs of your table and attach them to mine."

"How much?" Rummins asked.

"Not much, I'm afraid. This is just a reproduction," said Mr. Boggis.

"So how much?"

"Ten pounds."

"Ten? It's worth more than (A)that."

"How about fifteen?"

"(B)50으로 하지요."

"Well, thirty. This is my final offer."

"OK, it's yours, but how are you going to take it? This thing will not go in a car!"

"We'll see," Mr. Boggis said and went out to bring his car.

On his way to the car, Mr. Boggis couldn't help smiling. The table was what every dealer dreamed of. He couldn't believe his luck.

"Dad, what if this thing doesn't go in his car? He might not pay you," said Bert.

Rummins then had an idea. "＿＿ⓐ＿＿ he wants is only the legs. Let's cut the legs off for him," said Rummins. "Great idea!" said Bert. Bert then took out a saw and began to cut off the legs.

25 위 글의 빈칸 ⓐ에 들어갈 알맞은 말을 고르시오.

① That ② What

③ How ④ Why

⑤ Which

26 위 글의 밑줄 친 (A)that이 가리키는 것을 본문에서 찾아 쓰시오.

➡ ＿＿＿＿＿＿＿＿＿＿＿

27 위 글의 밑줄 친 (B)의 우리말에 맞게 주어진 어휘를 이용하여 3 단어로 영작하시오.

Make

➡ ＿＿＿＿＿＿＿＿＿＿＿

[28~29] 다음 글을 읽고 물음에 답하시오.

Review of the Story, One Lucky Sunday

This story was written by Roald Dahl. It is about Mr. Boggis, who was an antique furniture dealer. (①) In the story, he lied to Rummins that his table was a reproduction and offered 30 pounds to buy it. (②) Mr. Boggis said he only wanted the legs of the table, so Bert cut them off for him. (③) I think Mr. Boggis was not a good man because he lied to people. (④) What I like the most about this story is the surprising ending. (⑤) I think this story is very interesting.

28 위 글의 흐름으로 보아, 주어진 문장이 들어가기에 가장 적절한 곳은?

This surprised Mr. Boggis who really wanted the whole table.

① ② ③ ④ ⑤

29 위 글을 읽고 알 수 <u>없는</u> 것을 고르시오.

① Who is Mr. Boggis?

② What did Mr. Boggis tell Rummins?

③ How much did Mr. Boggis offer to Rummins?

④ What was the actual price of the table?

⑤ Why did Bert cut the legs of the table off?

01 다음 중 짝지어진 단어의 관계가 나머지와 다른 것은?

① play – replay
② tract – retract
③ act – react
④ use – reuse
⑤ view – review

02 다음 밑줄 친 부분의 의미로 알맞지 않은 것은?

① He is known for writing surprising endings. (~로 유명하다)
② Priceless antiques were destroyed in the fire. (대단히 귀중한)
③ She took advantage of the children's absence to tidy their rooms. (~을 이용했다)
④ He is depressed and cannot help crying. (~을 도울 수 없다)
⑤ On my way to school, I met Ms. Parker. (~로 가는 길에)

03 다음 빈칸에 공통으로 들어갈 알맞은 말을 쓰시오.

• Please _____ out the suitcase from the overhead bin.
• Right now forget the details and _____ a look at the big picture.

04 다음 주어진 우리말에 맞게 빈칸을 채우시오. (주어진 철자로 시작할 것.)

(1) 이탈리아 사람들은 대가족으로 알려져 있습니다.
➡ Italians are k_____ for having large families.

(2) 그 회사는 그에게 일자리를 제안해야 했지만 그는 거절했다.
➡ The company had to o_____ the man a job, but he refused.

(3) 그녀는 훌륭한 고가구를 소장하고 있다.
➡ She has a fine collection of a_____ f_____.

[05~06] 다음 대화를 읽고 물음에 답하시오.

G: Tim, congratulations on winning the gold medal in the school marathon.
B: Thanks, Suji. I'm very happy.
G: You must be very proud of yourself.
B: Yes, I am. I did my best.

05 위 대화를 읽고 대답할 수 없는 질문을 고르시오.

① Why is Tim happy?
② Why is Tim proud of himself?
③ What did Tim get in the school marathon?
④ When did Tim win the gold medal in the school marathon?
⑤ What does Suji congratulate Tim on?

06 How does Tim feel about himself? Answer with 7 English words.

➡ _____

[07~09] 다음 대화를 읽고 물음에 답하시오.

B: Mina, is anything wrong?

G: Well, I lost my smartphone. I'm ___(A)___ .

B: Oh, (a)I'm so sorry to hear that. (b)마지막으로 그것을 언제 사용했는지 기억하니? (it, remember, last, use)

G: Well, I remember taking it out of my bag at the snack shop.

B: Then, let's go back to the snack shop to look for it.

출제율 90%

07 빈칸 (A)에 알맞은 말을 고르시오.

① excited ② upset

③ confused ④ delighted

⑤ disappointed

출제율 100%

08 위 대화의 밑줄 친 (a)와 의도가 다른 것을 고르시오.

① You did a good job.

② That's too bad.

③ That's terrible.

④ That's really sad.

⑤ That's a pity.

출제율 95%

09 위 대화의 밑줄 친 (b)의 우리말에 맞게 주어진 어휘를 이용하여 영작하시오.

➡ _____

출제율 100%

10 다음 중 어법상 올바른 문장을 모두 고르면?

① Amy returned the books which she had borrowed from Mr. Johnson.

② The movie began when Jamie had arrived at the theater.

③ Harry's old friends were shocked that he has been designated as a terrorist.

④ The grass looked much greener than before as it had rained that morning.

⑤ I heard that your secretary has overworked to pass out three days before.

출제율 95%

11 다음 〈보기〉와 같이 관계대명사와 과거완료시제를 이용하여 두 문장을 한 문장으로 만드시오.

┌─ 보기 ─┐

• Mr. Boggis was very shocked at the thing.

• The thing was cut off by them.

→ Mr. Boggis was very shocked at what had been cut off by them.

└────────┘

(1) • Korea's national soccer team enjoyed the things.

• Many fans sent the things.

➡ _____

_____

(2) • We ate the thing.

• Mom cooked the thing for us.

➡ _____

(3) • My daughter read it.

• I wrote it.

➡ _____

(4) • The store didn't have the things.

• I always wanted to buy the things.

➡ _____

_____

출제율 100%

12 다음 주어진 문장의 밑줄 친 what과 같은 용법으로 쓰인 것을 모두 고르시오.

What made Mr. Boggis shocked was that the men had cut off the legs of the table.

① Everyone in the party wondered <u>what</u> the princess was interested in.

② This is <u>what</u> the professor has studied for almost 15 years so far.

③ <u>What</u> do you think the president meant to do for the next meeting?

④ <u>What</u> was regarded polite in the past is not always considered as such these days.

⑤ <u>What</u> has Brian come here for?

⑥ It was the book what he wrote for the poor children in England.

⑦ Rummins believed what Mr. Boggis mentioned about the value of the old table.

⑧ The table was what every dealer had dreamed of.

출제율 95%

13 다음 그림을 보고 자연스러운 문장이 되도록 괄호 안에 주어진 단어를 바르게 배열하여 빈칸을 완성하시오.

➡ When Mr. Boggis came back, _____ _____. (the table, already, the legs, off, been, of, cut, had)

출제율 95%

14 다음 중 어법상 <u>어색한</u> 문장을 <u>모두</u> 고르시오.

① Mr. Boggis is the only dealer what made a lot of villagers happy.

② When Mr. Boggis came back, the legs of the table had been cut off.

③ Mr. Boggis was so shocked what he couldn't say anything.

④ What happened when Mr. Boggis came to Bert's garden?

⑤ I was impressed by *Charlie and the Chocolate Factory* that Dahl had written in 1964.

출제율 95%

15 다음 〈보기〉처럼 괄호 안에 주어진 조건과 과거완료시제를 이용하여 두 문장을 한 문장으로 만드시오.

> ┤ 보기 ├
>
> Jonas decided to learn swimming. He saw his friend drown to death. (접속사 as 로 시작)
>
> → As he had seen his friend drown to death, Jonas decided to learn swimming.

(1) Mr. Boggis bought the good things at a low price. He sold them at a high price. (Before로 시작)

➡ _____

_____

(2) People said to him, "Where did you get the furniture?" (간접화법으로 전환)

➡ _____

[16~17] 다음 글을 읽고 물음에 답하시오.

This story was written by Roald Dahl. It is about Mr. Boggis, who was an antique furniture dealer. In the story, he lied to Rummins that his table was a reproduction and offered 30 pounds to buy it. ⓐMr. Boggis said he only wanted the legs of the table, so Bert cut off them for him. This surprised Mr.

Boggis who really wanted the whole table. I think Mr. Boggis was not a good man because he lied to people. What I like the most about this story is the surprising ending. I think this story is very interesting.

출제율 100%

16 위 글의 종류로 알맞은 것을 고르시오.

① biography ② manual
③ essay ④ book report
⑤ article

출제율 95%

17 위 글의 밑줄 친 ⓐ에서 어법상 틀린 부분을 찾아 고치시오.

_____ ➡ _____

[18~20] 다음 글을 읽고 물음에 답하시오.

Cyril Boggis was an antique furniture dealer in London. He was known for buying good things at a low price and then selling them at a high price. People asked him where he had got the furniture, but he just said, "(A)It's a secret."

Mr. Boggis' secret was simple. (B)He went to small towns every Sunday and knocked on doors. He told people that he was a furniture dealer. People didn't know how valuable their things were, so Mr. Boggis ___ⓐ___ them. He was able to buy things very cheaply.

출제율 95%

18 위 글의 빈칸 ⓐ에 들어갈 알맞은 말을 고르시오.

① educated ② took advantage of
③ looked on ④ encouraged
⑤ took a look

출제율 90%

19 위 글의 밑줄 친 (A)н이 가리키는 것을 본문에서 찾아 쓰시오.

➡ _____

출제율 95%

20 위 글의 밑줄 친 (B)를 다음과 같이 바꿔 쓸 때 빈칸에 들어갈 알맞은 단어를 쓰시오.

➡ He went to small towns on _____

[21~23] 다음 글을 읽고 물음에 답하시오.

Now it was another Sunday, and Mr. Boggis was in a small town again. At a house he visited, he met two men. One was Rummins, the owner, and the other was his son Bert.

"I buy old furniture. Do you have any?" asked Mr. Boggis.

"No, I don't," said Rummins.

"Can I just take a look?" asked Mr. Boggis.

"Sure. Please come in," said Rummins. (①)

Mr. Boggis first went to the kitchen, and there was nothing. (②) He then moved to the ⓐliving room. (③) A table which was a priceless piece of eighteenth-century English furniture. (④) He was so excited that he almost fell over. (⑤)

"What's wrong?" Bert asked.

"Oh, nothing. Nothing at all," Mr. Boggis lied. He then said with a straight face, "This table is a reproduction. It's worth only a few pounds."

출제율 95%

21 위 글의 흐름으로 보아, 주어진 문장이 들어가기에 가장 적절한 곳은?

And there it was!

① ② ③ ④ ⑤

22 위 글의 밑줄 친 ⓐliving과 문법적 쓰임이 같은 것을 모두 고르시오.

① He bought a swimming suit.
② Ann's uncle was a walking dictionary.
③ The lady is in a waiting room now.
④ Smoking is allowed only in a smoking room.
⑤ Look at the dancing girl.

23 위 글의 내용으로 보아 알 수 없는 것을 고르시오.

① When was Mr. Boggis in a small town again?
② At a house he visited, whom did Mr. Boggis meet?
③ Where did Mr. Boggis go first at Rummins' house?
④ What did Mr. Boggis find in the living room?
⑤ Where did Rummins buy the eighteenth-century English table?

[24~26] 다음 글을 읽고 물음에 답하시오.

　　　ⓐ　　　his way to the car, Mr. Boggis couldn't help smiling. The table was what every dealer dreamed of. He couldn't believe his luck.

"Dad, what if this thing doesn't go in his car? He might not pay you," said Bert.

Rummins then had an idea. "(A)What he wants is only the legs. Let's cut the legs off for him," said Rummins. "Great idea!" said Bert. Bert then took out a saw and began to cut off the legs.

　　When Mr. Boggis came back, the legs had been cut off. "Don't worry, this was a favor. I won't charge you 　ⓑ　 this," said Rummins. Mr. Boggis was so shocked that he couldn't say anything.

24 위 글의 빈칸 ⓐ와 ⓑ에 들어갈 전치사가 바르게 짝지어진 것은?

　　　ⓐ　ⓑ　　　　　　　ⓐ　ⓑ
① By – on　　　　② On – to
③ On – for　　　　④ By – to
⑤ To – for

25 위 글의 밑줄 친 (A)What과 문법적 쓰임이 같은 것을 모두 고르시오.

① Anderson is not what he was.
② What is the matter with you?
③ What time is it?
④ Kate always does what she believes is right.
⑤ Do you know what this is?

26 According to the passage, which is NOT true?

① On his way to the car, Mr. Boggis couldn't but smile.
② Mr. Boggis was satisfied with his good luck.
③ Rummins suggested to Bert that they should cut the legs of the table off.
④ Rummins said that what he did was a favor.
⑤ Mr. Boggis was so shocked that he could say nothing.

[01~03] 다음 대화를 읽고 물음에 답하시오.

B: Excuse me, Ms. Carter. Can I ask you a question? Did I get the main role in the play?

W: Yes, you were. Congratulations, Jiho! You're going to be Romeo in our school play, *Romeo and Juliet*.

B: Really? I'm so excited. Thank you so much, Ms. Carter.

W: I know how much you wanted the role. I'm so happy for you.

B: Thank you. What about Sumi? Did she get the role she wanted, too?

W: Unfortunately, no. She's very disappointed.

B: Oh, I'm sorry to hear that. Anyway, when is the first practice?

W: It's at 2 p.m. on September 20th, in the acting club room. You'll get a text message about it soon.

B: OK. I'll be there.

01 What will be Jiho's character in the school play, *Romeo and Juliet*? (4 words)

➡ _____

02 위 대화에서 어법상 <u>어색한</u> 것을 하나 찾아 바르게 고치시오.

_____ ➡ _____

03 Why does Jiho feel so excited? Answer by beginning with the word, 'Because'. (13 words)

➡ _____
_____

[04~05] 다음 중에서 <u>틀린</u> 문장을 각각 두 개씩 찾아, 순서대로 기호를 쓰고 바르게 고쳐 문장을 다시 쓰시오.

04 ① The mechanic said that someone had broken the tires on purpose.
② Louise had refused to go to the dentist as he already felt the pain of pulling teeth.
③ The old artist felt quite tired because she had repaired the statue since the day before yesterday.
④ The researchers had found out that somebody put the wrong data into the file.
⑤ The guard told us that he had already checked out the fences over there.

➡ _____

➡ _____
_____

05 ① What the students respected him was his extensive knowledge and good judgment.
② The antique dealer was careful about what he would buy from the villagers.
③ The windows were not what needed the special cleaning service.
④ The wrestler will show us what he could do on the stage.
⑤ These bags are not what the clerk has wanted to buy them.

➡ _____
_____

➡ _____
_____

Cyril Boggis was an antique furniture dealer in London. He was known for buying good things at a low price and then selling them at a high price. People asked him where he ___ⓐ___ the furniture, but he just said, "It's a secret."

Mr. Boggis' secret was simple. He went to small towns every Sunday and knocked on doors. He told people that he was a furniture dealer. ⓑ사람들은 자신들의 물건들이 얼마나 값진 것인지 몰랐다, so Mr. Boggis took advantage of them. He was able to buy things very cheaply.

06 위 글의 빈칸 ⓐ에 get을 알맞은 형태로 쓰시오.

➡ _____

07 위 글의 밑줄 친 ⓑ의 우리말에 맞게 주어진 어휘를 이용하여 8 단어로 영작하시오.

> how valuable, things

➡ _____

_____

08 What was Mr. Boggis' secret? Fill in the blanks (A) and (B) with suitable words.

> He bought good things at a (A)_____ price by taking advantage of people who didn't know the value of their things and then sold them at a (B)_____ price.

[09~11] 다음 글을 읽고 물음에 답하시오.

Now it was (A)[another / the other] Sunday, and Mr. Boggis was in a small town again. At a house he visited, he met two men. One was Rummins, the owner, and (B)[another / the other] was his son Bert.

"I buy old furniture. Do you have any?" asked Mr. Boggis.

"No, I don't," said Rummins.

"Can I just take a look?" asked Mr. Boggis.

"Sure. Please come in," said Rummins.

Mr. Boggis first went to the kitchen, and there was nothing. He then moved to the living room. And there it was! A table which was a priceless piece of eighteenth-century English furniture. He was so (C)[exciting / excited] that he almost fell over.

"What's wrong?" Bert asked.

"Oh, nothing. Nothing at all," Mr. Boggis lied. He then said with a straight face, "This table is a reproduction. ⓐIt's worth quite a few pounds."

09 위 글의 괄호 (A)~(C)에서 어법상 알맞은 낱말을 골라 쓰시오.

➡ (A) _____ (B) _____ (C) _____

10 위 글의 밑줄 친 ⓐ에서 흐름상 어색한 부분을 찾아 고치시오.

_____ ➡ _____

11 본문의 내용과 일치하도록 다음 빈칸 (A)와 (B)에 알맞은 단어를 쓰시오.

> Mr. Boggis told a (A)_____ with a straight face to deceive Bert about the real value of the priceless eighteenth-century English (B)_____.

01 다음 그림과 〈보기〉에 주어진 단어들을 활용하여, 빈칸에 들어갈 알맞은 내용을 3개 이상 자유롭게 영작하시오. 단, 과거완료시제를 반드시 사용하도록 한다.

(1)   (2)   (3)   (4)

┌ 보기 ┐
the grasshopper, Pinocchio, the rabbit, Pooh, play, lie, sleep, steal

- _____ regretted that _____
_____ .

(1) _____

(2) _____

(3) _____

(4) _____

02 다음 내용을 바탕으로 독후감을 쓰시오.

One Lucky Sunday

Q: Who is Mr. Boggis?

A: He was an antique furniture dealer.

Q: What happened to Mr. Boggis?

A: He lied to Rummins that his table was a reproduction and offered 30 pounds to buy it. Mr. Boggis said he only wanted the legs of the table, so Bert cut them off for him. This surprised Mr. Boggis who really wanted the whole table.

Q: What do you think of Mr. Boggis?

A: I think Mr. Boggis was not a good man.

Q: What makes you think so?

A: Because he lied to people.

Q: What do you like the most about this story?

A: What I like the most about this story is the surprising ending.

Review of the Story, *One Lucky Sunday*

This story was written by Roald Dahl. It is about Mr. Boggis, who was (A)_____ . In the story, he lied to Rummins that his table was (B)_____ and offered 30 pounds to buy it. Mr. Boggis said he only wanted (C)_____ , so Bert cut them off for him. This surprised Mr. Boggis who really wanted (D)_____ . I think Mr. Boggis was not a good man because he (E)_____ to people. What I like the most about this story is (F)_____ . I think this story is very interesting.

단원별 모의고사

01 다음 짝지어진 단어의 관계가 같도록 빈칸에 알맞은 말을 쓰시오. (주어진 철자로 시작할 것.)

> exact – precise : priceless – i_____

[02~03] 주어진 영어 설명에 알맞은 어휘를 빈칸에 쓰시오.

02 (2 단어)

> Branches were _____ from the tree by the wind.

> <영어 설명> to remove something by cutting it with a knife or a sharp tool

➡ _____

03 (1 단어)

> This vase is _____ several hundred dollars.

> <영어 설명> having a specific value

➡ _____

04 다음 빈칸에 알맞은 말로 짝지어진 것을 고르시오.

> • I _____ a beer and a sandwich.
> • There was a _____ of *the Mona Lisa* on the table.

① rejected – promotion
② objected – reproduction
③ objected – production
④ ordered – reproduction
⑤ ordered – production

05 다음 우리말을 주어진 어휘를 이용하여 영작하시오.

(1) 누군가가 당신의 약점을 이용하게 하지 마세요.
(let, anyone, take, weak points)

➡ _____
_____

(2) 나는 그를 비웃지 않을 수 없다. (help, laugh)

➡ _____

[06~07] 다음 대화를 읽고 물음에 답하시오.

> B: Sue, you look excited. What's up?
> G: I was elected as class president. I'm so excited.
> B: (a)That's wonderful. Congratulations!
> G: Thanks. I'm really happy to have a chance (b)to work for my class.

06 위 대화의 밑줄 친 (a)와 바꿔 쓸 수 <u>없는</u> 것은?

① Well done!
② Good job!
③ I suggest you do a nice job.
④ Great!
⑤ I'm glad to hear that.

07 위 대화의 밑줄 친 (b)to work와 같은 용법으로 쓰인 것은?

① He needs to work for the bank.
② I have some projects to work on.
③ Michelle went to her office to work.
④ How clever of you to work it out!
⑤ I'd like for us to work together.

[08~09] 다음 대화의 밑줄 친 부분을 괄호 안에 주어진 어휘를 이용하여 바꿔 쓰시오.

08

A: What's up?

B: I was chosen as the leader of the school band. I'm so excited.

A: <u>That's wonderful.</u> (hear, glad, that) Congratulations!

➡ _____

09

A: What's up?

B: My bike is broken. I'm very upset.

A: <u>That's too bad.</u> (hear, sorry, that)

➡ _____

[10~11] 다음 대화를 읽고 물음에 답하시오.

B: You don't look good, Sumi. What's the matter?

G: Well, I didn't get a role in the school play. I'm very disappointed.

B: Oh, I'm so sorry to hear that. But I'm sure you can get a role next time.

G: Thanks. I'll try harder next time.

10 Why is Sumi very disappointed? Answer by beginning with the word "Because".

➡ _____

11 위 대화의 내용과 일치하지 <u>않는</u> 것은?

① 수미는 기분이 안 좋아 보인다.

② 수미는 학교 연극에서 역할을 맡지 못 했다.

③ 수미는 정말 실망했다.

④ 소년은 수미에게 다음 기회에 역할을 맡을 수 있을 것이라고 위로한다.

⑤ 수미는 다음에는 포기할 것이다.

12 다음 그림의 상황에 맞게 〈보기〉에 주어진 어휘를 이용하여 대화의 빈칸을 알맞게 채우시오.

┤ 보기 ├

a toothache / too bad / see the doctor / taking medicine / feel better soon

A: What's up?

B: I _____.

A: _____. _____?

B: Yes. _____.

A: I hope _____.

B: Thanks.

13 두 문장을 같은 의미의 한 문장이 되도록 관계대명사 what을 사용하여 빈칸을 알맞게 채우시오.

(1) • Mr. Boggis was able to buy the things cheaply.

• They were very valuable.

= Mr. Boggis _____

_____.

(2) • Mr. Boggis wanted only the thing.

• It was the old vase.

= _____

_____.

14 다음 빈칸 (A)~(C)에 들어갈 알맞은 말이 차례대로 짝지어진 것은?

• Mr. Boggis had nothing to say when he saw Rummins (A)_____ the table.

• When Mr. Boggis (B)_____ Rummins, he had not known the value of his furniture.

• Bert showed Mr. Boggis the legs of the table after he (C)_____ the legs off.

	(A)	(B)	(C)
①	cut	had met	had cut
②	cut	met	has cut
③	had cut	has met	cut
④	cut	had met	was cut
⑤	had cut	met	cut

15 다음에 주어진 단어들을 모두 배열하여 우리말을 영작할 때, 세 번째와 여섯 번째에 오는 단어들을 쓰시오.

그는 그가 싼 가격에 구매한 것들을 판매했다.
(at, sold, low, he, he, what, bought, prices, had)

➡ 세 번째: _____ 여섯 번째: _____

16 다음 중 어법상 어색한 문장은?

① The wedding had already started when her friends got there.

② Have you ever listened to the song before I show you its music video?

③ Mr. Boggis doesn't have any money because he had lost his wallet.

④ They said that they had cut the legs of the table for free.

⑤ Alice had lived in Singapore for ten years before she moved to Seoul.

17 다음 중 어법상 옳은 문장끼리 바르게 짝지어진 것은?

ⓐ You could give me what you would like to throw away.

ⓑ Show Lisa the things what are in your backpack.

ⓒ That's not what Mike wanted for his high school graduation.

ⓓ Bossa Nova in Brazil music is that my brother enjoys listening to.

ⓔ A person what writes texts for advertising is called a copywriter.

ⓕ It's not that the police were looking for.

ⓖ Greg is not what he used to be.

① ⓐ, ⓒ, ⓓ, ⓖ ② ⓐ, ⓒ, ⓖ
③ ⓑ, ⓒ, ⓔ, ⓖ ④ ⓐ, ⓓ, ⓕ, ⓖ
⑤ ⓐ, ⓔ, ⓕ

18 다음 중 빈칸에 들어갈 것이 다른 하나는?

① Mr. Boggis sold _____ his neighbours regarded as a useless item.

② The baby girl was able to touch the mobile toys _____ her daddy had set up.

③ Did your secretary showed the host of the party _____ you had given to her?

④ Her neighbor forgot to tell Susan _____ she had heard about the missing puppy.

⑤ I'll show you _____ David has always studied in that little room.

19 다음 중 어법상 또는 의미상 모두 올바르게 쓰인 문장을 하나 고르시오.

① When Mr. Boggis had come to get the table, the legs were already cut off.

② Since Mr. Boggis recognized the value of the table, he had met the owner of the table.

③ By the time Rummins had arrived at his backyard, his son already cut the tree.

④ Because Bert had woken up late, he had to run to the subway station.

⑤ Though the villagers had not known the value of their items, they sold them at low prices.

[20~21] 다음 글을 읽고 물음에 답하시오.

Cyril Boggis was an ⓐ_____ furniture dealer in London. He was known for buying good things at a low price and then selling them at a high price. People asked him where he had got the furniture, but he just said, "It's a secret."

Mr. Boggis' secret was simple. He went to small towns every Sunday and knocked on doors. He told people that he was a furniture dealer. People didn't know how valuable their things were, so Mr. Boggis took advantage of them. He was able to buy things very cheaply.

20 주어진 영영풀이를 참고하여 빈칸 ⓐ에 철자 a로 시작하는 단어를 쓰시오.

| an old object such as a piece of china or furniture which is valuable because of its beauty or rarity   *rarity: 희귀성 |

➡ _____

21 How was it possible for Mr. Boggis to take advantage of people? Answer in English by beginning with "Because". (9 words)

➡ _____

_____

[22~23] 다음 글을 읽고 물음에 답하시오.

Now it was another Sunday, and Mr. Boggis was in a small town again. ⓐAt a house he visited, he met two men. One was Rummins, the owner, and the other was his son Bert.

"I buy old furniture. Do you have any?" asked Mr. Boggis.

"No, I don't," said Rummins.

"Can I just take a look?" asked Mr. Boggis.

"Sure. Please come in," said Rummins.

Mr. Boggis first went to the kitchen, and there was nothing. He then moved to the living room. And there it was! A table which was a priceless piece of eighteenth-century English furniture. He was so excited that he almost fell over.

"What's wrong?" Bert asked.

"Oh, nothing. Nothing at all," Mr. Boggis lied. He then said ⓑ정색하며, "This table is a reproduction. It's worth only a few pounds."

22 다음 문장의 빈칸에 위 글의 밑줄 친 ⓐ에 생략된 단어가 들어갈 수 있는 문장을 모두 고르시오.

① This is the house _____ he bought last year.

② I couldn't see the church from the place _____ I was standing.

③ Is there a shop _____ I can buy a pen?

④ Do you know the park _____ she likes most?

⑤ The library is the place _____ he spends most of his time.

23 위 글의 밑줄 친 ⓑ의 우리말에 맞게 주어진 어휘를 이용하여 4 단어로 영작하시오.

> face

➡ _____

[24~25] 다음 글을 읽고 물음에 답하시오.

He then added, "Hmm, I think I may buy it. The legs of my table at home are broken. I can cut off the legs of your table and attach them to mine."

"How much?" Rummins asked.

"Not much, I'm afraid. This is just a reproduction," said Mr. Boggis.

"So how much?"

"Ten pounds."

"Ten? It's worth more than that."

"How about fifteen?"

"Make it fifty."

"Well, thirty. This is my final offer."

"OK, it's yours, but how are you going to take it? This thing will not go in a car!"

"We'll see," Mr. Boggis said and went out to bring his car.

On his way to the car, Mr. Boggis couldn't help smiling. The table was what every dealer dreamed of. He couldn't believe his luck.

"(①) He might not pay you," said Bert. (②) Rummins then had an idea. "(③) What he wants is only the legs. (④) Let's cut the legs off for him," said Rummins. "(⑤) Great idea!" said Bert. Bert then took out a saw and began to cut off the legs.

24 위 글의 흐름으로 보아, 주어진 문장이 들어가기에 가장 적절한 곳은?

> Dad, what if this thing doesn't go in his car?

①   ②   ③   ④   ⑤

25 According to the passage, which is NOT true?

① Mr. Boggis said the legs of his table at home were broken.

② Mr. Boggis said the table was just a reproduction.

③ Rummins agreed to sell his table for thirty pounds.

④ Rummins was very happy with his luck.

⑤ Bert began to cut off the legs of the table with a saw.

[26~27] 다음 글을 읽고 물음에 답하시오.

"Dad, what if this thing doesn't go in his car? He ⓐ not pay you," said Bert.

Rummins then had an idea. "What he wants is only the legs. Let's cut the legs off for him," said Rummins. "Great idea!" said Bert. Bert then took out a saw and began to cut off the legs.

When Mr. Boggis came back, the legs had been cut off. "Don't worry, this was a favor. I won't charge you for ⓑthis," said Rummins. Mr. Boggis was so shocked that he couldn't say anything.

26 위 글의 빈칸 ⓐ에 알맞은 것을 고르시오.

① need   ② would

③ should   ④ could

⑤ might

27 위 글의 밑줄 친 ⓑthis가 가리키는 것을 우리말로 쓰시오.

➡ _____

MEMO

Lesson 7

Technology in Our Lives

 의사소통 기능

- 방법 · 절차 묻고 답하기

  A: Do you know how to return these books?

  B: Sure. First, insert the card. Then put the books in this box.

- 감사 표현하기

  I really appreciate your help.

 언어 형식

- 분사구문

  Using various methods, experts analyze big data.

- 접속사 as

  As information and communication technology develops, the amount of data we have is getting much greater than before.

교과서
Words & Expressions

Key Words

- **amount** [əmáunt] 명 총계, 총액
- **analyze** [ǽnəlàiz] 동 분석하다
- **appreciate** [əprí:ʃièit] 동 감사하다, 감상하다
- **as** [əz] 접 ~함에 따라, ~한 대로, ~ 때문에
- **avoid** [əvɔ́id] 동 피하다, 방지하다
- **communication** [kəmjù:nəkéiʃən] 명 의사소통, 연락
- **complex** [kəmpléks] 형 복잡한
- **crime** [kraim] 명 범죄
- **database** [déitəbeis] 명 데이터베이스
- **develop** [divéləp] 동 성장하다, 발달하다
- **endless** [éndlis] 형 끝없는, 무한한
- **expert** [ékspə:rt] 명 전문가
- **flu** [flu:] 명 독감
- **forecast** [fɔ́:rkæst] 동 예측하다, 예보하다
- **further** [fɔ́:rðər] 형 더 이상의, 추가의
- **huge** [hju:dʒ] 형 거대한, (크기·양·정도가) 막대한
- **identify** [aidéntəfài] 동 알아보다, 확인하다, 식별하다
- **improve** [imprú:v] 동 개선하다, 향상하다
- **include** [inklú:d] 동 포함하다
- **industry** [índəstri] 명 산업, 공업
- **influence** [ínfluəns] 동 영향을 미치다
- **insert** [insə́:rt] 동 삽입하다
- **mainly** [méinli] 부 주로
- **meaningful** [mí:niŋfəl] 형 의미 있는, 중요한
- **method** [méθəd] 명 방법
- **national** [nǽʃənl] 형 국가의, 전국적인
- **performance** [pərfɔ́:rməns] 명 경기력, 수행, 성과
- **predict** [pridíkt] 동 예측하다
- **prevention** [privénʃən] 명 예방
- **purchase** [pə́:rtʃəs] 명 구매
- **recommend** [rèkəménd] 동 추천하다, 권하다
- **rent** [rent] 동 빌리다
- **spread** [spred] 명 확산, 전파
- **symptom** [símptəm] 명 증상
- **trace** [treis] 명 자취, 발자국, 흔적
- **traffic** [trǽfik] 명 교통(량)
- **unlock** [ənlák] 동 잠금을 풀다
- **upload** [ʌplóud] 동 ~을 전송하다, 업로드하다
- **various** [véəriəs] 형 다양한
- **wisely** [wáizli] 부 현명하게, 지혜롭게

Key Expressions

- **be likely to ~** ~할 것 같다
- **be used to+동사원형** ~하는 데 사용되다
- **by ~ing** ~함으로써
- **get+비교급** 점점 더 ~해지다
- **focus on ~** ~에 초점을 맞추다
- **for sure** 확실히, 분명히
- **help+A(목적어)+동사원형** A가 ~하도록 돕다
- **hot spot** 다발 지역
- **just as** 꼭 ~처럼
- **make a decision** 결정하다
- **more and more** 점점 더 많이, 더욱 더
- **play a role** 역할을 하다
- **thanks to ~** ~ 덕분에, ~ 때문에
- **the amount of ~** ~의 양/수량
- **this kind of+명사** 이런 종류의 ~

Word Power

※ 서로 비슷한 뜻을 가진 어휘

- □ **complex** 복잡한 : **complicated** 복잡한
- □ **forecast** 예측하다, 예보하다 : **predict** 예측하다
- □ **mainly** 주로 : **mostly** 대개, 주로, 보통은

- □ **expert** 전문가 : **specialist** 전문가
- □ **influence** 영향을 주다 : **affect** 영향을 미치다
- □ **various** 다양한 : **diverse** 다양한, 여러 가지의

※ 서로 반대의 뜻을 가진 어휘

- □ **complex** 복잡한 ↔ **simple** 간단한, 단순한
- □ **likely** ~할 것 같은 ↔ **unlikely** ~할 것 같지 않은
- □ **unlock** 잠금을 풀다 ↔ **lock** 잠그다

- □ **include** 포함하다 ↔ **exclude** 제외하다
- □ **meaningful** 의미 있는 ↔ **meaningless** 무의미한
- □ **upload** 업로드하다 ↔ **download** 다운로드하다

※ 접미사 -ful → 명사+-ful

- □ awe+-ful → **awful** 끔찍한, 지독한
- □ help+-ful → **helpful** 도움이 되는
- □ power+-ful → **powerful** 강력한, 영향력 있는

- □ color+-ful → **colorful** 형형색색의
- □ peace+-ful → **peaceful** 평화로운
- □ use+-ful → **useful** 유용한, 쓸모 있는

English Dictionary

- □ **analyze** 분석하다
  → to examine something carefully
  어떤 것을 주의 깊게 조사하다
- □ **avoid** 피하다
  → to stay away from someone or something
  어떤 사람이나 사물로부터 떨어져 있다
- □ **communication** 의사소통
  → the process by which people exchange information or express their thoughts and feelings
  사람들이 정보를 교환하거나 생각, 감정 등을 표현하는 과정
- □ **database** 데이터베이스
  → a large amount of information stored in a computer system 컴퓨터 시스템에 저장되어 있는 많은 양의 정보
- □ **develop** 발전시키다, 성장하다
  → to grow and change into something bigger, better or more important
  더 크고 나은 또는 더 중요한 것으로 변화하고 성장하다
- □ **identify** 확인하다
  → to realize who someone is or what something is
  어떤 사람이 누구인지 또는 어떤 사물이 무엇인지 알아차리다
- □ **industry** 산업
  → the people or companies engaged in a particular kind of commercial enterprise
  특별한 종류의 상업적인 기업에 종사하는 사람들 또는 회사들
- □ **method** 방법
  → a way of doing something 어떤 것을 하는 방식

- □ **performance** 수행, 성과
  → the action or process of accomplishing a task or function 임무나 역할을 완수하는 행위 또는 과정
- □ **predict** 예측하다
  → to say that something is going to happen 어떤 일이 일어날 것이라고 말하다
- □ **rent** 빌리다
  → to pay someone for the use of something
  어떤 사람에게 물건을 사용하는 대가를 지불하다
- □ **spread** 확산, 전파
  → the growth or development of something, so that it affects a larger area or a larger number of people
  어떤 일의 성장이나 발전이 더 큰 지역이나 더 많은 수의 사람들에게 영향을 주는 것
- □ **recommend** 추천하다, 권하다
  → to suggest something to someone
  무엇인가를 누군가에게 제안하다
- □ **purchase** 구매, 구매품
  → the action of buying something; a thing that has been bought 무언가를 사는 행위; 산 물건
- □ **influence** 영향을 주다
  → to change or affect something
  어떤 것을 바꾸거나 영향을 미치다
- □ **symptom** 증상, 징후
  → something that shows you may have a particular illness
  특정한 질병을 갖고 있을지도 모른다는 것을 보여주는 어떤 것

01 다음 짝지어진 단어의 관계가 같도록 빈칸에 알맞은 말은?

| mainly – mostly : specialist – _____ |

① expert   ② purchase

③ crime   ④ complex

⑤ amount

서답형

02 주어진 영어 설명에 맞게 문장의 빈칸에 알맞은 말을 쓰시오.

| I can _____ big data and draw meaningful results from it. |

| <영어 설명> to examine something carefully |

➡ _____

03 밑줄 친 부분의 의미로 알맞지 <u>않은</u> 것은?

① When they <u>make a decision</u>, they depend not on emotion but on reason. (결정하다)

② We arrived <u>just as</u> the musicians were packing up their instruments. (마치 ~하듯이)

③ <u>Thanks to</u> the storm, all flights were canceled. (~ 때문에)

④ Experts say the West Sea will continue to <u>get warmer</u>. (점점 더 따뜻해지다)

⑤ Train fares are <u>likely to</u> remain unchanged. (~할 것 같다)

04 다음 빈칸에 들어갈 가장 알맞은 말을 고르시오.

| Telephone is an effective means of _____. |

① amount   ② transport

③ expert   ④ communication

⑤ database

05 다음 <보기>의 단어를 사용하여 자연스러운 문장을 만들 수 없는 것은?

| 보기 |
| unlock   influence   predict   improve |

① There is some hope that things will _____.

② The media has a powerful _____ on public opinion.

③ We will _____ a car for a week and explore the area.

④ I tried to _____ the door, but the key didn't fit.

⑤ It is impossible to _____ what the eventual outcome will be.

06 다음 빈칸에 공통으로 들어갈 말로 알맞은 것을 고르시오.

| • Everyone knows about it now, thanks _____ you!
• The test is used _____ diagnose a variety of diseases. |

① for   ② on   ③ at

④ with   ⑤ to

01 다음 영영풀이에 알맞은 어휘를 〈보기〉에서 찾아 쓰시오.

> ┤ 보기 ├
>
> identify   predict   develop   database

(1) to grow and change into something bigger, better or more important
(2) a large amount of information stored in a computer system
(3) to realize who someone is or what something is
(4) to say that something is going to happen

➡ (1) _____ (2) _____ (3) _____
　(4) _____

02 다음 짝지어진 두 단어의 관계가 같도록 빈칸에 알맞은 말을 쓰시오.

(1) angry – angrily : wise – _____
(2) peace – peaceful : awe – _____

03 다음 우리말에 맞도록 빈칸에 알맞은 말을 쓰시오. (철자가 주어진 경우 그 철자로 시작할 것.)

(1) 그것은 극도로 복잡한 주제에 대한 유용한 입문서이다.
　→ It's a useful introduction to an extremely c_____ subject.
(2) 그는 학교를 중퇴하자 범죄의 길로 들어섰다.
　→ He turned to c_____ when he dropped out of school.

(3) 경제가 어디로 향하고 있는지 예측이 되세요?
　→ Can you f_____ where the economy is heading?
(4) 당신 업무에는 새로운 컴퓨터 시스템을 설치하는 것도 들어간다.
　→ Your duties will i_____ setting up a new computer system.

04 우리말에 맞게 한 단어를 추가하여 주어진 어구를 알맞게 배열하시오.

(1) 저 실험은 수감자들에게만 초점이 맞춰져 있었다. (the prisoners, that test, focused, alone, on)
　➡ _____
　　_____

(2) 우리가 견딜 수 있는 고통의 양에는 한계가 있다. (we, a limit, pain, there, the, amount, bear, can, to, of)
　➡ _____
　　_____

(3) 점점 더 많은 사람들이 인터넷을 이용하고 있다. (the Internet, people, and, are, more, using)
　➡ _____
　　_____

(4) 그가 월요일에 돌아올 것인데 확실히 말할 수는 없다. (I, Monday, he'll, can't, be, say, back, sure, but, on)
　➡ _____
　　_____

Conversation

1 방법·절차 묻고 답하기

> **A** Do you know how to use this machine? 이 기계 어떻게 사용하는지 아시나요?
>
> **B** Yes. First, choose the dish you want. Then touch the ORDER button.
> 네. 우선 원하는 음식을 고르세요. 그 다음 '주문' 버튼을 누르세요.

■ 어떤 일을 하는 방법이나 절차를 물을 때 'Do you know how to ~?', 'Can[Could] you tell me how to ~?', 'Can[Could] you explain how to ~?' 등으로 물을 수 있다. 방법이나 절차를 말할 때 상대방이 이해하기 쉽도록 First, Second, Then 등과 같이 순서를 나타내는 말을 사용하여 설명할 수 있다.

■ 다음과 같은 표현을 이용할 수도 있다.
to begin with(처음에는, 우선, 먼저), secondly(두 번째로[둘째는]), next(그 다음에), also(또한), lastly(마지막으로, 끝으로), finally(마지막으로 (= lastly), 최종적으로) 등

■ 절차를 모르는 경우에는 'I'm sorry, I don't know.'라고 말할 수 있다.

방법·절차 묻고 답하기

- Do you know how to ~? ~하는 법을 아니?
- Can you tell me how to ~? ~하는 법을 말해 줄래?
- Could you tell me how to ~? ~하는 법을 말해 주시겠어요?
- Can you explain how to ~? ~하는 법을 설명해 줄래?
- Could you explain how to ~? ~하는 법을 설명해 주시겠어요?
- I'm sorry, I don't know. 죄송하지만 전 모릅니다.

핵심 Check

1. 다음 괄호 안의 단어들을 배열하여 문맥에 맞는 문장을 완성하시오.

A: I want to buy a snack. (this machine / you / use / explain / could / how to)?

B: Yes. First, choose the snack you want.

➡ _____

② 감사 표현하기

A I really appreciate your help. 도와줘서 매우 고맙습니다.

B It's my pleasure. 제가 좋아서 한 건데요.

■ 상대방에게 어떤 일에 대해 감사를 표현하고 싶을 때 'Thank you so much.'가 일반적이지만 'I really appreciate your help.', 'I can't thank you enough.', 'I'm grateful for ~.', 'I'm thankful for ~.' 등으로 말할 수도 있다.

■ 감사 표현에 대한 응답으로 'It's not a big deal.', 'It's my pleasure.', 'Don't mention it.', 'No problem.' 등으로 응답할 수 있다.

감사 표현하기

- Thank you so much. / Thanks a lot.
- I really appreciate your help.
- I'm thankful for helping me out.

- Thank you for your help.
- I'm grateful for your help.

감사에 응답하기

- It's my pleasure. 제가 좋아서 한 건데요.
- You're welcome. 천만에요.
- No worries. 괜찮아요.

- Don't mention it. 별말씀을요.
- No problem. 별거 아냐.

핵심 Check

2. 다음 중 빈칸에 들어갈 것으로 알맞지 <u>않은</u> 표현은?

A: Can you tell me how to make tea?

B: Sure. First, put a tea bag in a cup. Then, pour hot water in the cup and leave it for 3 minutes.

A: I got it. I really appreciate your help.

B: _____

① I don't mention it.　　② It's my pleasure.

③ You're welcome.　　④ No problem.

⑤ Don't mention it.

Listen and Talk A 1

B: Excuse me. ❶Can you tell me ❷how to add money to my transportation card?

G: Of course. ❸First, put your card in the machine. Second, choose the amount of money you want to add.

B: OK.

G: Last, insert your money into the machine.

B: That ❹sounds simple. ❺Thanks.

B: 실례합니다. 어떻게 교통카드에 돈을 충전하는지 알려주시겠어요?

G: 그럼요. 우선 기계에 카드를 넣으세요. 둘째로 충전하고 싶은 금액을 고르세요.

B: 네.

G: 마지막으로 기계에 돈을 넣으세요.

B: 간단해 보이는군요. 고맙습니다.

❶ 방법이나 절차를 물을 때 'Can[Could] you tell me how to ~?', 'Do you know how to ~?', 'Can[Could] you explain how to ~?' 등으로 물을 수 있다.

❷ 의문사+to부정사: tell의 직접목적어로 쓰였다.

❸ 방법이나 절차를 말할 때 상대방이 이해하기 쉽도록 First, Second, Then 등과 같이 순서를 나타내는 말을 사용하여 설명할 수 있다.

❹ sound+형용사: ~하게 들리다

❺ 감사를 표현하는 말이다. 'I really appreciate your help.', 'I can't thank you enough.', 'I'm grateful for ~.', 'I'm thankful for ~.' 등으로 말할 수도 있다.

Check(√) True or False

(1) The boy knows how to add money to a transportation card.　　T ☐ F ☐

(2) The girl explains how to add money to a transportation card.　　T ☐ F ☐

Listen and Talk A 2

B: I want to buy a snack. ❶Do you know how to use this snack machine?

G: Yeah. First, ❷choose the snack you want.

B: I already ❸did. What's ❹next?

G: Just put in the money. Then take the snack out.

B: ❺Got it. ❻Thanks.

B: 과자를 사고 싶어요. 이 과자 자판기를 어떻게 사용하는지 알려주시겠어요?

G: 네. 먼저 원하는 과자를 고르세요.

B: 이미 했어요. 그 다음은 뭔가요?

G: 돈을 넣으세요. 그리고 나서 과자를 꺼내세요.

B: 알겠어요. 고맙습니다.

❶ 방법이나 절차를 물을 때 'Do you know how to ~?', 'Can[Could] you tell me how to ~?', 'Can[Could] you explain how to ~?' 등으로 물을 수 있다.

❷ choose와 the snack 사이에 목적격 관계대명사가 생략되어 있다.

❸ did는 'chose the snack I want'를 대신하는 대동사이다.

❹ next는 '그 다음에'라는 의미로 순서를 밝히기 위해 사용된다.

❺ 이해했음을 나타내는 표현이다.

❻ 감사를 표현하는 말이다.

Check(√) True or False

(3) The boy wants to know how to use the snack machine.　　T ☐ F ☐

(4) The girl tells the boy to put in the money first.　　T ☐ F ☐

Listen and Talk A 3

G: Excuse me. I want to rent a bike. ❶Can you tell me how to use this application?

M: Sure. ❷First, log in to the application. Then find the RENT button and touch it.

G: Then what?

M: Then the application will give you a number ❸to unlock a bike with.

G: Thank you. ❹I really appreciate your help.

❶ 방법이나 절차를 묻는 표현이다.
❷ 방법이나 절차를 말할 때 상대방이 이해하기 쉽도록 First, Second, Then 등과 같이 순서를 나타내는 말을 사용하여 설명할 수 있다.
❸ 형용사적 용법의 to부정사이다.
❹ 감사를 표현하는 말이다.

Listen and Talk B

A: Excuse me. I want to return these books. ❶Do you know how to do it?

B: Sure. It's simple. First, ❷insert the library card into the machine. Second, put the books in this box.

A: OK.

B: Then just ❸take your card out.

A: I really appreciate your help.

❶ 방법이나 절차를 묻는 표현이다.
❷ insert A into B: A를 B에 넣다
❸ take A out: A를 꺼내다

Listen and Talk B

A: Excuse me. I want to ❶add money to my transportation card. Do you know how to do ❷it?

B: Sure. It's simple. First, put your card in the machine. Second, choose ❸the amount of money.

A: OK.

B: Then insert the money.

A: I really appreciate your help.

❶ add A to B: A를 B에 더하다, 추가하다
❷ it은 '교통카드에 돈을 충전하는 방법'을 가리킨다.
❸ the amount of: ~의 양[금액]

Listen and Talk B

A: Excuse me. I want ❶to buy a snack. Do you know how to do it?

B: Sure. It's simple. ❷First, choose the snack. Second, ❸put in the money.

A: OK.

B: Then ❹take the snack out.

A: ❺I really appreciate your help.

❶ want의 목적어로 to부정사가 쓰였다.
❷ 순서를 나타내는 말로 이해를 돕고 있다.
❸ put in the money = put the money in
❹ take out the snack = take the snack out
❺ 감사를 표현하는 말로 'Thank you so much.', 'I can't thank you enough.', 'I'm grateful for ~.', 'I'm thankful for ~.' 등으로 말할 수도 있다.

Listen and Talk C

G: Excuse me, but what's this robot for?

B: Oh, it's a robot ❶that finds books for you.

G: Really? Can you tell me how to use it?

B: Sure. First, ❷place your library card on the robot's screen.

G: OK.

B: Second, type the title of ❸the book you're looking for and then press ENTER.

G: Is ❹that all?

B: Yes. Then, the robot will find the book and take it to the front desk.

G: So I can just go to the front desk and get the book?

B: Right. It's so easy, ❺isn't it?

G: Yes, it's really ❻amazing. Thank you.

❶ that은 주격 관계대명사이다.
❷ place: 두다, 놓다
❸ the book과 you 사이에 목적격 관계대명사가 that[which]이 생략되어 있다.
❹ that은 앞에서 설명한 것을 가리킨다.
❺ 부가의문문으로 'right'로 바꿔 쓸 수 있다.
❻ 감정을 유발하는 것으로 감정을 나타내는 동사의 현재분사형이 쓰이고 있다.

Listen and Talk D

Let me tell you ❶how to use a drink machine. ❷First, insert money into the machine. Then, choose ❸the drink you want. Last, take the drink ❹out of the machine. ❺It's easy.

❶ 의문사+to부정사: tell의 직접목적어로 쓰였다.
❷ 방법이나 절차를 말할 때 상대방이 이해하기 쉽도록 First, Second, Then 등과 같이 순서를 나타내는 말을 사용하여 설명할 수 있다.
❸ the drink과 you 사이에 목적격 관계대명사가 생략되어 있다.
❹ out of = from
❺ It = how to use a drink machine

 Talk and Play

A: Do you know how to make tea?
B: Sure. First, ❶put a tea bag in a cup.
A: OK.
B: Then, pour hot water in the cup.
A: And ❷then?
B: Last, take the tea bag out after 3 minutes.
A: ❸I got it. ❹I really appreciate your help.

❶ put A in B: A를 B에 넣다
❷ then 뒤에는 'what should I do' 정도가 생략되어 있다고 볼 수 있다.
❸ I got it = I understand.
❹ 감사를 나타내는 표현이다.

 Talk and Play

A: Do you know how to boil eggs?
B: Sure. First, ❶put water and the eggs in a pot.
A: OK.
B: Then, ❷boil the water and eggs for 10 to 12 minutes.
A: And then?
B: Last, ❸take the eggs out and cool them.
A: I got it. I really appreciate your help.

❶ put A in B: A를 B에 넣다
❷ boil: (물이나 액체를) 끓이다
❸ take A out: A를 꺼내다, cool: 식히다, them은 eggs를 가리킨다.

 Talk and Play

A: ❶Do you know how to plant a potato?
B: Sure. First, cut the potato into small piece.
A: OK.
B: Then, ❷dig holes in the ground.
A: And then?
B: Third, ❸put the potato pieces in the holes.
A: Then what?
B: Last, cover the holes with ❹dirt.
A: I got it. I really appreciate your help.

❶ how+to부정사: ~하는 방법
❷ dig: (구멍 등을) 파다
❸ put A in B: A를 B에 넣다
❹ dirt: 흙

 Review 1

G: Can you tell me how to ❶plant a potato?
B: Sure. First, ❷cut a potato into small pieces. Second, dig holes in the ground.
G: Then?
B: Then put the potato pieces in the holes and ❸cover the holes with dirt.
G: ❹That sounds simple. Thanks.

❶ plant: (나무나 화초 등을) 심다
❷ cut A into small pieces: A를 잘게 썰다
❸ cover A with B: A를 B로 덮다
❹ sound+형용사: ~하게 들리다 simple: 단순한, 쉬운

 Review 2

B: ❶Excuse me. Can you tell me how ❷to use this machine?
G: Sure. First, put the paper on the copy machine. Then choose the paper size and ❸ the number of copies.
B: Then ❹what?
G: Press the START button.
B: ❺Thank you. I really appreciate your help.

❶ Excuse me. = I beg your pardon.
❷ '의문사+to부정사'로 명사적 용법이다.
❸ the number of: ~의 수, a number of = many
❹ what 뒤에는 'should I do' 정도가 생략되어 있다고 볼 수 있다.
❺ 감사를 표현하는 말로 'Thank you so much.', 'I can't thank you enough.', 'I'm grateful for ~.', 'I'm thankful for ~.' 등으로 말할 수도 있다.

다음 우리말과 일치하도록 빈칸에 알맞은 말을 쓰시오.

Listen and Talk A 1

B: Excuse me. Can you _____ me _____ _____ _____ money _____ my transportation card?

G: Of course. _____, _____ your card _____ the machine. _____, _____ the _____ of money you want to add.

B: OK.

G: _____, _____ your money _____ the machine.

B: That sounds _____. Thanks.

Listen and Talk A 2

B: I want to buy a snack. Do you _____ _____ _____ _____ this snack machine?

G: Yeah. _____, choose the snack you want.

B: I already _____. What's _____?

G: Just _____ _____ the money. Then _____ the snack _____.

B: _____ _____. Thanks.

Listen and Talk A 3

G: Excuse me. I want to _____ a bike. Can you _____ me _____ _____ _____ this application?

M: Sure. First, _____ _____ _____ the application. Then find the RENT button and touch _____.

G: Then _____?

M: Then the application will give you a number _____ _____ a bike _____.

G: Thank you. I really _____ your help.

Listen and Talk B

A: Excuse me. I want to _____ these books. Do you _____ _____ _____ it?

B: Sure. It's _____. First, _____ the library card _____ the machine. Second, _____ the books _____ this box.

A: OK.

B: _____ just _____ your card _____.

A: I really _____ your help.

A: Excuse me. I want to _____ money _____ my transportation card. Do you _____ _____ _____ _____ it?

B: Sure. It's _____. _____, put your card in the machine. _____, choose the _____ of money.

A: OK.

B: _____ _____ the money.

A: I really _____ your help.

A: Excuse me. I want _____ _____ a snack. Do you _____ _____ _____ _____ it?

B: Sure. It's _____. _____, choose the snack. _____, put in the money.

A: OK.

B: _____ take the snack out.

A: I really _____ your help.

Listen and Talk C

G: Excuse me, but _____ this robot _____?

B: Oh, it's a robot _____ finds books for you.

G: Really? Can you _____ me _____ _____ _____ it?

B: Sure. First, _____ your library card _____ the robot's screen.

G: OK.

B: Second, _____ the _____ of the book you're looking for and then _____ ENTER.

G: _____ _____ _____?

B: Yes. _____, the robot will find the book and take _____ to the front desk.

G: So I can just go to the front desk and _____ the book?

B: Right. It's so _____, _____ _____?

G: Yes, it's really _____. Thank you.

Listen and Talk D

Let me tell you _____ _____ _____ a drink machine. _____, insert money into the machine. _____, choose the drink you want. _____, take the drink _____ _____ the machine. It's easy.

해석

A: 실례합니다. 저는 교통카드에 돈을 충전하고 싶어요. 어떻게 하는지 아시나요?

B: 그럼요. 간단해요. 우선 기계에 카드를 넣으세요. 둘째로 금액을 고르세요.

A: 알겠어요.

B: 그러고 나서 돈을 넣으세요.

A: 도와주셔서 정말 고맙습니다.

A: 실례합니다. 저는 과자를 사고 싶어요. 어떻게 하는지 아시나요?

B: 그럼요. 간단해요. 우선 과자를 고르세요. 둘째로 돈을 넣으세요.

A: 알겠어요.

B: 그러고 나서 과자를 꺼내세요.

A: 도와주셔서 정말 고맙습니다.

G: 실례지만, 이 로봇은 용도가 뭔가요?

B: 아, 이 로봇은 당신을 위해 책을 찾아주는 로봇이에요.

G: 정말요? 어떻게 사용하는지 알려 주실래요?

B: 그럼요. 먼저, 당신의 도서 대출 카드를 로봇의 화면 위에 놓으세요.

G: 알겠어요.

B: 두 번째로, 당신이 찾으려는 책의 제목을 입력하고 나서 ENTER 키를 누르세요.

G: 그게 다인가요?

B: 네. 그러면 로봇이 책을 찾아서 안내 데스크로 가져다줄 거예요.

G: 그러면 저는 그냥 안내 데스크로 가서 책을 받을 수 있나요?

B: 맞아요. 정말 쉽죠, 그렇지 않나요?

G: 그러네요, 정말 놀라워요. 감사합니다.

음료 자판기를 어떻게 사용하는지 알려줄게. 먼저 기계에 돈을 넣어. 그러고 나서 원하는 음료를 골라. 마지막으로 기계에서 음료를 꺼내. 간단해.

Talk and Play

A: Do you _____ _____ _____ _____ tea?

B: Sure. _____, _____ a tea bag in a cup.

A: OK.

B: _____, _____ hot water in the cup.

A: And then?

B: _____, _____ the tea bag _____ after 3 minutes.

A: I _____ _____. I really _____ your help.

A: 차를 어떻게 만드는지 알고 있니?
B: 물론이지. 우선 컵에 티백을 넣어.
A: 알겠어.
B: 그런 후 컵에 뜨거운 물을 부어.
A: 그러고 나서는?
B: 마지막으로 3분 후에 티백을 꺼내.
A: 알겠어. 도와줘서 정말 고마워.

Review 1

G: Can you tell me _____ _____ _____ a potato?

B: Sure. First, _____ a potato _____ small _____. Second, _____ holes _____ the ground.

G: Then?

B: Then _____ the potato pieces _____ the holes and _____ the holes _____ dirt.

G: That _____ _____. Thanks.

G: 감자를 어떻게 심는지 알려주시겠어요?
B: 그럼요. 우선 감자를 작은 조각으로 자르세요. 둘째로 땅에 구멍을 파세요.
G: 그러고 나서요?
B: 그리고 나서 구멍에 감자 조각들을 넣고 흙으로 구멍을 덮으세요.
G: 간단한 것 같네요. 고맙습니다.

Review 2

B: Excuse me. Can you _____ me _____ _____ _____ this machine?

G: Sure. First, _____ the paper _____ the copy machine. Then choose the paper size and _____ _____ _____ copies.

B: Then _____?

G: Press the START button.

B: Thank you. I really _____ your help.

B: 실례합니다. 이 기계를 어떻게 사용하는지 알려주시겠어요?
G: 물론이죠. 우선 복사기에 종이를 올려놓으세요. 그리고 나서 종이 크기와 복사본 매수를 고르세요.
B: 그러고 나서 어떻게 해요?
G: START 버튼을 누르세요.
B: 감사합니다. 도와주셔서 고마워요.

01 다음 빈칸 (A)에 알맞지 <u>않은</u> 것은?

> B: Excuse me. _____(A)_____ how to add money to my transportation card?
> G: Of course. First, put your card in the machine. Second, choose the amount of money you want to add.
> B: OK.
> G: Last, insert your money into the machine.
> B: That sounds simple. Thanks.

① Can you tell me   ② Could you tell me   ③ Are you explaining

④ Can you explain   ⑤ Do you know

02 주어진 어휘를 이용하여 밑줄 친 우리말을 5 단어로 영작하시오.

> A: <u>도와주셔서 정말 감사해요</u>. (appreciate, really)
> B: It's my pleasure.

➡ _____

03 다음 대화의 밑줄 친 (a)의 의도와 <u>다르게</u> 쓰인 것을 고르시오.

> B: I want to buy a snack. (a)<u>Do you know how to use this snack machine?</u>
> G: Yeah. First, choose the snack you want.
> B: I already did. What's next?
> G: Just put in the money. Then take the snack out.
> B: Got it. Thanks.

① Can you explain how to use this snack machine?

② Could you explain how to use this snack machine?

③ Will you show me how to use this snack machine?

④ Can you tell me how to use this snack machine?

⑤ I'd like to tell you how to use this snack machine.

01 다음 중 짝지어진 대화가 <u>어색한</u> 것은?

① A: Do you know how to make tea?
  B: Sure. Last, put a tea bag in a cup.
② A: First, choose the snack you want.
  B: I already did. What's next?
③ A: Press the START button.
  B: Thank you. I really appreciate your help.
④ A: Then put the potato pieces in the holes and cover the holes with dirt.
  B: That sounds simple. Thanks.
⑤ A: Excuse me. Can you tell me how to add money to my transportation card?
  B: Of course. First, put your card in the machine.

[02~05] 다음 대화를 읽고 물음에 답하시오.

G: Excuse me, but what's this robot ___(A)___?
B: Oh, it's a robot that finds books for you.
G: Really? _____(B)_____?
B: Sure. First, (a)당신의 도서 대출 카드를 로봇의 화면 위에 놓으세요.(library card, screen, place)
G: OK.
B: Second, type the title of the book you're looking for and then press ENTER.
G: Is that all?
B: Yes. Then, the robot will find the book and take it to the front desk.
G: So I can just go to the front desk and get the book?
B: Right. It's so easy, isn't it?
G: Yes, it's really amazing. Thank you.

02 빈칸 (A)에 들어갈 말을 고르시오.

① in ② for ③ on
④ at ⑤ about

03 위 대화의 빈칸 (B)에 들어갈 알맞은 말을 주어진 어휘를 배열하여 쓰시오.

you, me, it, how, tell, can, use, to

➡ _____

04 밑줄 친 (a)의 우리말에 맞게 주어진 어휘를 이용하여 영작하시오.

➡ _____

05 도서 대출에 관한 위 대화의 내용과 일치하지 <u>않는</u> 것은?

① 로봇은 당신을 위해 책을 찾아 주는 로봇이다.
② 책을 대출하려면 먼저 도서 대출 카드를 로봇의 화면 위에 놓아야 한다.
③ 두 번째는 찾으려는 책의 제목을 입력하고 나서 ENTER 키를 눌러야 한다.
④ 그러면 로봇이 책을 찾아서 안내 데스크로 가져다준다.
⑤ 안내 데스크로 가면 로봇이 책을 건네준다.

06 대화가 자연스럽게 연결되도록 (A)~(C)를 적절하게 배열하시오.

A: Excuse me. I want to return these books. Do you know how to do it?
B: Sure. It's simple. First, insert the library card into the machine. Second, put the books in this box.
(A) Then just take your card out.
(B) OK.
(C) I really appreciate your help.

➡ _____

[07~08] 다음 대화를 읽고 물음에 답하시오.

> B: I want to buy a snack. _____(A)_____
> this snack machine?
> G: Yeah. First, choose the snack you want.
> B: I already ___(B)___ . What's next?
> G: Just put in the money. Then take the snack out.

07 위 대화의 빈칸 (A)에 들어갈 알맞은 말로 가장 적절한 것은?

① Why don't you know how to use
② Shall we know how to use
③ Do you know how to use
④ Do you know when to use
⑤ Will you know how to use

08 위 대화의 빈칸 (B)에 알맞은 대동사를 쓰시오.

➡ _____

[09~10] 다음 대화를 읽고 물음에 답하시오.

> A: Do you know how to make tea?
> B: Sure. First, (a)[pour / put] a tea bag in a cup.
> A: OK.
> B: Then, (b)[pour / put] hot water in the cup.
> A: And then?
> B: Last, (c)[make / take] the tea bag out after 3 minutes.
> A: I got it. _____(A)_____

09 위 대화의 빈칸 (A)에 들어갈 말로 알맞지 <u>않은</u> 것을 <u>모두</u> 고르시오.

① I really appreciate your help.
② It's not a big deal.
③ Thank you.
④ It's my pleasure.
⑤ I can't thank you enough.

10 위 대화의 괄호 (a)~(c)에서 알맞은 것을 골라 바르게 짝지은 것은?

	(a)	(b)	(c)
①	put	pour	take
②	put	pour	make
③	put	put	make
④	pour	put	make
⑤	pour	pour	take

[11~13] 다음 대화를 읽고 물음에 답하시오.

> A: Excuse me. (①) I want to add money to my transportation card. (②) Do you know how to do it?
> B: (③) It's simple. (④) First, put your card in the machine. (⑤) Second, choose the amount of money.
> A: OK.
> B: Then insert the money.
> A: (a)I really appreciate your help.

11 위 대화의 (①)~(⑤) 중 주어진 문장이 들어갈 곳은?

Sure.

①　　　②　　　③　　　④　　　⑤

12 위 대화의 밑줄 친 (a)의 의도로 적절한 것은?

① 절차 표현하기　② 축하 표현하기
③ 방법 답하기　④ 유감 표현하기
⑤ 감사 표현하기

서답형

13 위 대화에 나타난 교통카드에 돈을 충전하는 방법의 두 번째 단계를 10자 내외의 우리말로 쓰시오.

➡ _____

[01~04] 다음 대화를 읽고 물음에 답하시오.

G: Excuse me, but what's this robot for?

B: Oh, (a)이것은 당신을 위해 책을 찾아 주는 로봇이에요. (a robot, it, find)

G: Really? Can you tell me how to use it?

(A) Second, type the title of the book you're looking for and then press ENTER.

(B) Is that all?

(C) OK.

(D) Sure. First, place your library card on the robot's screen.

B: Yes. Then, the robot will find the book and take it to the front desk.

G: So I can just go to the front desk and get the book?

B: Right. It's so easy, ⓐ ?

G: Yes, it's really amazing. Thank you.

01 위 대화의 (A)~(D)를 알맞은 순서로 배열하시오.

➡ _____

02 빈칸 ⓐ에 알맞은 부가의문문을 쓰시오.

➡ _____

03 괄호 안에 주어진 어휘를 이용하여 밑줄 친 (a)를 8 단어로 쓰시오.

➡ _____

04 Where does this conversation happen?

➡ _____

[05~06] 다음 글을 읽고 물음에 답하시오.

Let me tell you how to use a drink machine. First, insert money into the machine. Then, choose the drink you want. Last, take the drink (a)out of the machine. It's easy.

05 밑줄 친 (a)out of를 한 단어로 바꿔 쓰시오.

➡ _____

06 위 글에 나타난 음료 자판기 사용하는 법 3 단계를 우리말로 쓰시오.

➡ (1) _____ (2) _____
   (3) _____

[07~08] 다음 대화를 읽고 물음에 답하시오.

B: Excuse me. Can you tell me how to use this machine?

G: Sure. First, put the paper on the copy machine. Then choose the paper size and the number of copies.

B: Then (a)what?

G: Press the START button.

B: Thank you. I really appreciate your help.

07 위 대화에서 주어진 영영풀이에 해당하는 말을 찾아 쓰시오.

to thank someone in a polite way or to say that you are grateful for something they have done

➡ _____

08 밑줄 친 (a)what 뒤에 생략되어 있는 것을 should를 포함한 3 단어로 쓰시오.

➡ _____

Grammar

① 분사구문

- **Using** various methods, experts analyze big data.
  다양한 방법들을 사용하여 전문가들은 빅데이터를 분석한다.

■ 분사구문은 종속접속사가 이끄는 부사절을 분사를 이용하여 간략한 부사구로 바꾼 것이다.

  - **While I was walking** along the street, I saw a man with five dogs.

  = **Walking** along the street, I saw a man with five dogs. 길을 걷다가, 나는 개 5마리와 함께 있는 남자를 보았다.

■ 부사구와 주절의 관계에 따라 양보, 동시동작, 이유, 시간, 조건 등의 의미로 쓰인다.

  (1) 양보: **Although she is** rich, the woman always buys second-hand goods.

  - **Being** rich, the woman always buys second-hand goods. 부유하지만, 그 여자는 늘 중고 물품을 산다.

  (2) 동시동작(부대상황): **While he waved** his hand, he walked out of the house.

  - **Waving** his hand, he walked out of the house. 손을 흔들며, 그는 집 밖으로 나왔다.

  (3) 이유: **Because she was** disappointed with him, Hannah said nothing.

  - **Being** disappointed with him, Hannah said nothing. 그에게 실망했기 때문에, Hannah는 아무 말도 하지 않았다.

  (4) 시간: **When he works** alone, he uses the special program.

  - **Working** alone, he uses the special program. 혼자 일할 때, 그는 그 특별한 프로그램을 사용한다.

  (5) 조건: **If you turn** left, you'll see the post office.

  - **Turning** left, you'll see the post office. 좌회전하면, 우체국이 보일 것이다.

■ 종속절의 시제가 주절보다 앞선 경우 완료분사구문을 사용한다.

  - **As he had read** the book before, Mike lent it to her.

  = **Having read** the book before, Mike lent it to her.

■ 주절과 종속절의 주어가 다를 경우 분사구문의 주어를 남겨 두는 것을 독립분사구문이라고 하며, 일반인이 주어일 경우에는 생략이 가능하다. (비인칭 독립분사구문)

  (1) 독립분사구문: **Since it is** windy, I can't play badminton.

  = **It being** windy, I can't play badminton. 바람이 불어서, 나는 배드민턴을 칠 수 없다.

  (2) 비인칭 독립분사구문: **generally speaking**(일반적으로 말해), **considering**(~를 고려하면)

  (3) with+목적어+분사: My uncle fell asleep **with the light turned on**. (불을 켠 채로)

핵심 Check

1. 다음 괄호 안에서 알맞은 말을 고르시오.

  (1) With summer (approaches / approaching), it got hotter and hotter.

  (2) (Feeling / Felt) nervous, the player drank a glass of water.

❷ 접속사 as

- **As** information and communication technology develops, the amount of data we have is getting much greater than before. 정보 통신 기술이 발달함에 따라, 우리가 갖고 있는 데이터의 양이 이전보다 훨씬 많아지고 있다.

■ as는 종속접속사로 부사절을 이끈다.
- **As** time goes by, I love her even more. 시간이 지날수록 나는 그녀를 더욱 사랑한다.
- Minho plays the piano **as** his brother sings. 민호는 형이 노래할 때 피아노를 친다.

■ 접속사 as의 역할
(1) '비례' ~함에 따라서
- **As** it got darker, she became more nervous. 어두워지면서, 그녀는 더 초조해졌다.
(2) '양태' ~하듯이, ~하는 것처럼, ~와 같이
- Do in Rome **as** the Romans do. 로마에서는 로마 사람들처럼 하라.
- She speaks as fast **as** her mother does. 그녀는 엄마만큼 빠르게 말한다.
(3) '이유' ~이기 때문에, ~이므로
- **As** the girl sings well, we will vote for her. 그녀가 노래를 잘해서, 우리는 그녀에게 투표할 것이다.
(4) '시간' ~할 때, ~하는 동안
- She showed up **as** I was talking. 내가 말하고 있을 때 그녀가 나타났다.
(5) '상태' ~인 채로, ~하는 대로
- Leave the thing **as** it is. 그것을 있는 그대로 두시오.
(6) '양보' ~라 할지라도, ~에도 불구하고
- Coward **as** he was, he didn't step back. 비록 겁쟁이였지만, 그는 뒤로 물러서지 않았다.
- Angry **as** she felt, she continued her work. 비록 화가 났지만, 그녀는 일을 계속했다.

■ 전치사 as: ~로, ~로서
- Shanon did well **as** his caretaker. Shanon은 그의 보호자로서 잘 해줬다.
- Mom treats me **as** a baby. 엄마는 나를 아기처럼 대한다.

핵심 Check

2. 다음 빈칸에 공통으로 들어갈 알맞은 단어를 고르시오. (대 · 소문자 구분 안 함)
- _____ I told you, we will meet at dawn at the bus stop.
- The girl got wiser _____ she grew.
- Thank you for your hard work _____ the leader of the team.

① when   ② because   ③ as   ④ until   ⑤ before

01 다음 각 문장의 빈칸에 As[as]를 넣을 때 <u>어색한</u> 것은?

① _____ it was late at night, she went back to her room.

② Stand still _____ I told you.

③ _____ James was very tired, he went to bed early.

④ It's so noisy _____ I can't read my book.

⑤ The boy got wiser _____ he got older.

02 다음 부사절을 분사구문으로 바꿔 쓸 때, 빈칸에 들어갈 말로 가장 적절한 것은?

> As she wanted to buy some snacks, Kay put some money in her pocket.
>
> → _____ to buy some snacks, Kay put some money in her pocket.

① As she wanting   ② She wanting   ③ Having wanted

④ Being wanting   ⑤ Wanting

03 다음 밑줄 친 부분 중 어법상 <u>어색한</u> 것을 고르시오.

① <u>As</u> Sam was intelligent, we relied on him.

② I was taking a shower <u>as</u> she visited my place.

③ Can you tell me <u>as</u> to use this snack machine?

④ Mary moved <u>as</u> the one in the screen danced.

⑤ <u>As</u> I was tired, I didn't arrange my desk.

04 다음 분사구문을 접속사가 이끄는 부사절로 만들 때, 빈칸에 알맞은 말을 써 넣으시오.

(1) Being absent from school, he couldn't take the test.

　➡ As _____ _____ _____ _____ _____, he couldn't take the test.

(2) Watching Utube videos, Susan did her homework.

　➡ While _____ _____ _____ _____, Susan did her homework.

(3) Feeling excited, she applied for the position.

　➡ As _____ _____, she applied for the position.

(4) Being short, Brian made a dunk shot.

　➡ _____ _____ _____ _____, Brian made a dunk shot.

[01~02] 다음 밑줄 친 as 중 나머지 넷과 쓰임이 다른 하나는?

01 ① As I didn't know how to add money to my card, I asked her.

② As Lynn talked with Tom, some people waved their hands to her.

③ Emma followed my step as I showed her the basic walking pose.

④ I asked him to recommend me a book as the owner of the bookstore.

⑤ The robot will find the book and take it to you as it is programmed.

02 ① As IT technology develops, the big data will do much for our society.

② As the CEO of the IT company, Peter Gates has much influence on the government policy.

③ Grace was loved by everyone in my college as she was kind and pretty.

④ Her confidence grew much bigger as she got accustomed to the position.

⑤ As the lady got ready for the party, her husband watched her silently.

[03~04] 다음 우리말을 어법상 알맞게 영작한 것을 고르시오.

03

> 그녀는 눈을 감은 채로 라디오에서 나오는 음악을 듣고 있었다.

① She was listening to music from the radio her eyes closing.

② She closed her eyes and listening to music from the radio.

③ She listened to music from the radio and closed her eyes.

④ She was listening to music from the radio with closed her eyes.

⑤ She was listening to music from the radio with her eyes closed.

04

> 많은 사람들을 행복하게 해줬는데도 불구하고, Chad는 외롭게 죽었다.

① Even though he having made many people happy, Chad died lonely.

② Although he making many people happy, Chad died lonely.

③ Having been made happy by many people, Chad died lonely.

④ Though having made many people happy, Chad died lonely.

⑤ He had made many people happy, though Chad died lonely.

05 다음 빈칸에 공통으로 들어갈 알맞은 말을 고르시오.

> (1) Jane started to exercise _____ she saw herself in the mirror.
>
> (2) David felt that it became harder to breathe _____ he tried to climb higher up.
>
> (3) The dog followed the movements _____ shown by the trainer.

① because   ② as

③ while   ④ when

⑤ what

서답형

06 다음 문장에서 어법상 <u>어색한</u> 단어 한 개를 찾아서 고치시오.

> Made sports more exciting, big data is improving the performance of the players.

_____ ➡ _____

07 다음 밑줄 친 as가 어법상 문장 속에서 옳게 쓰인 것을 고르시오.

① As smartphones have changed our lives, allowing us to watch movies on our phones.
② Do you know <u>as</u> to use this snack machine?
③ What happens <u>as</u> information and communication technology develops?
④ Did you know <u>as</u> health professionals can now forecast a disease just as weather experts forecast the weather?
⑤ With the help of this database, <u>as</u> Germany's national soccer team was able to improve its performance and win the 2014 World Cup.

08 다음 밑줄 친 분사구문을 같은 의미의 부사절로 바꿔 쓸 때 적절하지 <u>않은</u> 것은?

① <u>Walking along the street</u>, she saw a man with twelve cats.
   → When she walked along the street,
② <u>Waving her hands</u>, the singer walked out of the train.
   → While she was waving her hands,
③ <u>Eating a chicken sandwich</u>, Tom waited for the bus.
   → As he was eating a chicken sandwich,

④ <u>Using various methods</u>, experts have analyzed big data.
   → As they use various methods,
⑤ Big data improves the performance, <u>making sports more fun</u>.
   → though it makes sports more fun.

09 다음 주어진 문장에서 밑줄 친 as와 가장 가까운 뜻의 as가 쓰인 것을 고르시오.

> Health professionals can now forecast a disease just <u>as</u> weather experts forecast the weather.

① Mina got wiser <u>as</u> she got older.
② <u>As</u> it was late at night, Brian and Kevin went back to their places.
③ You should show up at the bus stop <u>as</u> I told you.
④ All the audience felt too hot <u>as</u> the air conditioning system broke down.
⑤ Would you turn off the TV <u>as</u> you go out this evening?

중요

10 다음 중 밑줄 친 분사구문의 용법이 〈보기〉와 같은 것은?

> ⊢ 보기 ⊢
> <u>Living in Korea for over 15 years</u>, Brian can't buy a thing at the supermarket.

① <u>Not knowing how long Susan waited for her,</u> Tracy was surprised at her cold face.
② <u>Finishing his homework,</u> Andrew went outside to play basketball.
③ <u>Having nothing unusual to do,</u> the boys lay on the playground.
④ <u>Born in Paris,</u> professor Sean Mika couldn't communicate well in French.
⑤ <u>Turning right at the second corner,</u> you will see the city hall.

11 다음 분사구문이 사용된 문장을 접속사를 이용한 부사절을 이용하여 바꿔 쓸 때, 가장 적절한 것은?

> The virus having come from his country, the Chinese diplomat criticized Korea for a slow response.

① Since the virus came from his country, the Chinese diplomat criticized Korea for a slow response.

② As the virus came from his country, the Chinese diplomat criticized Korea for a slow response.

③ If the virus had come from his country, the Chinese diplomat criticized Korea for a slow response.

④ Though the virus had come from his country, the Chinese diplomat criticized Korea for a slow response.

⑤ Before the virus had come from his country, the Chinese diplomat criticized Korea for a slow response.

서답형

[12~14] 우리말과 일치하도록 괄호 안에 주어진 단어들을 바르게 배열하시오.

12

> 그 축구 시합에서 부상을 당하고 싶지 않았기 때문에, Samuel은 천천히 경기했다.
> → (get, the, to, not, match, in, hurt, wanting, football), Samuel played slowly.

➡ _____

13

> 이상하게 들릴지 모르지만, 나는 결코 부자가 되고 싶지 않다.
> → (as, sound, strange, may, it), I never want to be rich.

➡ _____

14

> 천 년도 더 전에 건축되었음에도 불구하고, 그 사원은 몇 년 전에 지어진 것처럼 튼튼했다.
> → (been, than, having, more, though, built) a thousand years ago, the temple was as strong as it was built a few years ago.

➡ _____

[15~16] 다음 밑줄 친 부분이 어법상 옳지 <u>않은</u> 것을 고르시오.

15 ① <u>As</u> Carla lost her necklace at the hotel, she couldn't leave in time.

② <u>As</u> you lied to me, I could believe you more than ever.

③ <u>As</u> time went by, my uncle changed a lot after he became a lawyer.

④ <u>As</u> the passengers were talking on the road, the driver urged them to get on.

⑤ William took the medicine <u>as</u> he caught a cold.

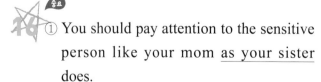

① You should pay attention to the sensitive person like your mom <u>as your sister does</u>.

② The president is speaking to the young lady <u>as a friend</u>.

③ J. K. Rowling is widely known <u>as the writer</u> of the Harry Potter series.

④ <u>As the couple was sitting</u> down to dinner, someone rang the bell.

⑤ We arrived at the toy store <u>so as they</u> were about to close.

01 다음 각 밑줄 친 부분 중 어법상 어색한 것은 고쳐 다시 쓰고, 어색하지 않은 것은 '고칠 필요 없음'이라고 쓰시오.

(1) A little being tired, Timothy went to bed earlier than usual.

➡ _____

(2) Found the ring she had lost, I called Sujin to come home early.

➡ _____

(3) Having rained the day before, the roads to the concert got all wet.

➡ _____

(4) Having not a car, Paul couldn't take his daughter to the interview.

➡ _____

(5) Frankly speaking, the prime minster of Japan talks like an idiot.

➡ _____

02 다음 〈보기〉에 있는 접속사를 한 번씩만 사용하여, 각 문장의 밑줄 친 분사구문을 부사절로 바꾸시오. (단, 진행형 불가, 주어는 가능한 대명사로 표현할 것.)

┌─ 보기 ┐
while / because / when / if / though / and
└──────┘

(1) Using various methods, experts analyze big data and draw results from it.

➡ _____

(2) Having a problem that you cannot talk to me, try sharing it with a stranger.

➡ _____

(3) Being sick through the weekend, I could hand in the report on Monday morning.

➡ _____

(4) Not wanting to wake the sleeping baby up, her daddy quietly stood up.

➡ _____
_____

(5) Big data improves the performance of players, making sports more exciting.

➡ _____

(6) Cleaning the windows of the kitchen, Sammy suddenly heard her cat meow from the front.

➡ _____
_____

03 다음 우리말과 일치하도록 괄호 안에 주어진 단어들을 바르게 배열하여 문장을 완성하시오.

(1) 정보와 통신 기술이 발달함에 따라, 우리가 가진 데이터의 양도 전보다 더 커진다. (develops, and, information, as, technology, communication)

➡ _____
_____, the amount of data we have is getting greater than before.

(2) 우리의 몸이 우리의 마음을 변화시키는 것과 같이, 우리의 마음도 우리의 행동을 변화시킨다. (our minds, just, our bodies, as, change)

➡ _____,
our minds also change our behavior.

(3) 그녀의 반에 친구들이 아무도 없있기 때문에, Jenny는 슬프고 외롭게 느꼈다. (her, friends, any, class, having, in, not)

➡ _____,
Jenny felt sad and lonely.

(4) 다양한 방법들을 사용해서, 전문가들은 빅데이터를 분석하고 그것으로부터 의미 있는 결과를 이끌어낸다. (experts, using, analyze, methods, various)

➡ _____
big data and draw meaningful results from it.

04 다음 각 문장에서 어법상 어색한 단어를 한 개씩 찾아, 다른 한 단어로 고치거나 생략하여 옳은 문장으로 다시 쓰시오.

(1) Did you know that health professionals can forecast a disease just if weather experts forecast the weather?

➡ _____

(2) Big data helps companies understand their customers' needs better, as assisting them sell more products.

➡ _____

(3) Can you tell me as to add money to my transportation card?

➡ _____

(4) Germany's national soccer team was able to improve its performance, won the 2014 World Cup.

➡ _____

05 다음 밑줄 친 As로 시작하는 부사절을 알맞은 분사구문으로 전환하여 빈칸을 채우시오.

> As she was singing to the radio music, Riley got a message from downstairs.

➡ _____

Riley got a message from downstairs.

06 다음 그림과 학생들의 발표 내용을 보고, 질문에 답하시오.

(A)설문 조사에 근거해서 우리는 경주를 골랐습니다. Ten students think that (B)수학 여행지를 고를 때, 가장 중요한 것은 '활동'이다. (C) After we searched for some data online, we found out that there are many things to see and do in Gyeongju.

(1) 밑줄 친 (A)의 우리말에 맞게 다음에 주어진 단어를 알맞은 순서로 배열하시오.
(survey, Gyeongju, on, we, chose, our, based)

➡ _____

(2) 밑줄 친 (B)의 우리말에 맞게 다음에 주어진 단어를 활용하여, 총 11 단어로 영작하시오. (동사 형태는 알맞게 변형 가능, 첫 단어는 activities로 시작할 것.)
(choose, be, a field trip place, when, important)

➡ _____

(3) 밑줄 친 (C)를 5 단어의 분사구문으로 전환하시오.

➡ _____

(4) 위의 발표 내용을 아래와 같이 한 문장으로 요약할 때, 빈칸에 공통으로 들어갈 알맞은 단어를 쓰시오.

> _____ students think it important to do activities, we selected Gyeongju _____ our field trip place.

Living with Big Data

Have you ever visited an online bookstore and been surprised by
the books that the store recommended for you? Many of them looked
interesting to you. So how did the bookstore know what you liked?
This is all possible because of big data.

What is big data?

Big data is data sets that are very big and complex. As information
and communication technology develops, the amount of data we have
is getting much greater than before. This is mainly because almost
everything that we do online leaves a trace. For example, the photos
you upload on your blog and the records of your purchases at online
stores are all part of big data.

Simply collecting data, however, is not enough. Big data has to be
analyzed, and this is done by big data experts. Using various methods,
experts analyze big data and draw meaningful results from it. These
results then can be used to make decisions or to predict the future.

How is big data influencing our lives?

Big data is influencing almost all parts of our lives. It
helps companies understand their customers' needs better and helps
them sell more products. It helps people avoid heavy traffic. Its uses
are endless, and here are some interesting examples.

---

communication 의사소통, 연락

develop 성장하다, 발달하다

amount 총계, 총액

trace 자취, 발자국, 흔적

purchase 구매

analyze 분석하다

method 방법

predict 예측하다

influence 영향을 미치다

avoid 피하다, 방지하다

traffic 교통(량)

endless 끝없는, 무한한

📎 **확인문제**

● 다음 문장이 본문의 내용과 일치하면 T, 일치하지 <u>않으면</u> F를 쓰시오.

1 Big data is data sets that are very big and complicated. ☐

2 Almost everything that we do offline leaves a trace. ☐

3 The photos you upload on your blog are all part of big data. ☐

4 Simply collecting data is enough. ☐

5 Big data is affecting almost all parts of our lives. ☐

6 The uses of big data are finite. ☐

Disease Forecast

Did you know that health professionals can now forecast a disease just as weather experts forecast the weather? This is possible thanks to big data. For example, when the flu season comes, people will buy more flu medicine. They will also search online about flu symptoms more. If this kind of data is analyzed wisely, the spread of the flu can be predicted.

Improving Performance in Sports

Are you a sports fan? Well, big data is improving the performance of players, making sports more exciting. A famous example is Germany's national soccer team. The team built a database by collecting and analyzing a huge amount of data on players. For example, the data included information about how much each player ran and how long he had the ball. With the help of this database, Germany's national soccer team was able to improve its performance and win the 2014 World Cup.

Crime Prevention

Thanks to big data, police can now predict crime before it happens. Through the analysis of big data about the type, time and place of crime, police can make a map of crime hot spots. This map identifies when and where crime is most likely to happen. Police can prevent further crime by focusing on the areas and the times this map predicts.

Big data has already changed the world greatly. So where will the big data industry go from here? Nobody knows for sure, but experts agree that big data will play a more and more important role in our lives.

flu 독감
symptom 증상
wisely 현명하게, 지혜롭게
spread 확산, 전파
improve 개선하다, 향상하다
performance 경기력, 수행, 성과
database 데이터베이스
huge 거대한, (크기·양·정도가) 막대한
include 포함하다
crime 범죄
prevention 예방
thanks to ~ ~ 덕분에
hot spot 다발 지역
identify 알아보다, 확인하다, 식별하다
be likely to ~할 것 같다
further 더 이상의, 추가의
focus on ~에 초점을 맞추다
play a role 역할을 하다
for sure 확실히

 확인문제

● 다음 문장이 본문의 내용과 일치하면 T, 일치하지 않으면 F를 쓰시오.

1 Health experts can now forecast a disease just as weather professionals forecast the weather. ☐

2 Germany's national soccer team built a database by collecting and analyzing a small amount of data on players. ☐

3 Police can make a map of crime hot spots by analyzing big data about the type, time and place of crime. ☐

4 Big data has not changed the world yet. ☐

우리말을 참고하여 빈칸에 알맞은 말을 쓰시오.

1 _____ _____ Big Data

2 Have you ever visited an online bookstore and been surprised by the books that the store _____ _____ you?

3 Many of them _____ _____ to you.

4 So how did the bookstore know _____ _____ _____ ?

5 This is all possible _____ _____ big data.

6 _____ _____ big data?

7 Big data is _____ _____ that are very big and _____ .

8 _____ information and communication technology develops, the amount of data we have is _____ _____ _____ than before.

9 This is mainly because almost everything that we do online _____ _____ _____ .

10 For example, the photos you _____ _____ _____ _____ and the records of _____ _____ at online stores are _____ _____ _____ big data.

11 _____ _____ , however, is not enough.

12 Big data _____ _____ _____ _____ , and this is done by big data experts.

13 _____ various methods, experts analyze big data and _____ meaningful results from it.

14 These results then _____ _____ _____ to make decisions or to predict the future.

15 _____ is big data influencing our lives?

16 Big data is influencing _____ _____ _____ of our lives.

17 It helps companies understand _____ _____ _____ better and helps them _____ _____ _____ .

18 It helps people _____ _____ _____ .

19 Its uses are _____ , and here are some _____ _____ .

20 Disease _____

---

1 빅데이터와 함께 살아가기

2 당신은 온라인 서점을 방문해서 그 서점이 당신을 위해 추천한 책들을 보고 놀란 적이 있는가?

3 그것들 중에 많은 것들이 당신에게 흥미로워 보였다.

4 그 서점은 당신이 무엇을 좋아하는지 어떻게 알았을까?

5 이것은 모두 빅데이터 때문에 가능하다.

6 빅데이터는 무엇인가?

7 빅데이터는 매우 크고 복잡한 데이터 집합이다.

8 정보 통신 기술이 발달함에 따라 우리가 갖고 있는 정보의 양도 이전보다 훨씬 더 많아지고 있다.

9 이것은 주로 우리가 온라인상에서 하는 거의 모든 것들이 흔적을 남기기 때문이다.

10 예를 들어, 당신이 블로그에 올린 사진들과 온라인 상점에서의 구매 기록들이 모두 빅데이터의 일부가 된다.

11 하지만 단순히 데이터를 수집하는 것만으로는 충분하지 않다.

12 빅데이터는 분석되어야 하고, 이것은 빅데이터 전문가들에 의해서 이루어진다.

13 다양한 방법들을 사용하여 전문가들은 빅데이터를 분석하고, 그것으로부터 의미 있는 결과들을 도출한다.

14 그런 다음, 이런 결과들은 결정을 하거나 또는 미래를 예측하는 데 사용될 수 있다.

15 빅데이터는 어떻게 우리 삶에 영향을 미치고 있는가?

16 빅데이터는 우리 삶의 거의 모든 부분에 영향을 미치고 있다.

17 그것은 회사들이 소비자들이 필요로 하는 것을 더 잘 이해하고 그들이 더 많은 상품을 팔도록 도와준다.

18 그것은 사람들이 교통 체증을 피하도록 도와주기도 한다.

19 그것의 활용은 끝이 없고, 여기에 몇 가지 흥미로운 예들이 있다.

20 질병 예측

21 Did you know that health professionals can now forecast a disease _____ _____ weather experts forecast the weather?

22 This is possible _____ _____ big data.

23 For example, when the flu season _____, people _____ _____ more flu medicine.

24 They will also _____ _____ _____ flu symptoms more.

25 If this kind of data _____ _____ _____, the spread of the flu can be predicted.

26 _____ _____ in Sports

27 Are you a _____ _____?

28 Well, big data is improving the performance of players, _____ sports more _____.

29 A famous example is Germany's _____ _____ _____.

30 The team built a database by _____ and _____ a huge amount of data on players.

31 For example, the data included information about _____ _____ each player ran and _____ _____ he had the ball.

32 _____ _____ _____ _____ this database, Germany's national soccer team was able to improve its performance and win the 2014 World Cup.

33 Crime _____

34 _____ _____ big data, police can now predict crime before it happens.

35 _____ the analysis of big data about the type, time and place of crime, police can make a map of _____ _____ _____.

36 This map identifies when and where crime _____ _____ _____ _____ _____.

37 Police can prevent _____ _____ by focusing on the areas and the times this map _____.

38 Big data _____ _____ _____ the world greatly.

39 So where will the big data industry _____ _____ _____?

40 Nobody knows for sure, but experts agree that big data will _____ a more and more important _____ in our lives.

21 당신은 날씨 전문가가 날씨를 예측하는 것과 같이 건강 전문가들이 현재 질병을 예측할 수 있다는 것을 알고 있는가?

22 이것은 빅데이터 덕분에 가능하다.

23 예를 들어서 독감의 계절이 오면, 사람들은 독감 약을 더 많이 구입할 것이다.

24 그들은 또한 온라인상에서 독감 증상들을 더 찾아볼 것이다.

25 만약 이런 종류의 데이터를 지혜롭게 분석한다면, 독감의 확산을 예측할 수 있다.

26 스포츠에서의 경기력 향상

27 당신은 스포츠 팬인가?

28 빅데이터는 스포츠를 더 흥미롭게 만들면서, 선수들의 경기력을 향상하고 있다.

29 유명한 사례로 독일 국가 대표 축구팀이 있다.

30 그 팀은 선수들에 관한 엄청난 양의 데이터를 모으고 분석함으로써, 데이터베이스를 구축했다.

31 예를 들어 데이터는 각각의 선수들이 얼마나 많이 달렸고, 얼마나 오랫동안 공을 소유했는지도 포함했다.

32 이 데이터베이스의 도움으로 독일 국가 대표 축구팀은 경기력을 향상할 수 있었고, 2014년 월드컵에서 우승할 수 있었다.

33 범죄 예방

34 빅데이터 덕분에 경찰은 이제 범죄가 발생하기 전에 범죄를 예측할 수 있다.

35 범죄의 유형, 시간 및 장소에 관한 빅데이터의 분석을 통해, 경찰은 범죄 다발 지역의 지도를 만들 수 있다.

36 이 지도는 범죄가 언제, 어디에서 가장 많이 발생할 것 같은지를 알려 준다.

37 경찰은 이 지도가 예측하는 장소들과 시간대에 집중함으로써, 추가 범죄를 예방할 수 있다.

38 빅데이터는 이미 세계를 크게 변화시켰다.

39 그러면 빅데이터 산업은 여기에서부터 어디로 가게 될까?

40 누구도 확실히 알지는 못하지만, 전문가들은 빅데이터가 우리 삶에서 더욱 더 중요한 역할을 할 것이라는 데에는 동의한다.

● 우리말을 참고하여 본문을 영작하시오.

1 빅데이터와 함께 살아가기
➡ _____

2 당신은 온라인 서점을 방문해서 그 서점이 당신을 위해 추천한 책들을 보고 놀란 적이 있는가?
➡ _____

3 그것들 중에 많은 것들이 당신에게 흥미로워 보였다.
➡ _____

4 그 서점은 당신이 무엇을 좋아하는지 어떻게 알았을까?
➡ _____

5 이것은 모두 빅데이터 때문에 가능하다.
➡ _____

6 빅데이터는 무엇인가?
➡ _____

7 빅데이터는 매우 크고 복잡한 데이터 집합이다.
➡ _____

8 정보 통신 기술이 발달함에 따라 우리가 갖고 있는 정보의 양도 이전보다 훨씬 더 많아지고 있다.
➡ _____

9 이것은 주로 우리가 온라인상에서 하는 거의 모든 것들이 흔적을 남기기 때문이다.
➡ _____

10 예를 들어, 당신이 블로그에 올린 사진들과 온라인 상점에서의 구매 기록들이 모두 빅데이터의 일부가 된다.
➡ _____

11 하지만 단순히 데이터를 수집하는 것만으로는 충분하지 않다.
➡ _____

12 빅데이터는 분석되어야 하고, 이것은 빅데이터 전문가들에 의해서 이루어진다.
➡ _____

13 다양한 방법들을 사용하여 전문가들은 빅데이터를 분석하고, 그것으로부터 의미 있는 결과들을 도출한다.
➡ _____

14 그런 다음, 이런 결과들은 결정을 하거나 또는 미래를 예측하는 데 사용될 수 있다.
➡ _____

15 빅데이터는 어떻게 우리 삶에 영향을 미치고 있는가?
➡ _____

16 빅데이터는 우리 삶의 거의 모든 부분에 영향을 미치고 있다.
➡ _____

17 그것은 회사들이 소비자들이 필요로 하는 것을 더 잘 이해하고 그들이 더 많은 상품을 팔도록 도와준다.
➡ _____

18 그것은 사람들이 교통 체증을 피하도록 도와주기도 한다.
➡ _____

19 그것의 활용은 끝이 없고, 여기에 몇 가지 흥미로운 예들이 있다.
➡ _____

20 질병 예측
➡ _____

21 당신은 날씨 전문가가 날씨를 예측하는 것과 같이 건강 전문가들이 현재 질병을 예측할 수 있다는 것을 알고 있는가?

➡ _____

22 이것은 빅데이터 덕분에 가능하다.

➡ _____

23 예를 들어서 독감의 계절이 오면, 사람들은 독감 약을 더 많이 구입할 것이다.

➡ _____

24 그들은 또한 온라인상에서 독감 증상들을 더 찾아볼 것이다.

➡ _____

25 만약 이런 종류의 데이터를 지혜롭게 분석한다면, 독감의 확산을 예측할 수 있다.

➡ _____

26 스포츠에서의 경기력 향상

➡ _____

27 당신은 스포츠 팬인가?

➡ _____

28 빅데이터는 스포츠를 더 흥미롭게 만들면서, 선수들의 경기력을 향상하고 있다.

➡ _____

29 유명한 사례로 독일 국가 대표 축구팀이 있다.

➡ _____

30 그 팀은 선수들에 관한 엄청난 양의 데이터를 모으고 분석함으로써, 데이터베이스를 구축했다.

➡ _____

31 예를 들어 데이터는 각각의 선수들이 얼마나 많이 달렸고, 얼마나 오랫동안 공을 소유했는지도 포함했다.

➡ _____

32 이 데이터베이스의 도움으로 독일 국가 대표 축구팀은 경기력을 향상할 수 있었고, 2014년 월드컵에서 우승할 수 있었다.

➡ _____

33 범죄 예방

➡ _____

34 빅데이터 덕분에 경찰은 이제 범죄가 발생하기 전에 범죄를 예측할 수 있다.

➡ _____

35 죄의 유형, 시간 및 장소에 관한 빅데이터의 분석을 통해, 경찰은 범죄 다발 지역의 지도를 만들 수 있다.

➡ _____

36 이 지도는 범죄가 언제, 어디에서 가장 많이 발생할 것 같은지를 알려 준다.

➡ _____

37 경찰은 이 지도가 예측하는 장소들과 시간대에 집중함으로써, 추가 범죄를 예방할 수 있다.

➡ _____

38 빅데이터는 이미 세계를 크게 변화시켰다.

➡ _____

39 그러면 빅데이터 산업은 여기에서부터 어디로 가게 될까?

➡ _____

40 누구도 확실히 알지는 못하지만, 전문가들은 빅데이터가 우리 삶에서 더욱 더 중요한 역할을 할 것이라는 데에는 동의한다.

➡ _____

[01~03] 다음 글을 읽고 물음에 답하시오.

ⓐHave you ever visited an online bookstore and been surprised by the books that the store recommended for you? Many of them looked interesting to you. So ⓑ그 서점은 당신이 무엇을 좋아하는지 어떻게 알았을까? ⓒThis is all possible because of big data.

01 위 글의 밑줄 친 ⓐ와 현재완료의 용법이 같은 것을 고르시오.

① Have you been to the bank yet?
② I have read this novel three times.
③ She has been sick since he came here.
④ He has gone to Seoul.
⑤ He has lived here for ten years.

서답형

02 위 글의 밑줄 친 ⓑ의 우리말에 맞게 주어진 어휘를 알맞게 배열하시오.

> the bookstore, you, how, what, know, liked, did

➡ _____

서답형

03 위 글의 밑줄 친 ⓒThis가 가리키는 것을 우리말로 쓰시오.

➡ _____
_____

[04~06] 다음 글을 읽고 물음에 답하시오.

_____ ⓐ _____

Thanks to big data, police can now predict crime before it happens. Through the analysis of big data about the type, time and place of crime, police can make a map of crime hot spots. This map identifies when and where crime is most likely to ⓑhappen. Police can prevent further crime by focusing on the areas and the times this map predicts.

Big data ⓒhas already changed the world greatly. So where will the big data industry go from here? Nobody knows for sure, but experts agree that big data will play a more and more important role in our lives.

중요

04 위 글의 빈칸 ⓐ에 들어갈 제목으로 알맞은 것을 고르시오.

① What is Big Data?
② How to Draw a Map Using Big Data
③ How Is Big Data Influencing Our Jobs?
④ Crime Prevention
⑤ Various Crime Hot Spots

05 위 글의 밑줄 친 ⓑhappen과 바꿔 쓸 수 없는 말을 고르시오.

① occur   ② take place
③ arise   ④ cause
⑤ come about

중요

06 아래 〈보기〉에서 위 글의 밑줄 친 ⓒhas already changed와 현재완료의 용법이 다른 것의 개수를 고르시오.

> — 보기 —
> ① I have been in Korea for five years.
> ② I have just finished my homework.
> ③ I have never seen such a strange thing before.
> ④ Has she done her homework yet?
> ⑤ She has lost her bag.

① 1개   ② 2개   ③ 3개   ④ 4개   ⑤ 5개

[07~09] 다음 글을 읽고 물음에 답하시오.

_____ ⓐ _____

Big data is influencing almost all parts of our lives. It helps companies understand their customers' needs better and helps them sell more products. It helps people avoid heavy traffic. Its uses are endless, and here are some interesting examples.

Disease Forecast

Did you know that health professionals can now forecast a disease just as weather experts forecast the weather? This is possible thanks to big data. ⓑFor example, when the flu season will come, people will buy more flu medicine. They will also search online about flu symptoms more. If this kind of data is analyzed wisely, the spread of the flu can be predicted.

7 위 글의 빈칸 ⓐ에 들어갈 제목으로 알맞은 것을 고르시오.

① How Does Big Data Help Companies?
② The Benefit of Big Data
③ How to Sell More Products by Using Big Data
④ How Is Big Data Influencing Our Lives?
⑤ The Best Way to Avoid Heavy Traffic

서답형

8 위 글의 밑줄 친 ⓑ에서 어법상 틀린 부분을 찾아 고치시오.

_____ ➡ _____

중요

9 Which question CANNOT be answered after reading the passage?

① What is big data influencing?

② How can companies understand their customers' needs better?
③ Can health professionals now forecast a disease?
④ How do weather experts forecast the weather?
⑤ How can the spread of the flu be predicted?

[10~12] 다음 글을 읽고 물음에 답하시오.

_____ ⓐ _____

Big data is data sets that are very big and complex. As information and communication technology develops, the amount of data we have is getting much greater than before. (①) This is mainly because almost everything that we do online leaves a trace. (②) For example, the photos you upload on your blog and the records of your purchases at online stores are all part of big data.

(③) Big data has to be analyzed, and this is done by big data experts. (④) Using various methods, experts analyze big data and draw meaningful results from it. (⑤) These results then can be used to make decisions or to predict the future.

10 위 글의 흐름으로 보아, 주어진 문장이 들어가기에 가장 적절한 곳은?

Simply collecting data, however, is not enough.

①　　　②　　　③　　　④　　　⑤

중요

11 위 글의 빈칸 ⓐ에 들어갈 제목으로 알맞은 것을 고르시오.

① The Increasing Amount of Data
② What is Big Data?
③ Our Online Activity Leaves a Trace
④ How to Record Online Purchases
⑤ How Is Big Data Influencing Our Lives?

12 According to the passage, which is NOT true?

① Big data is very big and complex data sets.
② Almost everything that we do online leaves a trace.
③ The records of your purchases at the street stalls are included in big data.
④ It is not enough to simply collect data.
⑤ Big data experts analyze big data.

[13~15] 다음 글을 읽고 물음에 답하시오.

Improving Performance in Sports

Are you a sports fan? Well, big data is improving the performance of players, (A) making sports more exciting. A famous example is Germany's national soccer team. The team built a database ___ⓐ___ collecting and analyzing a huge amount of data on players. For example, the data included information about how much each player ran and how long he had the ball. ___ⓑ___ the help of this database, Germany's national soccer team was able to improve its performance and win the 2014 World Cup.

13 위 글의 빈칸 ⓐ와 ⓑ에 들어갈 전치사가 바르게 짝지어진 것은?

① in – By   ② by – On
③ by – With   ④ in – On
⑤ on – With

서답형

14 위 글의 밑줄 친 (A)를 접속사와 주어, 동사를 포함하는 절로 바꾸시오.

➡ _____

중요

15 위 글의 주제로 알맞은 것을 고르시오.

① the reaction of big sports fans to big data
② the improvement of the team's performance thanks to the database
③ the way to make sports more exciting
④ how to collect and analyze a huge amount of data on players
⑤ the information that can be included in the data

[16~18] 다음 글을 읽고 물음에 답하시오.

Crime Prevention

___ⓐ___ big data, police can now predict crime before ⓑit happens. (A)[Though / Through] the analysis of big data about the type, time and place of crime, police can make a map of crime hot spots. This map identifies when and where crime is most likely to happen. Police can prevent (B)[farther / further] crime by focusing on the areas and the times this map predicts.

Big data has already changed the world greatly. So where will the big data industry go from here? Nobody knows for sure, but experts (C)[agree / disagree] that big data will play a more and more important role in our lives.

16 위 글의 빈칸 ⓐ에 들어갈 알맞은 말을 모두 고르시오.

① In spite of   ② Thanks to
③ Rather than   ④ Because of
⑤ Instead of

서답형

17 위 글의 밑줄 친 ⓑit이 가리키는 것을 본문에서 찾아 쓰시오.

➡ _____

서답형

18 위 글의 괄호 (A)~(C)에서 문맥이나 어법상 알맞은 낱말을 골라 쓰시오.

➡ (A) _____ (B) _____ (C) _____

[19~21] 다음 글을 읽고 물음에 답하시오.

Improving Performance in Sports

Are you a sports fan? Well, big data is improving the performance of players, ⓐmaking sports more exciting. A famous example is Germany's national soccer team. The team built a database by collecting and analyzing a ⓑhuge amount of data on players. For example, the data included information about ⓒ각각의 선수들이 얼마나 많이 달렸고, 얼마나 오랫동안 공을 소유했는지. With the help of this database, Germany's national soccer team was able to improve its performance and win the 2014 World Cup.

19 아래 〈보기〉에서 위 글의 밑줄 친 ⓐmaking과 문법적 쓰임이 다른 것의 개수를 고르시오.

┤ 보기 ├
① We liked eating pizza.
② I saw Linda crossing the street.
③ My hobby is playing baseball.
④ Walking to school makes me tired.
⑤ She watched TV eating some snacks.

① 1개   ② 2개   ③ 3개   ④ 4개   ⑤ 5개

20 위 글의 밑줄 친 ⓑhuge와 바꿔 쓸 수 없는 말을 모두 고르시오.

① enormous   ② tiny   ③ vast
④ tremendous   ⑤ minute

서답형

21 위 글의 밑줄 친 ⓒ의 우리말에 맞게 주어진 어휘를 알맞게 배열하시오.

each player / had / ran / how much / and / the ball / he / how long

➡ _____
_____

[22~24] 다음 글을 읽고 물음에 답하시오.

How is big data influencing our lives?

ⓐ빅데이터는 우리 삶의 거의 모든 부분에 영향을 미치고 있다. ⓑIt helps companies understand their customers' needs better and helps them sell more products. It helps people avoid heavy traffic. Its uses are endless, and here are some interesting examples.

서답형

22 위 글의 밑줄 친 ⓐ의 우리말에 맞게 주어진 어휘를 이용하여 10 단어로 영작하시오.

influencing, parts

➡ _____

서답형

23 위 글의 밑줄 친 ⓑIt이 가리키는 것을 본문에서 찾아 쓰시오.

➡ _____

서답형

24 위 글을 읽고 빅데이터의 활용 사례 3가지를 우리말로 쓰시오.

➡ (1) _____
(2) _____
(3) _____

[01~03] 다음 글을 읽고 물음에 답하시오.

What is big data?

Big data is data sets that are very big and complex. As information and communication technology develops, the amount of data we have is getting much greater than before. This is mainly because almost everything that we do online leaves a trace. For example, the photos you upload on your blog and the records of your purchases at online stores are all part of big data.

Simply collecting data, however, is not enough. Big data has to ____ⓐ____, and this is done by big data experts. Using various methods, experts analyze big data and draw meaningful results from ⓑit. These results then can be used to make decisions or to predict the future.

01 위 글의 빈칸 ⓐ에 analyze를 알맞은 형태로 쓰시오.

➡ _____

02 위 글의 밑줄 친 ⓑit이 가리키는 것을 본문의 단어를 변형하여 쓰시오.

➡ _____

03 본문의 내용과 일치하도록 다음 빈칸 (A)와 (B)에 알맞은 단어를 쓰시오.

Big data is (A)_____ _____ _____ _____ data sets and (B)_____ _____ _____ analyze big data and draw meaningful results from it.

[04~06] 다음 글을 읽고 물음에 답하시오.

How is big data influencing our lives?

Big data is influencing almost all parts of our lives. It helps companies understand their customers' needs better and helps them sell more products. It helps people avoid heavy traffic. ⓐIts uses are limited, and here are some interesting examples.

Disease Forecast

Did you know that health professionals can now forecast a disease just as weather experts forecast the weather? This is possible thanks to big data. For example, when the flu season comes, people will buy more flu medicine. They will also search online about flu symptoms more. ⓑIf this kind of data is analyzed wisely, the spread of the flu can be predicted.

04 위 글의 밑줄 친 ⓐ에서 흐름상 어색한 부분을 찾아 고치시오.

_____ ➡ _____ 또는

_____

05 How is it possible for health professionals to forecast a disease just as weather experts forecast the weather? Answer in English with 4 words.

➡ _____

06 위 글의 밑줄 친 ⓑ를 we를 주어로 하여 능동태로 고치시오.

➡ _____

_____

[07~10] 다음 글을 읽고 물음에 답하시오.

Improving Performance in Sports

Are you a sports fan? ⓐWell, big data is improving the performance of players, making sports more excited. A famous example is Germany's national soccer team. The team built a database by collecting and analyzing a huge amount of data on players. For example, ⓑthe data included information about how much each player ran and how long he had the ball. With the help of this database, Germany's national soccer team was able to improve ⓒits performance and win the 2014 World Cup.

07 위 글의 밑줄 친 ⓐ에서 어법상 틀린 부분을 찾아 고치시오.

_____ ➡ _____

08 위 글의 밑줄 친 ⓑthe data에 포함된 정보 두 가지를 우리말로 쓰시오.

➡ (1) _____
　(2) _____

09 위 글의 밑줄 친 ⓒits가 가리키는 것을 본문에서 찾아 쓰시오.

➡ _____

10 How was it possible for Germany's national soccer team to build a database? Fill in the blanks (A) and (B) with suitable words.

The team (A)_____ and (B)_____ a huge amount of data on players to build a database.

[11~14] 다음 글을 읽고 물음에 답하시오.

Crime Prevention

ⓐThanks to big data, police can now predict crime after it happens. Through the analysis of big data about the type, time and place of crime, police can make a map of crime hot spots. ⓑThis map identifies when and where crime is most likely to happen. Police can prevent further crime by focusing on the areas and the times this map predicts.

Big data has already changed the world greatly. So where will the big data industry go from here? Nobody knows for sure, but experts agree that big data will play a more and more important ⓒrole in our lives.

11 위 글의 밑줄 친 ⓐ에서 흐름상 어색한 부분을 찾아 고치시오.

_____ ➡ _____

12 위 글의 밑줄 친 ⓑThis map의 역할 두 가지를 우리말로 쓰시오.

➡ (1) _____
　　_____
　(2) _____
　　_____

13 위 글의 밑줄 친 ⓒrole과 바꿔 쓸 수 있는 한 단어를 쓰시오.

➡ _____

14 다음 빈칸 (A)와 (B)에 알맞은 단어를 넣어 경찰이 범죄 다발 지역의 지도를 만드는 방법을 완성하시오.

Police can make a map of crime hot spots by (A)_____ big data about the type, time and place of (B)_____.

After You Read B Read and Complete

Example 1

Health professionals can now forecast the spread of the flu by analyzing the
<u>= experts</u>   전치사 by의 목적어로 쓰인 동명사
sales of flu medicine and online searches about flu symptoms.

Example 2

By collecting and analyzing a huge amount of data on players, Germany's
collecting과 analyzing은 전치사 by의 목적어로 쓰인 동명사
national soccer team was able to improve its performance and win the 2014
Germany's national soccer team을 가리킨다.
World Cup.

Example 3

Through the analysis of big data, police can make a map of crime hot spots
police는 복수 형태의 명사는 아니지만 복수 취급한다.
and use it to prevent further crime.
to부정사의 부사적 용법(목적)

구문해설 · forecast 예측하다 · spread 확산, 전파 · flu 독감 · symptom 증상
· huge 거대한, (크기·양·정도가) 막대한 · performance 경기력, 수행, 성과
· crime 범죄 · hot spot 다발 지역 · prevent 예방하다 · further 더 이상의, 추가의

Around the World

Yuna: We're not late. The bus will arrive in 4 minutes.
in+시간: [경과] (지금부터) ~ 후에
Computer: Last time, you missed question numbers 3 and 5, so let's review

        them first.
= question numbers 3 and 5
Yuna: What's the weather like tomorrow?
= How's the weather tomorrow?
AI: It's going to rain. Take your umbrella.
= bring
Yuna: Big data is making my life so much easier!
비교급 수식 (= even. far. a lot. still)

구문해설 · review: 복습하다 · take: 가지고 가다, 휴대하다

Think and Write

Teens' Free Time Activities

We asked 100 teenagers about their free time activities. The results show
that the free time activity the teenagers want to do the most is traveling. 34%
접속사(명사절)   목적격 관계대명사 생략(which/that)   동명사(보어)
said that they want to travel in their free time. However, the free time activity
시제 일치 예외(현재 사실)
they actually do the most is watching TV. 39% said that they watch TV in
동명사(보어)   시제 일치 예외(현재 사실)
their free time. Looking at the results, we see that there is a big gap between
분사구문(= As/When we look at)   알게 되다(= find. learn)
what the teenagers want to do and what they actually do in their free time.
관계대명사절

구문해설 · actually: 실제로 · gap: 차이 · between A and B: A와 B 사이에

해석

사례 1
건강 전문가들은 독감 약 판매와 독감 증상에 관한 온라인 검색을 분석함으로써 이제 감기의 확산을 예측할 수 있다.

사례 2
독일 국가 대표 축구팀은 선수들에 관한 엄청난 양의 데이터를 모으고 분석함으로써, 경기력을 향상하고 2014년 월드컵에서 우승할 수 있었다.

사례 3
빅데이터의 분석을 통해서 경찰은 범죄 다발 지역의 지도를 만들 수 있고 그것을 추가 범죄를 예방하는 데에 사용할 수 있다.

유나: 늦지 않았네. 버스가 4분 후에 도착할 거야.

컴퓨터: 지난번에 당신은 3번과 5번 문제를 틀렸습니다. 그러니 우선 그것들부터 복습해 봅시다.

유나: 내일 날씨가 어때?

AI: 비가 올 예정입니다. 우산 챙기세요.

유나: 빅데이터는 내 삶을 훨씬 더 쉽게 만들고 있구나!

청소년들의 여가 활동들
우리는 100명의 청소년들에게 여가 활동에 관해 질문했습니다. 그 결과 청소년들이 가장 하고 싶은 여가 활동은 여행인 것으로 나타났습니다. 34%는 여가 시간에 여행을 가고 싶다고 답했습니다. 하지만 그들이 실제로 가장 많이 하는 여가 활동은 TV를 보는 것입니다. 39%는 여가 시간에 TV를 본다고 답했습니다. 결과로 봤을 때, 우리는 청소년들이 여가 시간에 하고 싶은 활동과 실제로 하는 활동 사이에 큰 차이가 있다는 것을 알 수 있습니다.

영역별 핵심문제

01 〈보기〉의 밑줄 친 identifies와 같은 의미로 쓰이지 않은 것을 고르시오.

┤ 보기 ├
This map identifies when and where crime is most likely to happen.

① You should not identify wealth with happiness.
② She was able to identify her attacker.
③ Many of those arrested refused to identify themselves.
④ They identify their members by a distinct smell.
⑤ Can you identify your umbrella among these?

02 다음 영영풀이에 해당하는 단어를 주어진 철자로 시작하여 빈칸에 쓰고, 알맞은 것을 골라 문장을 완성하시오.

- s_____ : the growth or development of something, so that it affects a larger area or a larger number of people
- i_____ : the people or companies engaged in a particular kind of commercial enterprise

(1) We hope to slow the _____ of the disease.
(2) His novels are a rich source of material for the movie _____ .

03 다음 문장의 빈칸에 〈영영풀이〉의 밑줄 친 this에 해당하는 어휘를 쓰시오.

The team built a database by collecting and analyzing a huge _____ of data on players.

<영영풀이> The this of something is how much there is, or how much you have, need, or get.

04 다음 빈칸 (A)~(C)에 알맞은 말을 쓰시오. (주어진 철자로 시작하여 쓸 것.)

- In this area oxen are (A)u_____ to pull carts.
- Some areas are (B)l_____ to have rain today.
- He (C)h_____ her focus only on her studying.

05 괄호 안에 주어진 어휘를 이용하여 빈칸에 알맞게 쓰시오.

(1) The garden was full of _____ flowers. (color)
(2) He offered some _____ advice. (use)
(3) She talks _____ about her problems. (endless)

Conversation

[06~07] 다음 대화를 읽고 물음에 답하시오.

> A: _____ (a) _____
> B: Sure. First, put a tea bag in a cup.
> (A) Then, pour hot water in the cup.
> (B) Last, take the tea bag out after 3 minutes.
> (C) And then?
> (D) OK.
> A: I got it. I really appreciate your help.

06 위 대화의 빈칸 (a)에 know를 이용하여 7 단어로 알맞은 말을 <u>쓰시오</u>.

➡ _____

07 주어진 문장 사이에 나올 대화의 순서로 알맞은 것은?

① (B) – (A) – (C) – (D)
② (C) – (B) – (A) – (D)
③ (D) – (A) – (C) – (B)
④ (D) – (B) – (A) – (C)
⑤ (D) – (B) – (C) – (A)

08 다음 중 짝지어진 대화가 <u>어색한</u> 것은?

① A: Then what?
   B: Then the application will give you a number to unlock a bike with.
② A: I want to return these books. Do you know how to do it?
   B: Thanks.
③ A: Then insert the money.
   B: I really appreciate your help.
④ A: What's this robot for?
   B: Oh, it's a robot that finds books for you.
⑤ A: It's so easy, isn't it?
   B: Yes, it's really amazing.

[09~10] 다음 대화를 읽고 물음에 답하시오.

> G: Excuse me, but what's this robot for?
> B: Oh, it's a robot that finds books for you.
> G: Really? Can you tell me how to use it?
> B: Sure. First, place your library card on the robot's screen.
> G: OK.
> B: Second, type the title of the book you're looking for and then press ENTER. (①)
> G: Is that all? (②)
> B: Yes. (③)
> G: So I can just go to the front desk and get the book? (④)
> B: Right. It's so easy, isn't it? (⑤)
> G: Yes, it's really amazing. Thank you.

09 위 대화의 (①)~(⑤) 중 주어진 문장이 들어갈 곳은?

> Then, the robot will find the book and take it to the front desk.

①   ②   ③   ④   ⑤

10 위 대화를 읽고 답할 수 <u>없는</u> 질문을 고르시오.

① What does the robot do?
② Does the boy know how to use the robot?
③ Should the girl type the title of the book she's looking for?
④ How can the robot find the book and take it to the front desk?
⑤ What does the girl think really amazing?

11 다음 문장의 밑줄 친 부사절을 분사구문으로 알맞게 바꾼 것을 고르시오.

> As he didn't have anyone around to help and save him, George Floyd was killed by the police.

① As he having not anyone around to help and save him,

② There being anyone around to help and save him,

③ Having not anyone around to help and save him,

④ As having not everyone around to help and save him,

⑤ Not having anyone around to help and save him,

12 다음 문장의 밑줄 친 as와 의미상 쓰임이 같은 것을 고르시오.

> The experts were analyzing the final data as the professor got ready to present their results.

① Take a rest in this place as you wish.

② As it gets hotter and hotter, my dog became weaker.

③ We were listening to music from the radio as my uncle drove us to the summer house in Seattle.

④ The researchers collected as much big data as they wanted in studying the unique psychology of the people online.

⑤ As I am mistaken for the actor, people often ask me to shake hands.

[13~14] 다음 문장의 밑줄 친 as와 의미상 쓰임이 다른 하나를 고르시오.

13

> As Tony lives alone in that big house, he must feel depressed and lonely.

① Big data can be useful as it helps our society in various ways.

② As almost everything that we do online leaves a trace, the amount of data is increasing much more than before.

③ What does the expert think happens as information technology develops?

④ Big data has to be analyzed as simply collecting data is not enough.

⑤ The spread of the flu can be predicted as people will search online more.

14

> Police use a map of crime hot spots as drivers are careful of the area where accident happens frequently.

① The sales of the product have gone up as the expert predicted.

② The puppies bark at me just as their mom does.

③ You can be happy as your mom and dad used to live happily.

④ She could succeed in the business as she built a database by collecting and analyzing a huge amount of data.

⑤ Health professionals can forecast a disease just as weather experts do.

15 다음 그림을 보고 괄호 안의 단어를 배열하여 빈칸을 알맞게 채우시오.

(1) (more, ate, eat, she, as, to)

➡ She felt too full _____
a whole pizza.

(2) (as, were, insects, the spider, caught)

➡ A few _____
planned.

Reading

[16~18] 다음 글을 읽고 물음에 답하시오.

What is big data?

Big data is data sets that are very big and complex. As information and communication technology develops, the amount of data we have is getting much greater than before. This is mainly because almost everything that we do online leaves a trace. For example, the photos you upload ⓐ your blog and the records of your purchases at online stores are all part of big data.

Simply collecting data, however, is not enough. Big data has to be analyzed, and this is done by big data experts. (A)Using various methods, experts analyze big data and draw

meaningful results ⓑ it. These results then can be used to make decisions or to predict the future.

16 위 글의 빈칸 ⓐ와 ⓑ에 들어갈 전치사가 바르게 짝지어진 것은?

ⓐ	ⓑ		ⓐ	ⓑ
① for	– to		② on	– from
③ in	– from		④ for	– with
⑤ on	– for			

17 주어진 영영풀이에 해당하는 단어를 본문에서 찾아 쓰시오.

a sign that something has happened or existed

➡ _____

18 위 글의 밑줄 친 (A)Using과 문법적 쓰임이 같은 것을 모두 고르시오.

① He answered smiling at me.
② The baby stopped crying.
③ Taking a walk, they talked about Bob's birthday.
④ Studying hard, he passed the exam.
⑤ Keeping pets has become popular.

[19~21] 다음 글을 읽고 물음에 답하시오.

How is big data influencing our lives?

Big data is influencing almost all parts of our lives. It helps companies understand their customers' needs better and helps them sell more products. It helps people avoid heavy traffic. Its uses are endless, and here are some interesting examples.

Disease Forecast

Did you know that health professionals can now forecast a disease just as weather experts forecast the weather? ⓐThis is possible thanks to big data. For example, when the flu season comes, people will buy more flu medicine. They will also search online about flu symptoms more. If this kind of data is analyzed wisely, the spread of the flu can be predicted.

19 위 글의 밑줄 친 ⓐThis가 가리키는 것을 본문에서 찾아 쓰시오.

➡ _____

_____

20 위 글의 주제로 알맞은 것을 고르시오.

① the way companies use big data
② how to avoid heavy traffic
③ health professionals who can now forecast a disease
④ the influence big data has on our lives
⑤ the effective way to predict the spread of the flu

21 According to the passage, which is NOT true?

① Big data is affecting almost all parts of our lives.
② Big data helps companies understand their customers' needs better.
③ People can avoid heavy traffic thanks to big data.
④ The uses of big data are infinite.
⑤ Health professionals can now cure a disease just as weather experts forecast the weather.

[22~23] 다음 글을 읽고 물음에 답하시오.

Teens' Free Time Activities

We asked 100 teenagers about their free time activities. The results show that the free time activity the teenagers want to do the most is traveling. 34% said that they want to travel in their free time. However, the free time activity they actually do the most is watching TV. 39% said that they watch TV in their free time. Looking at the results, we see that there is a big ___ⓐ___ between what the teenagers want to do and what they actually do in their free time.

22 위 글의 빈칸 ⓐ에 들어갈 알맞은 말을 고르시오.

① agreement   ② gap
③ harmony   ④ arrangement
⑤ correlation

23 According to the passage, which is NOT true?

① The free time activity the teenagers want to do the most is traveling.
② About a third of the teenagers want to travel in their free time.
③ The free time activity the teenagers actually do the most is watching TV.
④ More than two-fifths of the teenagers watch TV in their free time.
⑤ The survey shows that what the teenagers want to do is different from what they actually do in their free time.

출제율 90%

01 다음 중 짝지어진 단어의 관계가 나머지와 <u>다른</u> 것은?

① include – exclude
② complex – complicated
③ meaningful – meaningless
④ lock – unlock
⑤ borrow – lend

출제율 100%

02 밑줄 친 부분의 의미로 알맞지 <u>않은</u> 것은?

① The people cultivate <u>mainly</u> rice and beans. (주로)
② It is impossible to <u>predict</u> what will happen. (예측하다)
③ If he <u>improved</u> his IT skills, he'd easily get a job. (향상시키다)
④ <u>Prevention</u> plays a central role in traditional medicine. (훼방)
⑤ I would like to get advance <u>purchase</u> discount. (구매)

출제율 95%

03 다음 빈칸에 들어갈 알맞은 말을 쓰시오.

(1) Let your eyes _____ on objects that are further away from you.
(2) He is to _____ an important role in promoting Seoul's charm to the rest of the world.

[04~05] 다음 대화를 읽고 물음에 답하시오.

G: Can you tell me how to plant a potato?
B: Sure. First, cut a potato ___ⓐ___ small pieces. Second, dig holes in the ground.
G: Then?
B: Then put the potato pieces in the holes and cover the holes ___ⓑ___ dirt.
G: That sounds simple. Thanks.

출제율 90%

04 위 대화의 빈칸 ⓐ와 ⓑ에 알맞은 말을 쓰시오.

➡ ⓐ _____   ⓑ _____

출제율 100%

05 감자 심기에 관한 위 대화를 읽고 대답할 수 <u>없는</u> 질문을 고르시오.

① Does the boy know how to plant a potato?
② What is the first step?
③ What is the second step?
④ When will the girl plant a potato?
⑤ Does planting a potato seem simple?

[06~07] 다음 대화를 읽고 물음에 답하시오.

B: Excuse me. Can you tell me how to add money ___ⓐ___ my transportation card?
G: ___(A)___ First, put your card in the machine. Second, choose the amount of money you want to add.
B: OK.
G: Last, insert your money ___ⓑ___ the machine.
B: That sounds simple. Thanks.

출제율 95%

06 위 대화의 빈칸 (A)에 알맞지 <u>않은</u> 것을 <u>모두</u> 고르시오.

① Of course.   ② I don't know.
③ Why not?   ④ Sure.
⑤ Don't mention it.

07 위 대화의 빈칸 ⓐ와 ⓑ에 알맞은 말을 고르시오.

    ⓐ   ⓑ   ⓐ   ⓑ

① at – into   ② at – to

③ to – into   ④ to – to

⑤ on – in

08 다음 밑줄 친 부분 중 어법상 어색한 것을 고르시오.

① <u>Being sensitive to the feedback,</u> Mary was carefully checking her research paper.

② <u>Written quickly,</u> the novel has been praised as a masterpiece of all time.

③ <u>It being cold and windy,</u> all fishermen couldn't go fishing this morning.

④ <u>Being no money left in her pockets,</u> Robin started part-time job.

⑤ <u>Wanting to allow him to use his car,</u> Mr. Copper told his son to wait for him.

09 다음 주어진 문장의 부사절을 분사구문으로 적절히 전환한 것을 고르시오.

> As she had not been invited to the party, the girl stayed at home all day.

① Having not been invited to the party, the girl stayed at home all day.

② As she not being invited to the party, the girl stayed at home all day.

③ As she being not invited to the party, the girl stayed at home all day.

④ Not having been invited to the party, the girl stayed at home all day.

⑤ Not having invited to the party, the girl stayed at home all day.

10 다음 두 문장을 접속사 as를 활용하여, 한 문장으로 고친 것으로 알맞은 것은?

> • It was cold outside in the morning.
> • I nearly caught cold while running.

① As I nearly caught cold while running, it was cold outside in the morning.

② It was cold outside in the morning as I nearly caught cold while running.

③ As I was running, it was cold outside in the morning so that I nearly caught cold.

④ As it was cold outside in the morning, I nearly caught cold while running.

⑤ I nearly caught cold as running was cold outside in the morning.

11 다음 중 어법상 옳지 않은 문장을 고르면? (정답 2개)

① Worked hard to complete the report in time, Wendy was exhausted.

② Being looked much bigger than before, the flowers are in bloom.

③ The doctor succeeding in the heart operation, the patients in her clinic became even more dependent on her.

④ Living next door, I seldom see him.

⑤ There being no bus service, the crowd had to walk all the way home.

[12~14] 다음 글을 읽고 물음에 답하시오.

What is big data?

  Big data is data sets that are very big and complex. As information and communication technology develops, the amount of data we have is getting (A)<u>much</u> greater than before.

This is mainly because almost everything that we do online leaves a trace. ⓐ , the photos you upload on your blog and the records of your purchases at online stores are all part of big data.

Simply collecting data, ⓑ , is not enough. Big data has to be analyzed, and this is done by big data experts. Using various methods, experts analyze big data and draw meaningful results from it. These results then can be used to make decisions or to predict the future.

출제율 90%

12 위 글의 빈칸 ⓐ와 ⓑ에 들어갈 알맞은 말을 고르시오.

① For instance – therefore
② For example – however
③ In addition – however
④ However – as a result
⑤ That is – for example

출제율 100%

13 위 글의 밑줄 친 (A)much와 바꿔 쓸 수 없는 말을 고르시오.

① even   ② still
③ far   ④ very
⑤ a lot

출제율 100%

14 위 글의 주제로 알맞은 것을 고르시오.

① the very big and complex data
② the amount of data which is getting much greater than before
③ the popularity of big data experts
④ how to make decisions or to predict the future effectively
⑤ collecting and analyzing of big data and its use

[15~17] 다음 글을 읽고 물음에 답하시오.

Disease Forecast

(①) Did you know that health professionals can now forecast a disease just (A)as weather experts forecast the weather? (②) For example, when the flu season comes, people will buy more flu medicine. (③) They will also search online about flu symptoms more. (④) If this kind of data is analyzed wisely, the spread of the flu can be ⓐ . (⑤)

출제율 95%

15 위 글의 빈칸 ⓐ에 들어갈 알맞은 말을 고르시오.

① protected   ② improved
③ predicted   ④ produced
⑤ increased

출제율 95%

16 위 글의 흐름으로 보아, 주어진 문장이 들어가기에 가장 적절한 곳은?

> This is possible thanks to big data.

①   ②   ③   ④   ⑤

출제율 100%

17 위 글의 밑줄 친 (A)as와 같은 의미로 쓰인 것을 고르시오.

① As he was a child, he lived in England.
② As it was getting dark, we soon turned back.
③ Leave it as it is.
④ As rust eats iron, so care eats the heart.
⑤ Woman as she was, she was brave.

[18~20] 다음 글을 읽고 물음에 답하시오.

Crime Prevention

Thanks to big data, police can now predict crime before it happens. Through the analysis of big data about the type, time and place of crime, police can make a map of crime hot spots. ⓐ이 지도는 범죄가 언제, 어디에서 가장 많이 발생할 것 같은지를 알려 준다. Police can prevent further crime by focusing on the areas and the times this map predicts.

Big data has already changed the world greatly. So where will the big data industry go from here? Nobody knows for sure, but experts agree that big data will play a more and more important role in our lives.

18 위 글의 밑줄 친 ⓐ의 우리말에 맞게 주어진 어휘를 이용하여 12 단어로 영작하시오.

> identifies, most likely to, happen

➡ _____

_____

19 According to the second paragraph, what do experts agree about big data? Answer in English in a full sentence.

➡ _____

_____

20 According to the passage, which is NOT true?

① Even now, police can't predict crime before it happens.

② Police can make a map of crime hot spots by analyzing big data about the type, time and place of crime.

③ If the police focus on the areas and the times a map of crime hot spots predicts, they can prevent further crime.

④ The world has already changed greatly thanks to big data.

⑤ Nobody knows for sure where the big data industry will go from here.

[21~22] 다음 글을 읽고 물음에 답하시오.

Teens' Free Time Activities

We asked 100 teenagers about their free time activities. The results show that the free time activity the teenagers want to do the most is traveling. 34% said that they want to travel in their free time. However, the free time activity they actually do the most is watching TV. 39% said that they watch TV in their free time. ⓐ Looking at the results, we see that there is a big gap between what the teenagers want to do and what they actually do in their free time.

21 위 글의 밑줄 친 ⓐ를 접속사와 주어, 동사를 포함하는 절로 바꾸시오.

➡ _____

22 위 글을 읽고 알 수 없는 것을 고르시오.

① What free time activity do the teenagers want to do the most?

② What percent of the teenagers want to travel in their free time?

③ What free time activity do the teenagers actually do the most?

④ What percent of the teenagers watch TV in their free time?

⑤ Why is it difficult for the teenagers to do what they want to do the most in their free time?

[01~03] 다음 대화를 읽고 물음에 답하시오.

G: Excuse me, but what's this robot for?

B: Oh, it's a robot that finds books for you.

G: Really? Can you tell me how to use it?

B: Sure. First, place your library card on the robot's screen.

G: OK.

B: Second, type the title of the book you're looking for and then press ENTER.

G: Is that all?

B: Yes. Then, the robot will find the book and take it to the front desk.

G: So I can just go to the front desk and get the book?

B: Right. It's so easy, isn't it?

G: Yes, it's really amazed. Thank you.

01 위 대화의 로봇을 이용하여 책을 찾는 3 단계의 방법을 우리말로 쓰시오.

➡ 1. _____
　 2. _____
　 3. _____

02 위 대화에서 어법상 <u>어색한</u> 것을 하나 찾아 바르게 고치시오.

_____ ➡ _____

03 What does the robot do for people who are using it? Answer with the words, 'and, them'. (11 words)

➡ _____
_____

04 다음 우리말에 맞도록 괄호 안에 주어진 어휘를 알맞게 배열하여 빈칸을 채우시오.

(1) 비록 학생들이 선생님의 뜻을 알았지만, 그녀가 말한 대로 하지 않기로 결정했다. (what, meant, though, knowing, the teacher)

➡ _____,
the students decided not to do as she told.

(2) 그 열차에 남은 좌석이 있다면, 그녀는 다음 날 아침에 부산으로 갈 것이다. (seats, there, the train, left, any, on, being)

➡ _____,
she will go to Busan next morning.

(3) 집을 청소하고 싶었기 때문에, 나는 일을 하루 쉬겠다고 사장에게 말했다. (clean, wanting, house, to, my)

➡ _____,
I told the boss that I'd take a day off from work.

05 다음 우리말에 맞도록 괄호 안에 주어진 어휘를 알맞게 배열하여 빈칸을 채우시오.

(1) 그녀가 전에 말했듯이, 비데이터의 중요성은 더욱 커지고 있다. (the importance, is, said, growing, big data, she, of, before)

➡ As _____
_____ even more.

(2) 빅데이터가 세상을 이미 엄청나게 바꿔버렸기 때문에, 나는 미래가 더욱 궁금하다. (already, the world, big data, changed, greatly, as, has)

➡ _____
_____ I wonder more about the future.

What is big data?

Big data is data sets that are very big and complex. As information and communication technology develops, the amount of data we have is getting much greater than before. This is mainly because almost everything that we do online leaves a trace. For example, the photos you upload on your blog and the records of your purchases at online stores are all part of big data.

Simply collecting data, however, is not enough. Big data has to be analyzed, and this is done by big data experts. ⓐ다양한 방법들을 사용하여 전문가들은 빅데이터를 분석하고, 그것으로부터 의미 있는 결과들을 도출한다. These results then can be used to make decisions or to predict the future.

06 What's big data? Answer in English in a full sentence.

➡ _____

07 Why is the amount of data we have getting much greater than before? Answer in English in a full sentence beginning with "Because".

➡ _____

_____

08 위 글의 밑줄 친 ⓐ의 우리말에 맞게 주어진 어휘를 이용하여 13 단어로 영작하시오.

> Using, experts, draw, meaningful

➡ _____

_____

How is big data influencing our lives?

Big data is influencing almost all parts of our lives. It helps companies understand their customers' needs better and helps them sell more products. It helps people avoid heavy traffic. Its uses are endless, and here are some interesting examples.

Disease Forecast

Did you know that health professionals can now forecast a disease just as weather experts forecast the weather? This is possible thanks to big data. For example, when the flu season comes, people will buy more flu medicine. They will also search online about flu symptoms more. If ⓐthis kind of data is analyzed wisely, the spread of the flu can be predicted.

09 How does big data help companies? Answer in English in a full sentence beginning with "It".

➡ _____

_____

10 다음 빈칸에 알맞은 단어를 넣어 위 글의 밑줄 친 ⓐthis kind of data가 가리키는 것을 완성하시오.

> It is the data about people's behavior during _____ _____ _____ .

11 위 글의 내용을 다음과 같이 정리하고자 한다. 빈칸 (A)와 (B)에 들어갈 알맞은 단어를 본문에서 찾아 쓰시오.

> The big data is influencing (A)_____ _____ _____ of our lives and its (B)_____ are endless like health professionals can now forecast a disease thanks to big data.

01 다음 주어진 단어들 중에 자유롭게 선택하여, 아래의 그림과 연관되는 내용이 되도록 〈보기〉와 같이 ① 접속사 'as를 사용한 부사절'이 들어간 문장을 영작하고, ② 영작한 문장에 쓰인 부사절을 같은 의미의 분사구문으로 전환하여 두 세트 이상 쓰시오.

- read / talk / water / listen to / eat / watch / sit / dance / sing
- a book / plants / a sandwich / TV / music / the radio / a song

┌─ 보기 ────────────────────────────────┐
① As he talked on the phone, Minsu watched TV.
② Talking on the phone, Minsu watched TV.
└──┘

(1) _____

(2) _____

02 다음 내용을 바탕으로 정보를 설명하는 글을 쓰시오.

┌──┐
1. The survey is about teens' free time activities.
2. The free time activity the teenagers want to do the most is traveling.
3. 34% of the teenagers want to travel in their free time.
4. The free time activity the teenagers actually do the most is watching TV.
5. 39% of the teenagers watch TV in their free time.
6. The survey shows that there is a big gap between what the teenagers want to do and what they actually do in their free time.
└──┘

┌──┐
Teens' Free Time Activities

We asked 100 teenagers about their (A)_____. The results show that the free time activity the teenagers want to do the most is (B)_____. (C)_____ said that they want to travel in their free time. However, the free time activity they actually do the most is (D)_____. (E)_____ said that they watch TV in their free time. Looking at the results, we see that there is a big gap between (F)_____ and (G)_____ in their free time.
└──┘

단원별 모의고사

01 다음 짝지어진 단어의 관계가 같도록 빈칸에 알맞은 말을 쓰시오. (주어진 철자로 시작할 것.)

> spread – expansion : affect – i_____

[02~03] 주어진 영어 설명에 알맞은 어휘를 빈칸에 쓰시오. (주어진 철자로 시작할 것.)

02
> He made a quick exit to a_____ meeting her.

> <영어 설명> to stay away from someone or something

➡ _____

03
> If you are not satisfied with your p_____, we will give you a full refund.

> <영어 설명> the action of buying something; a thing that has been bought

➡ _____

04 다음 빈칸에 알맞은 말로 짝지어진 것을 고르시오.

> • Can you _____ a good hotel?
> • An early _____ of the disease is a fever.

① recollect – symphony
② reject – symptom
③ reject – sympathy
④ recommend – symptom
⑤ recommend – sympathy

05 다음 우리말을 주어진 어휘를 이용하여 영작하시오.

(1) 독감에 걸리거나 독감의 확산을 피하기 위해, 여러분은 거리를 두고 집에 머물러야 합니다. (the flu, spreading, catching, keep your distance, avoid, should, stay home)

➡ _____

_____

(2) 질문할 때 사용하는 말이 사람들이 대답하는 방식에 영향을 미칠 수 있다. (how, influence, the wording of questions)

➡ _____

_____

[06~07] 다음 대화를 읽고 물음에 답하시오.

G: Excuse me. I want to rent a bike. (a)Can you tell me how to use this application?
M: Sure. First, (b)앱에 로그인하세요. (log, the application) Then find the RENT button and touch it.
G: Then what?
M: Then the application will give you a number to unlock a bike with.
G: Thank you. I really appreciate your help.

06 위 대화의 밑줄 친 (a)를 me와 explain을 이용하여 바꿔 쓰시오.

➡ _____

_____

07 위 대화의 밑줄 친 (b)를 주어진 말을 이용하여 영작하시오.

➡ _____

[08~09] 다음 대화의 밑줄 친 부분을 괄호 안에 주어진 어휘를 이용하여 바꿔 쓰시오.

08

A: Excuse me. I want to return these books. Do you know how to do it?

B: Sure. It's simple. First, insert the library card into the machine. Second, put the books in this box.

A: OK.

B: Then just take your card out.

A: I really appreciate your help. (grateful)

➡ _____

09

B: I want to buy a snack. Do you know how to use this snack machine? (can, tell)

G: Yeah. First, choose the snack you want.

B: I already did. What's next?

G: Just put in the money. Then take the snack out.

B: Got it. Thanks.

➡ _____

[10~11] 다음 대화를 읽고 물음에 답하시오.

A: Do you know how to make tea?

B: Sure. First, put a tea bag in a cup.

A: OK.

B: Then, pour hot water in the cup.

A: And then?

B: Last, take the tea bag out after 3 minutes.

A: I got it. I really appreciate your help.

10 How long do you have to wait before you take out the tea bag? Answer by beginning with the word "We".

➡ _____

_____

11 위 대화의 내용과 일치하지 <u>않는</u> 것은?

① B는 차를 만드는 법을 알고 있다.

② 차를 만들려면 우선 티백을 컵에 넣어야 한다.

③ 티백을 넣은 후 컵에 뜨거운 물을 부어야 한다.

④ 차를 만드는 마지막 단계는 3분 후에 티백을 꺼내는 것이다.

⑤ B는 A에게 감사하고 있다.

12 다음 각 문장의 밑줄 친 분사구문을 부사절로 바꿀 때 어법상 <u>어색한</u> 것은?

① <u>Someone having broken down her bike,</u> Jessie may not use it this afternoon.

→ As someone has broken down her bike,

② <u>Speaking without a break for 2 hours,</u> the comedian got exhausted.

→ As he spoke without a break for 2 hours,

③ <u>Finding the tablet computer Anne had lost,</u> Jane cried out with joy.

→ As she found the tablet computer Anne had lost,

④ <u>Having heard much about the girl before,</u> he was hardly aware of her.

→ As he had heard much about the girl before,

⑤ <u>Composing the last scene of the film,</u> the writer was visited by a stranger.

→ As he was composing the last scene of the film,

13 다음 각 문장의 밑줄 친 부사절을 분사구문으로 바꾼 것 중 옳은 것은?

① If it rains tomorrow, we can't go to the zoo.
　→ Raining tomorrow,
② As William went to bed earlier this evening, he woke up at 3.
　→ William going to bed earlier this evening,
③ When they are seen from under water, the trees seem even taller.
　→ Seen from under water,
④ While Bentley was eating a beef steak, his little brothers fell asleep.
　→ Eating a beef steak,
⑤ If you put a coin on the box, the cat will take it away.
　→ Putting a coin on the box,

14 다음 문장에 공통으로 들어갈 알맞은 말을 고르시오. (대 · 소문자 구분 안 함.)

> • _____ I mentioned earlier, you should be careful when you upload the pictures or something private.
> • Messy used big data _____ a means of persuading his boss.
> • _____ the girl got older, she became a lot wiser than any other educated person.

① what　　② as　　③ when
④ since　　⑤ though

[15~16] 다음 글을 읽고 물음에 답하시오.

> Simply collecting data, however, is not enough. Big data has to be analyzed, and ⓐthis is done by big data experts. Using various methods, experts analyze big data and draw meaningful results from it. These results then can be used to make decisions or ⓑto predict the future.

15 위 글의 밑줄 친 ⓐthis가 가리키는 것을 우리말로 쓰시오.

➡ _____

16 아래 〈보기〉에서 위 글의 밑줄 친 ⓑto predict와 to부정사의 용법이 다른 것의 개수를 고르시오.

> ┤ 보기 ├
> ① I was sorry to hear about their problem.
> ② It is not good to spend so much time playing computer games.
> ③ He went to the library to study for the final exam.
> ④ I have so many friends to help me.
> ⑤ The teacher explained when to begin the test.

① 1개　② 2개　③ 3개　④ 4개　⑤ 5개

[17~18] 다음 글을 읽고 물음에 답하시오.

Disease Forecast

Did you know that health (A)professionals can now forecast a disease just as weather experts forecast the weather? This is possible thanks to big data. ____ⓐ____, when the flu season comes, people will buy more flu medicine. They will also search online about flu symptoms more. If this kind of data is analyzed wisely, the spread of the flu can be predicted.

17 위 글의 빈칸 ⓐ에 들어갈 알맞은 말을 고르시오.

① Whereas ② Therefore
③ In addition ④ For example
⑤ However

18 위 글의 밑줄 친 (A)professionals와 바꿔 쓸 수 있는 말을 본문에서 찾아 쓰시오.

➡ _____

[19~20] 다음 글을 읽고 물음에 답하시오.

ⓐ _____

Are you a sports fan? Well, big data is improving the performance of players, making sports more exciting. A famous example is Germany's national soccer team. The team built a database by collecting and analyzing a huge amount of data on players. For example, the data included information about how much each player ran and how long he had the ball. ⓑ _____ the help of this database, Germany's national soccer team was able to improve its performance and win the 2014 World Cup.

19 위 글의 빈칸 ⓐ에 들어갈 제목으로 알맞은 것을 고르시오.

① How Is Big Data Influencing Our Lives?
② Improving Performance in Sports
③ The Way to Build a Database
④ What is Big Data?
⑤ The Victory of Germany's National Soccer Team

20 위 글의 빈칸 ⓑ에 알맞은 전치사를 쓰시오.

➡ _____

[21~22] 다음 글을 읽고 물음에 답하시오.

Crime Prevention

Thanks to big data, police can now predict crime before it happens. (①) Through the analysis of big data about the type, time and place of crime, police can make a map of crime hot spots. (②) Police can prevent further crime by focusing on the areas and the times this map predicts. (③)

Big data has already changed the world greatly. (④) So where will the big data industry go from here? (⑤) Nobody knows for sure, but experts agree ⓐ빅데이터가 우리 삶에서 더욱 더 중요한 역할을 할 것이라는 것을.

21 위 글의 흐름으로 보아, 주어진 문장이 들어가기에 가장 적절한 곳은?

This map identifies when and where crime is most likely to happen.

①　　　②　　　③　　　④　　　⑤

22 위 글의 밑줄 친 ⓐ의 우리말에 맞게 주어진 어휘를 알맞게 배열하시오.

our lives / a / that / important role / big data / more and more / will play / in

➡ _____

_____

Lesson 8

The Joseon Dynasty Through Paintings

 ## 의사소통 기능

- 선호 표현하기

  A: Which food do you prefer, Tteokbokki or Gimbap?

  B: I prefer Tteokbokki.

- 의견 표현하기

  It seems to me that it's more delicious.

 ## 언어 형식

- to부정사의 의미상 주어

  It was impossible **for him to catch** any fish.

- 가정법 과거

  It **would** be wonderful **if I could** eat fresh fish.

Words & Expressions

Key Words

- **appear**[əpíər] 동 ~하게 보이다, 나타나다
- **attitude**[ǽtitjùːd] 명 태도, 자세
- **bamboo**[bæmbúː] 명 대나무
- **behavior**[bihéivjər] 명 행동
- **bend**[bend] 동 굽다, 구부러지다
- **bloom**[bluːm] 동 꽃을 피우다, 꽃이 피다
- **carp**[kɑːrp] 명 잉어(단·복수 동형)
- **cancel**[kǽnsəl] 동 취소하다
- **character**[kǽriktər] 명 글자
- **curvy**[kə́ːrvi] 형 굴곡이 많은
- **decoration**[dèkəréiʃən] 명 장식
- **despite**[dispáit] 전 ~에도 불구하고
- **difficulty**[dífikʌlti] 명 어려움, 고난
- **disappointed**[dìsəpɔ́intid] 형 실망한, 낙담한
- **dynasty**[dáinəsti] 명 시대, 왕조
- **effectively**[iféktivli] 부 효과적으로
- **folk painting** 민화
- **frozen**[fróuzn] 형 얼어붙은
- **greatly**[gréitli] 부 대단히, 크게
- **harmony**[hɑ́ːrməni] 명 조화
- **ill**[il] 형 아픈, 병든

- **impossible**[impásəbl] 형 불가능한
- **influence**[ínfluəns] 동 영향을 미치다
- **justice**[dʒʌ́stis] 명 정의, 공정성
- **lotus flower** 연꽃
- **loyalty**[lɔ́iəlti] 명 충성, 충실
- **melt**[melt] 동 녹다
- **muddy**[mʌ́di] 형 진흙투성이의, 탁한, 흙탕물의
- **object**[ábdʒikt] 명 물건, 물체
- **pond**[pand] 명 연못
- **prefer**[prifə́ːr] 동 선호하다, 더 좋아하다
- **represent**[rèprizént] 동 나타내다, 보여 주다, 상징하다
- **respect**[rispékt] 명 존경, 경의
- **society**[səsáiəti] 명 사회
- **suddenly**[sʌ́dnli] 부 갑자기
- **symbol**[símbəl] 명 상징, 기호
- **symbolic**[simbálik] 형 상징적인, 상징하는
- **symbolize**[símbəlàiz] 동 상징하다
- **thus**[ðʌs] 부 따라서, 그러므로
- **value**[vǽljuː] 명 가치, 중요성
- **will**[wil] 명 의지
- **wonderful**[wʌ́ndərfəl] 형 아주 훌륭한, 경이로운

Key Expressions

- **as follows** 다음과 같이
- **because of** ~ 때문에
- **for example** 예를 들어
- **for this reason** 이런 이유로
- **get well** 병이 나아지다, 회복하다
- **in particular** 특히, 특별히

- **look at** ~ ~을 보다
- **much more than** ~보다 훨씬 많이
- **once upon a time** 옛날에
- **remind ~ of** ... ~에게 …을 상기시키다
- **right after** ~ ~ 직후에
- **so ~ that** ... 너무 ~해서 …하다

Word Power

※ 서로 비슷한 뜻을 가진 어휘

- □ **despite** ~에도 불구하고 : **in spite of** ~에도 불구하고
- □ **ill** 아픈 : **sick** 아픈
- □ **object** 물건, 물체 : **item** 물품, 품목
- □ **society** 사회 : **community** 지역사회, 공동체

- □ **difficulty** 어려움, 고난 : **hardship** 곤란, 고충
- □ **loyalty** 충성, 충실 : **fidelity** 충성, 충실, 성실
- □ **represent** 나타내다, 상징하다 : **express** 나타내다, 표현하다
- □ **thus** 그러므로, 따라서 : **therefore** 그러므로

※ 서로 반대의 뜻을 가진 어휘

- □ **appear** 나타나다, 출현하다 ↔ **disappear** 사라지다, 없어지다
- □ **impossible** 불가능한 ↔ **possible** 가능한

- □ **ill** 아픈 ↔ **healthy** 건강한
- □ **justice** 정의, 공정 ↔ **injustice** 불평등, 부당함

※ 과거분사 (동사+ed)

- □ **bore**+ed → **bored** 지루해진
- □ **embarrass**+ed → **embarrassed** 당황한
- □ **fascinate**+ed → **fascinated** 마음을 뺏긴
- □ **shock**+ed → **shocked** 충격 받은

- □ **disappoint**+ed → **disappointed** 실망한
- □ **excite**+ed → **excited** 신이 난, 들뜬
- □ **interest**+ed → **interested** 흥미를 가진
- □ **surprise**+ed → **surprised** 놀란

English Dictionary

- □ **appear** 나타나다
  → to begin to be seen; come into existence or use
  보여지기 시작하다; 생기거나 쓰이게 되다
- □ **attitude** 태도, 자세
  → the way you think or feel about something
  어떤 것에 대해 생각하거나 느끼는 방식
- □ **behavior** 행동
  → the things that a person or animal does
  사람이나 동물이 하는 것들
- □ **bend** 굽다, 구부러지다
  → to shape or force something straight into a curve or angle 어떤 곧은 것을 구부러지거나 각이 지게 만들거나 힘을 가하다
- □ **bloom** 꽃을 피우다, 꽃이 피다
  → produce or yield flowers 꽃들이 생기게 하다
- □ **despite** ~에도 불구하고
  → although something happens or exists
  어떤 일이 일어나거나 존재하기는 하더라도
- □ **dynasty** 왕조
  → a period of time during which members of the same family rule a country or region
  일가족이 한 나라나 지역을 통치하는 기간
- □ **frozen** 얼어붙은
  → made into, covered with, or surrounded by ice
  얼음으로 만들어지거나 덮였거나 혹은 둘러쌓인

- □ **justice** 정의
  → the quality of being fair and reasonable; fairness in the way people are treated
  공평하고 합리적인 특성; 사람들이 대우 받는 방식에서의 공정함
- □ **loyalty** 충성, 충실
  → a feeling of support for someone or something
  어떤 사람이나 어떤 것에 대해 지지하는 감정
- □ **object** 물건, 물체
  → a thing that you can see and touch 보거나 만질 수 있는 것
- □ **remind** 상기시키다
  → to make someone remember something
  어떤 사람에게 어떤 것을 기억하게 만들다
- □ **represent** 나타내다
  → to show or mean something 어떤 것을 보여주거나 의미하다
- □ **society** 사회
  → all the people who live in a country, and the way they live 한 국가에 살고 있는 모든 사람과 그들이 사는 방식
- □ **symbol** 상징, 기호
  → a sign, picture, object etc. that represents something else 다른 어떤 것을 나타내는 기호, 그림, 물건 등
- □ **symbolic** 상징적인
  → representing a particular idea or quality
  특정한 생각이나 특성을 나타내는

01 다음 짝지어진 단어의 관계가 같도록 빈칸에 알맞은 말은?

> ill – sick : community – _____

① complex   ② influence

③ harmony   ④ society

⑤ symbol

02 주어진 영어 설명에 맞게 문장의 빈칸에 알맞은 말을 쓰시오.

> Sally's bad _____ began to annoy us.

> <영어 설명> the things that a person or animal does

➡ _____

03 밑줄 친 부분의 의미로 알맞지 <u>않은</u> 것을 고르시오.

① Let's <u>take a walk</u> in the bamboo forest. (산책하다)

② Did you figure out if your answers were <u>right after</u> the test? (~ 직후에)

③ <u>Despite</u> the fact that she was wearing a seat belt, she was thrown sharply forward. (~에도 불구하고)

④ <u>Once upon a time</u> there was a beautiful princess. (옛날 옛적에)

⑤ <u>In particular</u>, the museum has many Impressionist paintings. (특히)

04 다음 빈칸에 들어갈 가장 알맞은 말을 고르시오.

> You _____ me of your father when you say that.

① remind   ② expert

③ chase   ④ remember

⑤ memory

05 다음 빈칸에 공통으로 들어갈 말로 알맞은 것을 고르시오. (대 · 소문자 무시)

> • There is a similar word in many languages, _____ example in French and Italian.
>
> • _____ this reason, experts often compare sports to war.

① to   ② at   ③ on

④ by   ⑤ for

06 다음 <보기>의 단어를 사용하여 자연스러운 문장을 만들 수 <u>없는</u> 것은?

> ┤ 보기 ├
> object   frozen   respect   bend

① We once walked across a _____ pond at midnight.

② The _____ that he found was old.

③ No charge will be made if you _____ within 10 days.

④ The supports under the bridge were starting to _____.

⑤ We always show our _____ for teachers.

01 다음 영영풀이에 알맞은 어휘를 〈보기〉에서 찾아 쓰시오.

보기

remind   appear   bend   dynasty

(1) to begin to be seen; to come into existence or use
(2) to shape or force something straight into a curve or angle
(3) a period of time during which members of the same family rule a country or region
(4) to make someone remember something

➡ (1) _____ (2) _____ (3) _____
   (4) _____

02 다음 빈칸에 주어진 어휘를 알맞은 형태로 쓰시오.

(1) The local history of the area is _____. (fascinate)
(2) I was very _____ with myself. (disappoint)

03 다음 우리말에 맞도록 빈칸에 알맞은 말을 주어진 철자로 시작하여 쓰시오.

(1) 그 노래는 나의 아버지를 생각나게 한다.
   → The song r_____ me of my father.
(2) 하트 모양은 사랑을 상징한다.
   → The shape of a heart s_____ love.

(3) 학생들은 더운 날씨에도 불구하고 운동회를 즐겼다.
   → The students enjoyed the sports day d_____ the hot weather.
(4) 저 분홍 장미는 6월에 꽃이 필 것이다.
   → Those pink roses will b_____ in June.

04 우리말에 맞게 한 단어를 추가하여 주어진 단어를 알맞게 배열하시오.

(1) 저녁으로 특별히 뭐 먹고 싶은 거 있니? (anything, dinner, there, you'd, is, like, particular, for)

   ➡ _____
     _____

(2) 이런 이유로, 금요일은 결혼식 하기에 좋은 날로 여겨졌다. (Friday, reason, day, weddings, considered, be, was, a, this, good, for, to)

   ➡ _____
     _____

(3) 우리나라 민화에서 호랑이는 자주 등장하는 소재이다. (the tiger, paintings, subject, is, a, Korean, common, in)

   ➡ _____
     _____

(4) 그가 나를 찾아온 이유는 다음과 같다. (he, me, the reason, is, see, came, follows, to)

   ➡ _____
     _____

Conversation

1 선호 표현하기

> **A** Which food do you prefer, Tteokbokki or Gimbap?
> 떡볶이와 김밥 중에 어떤 음식을 더 좋아하니?
>
> **B** I prefer Tteokbokki. 난 떡볶이를 더 좋아해.

- A와 B 두 가지 중 어떤 것을 선호하는지 물을 때 prefer를 사용하여 'Which (one) do you prefer, A or B?'로 표현한다. 같은 표현으로 'Which (one) do you like better, A or B?', 'Which (one) do you like more, A or B?', 'Which one do you want to ~ more?' 등을 쓸 수 있다.

- 대답할 때는 'I prefer ~.' 또는 'I like 목적어 better.', 'I like 목적어 more.'라고 말한다. 'B보다 A를 더 선호한다.'라고 대답할 때는 'I prefer A to B.' 또는 'I like A better than B.', 'I like A more than B.'라고 말한다.

선호 묻고 대답하기

- Which (one) do you prefer, A or B?
- Which (one) do you like better, A or B?
- Which (one) do you like more, A or B?
- Which (one) do you want to ~ more?
- I prefer ~. / I prefer A to B.
- I like 목적어 better. / I like A better than B.
- I like 목적어 more. / I like A more than B.
- I want/would like 목적어 better.
- I want/would like 목적어 more.

핵심 Check

1. 다음 빈칸에 들어갈 알맞은 단어를 쓰시오.

   A: _____ painting do you prefer, the one with flowers _____ the one with animals?

   B: I prefer the one with flowers _____ the one with animals.

2 의견 표현하기

- It seems to me that it's more delicious. 난 그게 더 맛있는 것 같아.
- It seems that science is more interesting to learn. 과학이 더 배우기가 재밌는 것 같아.
- I think that taking a train is faster than taking a taxi. 택시 타는 것보다 기차 타는 게 더 빠른 것 같아.

- 자신의 의견을 말할 때 'It seems (to me) that+주어+동사 ~.'로 표현할 수 있다. that 뒤에는 주어와 동사를 갖춘 절로 말한다. 같은 의미의 표현으로 'I think that ~', 'I believe that ~', 'I feel that ~', 'In my opinion, ~(내 의견으로는, ~)', 'From my point of view, ~ (내 관점으로는, ~)' 등을 사용하여 말할 수 있다.

- 의견에 대해 동의하는 표현으로는 'I agree (with you).' 또는 'I think so.', 'I couldn't agree more.' 등을 쓸 수 있다. 반대로 의견에 동의하지 않는다는 표현으로는 'I disagree (with you).', 'I don't agree (with you).' 등이 있다.

의견 표현하기

- It seems to me that 주어+동사 ~.
- I think (that) 주어+동사 ~.
- I feel (that) 주어+동사 ~.

- In my opinion, 주어+동사 ~.
- I believe (that) 주어+동사 ~.

의견에 대한 동의/비동의 표현

- I think so. 내 생각도 그래.
- I agree (with you). 난 (네 의견에) 동의해.
- I couldn't agree (with you) more. 전적으로 동의해.
- I'm afraid I disagree (with you). 유감이지만 난 (네 의견에) 동의하지 않아.
- I'm sorry but I don't agree (with you). 유감이지만 난 (네 의견에) 동의하지 않아.

핵심 Check

2. 다음 주어진 문장을 자연스러운 대화로 배열하시오.

(A) Of course. And it seems to me that the mask exhibition will be much more interesting.

(B) I prefer the Korean mask exhibition. Is that okay?

(C) There are two exhibitions we can go to. Which do you want to see more?

➡ _____

Listen and Talk A 1

G: Minho, look at these two paintings of cats here. Aren't they great?

B: Yes, they are.

G: They ❶both are good, but I like ❷the one on the left more. How about you?

B: ❸I prefer the one on the right. ❹It seems to me that the cat in it is cuter. I also like the bird in it.

G: 민호야, 여기 고양이가 그려진 그림 두 점을 봐. 멋있지 않니?

B: 응, 그러네.

G: 그것들은 모두 멋있지만 난 왼쪽에 있는 그림이 더 좋아. 넌 어때?

B: 난 오른쪽에 있는 그림이 더 좋아. 그림 속 고양이가 더 귀여운 것 같아. 새도 마음에 들어.

❶ both는 대명사로 They와 동격이다.
❷ the one 다음에 which is가 생략되었다고 볼 수 있다.
❸ 선호를 표현할 때 쓰는 말로 문장의 마지막에 'to the one on the left'가 생략된 것이다. 'I like the one on the right more.'로 말할 수 있다.
❹ 자신의 의견을 말할 때 'It seems (to me) that ~'으로 말할 수 있다.

Check(√) True or False

(1) The girl likes the painting on the right more.　　T ☐ F ☐

(2) The boy thinks the cat in the painting on the right is cuter.　　T ☐ F ☐

Listen and Talk B

A: ❶Which food do you prefer, Tteokbokki or Gimbap?

B: ❷I prefer Tteokbokki. ❸It seems to me that it's more delicious. How about you?

A: I prefer Tteokbokki, too. / I prefer Gimbap. It seems to me that it's healthier.

A: 떡볶이와 김밥 중에 어떤 것을 더 좋아하니?

B: 난 떡볶이를 너 좋아해. 그것이 더 맛있을 것 같아. 너는 어때?

A: 나도 떡볶이를 더 좋아해. / 난 김밥을 더 좋아해. 그것이 더 건강에 좋은 것 같아.

❶ A와 B 두 가지 중에서 어떤 것을 선호하는지 물을 때 쓸 수 있는 표현이다. 'Which (one) do you like better, A or B?', 'Which (one) do you like more, A or B?', 'Which one do you want more?' 등으로 바꿔 쓸 수 있다.
❷ I like Tteokbokki more.로 바꿔 쓸 수 있다.
❸ 자신의 의견을 말할 때 쓰는 표현이다.

Check(√) True or False

(3) A wants to know if B prefers Tteokbokki or Gimbap.　　T ☐ F ☐

(4) B thinks Gimbap is more delicious.　　T ☐ F ☐

Listen and Talk A 2

G: We can have Bibimbap or Galbitang. ❶ Which do you prefer?

B: I prefer Bibimbap. ❷It seems to me that it's ❸the healthier choice.

G: I think so, too. I also like Bibimbap more.

B: Let's order, then. I'm very hungry.

❶ 선호를 묻는 표현이다.
❷ 의견을 말할 때 쓰는 표현이다.
❸ 비교급 앞에 the를 쓴 것은 두 개 중에서 비교하는 것이기 때문이다.

 Listen and Talk A 3

G: Look at these two old plates, Steve. Aren't they beautiful?

B: Yes. Which one do you prefer, the green plate or the white plate?

G: Well, it's hard ❶to choose, but I like the green one better. How about you?

B: Me, too. It seems to me that the green plate is more ❷unique.

❶ 부사적 용법의 to부정사이다. 명사적 용법으로 볼 수도 있다.
❷ unique: 독특한

 Listen and Talk A 4

G: Junsu, you said you're going to buy a gift for your sister. How about the bags here?

B: They look nice.

G: ❶Which one do you prefer, the one with flowers or the one with animals?

B: I prefer the one with flowers. It seems to me that my sister will like ❷it more.

❶ 선호를 묻는 표현이다.
❷ it은 the one with flowers를 받고 있다.

 Listen and Talk B

A: Which painting do you prefer, the one on the left or the one on the right?

B: I prefer the one on the right. It seems to me that the cat in it is cuter. How about you?

A: I prefer the one on the right, too. / I prefer the one on the left. It seems to me that it ❶looks more calm.

❶ looks+형용사(calm): ~하게 보이다

 Listen and Talk B

A: Which plate do you prefer, the green one or the white one?

B: I prefer the green one. It seems to me that it's more unique. ❶How about you?

A: I prefer the green one, too. / I prefer the white one. It seems to me that it's simple but beautiful.

❶ How about you? = What about you?

 Listen and Talk B

A: Which bag do you prefer, the one with fish or the one with stars?

B: I prefer the one with stars. It seems to me that ❶it's more my style. How about you?

A: I prefer the one with stars, too. / I prefer the one with fish. It seems to me that the fish are cute.

❶ it은 the one with stars를 받고 있다.

 Listen and Talk D

I prefer science. It seems to me that ❶it's more fun ❷to learn. I also prefer ❶it because I want to be a great inventor ❸like Edison.

❶ it = science
❷ 부사적 용법의 to부정사이다.
❸ like = such as

Listen and Talk C

G: There are two exhibitions ❶we can go to. Which one do you want to see more, Eric?

B: I prefer the Korean mask exhibition. Is that OK, Somi?

G: Of course. And it seems to me that the mask exhibition will be ❷much more interesting.

B: Do you think so?

G: Yes. Look at this poster. There isn't just an exhibition. There's also a mask dance show at 4:00 and 6:00.

B: Great! I've never seen a mask dance show before.

G: Well, I've seen a show before. I'm sure you'll like it.

B: So where is the show?

G: It's in Dasom Hall, ❸next to the exhibition room.

B: It's 4:30 now, so let's watch the 6 o'clock show.

G: OK. Let's go see the exhibition first.

❶ exhibitions와 we 사이에 목적격 관계대명사가 생략되어 있다.
❷ much로 비교급을 강조하고 있다.
❸ Hall과 next 사이에 '주격 관계대명사 which+is'가 생략되어 있다.

 Talk and Play

A: Which do you prefer, Ramyeon or spaghetti?

B: I prefer Ramyeon. It seems to me that ❶it's more delicious. How about you?

A: I prefer Ramyeon, too. / I prefer spaghetti. It seems to me that it's ❷healthier.

❶ it = Ramyeon
❷ healthier는 healthy의 비교급이다.

 Review 1

G: Joe, didn't you say you ❶needed to buy a cap? How about these caps here?

B: They look great.

G: Which one do you prefer, the one with triangles or the one with flowers?

B: I prefer the one with triangles. It seems to me that it's more unique.

❶ need는 to부정사를 목적어로 취한다.

 Review 2

B: We can have Gimbap or Tteokbokki. Which do you prefer, Jenny?

G: I prefer Gimbap. It seems to me that it's ❶the healthier choice. How about you, Minsu?

B: I'll have Tteokbokki. ❷I heard that the Tteokbokki here is very good.

G: Let's order, then. I'm very hungry.

❶ 두 개 중에서 비교하고 있기 때문에 비교급 앞에 the를 썼다.
❷ I heard = People say

Review 3

John: There are two movies we can see. ❶ Which one do you want to see more, Somi?

Somi: I prefer *Batman*. I saw *Spider-Man* last week. Is this OK, John?

John: Of course. ❷It seems to me that *Batman* will be much more fun.

Somi: Good. Then, let's go and see ❸it.

❶ 선호를 묻는 표현이다.
❷ 의견을 말할 때 쓰는 표현이다.
❸ it = *Batman*

다음 우리말과 일치하도록 빈칸에 알맞은 말을 쓰시오.

Listen and Talk A 1

G: Minho, look at these _____ _____ _____ _____ here. Aren't they great?

B: Yes, they _____.

G: They _____ are good, but I like _____ _____ on the left more. How about you?

B: I _____ the one on the right. It _____ to me that the cat in it is _____. I also like the bird in it.

G: 민호야, 여기 고양이가 그려진 그림 두 점을 봐. 멋있지 않니?
B: 응, 그러네.
G: 그것들은 모두 멋있지만 난 왼쪽에 있는 그림이 더 좋아. 넌 어때?
B: 난 오른쪽에 있는 그림이 더 좋아. 그림 속 고양이가 더 귀여운 것 같아. 새도 마음에 들어.

Listen and Talk A 2

G: We can have Bibimbap or Galbitang. _____ do you _____?

B: I _____ Bibimbap. _____ _____ to me that it's the healthier _____.

G: I think _____, too. I also _____ Bibimbap _____.

B: Let's order, then. I'm very hungry.

G: 우리는 비빔밥이나 갈비탕을 먹을 수 있어. 어떤 것이 더 좋니?
B: 난 비빔밥이 더 좋아. 그것이 더 건강에 좋은 선택인 것 같아.
G: 나도 그렇게 생각해. 난 비빔밥을 더 좋아하기도 해.
B: 그럼 주문하자. 난 정말 배고파.

Listen and Talk A 3

G: Look at these two old plates, Steve. Aren't they beautiful?

B: Yes. _____ _____ do you prefer, the green plate or the white plate?

G: Well, it's hard _____ _____, but I like the green one _____. How about you?

B: _____, _____. It _____ to me _____ the green plate is more unique.

G: Steve, 이 두 개의 옛날 접시들을 봐. 아름답지 않니?
B: 응. 초록색 접시와 흰색 접시 중 무엇이 더 좋니?
G: 음, 고르기가 어렵지만 난 초록색 접시가 더 좋아. 너는 어때?
B: 나도. 초록색 접시가 더 독특한 것 같아.

Listen and Talk A 4

G: Junsu, you said _____ _____ _____ buy a gift for your sister. How about the bags here?

B: They look _____.

G: _____ _____ do you _____, the one with flowers _____ the one with animals?

B: I _____ the one _____ flowers. _____ _____ _____ _____ that my sister will like it more.

G: 준수야, 너 여동생 줄 선물을 살 거라고 했잖아. 여기 이 가방들은 어때?
B: 좋아 보인다.
G: 가방에 꽃들이 있는 것과 동물들이 있는 것 중 무엇이 더 좋니?
B: 난 꽃들이 있는 것이 더 좋아. 내 여동생이 그것을 더 좋아할 것 같아.

Listen and Talk B

A: _____ food do you _____, Tteokbokki or Gimbap?

B: I _____ Tteokbokki. It seems to me that it's more delicious. How about you?

A: I _____ Tteokbokki, too. / I _____ Gimbap. It seems to me that it's healthier.

A: _____ painting do you _____, the one on the left _____ the one on the right?

B: I _____ the one on the right. It seems to me that the cat in it is cuter. How about you?

A: I _____ the one on the right, too. / I _____ the one on the left. It seems to me that it looks _____ _____.

A: _____ plate do you prefer, the green one _____ the white one?

B: I _____ the green one. It seems to me that it's _____ _____. How about you?

A: I _____ the green one, too. / I _____ the white one. It seems to me that it's simple _____ beautiful.

A: _____ bag do you _____, the one with fish _____ the one with stars?

B: I _____ the one with stars. It seems to me that it's _____ my style. How about you?

A: I _____ the one with stars, too. / I _____ the one with fish. It seems to me that the fish are cute.

Listen and Talk C

G: There are two exhibitions we can go to. _____ one do you want to see _____, Eric?

B: I _____ the Korean mask exhibition. Is _____ OK, Somi?

G: Of course. And it seems to me that the mask exhibition will be _____ more interesting.

B: Do you think _____?

G: Yes. Look at this poster. There isn't _____ an exhibition. There's _____ a mask dance show at 4:00 and 6:00.

B: Great! I've _____ seen a mask dance show _____.

G: Well, I've seen a show _____. I'm _____ you'll like it.

B: So where is the show?

G: It's in Dasom Hall, _____ _____ the exhibition room.

B: It's 4:30 now, so _____ _____ the 6 o'clock show.

G: OK. Let's go see the exhibition _____.

해석

A: 떡볶이와 김밥 중에 어떤 것을 더 좋아하니?

B: 난 떡볶이를 좋아해. 그것이 더 맛있을 것 같아. 너는 어때?

A: 나도 떡볶이를 좋아해. / 난 김밥을 좋아해. 그것이 더 건강에 좋은 것 같아.

A: 왼쪽 그림과 오른쪽 그림 중 어떤 것을 더 좋아하니?

B: 난 오른쪽 그림을 더 좋아해. 그림 속 고양이가 더 귀여운 것 같아. 너는 어때?

A: 나도 오른쪽 그림이 더 좋아. / 난 왼쪽 그림을 더 좋아해. 그것이 더 평화로워 보이거든.

A: 초록색 접시와 흰색 접시 중 어떤 것을 더 좋아하니?

B: 난 초록색 접시가 더 좋아. 그것이 더 독특하다고 생각해. 너는 어때?

A: 나도 초록색 접시가 더 좋아. / 난 흰색 접시가 더 좋아. 그것이 단순하지만 아름답다고 생각해.

A: 물고기가 있는 가방과 별들이 있는 가방 중 어떤 것을 더 좋아하니?

B: 난 별들이 있는 가방을 더 좋아해. 그것이 더 내 취향이야. 너는 어때?

A: 나도 별들이 있는 가방이 더 좋아. / 난 물고기가 있는 가방을 더 좋아해. 물고기가 귀여운 것 같아.

G: 우리가 갈 수 있는 전시회가 두 곳이 있어. 어느 것을 더 보고 싶니, Eric?

B: 나는 한국의 탈 전시회를 더 선호해. 소미야, 괜찮겠니?

G: 물론이지. 그리고 나도 탈 전시회가 더 흥미로울 것 같아.

B: 그렇게 생각하니?

G: 그래. 이 포스터를 봐. 단순히 전시회만 있는 것이 아니야. 탈춤 공연도 4시와 6시에 있어.

B: 좋아! 나는 전에 탈춤 공연을 본 적이 없어.

G: 음, 나는 전에 본 적이 있어. 네가 분명 좋아할 거야.

B: 그래서 공연은 어디서 해?

G: 전시관 옆 다솜 홀에서 해.

B: 지금 4시 30분이니까 6시 공연을 보자.

G: 그래. 우선 전시회부터 보자.

Listen and Talk D

I _____ science. It seems to me that it's _____ _____ _____ _____. I also _____ it because I want to be a great inventor _____ Edison.

난 과학을 더 좋아해. 그것을 배우는 것이 더 즐거운 것 같아. 난 Edison과 같은 훌륭한 발명가가 되고 싶어서 그것을 더 좋아하기도 해.

Talk and Play

A: _____ do you _____, Ramyeon or spaghetti?

B: I _____ Ramyeon. It seems to me that it's more delicious. How about you?

A: I _____ Ramyeon, too. / I _____ spaghetti. It seems to me that it's healthier.

A: 라면과 스파게티 중 어떤 걸 더 좋아하니?
B: 난 라면을 더 좋아해. 그것이 더 맛있는 것 같아. 너는 어때?
A: 나도 라면을 더 좋아해. / 난 스파게티를 더 좋아해. 그것이 건강에 더 좋을 것 같아.

Review 1

G: Joe, didn't you say you needed _____ _____ a cap? How about these caps here?

B: They look _____.

G: _____ _____ do you _____, the one with triangles _____ the one with flowers?

B: I _____ the one with triangles. It seems to me that it's more unique.

G: Joe, 모자를 사야 한다고 하지 않았니? 여기 있는 이 모자들은 어때?
B: 그것들은 좋아 보인다.
G: 삼각형이 있는 것과 꽃이 있는 것 중 어떤 것이 좋니?
B: 난 삼각형이 있는 것이 더 좋아. 그것이 더 독특한 것 같아.

Review 2

B: We can have Gimbap or Tteokbokki. _____ do you _____, Jenny?

G: I _____ Gimbap. It seems to me that it's _____ _____ _____. How about you, Minsu?

B: I'll have Tteokbokki. _____ _____ that the Tteokbokki here is very good.

G: Let's _____, then. I'm very hungry.

G: 우리는 김밥이나 떡볶이를 시킬 수 있어. 어떤 것이 더 좋니, Jenny?
B: 난 김밥이 더 좋아. 건강에 더 좋은 선택인 것 같거든. 민수야, 넌 어떠니?
G: 난 떡볶이 먹을래. 여기는 떡볶이가 더 맛있다고 들었거든.
B: 그럼 주문하자. 난 정말 배고파.

Review 3

John: There are two movies we can see. _____ _____ do you want to see _____, Somi?

Somi: I _____ *Batman*. I saw *Spider-Man* last week. Is _____ OK, John?

John: Of course. It seems to me that *Batman* will be _____ more fun.

Somi: Good. Then, let's go and see it.

John: 우리가 볼 수 있는 영화가 두 개 있어. 소미야, 어떤 것이 더 보고 싶니?
Somi: 난 "배트맨"이 더 좋아. 난 "스파이더맨"을 지난주에 봤거든. John, 괜찮니?
John: 물론이지. "배트맨"이 훨씬 더 재미있을 것 같아.
Somi: 좋아. 그럼 영화 보러 가자.

01 다음 빈칸 (A)에 알맞지 <u>않은</u> 것은?

> G: Minho, look at these two paintings of cats here. Aren't they great?
>
> B: Yes, they are.
>
> G: They both are good, but _____(A)_____. How about you?
>
> B: I prefer the one on the right. It seems to me that the cat in it is cuter. I also like the bird in it.

① I like the one on the left more   ② I like the one on the left better

③ I'd rather the one on the left   ④ I prefer the one on the left

⑤ I think the one on the left is better

02 주어진 어휘를 이용하여 밑줄 친 우리말을 8 단어로 영작하시오.

> G: Which cap do you prefer, the one with triangles or the one with flowers?
>
> B: I prefer the one with triangles. <u>그것이 더 독특한 것 같아.</u> (it, me, unique, seem)

➡ _____

03 다음 대화의 밑줄 친 (a)의 의도와 <u>다르게</u> 쓰인 것을 고르시오.

> G: Junsu, you said you're going to buy a gift for your sister. How about the bags here?
>
> B: They look nice.
>
> G: Which one do you prefer, the one with flowers or the one with animals?
>
> B: I prefer the one with flowers. (a)It seems to me that my sister will like it more.

① In my opinion, my sister will like it more.

② I think that my sister will like it more.

③ I feel that my sister will like it more.

④ I believe that my sister will like it more.

⑤ I hope that my sister will like it more.

01 다음 중 짝지어진 대화가 <u>어색한</u> 것은?

① A: Which movie do you want to see more, Somi?
   B: I like *Batman*.

② A: It seems to me that the mask exhibition will be much more interesting.
   B: Do you think so?

③ A: It seems to me that it's more my style. How about you?
   B: I prefer the one with stars, too.

④ A: I like the green one better. How about you?
   B: Me, too. It seems to me that the green plate is more unique.

⑤ A: Which do you prefer, dogs or cats?
   B: I prefer dogs. It seems to me that dogs are cuter.

[02~04] 다음 대화를 읽고 물음에 답하시오.

G: We can have Bibimbap or Galbitang. _____(A)_____? (prefer)
B: I prefer Bibimbap. It seems to me that it's the healthier choice.
G: I think so, too. I also like Bibimbap ___(B)___.
B: Let's order, then. I'm very hungry.

서답형

02 빈칸 (A)에 들어갈 알맞은 말을 주어진 어휘를 이용하여 4 단어로 쓰시오.

➡ _____

03 위 대화의 빈칸 (B)에 들어갈 말은?

① a lot   ② more   ③ many
④ much   ⑤ less

04 선호하는 것에 관한 위 대화의 내용과 일치하지 <u>않는</u> 것은?

① 여자 아이와 남자 아이는 비빔밥이나 갈비탕을 먹을 수 있다.
② 남자 아이는 비빔밥을 더 좋아한다.
③ 남자 아이는 비빔밥이 더 좋은 선택이라고 생각한다.
④ 여자 아이는 남자 아이의 의견에 동의하고 있다.
⑤ 여자 아이는 정말 배가 고프다.

서답형

05 대화가 자연스럽게 연결되도록 (A)~(C)를 순서대로 바르게 배열하시오.

G: Look at these two old plates, Steve. Aren't they beautiful?
(A) Well, it's hard to choose, but I like the green one better. How about you?
(B) Yes. Which one do you prefer, the green plate or the white plate?
(C) Me, too. It seems to me that the green plate is more unique.

➡ _____

[06~07] 다음 대화를 읽고 물음에 답하시오.

A: (a)넌 어떤 음식을 더 좋아하니, Tteokbokki ___(A)___ Gimbap?
B: I prefer Tteokbokki. It seems ___(B)___ me that it's more delicious. How about you?
A: I prefer Tteokbokki, too.

06 위 대화의 빈칸 (A)와 (B)에 들어갈 말로 알맞게 짝지어진 것은?

① and – for   ② and – to
③ or – to   ④ or – for
⑤ at – from

서답형

07 주어진 어휘를 이용하여 밑줄 친 (a)의 우리말을 5 단어로 영작하시오. (which)

➡ _____

[08~10] 다음 대화를 읽고 물음에 답하시오.

G: There are two exhibitions we can (a)[go / go to]. Which one do you want to see more, Eric?

B: I (b)[like / prefer] the Korean mask exhibition. Is that OK, Somi? (①)

G: Of course. (②) And it seems to me that the mask exhibition will be much more interesting.

B: Do you think so? (③)

G: Yes. Look at this poster. There isn't just an exhibition. (④)

B: Great! (⑤) I've never seen a mask dance show (c)[ago / before].

G: Well, I've seen a show (c)[ago / before]. I'm sure you'll like it.

B: So where is the show?

G: It's in Dasom Hall, next to the exhibition room.

B: It's 4:30 now, so let's watch the 6 o'clock show.

G: OK. Let's go see the exhibition first.

중요

08 위 대화의 (①)~(⑤) 중 주어진 문장이 들어갈 곳은?

> There's also a mask dance show at 4:00 and 6:00.

①   ②   ③   ④   ⑤

09 위 대화의 괄호 (a)~(c)에서 알맞은 것을 골라 바르게 짝지은 것은?

	(a)	(b)	(c)
①	go to	prefer	before
②	go to	like	before
③	go to	prefer	ago
④	go	like	ago
⑤	go	prefer	ago

10 위 대화의 내용과 일치하는 것은?

① Eric과 소미가 갈 수 있는 전시회는 탈 전시회뿐이다.

② Eric은 탈춤 공연을 더 선호한다.

③ 포스터에는 단순히 탈 전시회만 있었다.

④ 탈춤 공연은 전시관 옆 다솜 홀에서 한다.

⑤ Eric과 소미는 4시 30분 공연을 볼 것이다.

[11~12] 다음 대화를 읽고 물음에 답하시오.

A: Which do you prefer, Ramyeon or spaghetti?

B: I prefer Ramyeon. (a)It seems to me that it's more delicious. How about you?

A: I prefer spaghetti. It seems to me that it's healthier.

11 위 대화의 밑줄 친 (a)의 의도로 가장 적절한 것은?

① 선호 표현하기   ② 유감 표현하기

③ 동의하기   ④ 감정 표현하기

⑤ 의견 표현하기

중요

12 위 대화를 읽고 답할 수 있는 것을 고르시오. (정답 2개)

① Where are they talking?

② Does A prefer spaghetti to Ramyeon?

③ Why does B like Ramyeon?

④ What does A ask B to do?

⑤ Why does A think spaghetti is healthier?

[01~03] 다음 대화를 읽고 물음에 답하시오.

G: There are two exhibitions we can go to. (a) 어느 것을 더 보고 싶니, (one, see, more) Eric?

B: I prefer the Korean mask exhibition. Is that OK, Somi?

G: Of course. And it seems to me that the mask exhibition will be much more interesting.

B: Do you think so?

G: Yes. Look at this poster. There isn't just an exhibition. There's also a mask dance show at 4:00 and 6:00.

B: Great! I've never seen a mask dance show before.

(A) It's in Dasom Hall, next to the exhibition room.

(B) It's 4:30 now, so let's watch the 6 o'clock show.

(C) So where is the show?

(D) Well, I've seen a show before. I'm sure you'll like it.

G: OK. Let's go see the exhibition first.

01 위 대화의 (A)~(D)를 알맞은 순서로 배열하시오.

➡ _____

02 괄호 안에 주어진 어휘를 이용하여 밑줄 친 (a)를 8 단어로 쓰시오.

➡ _____

03 What are they talking about?

➡ _____

[04~05] 다음 글을 읽고 물음에 답하시오.

I prefer science. It seems to me that it's more fun to learn. I also prefer it because I want to be a great inventor (a)like Edison.

04 밑줄 친 (a)like를 두 단어로 바꿔 쓰시오.

➡ _____

05 Write the two reasons why the writer prefers science.

➡ (1) _____
(2) _____

[06~07] 다음 대화를 읽고 물음에 답하시오.

G: Minho, look at these two paintings of cats here. Aren't they great?

B: Yes, they ___(A)___ .

G: They both are good, but I like the one on the left more. How about you?

B: I prefer the one on the right. It seems to me that the cat in it is cuter. I also like the bird in it.

06 빈칸 (A)에 알맞은 동사를 쓰시오.

➡ _____

07 Why does the boy prefer the painting on the right? Write two reasons.

➡ _____
_____

Grammar

1 to부정사의 '의미상의 주어': 'for+목적격'

- It was impossible **for him to catch** any fish. 그가 어떤 물고기라도 잡는 것은 불가능했다.
- It is nice **of you to help** me. 네가 나를 돕다니 친절하구나.

■ 동작의 행위자(agent): 동사가 행하는 동작을 '누가' 하는지 나타내는 말을 동작의 행위자라고 한다. 주어가 대부분 행위자이지만 그렇지 않은 경우, '의미상의 주어'라고 한다.

- **Philip** wants to ride the car. Philip은 (그가) 그 차를 타기를 원한다.

  : 문장의 주어 Philip이 동사 wants와 to부정사 to ride의 행위자

  → Philip wants **me** to ride the car. Philip은 내가 그 차를 타기를 원한다.

  : me가 to ride의 행위자 = 의미상의 주어

■ 'It' 가주어, 'to' 진주어 문장에서 to부정사의 '의미상의 주어'는 'for+목적격' 형태로 표현한다.

- It is not easy **for me** to move this table. 내가 이 탁자를 옮기는 것은 쉽지 않다.
- It was impossible **for him** to solve the quiz. 그가 그 문제를 푸는 것은 불가능했다.
- It is necessary **for Sumin** to be honest with her friends. Sumin이 그녀의 친구들에게 솔직해지는 것이 필요하다.

■ to부정사의 의미상의 주어가 일반 사람을 가리킬 때는 생략할 수 있다.

- It is healthy **(for us)** to walk regularly. (우리가) 규칙적으로 걷는 것이 건강에 좋다.
- It is difficult **(for people)** to manage time effectively. (사람들이) 시간을 효과적으로 관리하는 일은 어렵다.
- It is easy to make egg scramble. 계란 스크램블을 만드는 것은 쉽다. (일반 사람)

  → It is easy **for my mom** to make egg scramble. 나의 엄마가 계란 스크램블을 만드는 것은 쉽다. (특정인)

■ 사람의 성격, 태도 등을 나타내는 형용사는 'of+목적격' 형태로 의미상의 주어를 표현한다.

- It was **kind of him** to help the blind. 그가 그 맹인들을 도운 것은 친절했다.
- It was **nice of the girls** to find the kid's parents. 그 소녀들이 그 아이의 부모님을 찾아준 것은 착한 일이었다.
- It was **foolish of me** to stay up all night watching foreign dramas. 내가 외국 드라마를 보느라 밤을 새운 것은 어리석은 것이었다.

핵심 Check

1. 다음 괄호 안에서 알맞은 말을 고르시오.

(1) It is stupid (for / of) Mike to spend all the money playing a card game.

(2) It was difficult (for / of) the employee not to fall asleep at work.

2 **가정법 과거: 'If+주어+동사 과거형 ~, 주어+would/could+동사원형 …'**

- It **would** be wonderful **if** I **could** eat fresh fish.
  신선한 물고기를 먹을 수 있다면, 정말 좋을 텐데.

■ 가정법 과거: '만약 ~라면 …할 텐데'의 뜻으로, 현재 사실을 반대로 가정하거나 실현 가능성이 없는 일에 대해서 가정할 때 쓰며, 'If+주어+동사 과거형 ~, 주어+would/could+동사원형 …'의 형태이다.

  - **If** I **knew** his phone number, I **would call** him. 내가 그의 전화번호를 안다면, 그에게 전화할 텐데. (가정법 과거, 현재 사실의 반대 가정)

    = **As** I **don't know** his phone number, I **won't call** him. 내가 그의 전화번호를 모르기 때문에, 나는 그에게 전화하지 않을 것이다.

■ 'be'동사는 주어의 인칭 및 수와 무관하게 'were'를 쓰지만, 1, 3인칭 단수의 경우 현대 영어에서는 'was'를 쓰기도 한다.

  - **If** she **were[was]** blind, she **couldn't see** me. 그녀가 눈이 안 보인다면, 나를 볼 수 없을 텐데.

■ 가정법 과거완료는 이미 일어난 과거 사실을 반대로 가정하는 데 사용하며, 'If+주어+had+과거분사 ~, 주어+would/could+have+과거분사 …'의 형태로 나타낸다.

  - **If** the teacher **had taught** us, we **would have succeeded**. 그 선생님이 우리를 가르쳐 주셨더라면, 우리는 성공했을 텐데.

■ **가정법의 다양한 표현들**

  - **As** the man **is** rich, he **can** buy me the expensive meal. (직설법)

    → **If** he **were[was]** not rich, he **couldn't buy** me the expensive meal. 그가 부유하지 않으면, 그 비싼 밥을 사줄 수 없을 텐데. (가정법)

    → **Were** he **not** rich, he **couldn't buy** the expensive meal. (If 생략 가능, 도치문으로 가정)

  - **Without[But for]** music, the world **would be** a dull place. 음악이 없다면, 세상은 따분한 곳일 텐데.

    → **If it were not for** music, the world **would be** a dull place.

    → **Were it not for** music, the world **would be** a dull place. (If 생략 후 도치)

핵심 Check

2. 다음 우리말에 맞게 괄호 안의 단어를 바르게 배열하여 빈칸을 채우시오.

  (1) 내가 당신이라면, 나를 뽑을 겁니다. (you, hire, would, were, I, me)

  ➡ If I _____.

  (2) 돈이 좀 있으면, James는 이사를 가지 않을 텐데. (if, money, move away, would, had, some, he, not)

  ➡ James _____.

01 다음 중 어법상 바르지 <u>않은</u> 것은?

① It was considerate of the girl to guide the old visitors.
② It can't be possible for him to learn the difficult yoga move.
③ It was a little easy of him to make such decisions.
④ It is interesting for Sean to take their pictures.
⑤ It is not good for you to live alone.

02 다음 각 가정법 문장에서 어법상 <u>어색한</u> 단어를 한 개씩만 찾아 고치시오.

(1) If we make lots of money, we would help poor children.
　　_____ ➡ _____

(2) If I had a talking teddy bear, I will take it everywhere.
　　_____ ➡ _____

(3) It would be good if he can eat some meat.
　　_____ ➡ _____

(4) I will learn Chinese characters if I were the boy.
　　_____ ➡ _____

03 다음 문장을 가주어 It과 to부정사를 이용하여 다시 쓰시오.

Riding a bike on the street was not easy for Suji.

➡ _____

04 다음 빈칸에 들어갈 말로 알맞은 것은?

If my mom _____ fresh fish, it would be wonderful.

① can eat　　② will eat　　③ had eaten
④ could eat　　⑤ eats

01 다음 문장의 밑줄 친 단어들 중 어법상 어색한 것은?

> It was ①very wise ②for the student to avoid the fight ③since it ④is hard ⑤to be patient.

02 다음 중 같은 뜻을 가진 문장끼리 짝지어진 것은?

① She could write a letter to the writer of the book if she knew her address.
　= She can't write a letter to the writer of the book though she knows her address.

② Brian would hand in the report in time if he had a computer.
　= Brian didn't have a computer, so he wouldn't hand in the report.

③ If she studied hard, she could pass the test.
　= She doesn't study hard, so she can't pass the test.

④ If Ted saw the car coming, he could avoid the accident.
　= Ted didn't see the car coming, so he couldn't avoid the accident.

⑤ If it rains this evening, Amanda would stay at home taking a rest.
　= It is raining this evening, so Amanda will stay at home taking a rest.

03 다음 중 빈칸에 들어갈 말이 나머지와 다른 것은?

① It seems easy _____ the soccer team to win the championship this year again.

② It is necessary _____ the thin girl to gain some weight.

③ It's not safe _____ the puppies to play near the stove.

④ It was rude _____ Jimmy to ask his teacher to get out of the room.

⑤ Is it okay _____ us to join you?

04 다음 중 어법상 어색한 문장은?

① If he were polite, he won't do a bad thing to old people.

② If the ants knew the way to their nest, they could cross the stream.

③ If she weren't in Egypt, she could attend her grandmother's funeral.

④ If it were not for the music by the singer, I would not able to live.

⑤ Ailey could be hurt, if the car didn't stop immediately.

05 다음 중 빈칸 ⓐ~ⓕ에 같은 단어가 들어가는 것끼리 바르게 짝지어진 것은?

> • It was wonderful ___ⓐ___ Dr. Jordan to win the award for the research.
> • It wasn't wise ___ⓑ___ the young lady to refuse the job offer.
> • It is possible ___ⓒ___ Pavien to get to the meeting place at 8 tomorrow evening.
> • It was difficult ___ⓓ___ the kids to understand the coach's instruction.
> • It is safe ___ⓔ___ the children to cut the cake with this plastic knife.
> • It is careless ___ⓕ___ Sujin to tell my secret plans to her friends.

① ⓐ, ⓑ, ⓕ　　　　② ⓐ, ⓒ, ⓕ
③ ⓑ, ⓓ, ⓔ　　　　④ ⓑ, ⓔ
⑤ ⓑ, ⓕ

서답형

[06~09] 다음 우리말과 일치하도록 괄호 안에 주어진 어구를 바르게 배열하시오.

06

내가 고기를 잡으면, 엄마가 그것을 드시게 할 텐데.

(let, the fish, eat, my mom, would, caught, if, it, I, I)

➡ _____

_____

07

문자도가 없었다면, 아이들은 조화의 중요성을 배울 수 없었을 텐데.

(the importance of harmony, couldn't, had, it, have, not, if, learned, been, Munjado, for, children)

➡ _____

_____

08

그 소년이 문자도를 사용해서, 한자를 배우는 것은 쉬웠다.

(learn, easy, Munjado, for, it, to, the boy, Chinese characters, was, using)

➡ _____

_____

09

그 소녀가 어떤 도움 없이 물고기를 잡는 것은 불가능했다.

(catch, impossible, for, any, without, fish, to, was, the girl, it, help)

➡ _____

_____

[10~11] 다음 중 밑줄 친 부분의 쓰임이 나머지 넷과 다른 것은?

10 ① It is too cold for the little kids to play outside all day long.
② It's good for the patient to walk for an hour every other day.
③ Isn't it difficult to understand the purpose of the city policy?
④ It is natural for a baby to cry.
⑤ I believe that it is unnecessary for you to go abroad to learn English.

중요

11 ① It is fun for her to speak in Chinese.
② It will soon be the lunch time.
③ It is not hard to search for much information on the Internet.
④ It was useful for you to bring the books here.
⑤ It was my pleasure to meet the beautiful person like you.

12 다음 문장의 빈칸 (A)~(C)에 들어갈 말로 가장 적절한 것은?

• If the movie ____(A)____ early, I would help you with the homework.
• Were it not for the air, all the living things in the planet ____(B)____ be dead.
• If I ____(C)____ some money, I could give it to you for helping the poor.

	(A)	(B)	(C)
①	ends	would	have
②	ends	could	have had
③	will end	could	had had
④	ended	would	had
⑤	ended	could	have

서답형

13 다음 대화가 자연스럽게 이루어지도록 주어진 단어를 활용하여 문장을 완성하시오. (어법에 맞게 1 단어를 추가할 것.)

> Teacher: Somebody gave so much water to the plants that they all died.
> Tony: Oh. I think it must be Jane.
> Teacher: _____.
> (too, give, careless, to, the plants, much, was, her, it, water)

➡ _____

_____

14 다음 중 어법상 옳은 문장은?

① It is hard of them to speak Spanish as well as English.
② It was very nice for Timothy to invite her to his presentation event.
③ It was cruel of her to mention his shameful experience in the past.
④ Is it okay for his to get a week off a little earlier than usual?
⑤ It isn't difficult of them to move that heavy furniture inside.

서답형

15 다음 우리말을 조건에 맞게 영작하시오.

> Munjado를 배우면, 그들이 한국을 더 이해할 수 있을 텐데.
> (learn, understand, much, can 활용. If로 시작, 총 9 단어로 할 것, 단어 변형 가능)

➡ _____

_____

서답형

16 다음 우리말을 영작할 때, 어법상 어색한 문장을 모두 고르시오.

> 사회 질서가 없다면, 우리는 이 세상 속에서 평화롭게 살아갈 수 없을 텐데.

① Without social order, we can't live peacefully in this world.
② If it were not for social order, we couldn't live peacefully in this world.
③ If there is no social order, we couldn't live peacefully in this world.
④ Were it not for social order, we couldn't live peacefully in this world.
⑤ If there were no social order, we couldn't live peacefully in this world.

17 다음 중 어법상 올바른 문장의 개수는?

> ⓐ It was pretty importantly for the teacher to make teaching easy to understand.
> ⓑ It was very stupid for Dean to lend money to Kate.
> ⓒ It was wise of Mary not to spend her money buying such a useless thing.
> ⓓ It is clever of Minsu using the equipment.
> ⓔ It is kind of the man to help the old lady to find the way to the subway.
> ⓕ It was impossible for me to arrive at the important business meeting on time.
> ⓖ It is not easy for the girls to pass by that *tteokbokki* restaurant.

① 1개 ② 2개 ③ 3개 ④ 4개 ⑤ 5개

서답형

18 다음 문장에서 어법상 어색한 부분을 찾아서 고치시오.

> If the ice didn't melt, the carp wouldn't have come out of the water.

_____ ➡ _____ 또는

_____ ➡ _____

01 다음 우리말과 일치하도록 괄호 안에 주어진 단어들을 바르게 배열하여 문장을 완성하시오.

(1) 그의 어머니가 잉어를 드시면, 곧 건강해질 수 있을 텐데.

➡ If his mother _____
soon. (could, carp, ate, she, well, get)

(2) 글자가 없다면, 우리가 지식을 전달하는 것이 어려워질 텐데.

➡ If there _____
_____ the knowledge.
(for, it, to, difficult, would, no, deliver, us, letters, be, were)

(3) 그의 어머니가 자신의 건강을 회복하는 것이 정말로 필요하다.

➡ It's really _____
_____. (health, to, for, his, mother, her, necessary, recover)

(4) 이렇게 추운 날씨에 그가 물고기를 잡으려고 하는 것은 매우 어리석었다.

➡ It was _____
_____. (try, catch, cold, stupid, this, weather, in, of, to, to, very, him, fish)

02 다음 〈보기〉의 문장과 같은 뜻이 되도록 괄호 안에 주어진 〈조건〉에 맞게 빈칸을 채우시오.

┌ 보기 ┐
Without computers, we could not find out much information easily.
└──────────────┘

(1) _____ computers, we could not find out much information easily. (it, be동사 활용, 5 단어)

(2) _____ computers, we could not find out much information easily. (there, no 활용, 4 단어)

(3) _____ computers, we could not find out much information easily. (it, be동사 활용, 4 단어)

(4) _____ find out much information easily. (직설법, there, 접속사 as 활용, 6 단어)

03 다음 그림을 보고, 우리말에 맞게 괄호 안의 단어를 활용하여 빈칸을 채우시오.

얼음이 녹지 않았다면, 그가 잉어 세 마리를 잡을 수 없었을 것이다.

→ If _____
_____.
(not, melt, catch, carp, ice, can) If 포함하여 총 13 단어, 어형 변화 가능, 축약형 불가)

04 다음 주어진 문장과 뜻이 같도록 빈칸을 알맞게 채우시오. (총 6 단어)

┌──────────────┐
Because Stacy doesn't sleep well enough, she can't be in good condition.
→ If Stacy _____
in good condition.
└──────────────┘

05 다음 우리말을 괄호 안에 주어진 단어들을 사용하여 영작하시오. (필요시 단어를 추가하거나 변형할 것)

(1) 전문가들조차 눈이 덮인 산을 등반하는 것은 매우 위험하다.

⇒ It is very ＿＿＿＿＿＿＿＿＿＿＿＿

＿＿＿＿＿＿＿＿＿＿＿＿＿＿ .

(experts, dangerous, up, with, even, cover, climb)

(2) 당신이 그 짐승을 죽이려고 시도했던 것은 어리석은 일이었다.

⇒ It was ＿＿＿＿＿＿＿＿＿＿＿＿

＿＿＿＿＿＿＿＿＿＿ . (attempt, the beast, foolish, kill, to)

(3) 그가 어제 사장님과 파티에 참석했던 것은 재미있었다.

⇒ It was ＿＿＿＿＿＿＿＿＿＿＿

＿＿＿＿＿＿＿＿＿＿ yesterday. (his boss, attend, fun, the party)

06 다음 각 가정법 문장에서 어법상 어색한 부분을 모두 찾아 바르게 고치시오.

(1) If I am the superman, I could save the people and defeat the evil aliens.

(2) If it is not for your support, I could not recover from the disaster.

(3) Michelle wouldn't be late for the wedding yesterday if she had caught the subway.

(4) If the girl is lying, I could not understand her situation.

(5) If I have a boy friend, I could go to the concert with him.

⇒ (1) ＿＿＿＿＿＿ (2) ＿＿＿＿＿＿

(3) ＿＿＿＿＿＿ (4) ＿＿＿＿＿＿

(5) ＿＿＿＿＿＿

07 다음 각 문장에서 어법상 어색한 단어를 한 개씩만 찾아 고치시오.

(1) It is necessary for the officers checked all the baggage at the airport.

(2) It was wise for the host of the program to make the actor tell the truth.

(3) It is interesting of Tiffany to meet the boy who could someday be a famous actor.

(4) It was fun for me and my family to sitting around the campfire.

(5) It is not easy for your friends let the eggs stand still.

⇒ (1) ＿＿＿＿＿＿ (2) ＿＿＿＿＿＿

(3) ＿＿＿＿＿＿ (4) ＿＿＿＿＿＿

(5) ＿＿＿＿＿＿

08 다음 〈보기〉와 같이 직설법 문장을 가정법으로 고치시오.

┌─── 보기 ───────────

As she isn't a dolphin, she can't swim well.

→ If she were a dolphin, she could swim well.

└──────────────────

(1) As he is not rich enough, he will go fishing in this cold weather.

⇒ ＿＿＿＿＿＿＿＿＿＿＿＿

＿＿＿＿＿＿＿＿＿＿＿＿

(2) As Bob isn't in Venice, he isn't happy.

⇒ ＿＿＿＿＿＿＿＿＿＿＿＿

＿＿＿＿＿＿＿＿＿＿＿＿

(3) As there is no time left, I will cross the road at a red light.

⇒ ＿＿＿＿＿＿＿＿＿＿＿＿

＿＿＿＿＿＿＿＿＿＿＿＿

(4) As we had Munjado, it was easy for children to learn Chinese characters.

⇒ ＿＿＿＿＿＿＿＿＿＿＿＿

＿＿＿＿＿＿＿＿＿＿＿＿

Munjado, a Window into the Joseon Dynasty

Look at the painting on the right. Do you see the Chinese character, *hyo*(孝)? Do you also see a carp, a geomungo, and a fan? This kind of painting is called Munjado, and it is a type of folk painting that was popular in the late Joseon dynasty. In Munjado, there is usually a Chinese character with some animals or objects.

One of eight Chinese characters appears in Munjado. They are *hyo*(孝), *je*(悌), *chung*(忠), *sin*(信), *ye*(禮), *ui*(義), *yeom*(廉), and *chi*(恥), and they represent the values that were important to people of the Joseon dynasty.

The animals or objects in Munjado are not just decorations. They often are symbolic. For example, carp in the paintings of *hyo* symbolize respect for parents because of an old story. The story goes as follows.

Once upon a time, a man lived with his old mother. One winter, the man's mother became ill and couldn't eat anything. On one very cold day, the mother said to the man, "It would be wonderful if I could eat fresh fish."

dynasty 시대, 왕조

character 글자

carp 잉어(단·복수 동형)

folk painting 민화

object 물건, 물체

appear 보이다, 나타나다

represent 나타내다, 보여 주다, 상징하다

value 가치

decoration 장식

symbolic 상징적인, 상징하는

symbolize 상징하다

because of ~ 때문에

once upon a time 옛날 옛적에

ill 아픈

fresh 신선한

확인문제

● 다음 문장이 본문의 내용과 일치하면 T, 일치하지 않으면 F를 쓰시오.

1 There is usually a Chinese character in Munjado. ☐

2 Munjado is a type of folk painting that was popular in the early Joseon dynasty. ☐

3 There are eight Chinese characters that appear in Munjado. ☐

4 The animals or objects in Munjado are only for decorations. ☐

5 The animals or objects in Munjado have meanings. ☐

The man went out to the river, but it was completely frozen. It was impossible for him to catch any fish. The man was so disappointed that he cried out to the sky, "What should I do? Please help me." Then the ice melted, and three carp suddenly came out of the water. The man went back home and cooked the fish for his mother. Then his mother got well.

There are other examples of symbolic objects in Munjado. They are bamboo in the paintings of the character *chung*(忠) and lotus flowers in the paintings of *ui*(義). Bamboo does not bend. It stays green in all kinds of weather. For these reasons, bamboo came to symbolize loyalty to the king. In the case of lotus flowers, they grow in muddy ponds but still bloom beautifully. They thus became a symbol of a person's will to fight for justice despite difficulties.

Munjado was much more than a painting to people of the Joseon dynasty. It reminded them of important values that greatly influenced their behaviors and attitudes. In particular, for children, Munjado was a study tool. Through it, children in the Joseon dynasty could learn the importance of harmony in family and society.

---

frozen 얼어붙은

disappointed 실망한, 낙담한

melt 녹다

suddenly 갑자기

get well 병이 낫다, 회복하다

bamboo 대나무

lotus flower 연꽃

bend 굽다, 구부러지다

for this reason 이런 이유로

loyalty 충성, 충실

muddy 진흙투성이의, 탁한, 흙탕물의

pond 연못

bloom 꽃을 피우다, 꽃이 피다

thus 따라서, 그러므로

will 의지

justice 정의, 공정성

despite ~에도 불구하고

remind A of B A에게 B를 상기시키다

influence 영향을 미치다

behavior 행동

attitude 태도, 자세

in particular 특히

harmony 조화

확인문제

● 다음 문장이 본문의 내용과 일치하면 T, 일치하지 않으면 F를 쓰시오.

1 The man went out to the sea to catch some fish. ☐

2 Three carp suddenly came out of the water in response to the man's cry. ☐

3 Bamboo symbolizes loyalty to the king. ☐

4 Children in the Joseon dynasty could learn the importance of harmony through family and society. ☐

● 우리말을 참고하여 빈칸에 알맞은 말을 쓰시오.

1 Munjado, a Window _____ the Joseon Dynasty

2 Look at the painting _____ _____ _____ .

3 Do you _____ the Chinese _____ , *hyo*(孝)?

4 Do you also _____ a carp, a geomungo, and a fan?

5 This kind of painting _____ _____ Munjado, and it is _____ _____ _____ _____ _____ _____ _____ _____ in the _____ Joseon dynasty.

6 In Munjado, there is _____ a Chinese character _____ some animals or objects.

7 _____ _____ eight Chinese _____ _____ in Munjado.

8 They are *hyo*(孝), *je*(悌), *chung*(忠), *sin*(信), *ye*(禮), *ui*(義), *yeom*(廉), and *chi*(恥), and they _____ the values _____ _____ _____ _____ people of the Joseon dynasty.

9 The animals or objects in Munjado are not _____ _____ .

10 They _____ are _____ .

11 For example, carp in the paintings of *hyo* _____ respect for parents _____ _____ an old story.

12 The story _____ _____ .

13 _____ _____ _____ _____ _____ , a man lived with his old mother.

14 One winter, the man's mother _____ _____ and couldn't eat _____ .

15 _____ one very cold day, the mother said to the man, "It _____ _____ _____ _____ _____ _____ fresh fish."

16 The man _____ _____ the river, but it _____ _____ _____ .

---

1 문자도, 조선 시대를 보는 창

2 오른쪽에 있는 그림을 보라.

3 한자 효(孝)가 보이는가?

4 잉어, 거문고, 그리고 부채가 보이는가?

5 이런 종류의 그림은 문자도이며, 조선 시대 후기에 인기 있었던 민화의 한 종류이다.

6 문자도에는 보통 한자 하나가 동물이나 사물과 함께 있다.

7 문자도에는 여덟 개의 한자 중 하나가 나온다.

8 그것들은 효(孝), 제(悌), 충(忠), 신(信), 예(禮), 의(義), 염(廉), 치(恥)이고, 그것들은 조선 시대 사람들에게 중요했던 가치들을 나타낸다.

9 문자도에 있는 동물이나 사물은 단순한 장식이 아니다.

10 그것들은 종종 상징적이다.

11 예를 들어, '효' 그림 속에 있는 잉어는 옛이야기 때문에 부모님에 대한 존경심을 상징한다.

12 그 이야기는 다음과 같다.

13 옛날 옛적에 한 남자가 나이 드신 어머니와 살았다.

14 어느 겨울, 남자의 어머니는 병이 들어서 어떤 것도 먹을 수 없었다.

15 무척 추운 어느 날, 어머니는 남자에게 말했다. "신선한 물고기를 먹을 수 있다면 좋겠구나."

16 그 남자는 강으로 나갔지만, 강은 완전히 얼어붙어 있었다.

17 _____ was impossible _____ _____ _____ _____
_____ fish.

18 The man was _____ _____ _____ he cried out _____
the sky, "What should I do? Please help me."

19 Then the ice _____, and three carp suddenly came _____
_____ the water.

20 The man went _____ _____ and cooked the fish for his
mother.

21 Then his mother _____ _____.

22 There are other examples of _____ _____ in Munjado.

23 They are bamboo _____ the paintings _____ the character
chung(忠) and lotus flowers _____ the paintings _____
_ui_(義).

24 Bamboo does not _____.

25 It _____ _____ _____ all kinds of weather.

26 _____ _____ _____, b a m b o o _____ _____
_____ loyalty _____ the king.

27 _____ _____ _____ _____ _____ lotus flowers, they grow in
muddy ponds _____ _____ bloom _____.

28 They _____ became a symbol of a person's _____ _____
_____ _____ justice _____ difficulties.

29 Munjado was _____ _____ _____ a painting _____
people of the Joseon dynasty.

30 It _____ them _____ important values _____ greatly
influenced their behaviors and attitudes.

31 _____ _____, _____ children, Munjado was a study tool.

32 _____ _____, children in the Joseon dynasty could learn the
_____ of _____ _____ family and society.

---

17 그가 그 어떤 물고기라도 잡는 것은 불가능했다.

18 남자는 몹시 낙담해서 하늘에 대고 외쳤다. "제가 어떻게 해야 하나요? 제발 저를 도와주세요."

19 그러자 얼음이 녹았고, 잉어 세 마리가 갑자기 물 밖으로 나왔다.

20 남자는 집으로 돌아가서 어머니를 위해 물고기들을 요리했다.

21 그러자 그의 어머니는 회복되었다.

22 문자도에 있는 상징적인 사물의 또 다른 예가 있다.

23 그것들은 글자 '충(忠)' 그림에 있는 대나무와 '의(義)' 그림에 있는 연꽃이다.

24 대나무는 구부러지지 않는다.

25 그것은 어떤 날씨에서도 푸르름을 유지한다.

26 이런 이유로 대나무는 왕에 대한 충성을 상징하게 되었다.

27 연꽃의 경우, 그것들은 진흙투성이의 연못에서 자라지만 여전히 아름답게 꽃을 피운다.

28 그래서 그 꽃들은 어려움에도 불구하고 정의를 위해 싸우는 사람의 의지를 상징하게 되었다.

29 문자도는 조선 시대 사람들에게 그림 그 이상이었다.

30 그것은 그들에게 자신들의 행동과 태도에 큰 영향을 미치는 중요한 가치를 상기시켰다.

31 특히 아이들에게 문자도는 학습 도구였다.

32 그것을 통해 조선 시대의 아이들은 가족과 사회에서의 조화의 중요성을 배울 수 있었다.

● 우리말을 참고하여 본문을 영작하시오.

1 문자도, 조선 시대를 보는 창

➡ _____

2 오른쪽에 있는 그림을 보라.

➡ _____

3 한자 효(孝)가 보이는가?

➡ _____

4 잉어, 거문고, 그리고 부채가 보이는가?

➡ _____

5 이런 종류의 그림은 문자도이며, 조선 시대 후기에 인기 있었던 민화의 한 종류이다.

➡ _____

_____

6 문자도에는 보통 한자 하나가 동물이나 사물과 함께 있다.

➡ _____

7 문자도에는 여덟 개의 한자 중 하나가 나온다.

➡ _____

8 그것들은 효(孝), 제(悌), 충(忠), 신(信), 예(禮), 의(義), 염(廉), 치(恥)이고, 그것들은 조선 시대 사람들에게 중요했던 가치들을 나타낸다.

➡ _____

_____

9 문자도에 있는 동물이나 사물은 단순한 장식이 아니다.

➡ _____

10 그것들은 종종 상징적이다.

➡ _____

11 예를 들어, '효' 그림 속에 있는 잉어는 옛이야기 때문에 부모님에 대한 존경심을 상징한다.

➡ _____

12 그 이야기는 다음과 같다.

➡ _____

13 옛날 옛적에 한 남자가 나이 드신 어머니와 살았다.

➡ _____

14 어느 겨울, 남자의 어머니는 병이 들어서 어떤 것도 먹을 수 없었다.

➡ _____

15 무척 추운 어느 날, 어머니는 남자에게 말했다. "신선한 물고기를 먹을 수 있다면 좋겠구나."

➡ _____

16 그 남자는 강으로 나갔지만, 강은 완전히 얼어붙어 있었다.

➡ _____

17 그가 그 어떤 물고기라도 잡는 것은 불가능했다.

➡ _____

18 남자는 몹시 낙담해서 하늘에 대고 외쳤다. "제가 어떻게 해야 하나요? 제발 저를 도와주세요."

➡ _____

19 그러자 얼음이 녹았고, 잉어 세 마리가 갑자기 물 밖으로 나왔다.

➡ _____

20 남자는 집으로 돌아가서 어머니를 위해 물고기들을 요리했다.

➡ _____

21 그러자 그의 어머니는 회복되었다.

➡ _____

22 문자도에 있는 상징적인 사물의 또 다른 예가 있다.

➡ _____

23 그것들은 글자 '충(忠)' 그림에 있는 대나무와 '의(義)' 그림에 있는 연꽃이다.

➡ _____

24 대나무는 구부러지지 않는다.

➡ _____

25 그것은 어떤 날씨에서도 푸르름을 유지한다.

➡ _____

26 이런 이유로 대나무는 왕에 대한 충성을 상징하게 되었다.

➡ _____

27 연꽃의 경우, 그것들은 진흙투성이의 연못에서 자라지만 여전히 아름답게 꽃을 피운다.

➡ _____

28 그래서 그 꽃들은 어려움에도 불구하고 정의를 위해 싸우는 사람의 의지를 상징하게 되었다.

➡ _____

29 문자도는 조선 시대 사람들에게 그림 그 이상이었다.

➡ _____

30 그것은 그들에게 자신들의 행동과 태도에 큰 영향을 미치는 중요한 가치를 상기시켰다.

➡ _____

31 특히 아이들에게 문자도는 학습 도구였다.

➡ _____

32 그것을 통해 조선 시대의 아이들은 가족과 사회에서의 조화의 중요성을 배울 수 있었다.

➡ _____

[01~03] 다음 글을 읽고 물음에 답하시오.

Munjado a Window into the Joseon Dynasty

Look at the painting on the right. Do you see the Chinese character, *hyo*(孝)? Do you also see a carp, a geomungo, and a fan? This ⓐkind of painting is called Munjado, and it is a type of folk painting that was popular in the late Joseon dynasty. In Munjado, there is usually a Chinese character with some animals or objects.

One of eight Chinese characters appears in Munjado. They are *hyo*(孝), *je*(悌), *chung*(忠), *sin*(信), *ye*(禮), *ui*(義), *yeom*(廉), and *chi*(恥), and ⓑ그것들은 조선 시대 사람들에게 중요했던 가치들을 나타낸다.

01 위 글의 밑줄 친 ⓐkind와 같은 의미로 쓰인 것을 고르시오.

① In the human kind there are varieties in the taste of beauty.
② He is not the kind of person to do things by halves.
③ I know her and her kind.
④ It is very kind of you to lend me the book.
⑤ The periods of kind weather were much too brief.

서답형

02 위 글의 밑줄 친 ⓑ의 우리말에 맞게 주어진 어휘를 알맞게 배열하시오.

> they, the Joseon dynasty, the values, people, that, represent, were, important, of, to

➡ _____

_____

03 According to the passage, which is NOT true?

① We see the Chinese character, *hyo,* at the painting on the right.
② The painting on the right is called Munjado.
③ Munjado is a type of traditional painting.
④ Munjado was popular in the late Joseon dynasty.
⑤ There are usually some animals or objects in Munjado.

[04~06] 다음 글을 읽고 물음에 답하시오.

The animals or objects in Munjado are not just decorations. They often are ⓐ_____ . For example, carp in the paintings of *hyo* symbolize respect for parents because of an old story. The story goes as follows.

Once upon a time, a man lived with his old mother. One winter, the man's mother became ill and couldn't eat anything. On one very cold day, the mother said to the man, "It would be wonderful if I could eat fresh fish." The man went out to the river, but it was completely frozen. ⓑIt was impossible for him to catch any fish. The man was so disappointed that he cried out to the sky, "What should I do? Please help me." Then the ice melted, and three carp suddenly came ⓒout of the water. The man went back home and cooked the fish for his mother. Then his mother got well.

04 위 글의 빈칸 ⓐ에 들어갈 알맞은 것은?

① characteristic   ② objective   ③ funny
④ symbolic   ⑤ simplistic

05 아래 〈보기〉에서 위 글의 밑줄 친 ⓑit과 용법이 다른 것의 개수를 고르시오.

┌─── 보기 ───
│ ① It was windy and chilly yesterday.
│ ② It was hard for me to hide my feelings.
│ ③ When the factory closes, it will mean 500 people losing their jobs.
│ ④ It was very kind of you to visit me when I was ill.
│ ⑤ I make it a rule to get up early in the morning.
└───

① 1개　② 2개　③ 3개　④ 4개　⑤ 5개

06 위 글의 밑줄 친 ⓒout of와 바꿔 쓸 수 있는 말을 고르시오.

① into　② on　③ at
④ among　⑤ from

[07~09] 다음 글을 읽고 물음에 답하시오.

There are other examples of symbolic objects in Munjado. They are bamboo in the paintings of the character *chung*(忠) and lotus flowers in the paintings of *ui*(義). Bamboo does not bend. It stays green in all kinds of weather. _____ⓐ_____, bamboo came to symbolize loyalty to the king. In the case of lotus flowers, they grow in muddy ponds but still bloom beautifully. They thus became a symbol of a person's will to fight for justice despite difficulties.

Munjado was much more than a painting to people of the Joseon dynasty. It reminded them of important values that greatly influenced their behaviors and attitudes. ⓑ특히, for children, Munjado was a study tool. Through it, children in the Joseon dynasty could learn the importance of harmony in family and society.

07 위 글의 빈칸 ⓐ에 들어갈 말로 알맞지 않은 것을 고르시오.

① However　② For these reasons
③ Therefore　④ Thus
⑤ Hence

서답형

08 위 글의 밑줄 친 ⓑ의 우리말을 두 단어로 쓰시오.

➡ _____

중요

09 위 글의 앞에 나올 내용으로 적절한 것을 고르시오.

① various Chinese characters that appear in Munjado
② how Munjado developed in the late Joseon dynasty
③ traditional painting skills used in Munjado
④ example of symbolic objects in Munjado
⑤ the use of Munjado

[10~12] 다음 글을 읽고 물음에 답하시오.

Look at the painting on the right. (①) Do you see the Chinese character, *hyo*(孝)? (②) This kind of painting is called Munjado, and it is a type of folk painting _____ⓐ_____ was popular in the late Joseon dynasty. (③) In Munjado, there is usually a Chinese character with some animals or objects. (④)
(A)문자도에는 여덟 개의 한자 중 하나가 나온다. (one, eight Chinese characters, Munjado) (⑤) They are *hyo*(孝), *je*(悌), *chung*(忠), *sin*(信), *ye*(禮), *ui*(義), *yeom*(廉), and *chi*(恥), and they represent the values _____ⓐ_____ were important to people of the Joseon dynasty.

10 위 글의 흐름으로 보아, 주어진 문장이 들어가기에 가장 적절한 곳은?

> Do you also see a carp, a geomungo, and a fan?

① ② ③ ④ ⑤

11 위 글의 빈칸 ⓐ에 공통으로 들어갈 알맞은 말을 <u>모두</u> 고르시오.

① which ② whom ③ who
④ what ⑤ that

서답형

12 밑줄 친 우리말 (A)를 주어진 어휘를 이용하여 영작하시오.

➡ _____

_____

[13~15] 다음 글을 읽고 물음에 답하시오.

The animals or objects in Munjado are not just decorations. They often are symbolic. _____(A)_____, carp in the paintings of *hyo* symbolize respect for parents because of an old story. The story goes as follows.

Once ___ⓐ___ a time, a man lived with his old mother. One winter, the man's mother became ill and couldn't eat anything. On one very cold day, the mother said to the man, "It would be wonderful if I could eat fresh fish."
The man went out to the river, but it was completely frozen. It was impossible for him to catch any fish. The man was so disappointed that he cried out ___ⓑ___ the sky, "What should I do? Please help me." Then the ice melted, and three carp suddenly came out of the water. The man went back home and cooked the fish for his mother. Then his mother got well.

13 위 글의 빈칸 (A)에 들어갈 말로 알맞은 것은?

① However ② Therefore
③ For example ④ In particular
⑤ For these reasons

14 위 글의 빈칸 ⓐ와 ⓑ에 들어갈 전치사가 바르게 짝지어진 것은?

ⓐ	ⓑ	ⓐ	ⓑ
① upon – from		② upon – to	
③ under – from		④ under – to	
⑤ on – at			

서답형

15 What are the animals or objects in Munjado? Answer by using 'not only A but also B', and 'meanings'.

➡ _____

_____

[16~17] 다음 글을 읽고 물음에 답하시오.

There are other examples of symbolic objects in Munjado. They are bamboo in the paintings of the character *chung*(忠) and lotus flowers in the paintings of *ui*(義). Bamboo does not bend. It stays green in all kinds of (A)[weather / whether]. For these reasons, bamboo came to symbolize (B) [royalty / loyalty] to the king. In the case of lotus flowers, they grow in muddy ponds but still bloom beautifully. They thus became a symbol of a person's will to fight (C)[against / for] justice despite difficulties.

서답형

16 What does bamboo stand for in Munjado?

➡ _____

17 위 글의 괄호 (A)~(C)에서 문맥이나 어법상 알맞은 낱말을 골라 쓰시오.

➡ (A) _____ (B) _____ (C) _____

[18~20] 다음 글을 읽고 물음에 답하시오.

Munjado was much more than a painting to people of the Joseon dynasty. It reminded them of important ___ⓐ___ that greatly influenced their behaviors and attitudes. In particular, for children, Munjado was ___ⓑ___. Through it, children in the Joseon dynasty could learn the importance of harmony in family and society.

18 위 글의 빈칸 ⓐ에 알맞은 말을 고르시오.

① values   ② tradition   ③ habit
④ experience   ⑤ experiment

19 위 글의 빈칸 ⓑ에 알맞은 말을 고르시오.

① an entertainment
② a free time activity
③ a playground
④ a study tool
⑤ a stage of practice

서답형

20 What could children in the Joseon dynasty learn from Munjado?

➡ _____

_____

[21~23] 다음 글을 읽고 물음에 답하시오.

Look at the painting on the right. Do you see the Chinese character, *hyo*(孝)? Do you also see a carp, a geomungo, and a fan? This kind of painting is called ⓐMunjado, and it is a type of folk painting that was popular in the late Joseon dynasty. In Munjado, there is usually a Chinese character with some animals or objects.

One of eight Chinese characters appears in Munjado. They are *hyo*(孝), *je*(悌), *chung*(忠), *sin*(信), *ye*(禮), *ui*(義), *yeom*(廉), and *chi*(恥), and they represent the values that were important to people of the Joseon dynasty.

서답형

21 How many Chinese characters appear in Munjado? Answer in a full sentence.

➡ _____

_____

서답형

22 다음 빈칸 (A)와 (B)에 알맞은 단어를 넣어, 밑줄 친 ⓐ Munjado에 대한 설명을 완성하시오.

Munjado is a type of (A)_____ painting that was popular in the late Joseon dynasty. In Munjado, there is usually a Chinese character with some animals or objects that represent the (B)_____ that were important to people of the Joseon dynasty.

서답형

23 우리가 문자도에서 볼 수 있는 것 두 가지를 본문에서 찾아 쓰시오.

➡ (1) _____
(2) _____

[01~03] 다음 글을 읽고 물음에 답하시오.

The animals or objects in Munjado are not just decorations. They often are symbolic. For example, carp in the paintings of ⓐ symbolize respect for parents because of an old story. The story goes as follows.

Once upon a time, a man lived with his old mother. One winter, the man's mother became ill and couldn't eat anything. On one very cold day, the mother said to the man, "_____ ⓑ _____" The man went out to the river, but it was completely frozen. It was impossible for him to catch any fish. The man was so disappointed that he cried out to the sky, "What should I do? Please help me." Then the ice melted, and three carp suddenly came out of the water. The man went back home and cooked the fish for his mother. Then his mother got well.

01 위 글의 빈칸 ⓐ에 알맞은 말을 쓰시오.

➡ _____

02 위 글의 빈칸 ⓑ에 'As I cannot eat fresh fish, it is not wonderful.'을 가정법으로 쓰시오. (It으로 시작할 것)

➡ _____

03 본문의 내용과 일치하도록 다음 빈칸 (A), (B)와 (C)에 알맞은 단어를 쓰시오.

Carp symbolize (A)_____ _____
_____. In an old story, a man caught (B)_____ _____ in a frozen river and cooked them for his (C)_____ _____.

[04~06] 다음 글을 읽고 물음에 답하시오.

Look at the painting on the right. Do you see the Chinese character, *hyo*(孝)? Do you also see a carp, a geomungo, and a fan? This kind of painting ⓐ Munjado, and it is a type of folk painting that was popular in the late Joseon dynasty. In Munjado, there is usually a Chinese character with some animals or objects.

One of eight Chinese characters appears in Munjado. They are *hyo*(孝), *je*(悌), *chung*(忠), *sin*(信), *ye*(禮), *ui*(義), *yeom*(廉), and *chi*(恥), and they represent the values that were worthless to people of the Joseon dynasty.

04 위 글의 빈칸 ⓐ에 call을 알맞은 형태로 쓰시오.

➡ _____

05 위 글에서 흐름상 어색한 한 단어를 찾아 고치시오.

_____ ➡ _____

06 위 글에 나타난 문자도의 특징을 '조선 시대 사람'을 반드시 넣어 45자 내외의 우리말로 쓰시오.

➡ _____

_____

[07~08] 다음 글을 읽고 물음에 답하시오.

Munjado was ⓐmuch more than a painting to people of the Joseon dynasty. (A)그것은 그들에게 자신들의 행동과 태도에 큰 영향을 미치는 중요한 가치를 상기시켰다. (behaviors and

attitudes, values, remind, influence, that)
In particular, for children, Munjado was a study tool. Through it, children in the Joseon dynasty could learn the importance of harmony in family and society.

07 위 글의 밑줄 친 ⓐ를 대신해서 쓸 수 있는 것을 3개 이상 쓰시오.

➡ _____

08 위 글의 밑줄 친 (A)의 우리말을 괄호 안에 주어진 어휘를 이용하여 13 단어로 영작하시오.

➡ _____

[09~12] 다음 글을 읽고 물음에 답하시오.

There are other examples of symbolic objects in Munjado. They are bamboo in the paintings of the character *chung*(忠) and lotus flowers in the paintings of *ui*(義). Bamboo does not bend. (A)It stays green in all kinds of weather. For ⓐthese reasons, bamboo ⓑcame to symbolize loyalty to the king. In the case of lotus flowers, they grow in muddy ponds but still bloom beautifully. (B)They thus became a symbol of a person's will to fight for justice despite difficulties.

09 위 글의 밑줄 친 (A)It과 (B)They가 각각 가리키는 것을 본문에서 찾아 쓰시오.

➡ (A) _____ (B) _____

10 위 글의 밑줄 친 ⓐthese reasons에 해당되는 사실 두 가지를 우리말로 쓰시오.

➡ (1) _____
  (2) _____

11 위 글의 밑줄 친 ⓑcame 대신 쓸 수 있는 단어를 쓰시오.

➡ _____

12 Why could lotus flowers become a symbol of a person's will to fight for justice despite difficulties?

➡ _____
  _____

[13~14] 다음 글을 읽고 물음에 답하시오.

The man went out to the river, but it was completely frozen. ⓐ그가 그 어떤 물고기라도 잡는 것은 불가능했다. The man was so disappointed that he cried out to the sky, "What should I do? Please help me." Then the ice melted, and three carp suddenly came out of the water. The man went back home and cooked the fish for his mother. Then his mother ___(A)___ .

13 위 글의 빈칸 (A)에 알맞은 말을 2 단어로 쓰시오.

➡ _____

14 위 글의 밑줄 친 ⓐ의 우리말을 it을 이용하여 9 단어로 영작하시오.

➡ _____

After You Read B Read and Complete

Paintings of *Hyo*(孝)

Carp symbolize respect for parents. In an old story, a man caught three carp in
> Carp를 복수 취급함.

a frozen river and cooked them for his sick mother.
> = three carp

Paintings of *Chung*(忠)

Bamboo symbolizes loyalty to the king. It does not bend and stays green in all
> stay+형용사: ~한 상태를 유지하다

kinds of weather.

Paintings of *Ui*(義)

Lotus flowers symbolize a person's will to fight for justice despite difficulties.
> ~을 위해 싸우다   though(×)

They grow in muddy ponds but still bloom beautifully.
> 연꽃이 자라는 환경과 꽃을 아름답게 피우는 모습이 대조적임을 나타냄.

구문해설
- carp: 잉어(단 · 복수 동형)   · respect: 존경, 존경심   · frozen: 얼어붙은
- loyalty: 충성, 충실   · will: 의지   · justice: 정의, 공정성   · despite: ~에도 불구하고
- muddy: 진흙투성이의, 탁한, 흙탕물의   · bloom: 꽃을 피우다, 꽃이 피다

Around the World

a: This painting shows the harvest time of a countryside in Europe in the 16th
> shows 다음에 접속사 that 생략

century.

b: This painting shows a ssireum competition in the late Joseon dynasty.
> 때 · 시간을 나타내는 전치사

c: This painting shows the marriage of an American farmer's daughter in the
> 시간을 나타내는 century 앞에 쓰인 전치사

19th century.

구문해설
- harvest time: 수확기   · countryside: 시골, 교외 지역   · century: 세기
- competition: 대회   · dynasty: 왕조   · marriage: 결혼, 결혼식

Think and Write

My Favorite Painting, *Water Lillies: The Clouds*

My favorite painting is *Water Lilies: The Clouds*. It was painted by Claude
> 수동태 be+p.p+by(행위자)

Monet. In the painting, I can see the reflection of clouds in the pond as well as
> B as well as A = not only A but also B

water lilies. I like this painting because the colors are beautiful and the scene

looks peaceful. I think it was very creative of the painter to draw the pond as a
> look+형용사 보어 peacefully (×)   가주어   사람의 성질+of+의미상 주어+진주어(to 부정사)

mirror so that the clouds in the sky are reflected in the pond.
> ~하도록(목적)   수의 일치 주의 is(×) (the clouds가 주어)

구문해설
- reflection: 반사, 반영, 비친 모습   · B as well as A: A뿐 아니라 B도
- so that: ~하기 위해서, ~하도록

해석

'효' 그림

잉어는 부모님에 대한 존경심을 상징한다. 옛이야기에서 한 남자가 얼어붙은 강에서 잉어 세 마리를 잡아 자신의 아픈 어머니를 위해 그것들을 요리했다.

'충' 그림

대나무는 왕에 대한 충성을 상징한다. 그것은 구부러지지 않고 어떤 날씨에서도 푸르름을 유지한다.

'의' 그림

연꽃은 어려움에도 불구하고 정의를 위해 싸우는 인간의 의지를 상징한다. 그 꽃들은 진흙투성이의 연못에서 자라지만 여전히 아름답게 꽃을 피운다.

a. 이 그림은 16세기 유럽 교외 지역의 수확기를 보여 준다.

b. 이 그림은 조선 시대 후기의 씨름 대회를 보여 준다.

c. 이 그림은 19세기 미국 농부의 딸의 결혼식을 보여 준다.

내가 가장 좋아하는 그림, '수련: 구름'

내가 가장 좋아하는 그림은 '수련: 구름'이다. 그것은 Claude Monet에 의해 그려졌다. 그림 속에서, 나는 수련뿐만 아니라 연못에 비친 구름도 볼 수 있다. 나는 색깔도 아름답고, 장면이 평화롭게 보여서 이 그림을 좋아한다. 나는 화가가 연못을 거울로 해서 하늘의 구름이 연못에 비치도록 한 것이 매우 창의적이라고 생각한다.

01 〈보기〉의 밑줄 친 character와 같은 의미로 쓰인 것을 고르시오.

┌─── 보기 ───┐
I found that every written character looks balanced and beautiful.
└─────────────┘

① Before we had our own letters, we had to use Chinese characters.
② The character of the neighbourhood hasn't changed at all
③ Eddie is the funniest character in the show.
④ Character is a habit long continued.
⑤ Just press the button to see your favourite character in action.

02 다음 영영풀이에 해당하는 단어를 주어진 철자로 시작하여 빈칸에 쓰고, 알맞은 것을 골라 문장을 완성하시오.

• a_____ : the way you think or feel about something
• t_____ : any instrument or simple piece of equipment that you hold in your hands and use to do a particular kind of work

(1) If you want to pass your exams, you'd better change your _____.
(2) Even in small companies, computers are an essential _____.

03 다음 문장의 빈칸에 〈영영풀이〉에 해당하는 어휘를 쓰시오.

They are demanding equal rights and _____.

<영영풀이> the quality of being fair and reasonable; fairness in the way people are treated

04 다음 빈칸 (A)~(C)에 알맞은 말을 쓰시오. (주어진 철자로 시작하여 쓸 것.)

• He goes to his mother and tells her not to worry and to (A)g_____ well soon.
• They might be worth (B)m_____ more than you think.
• You walk (C)s_____ fast that I can't keep up with you.

05 괄호 안에 주어진 어휘를 이용하여 빈칸에 알맞게 쓰시오.

(1) She looked _____ when I told her. (surprise)
(2) It can be very _____ to lose important matches. (disappoint)
(3) His speech was so _____. (bore)

Conversation

[06~08] 다음 대화를 읽고 물음에 답하시오.

> B: We can have Gimbap or Tteokbokki.
> _____(a)_____, Jenny?
> (A) Let's order, then. I'm very hungry.
> (B) I prefer Gimbap. (b)It seems to me that it's the healthier choice. How about you, Minsu?
> (C) I'll have Tteokbokki. I heard that the Tteokbokki here is very good.

06 위 대화의 빈칸 (a)에 like를 이용하여 5 단어로 알맞은 말을 쓰시오.

➡ _____

07 주어진 문장 다음에 나올 대화의 순서로 알맞은 것은?

① (A) – (C) – (B)   ② (B) – (A) – (C)
③ (B) – (C) – (A)   ④ (C) – (A) – (B)
⑤ (C) – (B) – (A)

08 위 대화의 밑줄 친 (b)를 think를 이용하여 바꿔 쓰시오. (7 words)

➡ _____

09 다음 중 짝지어진 대화가 어색한 것은?

① A: Look at these two old plates, Steve. Aren't they beautiful?
  B: Yes. Which one do you prefer, the green plate or the white plate?
② A: I'll have Tteokbokki. I heard that the Tteokbokki here is very good.
  B: Let's order, then. I'm very full.
③ A: Which one do you prefer, the one with flowers or the one with animals?
  B: I prefer the one with flowers.
④ A: I prefer Tteokbokki. It seems to me that it's more delicious. How about you?
  B: I prefer Tteokbokki, too.
⑤ A: Where is the show?
  B: It's in Dasom Hall, next to the exhibition room.

[10~11] 다음 대화를 읽고 물음에 답하시오.

> John: There are two movies we can see. Which one do you want to see more, Somi?
> Somi: I prefer *Batman*. I saw *Spider-Man* last week. Is this OK, John?
> John: Of course. It seems to me that *Batman* will be much more fun.
> Somi: Good. Then, let's go and see it.

10 위 대화를 읽고 답할 수 없는 질문을 고르시오.

① Do John and Somi want to see a movie?
② What movie did Somi see last week?
③ Does Somi prefer *Batman* to *Spider-Man*?
④ Does John think *Batman* will be much more fun?
⑤ When will John and Somi see *Batman*?

11 위 대화에서 주어진 영영풀이에 해당하는 단어를 찾아 쓰시오.

> to like someone or something more than someone or something else, so that you would choose it if you could

➡ _____

Grammar

12 다음 중 어법상 올바른 문장의 개수는 <u>모두</u> 몇 개인가?

> ⓐ It was exciting for the girl to going abroad to make her dreams come true.
> ⓑ It was possibly for me to paint the roof.
> ⓒ It is very polite of the baby to say hello to every adult she sees.
> ⓓ It's important for the attendants not be late for the event.
> ⓔ Was it interesting for they to watch the soccer game between the countries?
> ⓕ It is hard of the young ladies to become diligent all the time.

① 1개   ② 2개   ③ 3개   ④ 4개   ⑤ 5개

13 다음 주어진 문장을 가정법으로 바르게 고친 것은?

> Since Peterson didn't return the books in time, he couldn't borrow books from the library for a month.

① If Peterson returns the books in time, he can borrow books from the library for a month.

② If Peterson returned the books in time, he could borrow books from the library for a month.

③ If Peterson didn't return the books in time, he could borrow books from the library for a month.

④ If Peterson had returned the books in time, he could have borrowed books from the library for a month.

⑤ If Peterson hadn't returned the books in time, he could not have borrowed books from the library for a month.

[14~15] 다음 우리말에 맞게 영작한 것은?

14
> Munjado를 사용하여 자녀를 가르치는 것은 훨씬 더 유용할 것이다.

① It is quite more helpful for you to teach your children using Munjado.

② It will be much more helpful of you to teach your children using Munjado.

③ It is much more helpful for you to teach your children when you will use Munjado.

④ It will be much more helpful for you to teach your children using Munjado.

⑤ It would be quite more helpful for you to teach your children while using Munjado.

15
> 눈이 충분히 온다면 당신이 스키를 즐길 수 있을 텐데.

① If you have enough snow, you could enjoy skiing.

② Had you snow enough, you can enjoy skiing.

③ If it didn't snow much, you wouldn't enjoy skiing.

④ If it snows enough, you would enjoy skiing.

⑤ If it snowed enough, you could enjoy skiing.

16 다음 문장 중 어법상 어색한 것은?

① If Lucy got up early, she wouldn't be late for the meeting.

② If Jade had worn the coat, she wouldn't have got a cold.

③ If I were the president, I would make a new policy to respect each other.

④ If David told this to her, she would be mad at me.

⑤ If Smith succeeded in catching the school bus this morning, he would not have been late for school.

17 다음 우리말을 주어진 단어를 이용하여 가정법 문장으로 쓰고, 직설법 문장으로도 바꿔 쓰시오.

> 잉어들이 얼음 위로 올라오지 않았더라면, 그의 어머니가 그것들을 먹을 수 없었을 텐데.
> (the carp, come out, eat, can, over the ice)

➡ (1) If _____

_____ .

(2) 직설법: As _____

_____ .

Reading

[18~20] 다음 글을 읽고 물음에 답하시오.

There are other examples of symbolic objects in Munjado. They are bamboo in the paintings of the character *chung*(忠) and lotus flowers in the paintings of *ui*(義). Bamboo does not bend. It stays green in all kinds of weather. _____ⓐ_____ these reasons, bamboo came to symbolize loyalty to the king. In the case of lotus flowers, they grow in muddy ponds but still bloom

beautifully. They thus became a symbol of a person's will to fight _____ⓐ_____ justice despite difficulties.

18 위 글의 빈칸 ⓐ에 공통으로 들어갈 전치사는? (대 · 소문자 무시)

① on   ② from   ③ in
④ to   ⑤ for

19 주어진 영영풀이에 해당하는 단어를 본문에서 찾아 쓰시오.

> to express indirectly by an image, form, or model

➡ _____

20 본문의 내용과 일치하도록 다음 빈칸 (A), (B)와 (C)에 알맞은 단어를 쓰시오.

> Bamboo symbolizes (A)_____ to the king. It does not (B)_____ and stays (C)_____ in all kinds of weather.

[21~23] 다음 글을 읽고 물음에 답하시오.

Munjado was much more than a painting to people of the Joseon dynasty. It remained them of important values that greatly influenced their behaviors and attitudes. In particular, for children, Munjado was a study tool. Through it, children in the Joseon dynasty could learn the importance of harmony in family and society.

21 위 글에서 잘못 쓰인 어휘 하나를 찾아 바르게 고쳐 쓰시오.

_____ ➡ _____

22 위 글의 주제로 알맞은 것을 고르시오.

① the role of Munjado in the Joseon dynasty
② how to draw Munjado
③ the history of Munjado
④ why people of the Joseon dynasty liked Munjado
⑤ what is Munjado

23 According to the passage, which is NOT true?

① Munjado was much more than a painting to people of the Joseon dynasty.
② People of the Joseon dynasty had some important values.
③ Some important values greatly influenced behaviors and attitudes of people of the Joseon dynasty.
④ Children drew Munjado as a study tool.
⑤ Children in the Joseon dynasty could learn the importance of harmony in family and society through Munjado.

[24~25] 다음 글을 읽고 물음에 답하시오.

Look at the painting on the right. Do you see the Chinese character, *hyo*(孝)? Do you also see a carp, a geomungo, and a fan? This kind of painting is called Munjado, and it is a type of folk painting that was popular in the late Joseon dynasty. In Munjado, there is usually a Chinese character with some animals or objects.

One of eight Chinese characters appear in Munjado. They are *hyo*(孝), *je*(悌), *chung*(忠), *sin*(信), *ye*(禮), *ui*(義), *yeom*(廉), and *chi*(恥), and they represent the values that were important to people of the Joseon dynasty.

24 위 글에서 어법상 어색한 것을 찾아 바르게 고치시오.

_____ ➡ _____

25 What is usually there in Munjado?

➡ _____

_____

[26~27] 다음 글을 읽고 물음에 답하시오.

Ssireum was painted by Kim Hong Do. This is one of Kim Hong Do's most famous paintings. It shows two men in a ssireum competition. Many people are watching the competition.

The Country Wedding was painted by John Lewis Krimmel in 1820. The painting shows a wedding. There are two birds above the people getting married. These birds are symbols for peace and happiness.

The Harvesters was painted by Pieter Bruegel the Elder in 1565. It was painted on wood. The painting shows farmers working in the summer. Some workers are taking a rest and some are eating food.

26 What do the two birds above the people getting married in *The Country Wedding* symbolize?

➡ _____

27 Where and when was *The Harvesters* painted?

➡ _____

출제율 95%

01 다음 중 짝지어진 단어의 관계가 나머지와 다른 것은?

① ill – healthy
② represent – symbolize
③ possible – impossible
④ respect – disrespect
⑤ justice – injustice

출제율 100%

02 밑줄 친 부분의 의미로 알맞지 않은 것은?

① You thus need to stay alert and focused. (따라서, 그러므로)
② For this reason, we need signs in this area. (이런 이유로)
③ She puts great value on thrift. (가치, 중요성)
④ The people buried at Stonehenge might have been royalty. (충성, 충실)
⑤ A clover with four leaves is a symbol of luck. (상징)

출제율 90%

03 다음 빈칸에 들어갈 알맞은 어휘를 주어진 철자로 시작하여 쓰시오.

(1) Does this r_____ you of the mistake you made last time?
(2) The proposal will go ahead d_____ strong objections from the public.

출제율 90%

04 다음 주어진 우리말에 맞게 빈칸을 채우시오. (주어진 철자로 시작할 것)

(1) 그는 선생님들에게 좋은 태도를 보인다.
   ➡ He has a good a_____ towards his teachers.
(2) 조선 왕조는 1392년에 세워졌다.
   ➡ The Joseon d_____ was founded in 1392.

[05~06] 다음 대화를 읽고 물음에 답하시오.

> G: Joe, didn't you say you needed to buy a cap? (a)How about these caps here?
> B: They look great.
> G: Which one do you prefer, the one with triangles or the one with flowers?
> B: I prefer the one with triangles. It seems to me that it's more unique.

출제율 90%

05 위 대화의 밑줄 친 (a)를 what과 say를 이용하여 같은 뜻으로 쓰시오.

   ➡ _____

출제율 100%

06 위 대화의 내용과 일치하는 것을 고르시오.

① Joe didn't say he needed to buy a cap.
② These caps here don't look great.
③ Joe prefers the cap with flowers.
④ The cap with triangles seems more unique to Joe.
⑤ The girl prefers the cap with triangles.

[07~08] 다음 대화를 읽고 물음에 답하시오.

G: Look at these two old plates, Steve. Aren't they beautiful?

B: Yes. Which one do you prefer, the green plate or the white plate?

G: Well, it's hard to choose, but I like the green one better. How about you?

B: (a)Me, too. It seems to me that the green plate is more unique.

출제율 90%

07 Why does Steve prefer the green plate? Answer by using "It's because" and "seems to".

➡ _____

_____

출제율 95%

08 위 대화의 밑줄 친 (a)Me, too. 대신 쓸 수 있는 것을 고르시오.

① Me, neither.
② Neither am I.
③ Neither do I.
④ So am I.
⑤ So do I.

[09~10] 다음 대화를 읽고 물음에 답하시오.

G: Junsu, you said you're going to buy a gift for your sister. How about the bags here?

B: They look (a)[nice / nicely].

G: (b)[What / Which] one do you prefer, the one with flowers or the one with animals?

B: I prefer the one with flowers. It (c)[appears / looks] to me that my sister will like it more.

출제율 95%

09 위 대화의 괄호 (a)~(c)에서 알맞은 것을 골라 바르게 짝지은 것은?

	(a)	(b)	(c)
①	nice	Which	appears
②	nicely	What	looks
③	nice	What	appears
④	nicely	Which	looks
⑤	nice	What	appears

출제율 90%

10 What do you guess Junsu is going to do? Answer with 12 words.

➡ _____

_____

[11~12] 다음 중 어법상 옳은 것을 고르시오.

출제율 95%

11 ① It is impossible for they to master the Chinese grammar in two weeks.
② It was dangerous for the babies to jump on the thin board.
③ It is necessary of those inside the building to breathe in fresh air.
④ It was difficult for the boys to playing on the wet ground.
⑤ It was kind for the principal to help the poor students with his own money.

출제율 100%

12 ① What would Jimin do if it rained on his sister's marathon day?
② If there had been no Chinese characters, it would be difficult for us to communicate.
③ Mary will be sad if I left her.
④ If Nancy were not so hungry, she can share her meal with me.
⑤ Her father would feel happy if Susan makes it to the finals of the competition.

출제율 95%

13 다음 각 문장의 밑줄 친 It[it]이 어떤 용법으로 쓰였는지 〈보기〉에서 기호를 골라 괄호 안에 쓰시오.

> ┤ 보기 ├
> ⓐ 가주어-진주어 구문의 It[it]
> ⓑ It ~ that 강조 구문의 It[it]
> ⓒ 인칭대명사 It[it]
> ⓓ 비인칭 주어 It[it]

(1) It is over there. (　　　)

(2) It is for his daughters that David has worked so hard day and night. (　　　)

(3) It is not true that they will throw a surprise party tonight. (　　　)

(4) It is 6 miles from the store to the post office. (　　　)

(5) What was it that made the girl decide to lose weight in a short time? (　　　)

(6) It is wonderful for your neighbors to gather to celebrate your success. (　　　)

(7) It has rained since last weekend. (　　　)

(8) It was the graduation present that his uncle bought at the store. (　　　)

(9) It is clever of the students to make robots by recycling the waste. (　　　)

(10) She overcame her physical weakness, and it made people impressed. (　　　)

출제율 90%

14 괄호 안의 조건과 가정법을 이용하여 다음 대화의 빈칸을 알맞게 채우시오.

(1) A: Does he have my phone number?
　 B: No, but if he _____,
　　 he _____ you. (have, will, call 활용)

(2) A: Is the man on the right rich?
　 B: No, but if he _____, he _____ the car. (be, buy, can 활용)

(3) A: Didn't Amy attend the meeting?
　 B: Yes, but if she _____,
　　 she _____ the news. (not, attend, can, hear 활용, 축약형 쓸 것)

[15~17] 다음 글을 읽고 물음에 답하시오.

The animals or objects in Munjado are not just decorations. They often are symbolic. For example, carp in the paintings of hyo symbolize respect for parents because of an old story. The story goes (A)다음과 같이.

Once upon a time, a man lived with his old mother. One winter, the man's mother became ill and couldn't eat anything. On one very cold day, the mother said to the man, "It would be wonderful if I could eat fresh fish."

The man went out to the river, but it was completely frozen. (①) It was impossible for him to catch any fish. (②) The man was so disappointed that he cried out to the sky, "What should I do? (③) Please help me." (④) Then the ice ___ⓐ___, and three carp suddenly came out of the water. (⑤) Then his mother got well.

출제율 90%

15 위 글의 빈칸 ⓐ에 들어갈 알맞은 말을 고르시오.

① froze　　　　　② appeared
③ melted　　　　④ heightened
⑤ assembled

출제율 95%

16 위 글의 흐름으로 보아, 주어진 문장이 들어가기에 가장 적절한 곳은?

> The man went back home and cooked the fish for his mother.

①　　　②　　　③　　　④　　　⑤

✎ 출제율 90%

17 위 글의 밑줄 친 (A)의 우리말을 두 단어로 쓰시오.

➡ _____

[18~20] 다음 글을 읽고 물음에 답하시오.

There are other examples of symbolic objects in Munjado. They are bamboo in the paintings of the character (A)*chung*(忠) and lotus flowers in the paintings of (B)*ui*(義). Bamboo does not bend. It stays green in all kinds of weather. For these reasons, bamboo came to symbolize loyalty to the king. In the case of lotus flowers, they grow in muddy ponds but still bloom beautifully. They _____ⓐ_____ became a symbol of a person's will to fight for justice despite difficulties.

Munjado was much more than a painting to people of the Joseon dynasty. It reminded them of important values that greatly influenced their behaviors and attitudes. In particular, for children, Munjado was a study tool. Through it, children in the Joseon dynasty could learn the importance of harmony in family and society.

✎ 출제율 90%

18 위 글의 빈칸 ⓐ에 들어갈 알맞은 말을 고르시오.

① however   ② thus
③ for instance   ④ in addition
⑤ that is

✎ 출제율 95%

19 위 글의 밑줄 친 (A)와 (B)에 해당하는 그림을 고르시오.

①   ②   ③

➡ (A) _____ (B) _____

✎ 출제율 95%

20 What was Munjado to people of the Joseon dynasty? Fill in the blanks with suitable words.

Munjado (A)_____ them of important
(B)_____ that greatly influenced their
(C)_____ and (D)_____.

[21~22] 다음 글을 읽고 물음에 답하시오.

Look at the painting on the right. Do you see the Chinese character, *hyo*(孝)? Do you also see a carp, a geomungo, and a fan? This kind of painting is called Munjado, and it is a type of folk painting that was popular in the late Joseon dynasty. In Munjado, there is usually a Chinese character with some animals or objects.

One of eight Chinese characters appears in Munjado. They are *hyo*(孝), *je*(悌), *chung*(忠), *sin*(信), *ye*(禮), *ui*(義), *yeom*(廉), and *chi*(恥), and ⓐ그것들은 조선 시대 사람들에게 중요했던 가치들을 나타낸다.

✎ 출제율 95%

21 밑줄 친 ⓐ의 우리말에 맞게 주어진 어휘를 이용하여 13 단어로 영작하시오.

people of the Joseon dynasty, that, important, represent

➡ _____

✎ 출제율 100%

22 위 글을 읽고 답할 수 <u>없는</u> 것을 고르시오.

① Can you see the Chinese character, *hyo*(孝), in the painting on the right?
② Are there also a carp, a geomungo, and a fan in the painting?
③ Is Munjado a type of folk painting?
④ Was Munjado popular in the late Joseon dynasty?
⑤ Why does one of eight Chinese characters appear in Munjado?

[01~03] 다음 대화를 읽고 물음에 답하시오.

G: There are two exhibitions we can go to. Which one do you want to see more, Eric?

B: I prefer the Korean mask exhibition. Is that OK, Somi?

G: Of course. And it seems to me that the mask exhibition will be very more interesting.

B: Do you think so?

G: Yes. Look at this poster. There isn't just an exhibition. There's also a mask dance show at 4:00 and 6:00.

B: Great! I've never seen a mask dance show before.

G: Well, I've seen a show before. I'm sure you'll like it.

B: So where is the show?

G: It's in Dasom Hall, next to the exhibition room.

B: It's 4:30 now, so let's watch the 6 o'clock show.

G: OK. Let's go see the exhibition first.

01 Has Somi seen a mask dance show before?

➡ _____

02 Before watching the mask dance show what will they do? Answer with 6 words.

➡ _____

03 위 대화에서 어법상 어색한 것을 하나 찾아 바르게 고치시오.

_____ ➡ _____

04 다음 우리말과 같은 뜻이 되도록 괄호 안에 있는 단어들을 활용하여, 글자 수에 맞게 영작하시오. (의미에 맞게 주어진 단어들의 형태 변화 가능)

(1) 그들이 호랑이를 잡는 것은 불가능했다. (they, the tiger, catch, possible 활용, 총 9 단어)

➡ _____

(2) 그 여자들이 커다란 개를 향해 손을 내민 것은 정말로 부주의했다. (woman, care, real, reach out to, a big dog 활용, 총 14 단어)

➡ _____
_____

05 다음 그림을 보고, 주어진 단어를 알맞게 배열하여 대화를 완성하시오.

Tom: Kim, have you heard of an old story about the carp in Munjado?

Kim: Of course. In a cold day, a man caught the carp to save his mother, right?

Tom: Yeah, that's why the carp symbolized the love for parents.

Kim: Oh. If _____.

(in his situation, I, done, have, been, I, the same thing, never, had, could)

➡ _____
_____

The animals or objects in Munjado are not just decorations. They often are symbolic. For example, carp in the paintings of *hyo* symbolize respect for parents because of an old story. The story goes as follows.

Once upon a time, a man lived with his old mother. One winter, the man's mother became ill and couldn't eat anything. On one very cold day, the mother said to the man, "It would be wonderful if I could eat fresh fish."

The man went out to the river, but it was completely frozen. It was impossible for him to catch any fish. ⓐ남자는 몹시 낙담해서 하늘에 대고 외쳤다, "What should I do? Please help me." Then the ice melted, and three carp suddenly came out of the water. The man went back home and cooked the fish for his mother. Then his mother got well.

06 How could the man in the story catch three carp? Fill in the blanks (A) and (B) with suitable words.

> When he cried out to the sky, (A)_____ _____ _____, and three carp suddenly (B)_____ _____ _____ the water.

07 Why did the man go out to the river on one very cold winter day? Answer in English in a full sentence with to infinitive.

➡ _____

_____

08 Why was it impossible for the man to catch any fish? Answer in English in a full sentence beginning with "Because".

➡ _____

09 밑줄 친 ⓐ의 우리말에 맞게 주어진 어휘를 이용하여 12 단어로 영작하시오.

> disappointed, so, cried, the sky

➡ _____

_____

[10~11] 다음 글을 읽고 물음에 답하시오.

There are other examples of symbolic objects in Munjado. They are bamboo in the paintings of the character *chung*(忠) and lotus flowers in the paintings of *ui*(義). Bamboo does not bend. It stays green in all kinds of weather. For these reasons, bamboo came to symbolize loyalty to the king. In the case of lotus flowers, they grow in muddy ponds but still bloom beautifully. They thus became a symbol of a person's will to fight for justice ____ⓐ____ difficulties.

10 위 글의 빈칸 ⓐ에 알맞은 한 단어를 쓰시오.

➡ _____

11 본문의 내용과 일치하도록 다음 빈칸 (A), (B)와 (C)에 알맞은 단어를 쓰시오.

> Lotus flowers symbolize (A)_____ _____ _____ to fight for justice (B)_____ _____. They grow in muddy ponds but still (C)_____ _____.

01 주어진 표현을 이용하여 〈보기〉와 같이 대화를 완성하시오.

┌ 보기 ┐

A: Which bag do you prefer, the one with fish or the one with stars?

B: I prefer the one with stars. It seems to me that it's more my style. How about you?

A: I prefer the one with stars, too.

---

bag / plate / painting / food

the one with fish, the one with stars / the green one, the white one / the one on the left, the one on the right / Tteokbokki, Gimbap

my style / unique / cute / delicious

(1) _____

_____

_____

(2) _____

_____

_____

(3) _____

_____

_____

03 다음 내용을 바탕으로 미술 작품에 대해 감상문을 쓰시오.

1. My Favorite Painting: *Water Lilies: The Clouds*
2. name of the painter: Claude Monet
3. details about the painting: I can see the reflection of clouds in the pond as well as water lilies
4. why I like the painting: the colors are beautiful and the scene looks peaceful

---

My Favorite Painting, (A)_____

My favorite painting is (A)_____. It was painted by (B)_____. In the painting, I can see (C)_____ in the pond as well as (D)_____. I like this painting because (E)_____. I think it was very creative of the painter to draw the pond (F)_____ so that the clouds in the sky are reflected in the pond.

단원별 모의고사

01 다음 짝지어진 단어의 관계가 같도록 빈칸에 알맞은 말을 쓰시오. (주어진 철자로 시작할 것.)

> difficulty – hardship :
> community – s_____

[02~03] 주어진 영어 설명에 알맞은 어휘를 빈칸에 쓰시오. (주어진 철자로 시작할 것.)

02

> Soldiers swore their l_____ to the country.

> <영어 설명> a feeling of support for someone or something

➡ _____

03

> There's a strange o_____ in the sky.

> <영어 설명> a thing that you can see and touch

➡ _____

04 다음 빈칸에 알맞은 말로 짝지어진 것을 고르시오.

> • Notes _____ musical sounds.
> • The snow was beginning to _____.

① express – bloom
② hide – cancel
③ hide – melt
④ represent – cancel
⑤ represent – melt

05 다음 우리말을 주어진 어휘를 이용하여 영작하시오.

(1) 스트레칭을 할 때 무릎을 구부려라. (your knees, stretch, 6 단어)

➡ _____

(2) 그 소년은 나무 뒤에서 갑자기 나타났다. (from, the tree, behind, 8 단어)

➡ _____

(3) 비둘기는 평화를 상징한다. (the dove, represent, 4 단어)

➡ _____

[06~07] 다음 대화를 읽고 물음에 답하시오.

> **John:** There are two movies we can see. (a) Which one do you want to see more, Somi?
> **Somi:** I prefer *Batman*. I saw *Spider-Man* last week. Is this OK, John?
> **John:** Of course. (b)"배트맨"이 훨씬 더 재미있을 것 같아. (that, fun, me, seem, much)
> **Somi:** Good. Then, let's go and see it.

06 위 대화의 밑줄 친 (a)를 prefer를 이용하여 바꿔 쓰시오.

➡ _____

07 위 대화의 밑줄 친 (b)를 괄호 안에 주어진 어휘를 이용하여 영작하시오.

➡ _____
_____

[08~10] 다음 대화를 읽고 물음에 답하시오.

G: There are two exhibitions we can go to. Which one do you want to see more, Eric?

B: I prefer the Korean mask exhibition. Is that OK, Somi?

G: Of course. And it seems to me that the mask exhibition will be much more interesting.

B: Do you think so?

G: Yes. Look at this poster. There isn't just an exhibition. There's also a mask dance show at 4:00 and 6:00.

B: Great! I've never seen a mask dance show before.

G: Well, I've seen a show before. I'm sure you'll like it.

B: So where is the show?

G: It's in Dasom Hall, next to the exhibition room.

B: It's 4:30 now, so let's watch the 6 o'clock show.

G: OK. Let's go see the exhibition first.

08 What will they do right after the conversation?

➡ _____

09 What time will they watch the mask dance show?

➡ _____

10 위 대화의 내용과 일치하지 <u>않는</u> 것은?

① Eric은 한국의 탈 전시회를 더 선호한다.

② 소미는 탈 전시회가 더 흥미로울 것 같다고 말한다.

③ 포스터에는 전시회와 탈춤 공연이 나와 있다.

④ 공연은 전시관 옆 다솜 홀에서 한다.

⑤ Eric과 소미는 4시 30분에 탈춤 공연을 볼 것이다.

[11~12] 다음 중 밑줄 친 부분의 쓰임이 다른 것은?

11 ① <u>It</u> is nice of the police officer to help those kids cross the road.

② <u>It</u> is very important for you and your friends to manage time effectively.

③ <u>It</u> is foolish of the new staff to make the same mistake twice.

④ <u>It</u> is far from here, and the road is always packed with cars.

⑤ <u>It</u>'s very kind of the lady to help my son find his missing kitty.

12 ① <u>If</u> a burglar came into my room, I would throw something at him.

② <u>If</u> he were an actor in the film, we could see him at least once.

③ I'd go out to meet the friends <u>if</u> it stopped raining.

④ Dave has no idea <u>if</u> the rumor about Kelly would turn out true.

⑤ <u>If</u> Yuna practiced harder, she would get a full year scholarship.

13 다음 각 문장을 〈보기〉와 같이 바꿔 쓰시오.

┌─ 보기 ┐

To catch any fish was impossible. (the man)

→ It was impossible for the man to catch any fish.

└────────┘

(1) To move the heavy table alone is not easy. (she)

➡ _____

_____

(2) Taking animals on an airplane is impossible. (he)

➡ _____

_____

(3) Not showing respect for other players is rude. (Angelina)

➡ _____

_____

14 다음 중 〈보기〉의 밑줄 친 would와 쓰임이 같은 것은?

보기

Jacob would accept the job offer from the foreign companies if his wife agreed on their suggestion.

① Would you hold my umbrella a little while, please?

② The villagers said that they would visit the land full of honey and milk.

③ My family would go on a picnic to the lake park when my kids were young.

④ All the participants would like to meet the director of the *Academy* award film.

⑤ I would not buy those useless, expensive bags if I were you.

15 다음 중 내용상 〈보기〉의 밑줄 친 부분과 바꿔 쓸 수 없는 것은?

보기

If it were not for the carp from the lake, he could not help her mother to recover.

① Were it not for the carp from the lake

② Without the carp from the lake

③ If there were no carp from the lake

④ But for the carp from the lake

⑤ Had it not been for the carp from the lake

[16~18] 다음 대화를 읽고 물음에 답하시오.

Look at ⓐthe painting on the right. Do you see the Chinese character, *hyo*(孝)? Do you also see a carp, a geomungo, and a fan? This kind of painting is called Munjado, and it is a type of folk painting that was popular in the late Joseon dynasty. In Munjado, there is usually a Chinese character with some animals or objects.

One of eight Chinese characters appears in Munjado. They are ⓑ*hyo*(孝), *je*(悌), *chung*(忠), *sin*(信), *ye*(禮), *ui*(義), *yeom*(廉), and *chi*(恥), and they represent the values that were important to people of the Joseon dynasty.

16 위 글의 밑줄 친 ⓐ에 해당하는 것을 고르시오.

17 위 글의 밑줄 친 ⓑ에 대한 설명의 빈칸 (A)와 (B)를 알맞은 말로 써 넣으시오.

They are the eight Chinese characters that (A)_____ in Munjado and they represent (B)_____ _____ that were important to people of the Joseon dynasty.

18 When was Munjado popular? Answer in English in a full sentence.

➡ _____

[19~21] 다음 글을 읽고 물음에 답하시오.

The animals or objects in Munjado are not just decorations. They often are symbolic. For example, carp in the paintings of hyo symbolize respect for parents because of an old story. The story goes as follows.

Once upon a time, a man lived with his old mother. One winter, the man's mother became ill and couldn't eat anything. On one very cold day, the mother said to the man, "It would be wonderful if I could eat fresh fish."

The man went out to the river, but it was completely frozen. It was impossible for him to catch any fish. The man was so ⓐ that he cried out to the sky, "What should I do? Please help me." Then the ice melted, and three carp suddenly came out of the water. (A)The man went back home and cooked his mother the fish. Then his mother got well.

19 위 글의 빈칸 ⓐ에 들어갈 알맞은 말을 고르시오.

① excited
② delighted
③ disappointed
④ satisfied
⑤ indifferent

20 What happened after the man cried out to the sky?

➡ _____

_____

21 위 글의 밑줄 친 (A)를 다음과 같이 바꿔 썼을 때 빈칸에 알맞은 말을 쓰시오.

The man went back home and cooked _____ his mother.

[22~23] 다음 글을 읽고 물음에 답하시오.

There are other examples of symbolic objects in Munjado. They are bamboo in the paintings of the character *chung*(忠) and lotus flowers in the paintings of *ui*(義). Bamboo does not bend. It stays green in all kinds of weather. For these reasons, bamboo came to symbolize loyalty to the king. In the case of lotus flowers, they grow in muddy ponds but still bloom beautifully. They thus became a symbol of a person's will to fight against justice despite difficulties.

Munjado was much more than a painting to people of the Joseon dynasty. It reminded them of important values that greatly influenced their behaviors and attitudes. In particular, for children, Munjado was a study tool. Through it, children in the Joseon dynasty could learn the importance of

22 위 글에서 흐름상 어색한 부분을 하나 찾아 바르게 고치시오.

_____ ➡ _____

23 According to the passage, which is NOT true?

① There are some symbolic objects in Munjado.
② Bamboo symbolizes loyalty to the king in Munjado.
③ Lotus flowers in Munjado is a symbol of a person's will to fight for justice despite difficulties.
④ Munjado was just a normal folk painting to people of the Joseon dynasty.
⑤ Children in the Joseon dynasty could learn the importance of harmony in family and society through Munjado.

Reading for Fun 3

Finding the Good in Your Friends

Words & Expressions

Key Words

- **accident** [ǽksidənt] 명 사고
- **air** [ɛər] 명 공중, 허공
- **calm** [kɑ:m] 형 침착한, 차분한
- **cheerful** [tʃíərfəl] 형 발랄한, 쾌활한
- **compliment** [kámpləmənt] 명 칭찬, 찬사 동 칭찬하다
- **confidently** [kánfədəntli] 부 자신 있게
- **creative** [kriéitiv] 형 창의적인, 창조적인
- **fair** [fɛər] 형 공평한, 공정한
- **hesitate** [hézətèit] 동 망설이다, 주저하다
- **hurt** [həːrt] 동 ~을 다치게 하다, 아프다
- **list** [list] 명 목록, 명단

- **messy** [mési] 형 지저분한, 엉망인
- **pause** [pɔːz] 명 (일시적인) 중단
- **pick** [pik] 동 뽑다, 따다, 뜯다
- **point** [pɔint] 동 가리키다
- **scratch** [skrætʃ] 동 긁다
- **scream** [skri:m] 동 비명을 지르다
- **shyly** [ʃáili] 부 수줍게, 부끄러워하며
- **still** [stil] 형 가만히 있는, 고요한
- **stuck** [stʌk] 형 (~에 빠져) 움직일 수 없는
- **worried** [wə́:rid] 형 난처한, 딱한, 걱정[근심]스러운
- **work** [wə:rk] 동 효과가 있다

Key Expressions

- **a piece of** 하나의 ~, 한 조각의 ~
- **all day long** 하루 종일
- **bicycle stand** 자전거 거치대
- **come out of** ~에서 나오다
- **except for** ~을 제외하고

- **Just a minute.** 잠깐만.
- **pull out** 빠져나가다[나오다]
- **the other day** 일전에, 최근에
- **What made you ~?** 무엇 때문에 ~했니?
  = **Why did you ~?**

Word Power

※ 명사+y: 형용사

- **messy** 지저분한, 엉망인
- **stormy** 폭풍우의
- **foggy** 안개가 낀
- **milky** 유백색의, 젖의
- **sleepy** 졸린
- **dreamy** 꿈같은

- **cloudy** 구름이 낀
- **windy** 바람이 부는
- **salty** 짠, 소금기가 있는
- **fatty** 지방이 많은
- **dusty** 먼지투성이의
- **greedy** 욕심 많은

- **rainy** 비오는, 비가 많이 내리는
- **sunny** 햇빛이 잘 드는
- **oily** 기름의, 지성(脂性)의
- **spicy** 양념 맛이 강한, 매운
- **speedy** 빠른
- **thrifty** 검소한

※ 서로 비슷한 뜻을 가진 어휘

- **calm** 침착한, 차분한 : **cool** 냉정한, 침착한
- **fair** 공평한, 공정한 : **just** 올바른, 공정한
- **point** 가리키다 : **indicate** 가리키다

- **compliment** 칭찬 : **praise** 칭찬, 찬양
- **hurt** 다치게 하다 : **injure** 다치게 하다
- **messy** 지저분한, 엉망인 : **dirty** 더러운

※ 서로 반대의 뜻을 가진 어휘

- **compliment** 칭찬, 찬사 ↔ **criticism** 비평, 비판
- **hurt** 다치게 하다 ↔ **heal** 고치다, 낫게 하다

- **fair** 공평한, 공정한 ↔ **unfair** 불공평한
- **messy** 지저분한, 엉망인 ↔ **tidy** 단정한

English Dictionary

- **accident** 사고
  → an unfortunate mishap; especially one causing damage or injury
  불운한 일; 특히 손상이나 부상을 일으키는 것

- **compliment** 칭찬, 찬사
  → a polite remark that you say to someone to show that you like their appearance, appreciate their qualities, or approve of what they have done
  누군가에게 당신이 그의 외모를 좋아한다거나 그의 자질을 인정한다거나 그가 한 것을 지지한다는 것을 보여주기 위해 하는 공손한 언급

- **hesitate** 망설이다, 주저하다
  → to pause or hold back in uncertainty or unwillingness
  불확실하거나 내키지 않아서 잠시 멈추거나 억제하다

- **pause** 중단
  → a short period when you stop doing something before continuing
  계속하기 전에 하던 것을 멈추는 잠깐의 기간

- **point** 가리키다
  → to hold out your finger towards a person or thing in order to make someone notice them
  누군가가 그것을 알아채도록 하기 위해 손가락을 사람이나 물건을 향해 내밀다

- **scratch** 긁다
  → to rub your fingernails against your skin because it is itching
  가려워서 손톱을 피부에 대고 문지르다

- **scream** 비명을 지르다
  → to make a very loud, high-pitched cry
  매우 크고 높은 음조로 소리치다

- **work** 효과가 있다
  → to be successful, effective, or satisfactory
  성공적이거나 효과가 있거나 만족할 만 하다

- **list** 목록, 명단
  → a set of names or addresses which all belong to a particular category, written down one below the other
  모두 어떤 특정 범주에 속하는, 하나 밑에 다른 하나가 쓰여 있는 이름이나 주소의 모음

Reading

The Best Compliment Ever

Scene 1

It is the last week of school. Each student has just picked a piece of paper with a name on it.

It: 특별한 의미 없이 쓰인 비인칭 주어   paper: 셀 수 없는 명사. 단위를 나타내는 a piece of를 써서 수를 나타낸다.

Ms. Kemp: "Compliments for Classmates" will be our last activity of the school year. Did everyone pick a name?

Class: Yes, Ms. Kemp.

Students are talking to each other.

Beth: So, whose name did you pick?

Lucy: (*smiling*) I got Boyd. I have a lot to say about him. What about you, Beth?

to부정사의 형용사적 용법

Beth: (*looking worried*) Uh, I picked Peter's name.

Lucy: Peter? Oh, no! It won't be easy to find something to compliment him on.

가주어   진주어   compliment+목적어+on ~: ~에 대해 칭찬하다.
to compliment: to부정사의 형용사적 용법

Steve: Yeah. He doesn't talk much and just sits at his desk all day long.

Beth: (*scratching her head*) Well, I'll have to find something.

Scene 2

Beth is at home talking with her parents about the activity.

Beth: Everyone has long lists of compliments for other classmates, except for me. I don't know what to compliment Peter on.

everyone: 단수로 취급, 동사: has
~을 제외하고   = what I should compliment

Mom: Think carefully. There should be something.

Beth: Well, he's clean. He washes his face every day.

Mom: That's not a compliment. Everybody does that.

= He washes his face every day   everybody: 단수로 취급, 동사: does

Dad: Try again. I'm sure you can find something good to say about him.

I'm sure 다음에 명사절을   something과 같이 -thing으로   to부정사의 형용사적 용법
이끄는 접속사 that이 생략   끝나는 대명사는 형용사가 뒤에서 수식

Scene 3

The next day, there is an accident at school. Boyd's foot is stuck in a bicycle stand.

Boyd: (*with arms in the air*) Help! I need help!

Beth: Stay still. I'm trying to pull your foot out.

Boyd: (*screaming*) Ouch! That hurts!

Peter: Let me help. Just a minute.

 확인문제

● 다음 문장이 본문의 내용과 일치하면 T, 일치하지 <u>않으면</u> F를 쓰시오.

1   Lucy had a lot to say about Boyd. ☐

2   Dad wasn't sure Beth could find anything good to say about Peter. ☐

---

compliment 칭찬, 찬사; 칭찬하다

all day long 하루 종일

scratch 긁다

list 목록, 명단

except for ~을 제외하고

accident 사고

stuck (~에 빠져) 움직일 수 없는

air 공중, 허공

still 가만히 있는, 고요한

scream 비명을 지르다

Peter runs to the school's kitchen and comes back with butter.

Peter: I'm going to put this butter on your foot.

Boyd: What? Butter?

Peter: Just stay calm.

Beth: (*pointing to Boyd's foot*) Wow! It's working! Boyd's foot is coming out of the stand.

Scene 4

Beth is eating dinner with her parents. She tells them about what happened to Boyd.

Beth: There was a little accident at school today. Boyd's foot got stuck in a bicycle stand.

Mom: Oh, no! So how did he get his foot out?

Beth: Peter put butter on his foot and then pulled it out.

Dad: That was really creative. Messy but creative.

Beth: Hmm. Creative? Can that be a compliment, Dad?

Dad: Sure.

Scene 5

It is the last day of school, and the students are complimenting each other.

Ms. Kemp: Joanne, what compliment do you have for Beth?

Joanne: Beth, you're always cheerful. You're also kind and fair to everybody.

Beth: Thanks, Joanne. It's so nice of you to say so.

Ms. Kemp: Beth, let's hear from you now. You picked Peter's name.

Beth: (*hesitating*) Well, I think Peter is creative. Peter, you're … uh … creative.

Peter: (*shyly*) Really?

Ms. Kemp: What made you think Peter is creative?

Beth: (*after a long pause*) When Boyd's foot got stuck in the bicycle stand the other day, Peter got it out by using butter. That was creative.

Boyd: Yeah! Nobody else thought of doing that.

Steve: I didn't know that. Well, then, I also think he's creative.

Beth: (*confidently*) Yeah, Peter, you ARE creative!

Peter: Thanks, Beth! It's the best compliment ever!

calm 침착한, 차분한
point 가리키다
messy 지저분한, 엉망인
creative 창의적인, 창조적인
cheerful 발랄한, 쾌활한
fair 공평한, 공정한
hesitate 망설이다, 주저하다
shyly 수줍게, 부끄러워하며
pause (일시적인) 중단
the other day 일전에, 최근에
confidently 자신 있게

확인문제

다음 문장이 본문의 내용과 일치하면 T, 일치하지 <u>않으면</u> F를 쓰시오.

1 Peter put butter on Boyd's foot and then pulled it out. ☐

2 Steve thought Beth was creative. ☐

● 우리말을 참고하여 빈칸에 알맞은 말을 쓰시오.

1 The Best _____ Ever

2 Scene 1

3 *It is the _____ week of school.*

4 *Each student has just picked _____ _____ _____ _____ with a name on it.*

5 Ms. Kemp: "_____ _____ Classmates" will be our _____ _____ of the school year.

6 Did everyone _____ a name?

7 Class: Yes, Ms. Kemp.

8 *Students are talking to _____ _____.*

9 Beth: So, _____ _____ did you pick?

10 Lucy: (*smiling*) I _____ Boyd.

11 I have a lot _____ _____ about him.

12 _____ _____ you, Beth?

13 Beth: (_____ _____) Uh, I picked Peter's name.

14 Lucy: Peter? Oh, no! It won't be easy to find something to _____ _____ _____.

15 Steve: Yeah. He doesn't talk much and just _____ _____ _____ _____ all day long.

16 Beth: (*scratching her head*) Well, I'll _____ something.

17 Scene 2

18 *Beth is at home _____ _____ her parents about the activity.*

19 Beth: Everyone has long lists of compliments for other classmates, _____ _____ me.

20 I don't know _____ _____ _____ Peter on.

21 Mom: Think _____.

1 최고의 칭찬

2 〈장면 1〉

3 이번 주는 학교의 마지막 주이다.

4 각 학생들은 이름 하나가 쓰인 종이 한 장씩을 막 뽑았다.

5 Ms. Kemp: '학급 친구들 칭찬하기'는 이번 학년 우리의 마지막 활동이 될 거예요.

6 모두 이름을 뽑았나요?

7 Class: 네, Kemp 선생님.

8 학생들이 서로 이야기를 나누고 있다.

9 Beth: 너는 누구 이름을 뽑았니?

10 Lucy: (웃으며) Boyd를 뽑았어.

11 그 애에 관해 할 말이 많아.

12 너는 어때, Beth?

13 Beth: (걱정스러운 표정으로) 어, Peter 이름을 뽑았어.

14 Lucy: Peter? 아, 이런! 그 애에 관해서 칭찬할 것을 찾는 게 쉽지 않을 거야.

15 Steve: 그래. 그 애는 말을 많이 하지 않고 하루 종일 그냥 책상에 앉아만 있잖아.

16 Beth: (머리를 긁적이며) 음, 무언가를 찾아야 해.

17 〈장면 2〉

18 Beth는 집에서 그 활동에 대해 자신의 부모님과 이야기를 나누고 있다.

19 Beth: 저를 제외한 모두가 다른 친구들에 대해 긴 칭찬 목록을 가지고 있어요.

20 저는 Peter에 관해 무엇을 칭찬해야 할지 모르겠어요.

21 엄마: 잘 생각해 봐.

22 There _____ _____ something.

23 Beth: Well, _____ clean.

24 He _____ his face every day.

25 Mom: That's not _____ _____.

26 Everybody _____ _____.

27 Dad: Try _____.

28 _____ _____ you can find something good to say about him.

29 Scene 3

30 *The next day, there is _____ _____ at school.*

31 *Boyd's foot _____ _____ in a bicycle stand.*

32 Boyd: (_____ _____ _____ _____ _____) Help! I need help!

33 Beth: _____ _____. I'm trying to pull your foot out.

34 Boyd: (*screaming*) Ouch! That _____!

35 Peter: _____ me help. Just a minute.

36 *Peter runs to the school's kitchen and _____ _____ with butter.*

37 Peter: I'm going to _____ this butter _____ your foot.

38 Boyd: What? Butter?

39 Peter: Just stay _____.

40 Beth: (*pointing to Boyd's foot*) Wow! It's _____!

41 Boyd's foot is _____ _____ _____ the stand.

42 Scene 4

43 *Beth is _____ _____ with her parents.*

44 *She tells them about _____ _____ to Boyd.*

45 Beth: There was _____ _____ _____ at school today.

46 Boyd's foot _____ _____ _____ a bicycle stand.

47 Mom: Oh, no! So how did he _____ his foot _____?

22 뭔가 있을 거야.

23 Beth: 음, 그 애는 깔끔해요.

24 매일 세수를 해요.

25 엄마: 그건 칭찬이 아니야.

26 모든 사람들이 하는 거잖니.

27 아빠: 다시 생각해 보렴.

28 그 아이에 대해 말할 뭔가 좋은 것을 분명히 찾을 수 있을 거야.

29 〈장면 3〉

30 다음 날, 학교에서 사고가 생긴다.

31 Boyd의 발이 자전거 거치대에 끼었다.

32 Boyd: (공중에 양팔을 벌린 채) 도와줘! 도움이 필요해!

33 Beth: 가만히 있어. 네 발을 꺼내려고 노력 중이야.

34 Boyd: (비명을 지르며) 아! 아파!

35 Peter: 내가 도와줄게. 잠깐만.

36 Peter가 학교 주방으로 뛰어가 버터를 가지고 온다.

37 Peter: 네 발에 이 버터를 바를 거야.

38 Boyd: 뭐? 버터를?

39 Peter: 그냥 침착하게 있어.

40 Beth: (Boyd의 발을 가리키며) 와! 효과가 있어!

41 Boyd의 발이 거치대에서 빠져 나오고 있어.

42 〈장면 4〉

43 Beth는 부모님과 저녁 식사를 하고 있다.

44 그녀는 부모님께 Boyd에게 일어난 일에 대해 이야기한다.

45 Beth: 오늘 학교에서 작은 사고가 있었어요.

46 Boyd의 발이 자전거 거치대에 끼었어요.

47 엄마: 오, 저런! 그래서 발을 어떻게 뺐니?

48 Beth: Peter put butter on his foot and then _____ _____
_____.

49 Dad: That was really creative. _____ but _____.

50 Beth: Hmm. Creative? Can that be _____ _____, Dad?

51 Dad: _____.

52 Scene 5

53 *It is the last day of school, and the students are* _____ _____
_____.

54 Ms. Kemp: Joanne, _____ _____ do you have for Beth?

55 Joanne: Beth, you're always _____.

56 You're also kind and _____ to everybody.

57 Beth: Thanks, Joanne. It's so nice _____ _____ to say so.

58 Ms. Kemp: Beth, let's _____ _____ _____ now.

59 You _____ Peter's name.

60 Beth: (_____) Well, I think Peter is creative. Peter, you're … uh
… creative.

61 Peter: (_____) Really?

62 Ms. Kemp: _____ _____ _____ _____ Peter is
creative?

63 Beth: (*after a long* _____) When Boyd's foot got stuck in
the bicycle stand _____ _____ _____, Peter got it out
_____ _____ butter.

64 That was _____.

65 Boyd: Yeah! _____ _____ thought of doing that.

66 Steve: I didn't know that. Well, then, I _____ think he's
creative.

67 Beth: (_____) Yeah, Peter, you ARE creative!

68 Peter: Thanks, Beth! It's _____ _____ _____ _____!

---

48 Beth: Peter가 그 애 발에 버터를 바르고 나서 발을 당겨서 꺼냈어요.

49 아빠: 정말 창의적이구나. 지저분하지만 창의적이야.

50 Beth: 흠. 창의적이라고요? 아빠, 그것이 칭찬이 될 수 있어요?

51 아빠: 물론이지.

52 〈장면 5〉

53 오늘은 학교의 마지막 날이고 학생들은 서로를 칭찬하고 있다.

54 Ms. Kemp: Joanne, Beth에게 무슨 칭찬을 해 주겠니?

55 Joanne: Beth, 너는 항상 쾌활해.

56 또한 친절하고 모두에게 공정해.

57 Beth: 고마워, Joanne. 그렇게 말해 주다니 친절하구나.

58 Ms. Kemp: Beth, 이제 네 말을 들어 보자.

59 Peter의 이름을 뽑았구나.

60 Beth: (주저하며) 음, Peter는 창의적이라고 생각해요. Peter, 너는… 어… 창의적이야.

61 Peter: (수줍어하며) 정말?

62 Ms. Kemp: Peter가 왜 창의적이라고 생각하니?

63 Beth: (한참 있다가) 일전에 Boyd의 발이 자전거 거치대에 끼었을 때, Peter는 버터를 사용해서 그의 발을 꺼냈어요.

64 그것은 창의적이었어요.

65 Boyd: 맞아! 어느 누구도 그렇게 하는 것을 생각하지 못했어.

66 Steve: 난 몰랐어. 음, 그래, 나도 그가 창의적이라고 생각해.

67 Beth: (자신 있게) 그래, Peter, 너는 창의적이야!

68 Peter: 고마워, Beth! 그건 최고의 칭찬이야!

● 우리말을 참고하여 본문을 영작하시오.

1 최고의 칭찬
➡ _____

2 〈장면 1〉
➡ _____

3 이번 주는 학교의 마지막 주이다.
➡ _____

4 각 학생들은 이름 하나가 쓰인 종이 한 장씩을 막 뽑았다.
➡ _____

5 Ms. Kemp: '학급 친구들 칭찬하기'는 이번 학년 우리의 마지막 활동이 될 거예요.
➡ _____

6 모두 이름을 뽑았나요?
➡ _____

7 Class: 네, Kemp 선생님.
➡ _____

8 학생들이 서로 이야기를 나누고 있다.
➡ _____

9 Beth: 너는 누구 이름을 뽑았니?
➡ _____

10 Lucy: (웃으며) Boyd를 뽑았어.
➡ _____

11 그 애에 관해 할 말이 많아.
➡ _____

12 너는 어때, Beth?
➡ _____

13 Beth: (걱정스러운 표정으로) 어, Peter 이름을 뽑았어.
➡ _____

14 Lucy: Peter? 아, 이런! 그 애에 관해서 칭찬할 것을 찾는 게 쉽지 않을 거야.
➡ _____

15 Steve: 그래. 그 애는 말을 많이 하지 않고 하루 종일 그냥 책상에 앉아만 있잖아.
➡ _____

16 Beth: (머리를 긁적이며) 음, 무언가를 찾아야 해.
➡ _____

17 〈장면 2〉
➡ _____

18 Beth는 집에서 그 활동에 대해 자신의 부모님과 이야기를 나누고 있다.
➡ _____

19 Beth: 저를 제외한 모두가 다른 친구들에 대해 긴 칭찬 목록을 가지고 있어요.
➡ _____

20 저는 Peter에 관해 무엇을 칭찬해야 할지 모르겠어요.
➡ _____

21 엄마: 잘 생각해 봐.
➡ _____

22 뭔가 있을 거야.
➡ _____

23 Beth: 음, 그 애는 깔끔해요.
➡ _____

24 매일 세수를 해요.
➡ _____

25 엄마: 그건 칭찬이 아니야.
➡ _____

26 모든 사람들이 하는 거잖니.
➡ _____

27 아빠: 다시 생각해 보렴.
➡ _____

28 그 아이에 대해 말할 뭔가 좋은 것을 분명히 찾을 수 있을 거야.
➡ _____

29 〈장면 3〉
➡ _____

30 다음 날, 학교에서 사고가 생긴다.
➡ _____

31 Boyd의 발이 자전거 거치대에 끼었다.
➡ _____

32 Boyd: (공중에 양팔을 벌린 채) 도와줘! 도움이 필요해!
➡ _____

33 Beth: 가만히 있어. 네 발을 꺼내려고 노력 중이야.
➡ _____

34 Boyd: (비명을 지르며) 아! 아파!
➡ _____

35 Peter: 내가 도와줄게. 잠깐만.
➡ _____

36 Peter가 학교 주방으로 뛰어가 버터를 가지고 온다.
➡ _____

37 Peter: 네 발에 이 버터를 바를 거야.
➡ _____

38 Boyd: 뭐? 버터를?
➡ _____

39 Peter: 그냥 침착하게 있어.
➡ _____

40 Beth: (Boyd의 발을 가리키며) 와! 효과가 있어!
➡ _____

41 Boyd의 발이 거치대에서 빠져나오고 있어.
➡ _____

42 〈장면 4〉
➡ _____

43 Beth는 부모님과 저녁 식사를 하고 있다.
➡ _____

44 그녀는 부모님께 Boyd에게 일어난 일에 대해 이야기한다.
➡ _____

45 Beth: 오늘 학교에서 작은 사고가 있었어요.
➡ _____

46 Boyd의 발이 자전거 거치대에 끼었어요.

➡ _____

47 엄마: 오, 저런! 그래서 발을 어떻게 뺐니?

➡ _____

48 Beth: Peter가 그 애 발에 버터를 바르고 나서 발을 당겨서 꺼냈어요.

➡ _____

49 아빠: 정말 창의적이구나. 지저분하지만 창의적이야.

➡ _____

50 Beth: 흠. 창의적이라고요? 아빠, 그것이 칭찬이 될 수 있어요?

➡ _____

51 아빠: 물론이지.

➡ _____

52 〈장면 5〉

➡ _____

53 오늘은 학교의 마지막 날이고 학생들은 서로를 칭찬하고 있다.

➡ _____

54 Ms. Kemp: Joanne, Beth에게 무슨 칭찬을 해 주겠니?

➡ _____

55 Joanne: Beth, 너는 항상 쾌활해.

➡ _____

56 또한 친절하고 모두에게 공정해.

➡ _____

57 Beth: 고마워, Joanne. 그렇게 말해 주다니 친절하구나.

➡ _____

58 Ms. Kemp: Beth, 이제 네 말을 들어 보자.

➡ _____

59 Peter의 이름을 뽑았구나.

➡ _____

60 Beth: (주저하며) 음, Peter는 창의적이라고 생각해요. Peter, 너는… 어… 창의적이야.

➡ _____

61 Peter: (수줍어하며) 정말?

➡ _____

62 Ms. Kemp: Peter가 왜 창의적이라고 생각하니?

➡ _____

63 Beth: (한참 있다가) 일전에 Boyd의 발이 자전거 거치대에 끼었을 때, Peter는 버터를 사용해서 그의 발을 꺼냈어요.

➡ _____

64 그것은 창의적이었어요.

➡ _____

65 Boyd: 맞아! 어느 누구도 그렇게 하는 것을 생각하지 못했어.

➡ _____

66 Steve: 난 몰랐어. 음, 그래, 나도 그가 창의적이라고 생각해.

➡ _____

67 Beth: (자신 있게) 그래, Peter, 너는 창의적이야!

➡ _____

68 Peter: 고마워, Beth! 그건 최고의 칭찬이야!

➡ _____

[01~02] 다음 빈칸에 공통으로 들어갈 말을 쓰시오.

01
> • Come _____ of there, whoever you are.
>
> • The project became so expensive that we had to pull _____.

02
> • A car _____ happened last night.
>
> • We met by _____ at the airport.

03 다음 빈칸에 알맞은 단어를 〈보기〉에서 골라 쓰시오.

> ┌─── 보기 ───┐
> confidently   air   scratch   hesitate

(1) Smoke hung in the _____ above the city.

(2) He _____ said that he would take all the responsibility.

(3) I didn't _____ for a moment about taking the job.

(4) Dad saw you _____ the car.

04 다음 짝지어진 단어의 관계가 같도록 빈칸에 알맞은 말을 쓰시오.

(1) deep – shallow : criticism – _____

(2) appear – disappear : heal – _____

(3) long – lengthy : cool – _____

05 영영풀이를 보고 빈칸에 알맞은 단어를 주어진 철자로 시작하여 쓰시오.

> to be successful, effective, or satisfactory

> That medicine didn't w_____ at all.

06 다음 괄호 안의 단어를 알맞은 형으로 바꿔 빈칸에 쓰시오.

> 그 아이는 밥을 지저분하게 먹어서 자주 꾸지람을 듣는다.
> ➡ The boy is often scolded for his _____ way of eating. (mess)

07 다음 주어진 어휘를 알맞게 배열하여 우리말에 맞게 빈칸을 채우시오. (단어의 형태는 어법에 맞게 변화 가능함.)

(1) 당신이 누구의 이름을 뽑았는지 궁금하다.
(pick, name, wonder, whose, you)
➡ I _____.

(2) 나는 David에 대해 무엇을 칭찬해야 할지 모르겠다. (David, on, to, compliment, what)
➡ I don't know _____
_____.

(3) 너는 왜 Sarah가 창의적이라고 생각하게 되었니? (think, make, what, that, you)
➡ _____ Sarah is creative?

(4) 그녀는 부모님께 오늘 Tom에게 무슨 일이 일어났는지에 대해 말한다. (happen, about, what, to, Tom)
➡ She tells her parents _____
_____ today.

08 다음 문장에서 어법상 어색한 부분을 찾아 바르게 고치시오.

> It is so thoughtful for Beth to give Peter such a nice compliment.

_____ ➡ _____

[09~11] 다음 글을 읽고 물음에 답하시오.

It is the (A)[last / latest] week of school. Each student has just picked a piece of paper with a name on ⓐit.

Ms. Kemp: "(B)[Complements / Compliments] for Classmates" will be our last activity of the school year. Did everyone pick a name?

Class: Yes, Ms. Kemp.

Students are talking to each other.

Beth: So, whose name did you pick?

Lucy: (*smiling*) I got Boyd. I have a lot to say about him. What about you, Beth?

Beth: ((C)[*looking / looked*] *worried*) Uh, I picked Peter's name.

Lucy: Peter? Oh, no! It won't be easy to find something to compliment him on.

Steve: Yeah. He doesn't talk much and just sits at his desk all day long.

Beth: (*scratching her head*) Well, I'll have to find something.

09 위 글의 괄호 (A)~(C)에서 문맥이나 어법상 알맞은 낱말을 골라 쓰시오.

➡ (A) _____ (B) _____ (C) _____

10 위 글의 밑줄 친 ⓐ*it*이 가리키는 것을 본문에서 찾아 쓰시오.

➡ _____

11 Whose name did Lucy pick? Answer in English in a full sentence. (4 words)

➡ _____

[12~14] 다음 글을 읽고 물음에 답하시오.

The next day, there is an accident at school. Boyd's foot is ___ⓐ___ in a bicycle stand.

Boyd: (*with arms in the air*) Help! I need help!

Beth: Stay still. I'm trying to pull your foot out.

Boyd: (*screaming*) Ouch! That hurts!

Peter: Let me help. Just a minute.

Peter runs to the school's kitchen and comes back with butter.

Peter: I'm going to put this butter on your foot.

Boyd: What? Butter?

Peter: ⓑJust stay calmly.

Beth: (*pointing to Boyd's foot*) Wow! It's working! Boyd's foot is coming out of the stand.

12 위 글의 빈칸 ⓐ에 stick을 알맞은 형태로 쓰시오.

➡ _____

13 위 글의 밑줄 친 ⓑ에서 어법상 틀린 부분을 찾아 고치시오.

_____ ➡ _____

14 본문의 내용과 일치하도록 다음 빈칸 (A)와 (B)에 알맞은 단어를 쓰시오. (각각 한 단어로 쓰시오.)

> When Boyd's foot became unable to move further in a bicycle stand, Peter put (A)_____ on Boyd's foot. It (B)_____ and Boyd's foot came out of the stand.

01 출제율 90%

다음 빈칸에 알맞은 단어를 〈보기〉에서 골라 쓰시오.

┌─── 보기 ───┐
creative   stuck   compliment   work
└────────────┘

(1) We were _____ in a traffic jam.
(2) Let your imagination run wild and be _____.
(3) She took what he said as a _____.
(4) My plan _____ed, and I got them to agree.

02 출제율 95%

다음 단어의 영영풀이가 잘못된 것을 고르시오.

① accident: an unfortunate mishap; especially one causing damage or injury
② pull: to hold out your finger towards a person or thing in order to make someone notice them
③ compliment: a polite remark that you say to someone to show that you like their appearance, appreciate their qualities, or approve of what they have done
④ scream: to make a very loud, high-pitched cry
⑤ hesitate: to pause or hold back in uncertainty or unwillingness

03 출제율 95%

밑줄 친 부분과 바꿔 쓸 수 있는 말을 고르시오.

┌──────────────────────────────┐
That's maybe the best <u>compliment</u> of my life.
└──────────────────────────────┘

① indication   ② creation
③ thrift   ④ pause
⑤ praise

04 출제율 100%

빈칸에 들어갈 접미사가 나머지와 다른 하나를 고르시오.

① The sky looks storm____.
② I can't find anything on this mess____ desk.
③ The hotel staff are friend____ and attentive.
④ The greed____ man asked too much for the bag.
⑤ They have plenty of money now, but they still tend to be thrift____.

05 출제율 95%

다음 우리말에 맞도록 빈칸에 알맞은 말을 쓰시오. (철자가 주어진 것도 있음.)

(1) 약간의 실수를 제외하면 그것은 좋다.
➡ It is good _____ _____ a few mistakes.
(2) 나는 강물을 바라보며 하루 종일이라도 앉아 있을 수 있을 것 같아.
➡ I could sit and watch the river _____ _____ _____.
(3) 아이는 수줍게 웃었다.
➡ The child smiled _____.

06 빈칸 (A)와 (B)에 들어갈 말로 알맞은 것끼리 짝지어진 것을 고르시오.

- Our team was unable to _____(A)_____ out of slump during the first half of the game.
- You have to _____(B)_____ calm and patient.

	(A)	(B)
①	push	stay
②	push	keep
③	pull	take
④	pull	stay
⑤	pull	let

07 다음 중 〈보기〉의 밑줄 친 to부정사와 쓰임이 같지 <u>않은</u> 것은?

┌─ 보기 ┤

Mary has a lot <u>to say</u> about her boyfriend.

① Beth needs a piece of paper <u>to write</u> a letter on.
② Jake had no friends <u>to support</u> him.
③ Please bring the injured soldier some beverage <u>to drink</u>.
④ This is a great chance for you <u>to try</u> many kinds of chocolate in one place.
⑤ Clara was impressed <u>to see</u> Peter pull his foot out of the bicycle stand.

08 우리말에 맞게 주어진 어구를 알맞게 배열하시오.

(1) 버스는 나무를 들이박고, 모든 사람들이 비명을 지르며 도망간다. (the people, a tree, the bus, all, bumps, run away, scream, and, and)

➡ _____

_____

(2) 당신이 수의사를 직업으로 삼을 결심을 하게 된 계기는 무엇이었습니까? (a career, a vet, you, what, decide, made, as, on)

➡ _____

_____

(3) 일전에 그 문제에 대해서는 정말 미안해요. (I'm, day, the, that problem, awfully, other, sorry, about)

➡ _____

_____

09 다음 그림을 보고, 우리말에 맞게 괄호 안의 단어를 활용하고 필요한 단어를 추가하여 빈칸을 채우시오.

그녀에 대해 칭찬할 점을 찾기가 쉽지 않을 것이다.
→ It _____.
(compliment, something, find, her, easy, will, to, on, It을 포함하여 총 12 단어, 어형 변화 및 축약형 불가)

➡ _____

_____

10 다음 주어진 〈보기〉와 같이 빈칸에 알맞은 단어를 넣어 같은 의미의 문장을 완성하시오.

┌─ 보기 ┤

I don't know what to do next.
→ I don't know <u>what I should do</u> next.

(1) We're sure you will learn how to find something good about others.

➡ We're sure you will learn _____ _____.

(2) Jacob wondered what to put on his foot to pull it out of the bicycle stand.

➡ Jacob wondered _____ _____.

(3) Kate showed me how to open the safe.

➡ Kate showed me _____ _____.

11 다음 주어진 문장과 의미가 같은 문장을 고르시오. (출제율 95%)

> What makes you think the girl is brave?

① Do you think why the girl is brave?
② How you think is the girl brave?
③ How do you think is the girl brave?
④ Do you think why is the girl brave?
⑤ Why do you think the girl is brave?

12 다음 주어진 우리말에 맞게 괄호 안의 단어만을 사용하여, When을 포함한 총 15단어로 영작하시오. (어법에 맞게 단어의 형태 변화 가능, 단어 중복 사용 가능) (출제율 90%)

> 그녀의 손가락이 병에 끼었을 때, Brian이 버터를 사용해서 빼냈다.
> (Brian, get, use, stick, in, out, butter, it, finger, she, the bottle, by)

➡ When _____ _____.

[13~16] 다음 글을 읽고 물음에 답하시오.

> *Beth is at home talking with her parents about the activity.*
>
> Beth: ⓐEveryone has long lists of compliments for other classmates, including me. I don't know ⓑwhat to compliment Peter on.
> Mom: Think carefully. There should be something.
> Beth: Well, he's clean. He washes his face every day.
> Mom: That's not a compliment. Everybody ⓒdoes that.
> Dad: Try again. I'm sure you can find something good to say about him.

13 위 글의 밑줄 친 ⓐ에서 흐름상 어색한 부분을 찾아 고치시오. (출제율 95%)

_____ ➡ _____

14 위 글의 밑줄 친 ⓑ를 다음과 같이 바꿔 쓸 때 빈칸에 들어갈 알맞은 말을 두 단어로 쓰시오. (출제율 90%)

➡ what _____ _____ compliment

15 위 글의 밑줄 친 ⓒdoes that이 구체적으로 가리키는 것을 우리말로 쓰시오. (출제율 90%)

➡ _____

출제율 100%

16 According to the passage, which is NOT true?

① Beth didn't know what to compliment Peter on.

② Beth's mom advised her to think carefully.

③ Beth said Peter was clean.

④ Beth's mom said that it was a good compliment to say Peter washes his face every day.

⑤ Beth's dad was sure she could find something good to say about Peter.

[17~19] 다음 글을 읽고 물음에 답하시오.

The next day, there is an accident at school. Boyd's foot is stuck in a bicycle stand.

Boyd: (*with arms in the air*) Help! I need help!

Beth: Stay ⓐstill. I'm trying to pull your foot out.

Boyd: (*screaming*) Ouch! That hurts!

Peter: Let me help. Just a minute.

Peter runs to the school's kitchen and comes back with butter.

Peter: I'm going to put this butter on your foot.

Boyd: What? Butter?

Peter: Just stay calm.

Beth: (*pointing to Boyd's foot*) Wow! ⓑIt's working! Boyd's foot is coming out of the stand.

출제율 90%

17 위 글의 밑줄 친 ⓐstill과 같은 의미로 쓰인 것을 고르시오.

① I wrote to him last month and I'm still waiting for a reply.

② The next day was still warmer.

③ Still waters run deep.

④ We searched everywhere but we still couldn't find it.

⑤ Do you still live at the same address?

출제율 95%

18 위 글의 밑줄 친 ⓑIt이 가리키는 것을 영어로 쓰시오.

➡ _____

출제율 100%

19 Which question CANNOT be answered after reading the passage?

① The next day, what accident was there at school?

② Where was Boyd's foot stuck?

③ Who put butter on Boyd's foot?

④ How did Boyd's foot come out of the stand?

⑤ How did Boyd feel about Peter?

[20~22] 다음 글을 읽고 물음에 답하시오.

Beth is eating dinner with her parents. She tells them about what happened to Boyd.

Beth: There was a little accident at school today. (①)

Mom: Oh, no! (②) So how did he get his foot out? (③)

Beth: ⓐPeter put butter on his foot and then pulled out it. (④)

Dad: ⓑThat was really creative. (⑤) Messy but creative.

Beth: Hmm. Creative? Can that be a compliment, Dad?

Dad: Sure.

출제율 95%

20 위 글의 흐름으로 보아, 주어진 문장이 들어가기에 가장 적절한 곳은?

Boyd's foot got stuck in a bicycle stand.

①   ②   ③   ④   ⑤

21 위 글의 밑줄 친 ⓐ에서 어법상 틀린 부분을 찾아 고치시오.

ㅤ_____ ➡ _____

22 위 글의 밑줄 친 ⓑThat이 가리키는 것을 본문에서 찾아 쓰시오.

➡ _____

_____

23 위 글의 밑줄 친 ⓐ의 우리말에 맞게 so와 nice를 넣어 8 단어로 영작하시오.

➡ _____

24 위 글의 밑줄 친 ⓑ를 다음과 같이 바꿔 쓸 때 빈칸에 들어갈 알맞은 한 단어를 쓰시오.

➡ _____ did you think Peter is creative?

[23~25] 다음 글을 읽고 물음에 답하시오.

It is the last day of school, and the students are complimenting each other.

Ms. Kemp: Joanne, what compliment do you have for Beth?

Joanne: Beth, you're always cheerful. You're also kind and fair to everybody.

Beth: Thanks, Joanne. ⓐ그렇게 말해 주다니 친절하구나.

Ms. Kemp: Beth, let's hear from you now. You picked Peter's name.

Beth: (*hesitating*) Well, I think Peter is creative. Peter, you're … uh … creative.

Peter: (*shyly*) Really?

Ms. Kemp: ⓑWhat made you think Peter is creative?

Beth: (*after a long pause*) When Boyd's foot got stuck in the bicycle stand the other day, Peter got it out by using butter. That was creative.

25 본문의 내용과 일치하도록 다음 빈칸 (A)와 (B)에 알맞은 단어를 쓰시오.

Beth thought Peter is (A)_____ because Peter got Boyd's foot out by using butter when it (B)_____ _____ in the bicycle stand the other day.

중간+기말 plus

적중100

영어 기출문제집

영어 중 **3**

동아 | 윤정미

Best Collection

내용문의 중등영어발전소 적중100 편집부 TEL 070-7707-0457

INSIGHT
on the textbook

교과서 파헤치기

영어 기출 문제집

적중100 plus
2학기 전과정

영어 중 3

동아 | 윤정미

INSIGHT
on the textbook

교과서 파헤치기

Lesson **5** **The Team Behind the Team**

Lesson **6** **Stories for All Time**

Lesson **7** **Technology in Our Lives**

Lesson **8** **The Joseon Dynasty Through Paintings**

Lesson **S** **Finding the Good in Your Friends**

Step1

※ 다음 영어를 우리말로 쓰시오.

01	main	
02	hire	
03	invisible	
04	carry	
05	promote	
06	already	
07	crew	
08	recommendation	
09	expensive	
10	perfect	
11	manage	
12	several	
13	attention	
14	limit	
15	assistant	
16	hurt	
17	choose	
18	therefore	
19	especially	
20	tribe	
21	register	

22	activity	
23	direction	
24	experienced	
25	support	
26	tapper	
27	suggest	
28	particular	
29	breathe	
30	achieve	
31	harmony	
32	hidden	
33	allow	
34	windy	
35	in short	
36	most of all	
37	wear out	
38	have difficulty -ing	
39	sign up for	
40	on one's own	
41	keep track of	
42	in many ways	
43	depending on	

※ 다음 우리말을 영어로 쓰시오.

01	달성하다, 성취하다	
02	운반하다	
03	값비싼	
04	조화, 화합	
05	돕다, 지원하다	
06	주의, 주목	
07	숨쉬다	
08	그러므로	
09	보조자	
10	숨겨진	
11	응원하다	
12	제안하다	
13	경험 있는	
14	선택하다	
15	바람이 심한	
16	주된	
17	(눈에) 보이지 않는, 볼 수 없는	
18	홍보하다	
19	부족, 종족	
20	이끌다	
21	쏘다	

22	이미	
23	한계	
24	특정한	
25	팀, 조	
26	추천	
27	등록하다	
28	몇몇의	
29	방향	
30	특히	
31	관리하다	
32	완벽한	
33	허용하다	
34	두드리는 사람	
35	~에 따라	
36	끝나다	
37	간단히 말해서	
38	(낡아서) 떨어지다, 헤지다	
39	등록하다, 신청하다	
40	주목을 받다	
41	~을 돌보다	
42	~에 어려움을 겪다	
43	무엇보다도	

※ 다음 영영풀이에 알맞은 단어를 <보기>에서 골라 쓴 후, 우리말 뜻을 쓰시오.

1 _____ : to pay someone to work for you: _____

2 _____ : not able to be seen: _____

3 _____ : to make something more popular, well-known, etc.: _____

4 _____ : to succeed in doing or getting something you want: _____

5 _____ : to take air into your body and let it out again: _____

6 _____ : a group of people with a particular skill who work together: _____

7 _____ : to put someone's or something's name on an official list: _____

8 _____ : a person whose job is to help another person to do work: _____

9 _____ : to have something on your body as a piece of clothing, a decoration, etc.: _____

10 _____ : to say that you agree with a person, group, or idea: _____

11 _____ : a group of people who have their own language and ways of living: _____

12 _____ : to decide that a particular person or thing is the one that you want: _____

13 _____ : a metal cup or other object that someone gets for winning a game or race: _____

14 _____ : a set of clothes made of the same cloth, including a jacket and trousers or a skirt: _____

15 _____ : the area beside a race track where cars are repaired or get more gas during a race: _____

16 _____ : to use something a lot so that it no longer works, or can no longer be used: _____

suit	pit	assistant	crew
tribe	wear out	hire	invisible
trophy	support	register	breathe
wear	choose	promote	achieve

※ 다음 우리말과 일치하도록 빈칸에 알맞은 말을 쓰시오.

Listen and Talk A 1

B: How _____ do you _____ _____ ?

G: I play _____ a week, but I want to play _____ _____ .

B: I _____ you join my basketball club. We play _____ _____ a week.

G: That sounds _____ ! It'll be fun _____ _____ with you.

Listen and Talk A 2

B: I don't swim often. How _____ you, Kate? _____ _____ do you _____ ?

G: I swim _____ _____ _____ _____ .

B: _____ often? _____, _____ 'll be fun _____ together today.

G: Yes, but before we swim, I _____ we _____ _____ exercises.

B: That's a good idea.

Listen and Talk A 3

B: Suji, _____ _____ do you _____ bowling _____ ?

G: _____ a week. I'm just a _____ . I heard you're very good.

B: Well, I love bowling. Hmm. Your bowling ball looks _____ for you. I _____ you _____ a _____ _____ .

G: OK. I'll look _____ a lighter _____ , then.

Listen and Talk A 4

B: Mina, _____ _____ do you come here _____ _____ ?

G: _____ day.

B: Can I run _____ you today?

G: Sure, but I _____ you _____ running shoes. Your shoes aren't _____ _____ _____ .

Listen and Talk B

A: Minsu, _____ _____ do you _____ ?

B: I exercise _____ _____ _____ .

A: I _____ you _____ more often.

B: OK. I'll _____ .

Listen and Talk C

W: Hello. _____ _____ Sports World. May I help you?

B: Yes, I came _____ _____ _____ a swimming _____.

W: Is this your first time _____ _____ _____?

B: Yes, it is. I don't know _____ _____ _____ _____ _____.

W: I see. _____ _____ do you want to _____ classes?

B: I want to _____ classes _____ _____ _____. I'd like to _____ classes _____ weekdays and not _____ weekends.

W: Then, I suggest _____ you _____ the Beginner 2 class. This class meets _____ Tuesdays and Thursdays.

B: That _____ _____. I'd like to _____ _____ _____ that class. How big is the class?

W: The class has _____ _____ _____ 10 people.

B: That's _____.

Talk and Play

A: Jiho, _____ _____ do you _____?

B: I exercise _____ _____ _____ _____.

A: That's good.

Review 1

B: Mina, _____ _____ do you _____?

G: I swim _____ _____.

B: Can I _____ _____ _____ you this afternoon?

G: Sure, but I _____ you _____ a swimming cap. _____ a swimming cap, you _____ _____ in the pool.

Review 2

B: Somi, is your piano _____ _____?

G: Yes, it is.

B: _____ _____ do you _____?

G: I practice _____ _____ _____.

Review 3

W: Hello. May I help you?

B: Yes, I came to _____ _____ a _____ _____.

W: I see. _____ _____ do you want to _____ _____?

B: I want to _____ classes _____ _____ _____. I'd like to _____ classes _____ weekends.

W: Then, I _____ that you _____ the Beginner 1 class. This class meets _____ Saturdays and Sundays.

B: That sounds _____.

W: 안녕하세요. Sports World에 오신 것을 환영합니다. 무엇을 도와드릴 까요?

B: 네, 수영 수업을 등록하려고 왔어요.

W: 수영 수업을 받는 것이 이번이 처음 인가요?

B: 네. 저는 수영하는 법을 전혀 알지 못해요.

W: 알겠어요. 얼마나 자주 수업을 받고 싶으신가요?

B: 일주일에 두 번 수업을 듣길 원해요. 주말이 아니라 주중에 수업을 듣고 싶어요.

W: 그럼, 초급 2반을 들을 것을 권합니 다. 이 수업은 화요일과 목요일에 있 어요.

B: 좋아요. 그 수업으로 등록할게요. 그 수업은 몇 명이 듣나요?

W: 그 수업은 제한 인원이 열 명입니다.

B: 좋아요.

A: 지호야, 너는 얼마나 자주 운동을 하 니?

B: 나는 일주일에 세 번 운동을 해.

A: 좋다.

B: 미나야, 너는 얼마나 자주 수영을 하 니?

G: 나는 매일 수영을 해.

B: 오늘 오후에 너와 수영하러 가도 될 까?

G: 물론이지, 하지만 수영 모자를 챙기 는 것을 제안해. 수영 모자 없이 수 영장에 들어가는 것은 허락되지 않 아.

B: 소미야, 피아노 연습은 끝났니?

G: 응, 그래.

B: 얼마나 자주 연습을 하니?

G: 나는 일주일에 두 번 연습을 해.

W: 안녕하세요. 무엇을 도와드릴까요?

B: 네, 축구 수업을 등록하러 왔어요.

W: 알겠습니다. 얼마나 자주 수업을 수 강하기를 원하나요?

B: 일주일에 두 번 수강하고 싶어요. 주 말에 수업을 수강하는 게 좋아요.

W: 그럼, 초급 1반을 수강하기를 제안 드려요. 이 수업은 토요일과 일요일 에 있어요.

B: 좋아요.

※ 다음 우리말에 맞도록 대화를 영어로 쓰시오.

Listen and Talk A 1

B: _____

G: _____

B: _____

G: _____

B: 얼마나 자주 농구를 하니?

G: 일주일에 한 번 해. 그런데 더 자주 하고 싶어.

B: 네가 우리 농구 동아리에 들어오기를 제안해. 우리는 일주일에 세 번 농구를 해.

G: 좋은 생각이야! 같이 하면 재미있을 거야.

Listen and Talk A 2

B: _____

G: _____

B: _____

G: _____

B: _____

B: 난 수영을 자주 하지 않아. 넌 어떠니, Kate? 얼마나 자주 수영을 하러 가니?

G: 일주일에 네 번 수영을 해.

B: 그렇게 자주? 어쨌든 오늘 같이 수영을 하면 재미있을 거야.

G: 응, 그런데 우리가 수영하기 전에 스트레칭을 하는 것을 제안해.

B: 좋은 생각이다.

Listen and Talk A 3

B: _____

G: _____

B: _____

G: _____

B: 수지야, 너는 얼마나 자주 볼링 수업을 받니?

G: 일주일에 두 번 받아. 나는 초보야. 난 네가 볼링을 잘한다고 들었어.

B: 음, 난 볼링을 좋아해. 흠. 네 볼링공이 무거워 보인다. 더 가벼운 공을 쓰는 것을 제안해.

G: 알겠어. 그럼 더 가벼운 공을 찾아봐야겠다.

Listen and Talk A 4

B: _____

G: _____

B: _____

G: _____

B: 미나야, 넌 달리기를 하러 이곳에 얼마나 자주 오니?

G: 매일 와.

B: 오늘 너와 함께 달리기를 해도 될까?

G: 물론이야, 하지만 네가 운동화를 신는 것을 제안해. 네 신발은 달리기에 적합하지 않아.

Listen and Talk B

A: _____

B: _____

A: _____

B: _____

A: 민수야, 너는 얼마나 자주 운동을 하니?

B: 나는 일주일에 한 번 운동을 해.

A: 더 자주 운동하기를 제안해.

B: 알겠어. 시도해 볼게.

Listen and Talk C

W: _____

B: _____

W: _____

B: _____

W: _____

B: _____
_____

W: _____
_____

B: _____

W: _____

B: _____

Talk and Play

A: _____

B: _____

A: _____

Review 1

B: _____

G: _____

B: _____

G: _____

Review 2

B: _____

G: _____

B: _____

G: _____

Review 3

W: _____

B: _____

W: _____

B: _____

W: _____
_____

B: _____

W: 안녕하세요. Sports World에 오신 것을 환영합니다. 무엇을 도와드릴까요?

B: 네, 수영 수업을 등록하려고 왔어요.

W: 수영 수업을 받는 것이 이번이 처음인가요?

B: 네. 저는 수영하는 법을 전혀 알지 못해요.

W: 알겠어요. 얼마나 자주 수업을 받고 싶으신가요?

B: 일주일에 두 번 수업을 듣길 원해요. 주말이 아니라 주중에 수업을 듣고 싶어요.

W: 그럼, 초급 2반을 들을 것을 권합니다. 이 수업은 화요일과 목요일에 있어요.

B: 좋아요. 그 수업으로 등록할게요. 그 수업은 몇 명이 듣나요?

W: 그 수업은 제한 인원이 열 명입니다.

B: 좋아요.

A: 지호야, 너는 얼마나 자주 운동을 하니?

B: 나는 일주일에 세 번 운동을 해.

A: 좋다.

B: 미나야, 너는 얼마나 자주 수영을 하니?

G: 나는 매일 수영을 해.

B: 오늘 오후에 너와 수영하러 가도 될까?

G: 물론이지, 하지만 수영 모자를 챙기는 것을 제안해. 수영 모자 없이 수영장에 들어가는 것은 허락되지 않아.

B: 소미야, 피아노 연습은 끝났니?

G: 응, 그래.

B: 얼마나 자주 연습을 하니?

G: 나는 일주일에 두 번 연습을 해.

W: 안녕하세요. 무엇을 도와드릴까요?

B: 네, 축구 수업을 등록하러 왔어요.

W: 알겠습니다. 얼마나 자주 수업을 수강하기를 원하나요?

B: 일주일에 두 번 수강하고 싶어요. 주말에 수업을 수강하는 게 좋아요.

W: 그럼, 초급 1반을 수강하기를 제안드려요. 이 수업은 토요일과 일요일에 있어요.

B: 좋아요.

※ 다음 우리말과 일치하도록 빈칸에 알맞은 것을 골라 쓰시오.

1 _____ People _____ _____
   A. in   B. Hidden   C. Sports

2 In sports, _____ the players get a trophy or medal, _____ they don't win _____ their _____.
   A. own   B. only   C. on   D. but

3 _____ are people _____ help the _____.
   A. who   B. there   C. players

4 These people are _____ _____ and don't _____ _____.
   A. attention   B. often   C. get   D. hidden

5 _____, they are _____ _____ as the players.
   A. as   B. however   C. important

6 _____ _____ some _____.
   A. are   B. here   C. examples

7 _____ _____ a _____
   A. Marathon   B. in   C. Pacers

8 Pacers _____ _____ other _____ and _____ them in a marathon.
   A. lead   B. with   C. run   D. runners

9 Pacers are _____ runners, and their job is to help _____ runners _____ their race _____.
   A. manage   B. experienced   C. better   D. other

10 _____ _____ _____ several pacers in a race.
   A. be   B. can   C. there

11 Each pacer _____ at different _____ and _____ the race in different _____.
   A. times   B. speeds   C. runs   D. finishes

12 _____ usually _____ flags or balloons _____ their _____ time.
   A. showing   B. pacers   C. finish   D. have

13 Runners can _____ a pacer _____ _____ their finish time.
   A. depending   B. target   C. on   D. choose

14 For example, if a runner wants to _____ the race in four _____, the runner will _____ the four-hour _____.
   A. follow   B. hours   C. finish   D. pacer

15 _____ the pacer keeps _____ of the time, the runner can achieve his or her goal of _____ the marathon in a _____ time more easily.
   A. particular   B. since   C. finishing   D. track

16 _____ _____, pacers run but they don't run _____.
   A. short   B. to   C. in   D. win

17 They _____ _____ _____.
   A. for   B. run   C. others

18 _____ _____ in _____
   A. Crews   B. Racing   C. Car   D. Pit

19 You may only see the car and the driver _____ most car races, but _____ is a team _____ the _____.
   A. behind   B. during   C. driver   D. there

---

1 스포츠 속 숨은 조력자들

2 스포츠에서 선수들만 트로피나 메달을 받지만, 그들은 혼자 힘으로 이긴 것이 아니다.

3 그 선수들을 돕는 사람들이 있다.

4 이 사람들은 종종 숨겨져 있고 주목을 받지 못한다.

5 하지만 그들은 선수들만큼 중요하다.

6 여기 몇 가지 예가 있다.

7 마라톤의 페이서들

8 페이서들은 마라톤에서 다른 선수들과 함께 달리며 그들을 이끈다.

9 페이서들은 경험이 많은 선수들이며 그들의 역할은 다른 선수들이 경기를 더 잘 운영하도록 돕는 것이다.

10 한 경기에는 여러 명의 페이서들이 있을 수 있다.

11 각각의 페이서는 다른 속도로 달리고 다른 시간대에 경기를 마친다.

12 페이서들은 주로 자신들의 완주 시간을 나타내는 깃발이나 풍선들을 가지고 있다.

13 선수들은 자신들의 목표 완주 시간에 따라 페이서를 선택할 수 있다.

14 예를 들어, 한 선수가 4시간 안에 경기를 마치고 싶다면, 그 선수는 4시간 페이서를 따라갈 것이다.

15 페이서가 시간을 계속해서 파악하기 때문에, 선수는 특정 시간에 마라톤을 완주하려는 자신의 목표를 더 쉽게 달성할 수 있다.

16 요컨대, 페이서들은 달리지만 우승을 하기 위해 달리는 것은 아니다.

17 그들은 다른 선수들을 위해 달린다.

18 자동차 경주의 피트 크루

19 여러분은 대부분의 자동차 경주에서 자동차와 레이서만 보겠지만 그 레이서 뒤에는 팀이 있다.

20 This team _____ _____ a _____ _____.

    A. called   B. crew   C. pit   D. is

21 A pit is a place _____ the side _____ the race _____, and drivers stop there _____ times during a race.

    A. several   B. track   C. on   D. of

22 The _____ _____ of the pit crew is to _____ the car and _____ the tires.

    A. check   B. job   C. change   D. main

23 _____ the tires is especially important _____ the tires _____ easily in a high speed race.

    A. out   B. changing   C. wear   D. because

24 A pit stop can be _____ _____ as 2 _____, and there are as many as 20 members on a _____.

    A. seconds   B. crew   C. short   D. as

25 Therefore, the pit crew _____ to work _____ _____ _____.

    A. in   B. has   C. harmony   D. perfect

26 The driver may _____ all the _____, but as people say, "Races are _____ in the _____."

    A. attention   B. pits   C. get   D. won

27 Sherpas _____ _____ _____

    A. Climbing   B. in   C. Mountain

28 The word *Sherpa* _____ from the Sherpa _____, _____ lives in the _____ part of Nepal.

    A. tribe   B. eastern   C. which   D. comes

29 Sherpas have good _____ _____ and know their _____ the mountains well.

    A. around   B. climbing   C. way   D. skills

30 They also _____ _____ _____ _____ high up in the mountains.

    A. little   B. have   C. breathing   D. difficulty

31 Therefore, mountain climbers started to _____ Sherpas _____ _____ them _____ Mount Everest.

    A. help   B. hire   C. climb   D. to

32 Sherpas _____ mountain _____ _____ the _____ of the mountain.

    A. climbers   B. top   C. to   D. lead

33 They _____ climbers _____ many _____.

    A. in   B. support   C. ways

34 _____ example, they _____ _____ tents and _____ climbers' bags.

    A. carry   B. put   C. for   D. up

35 Sherpas are often called the _____ people of Mount Everest _____ people often see a picture of only the _____ at the _____ of the mountain.

    A. because   B. invisible   C. top   D. climbers

---

20 이 팀은 피트 크루라고 불린다.

21 피트는 경주 트랙의 한쪽에 있는 공간으로 레이서들은 경주 도중에 그곳에서 여러 번 정지한다.

22 피트 크루가 하는 주요 역할은 자동차를 점검하고 타이어를 교체하는 것이다.

23 빠른 속도의 경주에서는 타이어가 쉽게 마모되기 때문에 타이어를 교체하는 것이 특히 중요하다.

24 피트에서의 정지는 짧게는 2초 정도이고 한 팀에는 많게는 20명에 이르는 구성원이 있다.

25 그러므로 피트 크루는 완벽한 조화를 이루며 일해야 한다.

26 레이서만 주목을 받을지 모르지만 사람들이 말하는 것처럼, "경주의 우승은 피트에서 이루어진다."

27 등반에서의 셰르파

28 'Sherpa'라는 단어는 셰르파족에서 유래되었는데, 셰르파족은 네팔의 동쪽 지역에 산다.

29 셰르파는 훌륭한 등반 기량을 갖고 있으며 산 지리를 잘 안다.

30 그들은 또한 산의 높은 곳에서 호흡하는 데 어려움이 거의 없다.

31 그래서 등산가들은 자신들이 에베레스트산을 등반하는 것을 돕는 셰르파를 고용하기 시작했다.

32 셰르파는 등산가들을 산 정상까지 이끈다.

33 그들은 여러 방면에서 등산가들을 지원한다.

34 예를 들면, 그들은 텐트를 치고 등산가들의 가방을 운반한다.

35 셰르파는 종종 에베레스트산의 보이지 않는 사람들로 불리는데, 왜냐하면 사람들이 산 정상에서 등산가들만 찍힌 사진을 자주 보기 때문이다.

※ 다음 우리말과 일치하도록 빈칸에 알맞은 것을 골라 쓰시오.

1 _____ People in Sports

2 In sports, _____ the players get a trophy or medal, but they don't _____ _____ _____ _____.

3 There are _____ _____ _____ the players.

4 These people are often _____ and don't _____ _____.

5 _____, they are _____ _____ _____ the players.

6 _____ _____ some _____.

7 _____ in a Marathon

8 Pacers _____ _____ _____ _____ and _____ them in a marathon.

9 Pacers are _____ runners, and their job is _____ _____ other runners _____ _____ _____ _____.

10 _____ _____ _____ several pacers in a race.

11 Each pacer runs _____ _____ _____ and _____ the race _____ _____ _____.

12 Pacers usually have flags or balloons _____ their finish time.

13 Runners _____ _____ a pacer _____ _____ their target finish time.

14 For example, if a runner wants to finish the race _____ _____ _____, the runner will _____ the _____-hour pacer.

15 Since the pacer _____ _____ _____ the time, the runner _____ _____ his or her goal of finishing the marathon in a particular time more _____.

16 _____ _____, pacers run but they don't run _____ _____.

17 They run _____ _____.

18 Pit Crews in _____ _____

19 You may only see the car and the driver _____ most car races, but there is a team _____ _____ _____.

1 스포츠 속 숨은 조력자들
2 스포츠에서 선수들만 트로피나 메달을 받지만, 그들은 혼자 힘으로 이긴 것이 아니다.
3 그 선수들을 돕는 사람들이 있다.
4 이 사람들은 종종 숨겨져 있고 주목을 받지 못한다.
5 하지만 그들은 선수들만큼 중요하다.
6 여기 몇 가지 예가 있다.
7 마라톤의 페이서들
8 페이서들은 마라톤에서 다른 선수들과 함께 달리며 그들을 이끈다.
9 페이서들은 경험이 많은 선수들이며 그들의 역할은 다른 선수들이 경기를 더 잘 운영하도록 돕는 것이다.
10 한 경기에는 여러 명의 페이서들이 있을 수 있다.
11 각각의 페이서는 다른 속도로 달리고 다른 시간대에 경기를 마친다.
12 페이서들은 주로 자신들의 완주 시간을 나타내는 깃발이나 풍선들을 가지고 있다.
13 선수들은 자신들의 목표 완주 시간에 따라 페이서를 선택할 수 있다.
14 예를 들어, 한 선수가 4시간 안에 경기를 마치고 싶다면, 그 선수는 4시간 페이서를 따라갈 것이다.
15 페이서가 시간을 계속해서 파악하기 때문에, 선수는 특정 시간에 마라톤을 완주하려는 자신의 목표를 더 쉽게 달성할 수 있다.
16 요컨대, 페이서들은 달리지만 우승을 하기 위해 달리는 것은 아니다.
17 그들은 다른 선수들을 위해 달린다.
18 자동차 경주의 피트 크루
19 여러분은 대부분의 자동차 경주에서 자동차와 레이서만 보겠지만 그 레이서 뒤에는 팀이 있다.

20 This team _____ _____ a pit crew.

21 A pit is a place _____ _____ _____ _____ _____ _____, and drivers stop there _____ _____ during a race.

22 The _____ _____ of the pit crew is _____ _____ the car and change the tires.

23 _____ the tires _____ especially important because the tires _____ _____ _____ in a high speed race.

24 A pit stop can be _____ _____ _____ 2 _____, and there are _____ _____ _____ 20 members on a crew.

25 _____, the pit crew has to work _____ _____ _____.

26 The driver may _____ _____ _____ _____, but as people say, "Races are won _____ _____ _____."

27 Sherpas in _____ _____

28 The word *Sherpa* _____ _____ the Sherpa tribe, _____ lives in the _____ _____ of Nepal.

29 Sherpas have _____ _____ _____ and know their way around the mountains well.

30 They also _____ _____ _____ _____ high up in the mountains.

31 Therefore, mountain climbers started _____ _____ Sherpas _____ _____ _____ _____ Mount Everest.

32 Sherpas _____ mountain climbers _____ the top of the mountain.

33 They support climbers _____ _____ _____.

34 _____ example, they _____ _____ tents and _____ climbers' bags.

35 Sherpas are often called the _____ people of Mount Everest because people often see a picture of only the climbers _____ _____ _____ _____ the mountain.

---

20 이 팀은 피트 크루라고 불린다.

21 피트는 경주 트랙의 한쪽에 있는 공간으로 레이서들은 경주 도중에 그곳에서 여러 번 정지한다.

22 피트 크루가 하는 주요 역할은 자동차를 점검하고 타이어를 교체하는 것이다.

23 빠른 속도의 경주에서는 타이어가 쉽게 마모되기 때문에 타이어를 교체하는 것이 특히 중요하다.

24 피트에서의 정지는 짧게는 2초 정도이고 한 팀에는 많게는 20명에 이르는 구성원이 있다.

25 그러므로 피트 크루는 완벽한 조화를 이루며 일해야 한다.

26 레이서만 주목을 받을지 모르지만 사람들이 말하는 것처럼, "경주의 우승은 피트에서 이루어진다."

27 등반에서의 셰르파

28 'Sherpa'라는 단어는 셰르파족에서 유래되었는데, 셰르파족은 네팔의 동쪽 지역에 산다.

29 셰르파는 훌륭한 등반 기량을 갖고 있으며 산 지리를 잘 안다.

30 그들은 또한 산의 높은 곳에서 호흡하는 데 어려움이 거의 없다.

31 그래서 등산가들은 자신들이 에베레스트산을 등반하는 것을 돕는 셰르파를 고용하기 시작했다.

32 셰르파는 등산가들을 산 정상까지 이끈다.

33 그들은 여러 방면에서 등산가들을 지원한다.

34 예를 들면, 그들은 텐트를 치고 등산가들의 가방을 운반한다.

35 셰르파는 종종 에베레스트산의 보이지 않는 사람들로 불리는데, 왜냐하면 사람들이 산 정상에서 등산가들만 찍힌 사진을 자주 보기 때문이다.

※ 다음 문장을 우리말로 쓰시오.

본문 Test

1 ▷ Hidden People in Sports

➡ _____

2 ▷ In sports, only the players get a trophy or medal, but they don't win on their own.

➡ _____

3 ▷ There are people who help the players.

➡ _____

4 ▷ These people are often hidden and don't get attention.

➡ _____

5 ▷ However, they are as important as the players.

➡ _____

6 ▷ Here are some examples.

➡ _____

7 ▷ Pacers in a Marathon

➡ _____

8 ▷ Pacers run with other runners and lead them in a marathon.

➡ _____

9 ▷ Pacers are experienced runners, and their job is to help other runners manage their race better.

➡ _____

10 ▷ There can be several pacers in a race.

➡ _____

11 ▷ Each pacer runs at different speeds and finishes the race in different times.

➡ _____

12 ▷ Pacers usually have flags or balloons showing their finish time.

➡ _____

13 ▷ Runners can choose a pacer depending on their target finish time.

➡ _____

14 ▷ For example, if a runner wants to finish the race in four hours, the runner will follow the four-hour pacer.

➡ _____

15 ▷ Since the pacer keeps track of the time, the runner can achieve his or her goal of finishing the marathon in a particular time more easily.

➡ _____

16 ▷ In short, pacers run but they don't run to win.

➡ _____

17 ▷ They run for others.

➡ _____

18 Pit Crews in Car Racing
➡ _____

19 You may only see the car and the driver during most car races, but there is a team behind the driver.
➡ _____

20 This team is called a pit crew.
➡ _____

21 A pit is a place on the side of the race track, and drivers stop there several times during a race.
➡ _____

22 The main job of the pit crew is to check the car and change the tires.
➡ _____

23 Changing the tires is especially important because the tires wear out easily in a high speed race.
➡ _____

24 A pit stop can be as short as 2 seconds, and there are as many as 20 members on a crew.
➡ _____

25 Therefore, the pit crew has to work in perfect harmony.
➡ _____

26 The driver may get all the attention, but as people say, "Races are won in the pits."
➡ _____

27 Sherpas in Mountain Climbing
➡ _____

28 The word *Sherpa* comes from the Sherpa tribe, which lives in the eastern part of Nepal.
➡ _____

29 Sherpas have good climbing skills and know their way around the mountains well.
➡ _____

30 They also have little difficulty breathing high up in the mountains.
➡ _____

31 Therefore, mountain climbers started to hire Sherpas to help them climb Mount Everest.
➡ _____

32 Sherpas lead mountain climbers to the top of the mountain.
➡ _____

33 They support climbers in many ways.
➡ _____

34 For example, they put up tents and carry climbers' bags.
➡ _____

35 Sherpas are often called the invisible people of Mount Everest because people often see a picture of only the climbers at the top of the mountain.
➡ _____
_____

※ 다음 괄호 안의 단어들을 우리말에 맞도록 바르게 배열하시오.

1 (People / Hidden / Sports / in)
➡ _____

2 (sports, / in / the / only / get / players / a / or / trophy / medal, / they / but / win / don't / their / on / own.)
➡ _____

3 (are / there / who / people / help / players. / the)
➡ _____

4 (people / these / often / are / hidden / and / get / don't / attention.)
➡ _____

5 (they / however, / are / important / as / the / as / players.)
➡ _____

6 (are / here / examples. / some)
➡ _____

7 (in / Pacers / Marathon / a)
➡ _____

8 (run / pacers / other / with / and / runners / lead / in / them / marathon. / a)
➡ _____

9 (are / pacers / runners, / experienced / and / job / their / to / is / other / help / manage / runners / their / better. / race)
➡ _____

10 (can / there / several / be / in / pacers / race. / a)
➡ _____

11 (pacer / each / at / runs / speeds / different / and / the / finishes / race / different / in / times.)
➡ _____

12 (usually / pacers / flags / have / or / showing / balloons / finish / their / time.)
➡ _____

13 (can / runners / a / choose / pacer / on / depending / target / their / time. / finish)
➡ _____

14 (example, / for / a / if / wants / runner / finish / to / race / the / in / hours, / four / runner / the / follow / will / four-hour / the / pacer.)
➡ _____

15 (the / since / keeps / pacer / of / track / time, / the / runner / the / achieve / can / her / or / his / of / goal / the / finishing / in / marathon / a / time / particular / more / easily.)
➡ _____

16 (short, / in / run / pacers / they / but / don't / to / run / win.)
➡ _____

17 (run / they / others. / for)
➡ _____

18 (Crews / Pit / Car / in / Racing)
➡ _____

19 (may / you / see / only / car / the / and / driver / the / most / during / races, / car / there / but / is / team / a / the / behind / driver.)
➡ _____

1 스포츠 속 숨은 조력자들
2 스포츠에서 선수들만 트로피나 메달을 받지만, 그들은 혼자 힘으로 이긴 것이 아니다.
3 그 선수들을 돕는 사람들이 있다.
4 이 사람들은 종종 숨겨져 있고 주목을 받지 못한다.
5 하지만 그들은 선수들만큼 중요하다.
6 여기 몇 가지 예가 있다.
7 마라톤의 페이서들
8 페이서들은 마라톤에서 다른 선수들과 함께 달리며 그들을 이끈다.
9 페이서들은 경험이 많은 선수들이며 그들의 역할은 다른 선수들이 경기를 더 잘 운영하도록 돕는 것이다.
10 한 경기에는 여러 명의 페이서들이 있을 수 있다.
11 각각의 페이서는 다른 속도로 달리고 다른 시간대에 경기를 마친다.
12 페이서들은 주로 자신들의 완주 시간을 나타내는 깃발이나 풍선들을 가지고 있다.
13 선수들은 자신들의 목표 완주 시간에 따라 페이서를 선택할 수 있다.
14 예를 들어, 한 선수가 4시간 안에 경기를 마치고 싶다면, 그 선수는 4시간 페이서를 따라갈 것이다.
15 페이서가 시간을 계속해서 파악하기 때문에, 선수는 특정 시간에 마라톤을 완주하려는 자신의 목표를 더 쉽게 달성할 수 있다.
16 요컨대, 페이서들은 달리지만 우승을 하기 위해 달리는 것은 아니다.
17 그들은 다른 선수들을 위해 달린다.
18 자동차 경주의 피트 크루
19 여러분은 대부분의 자동차 경주에서 자동차와 레이서만 보겠지만 그 레이서 뒤에는 팀이 있다.

20 (team / this / called / is / pit / a / crew.)
➡ _____

21 (pit / a / is / place / a / the / on / side / the / of / track, / the / race / drivers / and / there / stop / several / during / times / race. / a)
➡ _____

22 (main / the / job / of / pit / the / is / crew / check / to / car / the / and / the / change / tires.)
➡ _____

23 (the / changing / tires / especially / is / because / important / tires / the / out / wear / easily / a / in / speed / high / race.)
➡ _____

24 (pit / a / stop / be / can / short / as / 2 / as / seconds, / there / and / as / are / many / 20 / as / members / a / on / crew.)
➡ _____

25 (the / therefore, / pit / has / crew / work / to / perfect / in / harmony.)
➡ _____

26 (driver / the / get / may / all / attention, / the / as / but / say, / people / are / "races / won / the / in / pits.")
➡ _____

27 (in / Sherpas / Climbing / Mountain)
➡ _____

28 (word / the / 'Sherpa' / from / comes / Sherpa / the / tribe, / lives / which / the / in / part / eastern / Nepal. / of)
➡ _____

29 (have / Sherpas / good / skills / climbing / and / their / know / around / way / mountains / the / well.)
➡ _____

30 (also / they / little / have / breathing / difficulty / up / high / the / in / mountains.)
➡ _____

31 (mountain / therefore, / started / climbers / hire / to / to / Sherpas / them / help / climb / Everest. / Mount)
➡ _____

32 (lead / Sherpas / climbers / mountain / the / to / of / top / mountain. / the)
➡ _____

33 (support / they / in / climbers / ways. / many)
➡ _____

34 (example, / for / put / they / tents / up / and / carry / bags. / climbers')
➡ _____

35 (are / Sherpas / called / often / invisible / the / of / people / Everest / Mount / people / because / see / often / picture / a / only / of / climbers / the / the / at / of / top / mountain. / the)
➡ _____

20 이 팀은 피트 크루라고 불린다.

21 피트는 경주 트랙의 한쪽에 있는 공간으로 레이서들은 경주 도중에 그곳에서 여러 번 정지한다.

22 피트 크루가 하는 주요 역할은 자동차를 점검하고 타이어를 교체하는 것이다.

23 빠른 속도의 경주에서는 타이어가 쉽게 마모되기 때문에 타이어를 교체하는 것이 특히 중요하다.

24 피트에서의 정지는 짧게는 2초 정도이고 한 팀에는 많게는 20명에 이르는 구성원이 있다.

25 그러므로 피트 크루는 완벽한 조화를 이루며 일해야 한다.

26 레이서만 주목을 받을지 모르지만 사람들이 말하는 것처럼, "경주의 우승은 피트에서 이루어진다."

27 등반에서의 셰르파

28 'Sherpa'라는 단어는 셰르파족에서 유래되었는데, 셰르파족은 네팔의 동쪽 지역에 산다.

29 셰르파는 훌륭한 등반 기량을 갖고 있으며 산 지리를 잘 안다.

30 그들은 또한 산의 높은 곳에서 호흡하는 데 어려움이 거의 없다.

31 그래서 등산가들은 자신들이 에베레스트산을 등반하는 것을 돕는 셰르파를 고용하기 시작했다.

32 셰르파는 등산가들을 산 정상까지 이끈다.

33 그들은 여러 방면에서 등산가들을 지원한다.

34 예를 들면, 그들은 텐트를 치고 등산가들의 가방을 운반한다.

35 셰르파는 종종 에베레스트산의 보이지 않는 사람들로 불리는데, 왜냐하면 사람들이 산 정상에서 등산가들만 찍힌 사진을 자주 보기 때문이다.

※ 다음 우리말을 영어로 쓰시오.

1 　스포츠 속 숨은 조력자들

➡ _____

2 　스포츠에서 선수들만 트로피나 메달을 받지만, 그들은 혼자 힘으로 이긴 것이 아니다.

➡ _____

3 　그 선수들을 돕는 사람들이 있다.

➡ _____

4 　이 사람들은 종종 숨겨져 있고 주목을 받지 못한다.

➡ _____

5 　하지만 그들은 선수들만큼 중요하다.

➡ _____

6 　여기 몇 가지 예가 있다.

➡ _____

7 　마라톤의 페이서들

➡ _____

8 　페이서들은 마라톤에서 다른 선수들과 함께 달리며 그들을 이끈다.

➡ _____

9 　페이서들은 경험이 많은 선수들이며 그들의 역할은 다른 선수들이 경기를 더 잘 운영하도록
돕는 것이다.

➡ _____

10 　한 경기에는 여러 명의 페이서들이 있을 수 있다.

➡ _____

11 　각각의 페이서는 다른 속도로 달리고 다른 시간대에 경기를 마친다.

➡ _____

12 　페이서들은 주로 자신들의 완주 시간을 나타내는 깃발이나 풍선들을 가지고 있다.

➡ _____

13 　선수들은 자신들의 목표 완주 시간에 따라 페이서를 선택할 수 있다.

➡ _____

14 　예를 들어, 한 선수가 4시간 안에 경기를 마치고 싶다면, 그 선수는 4시간 페이서를 따라갈 것이다.

➡ _____

15 　페이서가 시간을 계속해서 파악하기 때문에, 선수는 특정 시간에 마라톤을 완주하려는 자신의
목표를 더 쉽게 달성할 수 있다.

➡ _____

　_____

16 　요컨대, 페이서들은 달리지만 우승을 하기 위해 달리는 것은 아니다.

➡ _____

17 　그들은 다른 선수들을 위해 달린다.

➡ _____

18 자동차 경주의 피트 크루
➡ _____

19 여러분은 대부분의 자동차 경주에서 자동차와 레이서만 보겠지만 그 레이서 뒤에는 팀이 있다.
➡ _____

20 이 팀은 피트 크루라고 불린다.
➡ _____

21 피트는 경주 트랙의 한쪽에 있는 공간으로 레이서들은 경주 도중에 그곳에서 여러 번 정지한다.
➡ _____

22 피트 크루가 하는 주요 역할은 자동차를 점검하고 타이어를 교체하는 것이다.
➡ _____

23 빠른 속도의 경주에서는 타이어가 쉽게 마모되기 때문에 타이어를 교체하는 것이 특히 중요하다.
➡ _____

24 피트에서의 정지는 짧게는 2초 정도이고 한 팀에는 많게는 20명에 이르는 구성원이 있다.
➡ _____

25 그러므로 피트 크루는 완벽한 조화를 이루며 일해야 한다.
➡ _____

26 레이서만 주목을 받을지 모르지만 사람들이 말하는 것처럼, "경주의 우승은 피트에서 이루어진다."
➡ _____

27 등반에서의 셰르파
➡ _____

28 'Sherpa'라는 단어는 셰르파족에서 유래되었는데, 셰르파족은 네팔의 동쪽 지역에 산다.
➡ _____

29 셰르파는 훌륭한 등반 기량을 갖고 있으며 산 지리를 잘 안다.
➡ _____

30 그들은 또한 산의 높은 곳에서 호흡하는 데 어려움이 거의 없다.
➡ _____

31 그래서 등산가들은 자신들이 에베레스트산을 등반하는 것을 돕는 셰르파를 고용하기 시작했다.
➡ _____

32 셰르파는 등산가들을 산 정상까지 이끈다.
➡ _____

33 그들은 여러 방면에서 등산가들을 지원한다.
➡ _____

34 예를 들면, 그들은 텐트를 치고 등산가들의 가방을 운반한다.
➡ _____

35 셰르파는 종종 에베레스트산의 보이지 않는 사람들로 불리는데, 왜냐하면 사람들이 산 정상에서 등산가들만 찍힌 사진을 자주 보기 때문이다.
➡ _____
_____

※ 다음 우리말과 일치하도록 빈칸에 알맞은 말을 쓰시오.

After You Read B

1. Host: _____ _____ _____ _____ about your job?

2. Pacer: Pacers have flags or balloons _____ _____ _____ _____.

3. Pit Crew: A pit stop _____ _____ _____ _____ _____ _____ _____ _____.

4. So the pit crew _____ _____ _____ _____ _____.

5. Sherpa: Sherpas like me _____ _____ _____ _____ _____ _____ in the mountains.

1. 사회자: 여러분의 직업에 관해 어떤 흥미로운 것이 있나요?
2. 페이서: 페이서는 자신들의 완주 시간을 나타내는 깃발이나 풍선들을 가지고 있어요.
3. 피트 크루: 피트에서의 정지는 짧게는 2초 정도입니다.
4. 그래서 피트 크루는 완벽한 조화를 이루며 일해야 해요.
5. 셰르파: 저와 같은 셰르파는 산의 높은 곳에서 호흡하는 데 어려움이 거의 없어요.

Around the World

1. In swimming, a tapper uses a long pole _____ _____ _____ _____ _____ _____.

2. In a race, a guide runner _____ _____ _____ _____ _____ and _____ him or her _____ _____ _____ _____.

3. _____ _____ _____, _____ _____ _____ _____ tells his or her team players which _____ _____ _____.

1. 수영에서, tapper는 시각 장애인 수영 선수가 수영하는 것을 돕기 위해 장대를 사용한다.
2. 달리기에서, guide runner는 시각 장애인 선수와 함께 달리며 그들이 트랙에서 벗어나지 않도록 돕는다.
3. 시각 장애인 축구에서, shooting assistant는 자신의 팀 선수들에게 슛하는 방향을 말해 준다.

Think and Write

1. _____ in _____ _____ _____

2. _____ people _____ _____ _____ _____ that cheerleaders are _____ _____ a football team, they _____ _____ _____ _____ a football game.

3. _____ _____ at a game, they _____ _____ _____ _____.

4. They _____ _____ their team and fans.

5. _____ _____ _____ _____ _____, cheerleaders _____ _____ _____ and _____.

6. They also _____ _____ _____ _____ _____ and _____.

7. _____ _____ _____, they need to _____ _____ _____ _____.

1. 미식축구 경기에서의 치어리더
2. 사람들이 보통 치어리더는 미식축구팀의 일원이라고 생각하지 않을지라도 그들은 축구 경기에서 중요한 역할을 한다.
3. 경기에서 응원을 함으로써 그들은 공동체 정신을 만들어낸다.
4. 그들은 또한 팀과 팬들을 격려한다.
5. 자신의 역할을 잘 하기 위해, 치어리더들은 몸을 건강하게 관리하고 강해야 한다.
6. 그들은 또한 점프하는 것과 춤추는 것을 잘 해야 한다.
7. 무엇보다도, 그들은 선수들만큼이나 열심히 일해야 한다.

※ 다음 우리말을 영어로 쓰시오.

After You Read B

1. 사회자: 여러분의 직업에 관해 어떤 흥미로운 것이 있나요?
   ➡ _____

2. 페이서: 페이서는 자신들의 완주 시간을 나타내는 깃발이나 풍선들을 가지고 있어요.
   ➡ _____

3. 피트 크루: 피트에서의 정지는 짧게는 2초 정도입니다.
   ➡ _____

4. 그래서 피트 크루는 완벽한 조화를 이루며 일해야 해요.
   ➡ _____

5. 셰르파: 저와 같은 셰르파는 산의 높은 곳에서 호흡하는 데 어려움이 거의 없어요.
   ➡ _____

Around the World

1. 수영에서, tapper는 시각 장애인 수영 선수가 수영하는 것을 돕기 위해 장대를 사용한다.
   ➡ _____

2. 달리기에서, guide runner는 시각 장애인 선수와 함께 달리며 그들이 트랙에서 벗어나지 않도록 돕는다.
   ➡ _____

3. 시각 장애인 축구에서, shooting assistant는 자신의 팀 선수들에게 슛하는 방향을 말해 준다.
   ➡ _____

Think and Write

1. 미식축구 경기에서의 치어리더
   ➡ _____

2. 사람들이 보통 치어리더는 미식축구팀의 일원이라고 생각하지 않을지라도 그들은 축구 경기에서 중요한 역할을 한다.
   ➡ _____

3. 경기에서 응원을 함으로써 그들은 공동체 정신을 만들어낸다.
   ➡ _____

4. 그들은 또한 팀과 팬들을 격려한다.
   ➡ _____

5. 자신의 역할을 잘 하기 위해, 치어리더들은 몸을 건강하게 관리하고 강해야 한다.
   ➡ _____

6. 그들은 또한 점프하는 것과 춤추는 것을 잘 해야 한다.
   ➡ _____

7. 무엇보다도, 그들은 선수들만큼이나 열심히 일해야 한다.
   ➡ _____

※ 다음 영어를 우리말로 쓰시오.

01	accept	22	furniture
02	antique	23	order
03	attach	24	dealer
04	broken	25	price
05	reproduction	26	tightly
06	elect	27	cheaply
07	worth	28	unfortunately
08	endless	29	favor
09	pay	30	receive
10	exactly	31	role
11	priceless	32	while
12	add	33	prize
13	collection	34	shocked
14	disappointed	35	fall over
15	announcement	36	cut off
16	owner	37	on one's way
17	flu	38	be proud of ~
18	hug	39	remember -ing
19	charge	40	dream of ~
20	luckily	41	cannot help -ing
21	offer	42	be known for
		43	take advantage of

※ 다음 우리말을 영어로 쓰시오.

01 판매상, 중개인

02 지불하다

03 독감

04 끝없는

05 정확하게

06 가격

07 골동품

08 (금액을) 청구하다

09 복제품

10 값을 매길 수 없는, 대단히 귀중한

11 받아들이다

12 단단하게, 꽉

13 고장 난

14 불행하게도

15 가구

16 연습

17 실망한

18 붙이다, 첨부하다

19 지루한

20 호의

21 역할, 배역

22 가치; ~의 가치가 있는

23 끌어안다, 포옹하다

24 수집

25 아직

26 다행스럽게

27 제의, 제안

28 선출하다

29 싸게

30 주인

31 받다

32 주문하다, 지시하다

33 톱

34 발표

35 ~을 잘라내다

36 ~로 가는 길에

37 ~을 꺼내다

38 ~에 대하여 꿈꾸다

39 넘어지다

40 ~을 이용하다

41 ~로 유명하다

42 ~하지 않을 수 없다

43 ~을 자랑스러워하다

※ 다음 영영풀이에 알맞은 단어를 <보기>에서 골라 쓴 후, 우리말 뜻을 쓰시오.

1 _____ : extremely valuable: _____

2 _____ : a person who owns something: _____

3 _____ : no longer whole or working correctly: _____

4 _____ : to give money for goods or services: _____

5 _____ : to fasten or join to one thing to another: _____

6 _____ : a copy of something such as a picture: _____

7 _____ : the amount of money that you have to pay for something: _____

8 _____ : to use your authority to tell someone to do something: _____

9 _____ : someone who buys and sells a particular product: _____

10 _____ : to choose somebody to do a particular job by voting for them: _____

11 _____ : an infectious disease like a very bad cold, which causes fever, pains, and weakness: _____

12 _____ : an old object such as a piece of furniture or jewelry that has a high value: _____

13 _____ : to ask people to pay a particular amount of money for something: _____

14 _____ : to hit a door with your hand so that someone inside knows you are there: _____

15 _____ : a tool for cutting wood or materials, typically with a long, thin steel blade: _____

16 _____ : to put your arms around someone especially as a way of showing love or friendship: _____

보기			
hug	order	saw	price
elect	broken	flu	pay
knock	owner	charge	attach
dealer	priceless	antique	reproduction

※ 다음 우리말과 일치하도록 빈칸에 알맞은 말을 쓰시오.

Listen and Talk A 1

B: Sue, you look _____. What's _____?
G: I was _____ _____ class president. I'm so _____.
B: That's wonderful. Congratulations!
G: Thanks. I'm really happy _____ _____ a _____ _____ _____ for my class.

Listen and Talk A 2

G: Tim, congratulations _____ _____ the gold medal in the school marathon.
B: Thanks, Suji. I'm very happy.
G: You _____ be very _____ _____ _____.
B: Yes, I _____. I _____ my _____.

Listen and Talk A 3

B: Mina, is _____ _____?
G: Well, I _____ my smartphone. I'm _____.
B: Oh, I'm so _____ _____ _____ that. Do you remember _____ _____ _____ _____ last?
G: Well, I remember _____ it _____ of my bag at the snack shop.
B: Then, let's go back to the snack shop _____ _____ _____ it.

Listen and Talk A 4

G: You don't look so _____, Inho. What's _____ _____?
B: I have _____ _____.
G: That's too _____. Did you _____ the doctor?
B: Yes. I'm _____ _____.
G: Well, I hope you _____ _____ soon.
B: Thanks.

Listen and Talk B

A: What's _____?
B: I _____ _____ _____ in the English _____ _____. I'm so _____.
A: That's wonderful. _____!

A: What's _____?
B: My smartphone is _____. I'm very _____.
A: That's too _____. I'm _____ _____ _____ that.

Listen and Talk C

B: Excuse me, Ms. Carter. Can I ask you a question? Did I _____ the _____ _____ in the _____?

W: Yes, you did. Congratulations, Jiho! You're _____ _____ be Romeo in our school play, *Romeo and Juliet*.

B: Really? I'm so _____. Thank you so much, Ms. Carter.

W: I know _____ _____ _____ _____ the role. I'm so _____ _____ you.

B: Thank you. What _____ Sumi? Did she _____ the _____ she wanted, _____?

W: _____, no. She's very _____.

B: Oh, I'm _____ _____ _____ that. _____, when is the first _____?

W: It's _____ 2 p.m. _____ September 20th, _____ the acting club room. You'll _____ a text message _____ it soon.

B: OK. I'll be there.

Listen and Talk D

Last summer, I lost my dog, Bomi. She _____ _____ I was drinking water in the park. _____, I _____ _____ _____ find her two days _____. I was _____ _____ _____ I hugged her _____.

Talk and Play

A: What's up?

B: I was _____ as the leader of the school band. I'm so _____.

A: That's wonderful. Congratulations!

A: What's _____?

B: My bike is _____. I'm very _____.

A: That's _____ _____. I'm _____ _____ _____ _____.

Review 1

B: You look _____, Sally. What's _____?

G: I'm _____ _____ _____ to the Dream Concert.

B: Congratulations! I know _____ _____ _____ _____ _____ to go.

G: Thanks. I'm so happy _____ _____ a chance _____ _____ my favorite singer.

Review 2

B: You don't look _____, Sumi. What's _____ _____?

G: Well, I didn't get a role in the school play. I'm very _____.

B: Oh, I'm so _____ _____ _____ _____. But I'm sure you can _____ _____ _____ _____ next time.

G: Thanks. I'll _____ _____ next time.

B: 실례합니다. Carter 선생님. 질문 하나 해도 될까요? 제가 연극에서 주인공 역할을 맡게 됐나요?

W: 응, 그래. 축하해, 지호야! 너는 우리 학교 연극 "로미오와 줄리엣"에서 로미오를 하게 될 거야.

B: 정말요? 너무 신나요. 감사합니다, Carter 선생님.

W: 네가 얼마나 그 역할을 원했는지 내가 알지. 나도 정말 기쁘구나.

B: 감사합니다. 수미는 어떻게 됐어요? 수미도 원했던 역할을 맡게 됐나요?

W: 유감스럽게도 아니란다. 수미가 무척 실망했어.

B: 아, 정말 유감이네요. 그런데 첫 연습은 언제인가요?

W: 9월 20일 2시에 연극 동아리 방에서 할 거야. 그것에 관해서 문자 메시지를 곧 받게 될 거야.

B: 네. 연습 때 갈게요.

지난 여름에 나는 내 개 보미를 잃어버렸어. 보미는 내가 공원에서 물을 마시고 있는 동안 사라졌어. 다행히도, 나는 이틀 후에 그녀를 찾을 수 있었어. 나는 너무 행복해서 그녀를 품에 꼭 안았어.

A: 무슨 일이니?

B: 나는 학교 밴드의 리더로 뽑혔어. 정말 신이 나.

A: 멋지다. 축하해!

A: 무슨 일이니?

B: 내 자전거가 고장 났어. 아주 기분이 좋지 않아.

A: 참 안됐구나. 유감이야.

B: Sally, 너 신나 보인다. 무슨 일이니?

G: 나 Dream 콘서트에 가.

B: 축하해! 네가 얼마나 가고 싶어 했는지 알아.

G: 고마워. 나는 내가 가장 좋아하는 가수를 볼 기회를 얻어서 정말 기뻐.

B: 수미야, 너 기분 안 좋아 보인다. 무슨 일 있니?

G: 학교 연극에서 역할을 맡지 못 했어. 난 정말 실망했어.

B: 오, 정말 유감이야. 그렇지만 넌 분명 다음 기회에 역할을 맡을 수 있을 거야.

G: 고마워. 다음에는 더 많이 노력할 거야.

※ 다음 우리말에 맞도록 대화를 영어로 쓰시오.

Listen and Talk A 1

B: _____

G: _____

B: _____

G: _____

B: Sue, 신나 보인다. 무슨 일이니?
G: 나 학급 회장으로 당선되었어. 정말 신나.
B: 멋지다. 축하해!
G: 고마워. 우리 반을 위해서 일할 기회가 생겨서 정말 기뻐.

Listen and Talk A 2

G: _____

B: _____

G: _____

B: _____

G: Tim, 학교 마라톤에서 금메달을 딴 것을 축하해.
B: 고마워, 수지야. 정말 행복해.
G: 너 자신이 정말 자랑스럽겠다.
B: 응, 맞아. 난 최선을 다했어.

Listen and Talk A 3

B: _____

G: _____

B: _____

G: _____

B: _____

B: 미나야, 무슨 안 좋은 일 있니?
G: 스마트폰을 잃어버렸어. 기분이 안 좋아.
B: 오, 정말 유감이야. 마지막으로 그것을 언제 사용했는지 기억하니?
G: 음, 매점에서 그것을 가방에서 꺼냈던 것은 기억나.
B: 그러면, 그것을 찾으러 매점에 돌아가자.

Listen and Talk A 4

G: _____

B: _____

G: _____

B: _____

G: _____

B: _____

G: 인호야, 너 몸이 안 좋아 보인다. 무슨 문제 있니?
B: 나 독감에 걸렸어.
G: 참 안됐구나, 병원은 가 봤니?
B: 응. 약을 먹고 있어.
G: 얼른 나았으면 좋겠다.
B: 고마워.

Listen and Talk B

A: _____

B: _____

A: _____

A: _____

B: _____

A: _____

A: 무슨 일이니?
B: 영어 말하기 대회에서 1등 상을 받았어. 정말 신이 나.
A: 멋지다. 축하해!

A: 무슨 일이니?
B: 내 스마트폰이 고장 났어. 아주 기분이 좋지 않아.
A: 참 안됐구나. 유감이야.

Listen and Talk C

B: _____
_____
W: _____
_____
B: _____
W: _____
B: _____
W: _____
B: _____
W: _____
B: _____

Listen and Talk D

_____
_____

Talk and Play

A: _____
B: _____
A: _____
A: _____
B: _____
A: _____

Review 1

B: _____
G: _____
B: _____
G: _____

Review 2

B: _____
G: _____
B: _____
G: _____

B: 실례합니다. Carter 선생님. 질문 하나 해도 될까요? 제가 연극에서 주인공 역할을 맡게 됐나요?
W: 응, 그래. 축하해, 지호야! 너는 우리 학교 연극 "로미오와 줄리엣"에서 로미오를 하게 될 거야.
B: 정말요? 너무 신나요. 감사합니다, Carter 선생님.
W: 네가 얼마나 그 역할을 원했는지 내가 알지. 나도 정말 기쁘구나.
B: 감사합니다. 수미는 어떻게 됐어요? 수미도 원했던 역할을 맡게 됐나요?
W: 유감스럽게도 아니란다. 수미가 무척 실망했어.
B: 아, 정말 유감이네요. 그런데 첫 연습은 언제인가요?
W: 9월 20일 2시에 연극 동아리 방에서 할 거야. 그것에 관해서 문자 메시지를 곧 받게 될 거야.
B: 네. 연습 때 갈게요.

지난 여름에 나는 내 개 보미를 잃어버렸어. 보미는 내가 공원에서 물을 마시고 있는 동안 사라졌어. 다행히도, 나는 이틀 후에 그녀를 찾을 수 있었어. 나는 너무 행복해서 그녀를 품에 꼭 안았어.

A: 무슨 일이니?
B: 나는 학교 밴드의 리더로 뽑혔어. 정말 신이 나.
A: 멋지다. 축하해!

A: 무슨 일이니?
B: 내 자전거가 고장 났어. 아주 기분이 좋지 않아.
A: 참 안됐구나. 유감이야.

B: Sally, 너 신나 보인다. 무슨 일이니?
G: 나 Dream 콘서트에 가.
B: 축하해! 네가 얼마나 가고 싶어 했는지 알아.
G: 고마워. 나는 내가 가장 좋아하는 가수를 볼 기회를 얻어서 정말 기뻐.

B: 수미야, 너 기분 안 좋아 보인다. 무슨 일 있니?
G: 학교 연극에서 역할을 맡지 못 했어. 난 정말 실망했어.
B: 오, 정말 유감이야. 그렇지만 넌 분명 다음 기회에 역할을 맡을 수 있을 거야.
G: 고마워. 다음에는 더 많이 노력할 거야.

※ 다음 우리말과 일치하도록 빈칸에 알맞은 것을 골라 쓰시오.

1 _____ _____ Sunday
A. Lucky   B. One

2 Cyril Boggis was _____ _____ _____ _____ in London.
A. dealer   B. an   C. furniture   D. antique

3 He was known for _____ good things at a _____ and then selling them at a _____ price.
A. low   B. buying   C. high   D. price

4 People asked him where he _____ _____ the _____, but he just said, "It's a _____."
A. secret   B. got   C. furniture   D. had

5 Mr. Boggis' _____ was _____.
A. simple   B. secret

6 He _____ to small towns _____ Sunday and _____ _____ doors.
A. knocked   B. every   C. on   D. went

7 He told people _____ he was _____ _____ _____.
A. dealer   B. furniture   C. that   D. a

8 People didn't know how _____ their _____ were, so Mr. Boggis _____ _____ of them.
A. advantage   B. valuable   C. took   D. things

9 He was _____ to _____ _____ very _____.
A. cheaply   B. able   C. things   D. buy

10 Now it was _____ Sunday, and Mr. Boggis was _____ a small _____ _____.
A. town   B. another   C. in   D. again

11 _____ a _____ he _____, he met two _____.
A. men   B. house   C. visited   D. at

12 _____ was Rummins, the _____, and _____ was his son Bert.
A. other   B. one   C. the   D. owner

13 "I _____ _____ _____.
A. furniture   B. old   C. buy

14 Do you _____ _____?" _____ Mr. Boggis.
A. asked   B. any   C. have

15 "No, I _____," _____ Rummins.
A. said   B. don't

16 "Can I just _____ _____ _____?" asked Mr. Boggis.
A. look   B. a   C. take

1 어느 운수 좋은 일요일

2 Cyril Boggis는 런던의 골동품 가구 판매상이었다.

3 그는 좋은 물건을 낮은 가격에 사서 높은 가격에 파는 것으로 유명했다.

4 사람들은 그에게 어디서 가구를 구했는지 물어봤지만, 그는 "그건 비밀이에요."라고만 말했다.

5 Boggis 씨의 비밀은 단순했다.

6 그는 매주 일요일 작은 마을들을 방문해서 문을 두드렸다.

7 그는 사람들에게 자신이 가구 판매상이라고 말했다.

8 사람들은 자신들의 물건들이 얼마나 값진 것인지 몰랐으므로 Boggis 씨는 그들을 이용했다.

9 그는 물건들을 매우 싸게 살 수 있었다.

10 일요일이 또 찾아왔고 그날 Boggis 씨는 다시 어느 작은 마을에 있었다.

11 그는 방문한 집에서 두 남자를 만났다.

12 한 명은 주인인 Rummins였고, 다른 한 명은 그의 아들인 Bert 였다.

13 "저는 고가구를 삽니다.

14 고가구가 있으신가요?" Boggis 씨가 물었다.

15 "아니요." Rummins가 말했다.

16 "한번 둘러봐도 될까요?" Boggis 씨가 물었다.

17 "_____. _____ come _____," said Rummins.

    A. in   B. sure   C. please

18 Mr. Boggis first _____ to the kitchen, and _____ _____

    _____.

    A. nothing   B. went   C. was   D. there

19 He _____ _____ _____ the living room.

    A. then   B. to   C. moved

20 And _____ _____ _____!

    A. it   B. there   C. was

21 A table which was a _____ _____ _____ eighteenth-century English _____.

    A. furniture   B. piece   C. of   D. priceless

22 He was _____ excited _____ he almost _____ _____.

    A. over   B. so   C. fell   D. that

23 "What's _____?" Bert _____.

    A. asked   B. wrong

24 "Oh, _____. Nothing _____ _____," Mr. Boggis _____.

    A. lied   B. nothing   C. all   D. at

25 He then said _____ a _____ _____, "This table is a _____.

    A. reproduction   B. straight   C. with   D. face

26 It's _____ _____ a _____ pounds."

    A. only   B. worth   C. few

27 He then _____, "Hmm, I think I _____ _____ it.

    A. buy   B. added   C. may

28 The _____ of my _____ at home _____ _____.

    A. broken   B. legs   C. are   D. table

29 I can _____ _____ the legs of your table and _____ them to _____."

    A. off   B. mine   C. cut   D. attach

30 "_____ _____?" Rummins asked.

    A. much   B. how

31 "_____ much, I'm _____.

    A. afraid   B. not

32 This is _____ _____ _____," said Mr. Boggis.

    A. a   B. just   C. reproduction

33 "_____ how _____?"

    A. much   B. so

34 "_____ _____."

    A. pounds   B. ten

35 "Ten? It's _____ _____ that."

    A. than   B. worth   C. more

---

17 "그럼요. 들어오세요." Rummins가 말했다.

18 Boggis 씨는 먼저 부엌에 갔는데 아무것도 없었다.

19 그런 다음 그는 거실로 옮겼다.

20 그리고 그곳에 그것이 있었다!

21 18세기 영국 가구인 매우 귀중한 탁자가.

22 그는 몹시 흥분해서 거의 넘어질 뻔했다.

23 "무슨 일이세요?" Bert가 물었다.

24 "오. 아무것도 아니에요. 전혀 아무 일도 아닙니다." Boggis 씨는 거짓말을 했다.

25 그리고 나서 그는 정색하며 말했다 "이 탁자는 복제품입니다.

26 몇 파운드의 가치밖에 안 돼요."

27 그리고 그는 덧붙였다. "흠, 제 생각에 제가 살 수도 있을 것 같아요.

28 우리 집에 있는 탁자 다리가 부러졌거든요.

29 당신의 탁자 다리를 잘라서 제 탁자에 붙일 수 있겠어요."

30 "얼마 줄 거예요?" Rummins가 물었다.

31 "유감이지만 많이 줄 수는 없어요.

32 이것은 복제품일 뿐이니까요." Boggis 씨가 말했다.

33 "그래서 얼마 줄 수 있는데요?"

34 "10파운드요."

35 "10이요? 그것보다는 가치가 더 나가요."

36 "_____ _____ fifteen?"
    A. about   B. how

37 "_____ _____ fifty."
    A. it   B. make

38 "Well, thirty. This is _____ _____ _____."
    A. offer   B. my   C. final

39 "OK, it's _____, but how are you _____ to _____ it?
    A. going   B. yours   C. take

40 This _____ will not _____ _____ a car!"
    A. go   B. thing   C. in

41 "We'll see," Mr. Boggis said and _____ _____ _____ _____ his car.
    A. out   B. bring   C. went   D. to

42 _____ his _____ to the car, Mr. Boggis _____ _____ smiling.
    A. help   B. way   C. couldn't   D. on

43 The table was _____ every _____ dreamed _____.
    A. what   B. of   C. dealer

44 He _____ _____ his _____.
    A. luck   B. couldn't   C. believe

45 "Dad, _____ _____ this thing doesn't _____ _____ his car?
    A. if   B. in   C. what   D. go

46 He _____ _____ _____ you," said Bert.
    A. pay   B. not   C. might

47 Rummins then _____ _____ _____.
    A. idea   B. had   C. an

48 "_____ _____ _____ is only the legs.
    A. wants   B. what   C. he

49 Let's _____ _____ _____ _____ for him," said Rummins.
    A. off   B. the   C. cut   D. legs

50 "_____ _____!" said Bert.
    A. idea   B. great

51 Bert then _____ a saw and began to _____ _____ the legs.
    A. out   B. off   C. took   D. cut

52 When Mr. Boggis came _____, the legs _____ _____ cut _____.
    A. back   B. been   C. had   D. off

53 "Don't _____, this was a _____.
    A. favor   B. worry

54 I _____ _____ you _____ this," said Rummins.
    A. for   B. charge   C. won't

55 Mr. Boggis was _____ _____ _____ he couldn't say _____.
    A. anything   B. that   C. shocked   D. so

36 "15는 어때요?"

37 "50으로 하지요."

38 "음, 30이요. 이게 제 마지막 제 안입니다."

39 "그러죠, 이제 당신 겁니다. 그런데 이걸 어떻게 가져갈 건가요?

40 이게 차에 들어가지 않을 거예요!"

41 "한번 보죠." Boggis 씨가 말하고는 자신의 차를 가지러 밖으로 나갔다.

42 차로 가는 길에 Boggis 씨는 싱글벙글하지 않을 수 없었다.

43 그 탁자는 모든 판매상이 꿈꾸는 것이었다.

44 그는 자신의 운을 믿을 수 없었다.

45 "아버지, 만약 이게 차에 안 들어가면 어떻게 하죠?

46 그가 값을 지불하지 않을 수도 있어요." Bert가 말했다.

47 Rummins는 그때 생각이 떠올랐다.

48 "그가 원하는 건 오직 다리뿐이야.

49 그를 위해서 다리를 자르자." Rummins가 말했다.

50 "좋은 생각이에요!" Bert가 말했다.

51 그런 다음 Bert는 톱을 꺼내서 다리를 자르기 시작했다.

52 Boggis 씨가 돌아왔을 때, 다리는 잘려 있었다.

53 "걱정하지 마세요. 호의로 한 거예요.

54 이것에 대해 비용을 청구하지는 않을게요." Rummins가 말했다.

55 Boggis 씨는 너무 충격을 받아서 아무 말도 할 수 없었다.

※ 다음 우리말과 일치하도록 빈칸에 알맞은 말을 쓰시오.

1 _____ _____ Sunday

2 Cyril Boggis was _____ _____ _____ _____ in London.

3 He _____ _____ _____ buying good things _____ _____ _____ _____ and then selling them _____ _____ _____ _____.

4 People asked him _____ _____ _____ _____ the furniture, but he just said, "It's a _____."

5 Mr. Boggis' secret was _____.

6 He went to small towns _____ _____ and _____ on doors.

7 He told people that he was _____ _____ _____.

8 People didn't know _____ _____ _____ _____ _____, so Mr. Boggis _____ _____ _____ them.

9 He was _____ _____ buy things _____ _____.

10 Now it was _____ _____, and Mr. Boggis was in a small town again.

11 _____ _____ _____ he visited, he met two men.

12 _____ was Rummins, the _____, and _____ _____ was his son Bert.

13 "I buy _____ _____.

14 Do you have _____?" asked Mr. Boggis.

15 "No, I _____," said Rummins.

16 "Can I just _____ _____ _____?" asked Mr. Boggis.

17 "_____. Please come in," said Rummins.

18 Mr. Boggis first _____ _____ the kitchen, and _____ _____ _____.

19 He then _____ _____ the living room.

20 And _____ _____ _____!

21 A table which was _____ _____ _____ _____ eighteenth-century English _____.

22 He was _____ excited _____ he almost _____ _____.

23 "What's _____?" Bert asked.

24 "Oh, _____. Nothing _____ _____," Mr. Boggis lied.

25 He then said _____ _____ _____ _____, "This table is a _____.

26 _____ _____ only _____ _____ pounds."

27 He then _____, "Hmm, I think I _____ _____ it.

28 The legs of my table at home _____ _____.

29 I can _____ _____ the legs of your table and _____ _____ _____ _____."

30 "_____ _____?" Rummins asked.

31 "Not much, I'm _____.

32 This is just _____ _____," said Mr. Boggis.

33 "_____ how much?"

34 "Ten _____."

35 "Ten? _____ _____ _____ _____ that."

17	"그럼요. 들어오세요." Rummins가 말했다.
18	Boggis 씨는 먼저 부엌에 갔는데 아무것도 없었다.
19	그런 다음 그는 거실로 옮겼다.
20	그리고 그곳에 그것이 있었다!
21	18세기 영국 가구인 매우 귀중한 탁자가.
22	그는 몹시 흥분해서 거의 넘어질 뻔했다.
23	"무슨 일이세요?" Bert가 물었다.
24	"오, 아무것도 아니에요. 전혀 아무 일도 아닙니다." Boggis 씨는 거짓말을 했다.
25	그러고 나서 그는 정색하며 말했다 "이 탁자는 복제품입니다.
26	몇 파운드의 가치밖에 안 돼요."
27	그리고 그는 덧붙였다. "흠, 제 생각에 제가 살 수도 있을 것 같아요.
28	우리 집에 있는 탁자 다리가 부러졌거든요.
29	당신의 탁자 다리를 잘라서 제 탁자에 붙일 수 있겠어요."
30	"얼마 줄 거예요?" Rummins가 물었다.
31	"유감이지만 많이 줄 수는 없어요.
32	이것은 복제품일 뿐이니까요." Boggis 씨가 말했다.
33	"그래서 얼마 줄 수 있는데요?"
34	"10파운드요."
35	"10이요? 그것보다는 가치가 더 나가요."

36 "_____ _____ fifteen?"

37 "_____ _____ fifty."

38 "Well, _____. This is my _____ _____."

39 "OK, it's _____, but how are you _____ to _____ it?

40 This thing will not _____ _____ a car!"

41 "We'll see," Mr. Boggis said and _____ _____ _____ _____ his car.

42 _____ _____ _____ to the car, Mr. Boggis _____ _____.

43 The table was _____ every dealer _____ _____.

44 He _____ _____ his luck.

45 "Dad, _____ _____ this thing doesn't go in his car?

46 He might not _____ _____," said Bert.

47 Rummins then _____ _____ _____.

48 "_____ _____ _____ is only the legs.

49 Let's _____ _____ _____ _____ for him," said Rummins.

50 "_____ _____!" said Bert.

51 Bert then _____ _____ a saw and began to _____ _____ the legs.

52 When Mr. Boggis _____ _____, the legs _____ _____ _____ _____.

53 "Don't _____, this was _____ _____.

54 I won't _____ you _____ this," said Rummins.

55 Mr. Boggis was _____ shocked _____ he couldn't say _____.

36 "15는 어때요?"

37 "50으로 하지요."

38 "음, 30이요. 이게 제 마지막 제안입니다."

39 "그러죠. 이제 당신 겁니다. 그런데 이걸 어떻게 가져갈 건가요?

40 이게 차에 들어가지 않을 거예요!"

41 "한번 보죠." Boggis 씨가 말하고는 자신의 차를 가지러 밖으로 나갔다.

42 차로 가는 길에 Boggis 씨는 싱글벙글하지 않을 수 없었다.

43 그 탁자는 모든 판매상이 꿈꾸는 것이었다.

44 그는 자신의 운을 믿을 수 없었다.

45 "아버지, 만약 이게 차에 안 들어가면 어떻게 하죠?

46 그가 값을 지불하지 않을 수도 있어요." Bert가 말했다.

47 Rummins는 그때 생각이 떠올랐다.

48 "그가 원하는 건 오직 다리뿐이야.

49 그를 위해서 다리를 자르자." Rummins가 말했다.

50 "좋은 생각이에요!" Bert가 말했다.

51 그런 다음 Bert는 톱을 꺼내서 다리를 자르기 시작했다.

52 Boggis 씨가 돌아왔을 때, 다리는 잘려 있었다.

53 "걱정하지 마세요. 호의로 한 거예요.

54 이것에 대해 비용을 청구하지는 않을게요." Rummins가 말했다.

55 Boggis 씨는 너무 충격을 받아서 아무 말도 할 수 없었다.

※ 다음 문장을 우리말로 쓰시오.

1 One Lucky Sunday

➡ _____

2 Cyril Boggis was an antique furniture dealer in London.

➡ _____

3 He was known for buying good things at a low price and then selling them at a high price.

➡ _____

4 People asked him where he had got the furniture, but he just said, "It's a secret."

➡ _____

5 Mr. Boggis' secret was simple.

➡ _____

6 He went to small towns every Sunday and knocked on doors.

➡ _____

7 He told people that he was a furniture dealer.

➡ _____

8 People didn't know how valuable their things were, so Mr. Boggis took advantage of them.

➡ _____

9 He was able to buy things very cheaply.

➡ _____

10 Now it was another Sunday, and Mr. Boggis was in a small town again.

➡ _____

11 At a house he visited, he met two men.

➡ _____

12 One was Rummins, the owner, and the other was his son Bert.

➡ _____

13 "I buy old furniture.

➡ _____

14 Do you have any?" asked Mr. Boggis.

➡ _____

15 "No, I don't," said Rummins.

➡ _____

16 "Can I just take a look?" asked Mr. Boggis.

➡ _____

17 "Sure. Please come in," said Rummins.

➡ _____

18   Mr. Boggis first went to the kitchen, and there was nothing.

➡ _____

19   He then moved to the living room.

➡ _____

20   And there it was!

➡ _____

21   A table which was a priceless piece of eighteenth-century English furniture.

➡ _____

22   He was so excited that he almost fell over.

➡ _____

23   "What's wrong?" Bert asked.

➡ _____

24   "Oh, nothing. Nothing at all," Mr. Boggis lied.

➡ _____

25   He then said with a straight face, "This table is a reproduction.

➡ _____

26   It's worth only a few pounds."

➡ _____

27   He then added, "Hmm, I think I may buy it.

➡ _____

28   The legs of my table at home are broken.

➡ _____

29   I can cut off the legs of your table and attach them to mine."

➡ _____

30   "How much?" Rummins asked.

➡ _____

31   "Not much, I'm afraid.

➡ _____

32   This is just a reproduction," said Mr. Boggis.

➡ _____

33   "So how much?

➡ _____

34   "Ten pounds."

➡ _____

35   "Ten? It's worth more than that."

➡ _____

36   "How about fifteen?"

➡ _____

37 "Make it fifty."

➡ _____

38 "Well, thirty. This is my final offer."

➡ _____

39 "OK, it's yours, but how are you going to take it?

➡ _____

40 This thing will not go in a car!"

➡ _____

41 "We'll see," Mr. Boggis said and went out to bring his car.

➡ _____

42 On his way to the car, Mr. Boggis couldn't help smiling.

➡ _____

43 The table was what every dealer dreamed of.

➡ _____

44 He couldn't believe his luck.

➡ _____

45 "Dad, what if this thing doesn't go in his car?

➡ _____

46 He might not pay you," said Bert.

➡ _____

47 Rummins then had an idea.

➡ _____

48 "What he wants is only the legs.

➡ _____

49 Let's cut the legs off for him," said Rummins.

➡ _____

50 "Great idea!" said Bert.

➡ _____

51 Bert then took out a saw and began to cut off the legs.

➡ _____

52 When Mr. Boggis came back, the legs had been cut off.

➡ _____

53 "Don't worry, this was a favor.

➡ _____

54 I won't charge you for this," said Rummins.

➡ _____

55 Mr. Boggis was so shocked that he couldn't say anything.

➡ _____

※ 다음 괄호 안의 단어들을 우리말에 맞도록 바르게 배열하시오.

1 (Lucky / One / Sunday)
➡ _____

2 (Boggis / Cyril / an / was / furniture / antique / in / dealer / London.)
➡ _____

3 (was / he / for / known / buying / things / good / a / at / price / low / and / selling / then / at / them / a / price. / high)
➡ _____

4 (asked / people / where / him / had / he / got / furniture, / the / he / but / said, / just / a / "it's / secret.")
➡ _____

5 (Boggis' / Mr. / was / secret / simple.)
➡ _____

6 (went / he / small / to / towns / Sunday / every / and / on / knocked / doors.)
➡ _____

7 (told / he / that / people / was / he / a / dealer. / furniture)
➡ _____

8 (didn't / people / how / know / their / valuable / things / so / were, / Boggis / Mr. / advantage / took / them. / of)
➡ _____

9 (was / he / to / able / things / buy / cheaply. / very)
➡ _____

10 (it / now / another / was / Sunday, / Mr. / and / Boggis / in / was / small / in / again. / town)
➡ _____

11 (a / at / he / house / visited, / met / he / men. / two)
➡ _____

12 (was / one / Rummins, / owener, / the / and / other / the / his / was / Bert. / son)
➡ _____

13 (buy / "I / furniture. / old)
➡ _____

14 (you / do / any?" / have / Mr. / asked / Boggis.)
➡ _____

15 (I / "no, / said / don't," / Rummins.)
➡ _____

16 (I / "can / take / just / look?" / a / Mr. / asked / Boggis.)
➡ _____

1 어느 운수 좋은 일요일

2 Cyril Boggis는 런던의 골동품 가구 판매상이었다.

3 그는 좋은 물건을 낮은 가격에 사서 높은 가격에 파는 것으로 유명했다.

4 사람들은 그에게 어디서 가구를 구했는지 물어봤지만, 그는 "그 건 비밀이에요."라고만 말했다.

5 Boggis 씨의 비밀은 단순했다.

6 그는 매주 일요일 작은 마을들을 방문해서 문을 두드렸다.

7 그는 사람들에게 자신이 가구 판매상이라고 말했다.

8 사람들은 자신들의 물건들이 얼마나 값진 것인지 몰랐으므로 Boggis 씨는 그들을 이용했다.

9 그는 물건들을 매우 싸게 살 수 있었다.

10 일요일이 또 찾아왔고 그날 Boggis 씨는 다시 어느 작은 마을에 있었다.

11 그는 방문한 집에서 두 남자를 만났다.

12 한 명은 주인인 Rummins였고, 다른 한 명은 그의 아들인 Bert 였다.

13 "저는 고가구를 삽니다.

14 고가구가 있으신가요?" Boggis 씨가 물었다.

15 "아니요." Rummins가 말했다.

16 "한번 둘러봐도 될까요?" Boggis 씨가 물었다.

17 ("sure. // come / please / in," / Rummins. / said)

➡ _____

18 (Boggis / Mr. / went / first / the / to / kitchen, / there / and / nothing. / was)

➡ _____

19 (then / he / to / moved / the / room. / living)

➡ _____

20 (there / and / was! / it)

➡ _____

21 (table / a / was / which / priceless / a / piece / eighteenth-century / of / furniture. / English)

➡ _____

22 (was / he / excited / so / he / that / almost / over. / fell)

➡ _____

23 (wrong?" / "what's // asked. / Bert)

➡ _____

24 (nothing. / "oh, // at / nothing / all," / Boggis / lied. / Mr.)

➡ _____

25 (then / he / with / said / straight / a / face, / table / "this / a / is / reproduction.)

➡ _____

26 (worth / it's / a / only / pounds." / few)

➡ _____

27 (then / he / added, / "hmm, / think / I / may / I / it. / buy)

➡ _____

28 (legs / the / my / of / table / home / at / broken. / are)

➡ _____

29 (can / I / off / cut / legs / the / your / of / and / table / them / attach / mine." / to)

➡ _____

30 (much?" / "how / asked. / Rummins)

➡ _____

31 (much, / "not, / afraid. / I'm)

➡ _____

32 (is / this / a / just / reproduction," / Mr. / said / Boggis.)

➡ _____

33 (how / much?" / "so)

➡ _____

34 (pounds." / "ten)

➡ _____

35 ("ten? // worth / it's / than / more / that.")

➡ _____

17 "그럼요. 들어오세요." Rummins가 말했다.

18 Boggis 씨는 먼저 부엌에 갔는데 아무것도 없었다.

19 그런 다음 그는 거실로 옮겼다.

20 그리고 그곳에 그것이 있었다!

21 18세기 영국 가구인 매우 귀중한 탁자가.

22 그는 몹시 흥분해서 거의 넘어질 뻔했다.

23 "무슨 일이세요?" Bert가 물었다.

24 "오. 아무것도 아니에요. 전혀 아무 일도 아닙니다." Boggis 씨는 거짓말을 했다.

25 그러고 나서 그는 정색하며 말했다 "이 탁자는 복제품입니다.

26 몇 파운드의 가치밖에 안 돼요.

27 그리고 그는 덧붙였다. "흠, 제 생각에 제가 살 수도 있을 것 같아요.

28 우리 집에 있는 탁자 다리가 부러졌거든요.

29 당신의 탁자 다리를 잘라서 제 탁자에 붙일 수 있겠어요."

30 "얼마 줄 거예요?" Rummins가 물었다.

31 "유감이지만 많이 줄 수는 없어요.

32 이것은 복제품일 뿐이니까요." Boggis 씨가 말했다.

33 "그래서 얼마 줄 수 있는데요?"

34 "10파운드요."

35 "10이요? 그것보다는 가치가 더 나가요."

36 (about / fifteen?" / "how)

➡ _____

37 (it / "make / fifty.")

➡ _____

38 (thirty. / "well, // is / this / final / my / offer.")

➡ _____

39 ("ok, / yours, / it's / how / but / you / are / going / take / to / it?)

➡ _____

40 (thing / this / not / will / in / go / car!" / a)

➡ _____

41 (see," / "we'll / Boggis / Mr. / and / said / went / to / out / his / bring / car.)

➡ _____

42 (his / on / to / way / car, / the / Boggis / Mr. / help / couldn't / smiling.)

➡ _____

43 (table / the / what / was / dealer / every / of. / dreamed)

➡ _____

44 (couldn't / he / his / believe / luck.)

➡ _____

45 ("dad, / if / what / thing / this / go / doesn't / his / in / car?)

➡ _____

46 (might / he / pay / not / you," / Bert. / said)

➡ _____

47 (then / Rummins / an / had / idea.)

➡ _____

48 ("what / wants / he / only / is / legs. / the)

➡ _____

49 (cut / let's / legs / the / for / off / him," / Rummins. / said)

➡ _____

50 (idea!" / "great / Bert. / said)

➡ _____

51 (then / Bert / out / took / saw / a / and / to / began / cut / the / off / legs.)

➡ _____

52 (Mr. / when / came / Boggis / back, / legs / the / been / had / off. / cut)

➡ _____

53 (worry, / "don't / was / this / favor. / a)

➡ _____

54 (won't / I / charge / for / you / said / this," / Rummins.)

➡ _____

55 (Boggis / Mr. / so / was / that / shocked / he / say / couldn't / anything.)

➡ _____

36 "15는 어때요?"

37 "50으로 하지요."

38 "음, 30이요. 이게 제 마지막 제안입니다."

39 "그러죠. 이제 당신 겁니다. 그런데 이걸 어떻게 가져갈 건가요?

40 이게 차에 들어가지 않을 거예요!"

41 "한번 보죠." Boggis 씨가 말하고는 자신의 차를 가지러 밖으로 나갔다.

42 차로 가는 길에 Boggis 씨는 싱글벙글하지 않을 수 없었다.

43 그 탁자는 모든 판매상이 꿈꾸는 것이었다.

44 그는 자신의 운을 믿을 수 없었다.

45 "아버지, 만약 이게 차에 안 들어가면 어떻게 하죠?

46 그가 값을 지불하지 않을 수도 있어요." Bert가 말했다.

47 Rummins는 그때 생각이 떠올랐다.

48 "그가 원하는 건 오직 다리뿐이야.

49 그를 위해서 다리를 자르자." Rummins가 말했다.

50 "좋은 생각이에요!" Bert가 말했다.

51 그런 다음 Bert는 톱을 꺼내서 다리를 자르기 시작했다.

52 Boggis 씨가 돌아왔을 때, 다리는 잘려 있었다.

53 "걱정하지 마세요. 호의로 한 거예요.

54 이것에 대해 비용을 청구하지 않을게요." Rummins가 말했다.

55 Boggis 씨는 너무 충격을 받아서 아무 말도 할 수 없었다.

※ 다음 우리말을 영어로 쓰시오.

1 어느 운수 좋은 일요일

➡ _____

2 Cyril Boggis는 런던의 골동품 가구 판매상이었다.

➡ _____

3 그는 좋은 물건을 낮은 가격에 사서 높은 가격에 파는 것으로 유명했다.

➡ _____

4 사람들은 그에게 어디서 가구를 구했는지 물어봤지만, 그는 "그건 비밀이에요."라고만 말했다.

➡ _____

5 Boggis 씨의 비밀은 단순했다.

➡ _____

6 그는 매주 일요일 작은 마을들을 방문해서 문을 두드렸다.

➡ _____

7 그는 사람들에게 자신이 가구 판매상이라고 말했다.

➡ _____

8 사람들은 자신들의 물건들이 얼마나 값진 것인지 몰랐으므로 Boggis 씨는 그들을 이용했다.

➡ _____

9 그는 물건들을 매우 싸게 살 수 있었다.

➡ _____

10 일요일이 또 찾아왔고 그날 Boggis 씨는 다시 어느 작은 마을에 있었다.

➡ _____

11 그는 방문한 집에서 두 남자를 만났다.

➡ _____

12 한 명은 주인인 Rummins였고, 다른 한 명은 그의 아들인 Bert였다.

➡ _____

13 "저는 고가구를 삽니다.

➡ _____

14 고가구가 있으신가요?" Boggis 씨가 물었다.

➡ _____

15 "아니요." Rummins가 말했다.

➡ _____

16 "한번 둘러봐도 될까요?" Boggis 씨가 물었다.

➡ _____

17 "그럼요. 들어오세요." Rummins가 말했다.

➡ _____

18 Boggis 씨는 먼저 부엌에 갔는데 아무것도 없었다.

➡ _____

19 그런 다음 그는 거실로 옮겼다.

➡ _____

20 그리고 그곳에 그것이 있었다!

➡ _____

21 18세기 영국 가구인 매우 귀중한 탁자가.

➡ _____

22 그는 몹시 흥분해서 거의 넘어질 뻔했다.

➡ _____

23 "무슨 일이세요?" Bert가 물었다.

➡ _____

24 "오, 아무것도 아니에요. 전혀 아무 일도 아닙니다." Boggis 씨는 거짓말을 했다.

➡ _____

25 그러고 나서 그는 정색하며 말했다. "이 탁자는 복제품입니다.

➡ _____

26 몇 파운드의 가치밖에 안 돼요."

➡ _____

27 그리고 그는 덧붙였다. "흠, 제 생각에 제가 살 수도 있을 것 같아요.

➡ _____

28 우리 집에 있는 탁자 다리가 부러졌거든요.

➡ _____

29 당신의 탁자 다리를 잘라서 제 탁자에 붙일 수 있겠어요."

➡ _____

30 "얼마 줄 거예요?" Rummins가 물었다.

➡ _____

31 "유감이지만 많이 줄 수는 없어요.

➡ _____

32 이것은 복제품일 뿐이니까요." Boggis 씨가 말했다.

➡ _____

33 "그래서 얼마 줄 수 있는데요?"

➡ _____

34 "10파운드요."

➡ _____

35 "10이요? 그것보다는 가치가 더 나가요."

➡ _____

36 "15는 어때요?"

➡ _____

37 "50으로 하지요."
➡ _____

38 "음, 30이요. 이게 제 마지막 제안입니다."
➡ _____

39 "그러죠, 이제 당신 겁니다. 그런데 이걸 어떻게 가져갈 건가요?
➡ _____

40 이게 차에 들어가지 않을 거예요!"
➡ _____

41 "한번 보죠." Boggis 씨가 말하고는 자신의 차를 가지러 밖으로 나갔다.
➡ _____

42 차로 가는 길에 Boggis 씨는 싱글벙글하지 않을 수 없었다.
➡ _____

43 그 탁자는 모든 판매상이 꿈꾸는 것이었다.
➡ _____

44 그는 자신의 운을 믿을 수 없었다.
➡ _____

45 "아버지, 만약 이게 차에 안 들어가면 어떻게 하죠?
➡ _____

46 그가 값을 지불하지 않을 수도 있어요." Bert가 말했다.
➡ _____

47 Rummins는 그때 생각이 떠올랐다.
➡ _____

48 "그가 원하는 건 오직 다리뿐이야.
➡ _____

49 그를 위해서 다리를 자르자." Rummins가 말했다.
➡ _____

50 "좋은 생각이에요!" Bert가 말했다.
➡ _____

51 그런 다음 Bert는 톱을 꺼내서 다리를 자르기 시작했다.
➡ _____

52 Boggis 씨가 돌아왔을 때, 다리는 잘려 있었다.
➡ _____

53 "걱정하지 마세요. 호의로 한 거예요.
➡ _____

54 이것에 대해 비용을 청구하지는 않을게요." Rummins가 말했다.
➡ _____

55 Boggis 씨는 너무 충격을 받아서 아무 말도 할 수 없었다.
➡ _____

※ 다음 우리말과 일치하도록 빈칸에 알맞은 말을 쓰시오.

After You Read A Read and Complete

1. One Sunday, Mr. Boggis, an _____ _____ _____, went to a small town _____ _____ _____.

2. At Rummins and Bert's house, Mr. Boggis found a table, a _____ piece of _____ _____ _____ _____.

3. Mr. Boggis _____ to Rummins and Bert _____ the table was just a _____.

4. _____ _____ _____ for the table was thirty pounds and Rummins _____ _____.

5. _____ _____ Mr. Boggis wanted was _____ _____ _____ _____ the table, Bert _____ _____ _____.

6. Mr. Boggis _____ _____ _____ _____ _____ the table.

1. 골동품 가구 판매상인 Boggis 씨는 어느 일요일에 가구를 사기 위해 작은 마을로 갔다.
2. Boggis 씨는 Rummins와 Bert의 집에서 탁자 하나를 발견했는데, 그것은 18세기 영국 가구로 매우 귀중한 탁자였다.
3. Boggis 씨는 Rummins와 Bert에게 그 탁자가 복제품이라고 거짓말을 했다.
4. 그의 마지막 제안은 30파운드였고 Rummins는 그것을 수락했다.
5. Boggis 씨가 원했던 것은 탁자의 다리뿐이었기 때문에 Bert는 다리를 잘랐다.
6. Boggis 씨는 탁자를 보고 매우 충격을 받았다.

Around the World

1. Fantastic Mr. Fox: A fox _____ his family _____ three _____ _____.

2. Matilda: A girl uses her _____ _____ _____ _____ her friends.

3. Charlie and the Chocolate Factory: A boy visits _____ _____ _____ _____ _____ _____ _____ _____.

1. Fantastic Mr. Fox: 여우는 세 명의 못된 농부들로부터 자신의 가족을 지킨다.
2. Matilda: 한 소녀가 그녀의 친구들을 돕기 위해 자신의 특별한 힘을 사용한다.
3. Charlie and the Chocolate Factory: 한 소년이 세계 최고의 초콜릿 공장을 방문한다.

Think and Write

1. _____ of the story, _____ _____ *Sunday*

2. This story _____ _____ _____ Roald Dahl.

3. It is about Mr. Boggis, _____ was an _____ _____ _____.

4. In the story, he _____ _____ Rummins _____ his table was a _____ and _____ 30 pounds _____ _____ it.

5. Mr. Boggis _____ he _____ _____ the legs of the table, _____ Bert _____ _____ _____ _____ for him.

6. This _____ Mr. Boggis _____ really wanted _____ _____.

7. I think Mr. Boggis was not a good man _____ _____ _____ people.

8. _____ _____ _____ _____ _____ _____ about this story _____ _____ _____ _____ _____ _____.

9. _____ _____ this story is _____ _____.

1. 독후감, 어느 운수 좋은 일요일
2. 이 이야기는 Roald Dahl에 의해 쓰여졌다.
3. 골동품 가구 판매상이었던 Boggis 씨에 관한 이야기이다.
4. 이 이야기에서, 그는 Rummins에게 그의 탁자가 복제품이라고 거짓말을 하고, 그것을 사기 위해 30파운드를 제시했다.
5. Boggis 씨는 자기가 단지 탁자의 다리만을 원한다고 말했고, 그래서 Bert는 그를 위해 탁자 다리를 잘랐다.
6. 이것이 실제로는 탁자 전체를 원했던 Boggis 씨를 놀라게 했다.
7. 나는 Boggis 씨가 사람들에게 거짓말을 했기 때문에 좋은 사람이 아니라고 생각한다.
8. 이 이야기에서 내가 가장 좋아하는 것은 놀라운 결말이다.
9. 이 이야기는 매우 재미있다고 생각한다.

※ 다음 우리말을 영어로 쓰시오.

After You Read A Read and Complete

1. 골동품 가구 판매상인 Boggis 씨는 어느 일요일에 가구를 사기 위해 작은 마을로 갔다.
　➡ _____

2. Boggis 씨는 Rummins와 Bert의 집에서 탁자 하나를 발견했는데, 그것은 18세기 영국 가구로 매우 귀중한 탁자였다.
　➡ _____
　_____

3. Boggis 씨는 Rummins와 Bert에게 그 탁자가 복제품이라고 거짓말을 했다.
　➡ _____

4. 그의 마지막 제안은 30파운드였고 Rummins는 그것을 수락했다.
　➡ _____

5. Boggis 씨가 원했던 것은 탁자의 다리뿐이었기 때문에 Bert는 다리를 잘랐다.
　➡ _____

6. Boggis 씨는 탁자를 보고 매우 충격을 받았다.
　➡ _____

Around the World

1. Fantastic Mr. Fox: 여우는 세 명의 못된 농부들로부터 자신의 가족을 지킨다.
　➡ _____

2. Matilda: 한 소녀가 그녀의 친구들을 돕기 위해 자신의 특별한 힘을 사용한다.
　➡ _____

3. Charlie and the Chocolate Factory: 힌 소년이 세계 최고의 초콜릿 공장을 방문한다.
　➡ _____

Think and Write

1. 독후감, 어느 운수 좋은 일요일
　➡ _____

2. 이 이야기는 Roald Dahl에 의해 쓰여졌다.
　➡ _____

3. 골동품 가구 판매상이었던 Boggis 씨에 관한 이야기이다.
　➡ _____

4. 이 이야기에서, 그는 Rummins에게 그의 탁자가 복제품이라고 거짓말을 하고, 그것을 사기 위해 30파운드를 제시했다.
　➡ _____

5. Boggis 씨는 그가 단지 탁자의 다리만을 원한다고 말했고, 그래서 Bert는 그를 위해 탁자 다리를 잘랐다.
　➡ _____

6. 이것이 실제로는 탁자 전체를 원했던 Boggis 씨를 놀라게 했다.
　➡ _____

7. 나는 Boggis 씨가 사람들에게 거짓말을 했기 때문에 좋은 사람이 아니라고 생각한다.
　➡ _____

8. 이 이야기에서 내가 가장 좋아하는 것은 놀라운 결말이다.
　➡ _____

9. 이 이야기는 매우 재미있다고 생각한다.
　➡ _____

※ 다음 영어를 우리말로 쓰시오.

01 amount

02 predict

03 influence

04 mainly

05 complex

06 expert

07 flu

08 insert

09 rent

10 trace

11 forecast

12 analyze

13 prevention

14 crime

15 spread

16 unlock

17 symptom

18 meaningful

19 industry

20 appreciate

21 further

22 huge

23 identify

24 purchase

25 improve

26 develop

27 various

28 endless

29 avoid

30 method

31 recommend

32 upload

33 include

34 performance

35 for sure

36 focus on

37 by ~ing

38 be likely to ~

39 the amount of ~

40 thanks to ~

41 make a decision

42 play a role

43 be used to+동사원형

※ 다음 우리말을 영어로 쓰시오.

01 산업, 공업	22 의미 있는, 중요한
02 범죄	23 삽입하다
03 전문가	24 피하다, 방지하다
04 독감	25 추천하다, 권하다
05 (크기·양·정도가) 막대한	26 방법
06 알아보다, 식별하다	27 빌리다
07 다양한	28 확산, 전파
08 성장하다, 발달하다	29 영향을 미치다
09 예방	30 증상
10 현명하게	31 자취, 발자국, 흔적
11 개선하다, 향상하다	32 감사하다, 감상하다
12 분석하다	33 ~을 전송하다
13 포함하다	34 잠금을 풀다
14 총계, 총액	35 확실히, 분명히
15 예측하다, 예보하다	36 역할을 하다
16 교통(량)	37 ~의 양/수량
17 구매	38 ~할 것 같다
18 주로	39 ~에 초점을 맞추다
19 더 이상의, 추가의	40 결정하다
20 예측하다	41 ~ 덕분에
21 끝없는, 무한한	42 점점 더 많이
	43 ~하는 데 사용되다

※ 다음 영영풀이에 알맞은 단어를 <보기>에서 골라 쓴 후, 우리말 뜻을 쓰시오.

1 _____ : a way of doing something: _____

2 _____ : to change or affect something: _____

3 _____ : to examine something carefully: _____

4 _____ : to pay someone for the use of something: _____

5 _____ : to stay away from someone or something: _____

6 _____ : to realize who someone is or what something is: _____

7 _____ : to say that something is going to happen: _____

8 _____ : to suggest something to someone: _____

9 _____ : the action or process of accomplishing a task or function: _____

10 _____ : a large amount of information stored in a computer system: _____

11 _____ : the action of buying something; a thing that has been bought: _____

12 _____ : something that shows you may have a particular illness: _____

13 _____ : the people or companies engaged in a particular kind of commercial

enterprise: _____

14 _____ : to grow and change into something bigger, better or more important:

_____

15 _____ : the growth or development of something, so that it affects a larger area

or a larger number of people: _____

16 _____ : the process by which people exchange information or express their

thoughts and feelings: _____

보기			
predict	avoid	purchase	database
spread	analyze	develop	recommend
communication	method	identify	performance
symptom	rent	industry	influence

※ 다음 우리말과 일치하도록 빈칸에 알맞은 말을 쓰시오.

Listen and Talk A 1

B: Excuse me. Can you _____ me _____ _____ _____ money _____ my _____ card?

G: Of course. _____, _____ your card _____ the machine. _____, _____ the _____ of money you want _____ _____.

B: OK.

G: _____, _____ your money _____ the machine.

B: That sounds _____. Thanks.

B: 실례합니다. 어떻게 교통카드에 돈을 충전하는지 알려주시겠어요?
G: 그럼요. 우선 기계에 카드를 넣으세요. 둘째로 충전하고 싶은 금액을 고르세요.
B: 네.
G: 마지막으로 기계에 돈을 넣으세요.
B: 간단해 보이는군요. 고맙습니다.

Listen and Talk A 2

B: I want to buy a snack. Do you _____ _____ _____ _____ this snack machine?

G: Yeah. _____, _____ the snack you want.

B: I already _____. What's _____?

G: Just _____ _____ the money. Then _____ the snack _____.

B: _____ _____. Thanks.

B: 과자를 사고 싶어요. 이 과자 자판기를 어떻게 사용하는지 알려주시겠어요?
G: 네. 먼저 원하는 과자를 고르세요.
B: 이미 했어요. 그 다음은 뭔가요?
G: 돈을 넣으세요. 그리고 나서 과자를 꺼내세요.
B: 알겠어요. 고맙습니다.

Listen and Talk A 3

G: Excuse me. I want to _____ a bike. Can you _____ me _____ _____ _____ this _____?

M: Sure. First, _____ _____ _____ the application. Then find the RENT button and _____ _____.

G: Then _____?

M: Then the application will give you a number _____ _____ a bike _____.

G: Thank you. I really _____ your _____.

G: 실례합니다. 자전거를 빌리고 싶은데요. 이 앱을 어떻게 사용하는지 알려주시겠어요?
M: 그럼요. 우선 앱에 로그인하세요. 그러고 나서 RENT 버튼을 찾고 터치하세요.
G: 그러고 난 후엔 어떻게 하나요?
M: 그 후에는 앱이 자전거를 잠금 해제하는 번호를 알려 줄 거예요.
G: 고맙습니다. 도와주셔서 정말 감사해요.

Listen and Talk B

A: Excuse me. I want to _____ these books. Do you _____ _____ _____ _____ it?

B: Sure. It's _____. First, _____ the library card _____ the machine. Second, _____ the books _____ this box.

A: OK.

B: _____ just _____ your card _____.

A: I really _____ your help.

A: 실례합니다. 저는 이 책들을 반납하고 싶어요. 어떻게 하는지 아시나요?
B: 그럼요. 간단해요. 우선 도서 대출 카드를 기계에 넣으세요. 둘째로 이 상자 안에 책들을 넣으세요.
A: 알겠어요.
B: 그리고 나서 카드를 꺼내세요.
A: 도와주셔서 정말 고맙습니다.

A: Excuse me. I want to _____ money _____ my transportation card. Do you _____ _____ _____ _____ it?

B: Sure. It's _____. _____, put your card in the machine. _____, _____ the _____ of money.

A: OK.

B: _____ _____ the money.

A: I really _____ your _____.

A: Excuse me. I want _____ _____ a snack. Do you _____ _____ _____ _____ it?

B: Sure. It's _____. _____, choose the snack. _____, _____ _____ the money.

A: OK.

B: _____ _____ the snack _____.

A: I really _____ your help.

Listen and Talk C

G: Excuse me, but _____ this robot _____?

B: Oh, it's a robot _____ finds books for you.

G: Really? Can you _____ me _____ _____ _____ _____ it?

B: Sure. First, _____ your library card _____ the _____ _____.

G: OK.

B: Second, _____ the _____ of the book you're _____ _____ and then _____ ENTER.

G: _____ _____ _____ _____?

B: Yes. _____, the robot will find the book and take _____ to the _____ _____.

G: So I can just go to the front desk and _____ the book?

B: Right. It's so _____, _____ _____?

G: Yes, it's really _____. Thank you.

Listen and Talk D

_____ me tell you _____ _____ _____ a drink machine. _____, _____ money _____ the machine. _____, choose the drink you want. _____, take the drink _____ _____ the machine. It's easy.

A: 실례합니다. 저는 교통카드에 돈을 충전하고 싶어요. 어떻게 하는지 아시나요?

B: 그럼요. 간단해요. 우선 기계에 카드를 넣으세요. 둘째로 금액을 고르세요.

A: 알겠어요.

B: 그러고 나서 돈을 넣으세요.

A: 도와주셔서 정말 고맙습니다.

A: 실례합니다. 저는 과자를 사고 싶어요. 어떻게 하는지 아시나요?

B: 그럼요. 간단해요. 우선 과자를 고르세요. 둘째로 돈을 넣으세요.

A: 알겠어요.

B: 그러고 나서 과자를 꺼내세요.

A: 도와주셔서 정말 고맙습니다.

G: 실례지만, 이 로봇은 용도가 뭔가요?

B: 아, 이 로봇은 당신을 위해 책을 찾아 주는 로봇이에요.

G: 정말요? 어떻게 사용하는지 알려 주실래요?

B: 그럼요. 먼저, 당신의 도서 대출 카드를 로봇의 화면 위에 놓으세요.

G: 알겠어요.

B: 두 번째로, 당신이 찾으려는 책의 제목을 입력하고 나서 ENTER 키를 누르세요.

G: 그게 다인가요?

B: 네. 그러면 로봇이 책을 찾아서 안내 데스크로 가져다줄 거예요.

G: 그러면 저는 그냥 안내 데스크로 가서 책을 받을 수 있나요?

B: 맞아요. 정말 쉽죠, 그렇지 않나요?

G: 그러네요, 정말 놀라워요. 감사합니다.

음료 자판기를 어떻게 사용하는지 알려줄게. 먼저 기계에 돈을 넣어. 그러고 나서 원하는 음료를 골라. 마지막으로 기계에서 음료를 꺼내. 간단해.

Talk and Play

A: Do you _____ _____ _____ _____ tea?

B: Sure. _____, _____ a tea bag in a cup.

A: OK.

B: _____, _____ hot water in the cup.

A: And then?

B: _____, _____ the tea bag _____ _____ 3 _____.

A: I _____ _____. I really _____ your help.

A: 차를 어떻게 만드는지 알고 있니?
B: 물론이지. 우선 컵에 티백을 넣어.
A: 알겠어.
B: 그런 후 컵에 뜨거운 물을 부어.
A: 그리고 나서는?
B: 마지막으로 3분 후에 티백을 꺼내.
A: 알겠어. 도와줘서 정말 고마워.

Review 1

G: Can you tell me _____ _____ _____ a potato?

B: Sure. First, _____ a potato _____ small _____. Second, _____ holes _____ the ground.

G: Then?

B: Then _____ the potato _____ _____ the holes and _____ the holes _____ _____.

G: That _____ _____. Thanks.

G: 감자를 어떻게 심는지 알려주시겠어요?
B: 그럼요. 우선 감자를 작은 조각으로 자르세요. 둘째로 땅에 구멍을 파세요.
G: 그리고 나서요?
B: 그리고 나서 구멍에 감자 조각들을 넣고 흙으로 구멍을 덮으세요.
G: 간단한 것 같네요. 고맙습니다.

Review 2

B: Excuse me. Can you _____ me _____ _____ _____ this machine?

G: Sure. First, _____ the paper _____ the _____ _____. Then _____ the paper size and _____ _____ _____ copies.

B: Then _____?

G: _____ the START button.

B: Thank you. I really _____ your help.

B: 실례합니다. 이 기계를 어떻게 사용하는지 알려주시겠어요?
G: 물론이죠. 우선 복사기에 종이를 올려놓으세요. 그리고 나서 종이 크기와 복사본 매수를 고르세요.
B: 그리고 나서 어떻게 해요?
G: START 버튼을 누르세요.
B: 감사합니다. 도와주셔서 고마워요.

※ 다음 우리말에 맞도록 대화를 영어로 쓰시오.

Listen and Talk A 1

B: _____

G: _____

_____

B: _____

G: _____

B: _____

B: 실례합니다. 어떻게 교통카드에 돈을 충전하는지 알려주시겠어요?

G: 그럼요. 우선 기계에 카드를 넣으세요. 둘째로 충전하고 싶은 금액을 고르세요.

B: 네.

G: 마지막으로 기계에 돈을 넣으세요.

B: 간단해 보이는군요. 고맙습니다.

Listen and Talk A 2

B: _____

G: _____

B: _____

G: _____

B: _____

B: 과자를 사고 싶어요. 이 과자 자판기를 어떻게 사용하는지 알려주시겠어요?

G: 네. 먼저 원하는 과자를 고르세요.

B: 이미 했어요. 그 다음은 뭔가요?

G: 돈을 넣으세요. 그러고 나서 과자를 꺼내세요.

B: 알겠어요. 고맙습니다.

Listen and Talk A 3

G: _____

M: _____

G: _____

M: _____

G: _____

G: 실례합니다. 자전거를 빌리고 싶은데요. 이 앱을 어떻게 사용하는지 알려주시겠어요?

M: 그럼요. 우선 앱에 로그인하세요. 그러고 나서 RENT 버튼을 찾고 터치하세요.

G: 그러고 난 후엔 어떻게 하나요?

M: 그 후에는 앱이 자전거를 잠금 해제하는 번호를 알려 줄 거예요.

G: 고맙습니다. 도와주셔서 정말 감사해요.

Listen and Talk B

A: _____

B: _____

_____

A: _____

B: _____

A: _____

A: 실례합니다. 저는 이 책들을 반납하고 싶어요. 어떻게 하는지 아시나요?

B: 그럼요. 간단해요. 우선 도서 대출 카드를 기계에 넣으세요. 둘째로 이 상자 안에 책들을 넣으세요.

A: 알겠어요.

B: 그러고 나서 카드를 꺼내세요.

A: 도와주셔서 정말 고맙습니다.

A: _____

_____

B: _____

_____

A: _____

B: _____

A: _____

A: _____

B: _____

A: _____

B: _____

A: _____

A: 실례합니다. 저는 교통카드에 돈을 충전하고 싶어요. 어떻게 하는지 아시나요?

B: 그럼요. 간단해요. 우선 기계에 카드를 넣으세요. 둘째로 금액을 고르세요.

A: 알겠어요.

B: 그러고 나서 돈을 넣으세요.

A: 도와주셔서 정말 고맙습니다.

A: 실례합니다. 저는 과자를 사고 싶어요. 어떻게 하는지 아시나요?

B: 그럼요. 간단해요. 우선 과자를 고르세요. 둘째로 돈을 넣으세요.

A: 알겠어요.

B: 그러고 나서 과자를 꺼내세요.

A: 도와주셔서 정말 고맙습니다.

Listen and Talk C

G: _____

B: _____

G: _____

B: _____

G: _____

B: _____

G: _____

B: _____

G: _____

B: _____

G: _____

G: 실례지만, 이 로봇은 용도가 뭔가요?

B: 아, 이 로봇은 당신을 위해 책을 찾아 주는 로봇이에요.

G: 정말요? 어떻게 사용하는지 알려 주실래요?

B: 그럼요. 먼저, 당신의 도서 대출 카드를 로봇의 화면 위에 놓으세요.

G: 알겠어요.

B: 두 번째로, 당신이 찾으려는 책의 제목을 입력하고 나서 ENTER 키를 누르세요.

G: 그게 다인가요?

B: 네. 그러면 로봇이 책을 찾아서 안내 데스크로 가져다줄 거예요.

G: 그러면 저는 그냥 안내 데스크로 가서 책을 받을 수 있나요?

B: 맞아요. 정말 쉽죠, 그렇지 않나요?

G: 그러네요, 정말 놀라워요. 감사합니다.

Listen and Talk D

_____

_____

_____

음료 자판기를 어떻게 사용하는지 알려 줄게. 먼저 기계에 돈을 넣어. 그러고 나서 원하는 음료를 골라. 마지막으로 기계에서 음료를 꺼내. 간단해.

Talk and Play

A: _____

B: _____

A: _____

B: _____

A: _____

B: _____

A: _____

A: 차를 어떻게 만드는지 알고 있니?
B: 물론이지. 우선 컵에 티백을 넣어.
A: 알겠어.
B: 그런 후 컵에 뜨거운 물을 부어.
A: 그리고 나서는?
B: 마지막으로 3분 후에 티백을 꺼내.
A: 알겠어. 도와줘서 정말 고마워.

Review 1

G: _____

B: _____

G: _____

B: _____

G: _____

G: 감자를 어떻게 심는지 알려주시겠어
요?
B: 그럼요. 우선 감자를 작은 조각으로
자르세요. 둘째로 땅에 구멍을 파세
요.
G: 그리고 나서요?
B: 그리고 나서 구멍에 감자 조각들을
넣고 흙으로 구멍을 덮으세요.
G: 간단한 것 같네요. 고맙습니다.

Review 2

B: _____

G: _____

_____

B: _____

G: _____

B: _____

B: 실례합니다. 이 기계를 어떻게 사용
하는지 알려주시겠어요?
G: 물론이죠. 우선 복사기에 종이를 올
려놓으세요. 그리고 나서 종이 크기
와 복사본 매수를 고르세요.
B: 그리고 나서 어떻게 해요?
G: START 버튼을 누르세요.
B: 감사합니다. 도와주셔서 고마워요.

※ 다음 우리말과 일치하도록 빈칸에 알맞은 것을 골라 쓰시오.

1 _____ _____ , Big Data
A. with   B. Living

2 Have you ever visited an online bookstore and _____ by the books that the store _____ _____ you?
A. recommended   B. been   C. for   D. surprised

3 _____ of them _____ _____ to you.
A. looked   B. many   C. interesting

4 _____ how did the bookstore know _____ _____ _____ ?
A. you   B. so   C. liked   D. what

5 This is _____ _____ _____ _____ big data.
A. because   B. all   C. of   D. possible

6 _____ _____ big data?
A. is   B. what

7 Big data is _____ _____ that are very _____ and _____ .
A. sets   B. complex   C. data   D. big

8 _____ information and communication technology _____ , the _____ of data we have is getting _____ greater than before.
A. amount   B. develops C. much   D. as

9 This is _____ because _____ everything that we do online _____ a _____ .
A. trace   B. mainly   C. leaves   D. almost

10 For _____ , the photos you _____ on your blog and the records of your _____ at online stores are all _____ of big data.
A. purchases B. part   C. upload   D. example

11 _____ data, _____ , is not _____ .
A. collecting B. enough   C. simply   D. however

12 Big data _____ to be _____ , and this is _____ by big data _____ .
A. experts   B. has   C. analyzed D. done

13 Using various _____ , experts _____ big data and _____ meaningful _____ from it.
A. results   B. analyze   C. methods   D. draw

14 These _____ then can ne _____ to make _____ or to _____ the future.
A. predict   B. results   C. decisions D. used

15 _____ is big data _____ our _____ ?
A. influencing B. how   C. lives

16 Big data is _____ _____ all _____ of our _____ .
A. almost   B. lives   C. influencing D. parts

17 It helps companies understand their _____ _____ better and helps them _____ more _____ .
A. customers' B. products C. needs   D. sell

18 It helps people _____ _____ _____ .
A. heavy   B. avoid   C. traffic

19 Its _____ are _____ , and here are some _____ .
A. interesting B. endless C. examples D. uses

20 _____ _____
A. Forecast B. Disease

1 빅데이터와 함께 살아가기

2 당신은 온라인 서점을 방문해서 그 서점이 당신을 위해 추천한 책들을 보고 놀란 적이 있는가?

3 그것들 중에 많은 것들이 당신에게 흥미로워 보였다.

4 그 서점은 당신이 무엇을 좋아하는지 어떻게 알았을까?

5 이것은 모두 빅데이터 때문에 가능하다.

6 빅데이터는 무엇인가?

7 빅데이터는 매우 크고 복잡한 데이터 집합이다.

8 정보 통신 기술이 발달함에 따라 우리가 갖고 있는 정보의 양도 이전보다 훨씬 더 많아지고 있다.

9 이것은 주로 우리가 온라인상에서 하는 거의 모든 것들이 흔적을 남기기 때문이다.

10 예를 들어, 당신이 블로그에 올린 사진들과 온라인 상점에서의 구매 기록들이 모두 빅데이터의 일부가 된다.

11 하지만 단순히 데이터를 수집하는 것만으로는 충분하지 않다.

12 빅데이터는 분석되어야 하고, 이것은 빅데이터 전문가들에 의해서 이루어진다.

13 다양한 방법들을 사용하여 전문가들은 빅데이터를 분석하고, 그것으로부터 의미 있는 결과들을 도출한다.

14 그런 다음, 이런 결과들은 결정을 하거나 또는 미래를 예측하는 데 사용될 수 있다.

15 빅데이터는 어떻게 우리 삶에 영향을 미치고 있는가?

16 빅데이터는 우리 삶의 거의 모든 부분에 영향을 미치고 있다.

17 그것은 회사들이 소비자들이 필요로 하는 것을 더 잘 이해하고 그들이 더 많은 상품을 팔도록 도와준다.

18 그것은 사람들이 교통 체증을 피하도록 도와주기도 한다.

19 그것의 활용은 끝이 없고, 여기에 몇 가지 흥미로운 예들이 있다.

20 질병 예측

21 Did you know that health _____ can now _____ a _____ just as weather _____ forecast the weather?
　A. forecast　　　　B. professionals　C. experts　　　　D. disease

22 This is _____ _____ _____ big data.
　A. to　　　　　　B. possible　　　C. thanks

23 For example, when the flu season _____, people will _____ more _____ _____.
　A. flu　　　　　　B. buy　　　　　C. comes　　　　　D. medicine

24 They will also _____ _____ about _____ _____ more.
　A. symptoms　　　B. search　　　C. flu　　　　　　D. online

25 If this kind of data is _____ _____, the _____ of the flu can be _____.
　A. spread　　　　B. wisely　　　C. analyzed　　　D. predicted

26 _____ _____ in Sports
　A. Performance　　B. Improving

27 Are you a _____ _____?
　A. sports　　　　B. fan

28 Well, big data is _____ the _____ of players, _____ sports more _____.
　A. making　　　　B. performance　C. exciting　　　D. improving

29 A _____ _____ is _____ _____ soccer team.
　A. national　　　B. example　　　C. Germany's　　D. famous

30 The team built a database by _____ and _____ a _____ _____ of data on players.
　A. analyzing　　　B. amount　　　C. collecting　　D. huge

31 For example, the data _____ information about how _____ each player _____ and how _____ he had the ball.
　A. included　　　B. long　　　　C. much　　　　D. ran

32 _____ the _____ of this database, Germany's national soccer team was able to _____ its _____ and win the 2014 World Cup.
　A. improve　　　B. help　　　　C. performance　D. with

33 _____ _____
　A. Prevention　　B. Crime

34 _____ to big data, police can now _____ _____ before it _____.
　A. happens　　　B. thanks　　　C. crime　　　　D. predict

35 _____ the _____ of big data about the type, time and place of crime, police can make a map of crime _____ _____.
　A. hot　　　　　B. through　　　C. analysis　　　D. spots

36 This map _____ when and where _____ is most _____ to _____.
　A. likely　　　　B. identifies　　C. happen　　　D. crime

37 Police can _____ _____ crime by _____ on the areas and the times this map _____.
　A. focusing　　　B. predicts　　　C. further　　　D. prevent

38 Big data _____ _____ _____ the world _____.
　A. already　　　B. greatly　　　C. has　　　　　D. changed

39 So where will the big data _____ _____ _____ _____?
　A. go　　　　　B. here　　　　C. industry　　　D. from

40 Nobody knows for _____, but _____ agree that big data will _____ a more and more important _____ in our lives.
　A. sure　　　　　B. role　　　　C. experts　　　D. play

21 당신은 날씨 전문가가 날씨를 예측하는 것과 같이 건강 전문가들이 현재 질병을 예측할 수 있다는 것을 알고 있는가?

22 이것은 빅데이터 덕분에 가능하다.

23 예를 들어서 독감의 계절이 오면, 사람들은 독감 약을 더 많이 구입할 것이다.

24 그들은 또한 온라인상에서 독감 증상들을 더 찾아볼 것이다.

25 만약 이런 종류의 데이터를 지혜롭게 분석한다면, 독감의 확산을 예측할 수 있다.

26 스포츠에서의 경기력 향상

27 당신은 스포츠 팬인가?

28 빅데이터는 스포츠를 더 흥미롭게 만들면서, 선수들의 경기력을 향상하고 있다.

29 유명한 사례로 독일 국가 대표 축구팀이 있다.

30 그 팀은 선수들에 관한 엄청난 양의 데이터를 모으고 분석함으로써, 데이터베이스를 구축했다.

31 예를 들어 데이터는 각각의 선수들이 얼마나 많이 달렸고, 얼마나 오랫동안 공을 소유했는지도 포함했다.

32 이 데이터베이스의 도움으로 독일 국가 대표 축구팀은 경기력을 향상할 수 있었고, 2014년 월드컵에서 우승할 수 있었다.

33 범죄 예방

34 빅데이터 덕분에 경찰은 이제 범죄가 발생하기 전에 범죄를 예측할 수 있다.

35 범죄의 유형, 시간 및 장소에 관한 빅데이터의 분석을 통해, 경찰은 범죄 다발 지역의 지도를 만들 수 있다.

36 이 지도는 범죄가 언제, 어디에서 가장 많이 발생할 것 같은지를 알려 준다.

37 경찰은 이 지도가 예측하는 장소들과 시간대에 집중함으로써, 추가 범죄를 예방할 수 있다.

38 빅데이터는 이미 세계를 크게 변화시켰다.

39 그러면 빅데이터 산업은 여기에서부터 어디로 가게 될까?

40 누구도 확실히 알지는 못하지만, 전문가들은 빅데이터가 우리 삶에서 더욱 더 중요한 역할을 할 것이라는 데에는 동의한다.

※ 다음 우리말과 일치하도록 빈칸에 알맞은 말을 쓰시오.

1 _____ _____ Big Data

2 Have you ever visited an online bookstore and _____ _____ by the books that the store _____ _____ you?

3 Many of them _____ _____ to you.

4 So how did the bookstore know _____ _____ _____?

5 This is all _____ _____ _____ big data.

6 _____ _____ big data?

7 Big data is _____ _____ that _____ very big and _____.

8 _____ information and communication technology _____, the _____ _____ data we have is _____ _____ _____ than before.

9 This is _____ _____ almost everything that we do online _____ _____ _____.

10 For example, the photos you _____ _____ _____ _____ and the records of _____ _____ at online stores are _____ _____ _____ big data.

11 _____ _____ _____ _____, _____, is not enough.

12 Big data _____ _____ _____ _____, and this is _____ _____ big data experts.

13 _____ various methods, experts _____ big data and _____ _____ _____ from it.

14 These results then _____ _____ _____ to make decisions or _____ _____ the future.

15 _____ is big data _____ our _____?

16 Big data is influencing _____ _____ _____ of our lives.

17 It helps companies _____ _____ _____ _____ better and helps them _____ _____ _____.

18 It helps people _____ _____ _____.

19 Its uses are _____, and here are some _____ _____.

20 Disease _____

1 빅데이터와 함께 살아가기
2 당신은 온라인 서점을 방문해서 그 서점이 당신을 위해 추천한 책들을 보고 놀란 적이 있는가?
3 그것들 중에 많은 것들이 당신에게 흥미로워 보였다.
4 그 서점은 당신이 무엇을 좋아하는지 어떻게 알았을까?
5 이것은 모두 빅데이터 때문에 가능하다.
6 빅데이터는 무엇인가?
7 빅데이터는 매우 크고 복잡한 데이터 집합이다.
8 정보 통신 기술이 발달함에 따라 우리가 갖고 있는 정보의 양도 이전보다 훨씬 더 많아지고 있다.
9 이것은 주로 우리가 온라인상에서 하는 거의 모든 것들이 흔적을 남기기 때문이다.
10 예를 들어, 당신이 블로그에 올린 사진들과 온라인 상점에서의 구매 기록들이 모두 빅데이터의 일부가 된다.
11 하지만 단순히 데이터를 수집하는 것만으로는 충분하지 않다.
12 빅데이터는 분석되어야 하고, 이것은 빅데이터 전문가들에 의해서 이루어진다.
13 다양한 방법들을 사용하여 전문가들은 빅데이터를 분석하고, 그것으로부터 의미 있는 결과들을 도출한다.
14 그런 다음, 이런 결과들은 결정을 하거나 또는 미래를 예측하는 데 사용될 수 있다.
15 빅데이터는 어떻게 우리 삶에 영향을 미치고 있는가?
16 빅데이터는 우리 삶의 거의 모든 부분에 영향을 미치고 있다.
17 그것은 회사들이 소비자들이 필요로 하는 것을 더 잘 이해하고 그들이 더 많은 상품을 팔도록 도와준다.
18 그것은 사람들이 교통 체증을 피하도록 도와주기도 한다.
19 그것의 활용은 끝이 없고, 여기에 몇 가지 흥미로운 예들이 있다.
20 질병 예측

21 Did you know that health professionals can now forecast a disease _____ _____ weather experts _____ the weather?

22 This is possible _____ _____ big data.

23 For example, when the flu season _____, people _____ _____ more _____ _____.

24 They will also _____ _____ _____ _____ flu symptoms more.

25 If this kind of data _____ _____ _____ _____, the _____ of the flu can _____ _____.

26 _____ _____ in Sports

27 Are you a _____ _____?

28 Well, big data _____ _____ the performance of players, _____ sports more _____.

29 A famous example is Germany's _____ _____.

30 The team _____ a database by _____ and _____ a _____ _____ of data on players.

31 For example, the data included information about _____ _____ each player ran and _____ _____ _____ he had the ball.

32 _____ _____ _____ _____ this database, Germany's national soccer team was _____ _____ _____ its performance and win the 2014 World Cup.

33 Crime _____ _____

34 _____ _____ big data, police can now predict crime before it _____.

35 _____ the analysis of big data about the type, time and place of crime, police can make a map of _____ _____ _____.

36 This map _____ when and where crime _____ _____ _____ _____.

37 Police can prevent _____ _____ _____ _____ on the areas and the times this map _____.

38 Big data _____ _____ _____ the world _____.

39 So where will the big data industry _____ _____ _____?

40 Nobody knows for sure, but experts agree that big data will _____ a more and more important _____ in our _____.

21 당신은 날씨 전문가가 날씨를 예측하는 것과 같이 건강 전문가들이 현재 질병을 예측할 수 있다는 것을 알고 있는가?

22 이것은 빅데이터 덕분에 가능하다.

23 예를 들어서 독감의 계절이 오면, 사람들은 독감 약을 더 많이 구입할 것이다.

24 그들은 또한 온라인상에서 독감 증상들을 더 찾아볼 것이다.

25 만약 이런 종류의 데이터를 지혜롭게 분석한다면, 독감의 확산을 예측할 수 있다.

26 스포츠에서의 경기력 향상

27 당신은 스포츠 팬인가?

28 빅데이터는 스포츠를 더 흥미롭게 만들면서, 선수들의 경기력을 향상하고 있다.

29 유명한 사례로 독일 국가 대표 축구팀이 있다.

30 그 팀은 선수들에 관한 엄청난 양의 데이터를 모으고 분석함으로써, 데이터베이스를 구축했다.

31 예를 들어 데이터는 각각의 선수들이 얼마나 많이 달렸고, 얼마나 오랫동안 공을 소유했는지도 포함했다.

32 이 데이터베이스의 도움으로 독일 국가 대표 축구팀은 경기력을 향상할 수 있었고, 2014년 월드컵에서 우승할 수 있었다.

33 범죄 예방

34 빅데이터 덕분에 경찰은 이제 범죄가 발생하기 전에 범죄를 예측할 수 있다.

35 범죄의 유형, 시간 및 장소에 관한 빅데이터의 분석을 통해, 경찰은 범죄 다발 지역의 지도를 만들 수 있다.

36 이 지도는 범죄가 언제, 어디에서 가장 많이 발생할 것 같은지를 알려 준다.

37 경찰은 이 지도가 예측하는 장소들과 시간대에 집중함으로써, 추가 범죄를 예방할 수 있다.

38 빅데이터는 이미 세계를 크게 변화시켰다.

39 그러면 빅데이터 산업은 여기에서부터 어디로 가게 될까?

40 누구도 확실히 알지는 못하지만, 전문가들은 빅데이터가 우리 삶에서 더욱 더 중요한 역할을 할 것이라는 데에는 동의한다.

※ 다음 문장을 우리말로 쓰시오.

1 ▷ Living with Big Data
➡ _____

2 ▷ Have you ever visited an online bookstore and been surprised by the books that the store recommended for you?
➡ _____

3 ▷ Many of them looked interesting to you.
➡ _____

4 ▷ So how did the bookstore know what you liked?
➡ _____

5 ▷ This is all possible because of big data.
➡ _____

6 ▷ What is big data?
➡ _____

7 ▷ Big data is data sets that are very big and complex.
➡ _____

8 ▷ As information and communication technology develops, the amount of data we have is getting much greater than before.
➡ _____

9 ▷ This is mainly because almost everything that we do online leaves a trace.
➡ _____

10 ▷ For example, the photos you upload on your blog and the records of your purchases at online stores are all part of big data.
➡ _____

11 ▷ Simply collecting data, however, is not enough.
➡ _____

12 ▷ Big data has to be analyzed, and this is done by big data experts.
➡ _____

13 ▷ Using various methods, experts analyze big data and draw meaningful results from it.
➡ _____

14 ▷ These results then can be used to make decisions or to predict the future.
➡ _____

15 ▷ How is big data influencing our lives?
➡ _____

16 ▷ Big data is influencing almost all parts of our lives.
➡ _____

17 ▷ It helps companies understand their customers' needs better and helps them sell more products.
➡ _____

18 ▷ It helps people avoid heavy traffic.
➡ _____

19 ▷ Its uses are endless, and here are some interesting examples.
➡ _____

20 ▷ Disease Forecast
➡ _____

21 Did you know that health professionals can now forecast a disease just as weather experts forecast the weather?

➡ _____

22 This is possible thanks to big data.

➡ _____

23 For example, when the flu season comes, people will buy more flu medicine.

➡ _____

24 They will also search online about flu symptoms more.

➡ _____

25 If this kind of data is analyzed wisely, the spread of the flu can be predicted.

➡ _____

26 Improving Performance in Sports

➡ _____

27 Are you a sports fan?

➡ _____

28 Well, big data is improving the performance of players, making sports more exciting.

➡ _____

29 A famous example is Germany's national soccer team.

➡ _____

30 The team built a database by collecting and analyzing a huge amount of data on players.

➡ _____

31 For example, the data included information about how much each player ran and how long he had the ball.

➡ _____

32 With the help of this database, Germany's national soccer team was able to improve its performance and win the 2014 World Cup.

➡ _____

33 Crime Prevention

➡ _____

34 Thanks to big data, police can now predict crime before it happens.

➡ _____

35 Through the analysis of big data about the type, time and place of crime, police can make a map of crime hot spots.

➡ _____

36 This map identifies when and where crime is most likely to happen.

➡ _____

37 Police can prevent further crime by focusing on the areas and the times this map predicts.

➡ _____

38 Big data has already changed the world greatly.

➡ _____

39 So where will the big data industry go from here?

➡ _____

40 Nobody knows for sure, but experts agree that big data will play a more and more important role in our lives.

➡ _____

※ 다음 괄호 안의 단어들을 우리말에 맞도록 바르게 배열하시오.

1 (with / Living / Data / Big)
➡ _____

2 (you / have / visited / ever / online / an / bookstore / been / and / by / surprised / books / the / the / that / recommended / store / you? / for)
➡ _____
_____

3 (of / many / looked / them / to / interesting / you.)
➡ _____

4 (how / so / the / did / know / bookstore / you / what / liked?)
➡ _____

5 (is / this / possible / all / of / because / data. / big)
➡ _____

6 (is / what / data? / big)
➡ _____

7 (data / big / data / is / that / sets / are / big / very / complex. / and)
➡ _____

8 (information / as / and / technology / communication / develops, / amount / the / data / of / have / we / is / much / getting / greater / before. / than)
➡ _____

9 (is / this / because / mainly / almost / that / everything / do / we / online / a / leaves / trace.)
➡ _____

10 (example, / for / photos / the / upload / you / on / blog / your / the / and / records / your / of / at / purchases / online / are / stores / part / all / big / of / data.)
➡ _____

11 (collecting / simply / data, / is / however, / enough. / not)
➡ _____

12 (data / big / to / has / analyzed, / be / this / and / done / is / big / by / experts. / data)
➡ _____

1 빅데이터와 함께 살아가기

2 당신은 온라인 서점을 방문해서 그 서점이 당신을 위해 추천한 책들을 보고 놀란 적이 있는가?

3 그것들 중에 많은 것들이 당신에게 흥미로워 보였다.

4 그 서점은 당신이 무엇을 좋아하는지 어떻게 알았을까?

5 이것은 모두 빅데이터 때문에 가능하다.

6 빅데이터는 무엇인가?

7 빅데이터는 매우 크고 복잡한 데이터 집합이다.

8 정보 통신 기술이 발달함에 따라 우리가 갖고 있는 정보의 양도 이전보다 훨씬 더 많아지고 있다.

9 이것은 주로 우리가 온라인상에서 하는 거의 모든 것들이 흔적을 남기기 때문이다.

10 예를 들어, 당신이 블로그에 올린 사진들과 온라인 상점에서의 구매 기록들이 모두 빅데이터의 일부가 된다.

11 하지만 단순히 데이터를 수집하는 것만으로는 충분하지 않다.

12 빅데이터는 분석되어야 하고, 이것은 빅데이터 전문가들에 의해서 이루어진다.

13 (various / using / methods, / analyze / experts / data / big / and / meaningful / draw / from / results / it.)

➡ _____

_____

14 (results / these / can / then / used / be / to / decisions / make / to / or / the / predict / future.)

➡ _____

15 (is / how / data / big / our / influencing / lives?)

➡ _____

16 (data / is / big / influencing / all / almost / of / pasts / lives. / our)

➡ _____

17 (helps / it / understand / companies / customer's / their / better / needs / and / them / helps / more / sell / products.)

➡ _____

_____

18 (helps / it / avoid / people / traffic. / heavy)

➡ _____

19 (uses / its / endless, / are / here / and / some / are / examples. / interesting)

➡ _____

20 (Forecast / Disease)

➡ _____

21 (you / did / that / know / professionals / health / now / can / a / forecast / disease / as / just / experts / weather / the / forecast / weather?)

➡ _____

_____

22 (is / this / thanks / possible / big / to / data.)

➡ _____

23 (example, / for / the / when / season / flu / comes, / will / people / more / buy / medicine. / flu)

➡ _____

_____

24 (will / they / search / also / about / online / symptoms / flu / more.)

➡ _____

25 (this / if / of / kind / data / analyzed / is / wisely, / spread / the / the / of / can / flu / predicted. / be)

➡ _____

_____

13 다양한 방법들을 사용하여 전문가들은 빅데이터를 분석하고, 그것으로부터 의미 있는 결과들을 도출한다.

14 그런 다음, 이런 결과들은 결정을 하거나 또는 미래를 예측하는 데 사용될 수 있다.

15 빅데이터는 어떻게 우리 삶에 영향을 미치고 있는가?

16 빅데이터는 우리 삶의 거의 모든 부분에 영향을 미치고 있다.

17 그것은 회사들이 소비자들이 필요로 하는 것을 더 잘 이해하고 그들이 더 많은 상품을 팔도록 도와준다.

18 그것은 사람들이 교통 체증을 피하도록 도와주기도 한다.

19 그것의 활용은 끝이 없고, 여기에 몇 가지 흥미로운 예들이 있다.

20 질병 예측

21 당신은 날씨 전문가가 날씨를 예측하는 것과 같이 건강 전문가들이 현재 질병을 예측할 수 있다는 것을 알고 있는가?

22 이것은 빅데이터 덕분에 가능하다.

23 예를 들어서 독감의 계절이 오면, 사람들은 독감 약을 더 많이 구입할 것이다.

24 그들은 또한 온라인상에서 독감 증상들을 더 찾아볼 것이다.

25 만약 이런 종류의 데이터를 지혜롭게 분석한다면, 독감의 확산을 예측할 수 있다.

26 (Performance / Improving / Sports / in)

➡ _____

27 (you / are / sports / a / fan?)

➡ _____

28 (big / well, / data / improving / is / performance / the / players, / of / sports / making / exciting. / more)

➡ _____

29 (famous / a / is / example / national / Germany's / team. / soccer)

➡ _____

30 (team / the / a / built / by / database / collecting / and / a / analyzing / huge / of / amount / data / players. / on)

➡ _____

31 (example, / for / data / the / information / included / how / about / much / player / each / and / ran / long / how / had / he / ball. / the)

➡ _____

32 (the / with / of / help / database, / this / national / Germany's / team / soccer / able was / improve / to / performance / its / win / and / the / World / 2014 / Cup.)

➡ _____

33 (Prevention / Crime)

➡ _____

34 (to / thanks / data, / big / can / police / predict / now / before / crime / happens. / it)

➡ _____

35 (the / through / analysis / big / of / about / data / type, / the / and / time / of / place / crime, / can / police / make / map / a / crime / of / spots. / hot)

➡ _____

36 (map / this / when / identifies / and / crime / where / most / is / to / likely / happen.)

➡ _____

37 (can / police / further / prevent / by / crime / focusing / the / on / areas / the / and / this / times / predicts. / map)

➡ _____

38 (data / big / already / has / the / changed / greatly. / world)

➡ _____

39 (where / so / the / will / data / big / go / industry / here? / from)

➡ _____

40 (knows / nobody / sure, / for / experts / but / that / agree / big / will / data / play / more / a / and / important / more / in / role / lives. / our)

➡ _____

---

26 스포츠에서의 경기력 향상

27 당신은 스포츠 팬인가?

28 빅데이터는 스포츠를 더 흥미롭게 만들면서, 선수들의 경기력을 향상하고 있다.

29 유명한 사례로 독일 국가 대표 축구팀이 있다.

30 그 팀은 선수들에 관한 엄청난 양의 데이터를 모으고 분석함으로써, 데이터베이스를 구축했다.

31 예를 들어 데이터는 각각의 선수들이 얼마나 많이 달렸고, 얼마나 오랫동안 공을 소유했는지도 포함했다.

32 이 데이터베이스의 도움으로 독일 국가 대표 축구팀은 경기력을 향상할 수 있었고, 2014년 월드컵에서 우승할 수 있었다.

33 범죄 예방

34 빅데이터 덕분에 경찰은 이제 범죄가 발생하기 전에 범죄를 예측할 수 있다.

35 범죄의 유형, 시간 및 장소에 관한 빅데이터의 분석을 통해, 경찰은 범죄 다발 지역의 지도를 만들 수 있다.

36 이 지도는 범죄가 언제, 어디에서 가장 많이 발생할 것 같은지를 알려 준다.

37 경찰은 이 지도가 예측하는 장소들과 시간대에 집중함으로써, 추가 범죄를 예방할 수 있다.

38 빅데이터는 이미 세계를 크게 변화시켰다.

39 그러면 빅데이터 산업은 여기에서부터 어디로 가게 될까?

40 누구도 확실히 알지는 못하지만, 전문가들은 빅데이터가 우리 삶에서 더욱 더 중요한 역할을 할 것이라는 데에는 동의한다.

Step5

※ 다음 우리말을 영어로 쓰시오.

1 빅데이터와 함께 살아가기
➡ _____

2 당신은 온라인 서점을 방문해서 그 서점이 당신을 위해 추천한 책들을 보고 놀란 적이 있는가?
➡ _____

3 그것들 중에 많은 것들이 당신에게 흥미로워 보였다.
➡ _____

4 그 서점은 당신이 무엇을 좋아하는지 어떻게 알았을까?
➡ _____

5 이것은 모두 빅데이터 때문에 가능하다.
➡ _____

6 빅데이터는 무엇인가?
➡ _____

7 빅데이터는 매우 크고 복잡한 데이터 집합이다.
➡ _____

8 정보 통신 기술이 발달함에 따라 우리가 갖고 있는 정보의 양도 이전보다 훨씬 더 많아지고 있다.
➡ _____

9 이것은 주로 우리가 온라인상에서 하는 거의 모든 것들이 흔적을 남기기 때문이다.
➡ _____

10 예를 들어, 당신이 블로그에 올린 사진들과 온라인 상점에서의 구매 기록들이 모두 빅데이터의 일부가 된다.
➡ _____

11 하지만 단순히 데이터를 수집하는 것만으로는 충분하지 않다.
➡ _____

12 빅데이터는 분석되어야 하고, 이것은 빅데이터 전문가들에 의해서 이루어진다.
➡ _____

13 다양한 방법들을 사용하여 전문가들은 빅데이터를 분석하고, 그것으로부터 의미 있는 결과들을 도출한다.
➡ _____

14 그런 다음, 이런 결과들은 결정을 하거나 또는 미래를 예측하는 데 사용될 수 있다.
➡ _____

15 빅데이터는 어떻게 우리 삶에 영향을 미치고 있는가?
➡ _____

16 빅데이터는 우리 삶의 거의 모든 부분에 영향을 미치고 있다.
➡ _____

17 그것은 회사들이 소비자들이 필요로 하는 것을 더 잘 이해하고 그들이 더 많은 상품을 팔도록 도와준다.
➡ _____

18 그것은 사람들이 교통 체증을 피하도록 도와주기도 한다.
➡ _____

19 그것의 활용은 끝이 없고, 여기에 몇 가지 흥미로운 예들이 있다.
➡ _____

20 질병 예측
➡ _____

21 당신은 날씨 전문가가 날씨를 예측하는 것과 같이 건강 전문가들이 현재 질병을 예측할 수 있다는 것을 알고 있는가?
➡ _____

22 이것은 빅데이터 덕분에 가능하다.
➡ _____

23 예를 들어서 독감의 계절이 오면, 사람들은 독감 약을 더 많이 구입할 것이다.
➡ _____

24 그들은 또한 온라인상에서 독감 증상들을 더 찾아볼 것이다.
➡ _____

25 만약 이런 종류의 데이터를 지혜롭게 분석한다면, 독감의 확산을 예측할 수 있다.
➡ _____

26 스포츠에서의 경기력 향상
➡ _____

27 당신은 스포츠 팬인가?
➡ _____

28 빅데이터는 스포츠를 더 흥미롭게 만들면서, 선수들의 경기력을 향상하고 있다.
➡ _____

29 유명한 사례로 독일 국가 대표 축구팀이 있다.
➡ _____

30 그 팀은 선수들에 관한 엄청난 양의 데이터를 모으고 분석함으로써, 데이터베이스를 구축했다.
➡ _____

31 예를 들어 데이터는 각각의 선수들이 얼마나 많이 달렸고, 얼마나 오랫동안 공을 소유했는지도 포함했다.
➡ _____

32 이 데이터베이스의 도움으로 독일 국가 대표 축구팀은 경기력을 향상할 수 있었고, 2014년 월드컵에서 우승할 수 있었다.
➡ _____

33 범죄 예방
➡ _____

34 빅데이터 덕분에 경찰은 이제 범죄가 발생하기 전에 범죄를 예측할 수 있다.
➡ _____

35 죄의 유형, 시간 및 장소에 관한 빅데이터의 분석을 통해, 경찰은 범죄 다발 지역의 지도를 만들 수 있다.
➡ _____

36 이 지도는 범죄가 언제, 어디에서 가장 많이 발생할 것 같은지를 알려 준다.
➡ _____

37 경찰은 이 지도가 예측하는 장소들과 시간대에 집중함으로써, 추가 범죄를 예방할 수 있다.
➡ _____

38 빅데이터는 이미 세계를 크게 변화시켰다.
➡ _____

39 그러면 빅데이터 산업은 여기에서부터 어디로 가게 될까?
➡ _____

40 누구도 확실히 알지는 못하지만, 전문가들은 빅데이터가 우리 삶에서 더욱 더 중요한 역할을 할 것이라는 데에는 동의한다.
➡ _____
_____

※ 다음 우리말과 일치하도록 빈칸에 알맞은 말을 쓰시오.

After You Read B Read and Complete

Example 1

1. _____ _____ can now _____ _____ _____ of the flu _____ _____ the sales of flu medicine and online searches about _____ _____.

Example 2

2. _____ _____ a n d _____ _____ _____ _____ data on players, Germany's national soccer team _____ _____ _____ _____ its performance and win the 2014 World Cup.

Example 3

3. _____ _____ _____ of big data, police can make a map of _____ _____ _____ and use it _____ _____ _____ _____.

Around the World

1. Yuna: We're not _____ . The bus _____ _____ _____ _____ 4 _____ .

2. Computer: _____ _____, you _____ question numbers 3 and 5, _____ _____ _____ _____ _____ first.

3. Yuna: _____ _____ _____ _____ tomorrow?

4. AI: It's _____ _____ _____ . _____ your umbrella.

5. Yuna: Big data _____ _____ _____ _____ _____ so _____ _____ !

Think and Write

1. _____ _____ Time Activities

2. We asked 100 _____ about their _____ _____ _____ .

3. _____ _____ show that the free time activity the _____ _____ _____ _____ _____ _____ _____ _____ .

4. 34% said that they want _____ _____ _____ _____ _____ _____ .

5. However, _____ _____ _____ _____ _____ _____ they actually do the most _____ _____ _____ .

6. 39% said that they _____ TV _____ _____ _____ _____ .

7. _____ the results, we see that there is _____ _____ _____ between _____ _____ _____ _____ _____ do and _____ _____ _____ _____ in their free time.

사례 1

1. 건강 전문가들은 독감 약 판매와 독감 증상에 관한 온라인 검색을 분석함으로써 이제 감기의 확산을 예측할 수 있다.

사례 2

2. 독일 국가 대표 축구팀은 선수들에 관한 엄청난 양의 데이터를 모으고 분석함으로써, 경기력을 향상하고 2014년 월드컵에서 우승할 수 있었다.

사례 3

3. 빅데이터의 분석을 통해서 경찰은 범죄 다발 지역의 지도를 만들 수 있고 그것을 추가 범죄를 예방하는 데에 사용할 수 있다.

1. 유나: 늦지 않았네. 버스가 4분 후에 도착할 거야.

2. 컴퓨터: 지난번에 당신은 3번과 5번 문제를 틀렸습니다. 그러니 우선 그것들부터 복습해 봅시다.

3. 유나: 내일 날씨가 어때?

4. AI: 비가 올 예정입니다. 우산 챙기세요.

5. 유나: 빅데이터는 내 삶을 훨씬 더 쉽게 만들고 있구나!

1. 청소년들의 여가 활동들

2. 우리는 100명의 청소년들에게 여가 활동에 관해 질문했습니다.

3. 그 결과 청소년들이 가장 하고 싶은 여가 활동은 여행인 것으로 나타났습니다.

4. 34%는 여가 시간에 여행을 가고 싶다고 답했습니다.

5. 하지만 그들이 실제로 가장 많이 하는 여가 활동은 TV를 보는 것입니다.

6. 39%는 여가 시간에 TV를 본다고 답했습니다.

7. 결과로 봤을 때, 우리는 청소년들이 여가 시간에 하고 싶은 활동과 실제로 하는 활동 사이에 큰 차이가 있다는 것을 알 수 있습니다

※ 다음 우리말을 영어로 쓰시오.

After You Read B Read and Complete

사례 1

1. 건강 전문가들은 독감 약 판매와 독감 증상에 관한 온라인 검색을 분석함으로써 이제 감기의 확산을 예측할 수 있다.

➡ _____

_____

사례 2

2. 독일 국가 대표 축구팀은 선수들에 관한 엄청난 양의 데이터를 모으고 분석함으로써, 경기력을 향상하고 2014년 월드컵에서 우승할 수 있었다.

➡ _____

_____

사례 3

3. 빅데이터의 분석을 통해서 경찰은 범죄 다발 지역의 지도를 만들 수 있고 그것을 추가 범죄를 예방하는 데에 사용할 수 있다.

➡ _____

_____

Around the World

1. 유나: 늦지 않았네. 버스가 4분 후에 도착할 거야.

➡ _____

2. 컴퓨터: 지난번에 당신은 3번과 5번 문제를 틀렸습니다. 그러니 우선 그것들부터 복습해 봅시다.

➡ _____

3. 유나: 내일 날씨가 어때?

➡ _____

4. AI: 비가 올 예정입니다. 우산 챙기세요.

➡ _____

5. 유나: 빅데이터는 내 삶을 훨씬 더 쉽게 만들고 있구나!

➡ _____

Think and Write

1. 청소년들의 여가 활동들

➡ _____

2. 우리는 100명의 청소년들에게 여가 활동에 관해 질문했습니다.

➡ _____

3. 그 결과 청소년들이 가장 하고 싶은 여가 활동은 여행인 것으로 나타났습니다.

➡ _____

4. 34%는 여가 시간에 여행을 가고 싶다고 답했습니다.

➡ _____

5. 하지만 그들이 실제로 가장 많이 하는 여가 활동은 TV를 보는 것입니다.

➡ _____

6. 39%는 여가 시간에 TV를 본다고 답했습니다.

➡ _____

7. 결과로 봤을 때, 우리는 청소년들이 여가 시간에 하고 싶은 활동과 실제로 하는 활동 사이에 큰 차이가 있다는 것을 알 수 있습니다.

➡ _____

_____

※ 다음 영어를 우리말로 쓰시오.

01	melt	22	symbolic
02	suddenly	23	justice
03	curvy	24	lotus flower
04	thus	25	muddy
05	bend	26	bloom
06	represent	27	carp
07	despite	28	will
08	cancel	29	character
09	symbolize	30	disappointed
10	dynasty	31	respect
11	effectively	32	society
12	folk painting	33	decoration
13	value	34	difficulty
14	loyalty	35	in particular
15	behavior	36	as follows
16	frozen	37	get well
17	harmony	38	once upon a time
18	ill	39	much more than
19	appear	40	remind ~ of …
20	influence	41	for this reason
21	attitude	42	because of
		43	right after ~

※ 다음 우리말을 영어로 쓰시오.

01 시대, 왕조

02 효과적으로

03 ~하게 보이다, 나타나다

04 영향을 미치다

05 충성, 충실

06 정의, 공정성

07 꽃을 피우다, 꽃이 피다

08 잉어

09 나타내다, 보여 주다

10 굽다, 구부러지다

11 굴곡이 많은

12 장식

13 연꽃

14 어려움, 고난

15 갑자기

16 민화

17 존경, 경의

18 사회

19 가치, 중요성

20 글자

21 행동

22 상징하다

23 진흙투성이의, 흙탕물의

24 의지

25 취소하다

26 상징적인, 상징하는

27 조화

28 실망한, 낙담한

29 태도, 자세

30 대나무

31 얼어붙은

32 녹다

33 ~에도 불구하고

34 물건, 물체

35 병이 나아지다, 회복하다

36 ~ 직후에

37 특히, 특별히

38 다음과 같이

39 이런 이유로

40 ~보다 훨씬 많이

41 ~에게 …을 상기시키다

42 옛날에

43 너무 ~해서 …하다

※ 다음 영영풀이에 알맞은 단어를 <보기>에서 골라 쓴 후, 우리말 뜻을 쓰시오.

1 _____ : produce or yield flowers: _____

2 _____ : to show or mean something: _____

3 _____ : a sign, picture, object etc. that represents something else: _____

4 _____ : a thing that you can see and touch: _____

5 _____ : the way you think or feel about something: _____

6 _____ : to make someone remember something: _____

7 _____ : the things that a person or animal does: _____

8 _____ : representing a particular idea or quality: _____

9 _____ : although something happens or exists: _____

10 _____ : made into, covered with, or surrounded by ice: _____

11 _____ : a feeling of support for someone or something: _____

12 _____ : all the people who live in a country, and the way they live: _____

13 _____ : to begin to be seen; come into existence or use: _____

14 _____ : to shape or force something straight into a curve or angle: _____

15 _____ : the quality of being fair and reasonable; fairness in the way people are treated: _____

16 _____ : a period of time during which members of the same family rule a country or region: _____

보기

frozen	symbolic	loyalty	behavior
justice	object	dynasty	bloom
despite	attitude	society	remind
bend	represent	appear	symbol

※ 다음 우리말과 일치하도록 빈칸에 알맞은 말을 쓰시오.

Listen and Talk A 1

G: Minho, look at these _____ _____ _____ _____ here. _____ they great?

B: Yes, they _____.

G: They _____ are good, but I like _____ _____ on the left more. How _____ you?

B: I _____ the one on the right. It _____ _____ _____ _____ the cat in it is _____. I also like the bird in it.

G: 민호야, 여기 고양이가 그려진 그림 두 점을 봐. 멋있지 않니?
B: 응, 그러네.
G: 그것들은 모두 멋있지만 난 왼쪽에 있는 그림이 더 좋아. 넌 어때?
B: 난 오른쪽에 있는 그림이 더 좋아. 그림 속 고양이가 더 귀여운 것 같아. 새도 마음에 들어.

Listen and Talk A 2

G: We can have Bibimbap or Galbitang. _____ do you _____?

B: I _____ Bibimbap. _____ _____ to me that it's the _____ _____.

G: I think _____, too. I also _____ Bibimbap _____.

B: Let's _____, then. I'm very hungry.

G: 우리는 비빔밥이나 갈비탕을 먹을 수 있어. 어떤 것이 더 좋니?
B: 난 비빔밥이 더 좋아. 그것이 더 건강에 좋은 선택인 것 같아.
G: 나도 그렇게 생각해. 난 비빔밥을 더 좋아하기도 해.
B: 그럼 주문하자. 난 정말 배고파.

Listen and Talk A 3

G: Look at these two _____ _____, Steve. Aren't they beautiful?

B: Yes. _____ _____ do you _____, the green plate or the white plate?

G: Well, it's hard _____ _____, but I like the green one _____. How _____ you?

B: _____, _____. It _____ to me _____ the green plate is more _____.

G: Steve, 이 두 개의 옛날 접시들을 봐. 아름답지 않니?
B: 응. 초록색 접시와 흰색 접시 중 무엇이 더 좋니?
G: 음, 고르기가 어렵지만 난 초록색 접시가 더 좋아. 너는 어때?
B: 나도. 초록색 접시가 더 독특한 것 같아.

Listen and Talk A 4

G: Junsu, you said _____ _____ _____ buy a _____ for your sister. _____ _____ the bags here?

B: They _____ _____.

G: _____ _____ do you _____, the one with flowers _____ the one _____ animals?

B: I _____ the one _____ flowers. _____ _____ _____ _____ that my sister will like it more.

G: 준수야, 너 여동생 줄 선물을 살 거라고 했잖아. 여기 이 가방들은 어때?
B: 좋아 보인다.
G: 가방에 꽃들이 있는 것과 동물들이 있는 것 중 무엇이 더 좋니?
B: 난 꽃들이 있는 것이 더 좋아. 내 여동생이 그것을 더 좋아할 것 같아.

Listen and Talk B

A: _____ food do you _____, Tteokbokki or Gimbap?

B: I _____ Tteokbokki. _____ seems to me _____ it's more _____. How about you?

A: I _____ Tteokbokki, too. / I _____ Gimbap. It _____ _____ _____ that it's _____.

A: _____ painting do you _____, the one on the left _____ the one on the right?

B: I _____ the one on the right. It seems to me that the cat in it is cuter. How about you?

A: I _____ the one on the right, too. / I _____ the one on the left. It seems to me that it looks _____ _____.

A: _____ plate do you prefer, the green one _____ the white one?

B: I _____ the green one. It seems to me that it's _____ _____. How about you?

A: I _____ the green one, too. / I _____ the white one. It seems to me that it's _____ _____ beautiful.

A: _____ bag do you _____, the one with fish _____ the one _____ stars?

B: I _____ the one with stars. It seems to me that it's _____ my style. How about you?

A: I _____ the one with stars, _____. / I _____ the one with fish. It seems to me that the fish are _____.

Listen and Talk C

G: There are two _____ we can go to. _____ one do you want to see _____, Eric?

B: I _____ the Korean mask exhibition. Is _____ OK, Somi?

G: Of _____. And it seems to me that the mask exhibition will be _____ more interesting.

B: Do you think _____?

G: Yes. Look at this poster. There isn't _____ an exhibition. There's _____ a mask dance show at 4:00 and 6:00.

B: Great! I've _____ _____ a mask dance show _____.

G: Well, I've seen a show _____. I'm _____ you'll like it.

B: So where is the show?

G: It's in Dasom Hall, _____ _____ the exhibition room.

B: It's 4:30 now, so _____ _____ the 6 o'clock show.

G: OK. _____ go see the exhibition _____.

A: 떡볶이와 김밥 중에 어떤 것을 더 좋아하니?

B: 난 떡볶이를 좋아해. 그것이 더 맛있을 것 같아. 너는 어때?

A: 나도 떡볶이를 좋아해. / 난 김밥을 좋아해. 그것이 더 건강에 좋은 것 같아.

A: 왼쪽 그림과 오른쪽 그림 중 어떤 것을 더 좋아하니?

B: 난 오른쪽 그림을 더 좋아해. 그림 속 고양이가 더 귀여운 것 같아. 너는 어때?

A: 나도 오른쪽 그림이 더 좋아. / 난 왼쪽 그림을 더 좋아해. 그것이 더 평화로워 보이거든.

A: 초록색 접시와 흰색 접시 중 어떤 것을 더 좋아하니?

B: 난 초록색 접시가 더 좋아. 그것이 더 독특하다고 생각해. 너는 어때?

A: 나도 초록색 접시가 더 좋아. / 난 흰색 접시가 더 좋아. 그것이 단순하지만 아름답다고 생각해.

A: 물고기가 있는 가방과 별들이 있는 가방 중 어떤 것을 더 좋아하니?

B: 난 별들이 있는 가방을 더 좋아해. 그것이 더 내 취향이야. 너는 어때?

A: 나도 별들이 있는 가방이 더 좋아. / 난 물고기가 있는 가방을 더 좋아해. 물고기가 귀여운 것 같아.

G: 우리가 갈 수 있는 전시회가 두 곳이 있어. 어느 것을 더 보고 싶니, Eric?

B: 나는 한국의 탈 전시회를 더 선호해. 소미야, 괜찮겠니?

G: 물론이지. 그리고 나도 탈 전시회가 더 흥미로울 것 같아.

B: 그렇게 생각하니?

G: 그래. 이 포스터를 봐. 단순히 전시회만 있는 것이 아니야. 탈춤 공연도 4시와 6시에 있어.

B: 좋아! 나는 전에 탈춤 공연을 본 적이 없어.

G: 음, 나는 전에 본 적이 있어. 네가 분명 좋아할 거야.

B: 그래서 공연은 어디서 해?

G: 전시관 옆 다솜 홀에서 해.

B: 지금 4시 30분이니까 6시 공연을 보자.

G: 그래. 우선 전시회부터 보자.

Listen and Talk D

I _____ science. It seems to me that it's _____ _____ _____. I also _____ it because I want to be a great _____ _____ Edison.

Talk and Play

A: _____ do you _____, Ramyeon or spaghetti?

B: I _____ Ramyeon. _____ _____ _____ me that it's more delicious. How about you?

A: I _____ Ramyeon, too. / I _____ spaghetti. It seems to me that it's _____.

Review 1

G: Joe, didn't you say you needed _____ _____ a cap? How about these caps here?

B: They look _____.

G: _____ _____ do you _____, the one with triangles _____ the one _____ flowers?

B: I _____ the one _____ _____. It seems to me that it's _____ _____.

Review 2

B: We can have Gimbap or Tteokbokki. _____ do you _____, Jenny?

G: I _____ Gimbap. It seems to me that it's _____ _____ _____. How about you, Minsu?

B: I'll have Tteokbokki. _____ _____ that the Tteokbokki here is very good.

G: Let's _____, then. I'm very _____.

Review 3

John: There are two movies we can see. _____ _____ do you want to see _____, Somi?

Somi: I _____ *Batman*. I saw *Spider-Man* last week. Is _____ OK, John?

John: Of course. It seems to me that *Batman* will be _____ more fun.

Somi: Good. Then, _____ _____ and see it.

※ 다음 우리말에 맞도록 대화를 영어로 쓰시오.

Listen and Talk A 1

G: _____

B: _____

G: _____

B: _____

G: 민호야, 여기 고양이가 그려진 그림 두 점을 봐. 멋있지 않니?
B: 응, 그러네.
G: 그것들은 모두 멋있지만 난 왼쪽에 있는 그림이 더 좋아. 넌 어때?
B: 난 오른쪽에 있는 그림이 더 좋아. 그림 속 고양이가 더 귀여운 것 같아. 새도 마음에 들어.

Listen and Talk A 2

G: _____

B: _____

G: _____

B: _____

G: 우리는 비빔밥이나 갈비탕을 먹을 수 있어. 어떤 것이 더 좋니?
B: 난 비빔밥이 더 좋아. 그것이 더 건강에 좋은 선택인 것 같아.
G: 나도 그렇게 생각해. 난 비빔밥을 더 좋아하기도 해.
B: 그럼 주문하자. 난 정말 배고파.

Listen and Talk A 3

G: _____

B: _____

G: _____

B: _____

G: Steve, 이 두 개의 옛날 접시들을 봐. 아름답지 않니?
B: 응. 초록색 접시와 흰색 접시 중 무엇이 더 좋니?
G: 음, 고르기가 어렵지만 난 초록색 접시가 더 좋아. 너는 어때?
B: 나도. 초록색 접시가 더 독특한 것 같아.

Listen and Talk A 4

G: _____

B: _____

G: _____

B: _____

G: 준수야, 너 여동생 줄 선물을 살 거라고 했잖아. 여기 이 가방들은 어때?
B: 좋아 보인다.
G: 가방에 꽃들이 있는 것과 동물들이 있는 것 중 무엇이 더 좋니?
B: 난 꽃들이 있는 것이 더 좋아. 내 여동생이 그것을 더 좋아할 것 같아.

Listen and Talk B

A: _____

B: _____

A: _____

A: _____

B: _____

A: _____

A: _____

B: _____

A: _____

A: _____

B: _____

A: _____

A: 떡볶이와 김밥 중에 어떤 것을 더 좋아하니?

B: 난 떡볶이를 좋아해. 그것이 더 맛있을 것 같아. 너는 어때?

A: 나도 떡볶이를 좋아해. / 난 김밥을 좋아해. 그것이 더 건강에 좋은 것 같아.

A: 왼쪽 그림과 오른쪽 그림 중 어떤 것을 더 좋아하니?

B: 난 오른쪽 그림을 더 좋아해. 그림 속 고양이가 더 귀여운 것 같아. 너는 어때?

A: 나도 오른쪽 그림이 더 좋아. / 난 왼쪽 그림을 더 좋아해. 그것이 더 평화로워 보이거든.

A: 초록색 접시와 흰색 접시 중 어떤 것을 더 좋아하니?

B: 난 초록색 접시가 더 좋아. 그것이 더 독특하다고 생각해. 너는 어때?

A: 나도 초록색 접시가 더 좋아. / 난 흰색 접시가 더 좋아. 그것이 단순하지만 아름답다고 생각해.

A: 물고기가 있는 가방과 별들이 있는 가방 중 어떤 것을 더 좋아하니?

B: 난 별들이 있는 가방을 더 좋아해. 그것이 더 내 취향이야. 너는 어때?

A: 나도 별들이 있는 가방이 더 좋아. / 난 물고기가 있는 가방을 더 좋아해. 물고기가 귀여운 것 같아.

Listen and Talk C

G: _____

B: _____

G: _____

B: _____

G: _____

B: _____

G: _____

B: _____

G: _____

B: _____

G: _____

G: 우리가 갈 수 있는 전시회가 두 곳이 있어. 어느 것을 더 보고 싶니, Eric?

B: 나는 한국의 탈 전시회를 더 선호해. 소미야, 괜찮겠니?

G: 물론이지. 그리고 나도 탈 전시회가 더 흥미로울 것 같아.

B: 그렇게 생각하니?

G: 그래. 이 포스터를 봐. 단순히 전시회만 있는 것이 아니야. 탈춤 공연도 4시와 6시에 있어.

B: 좋아! 나는 전에 탈춤 공연을 본 적이 없어.

G: 음, 나는 전에 본 적이 있어. 네가 분명 좋아할 거야.

B: 그래서 공연은 어디서 해?

G: 전시관 옆 다솜 홀에서 해.

B: 지금 4시 30분이니까 6시 공연을 보자.

G: 그래. 우선 전시회부터 보자.

Listen and Talk D

_____

_____

Talk and Play

A: _____

B: _____

A: _____

Review 1

G: _____

B: _____

G: _____

B: _____

Review 2

B: _____

G: _____

B: _____

G: _____

Review 3

John: _____

_____

Somi: _____

John: _____

Somi: _____

난 과학을 더 좋아해. 그것을 배우는 것이 더 즐거운 것 같아. 난 Edison과 같은 훌륭한 발명가가 되고 싶어서 그것을 더 좋아하기도 해.

A: 라면과 스파게티 중 어떤 걸 더 좋아하니?

B: 난 라면을 더 좋아해. 그것이 더 맛있는 것 같아. 너는 어때?

A: 나도 라면을 더 좋아해. / 난 스파게티를 더 좋아해. 그것이 건강에 더 좋을 것 같아.

G: Joe, 모자를 사야 한다고 하지 않았니? 여기 있는 이 모자들은 어때?

B: 그것들은 좋아 보인다.

G: 삼각형이 있는 것과 꽃이 있는 것 중 어떤 것이 좋니?

B: 난 삼각형이 있는 것이 더 좋아. 그것이 더 독특한 것 같아.

G: 우리는 김밥이나 떡볶이를 시킬 수 있어. 어떤 것이 더 좋니, Jenny?

B: 난 김밥이 더 좋아. 건강에 더 좋은 선택인 것 같거든. 민수야, 넌 어떠니?

G: 난 떡볶이 먹을래. 여기는 떡볶이가 더 맛있다고 들었거든.

B: 그럼 주문하자. 난 정말 배고파.

John: 우리가 볼 수 있는 영화가 두 개 있어. 소미야, 어떤 것이 더 보고 싶니?

Somi: 난 "배트맨"이 더 좋아. 난 "스파이더맨"을 지난주에 봤거든. John, 괜찮니?

John: 물론이지. "배트맨"이 훨씬 더 재미있을 것 같아.

Somi: 좋아. 그럼 영화 보러 가자.

※ 다음 우리말과 일치하도록 빈칸에 알맞은 것을 골라 쓰시오.

1 Munjado, a _____ _____ the Joseon _____
A. into　　　　　B. Window　　　　C. Dynasty

2 Look _____ the painting _____ _____ _____.
A. on　　　　　B. right　　　　C. at　　　　D. the

3 Do you _____ the _____ _____, hyo(孝)?
A. character　　　B. see　　　　C. Chinese

4 Do you _____ _____ a _____, a geomungo, and a _____?
A. fan　　　　　B. also　　　　C. carp　　　　D. see

5 This kind of painting is _____ Munjado, and it is a _____ of folk painting that was _____ in the _____ Joseon dynasty.
A. popular　　　B. called　　　C. late　　　D. type

6 In Munjado, _____ is _____ a Chinese character _____ some animals or _____.
A. with　　　　B. objects　　　C. usually　　　D. there

7 _____ _____ eight Chinese _____ _____ in Munjado.
A. appears　　　B. one　　　C. characters　　　D. of

8 They are hyo(孝), je(悌), chung(忠), sin(信), ye(禮), ui(義), yeom(廉), and chi(恥), and they _____ the _____ that were _____ to people of the Joseon _____.
A. values　　　B. represent　　　C. important　　　D. dynasty

9 The _____ or _____ in Munjado are not _____ _____.
A. decorations　　B. objects　　C. animals　　D. just

10 They _____ are _____.
A. symbolic　　　B. often

11 For example, carp in the _____ of hyo _____ _____ for parents _____ of an old story.
A. because　　　B. symbolize　　　C. paintings　　　D. respect

12 The story _____ _____ _____.
A. as　　　　　B. goes　　　C. follows

13 _____ _____ a _____, a man lived _____ his old mother.
A. with　　　　B. time　　　C. once　　　D. upon

14 One winter, the man's mother _____ _____ and eat _____.
A. anything　　　B. ill　　　C. couldn't　　　D. became

15 _____ one very cold day, the mother said to the man, "It _____ be wonderful if I _____ eat _____ fish."
A. would　　　B. on　　　C. could　　　D. fresh

16 The man _____ _____ to the river, but it was _____ _____.
A. frozen　　　B. out　　　C. completely　　　D. went

---

1 문자도, 조선 시대를 보는 창

2 오른쪽에 있는 그림을 보라.

3 한자 효(孝)가 보이는가?

4 잉어, 거문고, 그리고 부채가 보이는가?

5 이런 종류의 그림은 문자도이며, 조선 시대 후기에 인기 있었던 민화의 한 종류이다.

6 문자도에는 보통 한자 하나가 동물이나 사물과 함께 있다.

7 문자도에는 여덟 개의 한자 중 하나가 나온다.

8 그것들은 효(孝), 제(悌), 충(忠), 신(信), 예(禮), 의(義), 염(廉), 치(恥)이고, 그것들은 조선 시대 사람들에게 중요했던 가치들을 나타낸다.

9 문자도에 있는 동물이나 사물은 단순한 장식이 아니다.

10 그것들은 종종 상징적이다.

11 예를 들어, '효' 그림 속에 있는 잉어는 옛이야기 때문에 부모님에 대한 존경심을 상징한다.

12 그 이야기는 다음과 같다.

13 옛날 옛적에 한 남자가 나이 드신 어머니와 살았다.

14 어느 겨울, 남자의 어머니는 병이 들어서 어떤 것도 먹을 수 없었다.

15 무척 추운 어느 날, 어머니는 남자에게 말했다. "신선한 물고기를 먹을 수 있다면 좋겠구나."

16 그 남자는 강으로 나갔지만, 강은 완전히 얼어붙어 있었다.

17 _____ was impossible _____ him _____ any fish.

A. for   B. it   C. catch   D. to

18 The man was _____ _____ _____ he cried out _____ the sky, "What should I do? Please help me."

A. that   B. so   C. to   D. disappointed

19 Then the ice _____, and three carp _____ came _____ _____ the water.

A. out   B. melted   C. suddenly   D. of

20 The man _____ _____ _____ and _____ the fish for his mother.

A. home   B. cooked   C. back   D. went

21 _____ his mother _____ _____.

A. well   B. got   C. then

22 There are _____ _____ of _____ _____ in Munjado.

A. objects   B. other   C. symbolic   D. examples

23 They are _____ in the _____ of the _____ _chung_(忠) and _____ flowers in the paintings of _ui_(義).

A. character   B. bamboo   C. paintings   D. lotus

24 _____ _____ not _____.

A. bend   B. bamboo   C. does

25 It _____ _____ all _____ of weather.

A. kinds   B. green   C. stays   D. in

26 _____ these _____, bamboo came to _____ _____ to the king.

A. symbolize   B. reasons   C. loyalty   D. for

27 In the _____ of lotus flowers, they _____ in _____ ponds but still _____ beautifully.

A. muddy   B. case   C. bloom   D. grow

28 They thus became a symbol of a person's _____ to _____ for justice _____ _____.

A. will   B. despite   C. fight   D. difficulties

29 Munjado was _____ _____ _____ a painting _____ people of the Joseon dynasty.

A. than   B. to   C. more   D. much

30 It _____ them of important values that greatly _____ their _____ and _____.

A. behaviors   B. reminded   C. attitudes   D. influenced

31 _____ _____, _____ children, Munjado was a study _____.

A. tool   B. in   C. for   D. particular

32 _____ it, children in the Joseon dynasty could learn the _____ of _____ in family and _____.

A. harmony   B. through   C. society   D. importance

---

17 그가 그 어떤 물고기라도 잡는 것은 불가능했다.

18 남자는 몹시 낙담해서 하늘에 대고 외쳤다. "제가 어떻게 해야 하나요? 제발 저를 도와주세요."

19 그러자 얼음이 녹았고, 잉어 세 마리가 갑자기 물 밖으로 나왔다.

20 남자는 집으로 돌아가서 어머니를 위해 물고기들을 요리했다.

21 그러자 그의 어머니는 회복되었다.

22 문자도에 있는 상징적인 사물의 또 다른 예가 있다.

23 그것들은 글자 '충(忠)' 그림에 있는 대나무와 '의(義)' 그림에 있는 연꽃이다.

24 대나무는 구부러지지 않는다.

25 그것은 어떤 날씨에서도 푸르름을 유지한다.

26 이런 이유로 대나무는 왕에 대한 충성을 상징하게 되었다.

27 연꽃의 경우, 그것들은 진흙투성이의 연못에서 자라지만 여전히 아름답게 꽃을 피운다.

28 그래서 그 꽃들은 어려움에도 불구하고 정의를 위해 싸우는 사람의 의지를 상징하게 되었다.

29 문자도는 조선 시대 사람들에게 그림 그 이상이었다.

30 그것은 그들에게 자신들의 행동과 태도에 큰 영향을 미치는 중요한 가치를 상기시켰다.

31 특히 아이들에게 문자도는 학습 도구였다.

32 그것을 통해 조선 시대의 아이들은 가족과 사회에서의 조화의 중요성을 배울 수 있었다.

※ 다음 우리말과 일치하도록 빈칸에 알맞은 말을 쓰시오.

1 Munjado, a Window _____ the Joseon _____

2 _____ _____ the painting _____ _____ _____ .

3 Do you _____ the _____ _____ , hyo(孝)?

4 Do you also _____ a _____ , a geomungo, and a fan?

5 This kind of painting _____ _____ Munjado, and it is _____ _____ _____ _____ _____ _____ in the _____ Joseon dynasty.

6 In Munjado, there is _____ a Chinese character _____ some animals or _____ .

7 _____ _____ eight Chinese _____ _____ in Munjado.

8 They are hyo(孝), je(悌), chung(忠), sin(信), ye(禮), ui(義), yeom(廉), and chi(恥), and they _____ the values _____ _____ _____ _____ people of the _____ _____ .

9 The animals or objects in Munjado are not _____ _____ .

10 They _____ are _____ .

11 For example, carp in the paintings of hyo _____ _____ for parents _____ _____ an old story.

12 The story _____ _____ _____ .

13 _____ _____ _____ _____ , a man lived with his old mother.

14 One winter, the man's mother _____ _____ and couldn't eat _____ .

15 _____ one very cold day, the mother said to the man, "It _____ _____ _____ _____ _____ _____ _____ _____ _____ ."

16 The man _____ _____ the river, but it _____ _____ _____ .

1 문자도, 조선 시대를 보는 창

2 오른쪽에 있는 그림을 보라.

3 한자 효(孝)가 보이는가?

4 잉어, 거문고, 그리고 부채가 보이는가?

5 이런 종류의 그림은 문자도이며, 조선 시대 후기에 인기 있었던 민화의 한 종류이다.

6 문자도에는 보통 한자 하나가 동물이나 사물과 함께 있다.

7 문자도에는 여덟 개의 한자 중 하나가 나온다.

8 그것들은 효(孝), 제(悌), 충(忠), 신(信), 예(禮), 의(義), 염(廉), 치(恥)이고, 그것들은 조선 시대 사람들에게 중요했던 가치들을 나타낸다.

9 문자도에 있는 동물이나 사물은 단순한 장식이 아니다.

10 그것들은 종종 상징적이다.

11 예를 들어, '효' 그림 속에 있는 잉어는 옛이야기 때문에 부모님에 대한 존경심을 상징한다.

12 그 이야기는 다음과 같다.

13 옛날 옛적에 한 남자가 나이 드신 어머니와 살았다.

14 어느 겨울, 남자의 어머니는 병이 들어서 어떤 것도 먹을 수 없었다.

15 무척 추운 어느 날, 어머니는 남자에게 말했다. "신선한 물고기를 먹을 수 있다면 좋겠구나."

16 그 남자는 강으로 나갔지만, 강은 완전히 얼어붙어 있었다.

17 _____ was impossible _____ _____ _____ _____
_____ fish.

18 The man was _____ _____ _____ he _____ _____
_____ the sky, "What should I do? Please help me."

19 Then the ice _____, and three carp _____ came _____
_____ the water.

20 The man went _____ _____ and cooked the fish for his
mother.

21 Then his mother _____ _____ .

22 There are other examples of _____ _____ in Munjado.

23 They are bamboo _____ the paintings _____ the character
chung(忠) and _____ _____ _____ the paintings _____
_ui_(義).

24 Bamboo does not _____ .

25 It _____ _____ _____ all _____ of weather.

26 _____ _____ _____, bamboo _____ _____ _____ _____
_____ _____ the king.

27 _____ _____ _____ _____ _____ lotus flowers, they grow in
muddy ponds _____ _____ _____ _____ _____ .

28 They _____ became a symbol of a person's _____ _____
_____ _____ justice _____ _____ .

29 Munjado was _____ _____ _____ a painting _____
people of the Joseon dynasty.

30 It _____ them _____ important values _____ greatly
influenced their _____ and _____ .

31 _____ _____, _____ children, Munjado was a study tool.

32 _____ _____, children in the Joseon dynasty could learn the
_____ of _____ _____ family and _____ .

---

17 그가 그 어떤 물고기라도 잡는
것은 불가능했다.

18 남자는 몹시 낙담해서 하늘에
대고 외쳤다. "제가 어떻게 해야
하나요? 제발 저를 도와주세요."

19 그러자 얼음이 녹았고, 잉어 세
마리가 갑자기 물 밖으로 나왔다.

20 남자는 집으로 돌아가서 어머니
를 위해 물고기들을 요리했다.

21 그러자 그의 어머니는 회복되었다.

22 문자도에 있는 상징적인 사물의
또 다른 예가 있다.

23 그것들은 글자 '충(忠)' 그림에
있는 대나무와 '의(義)' 그림에
있는 연꽃이다.

24 대나무는 구부러지지 않는다.

25 그것은 어떤 날씨에서도 푸르름
을 유지한다.

26 이런 이유로 대나무는 왕에 대
한 충성을 상징하게 되었다.

27 연꽃의 경우, 그것들은 진흙투
성이의 연못에서 자라지만 여전
히 아름답게 꽃을 피운다.

28 그래서 그 꽃들은 어려움에도
불구하고 정의를 위해 싸우는
사람의 의지를 상징하게 되었다.

29 문자도는 조선 시대 사람들에게
그림 그 이상이었다.

30 그것은 그들에게 자신들의 행동
과 태도에 큰 영향을 미치는 중
요한 가치를 상기시켰다.

31 특히 아이들에게 문자도는 학습
도구였다.

32 그것을 통해 조선 시대의 아이
들은 가족과 사회에서의 조화의
중요성을 배울 수 있었다.

※ 다음 문장을 우리말로 쓰시오.

1 Munjado, a Window into the Joseon Dynasty

➡ _____

2 Look at the painting on the right.

➡ _____

3 Do you see the Chinese character, *hyo*(孝)?

➡ _____

4 Do you also see a carp, a geomungo, and a fan?

➡ _____

5 This kind of painting is called Munjado, and it is a type of folk painting that was popular in the late Joseon dynasty.

➡ _____

6 In Munjado, there is usually a Chinese character with some animals or objects.

➡ _____

7 One of eight Chinese characters appears in Munjado.

➡ _____

8 They are *hyo*(孝), *je*(悌), *chung*(忠), *sin*(信), *ye*(禮), *ui*(義), *yeom*(廉), and *chi*(恥), and they represent the values that were important to people of the Joseon dynasty.

➡ _____

➡ _____

9 The animals or objects in Munjado are not just decorations.

➡ _____

10 They often are symbolic.

➡ _____

11 For example, carp in the paintings of *hyo* symbolize respect for parents because of an old story.

➡ _____

12 The story goes as follows.

➡ _____

13 Once upon a time, a man lived with his old mother.

➡ _____

14 One winter, the man's mother became ill and couldn't eat anything.

➡ _____

15 On one very cold day, the mother said to the man, "It would be wonderful if I could eat fresh fish."

➡ _____

16 The man went out to the river, but it was completely frozen.

➡ _____

17 It was impossible for him to catch any fish.

➡ _____

18 The man was so disappointed that he cried out to the sky, "What should I do? Please help me."

➡ _____

19 Then the ice melted, and three carp suddenly came out of the water.

➡ _____

20 The man went back home and cooked the fish for his mother.

➡ _____

21 Then his mother got well.

➡ _____

22 There are other examples of symbolic objects in Munjado.

➡ _____

23 They are bamboo in the paintings of the character *chung*(忠) and lotus flowers in the paintings of *ui*(義).

➡ _____

24 Bamboo does not bend.

➡ _____

25 It stays green in all kinds of weather.

➡ _____

26 For these reasons, bamboo came to symbolize loyalty to the king.

➡ _____

27 In the case of lotus flowers, they grow in muddy ponds but still bloom beautifully.

➡ _____

28 They thus became a symbol of a person's will to fight for justice despite difficulties.

➡ _____

29 Munjado was much more than a painting to people of the Joseon dynasty.

➡ _____

30 It reminded them of important values that greatly influenced their behaviors and attitudes.

➡ _____

31 In particular, for children, Munjado was a study tool.

➡ _____

32 Through it, children in the Joseon dynasty could learn the importance of harmony in family and society

➡ _____

※ 다음 괄호 안의 단어들을 우리말에 맞도록 바르게 배열하시오.

1 (a / Munjado / into / Window / Joseon / the / Dynasty)
➡ _____

2 (at / look / painting / the / the / on / right.)
➡ _____

3 (you / do / the / see / character, / Chinese / *hyo*(孝)?)
➡ _____

4 (you / do / see / also / carp, / a / geomungo / a / and / fan? / a)
➡ _____

5 (kind / this / painting / of / called / is / Munjado, / and / is / it / of / type / a / folk / that / painting / was / popular / the / in / Joseon / late / dynasty.)
➡ _____
_____

6 (Munjado, / in / is / there / a / usually / character / Chinese / some / with / or / animals / objects.)
➡ _____
_____

7 (of / one / Chinese / eight / appears / characters / Munjado. / in)
➡ _____

8 (are / they / *je*(悌), / *hyo*(孝), / *sin*(信), / *chung*(忠), / *ui*(義), / *ye*(禮), / *chi*(恥), / and / *yeom*(廉), / and / represent / they / values / the / were / that / to / important / of / people / the / dynasty. / Joseon)
➡ _____
_____

9 (animals / the / objects / or / Munjado / in / are / just / not / decorations.)
➡ _____

10 (often / they / symbolic. / are)
➡ _____

11 (example, / for / in / carp / paintings / the / *hyo* / of / respect / symbolize / parents / for / of / because / old / an / story.)
➡ _____
_____

12 (story / the / as / goes / follows.)
➡ _____

13 (upon / once / time, / a / man / a / with / lived / old / mother. / his)
➡ _____

14 (winter, / one / man's / the / became / mother / and / ill / eat / couldn't / anything.)
➡ _____

15 (one / on / cold / very / day, / mother / the / to / said / man, / the / would / "it / be / if / wonderful / eat / could / I / fish." / fresh)
➡ _____
_____

16 (man / the / out / went / the / to / river, / it / but / completely / was / frozen.)
➡ _____

1 문자도, 조선 시대를 보는 창

2 오른쪽에 있는 그림을 보라.

3 한자 효(孝)가 보이는가?

4 잉어, 거문고, 그리고 부채가 보이는가?

5 이런 종류의 그림은 문자도이며, 조선 시대 후기에 인기 있었던 민화의 한 종류이다.

6 문자도에는 보통 한자 하나가 동물이나 사물과 함께 있다.

7 문자도에는 여덟 개의 한자 중 하나가 나온다.

8 그것들은 효(孝), 제(悌), 충(忠), 신(信), 예(禮), 의(義), 염(廉), 치(恥)이고, 그것들은 조선 시대 사람들에게 중요했던 가치들을 나타낸다.

9 문자도에 있는 동물이나 사물은 단순한 장식이 아니다.

10 그것들은 종종 상징적이다.

11 예를 들어, '효' 그림 속에 있는 잉어는 옛이야기 때문에 부모님에 대한 존경심을 상징한다.

12 그 이야기는 다음과 같다.

13 옛날 옛적에 한 남자가 나이 드신 어머니와 살았다.

14 어느 겨울, 남자의 어머니는 병이 들어서 어떤 것도 먹을 수 없었다.

15 무척 추운 어느 날, 어머니는 남자에게 말했다. "신선한 물고기를 먹을 수 있다면 좋겠구나."

16 그 남자는 강으로 나갔지만, 강은 완전히 얼어붙어 있었다.

17 (was / it / for / impossible / to / him / any / catch / fish.)
➡ _____

18 (man / the / so / was / that / disappointed / cried / he / to / out / sky, / the / should / "what / I / do? / help / please / me.")
➡ _____

19 (the / then / melted, / ice / three / and / suddenly / carp / out / came / the / of / water.)
➡ _____

20 (man / the / back / went / home / and / the / cooked / for / fish / mother. / his)
➡ _____

21 (his / then / got / mother / well.)
➡ _____

22 (are / there / examples / other / symbolic / of / in / objects / Munjado.)
➡ _____

23 (are / they / in / bamboo / paintings / the / the / of / *chung*(忠) / character / lotus / and / in / flowers / paintings / the / *ui*(義) / of)
➡ _____

24 (does / bamboo / bend. / not)
➡ _____

25 (stays / it / in / green / kinds / all / weather. / of)
➡ _____

26 (these / for / reasons, / came / bamboo / symbolize / to / to / loyalty / king. / the)
➡ _____

27 (the / in / of / case / flowers, / lotus / grow / they / muddy / in / but / ponds / still / beautifully. / bloom)
➡ _____

28 (thus / they / a / became / symbol / of / person's / a / to / will / fight / justice / for / difficulties. / despite)
➡ _____

29 (was / Munjado / more / much / a / than / to / painting / of / people / the / dynasty. / Joseon)
➡ _____

30 (reminded / it / of / them / values / important / greatly / that / their / influenced / behaviors / attitudes. / and)
➡ _____

31 (particular, / in / children, / for / was / Munjado / study / a / tool.)
➡ _____

32 (it, / through / in / children / Joseon / the / could / dynasty / learn / the / of / importance / in / harmony / family / society. / and)
➡ _____

17 그가 그 어떤 물고기라도 잡는 것은 불가능했다.

18 남자는 몹시 낙담해서 하늘에 대고 외쳤다. "제가 어떻게 해야 하나요? 제발 저를 도와주세요."

19 그러자 얼음이 녹았고, 잉어 세 마리가 갑자기 물 밖으로 나왔다.

20 남자는 집으로 돌아가서 어머니를 위해 물고기들을 요리했다.

21 그러자 그의 어머니는 회복되었다.

22 문자도에 있는 상징적인 사물의 또 다른 예가 있다.

23 그것들은 글자 '충(忠)' 그림에 있는 대나무와 '의(義)' 그림에 있는 연꽃이다.

24 대나무는 구부러지지 않는다.

25 그것은 어떤 날씨에서도 푸르름을 유지한다.

26 이런 이유로 대나무는 왕에 대한 충성을 상징하게 되었다.

27 연꽃의 경우, 그것들은 진흙투성이의 연못에서 자라지만 여전히 아름답게 꽃을 피운다.

28 그래서 그 꽃들은 어려움에도 불구하고 정의를 위해 싸우는 사람의 의지를 상징하게 되었다.

29 문자도는 조선 시대 사람들에게 그림 그 이상이었다.

30 그것은 그들에게 자신들의 행동과 태도에 큰 영향을 미치는 중요한 가치를 상기시켰다.

31 특히 아이들에게 문자도는 학습 도구였다.

32 그것을 통해 조선 시대의 아이들은 가족과 사회에서의 조화의 중요성을 배울 수 있었다.

※ 다음 우리말을 영어로 쓰시오.

1 문자도, 조선 시대를 보는 창

➡ _____

2 오른쪽에 있는 그림을 보라.

➡ _____

3 한자 효(孝)가 보이는가?

➡ _____

4 잉어, 거문고, 그리고 부채가 보이는가?

➡ _____

5 이런 종류의 그림은 문자도이며, 조선 시대 후기에 인기 있었던 민화의 한 종류이다.

➡ _____

_____

6 문자도에는 보통 한자 하나가 동물이나 사물과 함께 있다.

➡ _____

7 문자도에는 여덟 개의 한자 중 하나가 나온다.

➡ _____

8 그것들은 효(孝), 제(悌), 충(忠), 신(信), 예(禮), 의(義), 염(廉), 치(恥)이고, 그것들은 조선 시대 사람들에게 중요했던 가치들을 나타낸다.

➡ _____

_____

9 문자도에 있는 동물이나 사물은 단순한 장식이 아니다.

➡ _____

10 그것들은 종종 상징적이다.

➡ _____

11 예를 들어, '효' 그림 속에 있는 잉어는 옛이야기 때문에 부모님에 대한 존경심을 상징한다.

➡ _____

12 그 이야기는 다음과 같다.

➡ _____

13 옛날 옛적에 한 남자가 나이 드신 어머니와 살았다.

➡ _____

14 어느 겨울, 남자의 어머니는 병이 들어서 어떤 것도 먹을 수 없었다.

➡ _____

15 무척 추운 어느 날, 어머니는 남자에게 말했다. "신선한 물고기를 먹을 수 있다면 좋겠구나."

➡ _____

16 그 남자는 강으로 나갔지만, 강은 완전히 얼어붙어 있었다.

➡ _____

17 그가 그 어떤 물고기라도 잡는 것은 불가능했다.

➡ _____

18 남자는 몹시 낙담해서 하늘에 대고 외쳤다. "제가 어떻게 해야 하나요? 제발 저를 도와주세요."

➡ _____

19 그러자 얼음이 녹았고, 잉어 세 마리가 갑자기 물 밖으로 나왔다.

➡ _____

20 남자는 집으로 돌아가서 어머니를 위해 물고기들을 요리했다.

➡ _____

21 그러자 그의 어머니는 회복되었다.

➡ _____

22 문자도에 있는 상징적인 사물의 또 다른 예가 있다.

➡ _____

23 그것들은 글자 '충(忠)' 그림에 있는 대나무와 '의(義)' 그림에 있는 연꽃이다.

➡ _____

24 대나무는 구부러지지 않는다.

➡ _____

25 그것은 어떤 날씨에서도 푸르름을 유지한다.

➡ _____

26 이런 이유로 대나무는 왕에 대한 충성을 상징하게 되었다.

➡ _____

27 연꽃의 경우, 그것들은 진흙투성이의 연못에서 자라지만 여전히 아름답게 꽃을 피운다.

➡ _____

28 그래서 그 꽃들은 어려움에도 불구하고 정의를 위해 싸우는 사람의 의지를 상징하게 되었다.

➡ _____

29 문자도는 조선 시대 사람들에게 그림 그 이상이었다.

➡ _____

30 그것은 그들에게 자신들의 행동과 태도에 큰 영향을 미치는 중요한 가치를 상기시켰다.

➡ _____

31 특히 아이들에게 문자도는 학습 도구였다.

➡ _____

32 그것을 통해 조선 시대의 아이들은 가족과 사회에서의 조화의 중요성을 배울 수 있었다.

➡ _____

※ 다음 우리말과 일치하도록 빈칸에 알맞은 말을 쓰시오.

After You Read B Read and Complete

1. Paintings of *Hyo*(孝): Carp _____ _____ _____ _____.

2. In an old story, a man caught _____ _____ _____ _____ _____ and cooked them _____ _____ _____.

3. Paintings of *Chung*(忠): Bamboo _____ _____ the king.

4. It does not _____ and _____ _____ in _____ _____ weather.

5. Paintings of *Ui*(義): Lotus flowers symbolize a _____ _____ _____ _____ justice _____ _____.

6. They grow _____ _____ _____ but still _____ _____.

1. '효' 그림: 잉어는 부모님에 대한 존경심을 상징한다.
2. 옛이야기에서 한 남자가 얼어붙은 강에서 잉어 세 마리를 잡아 자신의 아픈 어머니를 위해 그것들을 요리했다.
3. '충' 그림: 대나무는 왕에 대한 충성을 상징한다.
4. 그것은 구부러지지 않고 어떤 날씨에서도 푸르름을 유지한다.
5. '의' 그림: 연꽃은 어려움에도 불구하고 정의를 위해 싸우는 인간의 의지를 상징한다.
6. 그 꽃들은 진흙투성이의 연못에서 자라지만 여전히 아름답게 꽃을 피운다.

Around the World

1. This painting _____ _____ _____ _____ _____ in Europe in the 16th century.

2. This painting shows a ssireum competition _____ _____ _____ _____ _____.

3. This painting _____ _____ _____ _____ an American farmer's daughter _____ _____ _____ _____.

1. 이 그림은 16세기 유럽 교외 지역의 수확기를 보여 준다.
2. 이 그림은 조선 시대 후기의 씨름 대회를 보여 준다.
3. 이 그림은 19세기 미국 농부의 딸의 결혼식을 보여 준다.

Think and Write

1. My _____ Painting, *Water Lillies: The Clouds*

2. _____ _____ _____ is *Water Lilies: The Clouds*.

3. It _____ _____ _____ Claude Monet.

4. In the painting, I can see _____ _____ _____ _____ in the pond _____ _____ _____ water lilies.

5. I like this painting _____ the colors are beautiful and the _____ _____ _____.

6. I think _____ was very _____ _____ _____ _____ _____ the pond as a mirror _____ _____ the clouds in the sky _____ _____ in the pond.

1. 내가 가장 좋아하는 그림, '수련: 구름'
2. 내가 가장 좋아하는 그림은 '수련: 구름'이다.
3. 그것은 Claude Monet에 의해 그려졌다.
4. 그림 속에서, 나는 수련뿐만 아니라 연못에 비친 구름도 볼 수 있다.
5. 나는 색깔도 아름답고, 장면이 평화롭게 보여서 이 그림을 좋아한다.
6. 나는 화가가 연못을 거울로 해서 하늘의 구름이 연못에 비치도록 한 것이 매우 창의적이라고 생각한다.

구석구석 지문 Test

※ 다음 우리말을 영어로 쓰시오.

After You Read B Read and Complete

1. '효' 그림: 잉어는 부모님에 대한 존경심을 상징한다.

   ➡ _____

2. 옛이야기에서 한 남자가 얼어붙은 강에서 잉어 세 마리를 잡아 자신의 아픈 어머니를 위해 그것들을 요리했다.

   ➡ _____

3. '충' 그림: 대나무는 왕에 대한 충성을 상징한다.

   ➡ _____

4. 그것은 구부러지지 않고 어떤 날씨에서도 푸르름을 유지한다.

   ➡ _____

5. '의' 그림: 연꽃은 어려움에도 불구하고 정의를 위해 싸우는 인간의 의지를 상징한다.

   ➡ _____

6. 그 꽃들은 진흙투성이의 연못에서 자라지만 여전히 아름답게 꽃을 피운다.

   ➡ _____

Around the World

1. 이 그림은 16세기 유럽 교외 지역의 수확기를 보여 준다.

   ➡ _____

2. 이 그림은 조선 시대 후기의 씨름 대회를 보여 준다.

   ➡ _____

3. 이 그림은 19세기 미국 농부의 딸의 결혼식을 보여 준다.

   ➡ _____

Think and Write

1. 내가 가장 좋아하는 그림, '수련: 구름'

   ➡ _____

2. 내가 가장 좋아하는 그림은 '수련: 구름'이다.

   ➡ _____

3. 그것은 Claude Monet에 의해 그려졌다.

   ➡ _____

4. 그림 속에서, 나는 수련뿐만 아니라 연못에 비친 구름도 볼 수 있다.

   ➡ _____

5. 나는 색깔도 아름답고, 장면이 평화롭게 보여서 이 그림을 좋아한다.

   ➡ _____

6. 나는 화가가 연못을 거울로 해서 하늘의 구름이 연못에 비치도록 한 것이 매우 창의적이라고 생각한다.

   ➡ _____

   _____

※ 다음 영어를 우리말로 쓰시오.

01 still _____

02 accident _____

03 pick _____

04 confidently _____

05 fair _____

06 compliment _____

07 list _____

08 hesitate _____

09 stuck _____

10 worried _____

11 creative _____

12 work _____

13 cheerful _____

14 point _____

15 scratch _____

16 messy _____

17 hurt _____

18 pause _____

19 scream _____

20 air _____

21 calm _____

22 shyly _____

23 bicycle stand _____

24 except for _____

25 all day long _____

26 Just a minute. _____

27 pull out _____

28 the other day _____

29 a piece of _____

30 come out of _____

31 What made you ~? _____

※ 다음 영어를 우리말로 쓰시오.

※ 다음 우리말을 영어로 쓰시오.

01 효과가 있다

02 가만히 있는, 고요한

03 사고

04 칭찬, 찬사; 칭찬하다

05 공평한, 공정한

06 망설이다, 주저하다

07 수줍게, 부끄러워하며

08 난처한, 걱정[근심]스러운

09 자신 있게

10 목록, 명단

11 ~을 다치게 하다, 아프다

12 지저분한, 엉망인

13 창의적인, 창조적인

14 (일시적인) 중단

15 (~에 빠져) 움직일 수 없는

16 발랄한, 쾌활한

17 가리키다

18 긁다

19 공중, 허공

20 뽑다, 따다, 뜯다

21 침착한, 차분한

22 비명을 지르다

23 자전거 거치대

24 일전에, 최근에

25 빠져나가다[나오다]

26 ~을 제외하고

27 하루 종일

28 잠깐만.

29 하나의 ~, 한 조각의 ~

30 ~에서 나오다

31 무엇 때문에 ~했니?

※ 다음 영영풀이에 알맞은 단어를 <보기>에서 골라 쓴 후, 우리말 뜻을 쓰시오.

1 _____ : dirty and/or not neat: _____

2 _____ : not excited, nervous, or upset: _____

3 _____ : the space or sky that is filled with air: _____

4 _____ : to make a very loud, high-pitched cry: _____

5 _____ : feeling or showing happiness: _____

6 _____ : to be successful, effective, or satisfactory: _____

7 _____ : to rub your fingernails against your skin because it is itching: _____

8 _____ : involving the use of imagination to produce new ideas or things:
_____

9 _____ : an unfortunate mishap; especially one causing damage or injury:
_____

10 _____ : to pause or hold back in uncertainty or unwillingness: _____

11 _____ : a short period when you stop doing something before continuing:
_____

12 _____ : treating people in a way that does not favor some over others: _____

13 _____ : to hold out your finger towards a person or thing in order to make someone
notice them: _____

14 _____ : a set of names or addresses which all belong to a particular category,
written down one below the other: _____

15 _____ : in a way that shows that you feel sure about your own ability to do
things and be successful: _____

16 _____ : a polite remark that you say to someone to show that you like their
appearance, appreciate their qualities, or approve of what they have
done: _____

보기			
pause	work	hesitate	list
compliment	calm	air	messy
fair	cheerful	point	creative
accident	scream	scratch	confidently

※ 다음 우리말과 일치하도록 빈칸에 알맞은 것을 골라 쓰시오.

1 The _____ _____ _____
    A. Best   B. Ever   C. Compliment

2 Scene 1

3 *It is _____ _____ _____ of school.*
    A. week   B. last   C. the

4 _____ *student has just* _____ *a* _____ *of paper* _____
a name on it.
    A. piece   B. each   C. with   D. picked

5 Ms. Kemp: "_____ _____ Classmates" will be our _____
_____ of the school year.
    A. activity   B. Compliments   C. last   D. for

6 Did _____ _____ a _____?
    A. pick   B. name   C. everyone

7 Class: _____, _____ Kemp.
    A. Ms.   B. yes

8 *Students are* _____ *to* _____ _____.
    A. other   B. talking   C. each

9 Beth: So, _____ _____ did you _____?
    A. pick   B. whose   C. name

10 Lucy: (_____) I _____ Boyd.
    A. got   B. smiling

11 I have a _____ _____ _____ about him.
    A. say   B. lot   C. to

12 _____ _____ you, Beth?
    A. about   B. what

13 Beth: (_____ _____) Uh, I _____ Peter's name.
    A. worried   B. picked   C. looking

14 Lucy: Peter? Oh, no! It won't be _____ to find _____ to
_____ him _____.
    A. compliment   B. on   C. easy   D. something

15 Steve: Yeah. He doesn't talk much and just _____ _____ his
desk _____ day _____.
    A. long   B. sits   C. all   D. at

16 Beth: (_____ *her head*) Well, I'll _____ _____ _____
something.
    A. to   B. scratching   C. have   D. find

17 Scene 2

---

1 최고의 칭찬

2 〈장면 1〉

3 이번 주는 학교의 마지막 주이다.

4 각 학생들은 이름 하나가 쓰인 종이 한 장씩을 막 뽑았다.

5 Ms. Kemp: '학급 친구들 칭찬하기'는 이번 학년 우리의 마지막 활동이 될 거예요.

6 모두 이름을 뽑았나요?

7 Class: 네, Kemp 선생님.

8 학생들이 서로 이야기를 나누고 있다.

9 Beth: 너는 누구 이름을 뽑았니?

10 Lucy: (웃으며) Boyd를 뽑았어.

11 그 애에 관해 할 말이 많아.

12 너는 어때, Beth?

13 Beth: (걱정스러운 표정으로) 어, Peter 이름을 뽑았어.

14 Lucy: Peter? 아, 이런! 그 애에 관해서 칭찬할 것을 찾는 게 쉽지 않을 거야.

15 Steve: 그래. 그 애는 말을 많이 하지 않고 하루 종일 그냥 책상에 앉아만 있잖아.

16 Beth: (머리를 긁적이며) 음, 무언가를 찾아야 해.

17 〈장면 2〉

18 *Beth is _____ home _____ _____ her parents about the _____.*

A. activity   B. with   C. at   D. talking

19 Beth: Everyone has long _____ of _____ for classmates, _____ for me.

A. except   B. lists   C. other   D. compliments

20 I don't know _____ _____ _____ Peter _____.

A. to   B. on   C. compliment   D. what

21 Mom: _____ _____.

A. carefully   B. think

22 _____ _____ be _____.

A. something   B. there   C. should

23 Beth: Well, _____ _____.

A. clean   B. he's

24 He _____ his _____ _____ day.

A. face   B. washes   C. every

25 Mom: That's _____ _____ _____.

A. not   B. compliment   C. a

26 Everybody _____ _____.

A. that   B. does

27 Dad: _____ _____.

A. again   B. try

28 I'm _____ you can find _____ _____ to _____ about him.

A. say   B. good   C. sure   D. something

29 Scene 3

30 *The _____ day, _____ is _____ _____ at school.*

A. accident   B. next   C. there   D. an

31 *Boyd's _____ _____ _____ in a bicycle _____.*

A. stand   B. stuck   C. is   D. foot

32 Boyd: (_____ _____ in the _____) Help! I need _____!

A. air   B. with   C. help   D. arms

33 Beth: _____ _____. I'm trying to _____ your foot _____.

A. pull   B. stay   C. out   D. still

34 Boyd: (_____) Ouch! That _____!

A. hurts   B. screaming

35 Peter: _____ me _____. Just a _____.

A. help   B. let   C. minute

---

18 Beth는 집에서 그 활동에 대해 자신의 부모님과 이야기를 나누고 있다.

19 Beth: 저를 제외한 모두가 다른 친구들에 대해 긴 칭찬 목록을 가지고 있어요.

20 저는 Peter에 관해 무엇을 칭찬해야 할지 모르겠어요.

21 엄마: 잘 생각해 봐.

22 뭔가 있을 거야.

23 Beth: 음. 그 애는 깔끔해요.

24 매일 세수를 해요.

25 엄마: 그건 칭찬이 아니야.

26 모든 사람들이 하는 거잖니.

27 아빠: 다시 생각해 보렴.

28 그 아이에 대해 말할 뭔가 좋은 것을 분명히 찾을 수 있을 거야.

29 〈장면 3〉

30 다음 날. 학교에서 사고가 생긴다.

31 Boyd의 발이 자전거 거치대에 끼었다.

32 Boyd: (공중에 양팔을 벌린 채) 도와줘! 도움이 필요해!

33 Beth: 가만히 있어. 네 발을 꺼내려고 노력 중이야.

34 Boyd: (비명을 지르며) 아! 아파!

35 Peter: 내가 도와줄게. 잠깐만.

36 *Peter _____ to the school's kitchen and _____ _____ _____ butter.*

    A. back   B. runs   C. comes   D. with

37 Peter: I'm _____ to _____ this butter _____ your _____ .

    A. on   B. put   C. foot   D. going

38 Boyd: _____ ? _____ ?

    A. butter   B. what

39 Peter: Just _____ _____ .

    A. calm   B. stay

40 Beth: (_____ *to Boyd's* _____) Wow! It's _____ !

    A. working   B. pointing   C. foot

41 Boyd's foot is _____ _____ _____ the _____ .

    A. of   B. stand   C. out   D. coming

42 Scene 4

43 *Beth is _____ _____ _____ her parents.*

    A. with   B. dinner   C. eating

44 *She tells them _____ _____ _____ to Boyd.*

    A. happened   B. what   C. about

45 Beth: _____ was a _____ _____ at school today.

    A. little   B. there   C. accident

46 Boyd's foot _____ _____ _____ a bicycle stand.

    A. stuck   B. in   C. got

47 Mom: Oh, no! _____ how did he _____ his foot _____ ?

    A. get   B. so   C. out

48 Beth: Peter _____ butter _____ his foot and then _____ it _____ .

    A. on   B. pulled   C. put   D. out

49 Dad: That was really _____ . _____ _____ creative.

    A. creative   B. messy   C. but

50 Beth: Hmm. _____ ? Can that _____ a _____ , Dad?

    A. compliment   B. creative   C. be

51 Dad: _____ .

---

36 Peter가 학교 주방으로 뛰어가 버터를 가지고 온다.

37 Peter: 네 발에 이 버터를 바를 거야.

38 Boyd: 뭐? 버터를?

39 Peter: 그냥 침착하게 있어.

40 Beth: (Boyd의 발을 가리키며) 와! 효과가 있어!

41 Boyd의 발이 거치대에서 빠져 나오고 있어.

42 〈장면 4〉

43 Beth는 부모님과 저녁 식사를 하고 있다.

44 그녀는 부모님께 Boyd에게 일 어난 일에 대해 이야기한다.

45 Beth: 오늘 학교에서 작은 사고 가 있었어요.

46 Boyd의 발이 자전거 거치대에 끼었어요.

47 엄마: 오, 저런! 그래서 발을 어 떻게 뺐니?

48 Beth: Peter가 그 애 발에 버터 를 바르고 나서 발을 당겨서 꺼 냈어요.

49 아빠: 정말 창의적이구나. 지저 분하지만 창의적이야.

50 Beth: 흠. 창의적이라고요? 아빠, 그것이 칭찬이 될 수 있어요?

51 아빠: 물론이지.

52 Scene 5

53 *It is the _____ day of school, and the students are _____ _____ _____.*

    A. complimenting   B. last   C. other   D. each

54 Ms. Kemp: Joanne, _____ _____ do you have _____ Beth?

    A. what   B. for   C. compliment

55 Joanne: Beth, you're _____ _____.

    A. cheerful   B. always

56 You're also _____ and _____ to _____.

    A. fair   B. kind   C. everybody

57 Beth: Thanks, Joanne. It's _____ nice _____ _____ _____ say so.

    A. you   B. to   C. of   D. so

58 Ms. Kemp: Beth, _____ _____ _____ you now.

    A. from   B. let's   C. hear

59 You _____ Peter's _____.

    A. name   B. picked

60 Beth: (_____) Well, I _____ Peter is _____. Peter, you're … uh … creative.

    A. creative   B. hesitating   C. think

61 Peter: (_____) _____?

    A. really   B. shyly

62 Ms. Kemp: _____ _____ _____ _____ Peter is creative?

    A. think   B. what   C. you   D. made

63 Beth: (*after a long _____*) When Boyd's foot got _____ in the bicycle stand the _____ day, Peter got it out by _____ butter.

    A. using   B. other   C. pause   D. stuck

64 _____ was _____.

    A. creative   B. that

65 Boyd: Yeah! _____ _____ _____ of _____ that.

    A. doing   B. else   C. thought   D. nobody

66 Steve: I didn't know that. Well, _____, I _____ think he's _____.

    A. also   B. creative   C. then

67 Beth: (_____) Yeah, Peter, you ARE _____!

    A. creative   B. confidently

68 Peter: Thanks, Beth! It's _____ _____ _____ _____!

    A. best   B. ever   C. the   D. compliment

52 〈장면 5〉

53 오늘은 학교의 마지막 날이고 학생들은 서로를 칭찬하고 있다.

54 Ms. Kemp: Joanne, Beth에게 무슨 칭찬을 해 주겠니?

55 Joanne: Beth, 너는 항상 쾌활해.

56 또한 친절하고 모두에게 공정해.

57 Beth: 고마워, Joanne. 그렇게 말해 주다니 친절하구나.

58 Ms. Kemp: Beth, 이제 네 말을 들어 보자.

59 Peter의 이름을 뽑았구나.

60 Beth: (주저하며) 음, Peter는 창의적이라고 생각해요. Peter, 너는… 어… 창의적이야.

61 Peter: (수줍어하며) 정말?

62 Ms. Kemp: Peter가 왜 창의적이라고 생각하니?

63 Beth: (한참 있다가) 일전에 Boyd의 발이 자전거 거치대에 끼었을 때, Peter는 버터를 사용해서 그의 발을 꺼냈어요.

64 그것은 창의적이었어요.

65 Boyd: 맞아! 어느 누구도 그렇게 하는 것을 생각하지 못했어.

66 Steve: 난 몰랐어. 음, 그래, 나도 그가 창의적이라고 생각해.

67 Beth: (자신 있게) 그래, Peter, 너는 창의적이야!

68 Peter: 고마워, Beth! 그건 최고의 칭찬이야!

※ 다음 우리말과 일치하도록 빈칸에 알맞은 것을 골라 쓰시오.

1 The ＿＿＿＿＿ ＿＿＿＿＿ Ever

2 Scene 1

3 *It is the ＿＿＿＿ ＿＿＿＿ of school.*

4 ＿＿＿＿ *student has just picked* ＿＿＿ ＿＿＿ ＿＿＿ ＿＿＿ ＿＿＿ *a name on it.*

5 Ms. Kemp: "＿＿＿ ＿＿＿ Classmates" will be our ＿＿＿ ＿＿＿ of the school year.

6 Did everyone ＿＿＿＿ a name?

7 Class: Yes, Ms. Kemp.

8 *Students are ＿＿＿＿ to ＿＿＿ ＿＿＿.*

9 Beth: So, ＿＿＿ ＿＿＿ did you ＿＿＿?

10 Lucy: (＿＿＿) I ＿＿＿ Boyd.

11 I have ＿＿＿ ＿＿＿ ＿＿＿ ＿＿＿ about him.

12 ＿＿＿ ＿＿＿ you, Beth?

13 Beth: (＿＿＿ ＿＿＿) Uh, I ＿＿＿ Peter's name.

14 Lucy: Peter? Oh, no! It won't be easy ＿＿＿ ＿＿＿ something to ＿＿＿ ＿＿＿ ＿＿＿.

15 Steve: Yeah. He doesn't talk much and just ＿＿＿ ＿＿＿ ＿＿＿ ＿＿＿ ＿＿＿ ＿＿＿ ＿＿＿.

16 Beth: (*scratching her head*) Well, I'll ＿＿＿ ＿＿＿ something.

17 Scene 2

18 *Beth is at home ＿＿＿ ＿＿＿ her parents about the activity.*

19 Beth: Everyone has long lists of ＿＿＿ for ＿＿＿ classmates, ＿＿＿ ＿＿＿ me.

20 I don't know ＿＿＿ ＿＿＿ ＿＿＿ Peter ＿＿＿.

21 Mom: Think ＿＿＿.

1 최고의 칭찬

2 〈장면 1〉

3 이번 주는 학교의 마지막 주이다.

4 각 학생들은 이름 하나가 쓰인 종이 한 장씩을 막 뽑았다.

5 Ms. Kemp: '학급 친구들 칭찬하기'는 이번 학년 우리의 마지막 활동이 될 거예요.

6 모두 이름을 뽑았나요?

7 Class: 네, Kemp 선생님.

8 학생들이 서로 이야기를 나누고 있다.

9 Beth: 너는 누구 이름을 뽑았니?

10 Lucy: (웃으며) Boyd를 뽑았어.

11 그 애에 관해 할 말이 많아.

12 너는 어때, Beth?

13 Beth: (걱정스러운 표정으로) 어, Peter 이름을 뽑았어.

14 Lucy: Peter? 아, 이런! 그 애에 관해서 칭찬할 것을 찾는 게 쉽지 않을 거야.

15 Steve: 그래. 그 애는 말을 많이 하지 않고 하루 종일 그냥 책상에 앉아만 있잖아.

16 Beth: (머리를 긁적이며) 음, 무언가를 찾아야 해.

17 〈장면 2〉

18 Beth는 집에서 그 활동에 대해 자신의 부모님과 이야기를 나누고 있다.

19 Beth: 저를 제외한 모두가 다른 친구들에 대해 긴 칭찬 목록을 가지고 있어요.

20 저는 Peter에 관해 무엇을 칭찬해야 할지 모르겠어요.

21 엄마: 잘 생각해 봐.

22 There _____ _____ something.

23 Beth: Well, _____ _____ .

24 He _____ his face _____ _____ .

25 Mom: That's not _____ _____ .

26 Everybody _____ _____ .

27 Dad: _____ _____ .

28 _____ _____ you can find _____ _____ to say about him.

29 Scene 3

30 *The next day, there is _____ _____ at school.*

31 *Boyd's foot _____ _____ in a bicycle _____ .*

32 Boyd: (_____ _____ _____ _____ _____ _____) Help! I need help!

33 Beth: _____ _____ . I'm trying to _____ your foot _____ .

34 Boyd: (_____) Ouch! That _____ !

35 Peter: _____ me help. Just a _____ .

36 *Peter runs to the school's kitchen and _____ _____ with butter.*

37 Peter: I'm going to _____ this butter _____ your _____ .

38 Boyd: _____ ? Butter?

39 Peter: Just stay _____ .

40 Beth: (_____ _____ *Boyd's foot*) Wow! It's _____ !

41 Boyd's foot is _____ _____ _____ the stand.

42 Scene 4

43 *Beth is _____ _____ _____ her parents.*

44 *She tells them about _____ _____ to Boyd.*

45 Beth: There was _____ _____ _____ at school today.

46 Boyd's foot _____ _____ _____ a bicycle stand.

47 Mom: Oh, no! So how did he _____ his foot _____ ?

---

22 뭔가 있을 거야.

23 Beth: 음, 그 애는 깔끔해요.

24 매일 세수를 해요.

25 엄마: 그건 칭찬이 아니야.

26 모든 사람들이 하는 거잖니.

27 아빠: 다시 생각해 보렴.

28 그 아이에 대해 말할 뭔가 좋은 것을 분명히 찾을 수 있을 거야.

29 〈장면 3〉

30 다음 날, 학교에서 사고가 생긴다.

31 Boyd의 발이 자전거 거치대에 끼었다.

32 Boyd: (공중에 양팔을 벌린 채) 도와줘! 도움이 필요해!

33 Beth: 가만히 있어. 네 발을 꺼내려고 노력 중이야.

34 Boyd: (비명을 지르며) 아! 아파!

35 Peter: 내가 도와줄게. 잠깐만.

36 Peter가 학교 주방으로 뛰어가 버터를 가지고 온다.

37 Peter: 네 발에 이 버터를 바를 거야.

38 Boyd: 뭐? 버터를?

39 Peter: 그냥 침착하게 있어.

40 Beth: (Boyd의 발을 가리키며) 와! 효과가 있어!

41 Boyd의 발이 거치대에서 빠져 나오고 있어.

42 〈장면 4〉

43 Beth는 부모님과 저녁 식사를 하고 있다.

44 그녀는 부모님께 Boyd에게 일어난 일에 대해 이야기한다.

45 Beth: 오늘 학교에서 작은 사고가 있었어요.

46 Boyd의 발이 자전거 거치대에 끼었어요.

47 엄마: 오, 저런! 그래서 발을 어떻게 뺐니?

48 Beth: Peter _____ butter _____ his foot and then _____ _____ _____.

49 Dad: That was really creative. _____ but _____.

50 Beth: Hmm. Creative? Can that be _____ _____, Dad?

51 Dad: _____.

52 Scene 5

53 *It is _____ _____ _____ of school, and the students are _____ _____ _____.*

54 Ms. Kemp: Joanne, _____ _____ do you have for Beth?

55 Joanne: Beth, you're always _____.

56 You're _____ kind and _____ to everybody.

57 Beth: Thanks, Joanne. It's so nice _____ _____ to say so.

58 Ms. Kemp: Beth, let's _____ _____ _____ now.

59 You _____ Peter's name.

60 Beth: (_____) Well, I think Peter is _____. Peter, you're … uh … creative.

61 Peter: (_____) Really?

62 Ms. Kemp: _____ _____ _____ _____ Peter is creative?

63 Beth: (*after a long* _____) When Boyd's foot _____ _____ in the bicycle stand _____ _____ _____, Peter _____ it _____ _____ _____ butter.

64 That was _____.

65 Boyd: Yeah! _____ _____ _____ _____ doing that.

66 Steve: I didn't know that. Well, then, I _____ think he's creative.

67 Beth: (_____) Yeah, Peter, you ARE _____!

68 Peter: Thanks, Beth! It's _____ _____ _____ _____ _____!

---

48 Beth: Peter가 그 애 발에 버터를 바르고 나서 발을 당겨서 꺼냈어요.

49 아빠: 정말 창의적이구나. 지저분하지만 창의적이야.

50 Beth: 흠. 창의적이라고요? 아빠, 그것이 칭찬이 될 수 있어요?

51 아빠: 물론이지.

52 〈장면 5〉

53 오늘은 학교의 마지막 날이고 학생들은 서로를 칭찬하고 있다.

54 Ms. Kemp: Joanne, Beth에게 무슨 칭찬을 해 주겠니?

55 Joanne: Beth, 너는 항상 쾌활해.

56 또한 친절하고 모두에게 공정해.

57 Beth: 고마워, Joanne. 그렇게 말해 주다니 친절하구나.

58 Ms. Kemp: Beth, 이제 네 말을 들어 보자.

59 Peter의 이름을 뽑았구나.

60 Beth: (주저하며) 음, Peter는 창의적이라고 생각해요. Peter, 너는… 어… 창의적이야.

61 Peter: (수줍어하며) 정말?

62 Ms. Kemp: Peter가 왜 창의적이라고 생각하니?

63 Beth: (한참 있다가) 일전에 Boyd의 발이 자전거 거치대에 끼었을 때, Peter는 버터를 사용해서 그의 발을 꺼냈어요.

64 그것은 창의적이었어요.

65 Boyd: 맞아! 어느 누구도 그렇게 하는 것을 생각하지 못했어.

66 Steve: 난 몰랐어. 음, 그래, 나도 그가 창의적이라고 생각해.

67 Beth: (자신 있게) 그래, Peter, 너는 창의적이야!

68 Peter: 고마워, Beth! 그건 최고의 칭찬이야!

본문 Test **97**

※ 다음 문장을 우리말로 쓰시오.

1 The Best Compliment Ever
➡ _____

2 Scene 1
➡ _____

3 It is the last week of school.
➡ _____

4 Each student has just picked a piece of paper with a name on it.
➡ _____

5 Ms. Kemp: "Compliments for Classmates" will be our last activity of the school year.
➡ _____

6 Did everyone pick a name?
➡ _____

7 Class: Yes, Ms. Kemp.
➡ _____

8 Students are talking to each other.
➡ _____

9 Beth: So, whose name did you pick?
➡ _____

10 Lucy: (smiling) I got Boyd.
➡ _____

11 I have a lot to say about him.
➡ _____

12 What about you, Beth?
➡ _____

13 Beth: (looking worried) Uh, I picked Peter's name.
➡ _____

14 Lucy: Peter? Oh, no! It won't be easy to find something to compliment him on.
➡ _____

15 Steve: Yeah. He doesn't talk much and just sits at his desk all day long.
➡ _____

16 Beth: (scratching her head) Well, I'll have to find something.
➡ _____

17 Scene 2
➡ _____

18 Beth is at home talking with her parents about the activity.
➡ _____

19 Beth: Everyone has long lists of compliments for other classmates, except for me.
➡ _____

20 I don't know what to compliment Peter on.
➡ _____

21 Mom: Think carefully.
➡ _____

22 There should be something.
➡ _____

23 Beth: Well, he's clean.
➡ _____

24 He washes his face every day.
➡ _____

25 Mom: That's not a compliment.
➡ _____

26 Everybody does that.
➡ _____

27 Dad: Try again.
➡ _____

28 I'm sure you can find something good to say about him.
➡ _____

29 Scene 3
➡ _____

30 The next day, there is an accident at school.
➡ _____

31 Boyd's foot is stuck in a bicycle stand.
➡ _____

32 Boyd: (with arms in the air) Help! I need help!
➡ _____

33 Beth: Stay still. I'm trying to pull your foot out.
➡ _____

34 Boyd: (screaming) Ouch! That hurts!
➡ _____

35 Peter: Let me help. Just a minute.
➡ _____

36 Peter runs to the school's kitchen and comes back with butter.
➡ _____

37 Peter: I'm going to put this butter on your foot.
➡ _____

38 Boyd: What? Butter?
➡ _____

39 Peter: Just stay calm.
➡ _____

40 Beth: (pointing to Boyd's foot) Wow! It's working!
➡ _____

41 Boyd's foot is coming out of the stand.
➡ _____

42 Scene 4
➡ _____

43 Beth is eating dinner with her parents.
➡ _____

44 She tells them about what happened to Boyd.
➡ _____

45 Beth: There was a little accident at school today.
➡ _____

46 Boyd's foot got stuck in a bicycle stand.
➡ _____

47 Mom: Oh, no! So how did he get his foot out?
➡ _____

48 Beth: Peter put butter on his foot and then pulled it out.
➡ _____

49 Dad: That was really creative. Messy but creative.
➡ _____

50 Beth: Hmm. Creative? Can that be a compliment, Dad?
➡ _____

51 Dad: Sure.
➡ _____

52 Scene 5
➡ _____

53 It is the last day of school, and the students are complimenting each other.
➡ _____

54 Ms. Kemp: Joanne, what compliment do you have for Beth?
➡ _____

55 Joanne: Beth, you're always cheerful.
➡ _____

56 You're also kind and fair to everybody.
➡ _____

57 Beth: Thanks, Joanne. It's so nice of you to say so.
➡ _____

58 Ms. Kemp: Beth, let's hear from you now.
➡ _____

59 You picked Peter's name.
➡ _____

60 Beth: (hesitating) Well, I think Peter is creative. Peter, you're … uh … creative.
➡ _____

61 Peter: (shyly) Really?
➡ _____

62 Ms. Kemp: What made you think Peter is creative?
➡ _____

63 Beth: (after a long pause) When Boyd's foot got stuck in the bicycle stand the other day, Peter got it out by using butter.
➡ _____

64 That was creative.
➡ _____

65 Boyd: Yeah! Nobody else thought of doing that.
➡ _____

66 Steve: I didn't know that. Well, then, I also think he's creative.
➡ _____

67 Beth: (confidently) Yeah, Peter, you ARE creative!
➡ _____

68 Peter: Thanks, Beth! It's the best compliment ever!
➡ _____

Step4

※ 다음 괄호 안의 단어들을 우리말에 맞도록 바르게 배열하시오.

1 (Best / The / Ever / Compliment)
➡ _____

2 (1 / Scene)
➡ _____

3 (is / it / last / the / of / week / school.)
➡ _____

4 (student / each / just / has / picked / piece / a / paper / of / with / name / a / it. / on)
➡ _____

5 (Ms. Kemp: / for / "Compliments / Classmates" / be / will / last / our / of / activity / school / year. / the)
➡ _____
_____

6 (everyone / did / a / pick / name?)
➡ _____

7 (Class: / Ms. / Yes, / Kemp.)
➡ _____

8 (are / students / to / talking / other. / each)
➡ _____

9 (Beth: / whose / so, / did / name / pick? / you)
➡ _____

10 (Lucy: / (smiling) / got / Boyd. / I)
➡ _____

11 (have / I / lot / a / about / say / to / him.)
➡ _____

12 (about / what / Beth? / you,)
➡ _____

13 (Beth: / worried) / (looking / I / uh, / Peter's / picked / name.)
➡ _____

14 (Lucy: / Peter? // no! / oh, // won't / it / easy / be / find / to / to / something / complement / on. / him)
➡ _____

15 (Steve: / Yeah. // doesn't / he / much / talk / and / sits / just / at / desk / his / all / long. / day)
➡ _____

16 (Beth: / her / (scratching / head) / I'll / well, / to / have / something. / find)
➡ _____

17 (2 / Scene)
➡ _____

1 최고의 칭찬

2 〈장면 1〉

3 이번 주는 학교의 마지막 주이다.

4 각 학생들은 이름 하나가 쓰인 종이 한 장씩을 막 뽑았다.

5 Ms. Kemp: '학급 친구들 칭찬하기'는 이번 학년 우리의 마지막 활동이 될 거예요.

6 모두 이름을 뽑았나요?

7 Class: 네, Kemp 선생님.

8 학생들이 서로 이야기를 나누고 있다.

9 Beth: 너는 누구 이름을 뽑았니?

10 Lucy: (웃으며) Boyd를 뽑았어.

11 그 애에 관해 할 말이 많아.

12 너는 어때, Beth?

13 Beth: (걱정스러운 표정으로) 어, Peter 이름을 뽑았어.

14 Lucy: Peter? 아, 이런! 그 애에 관해서 칭찬할 것을 찾는 게 쉽지 않을 거야.

15 Steve: 그래. 그 애는 말을 많이 하지 않고 하루 종일 그냥 책상에 앉아만 있잖아.

16 Beth: (머리를 긁적이며) 음, 무언가를 찾아야 해.

17 〈장면 2〉

18 ► (is / Beth / home / at / with / talking / parents / her / the / about / activity.)

➥ _____

19 ► (Beth: / has / everyone / lists / of / long / compliments / other / for / classmates, / for / except / me.)

➥ _____

20 ► (don't / I / what / know / complement / to / on. / Peter)

➥ _____

21 ► (Mom: / carefully. / think)

➥ _____

22 ► (should / there / something. / be)

➥ _____

23 ► (Beth: / he's / well, / clean.)

➥ _____

24 ► (washes / he / face / his / day. / every)

➥ _____

25 ► (Mom: / not / that's / complement. / a)

➥ _____

26 ► (does / everybody / that.)

➥ _____

27 ► (Dad: / again. / try)

➥ _____

28 ► (sure / I'm / can / you / something / find / to / good / about / say / him.)

➥ _____

29 ► (3 / Scene)

➥ _____

30 ► (next / the / there / day, / an / is / accident / school. / at)

➥ _____

31 ► (foot / Boyd's / stuck / is / a / in / stand. / bicycle)

➥ _____

32 ► (Boyd: / arms / (with / the / in / air) / help! // help! / need / I)

➥ _____

33 ► (Beth: / still. / stay // trying / I'm / pull / to / foot / your / out.)

➥ _____

34 ► (Boyd: / Ouch! / (screaming) // hurts! / that)

➥ _____

35 ► (Peter: / me / let / help. // a / just / minute.)

➥ _____

18 Beth는 집에서 그 활동에 대해 자신의 부모님과 이야기를 나누고 있다.

19 Beth: 저를 제외한 모두가 다른 친구들에 대해 긴 칭찬 목록을 가지고 있어요.

20 저는 Peter에 관해 무엇을 칭찬해야 할지 모르겠어요.

21 엄마: 잘 생각해 봐.

22 뭔가 있을 거야.

23 Beth: 음, 그 애는 깔끔해요.

24 매일 세수를 해요.

25 엄마: 그건 칭찬이 아니야.

26 모든 사람들이 하는 거잖니.

27 아빠: 다시 생각해 보렴.

28 그 아이에 대해 말할 뭔가 좋은 것을 분명히 찾을 수 있을 거야.

29 〈장면 3〉

30 다음 날, 학교에서 사고가 생긴다.

31 Boyd의 발이 자전거 거치대에 끼었다.

32 Boyd: (공중에 양팔을 벌린 채) 도와줘! 도움이 필요해!

33 Beth: 가만히 있어. 네 발을 꺼내려고 노력 중이야.

34 Boyd: (비명을 지르며) 아! 아파!

35 Peter: 내가 도와줄게. 잠깐만.

36 (runs / Peter / the / to / kitchen / school's / comes / and / with / back / butter.)

➡ _____

37 (Peter: / going / I'm / put / to / butter / this / your / on / foot.)

➡ _____

38 (Boyd: / butter? // what?)

➡ _____

39 (Peter: / stay / just / calm.)

➡ _____

40 (Beth: / to / (pointing / foot) / Boyd's / wow! // working! / it's)

➡ _____

41 (foot / Boyd's / coming / is / of / out / stand. / the)

➡ _____

42 (4 / Scene)

➡ _____

43 (is / Beth / dinner / eating / her / with / parents.)

➡ _____

44 (tells / she / about / them / happened / what / Boyd. / to)

➡ _____

45 (Beth: / was / there / little / a / at / accident / today. / school)

➡ _____

46 (Boyd's / got / foot / in / stuck / a / stand. / bicycle)

➡ _____

47 (Mom: / no! / oh, // how / so / he / did / his / get / out? / foot)

➡ _____

48 (Beth: / put / Peter / on / butter / foot / his / then / and / it / pulled / out.)

➡ _____

49 (Dad: / was / that / creative. / really // but / creative. / messy)

➡ _____

50 (Beth: / Creative? // hmm. // that / can / a / be / Dad? / compliement)

➡ _____

51 (Dad: / sure.)

➡ _____

36 Peter가 학교 주방으로 뛰어가 버터를 가지고 온다.

37 Peter: 네 발에 이 버터를 바를 거야.

38 Boyd: 뭐? 버터를?

39 Peter: 그냥 침착하게 있어.

40 Beth: (Boyd의 발을 가리키며) 와! 효과가 있어!

41 Boyd의 발이 거치대에서 빠져 나오고 있어.

42 〈장면 4〉

43 Beth는 부모님과 저녁 식사를 하고 있다.

44 그녀는 부모님께 Boyd에게 일어난 일에 대해 이야기한다.

45 Beth: 오늘 학교에서 작은 사고가 있었어요.

46 Boyd의 발이 자전거 거치대에 끼었어요.

47 엄마: 오, 저런! 그래서 발을 어떻게 뺐니?

48 Beth: Peter가 그 애 발에 버터를 바르고 나서 발을 당겨서 꺼냈어요.

49 아빠: 정말 창의적이구나. 지저분하지만 창의적이야.

50 Beth: 흠. 창의적이라고요? 아빠, 그것이 칭찬이 될 수 있어요?

51 아빠: 물론이지.

52 (5 / Scene)
➡ _____

53 (is / it / last / the / of / day / school, / the / and / are / students / each / complementing / other.)
➡ _____

54 (Ms. Kemp: / what / Joanne, / do / compliment / have / you / Beth? / for)
➡ _____

55 (Joanne: / you're / Beth / cheerful. / always)
➡ _____

56 (also / you're / and / kind / to / fair / everybody.)
➡ _____

57 (Beth: / Joanne. / thanks, // so / it's / of / nice / to / you / so. / say)
➡ _____

58 (Ms. Kemp: / let's / Beth, / from / hear / now. / you)
➡ _____

59 (picked / you / name. / Peter's)
➡ _____

60 (Beth: / (hesitating) / I / well, / Peter / think / creative. / is // you're / Peter, / … / creative. / … / uh)
➡ _____

61 (Peter: / really? / (shyly))
➡ _____

62 (Ms. Kemp: / made / what / think / you / is / Peter / creative?)
➡ _____

63 (Beth: / a / (after / pause) / long / Boyd's / when / got / foot / stuck / the / in / stand / bicycle / other / the / Peter / day, / it / got / out / using / by / butter.)
➡ _____

64 (was / that / creative.)
➡ _____

65 (Boyd: / yeah! // else / nobody / of / thought / that. / doing)
➡ _____

66 (Steve: / didn't / I / that. / know // then, / well, / also / I / he's / think / creative.)
➡ _____

67 (Beth: / yeah, / (confidently) / you / Peter, / creative! / ARE)
➡ _____

68 (Peter: / Beth! / thanks, // the / it's / compliment / best / ever!)
➡ _____

52 〈장면 5〉

53 오늘은 학교의 마지막 날이고 학생들은 서로를 칭찬하고 있다.

54 Ms. Kemp: Joanne, Beth에게 무슨 칭찬을 해 주겠니?

55 Joanne: Beth, 너는 항상 쾌활해.

56 또한 친절하고 모두에게 공정해.

57 Beth: 고마워, Joanne. 그렇게 말해 주다니 친절하구나.

58 Ms. Kemp: Beth, 이제 네 말을 들어 보자.

59 Peter의 이름을 뽑았구나.

60 Beth: (주저하며) 음, Peter는 창의적이라고 생각해요. Peter, 너는… 어… 창의적이야.

61 Peter: (수줍어하며) 정말?

62 Ms. Kemp: Peter가 왜 창의적이라고 생각하니?

63 Beth: (한참 있다가) 일전에 Boyd의 발이 자전거 거치대에 끼었을 때, Peter는 버터를 사용해서 그의 발을 꺼냈어요.

64 그것은 창의적이었어요.

65 Boyd: 맞아! 어느 누구도 그렇게 하는 것을 생각하지 못했어.

66 Steve: 난 몰랐어. 음, 그래, 나도 그가 창의적이라고 생각해.

67 Beth: (자신 있게) 그래, Peter, 너는 창의적이야!

68 Peter: 고마워, Beth! 그건 최고의 칭찬이야!

※ 다음 우리말을 영어로 쓰시오.

1 최고의 칭찬
➡ _____

2 〈장면 1〉
➡ _____

3 이번 주는 학교의 마지막 주이다.
➡ _____

4 각 학생들은 이름 하나가 쓰인 종이 한 장씩을 막 뽑았다.
➡ _____

5 Ms. Kemp: '학급 친구들 칭찬하기'는 이번 학년 우리의 마지막 활동이 될 거예요.
➡ _____

6 모두 이름을 뽑았나요?
➡ _____

7 Class: 네, Kemp 선생님.
➡ _____

8 학생들이 서로 이야기를 나누고 있다.
➡ _____

9 Beth: 너는 누구 이름을 뽑았니?
➡ _____

10 Lucy: (웃으며) Boyd를 뽑았어.
➡ _____

11 그 애에 관해 할 말이 많아.
➡ _____

12 너는 어때, Beth?
➡ _____

13 Beth: (걱정스러운 표정으로) 어, Peter 이름을 뽑았어.
➡ _____

14 Lucy: Peter? 아, 이런! 그 애에 관해서 칭찬할 것을 찾는 게 쉽지 않을 거야.
➡ _____

15 Steve: 그래. 그 애는 말을 많이 하지 않고 하루 종일 그냥 책상에 앉아만 있잖아.
➡ _____

16 Beth: (머리를 긁적이며) 음, 무언가를 찾아야 해.
➡ _____

17 〈장면 2〉
➡ _____

18 Beth는 집에서 그 활동에 대해 자신의 부모님과 이야기를 나누고 있다.
➡ _____

19 Beth: 저를 제외한 모두가 다른 친구들에 대해 긴 칭찬 목록을 가지고 있어요.
➡ _____

20 저는 Peter에 관해 무엇을 칭찬해야 할지 모르겠어요.
➡ _____

21 엄마: 잘 생각해 봐.
➡ _____

22 뭔가 있을 거야.
➡ _____

23 Beth: 음, 그 애는 깔끔해요.
➡ _____

24 매일 세수를 해요.
➡ _____

25 엄마: 그건 칭찬이 아니야.
➡ _____

26 모든 사람들이 하는 거잖니.
➡ _____

27 아빠: 다시 생각해 보렴.
➡ _____

28 그 아이에 대해 말할 뭔가 좋은 것을 분명히 찾을 수 있을 거야.
➡ _____

29 〈장면 3〉
➡ _____

30 다음 날, 학교에서 사고가 생긴다.
➡ _____

31 Boyd의 발이 자전거 거치대에 끼었다.
➡ _____

32 Boyd: (공중에 양팔을 벌린 채) 도와줘! 도움이 필요해!
➡ _____

33 Beth: 가만히 있어. 네 발을 꺼내려고 노력 중이야.
➡ _____

34 Boyd: (비명을 지르며) 아! 아파!
➡ _____

35 Peter: 내가 도와줄게. 잠깐만.
➡ _____

36 Peter가 학교 주방으로 뛰어가 버터를 가지고 온다.
➡ _____

37 Peter: 네 발에 이 버터를 바를 거야.
➡ _____

38 Boyd: 뭐? 버터를?
➡ _____

39 Peter: 그냥 침착하게 있어.
➡ _____

40 Beth: (Boyd의 발을 가리키며) 와! 효과가 있어!
➡ _____

41 Boyd의 발이 거치대에서 빠져나오고 있어.
➡ _____

42 〈장면 4〉
➡ _____

43 Beth는 부모님과 저녁 식사를 하고 있다.
➡ _____

44 그녀는 부모님께 Boyd에게 일어난 일에 대해 이야기한다.
➡ _____

45 Beth: 오늘 학교에서 작은 사고가 있었어요.
➡ _____

46 Boyd의 발이 자전거 거치대에 끼었어요.
➡ _____

47 엄마: 오, 저런! 그래서 발을 어떻게 뺐니?
➡ _____

48 Beth: Peter가 그 애 발에 버터를 바르고 나서 발을 당겨서 꺼냈어요.
➡ _____

49 아빠: 정말 창의적이구나. 지저분하지만 창의적이야.
➡ _____

50 Beth: 흠. 창의적이라고요? 아빠, 그것이 칭찬이 될 수 있어요?
➡ _____

51 아빠: 물론이지.
➡ _____

52 〈장면 5〉
➡ _____

53 오늘은 학교의 마지막 날이고 학생들은 서로를 칭찬하고 있다.
➡ _____

54 Ms. Kemp: Joanne, Beth에게 무슨 칭찬을 해 주겠니?
➡ _____

55 Joanne: Beth, 너는 항상 쾌활해.
➡ _____

56 또한 친절하고 모두에게 공정해.
➡ _____

57 Beth: 고마워, Joanne. 그렇게 말해 주다니 친절하구나.
➡ _____

58 Ms. Kemp: Beth, 이제 네 말을 들어 보자.
➡ _____

59 Peter의 이름을 뽑았구나.
➡ _____

60 Beth: (주저하며) 음, Peter는 창의적이라고 생각해요. Peter, 너는… 어… 창의적이야.
➡ _____

61 Peter: (수줍어하며) 정말?
➡ _____

62 Ms. Kemp: Peter가 왜 창의적이라고 생각하니?
➡ _____

63 Beth: (한참 있다가) 일전에 Boyd의 발이 자전거 거치대에 끼었을 때, Peter는 버터를 사용해서 그의 발을 꺼냈어요.
➡ _____
_____

64 그것은 창의적이었어요.
➡ _____

65 Boyd: 맞아! 어느 누구도 그렇게 하는 것을 생각하지 못했어.
➡ _____

66 Steve: 난 몰랐어. 음, 그래, 나도 그가 창의적이라고 생각해.
➡ _____

67 Beth: (자신 있게) 그래, Peter, 너는 창의적이야!
➡ _____

68 Peter: 고마워, Beth! 그건 최고의 칭찬이야!
➡ _____

MEMO

영어 기출 문제집

적중100 plus
2학기 전과정

2학기 전과정

2학기

정답 및 해설

동아 | 윤정미

중 3

적중100

영어 기출 문제집

적중100

2학기

정답 및 해설

동아 | 윤정미

중 **3**

The Team Behind the Team

시험대비 실력평가   p.08

01 ①   02 invisible   03 ②   04 ④
05 ③   06 ⑤

01 동의어 관계이다. impolite: 무례한, rude: 버릇없는, 무례한, achieve: 달성하다, accomplish: 성취하다 accompany: ~에 동반하다

02 '볼 수 없는'은 'invisible'이 적절하다. 많은 별은 눈에 보이지 않는다.

03 ① be good for: ~에 좋다. 때때로 비판을 좀 받는 것이 좋을 수도 있다. ② keep track of: ~을 파악하다. 아이들이 드나드는 것을 계속 파악하기는 어렵다. ③ in short: 간단히 말해서. 간단히 말해서, 아이들에게 벌을 주는 가장 좋은 방법에 대하여 많은 의견의 불일치가 있다. ④ get attention: 주목을 받다. 여러분이 특이한 일을 한다면 주목 받을 것이고 예술가는 주목 받기를 원한다. ⑤ depending on: ~에 따 라. 차 종류에 따라서 임대료가 달라집니까?

04 register: 등록하다. 몇 명의 학생이 영어 수업에 등록했나요?

05 ① give a speech: 연설하다. 나는 왜 그들이 그가 연설하기를 원했는지 이해할 수가 없어. ② cheer: 응원하다. 나는 언제나 나의 지역 팀을 응원해. ③ limit: 한계. 내 인내심도 한계에 다다랐다. ④ target: 목표. 누구를 목표 시장으로 삼고 있는가? ⑤ tribe: 부족, 종족. 그들은 12세기에 하나의 부족으로 시작했다.

06 support: 돕다, 지원하다. 많은 학생들이 교복을 바꾸는 계획을 지지한다. promote: 홍보하다. 그 밴드는 새 앨범 홍보를 위해 순회 공연을 떠났다.

서술형 시험대비   p.09

01 (1) support (2) achieve (3) hire (4) register
02 (1) independent (2) breath
03 (1) wear (2) (s)everal (3) (a)chieve
    (4) (r)ecommendation
04 (1) I followed the map, keeping track of our position.
    (2) My personality changes depending on the person.
    (3) The house was hidden from sight behind some trees.
    (4) He managed to fix the problem on his own.

01 (1) support: 돕다, 지원하다. 어떤 사람, 그룹 또는 생각에 동의한다고 말하다 (2) achieve: 달성하다, 성취하다. 원하는 것을 하거나 얻는 것에 성공하다 (3) hire: 고용하다. 당신을 위해 일을 하도록 누군가에게 돈을 지불하다 (4) register: 등록하다. 공식적인 명단에 이름을 올리다

02 (1) '반의어'의 관계이다. possible: 가능한, impossible: 불가능한, dependent: 의존하는, independent: 독립적인 (2) '동사 - 명사'의 관계이다. achieve: 달성하다, achievement: 성취, breathe: 숨쉬다, breath: 호흡

03 (1) wear out: (낡아서) 떨어지다, 헤지다 (2) several: 몇몇의 (3) achieve: 달성하다, 성취하다 (4) recommendation: 추천

04 (1) keep track of: ~을 파악하다. track을 추가한다. (2) depending on: ~에 따라. on을 추가한다. (3) hidden: 숨겨진. 수동태가 되어야 하므로 was를 추가한다. (4) on one's own: 혼자서. own을 추가한다.

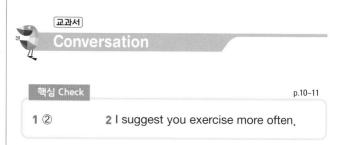

교과서 Conversation

핵심 Check   p.10~11

1 ②   2 I suggest you exercise more often.

교과서 대화문 익히기

Check(√) True or False   p.12

1 T   2 F   3 T   4 T

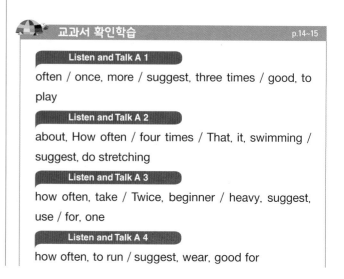

교과서 확인학습   p.14~15

Listen and Talk A 1
often / once, more / suggest, three times / good, to play

Listen and Talk A 2
about, How often / four times / That, it, swimming / suggest, do stretching

Listen and Talk A 3
how often, take / Twice, beginner / heavy, suggest, use / for, one

Listen and Talk A 4
how often, to run / suggest, wear, good for

시험대비 기본평가   p.16

01 ③

02 I suggest we do stretching exercises

03 ③   04 Twice a week

01 이어지는 대화에서 일주일에 한 번 한다고 하고 있으므로 얼마나 자주 하는지 묻는 표현이 적절하다.

02 상대방에게 제안하거나 권유할 때는 'I suggest (that)+주어+(should)+동사원형' 구문으로 말한다.

03 '제안하다'는 'suggest'이다.

04 twice는 '2회, 두 번; 2배로'라는 뜻이다.

시험대비 실력평가   p.17~18

01 ①   02 ②

03 I suggest that you take

04 I don't know how to swim at all.

05 ⑤   06 ②   07 ②, ④   08 ①

09 ④   10 ③   11 ⑤   12 ⑤

13 He will take the class twice a week.

01 빈도를 묻는 질문에 '많이 했다'고 답하는 것은 어색하다. 'I exercise twice a week.' 등으로 답하는 것이 적절하다.

02 weekdays나 weekends 앞에는 전치사 on이 쓰인다.

03 상대방에게 제안하거나 권유할 때는 'I suggest (that)+주어+(should)+동사원형' 구문으로 말한다.

04 not ~ at all = never: 결코 ~ 아닌

05 등록하고 싶다고 했지만 이미 등록한 것은 아니다.

06 얼마나 자주 하는지 빈도를 묻는 (B)에 이어, (C)에서 매일 한

다고 빈도에 대한 답을 하고, (A)에서 덜 하기를 제안하고, (D)에서 시도해 보겠다는 말로 마무리하는 것이 자연스럽다.

07 'OK. I'll try.'와 'I'll give it a try.'는 모두 '시도해 보겠다.'라는 의미이다.

08 (a)에는 대답으로 twice가 나오고 있으므로 빈도를 묻는 often이 적절하다. (b)에는 'per'의 의미로 쓰인 a가 적절하다. (c)에는 suggest가 '제안하다'라는 뜻으로 사용될 때 '주어+suggest+(that)+주어+(should)+동사원형 ~'의 구문으로 나타내므로 should가 생략된 read가 적절하다.

09 be over: 끝나다. 여기에 쓰인 over는 '부사'로 '끝나, 지나'라는 뜻이며 '부사'가 아닌 '형용사'로 볼 수도 있다.

10 빈도를 묻는 질문에 대한 답이므로 'always, usually, often, sometimes, never' 등과 같은 빈도부사를 사용하여 답하거나, 구체적인 빈도를 나타내는 '횟수+a+특정 기간(day/week/month/year 등)'으로 답하는 것이 적절하다.

11 밑줄 친 문장은 빈도를 물어 볼 때 쓰는 표현이다.

12 ⑤번 다음 문장의 'This class'가 주어진 문장의 'the Beginner 1 class'를 가리키므로 ⑤번이 적절하다.

13 소년은 '일주일에 두 번 수강하고 싶어요.'라고 하고 있다.

서술형 시험대비   p.19

01 (D) → (C) → (A) → (B)

02 I'd like to take classes on weekdays and not on weekends.

03 The class can have up to 10 people.

04 The writer suggests joining the club, Fun Wheels.

05 It's fun to ride bikes together.

06 (1) Sure   (2) Of course

07 I suggest you bring a swimming cap

01 (C)의 That이 (D)의 내용을 가리키므로 (D) 다음에 (C)가 이어지고, (A)는 (C)의 질문에 대한 답이므로 (C) 다음에 (A)가 나오고, (B)의 That이 (A)의 내용을 가리키므로 (A) 다음에 (B)가 나오는 순서가 적절하다.

02 I'd like to: ~하고 싶다, take classes: 수업을 듣다, on weekdays: 주중에 on weekends: 주말에, B and not A: A가 아니라 B

03 up to: (특정한 수·정도 등)까지

05 가주어 It과 진주어로 'to ride bikes together'를 쓴다.

06 이어지는 내용으로 보아 긍정의 대답인 'Sure'나 'Of course'가 적절하다.

07 상대방에게 어떤 일이나, 행동을 제안하거나 권유할 때는 동사 'suggest(제안하다)'를 사용하여 'I suggest (that)+주어+(should)+동사원형 ~'의 구문으로 나타낼 수 있으며, 이때 that과 should는 생략할 수 있다.

Grammar

핵심 Check
p.20~21

1 (1) wearing (2) broken

2 (1) Today is as windy as yesterday.
(2) The lamp is not so tall as the stool.

시험대비 기본평가
p.22

01 (1) more expensive → expensive
(2) earliest → early (3) than → as
(4) them → those

02 ⑤　　　**03** ④

04 (1) The girl waving across the street is Sarah.
(2) The storm approaching our country has a strong force.

01 (1) as ~ as를 이용한 표현에서는 비교급을 쓸 수 없다. (2) as ~ as 사이에는 형용사/부사의 원급만 가능하다. 비교급/최상급은 부적절하다. (3) as ~ as에 than은 부적절하다. than은 비교급 뒤에 사용한다. (4) 원급 비교에서 비교 대상을 일치시켜야 한다. the villagers in other towns를 대명사로 받을 때, those in other towns를 쓰는 것이 적절하다.

02 벌레들이 가득한 방은 '능동'이 아닌 '수동'이다. crowded가 적절하다.

03 not so[as] ~ as 구문은 원급을 써야 한다.

04 명사 주어를 뒤에서 수식하는 현재분사를 활용하여, 주어진 단어를 알맞게 배열한다. (1) wave를 waving으로, (2) approach를 approaching으로 어형을 바꾸는 것에 유의한다.

시험대비 실력평가
p.23~25

01 ④　　**02** taking → taken　　**03** ③

04 ③　　**05** ②　　**06** ④　　**07** ④

08 ⑤　　**09** ①, ③

10 (1) sung → singing (2) using → used
(3) ran → running

11 ②, ③, ④　　**12** ⑤

13 (1) made by my ancestors is
(2) were some flies buzzing around

14 men wearing black sunglasses got on

15 ④　　**16** ②　　**17** ④　　**18** ②

01 'as ~ as'의 부정은 not을 앞에 쓰며, 그 경우 not 바로 뒤의 as는 so로 쓸 수 있다.

02 런던에서 촬영된 사진들이므로 과거분사가 적절하다.

03 John이 더 무겁기 때문에 'Sam만큼 무게가 나가지 않다(Sam보다 가볍다)'는 것은 표의 내용과 일치하지 않는다.

04 (1) 강의에 참석한 청중(능동) (2) 컴퓨터 게임에 쓰인 시간(수동) (3) 흥미진진한 콘서트(능동)이므로 정답은 ③

05 '그 지팡이는 그 뱀만큼 길다.' ① harder → hard ③ faster → fast ④ tallest → tall ⑤ heavier → heavy

06 ④는 forgot의 목적어로 쓰인 '동명사'이고, 나머지는 모두 명사를 앞 또는 뒤에서 수식하는 '현재분사'이다.

07 My backpack과 Sujin's backpack(= Sujin's)을 'as 원급 as'로 비교하는 문장이다.

08 'not as ~ as'는 비교급의 의미와 같게 사용되지만, not이 없는 'as ~ as'는 비교의 의미가 없다.

09 ① 영화가 감동적이었다. touched → touching ③ 축구 경기가 가장 흥미진진했다. excited → exciting

10 (1) 노래를 부르는 소녀(진행) (2) 사용된 조개껍질(수동) (3) 달리는 선수들(진행)

11 ② '내가 만난 사람들'로서 '관계대명사 목적격'이 생략된 '주어+동사'의 관계이므로 meeting → met ③ '도둑맞은 그림들이 다른 나라에서 발견되었다'는 뜻으로 앞부분의 동사 got을 삭제하고, 과거분사의 수식을 활용한다. ④ '넓은 수영장에서 빠르게 수영하고 있는 소년'이므로, The boy swimming fast in a wide pool로 고치는 것이 적절하다.

12 아기 펭귄 5마리가 어른 둘만큼 먹는다는 문장이므로 내용상 '많이'라는 의미의 부사가 필요하다. as와 as 사이에는 원급을 써야 하므로 much가 적절하다.

13 분사가 명사의 뒤에서 수식하는 것을 적절히 활용한다. (1) made by my ancestors가 The table을 수식(수동), (2) buzzing around the jam이 some flies를 수식(진행)

14 분사가 명사를 뒤에서 꾸며주는 것을 활용한다. 능동이므로 wearing을 사용하고, 과거시제이므로 get을 got으로 고치는 것에 유의한다.

15 ⓐ, ⓔ는 '동명사', ⓑ, ⓒ, ⓓ는 '현재분사'이다.

16 ②는 '가능한 한 많은 물을 마시는 것이 좋다'이므로, '수'를 나타내는 many가 아닌, '양'을 뜻하는 much가 적절하다.

17 'ⓐ producing → produced(생산된) ⓑ calling → called(~라고 불린) ⓒ walked → walking(걷고 있는) ⓔ taken → taking(찍는)

18 Alicia는 그녀의 학급에서 가장 힘이 센 학생이다, = 다른 어떤 학생도 그녀의 학급에서 Alicia만큼 힘이 세지 않다.

4 정답 및 해설

01 (1) is as old as Key   (2) is not so old as Key

(3) is as tall as Dave   (4) is not so tall as Key

(5) is so heavy as Sean   (6) is so tall as Key

02 (A) holding   (B) looking

03 (1) can speak English as freely as her teacher

(2) sang as well as the singer

(3) does the dishes as often as my mom

(4) was not so interesting as the original novel

04 (1) the flowers planted in my garden

(2) girls standing near the post office

(3) written by Mark Twain is exciting

(4) gentlemen dancing to the disco music

05 (1) could not write as neatly as his mother cut

(2) didn't lose as much weight as he thought

06 (A) written   (B) known   (C) covering

(D) making   (E) appearing

07 (1) a lady wearing a colorful skirt

(2) are the illegally copied books

(3) an airplane flying between the clouds

(4) made by the master craftsman is so

expensive

(5) careful not to wake up the sleeping baby

08 sleeping, wearing

01 (1) Dave는 Key와 같은 나이이다. (2) Sean은 Key만큼의 나이가 아니다. (3) Sean은 Dave만큼 키가 크다. (4) Dave는 Key만큼 키가 크지 않다. (5) 누구도 Sean만큼 몸무게가 나가지 않는다. (6) 누구도 Key만큼 키가 크지 않다.

02 진행의 분사가 명사의 뒤에서 수식하는 것을 활용한다.

03 (1) 부사 freely에 유의. (3) 3인칭 현재 does에 유의. (4) 과거시제 was, 현재분사형 형용사 interesting에 유의.

04 명사를 뒤에서 꾸미는 분사 활용 (1) Daisy는 나의 정원에 '심어진 꽃들'(수동)을 보고 있었다. (2) 우체국 가까이에 '서 있는 소녀들'(진행)은 그들의 선생님을 기다리고 있다. (3) Mark Twain에 의해 '쓰여진 책'(수동)은 '흥미로웠다'. (4) 그 디스코 음악에 맞춰 '춤을 추는 신사들'(진행)은 누구입니까?

05 (1) neatly: 반듯하게, 깔끔하게 (2) lose weight: 살이 빠지다, 체중이 줄다

06 (A) 쓰여진 영화 (B) ~로서 알려진 (C) 덮고 있는 (D) (영화를 더욱 미스테리하게) 만드는 (E) 등장하는

07 (1) 화려한 스커트를 입은 숙녀 (2) 불법 복제된 책들 (3) 구름들 사이로 날아가는 비행기 (4) 그 명장에 의해 만들어진 바이올린 (5) 잠자는 아기

08 Minho는 아버지가 퇴근하고 집에 오시자마자 양복을 입은 채로 소파에서 주무시는 것을 발견했다.

교과서
Reading

확인문제 p.28

1 T 2 F 3 T 4 F 5 T 6 F

확인문제 p.29

1 T 2 F 3 T 4 F 5 T 6 F

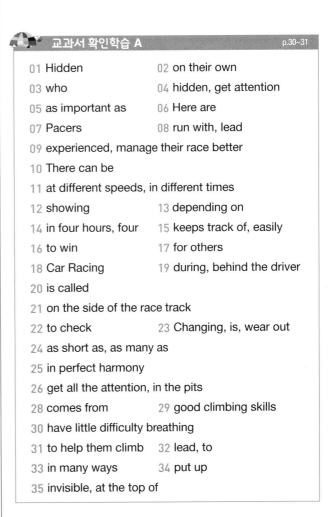

교과서 확인학습 A p.30~31

01 Hidden   02 on their own
03 who   04 hidden, get attention
05 as important as   06 Here are
07 Pacers   08 run with, lead
09 experienced, manage their race better
10 There can be
11 at different speeds, in different times
12 showing   13 depending on
14 in four hours, four   15 keeps track of, easily
16 to win   17 for others
18 Car Racing   19 during, behind the driver
20 is called
21 on the side of the race track
22 to check   23 Changing, is, wear out
24 as short as, as many as
25 in perfect harmony
26 get all the attention, in the pits
28 comes from   29 good climbing skills
30 have little difficulty breathing
31 to help them climb   32 lead, to
33 in many ways   34 put up
35 invisible, at the top of

교과서 확인학습 B p.32~33

1 Hidden People in Sports

2 In sports, only the players get a trophy or medal, but they don't win on their own.

3 There are people who help the players.

4 These people are often hidden and don't get attention.

5 However, they are as important as the players.

6 Here are some examples.

7 Pacers in a Marathon

8 Pacers run with other runners and lead them in a marathon.

9 Pacers are experienced runners, and their job is to help other runners manage their race better.

10 There can be several pacers in a race.

11 Each pacer runs at different speeds and finishes the race in different times.

12 Pacers usually have flags or balloons showing their finish time.

13 Runners can choose a pacer depending on their target finish time.

14 For example, if a runner wants to finish the race in four hours, the runner will follow the four-hour pacer.

15 Since the pacer keeps track of the time, the runner can achieve his or her goal of finishing the marathon in a particular time more easily.

16 In short, pacers run but they don't run to win.

17 They run for others.

18 Pit Crews in Car Racing

19 You may only see the car and the driver during most car races, but there is a team behind the driver.

20 This team is called a pit crew.

21 A pit is a place on the side of the race track, and drivers stop there several times during a race.

22 The main job of the pit crew is to check the car and change the tires.

23 Changing the tires is especially important because the tires wear out easily in a high speed race.

24 A pit stop can be as short as 2 seconds, and there are as many as 20 members on a crew.

25 Therefore, the pit crew has to work in perfect harmony.

26 The driver may get all the attention, but as people say, "Races are won in the pits."

27 Sherpas in Mountain Climbing

28 The word *Sherpa* comes from the Sherpa tribe, which lives in the eastern part of Nepal.

29 Sherpas have good climbing skills and know their way around the mountains well.

30 They also have little difficulty breathing high up in the mountains.

31 Therefore, mountain climbers started to hire Sherpas to help them climb Mount Everest.

32 Sherpas lead mountain climbers to the top of the mountain.

33 They support climbers in many ways.

34 For example, they put up tents and carry climbers' bags.

35 Sherpas are often called the invisible people of Mount Everest because people often see a picture of only the climbers at the top of the mountain.

시험대비 실력평가 p.34~37

01 ① 02 ②, ③ 03 ① 04 ②
05 ③, ⑤ 06 ④ 07 ②
08 (A) check (B) change 09 ②
10 A pit stop can be as short as 2 seconds, and there are as many as 20 members on a crew.
11 ④ 12 ③ 13 ⑤ 14 ①
15 ② 16 (A) climbers 17 hidden
18 win → don't win
19 people who help the players 20 ③
21 (a) checking (b) changing
22 shorter → short, much → many
23 (A) eastern (B) little (C) invisible
24 mountain climbers started to hire Sherpas to help them climb Mount Everest
25 ④

01 ⓐ at different speeds: 다른 속도로, ⓑ in different times: 다른 시간대에

02 (A)와 ②, ③: 명사적 용법, ①, ⑤: 부사적 용법, ④: 형용사적 용법

03 페이서들은 마라톤에서 다른 선수들을 '이끈다.'

04 앞에 나오는 내용과 상반되는 내용이 뒤에 이어지므로 However가 가장 적절하다. ① 즉[말하자면], ③ 비슷하게, ④ 그 결과, ⑤ 게다가, 더욱이

05 on one's own: 혼자서, 혼자 힘으로(= alone, by oneself), ① 외로운, 쓸쓸한, ② 이성을 잃고, 어찌할 바를 모르고, ④ on behalf of: ~을 대신하여, ~을 대표하여, ~을 위해서

06 종종 숨겨져 있고 주목을 받지 못하지만 선수들만큼 중요한, 선수들을 돕는 사람들이 있다고 말하면서, 여기 몇 가지 예가 있다고 했으므로, 뒤에 올 내용으로는 '스포츠 속 숨은 조력자들'이 적절하다. ⑤ noticeable: 눈에 띄는, 주목할 만한

07 빠른 속도의 경주에서는 타이어가 쉽게 마모되기 때문에 타이어를 교체하는 것이 특히 중요한데 '피트'에서 피트 크루가 자동차를 점검하고 타이어를 교체해 주기 때문에, "경주의 우승은 '피트'에서 이루어진다."고 하는 것이 적절하다. ⑤ 응원석

08 자동차를 '점검하고' 타이어를 '교체하기' 위해서이다.

09 ⓐ와 ②, ⑤: 동명사, ①, ③, ④: 현재분사

10 as+형용사/부사의 원급+as: '~만큼 …한/하게'(동등 비교)

11 앞의 내용을 요약해서 설명하고 있으므로 In short가 가장 적절하다. in short: 요컨대, 요약하면, ② 게다가, ⑤ 다른 한편으로는

12 ③번 다음 문장의 For example에 주목한다. 주어진 문장의 예에 해당하므로 ③번이 적절하다.

13 이 글은 '마라톤에서 페이서들이 하는 역할'에 대한 글이므로, 주제로는 ⑤번 '마라톤에서 페이서들의 역할'이 적절하다.

14 have difficulty/trouble -ing: '~하는 데 어려움이 있다'

15 put up: (천막 따위를) 치다, 세우다

16 왜냐하면 그것은 사람들이 자주 보는 산 정상에 있는 '등산가들'만 찍힌 사진이기 때문이다.

17 이 사람들은 종종 숨겨져 있다고 해야 하므로 과거분사로 써서 수동태를 만드는 것이 적절하다.

18 스포츠에서 선수들만 트로피나 메달을 받지만, 그들은 '혼자 힘으로 이기는 것이 아니다'라고 해야 하므로, win을 don't win으로 고치는 것이 적절하다.

19 '선수들을 돕는 사람들'을 가리킨다.

20 피트에서의 정지는 짧게는 2초 정도인데 한 팀에는 많게는 20명에 이르는 구성원이 있으므로, 피트 크루는 '완벽한 조화를 이루며' 일해야 한다고 하는 것이 적절하다. ② 차례로, 이어서, ④ 가끔[이따금], ⑤ 조금씩, 천천히

21 보어로 쓰인 to부정사를 동명사로 바꾸는 것이 적절하다.

22 '동등 비교'는 as+형용사/부사의 원급+as로 써야 하고, '20명에 이르는 구성원'이라고 해야 하므로, 양을 나타내는 much가 아니라 수를 나타내는 many로 고치는 것이 적절하다.

23 (A) part를 수식하는 형용사가 와야 하므로 eastern이 적절하다. (B) 셰르파는 산의 높은 곳에서 호흡하는 데 어려움이 '거의 없다'고 해야 하므로 little이 적절하다. (C) 사람들이 산 정상에서 등산가들만 찍힌 사진을 자주 보기 때문에 셰르파는 종종 에베레스트산의 '보이지 않는' 사람들로 불린다고 해야 하므로 invisible이 적절하다. invisible 보이지 않는, 볼 수 없는

24 help+목적어+(to+)동사원형; ~가 …하는 것을 돕다

25 셰르파가 어떻게 산의 높은 곳에서 호흡하는 데 어려움이 거의 없는지는 알 수 없다. ① No, it is named after the Sherpa tribe. ② It lives in the eastern part of Nepal. ③ They have good climbing skills. ⑤ No, they often see a picture of only the climbers.

🦉 **서술형 시험대비** p.38~39

01 as 02 (a) hidden (b) attention
03 the same → different 04 which[that] show

05 pacers run but they don't run to win
06 (A) a particular time (B) keeps track of
07 (A) during (B) change (C) short
08 after → during
09 (A) pit crew (B) pit crew
10 breathing 11 and it
12 the sherpas → the climbers
13 (A) lead (B) good climbing skills

01 동등한 두 대상을 비교할 때는 'as+형용사/부사+as'의 형태로 '~만큼 …한/하게'라는 뜻이다.

02 그들은 스포츠에서 선수들이 이기도록 돕지만, '주목'을 받지 못한 채 종종 '숨겨져' 있다.

03 각각의 페이서는 '다른' 속도로 달리고 다른 시간대에 경기를 마친다고 했으므로, the same을 different로 고치는 것이 적절하다.

04 현재분사 showing을 '주격 관계대명사 which[that] show'로 바꿔 쓰는 것이 적절하다.

05 to win: to부정사의 부사적 용법(목적)

06 페이서가 시간을 '계속해서 파악하기' 때문에, 선수들은 자신들의 목표 완주 시간에 따라 페이서를 선택함으로써 선수는 '특정 시간에' 마라톤을 완주하려는 자신의 목표를 더 쉽게 달성할 수 있다.

07 (A) during+기간을 나타내는 명사, while+주어+동사, (B) to check와 병렬을 이루도록 (to) change라고 하는 것이 적절하다. (C) be동사의 보어이므로 형용사 short가 적절하다. shortly: (시간상으로) 얼마 안 되어, 곧(부사)

08 레이서들은 경주 '도중에' 피트에서 여러 번 정지한다.

09 레이서들이 자동차를 점검하고 타이어를 교체하기 위해 피트에 정지할 때, '피트 크루'는 매우 짧은 시간 내에 완벽한 조화를 이루며 일해야 하므로, '피트 크루'의 완벽한 작업이 레이스의 승리에 매우 중요한 역할을 한다.

10 have difficulty -ing: ~하는 데 어려움이 있다

11 계속적 용법의 관계대명사는 '접속사+대명사'로 바꿔 쓸 수 있다. 관계대명사가 who가 아닌 which이므로 and he(she)가 아니라 'and it'으로 고치는 것이 적절하다.

12 사람들이 산 정상에서 '등산가들'만 찍힌 사진을 자주 보기 때문에 셰르파는 종종 에베레스트산의 보이지 않는 사람들로 불린다고 해야 하므로, the sherpas를 the climbers로 고치는 것이 적절하다.

13 셰르파족은 네팔의 동쪽 지역에 살고 있고, 셰르파는 '훌륭한 등반 기량'을 갖고 있으며 산 지리를 잘 알기 때문에 등산가들을 산 정상까지 '이끈다.'

01 ①

02 (c)rew / (p)articular / (d)irection

   (1) particular   (2) crew   (3) direction

03 wear out

04 (A) (h)armony   (B) (d)ifficulty   (C) (r)ole

05 (1) invisible   (2) inexperienced   (3) impatient

06 ④	07 ③	08 ②	09 limit
10 register	11 ④	12 ①	13 ①
14 ②	15 written by Susan is for		16 ⑤
17 ⑤	18 ②, ⑤, ⑦		19 ③

20 themselves → others 또는 other runners

21 ⑤	22 ②	23 ④	24 ③
25 ②			

01 <보기>와 ①번은 '가입하다'라는 의미로 쓰였다. <보기> 그는 나름대로 이유가 있어서 그 클럽 가입을 거절했다. ① 새로 가입한 체육관은 어때요? ② 그는 파이프 한 쪽을 그 다음 것과 연결했다. ③ 목요일에 저희와 함께 저녁식사하실 시간 있으세요? ④ 1189년, 리차드는 프랑스의 필립 II세와 힘을 합쳐 그의 아버지와 맞서 싸웠다. ⑤ 단단히 붙여서 이음새를 찾을 수 없었다.

02 (1) particular: 특정한. 특별한, 또는 보통 이상의. 그가 즐기는 특정한 종류의 책이 있나요? (2) crew: 팀, 조. 함께 일하는 특정한 기술을 가진 한 무리의 사람들. 촬영 팀이 그 장면을 찍으려고 바다로 들어갔다. (3) direction: 방향. 무언가 또는 누군가가 움직이거나, 향하는 길. 나는 모든 방향 감각을 상실해 버렸다.

03 '어떤 것을 많이 사용하여 더 이상 작동하지 않거나 더 이상 사용될 수 없다'라는 의미로 'wear out((낡아서) 떨어지다, 헤지다)'이 적절하다.

04 (A) harmony: 조화, 화합. 그들은 서로 사이 좋게 살았다. (B) have difficulty -ing: ~하는 데 어려움을 겪다. 십대들은 흔히 의사[감정] 표현에 어려움을 겪는다. (C) play an important role: 중요한 역할을 하다. 관광 산업이 국가 경제 발전에 중요한 역할을 할 것으로 예상된다.

05 (1) 접두사 'in'을 붙여 반의어가 되는 어휘이다. invisible: 보이지 않는. 선의는 무형의 자산이다. (2) 동사 experience의 과거분사에 'in'을 붙여 반의어가 된 어휘이다. inexperienced: 경험이 없는. 그녀는 경험이 없어서 지도의 손길[지도해 줄 사람]이 필요하다. (3) 접두사 'im'을 붙여 반의어가 되는 어휘이다. impatient: 초조해 하는. 시간이 흐를수록 그는 더욱 더 조급해졌다.

06 (D)의 얼마나 자주 수영을 하는지 묻는 말에 이어, (B)에서 일주일에 네 번 수영을 한다고 답하고, (A)에서 '그렇게 자주?'라며 (B)의 내용을 확인하며 묻고, (C)에서 수영하기 전에 스트레

칭을 하는 것을 제안한 후, 좋은 생각이라는 주어진 문장으로 이어지는 것이 적절하다.

07 (a)와 ③: 지시부사. [수량·정도를 나타내는 말을 한정하여] 그만큼, 그렇게 ① 지시형용사 저(말하는 이 가까이에 있지 않은 사람이나 사물을 가리킬 때 씀) ② 접속사. so ~ that ...: 너무 ~해서 …하다 ④ 관계대명사 ⑤ 접속사. [동격절을 이끌어] ~이라는, ~하다는

08 'I eat fast food three times a week.'이라고 대답하고 있으므로 빈도를 묻는 'How often do you eat fast food?'가 적절하다.

09 규칙, 법 등 때문에 허용되는 시간이나 돈의 가장 크거나 작은 양'은 'limit(한계)'이다.

10 sign up for = register for: ~에 등록하다

11 ① Bong에 의해 '연출된 영화'가 되어야 하므로 directed를 써야 한다. ② which 뒤에 be동사를 써주거나, which를 생략해서 뒤에서 명사를 꾸미는 형태로 쓰는 것이 적절하다. ③ Bow라고 '이름 불리는 개'이므로 named가 적절하다. ⑤ 회의에 '초대받은 정치인들'이므로 invited가 적절하다.

12 각각 '프랑스어로 쓰여진 편지(수동)', '기타를 연주하는 남자(진행)', '자전거를 고치는 소년(진행)'이다.

13 'as ~ as'에는 수식어의 원급을 쓴다. 비교급이나 최상급은 쓸 수 없으며, high(높은; 높게)와 highly(상당히)의 쓰임새 구분을 명확하게 해야 한다.

14 'with+A+형용사/분사' 형태는 A의 능동/수동 여부에 따라 현재분사 또는 과거분사를 활용한다. ② '다리를 꼰 채로'는 'with one's legs crossed'로 써야 한다. ① with the TV on: TV를 켠 채로 ③ with one's arms folded: 팔짱을 낀 채로 ④ with one's eyes closed: 눈을 감은 채로 ⑤ with one's clothes wet with sweat: 옷이 땀에 젖은 채로

15 Susan이 카드를 썼으므로, 한 문장으로 만들 때, 'The card that Susan wrote' 또는 'The card (that was) written by Susan'이 가능하다. 분사를 이용해야 하므로 후자를 쓴다.

16 be busy ~ing는 '~하느라 바쁘다'라는 뜻의 동명사의 관용적 표현이다. 다른 문장들에서는 밑줄 친 부분들 모두가 현재분사로 사용되었다.

17 'as ~ as'에는 수식어의 원급을 쓴다. 비교급이나 최상급은 쓸 수 없다. more valuable → valuable

18 명사를 꾸미는 분사가 다른 어구와 결합해서 뒤에서 꾸밀 때는 '관계대명사+be동사'가 생략된 것으로 볼 수 있다. 따라서, 명사를 앞에서 꾸미거나, 서술적 용법으로 사용된 분사를 찾으면, '관계대명사+be동사'가 생략된 것이 아닌 경우에 해당한다. ②는 분사가 앞에서 수식 ⑤, ⑦은 서술적 용법으로 사용되었다.

19 ⓐ와 ③: 동격 관계(~이라고 하는, ~인), ① [거리·위치·시간] ~의, ~부터, ② [재료·구성 요소] ~으로 (만든), ④ [목적격 관계] ~을, ~에 대한, ⑤ [성질·상태] ~의, ~을 지닌

20 그들은 '다른 선수들'을 위해 달린다고 하는 것이 적절하다.

21 앞의 내용의 결과가 나오고 있으므로 Therefore가 가장 적절하다. ② 그렇기는 하지만, 그렇더라도, ③ 즉[말하자면], ④ 그 대신에

22 ⓑ와 ②: ~하는 것처럼(접속사), ① ~함에 따라(접속사), ③ ~로서(전치사), ④ ~이므로(접속사), ⑤ [보통 as ~ as ...로 형용사·부사 앞에서] …와 같은 정도로, (as ~ as ...에서, 앞의 as는 지시부사, 뒤의 as는 접속사)

23 피트에서의 정지는 짧게는 '2초' 정도이다.

24 ③them은 등산가들을 가리키고, 나머지는 다 Sherpas를 가리킨다.

25 이 글은 '등산가들이 등반할 때 세르파가 하는 역할'에 대한 글이므로, 주제로는 ②번 '등산에서의 세르파의 역할'이 적절하다.

단원별 예상문제
p.46~49

01 ②　　　　　　　　　**02** ④

03 (1) (h)ired　(2) (o)ver　(3) (a)ttention

04 of / of　　　　　　**05** ①

06 토요일과 일요일에 수업이 있는 초급 1반을 수강하는 것.

07 ④

08 It's because Suji's bowling ball looks heavy for her.

09 bowling ball　　**10** embarrassed, broken

11 ③　　　　**12** ④　　　　**13** ③

14 experiencing → experienced

15 ②, ⑤　　**16** ②　　**17** ④　　　**18** ①

19 ③　　　　**20** tribe　　**21** ①

22 ⓐ a blind runner　ⓑ a shooting assistant

12 they should

24 (A) A tapper　(B) a guide runner
　　(C) a shooting assistant

01 ②번은 동의어 관계이다. 나머지는 모두 반의어 관계이다. allow: 허용하다, permit: 허가하다 ① perfect: 완전한, imperfect: 불완전한 ③ complete: 완전한, incomplete: 불완전한 ④ hire: 고용하다, fire: 해고하다 ⑤ full: 가득 찬, empty: 비어 있는

02 ① 달리기에서, guide runner는 시각 장애인 선수와 함께 달리며 그들이 트랙에서 벗어나지 않도록 돕는다. ② 마일리지 프로그램은 어떻게 신청합니까? ③ 손님을 상대하는 일은 결코 쉬운 일이 아니다. ④ most of all: 무엇보다도. 그것은 그녀가 무엇보다도 원하던 것이었다. ⑤ 그녀는 연설을 하느니 차라리 죽는 게 나을 것 같았다.

03 (1) hire: 고용하다 (2) be over: 끝나다 (3) attention: 주의, 주목

04 • take care of: ~을 돌보다. 그는 스스로를 돌볼 수 있다. • keep track of: ~을 파악하다. 은행 입출금 내역서는 당신의 돈이 어디에 쓰이고 있는지를 계속 파악하는 데 도움이 된다.

05 ① 소년이 언제 방문했는지는 알 수 없다. ② Twice a week. ③ On weekends. ④ On Saturdays and Sundays. ⑤ The Beginner 1 class.

06 여자가 앞에서 한 말의 내용을 요약해서 쓰면 된다.

07 '볼링공이 무거워 보인다.'라고 한 후, 더 가벼운 공을 쓰는 것을 제안하는 것이 자연스러우므로 ④번이 적절하다.

08 Suji의 볼링공이 무거워 보인다며 더 가벼운 공을 쓸 것을 제안하고 있다.

09 one은 'bowling ball'을 대신하는 부정대명사이다.

10 Jeffrey는 자전거를 어떻게 수리할지 몰랐기 때문에 그의 고장 난 자전거에 당황했다.

11 'as ~ as'에는 수식어의 원급을 쓴다. ③ 내용상 '배우기 어렵지 않다'는 뜻이므로 hardly가 아닌 hard로 쓰는 것이 적절하다.

12 ④번은 help의 목적어로 쓰인 동명사(can't help ~ing: ~하지 않을 수 없다)이다. 나머지는 모두 명사의 뒤에서 꾸미는 분사로 사용되었다.

13 ③ Jim이 Mary, Steve와 함께 가장 나이가 많으므로, 'Jim이 Paul만큼 나이 들지 않았다'는 문장은 'Jim이 Paul보다 어리다'는 뜻과 같기 때문에 적절하지 않다.

14 페이서들은 '경험이 많은' 선수들이라고 해야 하므로, experiencing을 experienced로 고치는 것이 적절하다. experienced: (특정 분야에) 경험[경력]이 있는, experiencing: 경험하는

15 in short = in brief = to put it shortly[briefly] = in a word: 요약하면, 요컨대, ② in addition: 게다가 ⑤ in other words: 바꿔 말하면

16 처음에 페이서들이 어떻게 그들의 달리는 속도를 결정하는지는 알 수 없다. ① They help other runners manage their race better by running with them and leading them in a marathon. ③ They usually have flags or balloons showing their finish time. ④ Depending on their target finish time. ⑤ By choosing a pacer depending on their target finish time and following the pacer.

17 ⓐ on: '소속'을 나타냄, ⓑ in harmony: 조화를 이루며

18 우리는 대부분의 자동차 경주에서 자동차와 레이서만 보게 되고, 그 레이서 뒤에 있는 팀이 피트 크루이다.

19 이 글은 '자동차 경주에서 피트 크루가 하는 역할'에 대한 글이므로, 제목으로는 ③번 '피트 크루는 주로 무슨 일을 하는가?'가 적절하다.

20 tribe: 부족, 종족. 같은 인종의, 같은 언어와 풍습을 가진 사람들의 집단

21 ①번 다음 문장의 also에 주목한다. 주어진 문장의 내용에 이어

세르파에 대한 설명을 계속하는 것이므로 ①번이 적절하다.

22 ⓐ '시각 장애인 선수', ⓑ '슈팅 보조원'을 가리킨다.

23 의문사+to부정사 = 의문사+주어+should+동사

24 'tapper', 'guide runner', 그리고 'shooting assistant'는 모두 패럴림픽의 조력자들이다.

01 Because he wants to take classes twice a week on weekdays.

02 He wants to take the lessons twice a week.

03 He will take the swimming classes on Tuesdays and Thursdays.

04 (1) India's population growth rate is as fast as that of China.
　　(2) The Chinese government is as unashamed as the Japanese political leaders.

05 ⓐ boiling　ⓑ written　ⓒ leaving　ⓓ covered
　　ⓔ crying　ⓕ sleeping　ⓖ composed
　　이유: ⓕ는 동명사이고, 나머지는 모두 분사이다.

06 (A) pacer runs　(B) four hours　(C) four-hour

07 the runner can achieve his or her goal of finishing the marathon in a particular time more easily

08 It is to help other runners manage their race better.

09 is called　　　　　　　　　10 are → is

11 (A) the side　(B) a race

01 소년이 일주일에 두 번 주중에 수업을 듣길 원하기 때문이다.

02 소년은 일주일에 두 번 수업을 듣길 원한다.

03 초급 2반의 수업은 화요일과 목요일에 있다고 했다.

04 'as ~ as' 원급 비교 표현을 사용하여, 주어진 단어들을 알맞게 배열한다. *a population growth rate: 인구 성장률 *unashamed: 부끄러움을 모르는

05 ⓐ '끓는 물'(능동) ⓑ '운동주에 의해 쓰여진 시'(수동) ⓒ '뉴욕행 열차'(능동) ⓓ '눈으로 덮인 산'(수동) ⓔ '울고 있는 아기'(능동) ⓕ '침낭'은 '잠을 자기 위한 용도의 가방'이므로 동명사 ⓖ '작곡된 음악'(수동)

06 (A) each는 단수 취급해야 하므로 pacer runs가 적절하다.
(B) in four hours: 4시간 안에, (C) 명사 pacer를 수식하는 형용사로 쓰인 것이므로 four-hour가 적절하다.

07 동격을 나타내는 전치사 of를 보충하여, 'his or her goal'이 'finishing the marathon in a particular time'임을 나타내도록 하는 것이 적절하다.

08 페이서의 역할은 다른 선수들이 경기를 더 잘 운영하도록 돕는 것이다.

09 피트 크루라고 '불린다'고 해야 하므로 수동태로 쓰는 것이 적절하다..

10 주어가 동명사 Changing이므로, 동사를 is로 고치는 것이 적절하다.

11 '피트'는 레이서들이 경주 도중에 자동차를 점검하고 타이어를 교체하기 위해 여러 번 정지하는, 경주 트랙의 한쪽에 있는 공간이다.

|모범답안|

01 (1) often do you play computer games, play computer games three times a week
　　(2) often do you eat late at night, eat late at night five times a week
　　(3) often do you take swimming classes, take swimming classes twice a week

02 (1) Sein runs as fast as Bona.
　　(2) Minju is not so fast as Sein.
　　(3) Bona jumps as high as Minju.
　　(4) Seohyun can throw the ball as far as Ahrin.

03 (A) cheering　(B) team spirit
　　(C) their team and fans　(D) fit and strong
　　(E) jumping and dancing

01 hire　　　02 breathe　　　03 tribe　　　04 ④

05 (1) My boots are beginning to wear out.
　　(2) There is heavy traffic, therefore, we should take the subway.
　　(3) Do you have a particular restaurant in mind?

06 I suggest you bring a swimming cap.

07 ②

08 I suggest that you should wear running shoes

09 She comes here every day to run.

10 how to swim　　　　11 ①　　　　12 ④

13 have flags or balloons showing their start time / since a pit stop can be as short as 2 minutes

14 ④

15 (1) My pencil case is as light as Mina's.
　　(2) Isabelle is as tall as John, but she isn't so heavy as he.

16 ⑤

17 Mom makes as delicious dishes as a man called 'Housewife Baek.'

18 ④　　　　　19 ④　　　　　20 ③　　　　　21 ③

22 win → are won

23 (A) the attention   (B) pit crew   24 ①

25 because people often see a picture of only the climbers at the top of the mountain

26 ④

27 (A) Although   (B) at (C) hard

28 ②, ④, ⑤   29 ④

01 동의어 관계이다. suggest: 제안하다 – propose: 제안하다, employ: 고용하다 – hire: 고용하다

02 breathe: 숨을 쉬다. 공기를 체내로 빨아들이고 다시 내보내다

03 tribe: 부족, 종족. 자신들의 언어와 생활 방식을 가지고 있는 사람들의 집단. 이 수업에서 우리는 마사이 부족의 문화를 배울 수 있다.

04 allow: 허용하다. 홀 안에서는 흡연을 허용하지 않습니다. suggest: 제안하다. 전 나가서 외식할 것을 제안해요.

05 (1) wear out: (낡아서) 떨어지다, 헤지다 (2) therefore: 그러므로 (3) particular: 특정한, have ~ in mind: ~을 생각하고 있다

06 suggest 다음에 나오는 that절에서 '주어+(should)+동사원형 ~'으로 쓰는 것에 주의한다.

07 ⓑ의 'to swim'을 swimming으로 고치는 것이 적절하다. go ~ing: ~하러 가다

08 suggest 다음에 나오는 that 절에서 '주어+(should)+동사원형 ~'으로 쓴다. that과 should는 생략할 수 있다.

09 '여기에 얼마나 자주 달리기를 하러 오니?'라는 질문에 '매일 와.'라고 답하고 있다.

10 의문사+to부정사 = 의문사+주어+should+동사원형

11 '제한 인원이 열 명'이라는 의미이므로 limit이 알맞다.

12 소년은 주말이 아니라 주중에 수업을 듣고 싶다고 말하고 있다.

13 (A) 현재분사가 이끄는 형용사구 'showing their start time'이 앞의 명사들을 뒤에서 수식하는 것에 유의한다. (B) 'as ~ as 구문'을 활용하되, 조동사 can 뒤에 be동사의 '원형'을 쓰는 것에 유의한다.

14 included → including ④ '종이, 연필, 지우개 등을 포함한 많은 문구류'(능동)

15 'as 원급 as'를 활용하여, 주어진 단어를 알맞게 배열한다.

16 주어진 문장과 ①, ②, ③, ④는 모두 수동의 의미로 명사를 뒤에서 꾸미는 과거분사를 써야 한다. ⑤번만 현재분사이다. 'the elderly living alone: 독거 노인들'(능동)

17 주어가 3인칭 단수 현재이므로 makes, '~라고 불리는 남자'이므로 'a man called'를 쓰는 것에 유의하여, 'as ~ as'를 활용하여 알맞게 배열한다.

18 명사를 뒤에서 꾸며주는 분사의 능동/수동을 적절하게 구분해야 한다. ④ '옛날에 만들어진 오래된 동전들'이므로 '수동'의 의미를 가진 made가 적절하다.

19 페이서가 시간을 '계속해서 파악한다'고 하는 것이 적절하다. keep track of: (계속해서) ~을 파악하다, ~에 주의를 기울이다. ① (먼저 간 사람을) 따라 잡다[따라가다], (정도나 수준이 앞선 것을) 따라잡다, ② ~을 참다, ③ ~을 생각해 내다, ⑤ (손실 따위를) 보상하다

20 ⓑ와 ②, ⑤: 부사적 용법, ①, ④: 명사적 용법, ③: 형용사적 용법

21 ③번 다음 문장의 Changing the tires에 주목한다. 주어진 문장의 change the tires를 가리키는 것이므로 ③번이 적절하다.

22 '경주의 우승은 피트에서 이루어진다'고 해야 하므로, 수동태로 고치는 것이 적절하다.

23 자동차 경주에서 레이서만 '주목'을 받을지 모르지만, '피트 크루'라고 불리는 팀이 레이서가 경주에서 이기도록 레이서 뒤에서 도와주는 중요한 역할을 한다.

24 ⓐ: 앞의 내용의 결과가 나오고 있으므로 Therefore가 가장 적절하다. ⓑ: 앞의 내용의 예가 나오고 있으므로 For example이 가장 적절하다. ② 다시 말해서 - 그에 반해서, ③ 게다가 - 따라서, ④ ~임에 비하여[반하여] - 게다가, ⑤ 예를 들어 - 똑같이

25 a picture of only the climbers at the top of the mountain: 산 정상에서 등산가들만 찍힌 사진

26 셰르파는 산의 높은 곳에서 호흡하는 데 '어려움이 거의 없다.'

27 (A) 사람들이 보통 치어리더는 미식축구팀의 일원이라고 생각하지 '않을지라도' 그들은 축구 경기에서 중요한 역할을 한다고 해야 하므로 Although가 적절하다. (B) be good at: ~을 잘하다, be good for: ~에 좋다, (C) 선수들만큼이나 '열심히' 일해야 한다고 해야 하므로 hard가 적절하다. hardly: 거의 ~ 아니다[없다]

28 most of all = first of all = above all = more than anything else: 무엇보다, ① 처음에는, ③ 결국에는

29 점프하는 것과 '춤추는 것'을 잘해야 한다.

Stories for All Time

01 동의어 관계이다. broken: 고장 난 – damaged: 손상된, precisely: 정확하게 – exactly: 정확하게

02 '무언가를 더 잘 할 수 있도록 규칙적으로 하기'는 'practice(연습, 훈련)'가 적절하다. 너 알잖아, 연습하면 숙달한다는 거.

03 ① cannot help –ing: ~하지 않을 수 없다. 나는 그녀와 사랑에 빠질 수밖에 없다. ② remember –ing: ~한 것을 기억하다. remember to: ~할 것을 기억하다 ③ dream of: ~에 대한 꿈. 그녀는 자신의 사업체를 경영하는 꿈을 실현하고자 했다. ④ on one's way to: ~로 가는 길에. 프란치스코 교황은 5일간의 일정으로 멕시코를 방문하러 가는 길이었다. ⑤ with a straight face: 정색하며, 무표정한 얼굴로. 그러고 나서 그는 정색하며 말했다. "이 탁자는 복제품입니다. 몇 파운드의 가치밖에 안 돼요."

04 reproduction: 복제품. 이 그림은 Van Gogh의 '해바라기'의 복제품이다.

05 ① saw: 톱. 금속을 자르려면 강력한 톱이 있어야 한다. ② offer: 제의, 제안. 그 제의는 이번 주말에 마감됩니다. ③ attach: 붙이다, 첨부하다. 그 파일들을 첨부하는 것을 잊지 마라. ④ charge: (요금을) 청구하다. 그들은 회원 자격으로 100달러를 청구한다. ⑤ dealer: 판매상, 중개인. 그녀의 아빠는 차 중개인에게서 트럭을 사셨다.

06 be known for: ~로 유명하다. 그녀는 인내심이 강하기로 유명하다. be known as: ~으로 알려지다. be known to: ~에게 알려지다. take out: 꺼내다. 쓰레기 내다 놓는 거 잊지 마. take on: 떠맡다

01 (1) saw   (2) attach   (3) knock   (4) antique
02 (1) reject   (2) valuable 또는 invaluable
03 (1) (p)riceless   (2) (h)ug   (3) attach   (4) furniture
04 (1) I can't help feeling sorry for the lost dog.
　 (2) The woman began to cut off my long blond hair
　 (3) Congratulations on making a dream come true.

(4) This may cause balance problems and the person may fall over frequently.

01 (1) saw: 톱. 전형적으로 길고 얇은 강철 날이 있는 나무나 재료를 자르는 도구 (2) attach: 붙이다, 첨부하다. 무언가를 다른 것에 고정하거나 결합하다 (3) knock: 두드리다. 안에 있는 사람이 밖에 누군가가 있다는 것을 알도록 손으로 문을 두드리다 (4) antique: 골동품. 높은 가치가 있는 가구나 보석 같은 오래된 물품

02 '반의어'의 관계이다. (1) add: 더하다 – subtract: 빼다, accept: 받아들이다 – reject: 거절하다 (2) hopeful: 희망이 있는 – hopeless: 절망적인, valueless: 가치 없는 – valuable: 귀중한, invaluable: 매우 귀중한

03 (1) priceless: 값을 매길 수 없는, 대단히 귀중한 (2) hug: 끌어안다, 포옹하다 (3) attach: 붙이다, 첨부하다 (4) furniture: 가구

04 (1) cannot help -ing: ~하지 않을 수 없다. help를 추가한다. (2) cut off: ~을 잘라내다. off를 추가한다. (3) congratulations on: ~에 대하여 축하하다. on을 추가한다. (4) fall over: 넘어지다. over를 추가한다.

교과서
Conversation

교과서 대화문 익히기

교과서 확인학습

Listen and Talk A 1
excited, up / elected, excited / to have, to work

Listen and Talk A 2
on / must, proud of yourself / am, best

Listen and Talk A 3
anything wrong / upset / sorry to hear, when you used it / taking, out / to look

Listen and Talk A 4
good, the matter / the flu / bad / taking medicine / feel better

Listen and Talk B
up / first prize, excited / Congratulations / up / broken, upset / bad, sorry to hear

Listen and Talk C
get, main role / excited / how much you wanted, happy for / about, get, role / disappointed / sorry to hear, Anyway / at, on, in, get, about

Listen and Talk D
while / was able to / so happy that

Talk and Play
chosen, excited / broken, upset / too bad, sorry to hear that

Review 1
excited, up / how much you wanted / to get, to see

Review 2
good, the matter / disappointed / sorry to hear that / try harder

---

시험대비 기본평가　　　　　　　　　　p.70

01 ③
02 congratulations on winning the gold medal
03 medicine　　　　　04 I'm sorry to hear that.

01 이어지는 말로 보아 무슨 일인지 묻는 What's up?이 자연스럽다.
02 'Congratulations.'만 가지고도 축하의 의미를 전달하지만 보통 뒤에 전치사 on을 써서 무엇에 대하여 축하하는지 구체적으로 덧붙인다.
03 '병을 치료하기 위해 마시거나 삼키는 물질'은 'medicine(약)'이다.
04 유감이나 안타까움을 나타내는 표현으로 'I'm sorry to hear ~.', 'That's too bad.', 'That's terrible.', 'That's really sad.' 등이 있다.

시험대비 실력평가　　　　　　　　　　p.71~72

01 ①　　　　02 ②
03 I'm sorry to hear that
04 I know how much you wanted the role.
05 ⑤　　　06 (B) - (A) - (C)　　　07 ③
08 taking　　09 ③, ⑤　　10 ①　　11 ⑤
12 ②　　　13 Because he has the flu.

---

01 무척 실망했다는 말에 '멋지다. 축하해!'라고 답하는 것은 어색하다. 'Oh, I'm sorry to hear that.' 등으로 답하는 것이 적절하다.
02 What about ~?: '~는 어떻게 됐어요?' about: ~에 관하여(전치사)
03 'I'm sorry to hear that.'은 유감이나 안타까움을 나타내는 표현이다.
04 know의 목적어로 간접의문문 'how much you wanted the role'을 쓴다.
05 Jiho는 '첫 연습은 언제인가요?'라고 묻고 있다.
06 무슨 일인지 묻는 (B)에 이어, (A)에서 1등상을 받아서 신이 난다고 답하고, (C)에서 축하하는 순서가 자연스럽다.
07 앞에서 스마트폰을 잃어버려서 기분이 안 좋다고 하고 있으므로 유감을 표시하는 ③번이 적절하다. 나머지는 모두 축하하거나 기쁨을 나타내는 말이다.
08 remember+ing: ~한 것을 기억하다, remember+to부정사: ~할 것을 기억하다
09 'I'm sorry to hear that.'과 'That's terrible.'은 모두 유감을 나타내는 표현이다.
10 (a) 감정을 나타내는 동사의 경우 감정을 유발할 때는 현재분사, 감정을 느낄 때는 과거분사를 쓰는 것이 적절하다. (b) 동사 'know'의 목적어로 쓰인 간접의문문이므로 you wanted가 적절하다. (c) happy의 원인을 나타내는 부정사 to get이 적절하다.
11 밑줄 친 문장은 유감을 나타낼 때 쓰는 표현이다.
12 주어진 문장은 유감을 나타내는 문장으로 That이 ②번 앞 문장의 'I have the flu.'를 가리키므로 ②번이 적절하다.
13 인호는 '독감에 걸렸어.'라고 하고 있다.

서술형 시험대비　　　　　　　　　　p.73

01 (D) → (C) → (A) → (B)
02 I'm so happy for you.
03 He will visit the club acting room at 2 p.m. on September 20th.
04 The writer lost his or her dog.
05 I was so happy that I hugged her tightly.
06 role
07 I didn't get a role in the school play.

---

01 수미에 관한 질문에 이어서, (D)에서 실망했다고 답하고, (C)에서 그에 대한 유감을 나타내고 이어서 첫 연습은 언제인지 묻고, (A)에서 (C)의 질문에 대해 답하고, (B)에서 there가 (A)의 the acting club room을 가리키므로 (A) 다음에 (B)가 나오는 순서가 적절하다.

13

02 be happy for: ~ 때문에 기쁘다. 전치사 for가 이유를 나타내고 있다.

03 시간 앞에는 전치사 at을 쓰고, 날짜 앞에는 전치사 on을 쓴다.

04 첫 문장에서 'Last summer, I lost my dog, Bomi.'라고 하고 있다.

05 so ~ that ...: 너무 ~해서 …하다

06 '배우나 가수가 영화, 연극 또는 오페라에서 연기할 수 있는 등장인물의 하나'를 가리키는 말은 'role(역할)'이다.

07 앞에서 수미가 '학교 연극에서 역할을 맡지 못했어.'라고 한 말에 대해 유감을 나타내는 말로 여기서 that은 '학교 연극에서 역할을 맡지 못한 것'이다.

교과서 Grammar

p.74~75

핵심 Check

1 (1) had　(2) met

2 (1) This candy is what I wanted to eat.

(2) She liked what her husband brought home.

시험대비 기본평가

p.76

01 ⑤

02 (1) which → what

(2) what → that, 또는 All what → What

(3) That → What

03 ③　　　　　　　　　　　　04 what

01 부사절의 시제가 과거이고, my sister가 잠자리에 든 것은 그 이전에 일어난 일이므로 과거완료시제를 쓴다.

02 (1) 전치사 at의 목적어와 동사 showed의 목적어 두 개의 명사가 필요한 자리이므로 관계대명사 what을 쓴다. (2) 선행사 all 뒤에는 관계대명사 that을 쓴다. All을 삭제하는 것도 어법상 적절하다. (3) 내용상 '학생들이 가장 좋아한 것'이라는 의미이므로, What이 적절하다.

03 ① until now가 있으므로 현재완료시제를 써야 한다. had lived → have lived ② 파일을 찾아낸 것이 나중의 시제이므로 과거형으로 쓴다. had found → found ④ When은 '시점'을 묻는 의문사이므로 완료시제와 함께 쓸 수 없다. ⑤ 부모님이 도착한 시점이 과거시제이므로 그 전에 Singapore로 간 것은 과거완료시제를 써야 한다. has left → had left

04 선행사인 the things와 관계대명사 that을 한 단어로 바꾸려면, 선행사를 포함하는 관계대명사 what을 쓰는 것이 적절하다.

시험대비 실력평가

p.77~79

01 ⑤　　　02 ④　　　03 ②　　　04 ④

05 has left → had left 또는 left　　　06 ③

07 ⑤　　　08 ④　　　09 ①　　　10 ③

11 ①　　　12 ⑤　　　13 ②

14 네 번째 / 일곱 번째

15 had been playing, four　　16 what, was

17 ⓐ, ⓑ, ⓒ, ⓔ, ⓖ

18 told me to write down one good thing that had happened recently

01 드론이 고장 난 것은 과거 시점 이전에 발생한 일이다. has broken → had broken

02 두 문장을 합친 의문문이므로, 앞 문장의 보어와 뒤 문장에서의 목적어 역할을 하는 명사 두 개가 필요한데, 이 조건을 충족시키는 것은 관계대명사 what이다.

03 ② 오답률이 비교적 높은 고난도 문제로서 정답을 평서문으로 바꿔보면 what이 옳게 쓰였다는 것을 쉽게 이해할 수 있다. This hat is what he is looking for. ① 선행사가 있다. what → that[which] ③ 내용상 접속사가 필요하다. what → that ④ 선행사가 있다. what → which[that] ⑤ '그 소녀가 그에게 거짓말을 했다는 것은 놀랍지 않았다.'라는 내용이다. 접속사가 필요하다. What → That

04 ① 수학 선생님이 시험을 끝내라고 요구한 것이므로 had finished → (should) finish ② Ann과 Kate가 그들이 그 도시로 이주하기 전에 살았다는 문장이므로 Ann and Kate had lived in the city before they moved there.가 옳은 문장이다. ③ had read → has read ⑤ had not eaten → has not eaten

05 과거 특정 시점 이전에 발생한 일은 과거완료시제이다. 접속사 after가 있어서 전후 관계가 명확할 경우 과거시제로 쓸 수도 있다.

06 첫 문장의 빈칸은 'Mr. Boggis가 원했던 것'으로서 선행사를 포함한 관계대명사 what이 적절하고, 두 번째 문장에는 the table이 선행사로 있으므로, 관계대명사 which 또는 that이 들어가야 한다.

07 선행사를 포함하는 관계대명사 what을 선행사 the song 뒤에 쓸 수 없다. which나 that으로 고치는 것이 적절하다.

08 ④ '연출자가 무대 위에서 그들에게 말했던 것이 그들이 계속 동기가 부여되도록 했다.' Which → What

09 <보기>의 had solved는 과거완료시제 중 '완료' 용법으로 쓰였다. ②, ③, ④는 '계속' ⑤는 '경험' 용법이다.

10 관계대명사 what과 의문대명사 what의 문장 구조는 거의 동일하다. 구분의 기준은 해석으로서 관계대명사는 '~하는 것'으로, 의문대명사는 '무엇(이을) ~지'로 한다. ③ 그 기자는 그 배

우에게 '무엇을 계획 중인지' 물어보았다.

11 관계대명사 what과 의문대명사 what을 구분하는 문제이다. 명백하게 '무엇이(을) ~하는지'로 해석되면 의문사이다. ① 내 친구들 모두가 Tiffany가 선물로 나에게 무엇을 줬는지 궁금해 했다.

12 ① which → that[in which] 또는 which 생략 ② which → why[that] ③ what → (the place) where ④ what → which[that] 또는 the thing 생략

13 ① has → had ③ had killed → has killed 또는 killed ④ had been given → had given ⑤ has → had

14 Pay attention to what the teacher is showing.

15 과거의 특정 시점을 기준으로 그 전에 시작된 일이 과거 시점까지 진행되고 있을 때, 과거완료진행시제로 표현한다. 동사는 had been playing이 적절하고, 기간(~ 동안)을 나타내는 전치사 for 뒤에, 2년 전을 기준으로 연주 경력이 총 몇 년인지 유의하도록 한다.

16 과거의 그녀: what she was, 과거의 재산: what she had, 현재의 그녀: what she is, 현재의 재산: what she has

17 ⓐ The thing → The thing that[which] 또는 What ⓑ what → which[that] ⓒ which → what ⓔ That → What ⓖ that → what *participant: 참가자

18 과거완료시제를 활용하는 문제이다. '최근에 일어났던 좋은 일 하나'는 'one good thing that had happened recently'로 표현한다.

서술형 시험대비
p.80~81

01 (1) Irene believed what the professor explained.
(2) What was discussed in the meeting was boring.
(3) Mom bought what were much cheaper than I thought.

02 (1) the thief had broken into the house
(2) the furniture whose value people had not realized
(3) him where he had got the furniture
(4) found Sunny had fed the cat

03 to sell the table, Rummins had not known its value

04 (1) What Minho saw at the museum were world-famous paintings.
(2) Jisu was surprised at what her mother had bought for her birthday.

---

(3) When Grandma came back, we had already eaten all the cookies.
(4) Rachel found Harry had already washed the dishes and had finished his meal.

05 (1) Sean didn't recognize Janet as he hadn't met her before.
(2) Please show us what you put in your bag.
(3) That the doctor asked me to help the patient was not surprising.
(4) I don't believe what you told me.
(5) Sue was shocked that somebody had stolen her laptop during the lunchtime.

06 (1) What people believed in the past is not believed today.
(2) That is far different from what Brian has been expecting.
(3) That she met Chris yesterday is true.
(4) Martin succeeded in business, and what was better, he was engaged to his girl friend.

---

01 (1) Irene은 그 교수님이 설명한 것을 믿었다. (2) 회의에서 논의된 것은 지루했다. (3) 엄마는 내 생각보다 훨씬 싼 것들을 구매했다. 관계대명사 what은 문맥에 따라 단/복수 취급에 유의해야 한다.

02 과거의 특정 시점 이전에 일어난 일은 '과거완료시제'로 사용한다. *break into: 침입하다

03 과거의 어느 특정 시점을 기준으로 그 전에 시작된 동작이나 상태를 과거완료시제로 표현한다. Mr. Boggis가 테이블을 팔라고 요구한 것은 과거시제이고, 그 때까지 Rummins는 그 가치를 알지 못한 것이므로 'had not known'이 적절하다.

04 (1), (2) 관계대명사 what을 활용한다. (3), (4) 과거완료시제를 활용한다.

05 (1) 'Sean이 Janet을 전에 만난 적이 없기 때문에, 그녀를 알아보지 못했다'는 문장이다. 기준이 과거시제이므로 과거완료시제는 종속절에 나타나는 것이 내용상 알맞다. (2) 우리에게 '당신이 가방에 넣은 것'을 보여 달라는 문장이므로 접속사 that을 관계대명사 what으로 바꾼다. (3) What 뒤에는 불완전한 절의 구조가 나온다. '의사가 나에게 환자를 도와달라고 요청한 것'은 완전한 절의 구조이므로, 주어 역할을 하는 명사절을 이끄는 접속사 that이 적절하다. (4) believe의 목적어와 told me의 목적어 두 개의 역할을 할 수 있는 what이 적절하다. (5) Sue가 충격을 받은 과거시제를 기준으로 누군가가 노트북을 훔쳐간 것은 과거완료시제가 적절하다.

06 (1) That → What (2) which → what (3) What → That (4) that → what *what was better: 더 좋은 것은

확인문제 p.82

1 T 2 F 3 T 4 F 5 T 6 F

확인문제 p.83

1 T 2 F 3 T 4 F 5 T 6 F

확인문제 p.84

1 T 2 F 3 T 4 F 5 T 6 F

교과서 확인학습 A p.85~87

01 Lucky
02 an antique furniture dealer
03 at a low price, at a high price
04 where he had got   05 simple
06 every Sunday   07 a furniture dealer
08 how valuable their things were, took advantage of
09 very cheaply   10 another Sunday
11 At a house   12 One, the other
13 old furniture   14 any
15 don't   16 take a look
17 Sure   18 there was nothing
19 moved to   20 there it was
21 a priceless piece of 22 so, that
23 wrong   24 nothing
25 with a straight face 26 It's worth
27 may buy   28 are broken
29 attach them to mine   30 How much
31 afraid   32 a reproduction
33 So   34 pounds
35 It's worth   36 How about
37 Make it   38 final offer
39 yours   40 go in
41 to bring
42 On his way, couldn't help smiling
43 what, of   44 couldn't believe
45 what if   46 pay you
47 had an idea   48 What he wants
49 cut the legs off   50 Great idea
51 took out   52 had been cut off
53 a favor   54 charge, for
55 so, that

교과서 확인학습 B p.88~90

1 One Lucky Sunday
2 Cyril Boggis was an antique furniture dealer in London.
3 He was known for buying good things at a low price and then selling them at a high price.
4 People asked him where he had got the furniture, but he just said, "It's a secret."
5 Mr. Boggis' secret was simple.
6 He went to small towns every Sunday and knocked on doors.
7 He told people that he was a furniture dealer.
8 People didn't know how valuable their things were, so Mr. Boggis took advantage of them.
9 He was able to buy things very cheaply
10 Now it was another Sunday, and Mr. Boggis was in a small town again.
11 At a house he visited, he met two men.
12 One was Rummins, the owner, and the other was his son Bert.
13 "I buy old furniture.
14 Do you have any?" asked Mr. Boggis.
15 "No, I don't," said Rummins.
16 "Can I just take a look?" asked Mr. Boggis.
17 "Sure. Please come in," said Rummins.
18 Mr. Boggis first went to the kitchen, and there was nothing.
19 He then moved to the living room.
20 And there it was!
21 A table which was a priceless piece of eighteenth-century English furniture.
22 He was so excited that he almost fell over.
23 "What's wrong?" Bert asked.
24 "Oh, nothing. Nothing at all," Mr. Boggis lied.
25 He then said with a straight face, "This table is a reproduction
26 It's worth only a few pounds."
27 He then added, "Hmm, I think I may buy it.
28 The legs of my table at home are broken.
29 I can cut off the legs of your table and attach them to mine."
30 "How much?" Rummins asked.
31 "Not much, I'm afraid
32 This is just a reproduction," said Mr. Boggis
33 "So how much?
34 "Ten pounds."
35 "Ten? It's worth more than that."
36 "How about fifteen?"

37 "Make it fifty."

38 "Well, thirty. This is my final offer."

39 "OK, it's yours, but how are you going to take it?

40 This thing will not go in a car!"

41 "We'll see," Mr. Boggis said and went out to bring his car.

42 On his way to the car, Mr. Boggis couldn't help smiling.

43 The table was what every dealer dreamed of.

44 He couldn't believe his luck.

45 "Dad, what if this thing doesn't go in his car?

46 He might not pay you," said Bert.

47 Rummins then had an idea.

48 "What he wants is only the legs.

49 Let's cut the legs off for him," said Rummins.

50 "Great idea!" said Bert.

51 Bert then took out a saw and began to cut off the legs.

52 When Mr. Boggis came back, the legs had been cut off.

53 "Don't worry, this was a favor.

54 I won't charge you for this," said Rummins

55 Mr. Boggis was so shocked that he couldn't say anything.

시험대비 실력평가

p.91~95

01 ①, ②, ④ 02 ④ 03 ②, ⑤ 04 ③
05 (A) good things (B) a low price
06 ② 07 ④ 08 ②
09 what if this thing doesn't go in his car?
10 People asked him where he had got the furniture
11 expensively → cheaply 12 ④
13 (A) are (B) yours (C) what 14 ②
15 ④ 16 ② 17 ②, ③, ⑤
18 ④ 19 ①, ⑤
20 a table which was a priceless piece of eighteenth-century English furniture
21 lay → lied
22 The table was what every dealer dreamed of
23 ② 24 ③ 25 ⑤

01 ① invaluable: 값을 헤아릴 수 없는, 매우 귀중한, ② priceless: 값을 매길 수 없는, 대단히 귀중한, ③ valueless: 가치 없는, ④ precious: 귀중한, ⑤ worthless: 가치 없는, 보잘 것 없는, 무익한

02 이 글은 '고가구 판매상인 Boggis 씨가 Rummins의 거실에

있는 탁자가 18세기 영국 가구인 매우 귀중한 탁자라는 것을 알아차렸음에도 불구하고 그 탁자를 복제품이라고 거짓말을 하면서 몇 파운드의 가치밖에 안 된다'고 말하는 내용의 글이므로, 주제로는 ④번 '더 큰 수익을 얻기 위한 가구 판매상의 거짓말'이 적절하다.

03 Boggis 씨는 Rummins의 거실에 있는 탁자가 18세기 영국 가구인 매우 귀중한 탁자라는 것을 알아차렸음에도 불구하고 몇 파운드의 가치밖에 안 되는 복제품이라고 거짓말을 한 것으로 보아 '교활한' 그리고 '부정직한' 성격이라고 하는 것이 적절하다. ① 진실된, 진정한, ② 교활한, ③ 정직한, 솔직한, ④ 솔직한, 숨김없는

04 주어진 문장의 Mr. Boggis' secret에 주목한다. ③번 앞 문장의 a secret을 받고 있으므로 ③번이 적절하다.

05 Cyril Boggis가 '낮은 가격'에 산 '좋은 물건들'을 가리킨다.

06 ② 사람들은 Boggis 씨에게 어디서 가구를 구했는지 물어봤지만, 그는 "그건 비밀이에요."라고만 말했다. ① deal in: 사고팔다, ③ on Sundays = every Sunday

07 ④는 Rummins를 가리키고, 나머지는 다 Boggis 씨를 가리킨다.

08 ⓐ와 ①, ④: 부사적 용법, ②, ⑤: 명사적 용법, ③: 형용사적 용법

09 what if ~?: ~면 어쩌지, ~라면 어떻게 될까?

10 사람들이 물어본 시점보다 가구를 산 시점이 앞서 있으므로, 과거완료시제인 had got으로 쓰는 것이 적절하다.

11 Boggis 씨는 사람들을 이용해서 물건들을 매우 '싸게' 살 수 있었다고 하는 것이 적절하다.

12 Boggis 씨가 얼마나 오래 그의 일을 했는지는 대답할 수 없다. ① He was an antique furniture dealer. ② Yes, it was. profitable: 수익성이 있는, ③ No, he didn't. ⑤ No, they didn't.

13 (A) 주어가 The legs이므로 'are'가 적절하다. (B) 30파운드에 팔겠다고 동의한 다음이니까, '그러죠, 이제 당신 겁니다.'라고 해야 하므로 yours가 적절하다. (C) 선행사가 없으므로 the thing which를 나타내는 관계대명사 what(~인 것, ~하는 것)이 적절하다.

14 mine은 my table을 의미한다.

15 이 글은 'Boggis 씨가 Rummins와 Bert를 속여 싼 값으로 귀한 탁자를 구입하려다 낭패를 당하는' 내용의 글이므로, 제목으로는 ④번 '제 꾀에 넘어 간 남자'가 적절하다. have something undone by one's own trick: 제 꾀에 (제가) 넘어가다

16 ⓐ at a low[high] price: 낮은[높은] 가격에, ⓑ knock on[at] the door: 문을 (똑똑) 두드리다

17 (A)의 selling: 전치사 for 다음에 동명사 buying과 selling이 연결되었다. (A)와 ②, ③, ⑤: 동명사, ①, ④: 현재분사

18 이 글은 '자신들의 물건들이 얼마나 값진 것인지를 모르는 사람

17

들을 이용하여 Boggis 씨가 사업에서 수익을 얻는 것'에 관한 글이므로, 제목으로는 ④번 'Boggis 씨의 수익성이 있는 사업의 비밀'이 적절하다.

19 have[take] a look: 한 번 슬쩍 보다

20 '18세기 영국 가구인 매우 귀중한 탁자'를 가리킨다.

21 lie-lay-lain: 누워 있다, 눕다, lie-lied-lied: 거짓말하다, 고가구 판매상인 Boggis 씨는 Rummins의 거실에 있는 탁자를 복제품이라고 '거짓말을 했다'고 하는 것이 적절하다.

22 what은 관계대명사로 쓰여 '~인 것, ~하는 것'이라는 뜻이다. 관계대명사 what에는 선행사가 포함되어 있으며 the thing that과 같은 의미로 쓰인다.

23 ⓑ와 ②: (요금, 값을) 청구하다, ① 장전하다, powder: 화약, ③ 책임, 담당(명사), ④ (의무·책임 따위를) ~에 지우다, ⑤ 요금, 대금(명사)

24 이 글은 'Boggis 씨가 모든 판매상이 꿈꾸는 탁자를 구입하게 된 자신의 운에 기뻐하다가, "Boggis 씨가 원하는 건 오직 다리뿐이야."라고 믿고 있던 Rummins와 Bert가 탁자의 다리를 잘라버린 것을 보고 충격을 받게 되는' 내용의 글이므로, 어울리는 속담으로는 ③번 '(욕심 부려) 다 잡으려다가는 몽땅 놓친다.(너무 욕심을 부리면 아무것도 얻지 못한다)'가 적절하다. ① 뛰기 전에 잘 봐라.(유비무환), ② 한 푼을 아끼면 한 푼을 번다. ④ 과감히 하지 않으면 아무것도 얻지 못한다. ⑤ 부전자전

25 전반부의 'He couldn't believe his luck.'을 통해 'delighted(아주 기뻐[즐거워]하는)'를, 마지막 부분의 'Mr. Boggis was so shocked that he couldn't say anything.'를 통해 'disappointed(실망한)'를 찾을 수 있다. ① upset: 속상한, frustrated 좌절감을 느끼는, 불만스러워 하는, ② nervous: 초조한, ③ bored: 지루한

서술형 시험대비   p.96~97

01 (A) for   (B) low   (C) high
02 people   03 (A) cheaply   (B) valuable
04 He was so excited that he almost fell over.
05 reproduction
06 (A) only a few   (B) value
07 My table
08 (1) couldn't but   (2) had no choice but
09 (1) happen   (2) do   10 had been cut off
11 too, to   12 Because the legs had been cut off.

01 (A) 그는 좋은 물건을 낮은 가격에 사서 높은 가격에 파는 것으로 '유명했다'고 해야 하므로 for가 적절하다. be known for: ~으로 유명하다, be known by: ~에 의해 알 수 있다, (B)와 (C): '낮은 가격'에 사서 '높은 가격'에 파는 것으로 유명했다고 해야 하므로, (B)에는 low, (C)에는 high가 적절하다. 그리고

price를 수식할 때는, 일반적으로 'low'와 'high'를 사용하는 것이 적절하다.

02 Boggis 씨가 방문한 '사람들'을 가리킨다.

03 take advantage of something/somebody: ~을 이용하다 (make use of somebody/something in a way that is unfair or dishonest), Boggis 씨는 자신들의 물건들이 얼마나 '값진' 것인지 모르는 사람들을 부정직한 방식으로 이용함으로써 매우 '싸게' 좋은 물건을 살 수 있었다.

04 so＋형용사＋that＋주어＋동사: 매우 ~해서 …하다

05 reproduction (예술 작품의) 복제품, 복제화, 가구나 예술 작품과 같은 것의 복제품

06 Boggis 씨는 탁자의 진정한 '가치'를 알아차렸음에도 불구하고, 그 탁자가 복제품이고 '몇 파운드'의 가치밖에 안 된다고 말했다.

07 It은 Rummins의 탁자를 가리킨다.

08 cannot help ~ing = cannot but 동사원형 = have no choice but to부정사: ~하지 않을 수 없다

09 'what if'는 'what will happen if' 또는 'what should we do if'로 바꿔 쓸 수 있다. what if ~?: ~하면 어쩌지, ~라면 어떻게 될까?

10 탁자 다리를 자른 것이 Boggis 씨가 돌아온 시점보다 앞서 일어난 일이기 때문에 과거완료시제로 쓰고, 탁자 다리는 Rummins와 Bert에 의해 잘려진 것이기 때문에 수동태로 쓰는 것이 적절하다.

11 so ~ that ... can't = too ~ to

12 다리가 잘려 있었기 때문이다.

영역별 핵심문제   p.99~104

01 ①
02 (v)aluable / (o)ffer / (f)urniture
    (1) furniture   (2) offer   (3) valuable
03 advantage
04 (A) (t)ake   (B) (t)hat   (C) (p)roud
05 (1) reproduce   (2) recycle   (3) countless
06 ④   07 ③   08 ②   09 ⑤
10 ④   11 what   12 had not known
13 (1) ⓐ (2) ⓑ (3) ⓐ (4) ⓓ (5) ⓒ (6) ⓑ (7) ⓐ
   (8) ⓓ
14 ④   15 ②   16 what   17 ③
18 (1) Her neighbors know what Sarah did five years ago.
   (2) These are not what Jinwoo has always wanted.
   (3) Tell your teacher what have bothered you.
19 (1) had cut   (2) wrote   (3) had gone
   (4) had been   (5) had hidden   (6) got

20 selling	21 As[Because]	22 ③
23 ④	24 ③	25 ②
26 ten pounds	27 Make it fifty.	
28 ③	29 ④	

01 <보기>와 ①번은 '청구하다'라는 의미로 쓰였다. <보기> 그는 비교적 비싸지 않은 수수료를 청구했다. ① 이런 종류의 작업에는 얼마를 청구하나요? ② 그의 임무는 특수한 정보를 입수하는 것이었다. ③ 그녀는 밧데리 충전하는 것을 잊어버렸어요. ④ 당신에게 이 편지를 전하도록 분부받았습니다. ⑤ 그 계산서에는 15%의 서비스료가 추가되었다.

02 (1) furniture: 가구. 의자, 침대, 탁자, 찬장 등과 같은 것들. 우리는 낡은 가구를 모두 처리했다. (2) offer: 제안, 제의. 누군가를 위해 어떤 것을 기꺼이 하겠다거나 누군가에게 무엇인가를 주겠다는 언급. 그 일자리 제안은 그저 너무 좋아서 거절할 수가 없었다. (3) valuable: 귀중한. 많은 돈의 가치가 있는. 그 책은 최근의 동향에 대해 귀중한 정보를 제공한다.

03 '어떤 것이나 기회를 잘 활용하다'라는 의미로 'take advantage of(이용하다)'가 적절하다.

04 (A) take a look: 살펴보다. 빨리 이리 와서 창 밖 좀 봐. (B) so ~ that ...: 너무 ~해서 …하다. 날씨가 너무 안 좋아져서 그들은 되돌아와야 했다. (C) be proud of ~: ~을 자랑스러워하다. 그들은 자식들이 이뤄 낸 일들이 자랑스러웠다.

05 (1), (2) 접두사 're'를 붙여 '다시, 재-'의 뜻을 첨가한 어휘이다. reproduce: 복제하다, 번식하다. 사진 복사기는 서류를 복사할 수 있다. recycle: 재활용하다. 우리는 중고품들을 재활용해야 해. (3) 접미사 'less'를 붙여 형용사가 된 어휘이다. 'less'가 붙으면 보통 '~이 없는'의 뜻이지만 몇몇 단어는 '너무 ~해서 …할 수 없는'의 의미가 첨가되기도 한다. (예: priceless: (너무 값이 나가서) 값을 매길 수 없는) countless: 셀 수 없이 많은 (너무 많아서 셀 수 없는). 밤하늘에는 셀 수 없이 많은 별들이 있습니다.

06 '무슨 문제 있니?'라는 질문에 (D)에서 독감에 걸렸다고 답하고, (B)에서 안됐다고 유감을 나타내며 병원은 가 봤느냐고 묻고, (A)에서 '그렇다'며 약을 먹고 있다고 하자, (C)에서 얼른 낫기를 바란다고 한 후, 고맙다고 하는 주어진 문장으로 이어지는 것이 적절하다.

07 ③은 얼른 나을지 의심스럽다는 내용으로 어울리지 않는다. 나머지는 모두 얼른 낫기를 바라는 내용이다.

08 'That's a shame.(그거 유감이다, 그거 아쉽다)'은 유감을 나타내는 말이므로 축하하는 'Congratulations.'나 'Good for you.' 등이 적절하다.

09 ⑤번 다음 문장에서 주어진 문장의 when에 대한 시간을 답하고 있으므로 ⑤번이 적절하다.

10 왜 수미가 원했던 역할을 맡지 못했는지는 알 수 없다.

11 Lisa는 사장이 제시한 승진에 기뻐하고 있다. 전치사 about과 동사 offer의 목적어 자리에 관계대명사 what이다.

12 James를 만난 과거 시점을 기준으로 그 이전에는 그를 몰랐으므로 과거완료시제를 쓰는 것이 적절하다.

13 (1) Bert가 그를 만나러 왔을 때, Mr. Boggis는 이미 마을을 떠났다. (2) Belinda는 Hokkaido에 올 때까지는 눈을 본 적이 없었다. (3) Mr. Boggis가 집에 도착했을 무렵, 그들은 이미 의자의 다리를 잘라냈다. (4) Sam은 지난달까지 10년째 대구에서 살아왔다. (5) 나는 누군가가 내 차의 문을 부순 것을 알았다. (6) April은 그 사업가를 전에 만난 적이 없어서 그를 알아보지 못했다. (7) 공주가 깨어났을 때, 일곱 명의 작은 남자들이 식사를 준비했다. (8) 나는 시사회가 시작되기 전에 그 배우를 거의 하루 동안 기다렸다.

14 ④ so ~that 구문이다. what → that

15 내용상 과거완료시제 문장이다. has → had

16 the thing(s)+that[which] = what

17 첫 번째 문장에서는 '그들이 찍은 사진들'이라는 선행사가 있으므로, what은 부적절하다. that 또는 which를 쓴다. 두 번째 문장에서는 식사를 하지 않은 이유이므로 과거 또는 과거완료시제가 적절하다.

18 관계대명사 what은 선행사를 포함하며, 문맥에 따라 단/복수 취급한다. (1) 그녀의 이웃들은 Sarah가 5년 전에 한 것을 알고 있다. (2) 이것들은 진우가 항상 원해 왔던 것들이 아니다. (3) 너의 선생님에게 너를 괴롭혀 온 것들을 말해라.

19 (1), (3), (4), (5) 과거의 어느 특정 시점을 기준으로 그 이전에 시작된 일은 과거완료시제로 표현한다. (2) 역사적 사실은 주절의 동사 시제와 상관없이 과거시제를 쓴다. (6) 간접의문문에서 when이 이끄는 절은 완료시제로 표현할 수 없다.

20 전치사 for의 목적어로, 동명사 buying과 병렬구문을 이루도록 selling으로 쓰는 것이 적절하다.

21 문장 중간의 so 대신에, 문장 맨 앞에 As[Because, Since]를 쓰는 것이 적절하다.

22 '그가 자신의 일로 얼마나 많은 돈을 벌었는지'는 알 수 없다. ① He was an antique furniture dealer. occupation: 직업 ② He lived in London. ④ It was that he sold his things that he bought cheaply at a high price. ⑤ He went to small towns every Sunday.

23 이 글은 '고가구 판매상인 Boggis 씨가 Rummins의 거실에 있는 탁자가 18세기 영국 가구인 매우 귀중한 탁자라는 것을 알아차렸음에도 불구하고 그 탁자를 복제품이라고 거짓말을 하면서 몇 파운드의 가치밖에 안 된다'고 말하는 내용의 글이므로, 제목으로는 ④번 '더 많은 수익을 얻기 위한 교활한 거짓말'이 적절하다.

24 ③ Boggis 씨가 18세기의 영국 가구인 매우 귀중한 탁자를 발견한 곳은 '거실'이었다.

25 선행사를 포함하는 관계대명사 what을 쓰는 것이 적절하다. What he wants: 그가 원하는 것

26 that은 10파운드를 가리킨다.

27 make: …일 거라고 생각[계산]하다, ~을 …로 정하다

28 주어진 문장의 This에 주목한다. ③번 앞 문장의 'Bert cut them off for him'을 받고 있으므로 ③번이 적절하다.

29 탁자의 실제 가격이 얼마인지는 알 수 없다. ① He was an antique furniture dealer. ② He lied to Rummins that his table was a reproduction. ③ 30 pounds. ⑤ Because Mr. Boggis said he only wanted them.

단원별 예상문제 p.105~109

01 ②　　　　02 ④　　　　03 take / take
04 (1) (k)nown　(2) (o)ffer　(3) (a)ntique (f)urniture
05 ④
06 He feels happy and proud of himself.
07 ②　　　　08 ①
09 Do you remember when you used it last?
10 ①, ④
11 (1) Korea's national soccer team enjoyed what many fans had sent.
　　(2) We ate what Mom had cooked for us.
　　(3) My daughter read what I had written.
　　(4) The store didn't have what I had always wanted to buy.
12 ②, ④
13 the legs of the table had already been cut off
14 ①, ③, ⑤, ⑥
15 (1) Before Mr. Boggis sold the good things at a high price, he had bought them at a low price.
　　(2) People asked him where he had got the furniture.
16 ④　　　　17 cut off them → cut them off
18 ②　　　　19 where he had got the furniture
20 Sundays　　21 ③　　　22 ①, ③, ④　　23 ⑤
24 ③　　　　25 ①, ④　　　26 ②

01 ②번은 명사와 동사로 서로 관련이 없는 단어이다. 나머지는 모두 접두사 re를 붙여 만들어진 단어이다. tract: 넓은 지면, 토지, retract: 취소[철회]하다. ① play: 연주하다, replay: 재생[재연]하다 ③ act: 작용하다, react: 반응하다 ④ use: 이용하다, reuse: 다시 이용하다 ⑤ view: 보다, 조사하다, review: 재검토하다, 회고하다

02 ① 그는 놀라운 결말을 쓰는 것으로 유명하다. ② 그 화재로 대단히 귀중한 골동품들이 소실되었다. ③ 그녀는 아이들이 없는 것을 기회 삼아 애들 방을 청소했다. ④ cannot help -ing: ~하지 않을 수 없다. 그는 의기소침해져서 울지 않을 수가 없다. ⑤ 나는 학교 가는 길에 Ms. Parker를 만났다.

03 • take out: 꺼내다. 객실 위에 있는 짐칸에서 짐을 꺼내세요. • take a look: 살펴보다. 지금 당장은 세부적인 사항들은 잊어버

리고 전체적인 상황을 한번 보세요.

04 (1) be known for: ~로 알려져 있다, ~로 유명하다 (2) offer: 제안[제의]하다 (3) antique: 골동품; 고대 양식의 furniture: 가구

05 Tim이 언제 학교 마라톤에서 금메달을 땄는지는 알 수 없다.

06 Tim이 'I'm very happy.'라고 했고 'You must be very proud of yourself.'라는 말에 'Yes, I am.'이라고 했다.

07 스마트폰을 잃어버렸으므로 '기분이 안 좋다'고 하는 것이 가장 적절하다. confused: 당황한; 혼란한, delighted: 아주 기뻐하는

08 ①번을 제외한 나머지는 모두 유감을 나타내는 표현이다. ①번은 상대를 칭찬할 때 쓰는 말이다.

09 remember의 목적어로 간접의문문 'when you used it last'를 쓴다.

10 ②번 문장은 내용의 인과관계상 사건의 발생 순서를 바로잡아야 한다. 'Jamie가 영화관에 도착했을 때, 영화가 (벌써) 시작되었다'는 내용이므로 The movie had begun when Jamie arrived at the theater.가 적절하다. ③ 과거 이전에 발생한 일은 과거완료시제로 표현한다. has been → had been ⑤ has overworked → had overworked

11 선행사와 그 선행사를 받는 대명사를 합쳐 관계대명사 what으로 표현하고, 문제에서 과거완료시제를 이용하라고 했으므로, 전후 관계상 앞선 내용을 과거완료로 하여 영작한다.

12 what이 관계대명사인지 의문사인지 구분하는 것은 보통 해석을 기준으로 한다. 때로, 구분이 모호한 경우도 많지만 일반적으로 의문사 what은 '무엇을[이] ~인지'로, 관계대명사 what은 '~하는 것'으로 해석한다. ① 의문사 ② 관계대명사 ③ 의문사 ④ 관계대명사 (과거에 예의 바르게 여겨지던 것이 오늘날에는 항상 그렇게 간주되는 것은 아니다.) ⑤ 의문사 (Brian은 무엇 때문에 여기 왔나?)

13 과거완료시제와 수동태 표현, 부사 already의 위치 등에 유의하여 단어를 배열한다.

14 ① 선행사가 있고, 사람이므로 what이 아닌, who 또는 that이 적절하다. ③ so ~ that ... 구문이므로 접속사 that이 적절하다. ⑤ 1964년 작가가 소설을 쓴 역사적 사실이므로 과거완료가 아닌 과거시제로 표현해야 한다. had written → wrote ⑥ 'It ~ that ...' 강조 구문이다. what을 that으로 바꾸는 것이 적절하다.

15 (1) 'Mr. Boggis가 고가에 좋은 물건들을 팔기 전에 그는 그것들을 저렴하게 구입했다.' (2) '사람들은 그에게 어디에서 그 가구를 구입했는지 물어보았다.'

16 위 글은 '독후감'이다. ① 전기, ② (특히 기계 등을 사면 따라 나오는) 설명서, ③ 수필, ⑤ (신문·잡지의) 글, 기사

17 구동사의 목적어가 인칭대명사일 경우, 목적어를 부사 앞에 쓰는 것이 적절하다.

18 사람들은 자신들의 물건들이 얼마나 값진 것인지 몰랐다고 한

말과 그는 물건들을 매우 싸게 살 수 있었다고 한 말로 미루어, Boggis 씨는 그들을 '이용했다'고 하는 것이 적절하다. ③ look on: 방관하다, ④ encourage: 격려하다, 용기를 북돋우다, ⑤ take a look: 살펴보다

19 '어디서 그가 가구를 구했는지'를 가리킨다.

20 every Sunday = on Sundays: 매주 일요일, 일요일마다

21 주어진 문장의 there와 it에 주목한다. there는 ③번 앞 문장의 the living room을 가리키고, it은 ③번 다음 문장의 A table which was a priceless piece of eighteenth-century English furniture를 가리키므로 ③번이 적절하다.

22 ⓐ와 ①, ③, ④: 동명사(목적, 용도), ②, ⑤: 현재분사(동작의 진행)

23 Rummins가 18세기 영국 탁자를 구입한 장소는 알 수 없다. ① Another Sunday. ② He met two men. ③ He first went to the kitchen. ④ A table which was a priceless piece of eighteenth-century English furniture.

24 ⓐ on one's way to ~: ~에 가는 길[도중]에, ⓑ charge A for B: B에 대해 A에게 (요금·값을) 청구하다

25 (A)와 ①, ④: 관계대명사, ②와 ⑤: 의문대명사, ③ 의문형용사

서술형 실전문제　　p.110~111

01 It will be Romeo.

02 Yes, you were. → Yes, you did

03 Because he got the main role in his school play, *Romeo and Juliet*.

04 ② Louise refused to go to the dentist as he had already felt the pain of pulling teeth.
④ The researchers found out that somebody had put the wrong data into the file.

05 ① What the students respected him for was his extensive knowledge and good judgment.
⑤ These bags are not what the clerk has wanted to buy.

06 had got[gotten]

07 People didn't know how valuable their things were

08 (A) low　(B) high

09 (A) another　(B) the other　(C) excited

10 quite a few → only a few

11 (A) lie　(B) furniture[table]

01 Carter 선생님이 '너는 우리 학교 연극 "로미오와 줄리엣"에서 로미오를 하게 될 거야.'라고 하고 있다.

02 'Yes, you got the main role in the play.'를 대동사를 이용하여 쓴 것이므로 be동사가 아닌 do동사를 이용하여 'Yes,

you did.'로 써야 한다.

03 Carter 선생님이 지호에게 '너는 우리 학교 연극 "로미오와 줄리엣"에서 로미오를 하게 될 거야.'라고 하고 있다.

04 ② Louise가 치과에 가기를 거부하는 것과 이를 뽑는 고통을 느낀 것의 전후 관계를 정리하면 'Louise는 이미 이를 뽑는 고통을 느꼈기 때문에, 치과에 가기를 거부했다.'이다. ④ 연구원들이 알아낸 것과 누군가 잘못된 자료를 파일에 입력한 것의 전후 관계를 정리하면, '연구원들은 누군가가 파일에 잘못된 자료를 입력했다는 것을 알아냈다'가 된다.

05 what은 관계대명사이므로 뒤에 불완전한 절이 온다. ①의 경우, 학생들이 그를 존경한 이유에 대한 내용이므로 전치사 for를 추가해야 한다. ⑤ them을 삭제하는 것이 적절하다.
*extensive: 폭넓은

06 사람들이 물어본 시점보다 가구를 산 시점이 더 먼저 일어난 일이므로, 과거완료시제로 쓰는 것이 적절하다.

07 People didn't know 뒤에 간접의문문의 순서로 쓰는 것이 적절하다.

08 그는 자신들의 물건들의 가치를 모르는 사람들을 이용함으로써 좋은 물건을 '낮은' 가격에 사서 그것들을 '높은' 가격에 팔았다.

09 (A) 셋 이상 중에서 '또 하나의 일요일'을 나타내므로 another가 적절하다. (B) 둘 중에서 '다른 한 명'을 나타내므로 the other가 적절하다. (C) 감정을 나타내는 동사는 감정을 느끼게 되는 경우에 과거분사를 쓰므로 excited가 적절하다.

10 이 탁자는 복제품이라서 '몇 파운드의' 가치밖에 안 된다고 해야 하므로, quite a few를 only a few로 고치는 것이 적절하다. quite a few: 상당수의, only a few: 다만, 몇 안 되는

11 Boggis 씨는 18세기 영국의 매우 귀중한 '가구[탁자]'의 진정한 가치에 대해 Bert를 속이기 위해 정색하며 '거짓말'을 했다.

창의사고력 서술형 문제　　p.112

|모범답안|

01 (1) The grasshopper regretted that he had played through the summer.
(2) Pinocchio regretted that he had lied.
(3) The rabbit regretted that he had slept during the race.
(4) Pooh regretted that he had stolen the honey from bees.

02 (A) an antique furniture dealer
(B) a reproduction　(C) the legs of the table
(D) the whole table　(E) lied
(F) the surprising ending

01 어법과 그림에 어울리는 내용으로 과거완료시제를 사용하여 적절하게 영작한다.

01 (i)nvaluable
02 cut off
03 worth
04 ④
05 (1) Don't let anyone take advantage of your weak points.
　　(2) I cannot help laughing at him.
06 ③
07 ②
08 I'm glad to hear that.
09 I'm sorry to hear that.
10 Because she didn't get a role in the school play.
11 ⑤
12 have a toothache / That's too bad. Did you see the doctor / I'm taking medicine / you feel better soon
13 (1) was able to buy what were very valuable cheaply
　　(2) What Mr. Boggis wanted was only the old vase
14 ⑤
15 what, bought
16 ③
17 ②
18 ②
19 ④
20 antique
21 Because people didn't know how valuable their things were.
22 ①, ④
23 with a straight face
24 ①
25 ④
26 ⑤
27 Bert가 탁자 다리를 자른 일

01 동의어 관계이다. exact: 정확한 – precise: 정확한, priceless: 값을 매길 수 없는 – invaluable: 매우 귀중한

02 '무엇인가를 칼이나 날카로운 도구로 자름으로써 제거하다'는 'cut off(~을 잘라내다)'가 적절하다. 바람에 나뭇가지가 잘려나갔다.

03 '특정한 가치가 있는'은 'worth(~의 가치가 있는)'가 적절하다. 이 화병은 가치가 수백 달러 된다.

04 • order: 주문하다, 지시하다. 나는 맥주 한 잔과 샌드위치를 주문했다. • reproduction: 복제품. '모나리자' 복제품인 점이 탁자 위에 있었다.

05 (1) take advantage of: ~을 이용하다 (2) cannot help -ing ~하지 않을 수 없다, ~할 수밖에 없다

06 ③번은 제안을 하는 것으로 '잘했다'라고 칭찬하는 것과는 거리가 멀다.

07 (a)와 ②: 형용사적 용법 ①, ⑤: 명사적 용법 ③, ④: 부사적 용법

08 'That's wonderful.'은 '멋지다!' 정도의 뜻으로 축하나 칭찬하는 표현이며 'I'm glad to hear that.'으로 바꿔 쓸 수 있다.

09 "That's too bad."는 '참 안됐구나.' 정도의 뜻으로 유감이나 안타까움을 나타내는 표현이며 'I'm sorry to hear that.'으로 바꿔 쓸 수 있다.

10 '무슨 일이니?'라는 질문에 수미는 '학교 연극에서 역할을 맡지 못 했어. 난 정말 실망했어.'라고 답하고 있다.

11 수미는 '다음에는 더 많이 노력할 거야.'라고 말하고 있다.

13 관계대명사 what은 선행사가 the thing인지 the things인지에 따라 뒤에 동사의 수 일치에 유의해야 한다. (1)은 복수, (2)는 단수 취급에 유의하여 문장을 완성한다.

14 (A)는 내용상 cut/had cut 모두 가능하다. (B)는 특정 시점을 가리키는 when으로 시작하므로 완료시제는 불가하고, 과거동사 met만 가능하다. (C)는 접속사 after는 내용의 전후 관계를 알 수 있으므로, 과거시제 cut과 과거완료 had cut 둘 다 가능한데, 이 세 가지 조건을 만족하는 답은 ⑤뿐이다.

15 He sold what he had bought at low prices.

16 ③ doesn't를 didn't로 고쳐서 과거완료시제와 맞추거나, had lost를 has lost로 바꿔 현재완료시제로 표현하는 것이 적절하다.

17 ⓑ what → that[which] ⓓ that → what ⓔ what → who[that] ⓕ that → what

18 ①, ③, ④, ⑤는 모두 what이 들어가면 된다. ②는 선행사가 있으므로, which 또는 that을 써야 한다.

19 ④ Bert는 늦게 일어나서, 지하철까지 뛰어야 했다. ① had come → came, were already → had already been ② recognized → had recognized, had met → met ③ had arrived → arrived, already cut → had already cut ⑤ 시제는 크게 문제가 없으나, 내용상 접속사 though가 부적절하다. Though → As[Since, Because]로 하거나, 아니면 종속절의 not을 삭제하는 것도 좋다.

20 antique: 골동품의; (귀중한) 골동품, 그것의 아름다움이나 희귀성 때문에 귀중한 도자기나 가구와 같은 오래된 물건

21 '사람들은 자신들의 물건들이 얼마나 값진 것인지 몰랐으므로' Boggis 씨가 그들을 이용하는 것이 가능했다.

22 ⓐ: 관계대명사 that[which]이 생략되어 있음, ①, ④: 관계대명사 that[which], ②, ③, ⑤: 관계부사 where

23 with a straight face: 정색하며, 무표정한 얼굴로

24 ①번 다음 문장의 내용에 주목한다. 주어진 문장의 결과에 해당하므로 ①번이 적절하다.

25 자신의 운에 기뻐한 사람은 'Boggis 씨'였다.

26 문맥상 추측을 나타내는 조동사 might가 알맞다.

27 this는 'Bert가 탁자 다리를 자른 일'을 가리킨다.

Technology in Our Lives

Lesson 7

시험대비 실력평가
p.122

01 ① 02 analyze 03 ② 04 ④
05 ③ 06 ⑤

01 동의어 관계이다. mainly: 주로 – mostly: 대개, 주로, specialist: 전문가 – expert: 전문가

02 '어떤 것을 주의 깊게 조사하다'는 'analyze(분석하다)'가 적절하다. 저는 빅데이터를 분석하고 그것으로부터 의미 있는 결과들을 도출할 수 있어요.

03 ① make a decision: 결정하다. 어떤 결정을 할 때 그들은 감정이 아니라 이성에 의지한다. ② just as ~: 바로 ~할 때. 우리는 바로 그 연주자들이 악기를 챙기고 있을 때 도착했다. ③ thanks to ~: ~ 덕분에, ~ 때문에. 폭풍 때 문에 모든 항공편이 취소됐다. ④ get+비교급: 점점 더 ~해지다. 전문가들은 서해가 계속해서 더 따뜻해질 것이라고 말한다. ⑤ be likely to ~: ~할 것 같다. 기차 요금은 계속 변하지 않을 것 같다.

04 communication: 의사소통, 연락. 전화는 효율적인 의사전달 수단이다.

05 ① improve: 개선하다, 향상하다. 사정이 나아질 희망이 약간 있다. ② influence: 영향을 미치다. 미디어[대중 매체]는 여론에 강력한 영향력이 있다. ③ rent: 빌리다. 우리는 한 주 동안 자동차를 한 대 빌려 그 지역을 탐사할 것이다. ④ unlock: 잠금을 풀다. 문을 열려고 했지만 열쇠가 맞지 않았다. ⑤ predict: 예측하다. 최종 결과가 어떻게 될지 예견하기는 불가능하다.

06 thanks to ~: ~ 덕분에, ~ 때문에. 이젠 모든 사람들이 그것에 대해 알아, 너 때문에 말야! be used to+동사원형: ~하는 데 사용되다. 그 테스트는 다양한 질병들을 진단하는 데 이용된다. diagnose: 진단하다

서술형 시험대비
p.123

01 (1) develop (2) database (3) identify (4) predict
02 (1) wisely (2) awful
03 (1) (c)omplex (2) (c)rime (3) (f)orecast
   (4) (i)nclude
04 (1) That test was focused on the prisoners alone.
   (2) There is a limit to the amount of pain we can bear.
   (3) More and more people are using the Internet.

(4) He'll be back on Monday, but I can't say for sure.

01 (1) develop: 발전시키다, 성장하다. 더 크고 나은, 또는 더 중요한 것으로 변화하고 성장하다 (2) database: 데이터베이스. 컴퓨터 시스템에 저장되어 있는 많은 양의 정보 (3) identify: 확인하다. 어떤 사람이 누구인지 또는 어떤 사물이 무엇인지 알아차리다 (4) predict: 예측하다. 어떤 일이 일어날 것이라고 말하다

02 (1) '형용사+ly = 부사'의 관계이다. angry: 화난 – angrily: 노하여, 성내서, wise: 현명한 – wisely: 현명하게 (2) '명사+ful = 형용사'의 관계이다. peace: 평화 – peaceful 평화로운, awe: 경외(敬畏), 두려움 – awful: 끔찍한, 지독한

03 (1) complex: 복잡한 (2) crime: 범죄 (3) forecast: 예측하다, 예보하다 (4) include: 포함하다

04 (1) focus on: ~에 초점을 맞추다. 수동태가 적절하므로 was를 추가한다. (2) the amount of: ~의 양/수량. 주어가 단수이므로 is를 추가한다. (3) more and more: 점점 더 많이, 갈수록 더. more를 추가한다. (4) for sure: 확실히, 분명히. for를 추가한다.

교과서
Conversation

핵심 Check
p.124~125

1 Could you explain how to use this machine?
2 ①

교과서 대화문 익히기

Check(√) True or False
p.126

1 F 2 T 3 T 4 F

교과서 확인학습
p.129~131

Listen and Talk A 1

tell, how to add, to / First, put, in, Second, choose, amount / Last, insert, into, simple

Listen and Talk A 2

know how to use / First / did, next / put in, take, out / Got it rent, tell, how to use / log in to / it / what / to unlock, with / appreciate

Listen and Talk B

return, know how to do / simple, insert, into, put, in / Then, take, out / appreciate / add, to, know how to do / simple, First, Second, amount / Then insert / appreciate / to buy, know how to do / simple, First, Second / Then / appreciate

Listen and Talk C

what's, for / that / tell, how to use / place, on / type, title, press / Is that all / Then, it / get / easy, isn't it / amazing

Listen and Talk D

how to use, First, Then, Last, out of

Talk and Play

know how to make / First, put / Then, pour / Last, take, out / got it, appreciate

Review 1

how to plant / cut, into, pieces, dig, in / put, in, cover, with / sounds simple

Review 2

tell, how to use / put, on, the number of / what / appreciate

---

시험대비 기본평가   p.132

01 ③

02 I really appreciate your help.   03 ⑤

01 'Are you explaining ~?'은 '~을 설명하는 중이니?'라는 의미로 방법이나 절차를 물 때 쓰는 표현이 아니다.

02 'I really appreciate your help.'는 상대방에게 감사를 표현할 때 사용하는 말이다.

03 (a)와 나머지는 방법이나 절차를 묻는 것이지만 ⑤번은 사용법을 알려주겠다는 것이다.

시험대비 실력평가   p.133~134

01 ①   02 ②

03 Can you tell me how to use it

04 place your library card on the robot's screen

05 ⑤   06 (B) – (A) – (C)   07 ③

08 did   09 ②, ④   10 ①   11 ③

12 ⑤   13 충전할 금액을 고른다.

---

01 방법이나 절차를 묻는 말에 '물론'이라고 답하고 '마지막으로'라며 설명을 시작하는 것은 어색하다. Last를 First로 바꾸는 것이 적절하다.

02 용도를 나타내는 전치사 for가 적절하다.

03 'Can you tell me how to use it'은 방법이나 절차를 물을 때 쓰는 표현이다.

04 place: ~에 두다, 놓다 on the screen: 화면 위에

05 그냥 안내 데스크로 가서 책을 받을 수 있고 로봇이 책을 건네준다는 말은 없다.

06 반납에 대한 순서를 설명하는 주어진 글에 이어 (B)에서 '알았다'고 답하고, (A)에서 마지막 순서를 설명하고, (C)에서 감사하는 말이 자연스럽다.

07 뒤에 나오는 대답으로 보아 방법이나 절차를 묻는 질문이 적절하다.

08 'choose the snack I want'를 대신하는 대동사이므로 did가 적절하다.

09 'It's not a big deal.'과 'It's my pleasure.'는 모두 감사 표현에 대한 응답이다.

10 (a) put A in B: A를 B에 넣다 (b) pour A in B: A를 B에 붓다 (c) take A out: A를 꺼내다

11 방법을 아느냐는 질문에 대한 답으로 이어서 First, ~. Second ~.로 순서대로 설명하고 있으므로 ③번이 적절하다.

12 밑줄 친 문장은 감사를 나타낼 때 쓰는 표현이다. appreciate: 감사하다, 감상하다

13 'Second, choose the amount of money.'라고 하고 있다.

서술형 시험대비   p.135

01 (D) → (C) → (A) → (B)   02 isn't it

03 it's a robot that[which] finds books for you

04 This conversation happens in a library.

05 from

06 (1) 기계에 돈을 넣는다.   (2) 원하는 음료를 고른다.

  (3) 기계에서 음료를 꺼낸다.

07 appreciate   08 should I do

01 방법을 묻는 질문에 이어, (D)에서 첫 번째 순서를 설명하고, (C)에서 알겠다고 답하고 이어서, (A)에서 두 번째 순서에 대해 설명하고, (B)에서 그게 다인지 묻자 그렇다고 답하는 순서가 적절하다.

02 앞에서 긍정의 be동사 is가 쓰였으므로 isn't를 쓰고 대명사 주어 it을 쓴다.

03 주격 관계대명사로 that이나 which를 쓴다. find A for B: B를 위해 A를 찾아 주다

04 이 대화는 '당신의 도서 대출 카드(library card)를 로봇의 화면 위에 놓으라'는 말로 보아 도서관이라고 할 수 있다.

14 Though having been built more than

15 ②   16 ⑤

05 'out of'는 (1) ~의 안에서 밖으로, ~의 밖으로 (2) ~ 바깥에, (3) ~ 중에(서) (4) ~에서(from) 등의 뜻이 있다.

06 First: 우선, 맨 먼저, Then: 그 다음에, 그리고 나서, Last: 마지막으로

07 '누군가에게 공손하게 감사하거나 해준 것에 대해 고맙다고 말하다'를 가리키는 말은 'appreciate(감사하다)'이다.

08 다음에 무엇을 해야 하는지 묻는 것이므로 'what should I do?'에서 should I do를 생략했다고 보는 것이 적절하다.

교과서 Grammar

핵심 Check   p.136~137

1 (1) approaching   (2) Feeling   2 ③

시험대비 기본평가   p.138

01 ④   02 ⑤   03 ③

04 (1) he was absent from school
   (2) she watched Utube videos
   (3) she felt excited
   (4) Though[Although] he is short

01 ④는 결과의 부사절을 나타내는 접속사 that이 적절하다.

02 부사절을 분사구문으로 바꿀 때, 주어가 같으면 주어를 생략하고 분사를 쓴다. ③의 완료분사구문은 종속절의 시제가 주절의 시제보다 앞설 때 써야 한다.

03 ③ 접속사 또는 전치사로서 as가 들어갈 수 없다. 내용상 '의문사+to부정사' 형태의 구조로서 how가 적절하며, 'as to'는 '~에 대한'이라는 뜻의 전치사구로, 뒤에 명사/동명사가 와야 한다.

04 분사구문은 분사를 활용하여 부사절을 부사구로 줄인 표현이다. 대개 양보, 동시동작, 이유, 시간, 조건 등의 부사절이며, 절과 구의 전환시 동사의 시제 등에 유의해야 한다. (4)는 내용상 양보이므로 Though 외에도 Although, Even though 등의 접속사가 가능하다.

시험대비 실력평가   p.139~141

01 ④   02 ②   03 ⑤   04 ④
05 ②   06 Made → Making   07 ③
08 ⑤   09 ③   10 ④   11 ④
12 Not wanting to get hurt in the football match
13 Strange as it may sound

01 ④는 전치사 as로 쓰였으며, '~로서'라는 뜻이다. 그 외에는 모두 접속사 as로 사용되었다.

02 ②는 전치사 as로 쓰였으며, '~로서'라는 뜻이다. 그 외에는 모두 접속사 as로 사용되었다.

03 'with+목적어+분사' 구문은 '목적어의 능동/수동' 여부가 중요하다. 눈이 '감겨진 것'이므로 과거분사 closed가 적절하다.

04 부사절로 영작하면, 'Though he had made many people happy, Chad died lonely.'이다. 분사구문 Having made에 분사구문의 의미를 명확하게 하기 위해 Though를 추가한 문장이 ④이다. ①의 경우, 접속사와 주어가 동시에 있는 경우에는 분사구문을 쓸 수 없음에 유의한다.

05 각 문장을 해석하면, (1) 'Jane은 거울에 비친 자신의 모습을 보았을 때 운동을 시작했다.', (2) 'David은 그가 더 높이 올라가려고 할수록 숨 쉬기가 더 힘들어지는 것을 느꼈다.', (3) '그 개는 훈련사가 보여준 대로 움직임을 따랐다.'가 된다.

06 '스포츠를 더욱 흥미진진하게 만들면서'(능동의 분사구문)이므로 Made를 Making으로 고치는 것이 적절하다.

07 ① 접속사로도 전치사로도 쓸 수 없다.(As → 삭제) ② 내용상 '의문사+to부정사'의 구조.(as → how 또는 when이나 where 등 의문부사가 적절하다.) ④ 명사절 접속사가 필요하다.(as → that) ⑤ '부사구'로 시작해서 완전한 절이 왔으므로, as는 접속사로도 전치사로도 무의미하다.(as → 삭제)

08 내용상 though의 역접 관계가 아닌, and 또는 so와 같은 순접 관계의 접속사가 적절하다.

09 주어진 문장의 as는 '~하는 것과 같이'라는 뜻으로서 '양태'를 나타낸다. 나머지는 각각 ① ~함에 따라서(비례) ② ~ 때문에(이유) ④ 이유 ⑤ ~할 때(시간) 등이다.

10 <보기>와 ④는 '양보'의 의미로 사용되었다.

11 완료분사구문과 양보 의미의 부사구가 쓰였으므로, 접속사는 Though 또는 Although를, 시제는 had come을 쓰는 것이 적절하다. '그 바이러스가 자국에서 왔음에도 불구하고, 그 중국 외교관은 한국의 늑장 대응을 비난했다.'

12 분사구문의 부정은 분사 앞에 not이나 never를 쓴다. 'As he didn't want to get hurt in the football match,'이다.

13 접속사 as의 양보 의미는 형용사를 앞에 두어 표현한다.

14 주절보다 종속절 시제가 앞서고, 수동태이므로 완료분사구문의 수동형인 'Having been p.p.'를 활용한다.

15 접속사 as의 용법이 알맞게 쓰였는지 묻고 있다. ②를 해석해 보면, '당신이 거짓말을 했기 때문에, 나는 그 어느 때보다 당신을 더 믿을 수 있었다.'가 되어 어색하다. As를 양보의 접속사 Though 또는 Although 등으로 바꾸는 것이 적절하다.

16 접속사 또는 전치사로 쓰인 as와 적절하게 어법상 어울리는지 묻는 문제이다. ①은 '언니가 하듯이 엄마에게 관심을 가지라'는

내용으로서 옳다. ②와 ③은 전치사로 쓰였고, 문제없다. ④의 'couple'은 '단/복수 취급이 가능'하며, as도 알맞게 쓰였다. ⑤의 경우, '그 장난감 가게가 막 문을 닫으려고 할 때, 우리가 도착했다.'는 내용으로 so as는 의미가 맞지 않는다. so as → just as 로 바꾸는 것이 적절하다.

서술형 시험대비 p.142~143

01 (1) Being a little tired,

(2) Finding the ring she had lost,

(3) It having rained the day before,

(4) Not having a car,

(5) 고칠 필요 없음

02 (1) While they use various methods,

(2) If you have a problem that you cannot talk to me,

(3) Though I was sick through the weekend,

(4) Because he did not want to wake the sleeping baby up,

(5) and it makes sports more exciting

(6) When she cleaned the windows of the kitchen,

03 (1) As information and communication technology develops

(2) Just as our bodies change our minds

(3) Not having any friends in her class

(4) Using various methods, experts analyze

04 (1) Did you know that health professionals can forecast a disease just as weather experts forecast the weather?

(2) Big data helps companies understand their customers' needs better, assisting them sell more products.

(3) Can you tell me how to add money to my transportation card? (how 대신 when 또는 where도 가능)

(4) Germany's national soccer team was able to improve its performance, winning the 2014 World Cup.

05 Singing to the radio music,

06 (1) Based on our survey, we chose Gyeongju.

(2) activities are the most important when choosing a field trip place

(3) Searching for some data online,

(4) As, as

01 (1) 내용상 부사구 a little은 tired를 수식하기 때문에, 분사 being 앞에 쓰지 않는다. (2) 능동이므로 Found → Finding 이 적절하다. (3) 분사구문에서의 비인칭 주어 It과 주절의 주어가 다르므로, 'It having rained'와 같이 독립분사구문 형태로

표현하는 것이 적절하다. (4) 분사구문의 부정은 Not을 분사 앞에 쓴다. *Frankly speaking:솔직히 말해서

02 문제에 쓰인 분사구문은 각각 동시동작, 조건, 양보, 이유, 병렬, 시간 등의 의미로 쓰였다. (1) 다양한 방법을 사용하여, (2) 나에게 말할 수 없는 문제가 있다면, (3) 주말 내내 아팠지만, (4) 잠자는 아기를 깨우고 싶지 않아서, (5) 그리고 스포츠를 더욱 흥미롭게 만든다. (6) 부엌 창문을 청소할 때,

03 (1), (2)는 '접속사 as'를, (3), (4)는 분사구문을 활용하는 문제이다. 의미에 맞게 단어를 배열하도록 한다.

04 (1) just if → just as (2) 내용상 as는 접속사로도 전치사로도 의미가 없으며, 생략하면 적절한 분사구문이 된다. (3) as to → how(when/where) to (4) 접속사 없이 동사 두 개가 있으므로, won을 winning으로 바꿔 분사구문을 만드는 것이 적절하다.

05 부사절의 주어와 주절의 주어가 같으므로 부사절의 접속사와 주어를 생략한다.

06 (1) 과거분사로 시작하는 분사구문이다. (2) when choosing은 분사구문 앞에 접속사를 넣어 의미를 명확하게 한 것이다. (3) 종속절과 주절의 주어가 같으므로, 접속사와 주어를 생략하고, 동사를 현재분사 형태로 전환하면 된다. (4) 접속사와 전치사 역할을 하며, 내용상 알맞은 것은 as 뿐이다.

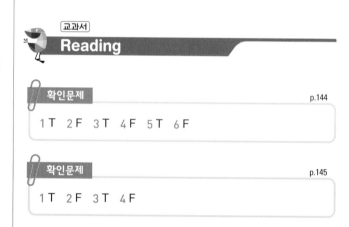
교과서 Reading

확인문제 p.144

1 T 2 F 3 T 4 F 5 T 6 F

확인문제 p.145

1 T 2 F 3 T 4 F

교과서 확인학습 A p.146~147

01 Living with

02 recommended for

03 looked interesting

04 what you liked

05 because of

06 What is

07 data sets, complex

08 As, getting much greater

09 leaves a trace

10 upload on your blog, your purchases, all part of

11 Simply collecting data

12 has to be analyzed

13 Using, draw

14 can be used

15 How

16 almost all parts

17 their customers' needs, sell more products

18 avoid heavy traffic

19 endless, interesting examples

20 Forecast

21 just as

22 thanks to

23 comes, will buy

24 search online about

25 is analyzed wisely

26 Improving Performance

27 sports fan

28 making, exciting

29 national soccer team

30 collecting, analyzing

31 how much, how long

32 With the help of

33 Prevention

34 Thanks to

35 Through, crime hot spots

36 is most likely to happen

37 further crime, predicts

38 has already changed

39 go from here

40 play, role

1 Living with Big Data

2 Have you ever visited an online bookstore and been surprised by the books that the store recommended for you?

3 Many of them looked interesting to you.

4 So how did the bookstore know what you liked?

5 This is all possible because of big data.

6 What is big data?

7 Big data is data sets that are very big and complex.

8 As information and communication technology develops, the amount of data we have is getting much greater than before.

9 This is mainly because almost everything that we do online leaves a trace.

10 For example, the photos you upload on your blog and the records of your purchases at online stores are all part of big data.

11 Simply collecting data, however, is not enough.

12 Big data has to be analyzed, and this is done by big data experts.

13 Using various methods, experts analyze big data and draw meaningful results from it.

14 These results then can be used to make decisions or to predict the future.

15 How is big data influencing our lives?

16 Big data is influencing almost all parts of our lives.

17 It helps companies understand their customers' needs better and helps them sell more products.

18 It helps people avoid heavy traffic.

19 Its uses are endless, and here are some interesting examples.

20 Disease Forecast

21 Did you know that health professionals can now forecast a disease just as weather experts forecast the weather?

22 This is possible thanks to big data.

23 For example, when the flu season comes, people will buy more flu medicine.

24 They will also search online about flu symptoms more.

25 If this kind of data is analyzed wisely, the spread of the flu can be predicted.

26 Improving Performance in Sports

27 Are you a sports fan?

28 Well, big data is improving the performance of players, making sports more exciting.

29 A famous example is Germany's national soccer team.

30 The team built a database by collecting and analyzing a huge amount of data on players.

31 For example, the data included information about how much each player ran and how long he had the ball.

32 With the help of this database, Germany's national soccer team was able to improve its performance and win the 2014 World Cup.

33 Crime Prevention

34 Thanks to big data, police can now predict crime before it happens.

35 Through the analysis of big data about the type, time and place of crime, police can make a map of crime hot spots.

36 This map identifies when and where crime is most likely to happen.

37 Police can prevent further crime by focusing on the areas and the times this map predicts.

38 Big data has already changed the world greatly.

39 So where will the big data industry go from here?

40 Nobody knows for sure, but experts agree that big data will play a more and more important role in our lives.

01 ②

02 how did the bookstore know what you liked

03 온라인 서점이 당신을 위해 추천한 책들 중에 많은 것들이 당신에게 흥미로워 보이는 것

04 ④	05 ④	06 ③	07 ④

08 will come → comes   09 ④   10 ③

11 ②   12 ③   13 ③

14 and it makes sports more exciting

15 ②   16 ②, ④   17 crime

18 (A) Through (B) further (C) agree

19 ③   20 ②, ⑤

21 how much each player ran and how long he had the ball

22 Big data is influencing almost all parts of our lives.

23 Big data

24 (1) 회사들이 소비자들이 필요로 하는 것을 더 잘 이해하도록 도와준다.
   (2) 회사들이 더 많은 상품을 팔도록 도와준다.
   (3) 사람들이 교통 체증을 피하도록 도와준다.

---

01 ⓐ와 ②: 경험 용법, ① 완료 용법, ③, ⑤: 계속 용법, ④ 결과 용법

02 know의 목적어를 간접의문문으로 써서 what you like로 쓰는 것이 적절하다.

03 'Many of the books that the online bookstore recommended for you looked interesting to you.'를 가리킨다.

04 이 글의 전반부는 '빅데이터 덕분에 경찰은 이제 범죄가 발생하기 전에 범죄를 예측할 수 있다'는 내용의 글이므로, 제목으로는 ④번 '범죄 예방'이 적절하다.

05 happen/occur/take place/arise/come about: (사건 등이) 발생하다, ④ cause: ~을 야기하다[초래하다]

06 ⓒ와 ②, ④: 완료 용법, ① 계속 용법, ③ 경험 용법, ⑤ 결과 용법

07 이 글은 '빅데이터가 우리 삶에 영향을 미치고 있는 부분들'에 대한 글이므로, 제목으로는 ④번 '빅데이터는 어떻게 우리 삶에 영향을 미치고 있는가?'가 적절하다. ② benefit: 혜택, 이득

08 when절에서는 미래의 일이라고 해도 현재시제로 쓰는 것이 적절하다.

09 '날씨 전문가가 어떻게 날씨를 예측하는지'는 대답할 수 없다. ① It is influencing almost all parts of our lives. ② Thanks to big data, they can do so. ③ Yes, they can. ⑤ If the data about people's behavior during the flu season is analyzed wisely, the spread of the flu can be predicted.

10 ③번 다음 문장의 Big data has to be analyzed에 주목한다. 주어진 문장의 내용을 보충 설명하는 것이므로 ③번이 적절하다.

11 이 글은 '빅 데이터에 대한 소개와 빅데이터의 수집과 분석 및 활용'에 대한 글이므로, 제목으로는 ②번 '빅데이터는 무엇인

가?'가 적절하다.

12 '온라인 상점'에서의 구매 기록들이 빅데이터의 일부가 된다고 했다. street stall: 노점

13 ⓐ by ~ing: ~함으로써, ⓑ With the help of ~: ~의 도움으로

14 making을 makes로 바꿔 쓰는 것이 적절하다.

15 위 글은 '데이터베이스의 도움으로 스포츠에서 경기력을 향상시키는' 내용의 글이므로, 주제로는 ②번 '데이터베이스의 도움에 의한 팀의 경기력 향상'이 적절하다.

16 빅데이터 '때문에' 경찰은 이제 범죄가 발생하기 전에 범죄를 예측할 수 있다고 하는 것이 적절하다. ① ~에도 불구하고, ③ ~라기 보다는, ⑤ ~ 대신에

17 '범죄'를 가리킨다.

18 (A) 빅데이터의 분석을 '통해서'라고 해야 하므로 Through가 적절하다. Though: 비록 ~이지만(뒤에 주어+동사), (B) '추가' 범죄라고 해야 하므로 further가 적절하다. further: 더 이상의, 추가의, farther: (공간, 시간상으로) 더 먼, (C) 전문가들은 빅데이터가 우리 삶에서 더욱더 중요한 역할을 할 것이라는 데에 '동의한다.'고 해야 하므로 agree가 적절하다. disagree: 동의하지 않다

19 ⓐ와 ②, ⑤: 현재분사, ①, ③, ④: 동명사

20 huge: 거대한, (크기·양·정도가) 막대한, ② 작은, 조그마한, ⑤ 미소한, 미세한, ① 거대한, 막대한, 엄청난, ③ 광대한, ④ 거대한

21 전치사 about의 목적어이므로 간접의문문(의문사+주어+동사)의 어순으로 쓰는 것이 적절하다.

22 almost all parts: 거의 모든 부분

23 '빅데이터'를 가리킨다.

24 'Big data is influencing almost all parts of our lives.' 뒤에 이어지는 내용을 쓰는 것이 적절하다.

🦉 서술형 시험대비
p.154~155

01 be analyzed   02 analyzing big data

03 (A) very big and complex   (B) big data experts

04 limited → endless 또는 limitless/unlimited/infinite

05 Thanks to big data.

06 If we analyze this kind of data wisely, we can predict the spread of the flu.

07 excited → exciting

08 (1) 각각의 선수들이 얼마나 많이 달렸는가?
   (2) 각각의 선수들이 얼마나 오랫동안 공을 소유했는가?

09 Germany's national soccer team

10 (A) collected   (B) analyzed

11 after → before

12 (1) 범죄가 언제, 어디에서 가장 많이 발생할 것 같은지를 알려 준다.

(2) 경찰은 이 지도가 예측하는 장소들과 시간대에 집중함으로써, 추가 범죄를 예방할 수 있다.

13 part   14 (A) analyzing   (B) crime

01 '빅데이터는 분석되어야 한다.'라고 해야 하므로 수동태로 써서 'be analyzed'로 쓰는 것이 적절하다.

02 '빅데이터를 분석한 것'을 가리킨다.

03 빅데이터는 '매우 크고 복잡한' 데이터 집합이고 '빅데이터 전문가들'은 빅데이터를 분석하고, 그것으로부터 의미 있는 결과들을 도출한다.

04 '빅데이터는 우리 삶의 거의 모든 부분에 영향을 미치고 있다.'고 했으므로, '그것(빅데이터)의 활용은 끝이 없다'고 하는 것이 적절하다.

05 '빅데이터 덕분에' 가능하다.

06 this kind of data와 the spread of the flu를 각각 목적어로 사용하여 능동태로 고치는 것이 적절하다.

07 감정을 나타내는 동사는 감정을 유발할 때 현재분사를 쓰는 것이 적절하다.

08 바로 뒤에 이어지는 내용을 쓰는 것이 적절하다.

09 '독일 국가 대표 축구팀'을 가리킨다.

10 그 팀은 데이터베이스를 구축하기 위해 선수들에 관한 엄청난 양의 데이터를 '모으고' '분석했다.'

11 빅데이터 덕분에 경찰은 이제 범죄가 발생하기 '전에' 범죄를 예측할 수 있다고 하는 것이 적절하다.

12 바로 뒤에 이어지는 내용을 쓰는 것이 적절하다.

13 play a role = play a part: 역할을 맡다, 한몫을 하다

14 '범죄'의 유형, 시간 및 장소에 관한 빅데이터를 '분석'함으로써, 경찰은 범죄 다발 지역의 지도를 만들 수 있다.

영역별 핵심문제   p.157~161

01 ①

02 (s)pread / (i)ndustry / (1) spread   (2) industry

03 amount

04 (A) (u)sed   (B) (l)ikely   (C) (h)elped(helps)

05 (1) colorful   (2) useful   (3) endlessly

06 Do you know how to make tea?

07 ③   08 ②   09 ③   10 ④

11 ⑤   12 ③   13 ③   14 ④

15 (1) to eat more as she ate

   (2) insects were caught as the spider

16 ②   17 trace   18 ①, ③, ④

19 health professionals can now forecast a disease just as weather experts forecast the weather

20 ④   21 ⑤   22 ②   23 ④

01 ①번은 '동일시하다'라는 의미로 쓰였지만 <보기>와 나머지는 모두 '알아보다'라는 의미로 쓰였다. <보기> 이 지도는 범죄가 언제, 어디에서 가장 많이 발생할 것 같은지를 알려 준다. ① 부를 행복과 동일시해서는 안 된다. ② 그녀는 자신을 공격한 범인을 알아볼 수 있었다. ③ 체포된 사람들 중 많은 이들이 자신의 신분을 밝히기를 거부했다. ④ 그들은 각기 구별되는 냄새로 구성원을 알아봅니다. ⑤ 이 중에서 당신 우산을 알아볼 수 있습니까?

02 (1) spread: 확산, 전파. 어떤 것이 더 큰 지역이나 더 많은 수의 사람들에게 영향을 주도록 성장하거나 발전하는 것 / 우리는 그 질병의 확산을 둔화시키게 되기를 바라고 있습니다. (2) industry: 산업. 특별한 종류의 상업적인 기업에 종사하는 사람들 또는 회사들 / 그의 소설들은 영화 산업을 위한 풍성한 자료의 원천이다.

03 '어떤 것의 이것은 얼마나 있는지 또는 얼마나 갖고 있거나 필요한지이다.'라는 의미로 'amount(양)'가 적절하다.

04 (A) be used to+동사원형: ~하는 데 이용되다. 이 지역에서는 소가 달구지를 끄는 데 이용된다. (B) be likely to: ~할 것 같다. 오늘은 곳에 따라 비가 오겠습니다. (C) help+A(목적어)+동사원형: A(목적어)가 ~하도록 돕다, 하게 하다. 목적격보어로 동사원형이 나왔으므로 사역동사나 준사역동사 help가 나와야 한다. 그는 그녀가 공부에만 전념할 수 있게 도와주었다.

05 (1), (2) 접미사 'ful'을 붙여 형용사가 된 어휘이다. colorful: 형형색색의. 그 정원은 형형색색의 꽃들로 가득 차 있었다. useful: 유용한, 쓸모 있는. 그는 유용한 충고를 좀 해 주었다. (3) 접미사 'ly'를 붙여 '부사'가 된 어휘이다. endlessly: 무한히, 영원히. 그녀는 자기 문제에 대해 끝도 없이 얘기를 한다.

06 뒤에 이어지는 내용으로 보아 차를 만드는 방법을 묻는 질문이 적절하다.

07 '우선 컵에 티백을 넣어'라는 말에 이어 (D)에서 알겠다고 반응하고, (A)에서 Then(그런 후)으로 이어서 설명하고, (C)에서 '그러고 나서는?'이라고 묻자, (B)에서 '마지막으로 3분 후에 티백을 꺼내.'라고 한 후, 알겠다며 고맙다고 하는 주어진 문장으로 이어지는 것이 적절하다.

08 방법을 묻고 있는 질문에 '고맙다'고 답하는 것은 어색하다. Sure. 정도가 적절하다.

09 ③번 다음 문장의 So에 주목한다. 주어진 문장의 결과를 이끄는 내용이 나오고 있으므로 ③번이 적절하다.

10 로봇이 어떻게 책을 찾아서 안내 데스크로 가져다주는지는 알 수 없다.

11 분사구문의 부정은 분사 앞에 not을 쓴다. 접속사를 쓸 경우, 접속사 뒤에 주어가 오면 분사구문은 쓸 수 없다.

12 주어진 문장의 접속사 As는 '~할 때, ~하는 동안'의 의미로서 '시간'을 나타낸다. ③을 제외한 나머지는 각기 ① '양태-당신이 바라는 대로' ② '비례-날씨가 더욱 더 더워지면서' ④ '비교-그

13 주어진 문장의 접속사 As는 '이유'로 사용되었다. ③은 '~함에 따라서'로 해석되어, '비례'의 의미이다.

14 주어진 문장의 접속사 as는 '~하듯이, ~하는 것처럼'으로 해석되어 '양태'로 사용되었다. ④는 '~이기 때문에'로 해석되어, '이유'로 쓰였다.

15 접속사 as를 활용하는 문장이다. (1) '그녀는 피자 한 판을 다 먹었기 때문에 배가 너무 불러 더 먹을 수가 없었다.' (2) '거미가 계획한 대로 곤충 몇 마리가 잡혔다.'

16 ⓐ on your blog: 블로그에, ⓑ draw A from B: B로부터 A를 끌어내다

17 trace: 흔적, 어떤 것이 발생했거나 존재했다는 신호

18 (A)와 ①, ③, ④: 현재분사, ②, ⑤: 동명사

19 '날씨 전문가가 날씨를 예측하는 것과 같이 건강 전문가들이 현재 질병을 예측할 수 있다는 것'을 가리킨다.

20 이 글은 '빅데이터가 어떻게 우리 삶에 영향을 미치고 있는지'에 관한 글이므로, 주제로는 ④번 '빅데이터가 우리 삶에 끼치는 영향'이 적절하다.

21 건강 전문가들은 현재 질병을 '치유'할 수 있는 것이 아니라, 날씨 전문가가 날씨를 예측하는 것과 같이 현재 질병을 '예측'할 수 있다. cure: 치유하다

22 ② 십대들이 여가 시간에 가장 하고 싶어 하는 활동은 여행이지만 실제로 그들이 가장 많이 하는 활동은 TV 시청이므로, 십대들이 여가 시간에 가장 하고 싶어 하는 활동과 실제로 그들이 가장 많이 하는 활동 사이에는 큰 '차이'가 있다고 하는 것이 적절하다. gap: 차이, ① 합의, 일치, ③ 조화, 일치, ④ 정돈, 정리, ⑤ 상호 관련, 상관

23 ④ 39%의 학생들이 여가 시간에 TV를 시청하므로, 5분의 2 미만의 학생들(Less than two-fifths)이라고 하는 것이 적절하다. two-fifths: 5분의 2

단원별 예상문제
p.162~165

01 ②	02 ④	03 (1) focus (2) play
04 ⓐ into ⓑ with	05 ④	
06 ②, ⑤	07 ③	08 ④ 09 ④
10 ④	11 ①, ②	12 ② 13 ④
14 ⑤	15 ③	16 ② 17 ④

18 This map identifies when and where crime is most likely to happen.

19 They agree that big data will play a more and more important role in our lives.

20 ①   21 When[If] we look at the results

22 ⑤

01 ②번은 동의어의 관계이며 나머지는 모두 반의어의 관계이다. complex: 복잡한, complicated: 복잡한 ① include: 포함하다, exclude: 제외하다 ③ meaningful: 의미 있는, meaningless: 무의미한 ④ lock: 잠그다, unlock: 잠금을 풀다 ⑤ borrow: 빌리다, lend: 빌려주다

02 ① 그 사람들은 주로 쌀과 콩을 재배한다. ② 무슨 일이 일어날지 예견하기는 불가능하다. ③ 그가 IT 기술을 향상시키면 직장을 쉽게 구할 텐데. ④ prevention: 예방. 전통 의학에서는 예방이 중요한 역할을 한다. ⑤ 사전 구매 할인을 받고 싶어요.

03 (1) focus on: ~에 초점을 맞추다. 자신으로부터 더 멀리 있는 물체에 눈의 초점을 맞추어라. (2) play a role: 역할을 하다. 그는 서울의 매력을 전 세계에 알리는 데 중요한 역할을 할 것이다.

04 ⓐ cut A into small pieces: A를 잘게 썰다, ⓑ cover A with B: A를 B로 덮다

05 언제 소녀가 감자를 심는지는 알 수 없다.

06 'Don't mention it.(별일 아닌 걸요., 천만에요.)'은 상대방의 감사 표현에 대한 응답으로 주로 사용된다.

07 ⓐ add A to B: A를 B에 더하다[추가하다] ⓑ insert A into B: A를 B에 끼우다[삽입하다]

08 ④ 부사절로 고쳐보면, 'As there was no money left in her pockets'가 된다. 주어가 다르므로, 유도부사 there는 생략할 수 없다. 'Being no money left in her pockets → There being no money left in her pockets'가 적절하다.

09 종속절이 주절보다 앞선 시제이므로, 완료분사구문이 필요하다. 준동사의 부정은 not을 앞에 쓴다.

10 내용상 '오전에 밖은 추워서 뛰다가 거의 감기에 걸릴 뻔했다'라는 문장이다. 접속사 as의 위치에 유의한다.

11 ① '보고서를 제시간에 완성하기 위해 열심히 일하고 녹초가 되었다'는 내용이므로, 능동의 분사구문이 되어야 한다. 'Worked → Working' ② 'look'이 자동사로 쓰였으므로 수동태로 쓸 수 없다. 'Being looked → Looking'

12 ⓐ 앞의 내용의 예가 나오고 있으므로 For example이 가장 적절하다. ⓑ 앞에 나오는 내용과 상반되는 내용이 뒤에 이어지므로 however가 가장 적절하다.

13 very는 비교급을 강조할 수 없다.

14 이 글은 '빅 데이터에 대한 소개와 빅데이터의 수집과 분석 및 활용'에 관한 글이므로, 주제로는 ⑤번 '빅데이터의 수집과 분석 및 활용'이 적절하다.

15 건강 전문가들이 현재 질병을 예측할 수 있다고 했으므로, 이런 종류의 데이터를 지혜롭게 분석한다면, 독감의 확산을 '예측할 수 있다'고 하는 것이 적절하다. ① protect: 보호하다, ② improve: 개선되다, ④ produce: 생산하다, ⑤ increase: 증가하다

16 주어진 문장의 This에 주목한다. ②번 앞 문장의 내용을 받고 있으므로 ②번이 적절하다.

17 (A)와 ④: '~하는 것처럼'(접속사), 녹이 쇠를 좀먹듯이 근심은 마음을 좀먹는다. ① 때(접속사), ② 이유(접속사), ③ ~한 대로, ~인 채로(접속사), ⑤ (양보) ~이지만, ~이면서도(접속사, as 앞의 명사는 관사가 없음)

18 identify: 알아보다, 확인하다, 식별하다, be likely to: ~할 것 같다

19 전문가들은 '빅데이터가 우리 삶에서 더욱 더 중요한 역할을 할 것이라는 데에' 동의한다.

20 빅데이터 덕분에 경찰은 이제 범죄가 발생하기 전에 '범죄를 예측할 수 있다.' ③ the police: 복수 취급함. ④ change: 변하다, 변화시키다

21 접속사 When이나 If를 사용하여 바꿔 쓰는 것이 적절하다.

22 십대들이 여가 시간에 가장 하고 싶어 하는 활동을 하는 것이 어려운 이유는 알 수 없다. ① What they want to do the most is traveling. ② 34%. ③ Watching TV. ④ 39%.

서술형 실전문제　　　　　　　　p.166~167

01 1. 도서 대출 카드를 로봇의 화면 위에 놓는다.
　 2. 찾으려는 책의 제목을 입력하고 나서 ENTER 키를 누른다.
　 3. 안내 데스크로 가서 책을 받는다

02 amazed → amazing

03 The robot finds books and take them to the front desk.

04 (1) Though knowing what the teacher meant
　 (2) There being any seats left on the train
　 (3) Wanting to clean my house

05 (1) she said before, the importance of big data is growing
　 (2) As big data has already changed the world greatly,

06 It is data sets that are very big and complex.

07 Because information and communication technology develops.

08 Using various methods, experts analyze big data and draw meaningful results from it.

09 It helps them understand their customers' needs better and helps them sell more products.

10 the flu season

11 (A) almost all parts　(B) uses

01 대화의 First ~, Second ~, Then ~에 이어지는 내용을 쓰면 된다.

02 감정동사의 경우 감정을 느끼게 하면 현재분사형으로 쓰고, 감정을 느끼면 과거분사형으로 쓴다. 보통 사람이 주어인 경우 과거분사형이 나오고, 사물이 주어인 경우 현재분사형이 나온다.

03 로봇은 사람들이 찾으려는 책을 찾아 안내 데스크로 가져다준다.

04 주어진 어휘에 접속사들이 없으므로, 분사구문을 배열하는 문제이다. 각각 (1) '양보', (2) '조건', (3) '이유' 등의 부사절을 분사구문으로 만든 것이며, (2)의 경우 주절과 종속절의 주어가 다르기 때문에, 유도부사 There를 문두에 써야 한다.

05 접속사 as가 각각 (1) '양태', (2) '이유' 등의 의미로 사용된 문장들이다.

06 빅데이터는 매우 크고 복잡한 데이터 집합이다.

07 정보 통신 기술이 발달하기 때문이다.

08 Using various methods는 분사구문으로 '다양한 방법들을 사용하여'라는 의미이다.

09 그것은 회사들이 소비자들이 필요로 하는 것을 더 잘 이해하고 그들이 더 많은 상품을 팔도록 도와준다.

10 '독감 계절 동안 사람들의 행동에 관한 데이터'를 가리킨다.

11 빅데이터는 우리 삶의 '거의 모든 부분'에 영향을 미치고 있고, 빅데이터 덕분에 건강 전문가들이 현재 질병을 예측할 수 있는 것과 같이 빅데이터의 '활용'은 끝이 없다.

창의사고력 서술형 문제　　　　　　　p.168

|모범답안|

01 (1) ① As she was eating a sandwich, Jisu read a book.
　　　② Eating a sandwich, Jisu read a book.
　 (2) ① As he watered the plants, Brian danced.
　　　② Watering the plants, Brian danced.

02 (A) free time activities　(B) traveling　(C) 34%
　 (D) watching TV　(E) 39%
　 (F) what the teenagers want to do
　 (G) what they actually do

01 단어들을 적절히 조합하여 내용과 어법에 맞게 영작한 답이면 된다.

단원별 모의고사　　　　　　　　　p.169~172

01 (i)nfluence　02 avoid　03 purchase　04 ④

05 (1) To avoid spreading or catching the flu, you should keep your distance and stay home.
　 (2) The wording of questions can influence how people answer.

06 Can you explain to me how to use this application?

07 log in to the application

08 I'm really grateful to you for your help.

09 Can you tell me how to use this snack machine?

10 We have to wait for 3 minutes before we take out the tea bag.

11 ⑤ 12 ④ 13 ③ 14 ②

15 빅데이터를 분석하는 것 16 ③ 17 ④

18 experts 19 ② 20 With 21 ②

22 that big data will play a more and more important role in our lives

---

01 동의어 관계이다. spread: 확산, 전파 – expansion: 확장, 확대, affect: 영향을 미치다 – influence: 영향을 주다

02 '어떤 사람이나 사물로부터 떨어져 있다'는 'avoid(피하다)'가 적절하다. 그는 그녀를 만나는 것을 피하려고 급히 나갔다.

03 '무언가를 사는 행위; 산 물건'은 'purchase(구매(품))'가 적절하다. 구입한 물건이 마음에 들지 않으시면 전액 환불해 드립니다.

04 • recommend: 추천하다[권하다]. 좋은 호텔을 좀 추천해 주실 수 있으세요? • symptom: 증상[징후]. 그 질병의 초기 증세는 열이 나는 것. sympathy: 동정

05 (1) avoid: 피하다, spreading: 확산, catch the flu: 독감에 걸리다, keep distance: 거리를 두다 (2) influence: 영향을 주다

06 explain은 4형식으로 쓰이지 않고 'explain+to 사람+목적어' 형식으로 쓰인다.

07 log in to: ~에 접속하다. 전치사 to를 빠뜨리지 않도록 주의한다.

08 be grateful to A for B: B에 대해 A에게 감사하다

09 tell은 'tell+간접목적어+직접목적어' 형식으로 쓰는 것이 일반적이다.

10 '3분 후에 티백을 꺼내.'라고 하고 있으므로 3분을 기다렸다가 꺼내야 한다.

11 A가 B에게 감사하고 있다.

12 '전에 그녀에 대해 많이 들었다.'는 내용과, '그녀에 대해 거의 알지 못했다.'는 내용은 접속사 As로 표현하면 맞지 않는다. '양보'로 표현하는 것이 좋다. As → (Al)though 또는 Even though 가 적절하다.

13 ①, ④, ⑤는 주절과 종속절의 주어가 다르므로, 분사구문의 주어를 쓴다. ① Raining → It raining, ④ Eating → Bentley eating ⑤ Putting → You putting, ②번은 주절과 종속절의 주어가 같기 때문에, 주어를 생략해야 한다. William going → Going

14 각 부분은, '내가 전에 언급했듯이', '그의 상사를 설득하는 수단으로서', '그 여자가 나이를 먹어감에 따라' 등으로 해석할 수 있다. '양태'와 '비례'의 접속사, '자격, 도구'의 전치사로 모두 쓸 수 있는 것은 as뿐이다.

15 'to analyze big data'를 가리킨다.

16 ⓑ와 ①, ③: 부사적 용법, ②, ⑤: 명사적 용법, ④: 형용사적

용법

17 앞의 내용의 예가 나오고 있으므로 For example이 가장 적절하다. ① …임에 비하여[반하여], ② 그러므로, ③ 게다가, 더욱이

18 professional = expert: 전문가

19 이 글은 '데이터베이스의 도움으로 스포츠에서 경기력을 향상시키는' 내용의 글이므로, 제목으로는 ②번 '스포츠에서의 경기력 향상'이 적절하다.

20 with the help of: ~의 도움으로

21 주어진 문장의 This map에 주목한다. ②번 앞 문장의 a map of crime hot spots를 받고 있으므로 ②번이 적절하다.

22 play an important role: 중요한 역할을 하다

The Joseon Dynasty Through Paintings

시험대비 실력평가 p.176

01 ④　　02 behavior[behaviour]　　03 ②
04 ①　　05 ⑤　　06 ③

01 동의어 관계이다. ill: 아픈 – sick: 아픈, community 지역사회, 공동체 – society 사회

02 '사람이나 동물이 하는 것들'은 'behavior(행동)'가 적절하다. Sally의 안 좋은 행동은 우리를 짜증나게 하기 시작했다.

03 ① take a walk: 산책하다. 대나무 숲에서 산책하자. ② right: 옳은. 시험 끝나고 답 맞춰 봤어요? 이 문장에서는 '~후에 옳은지' 정도의 뜻으로 'right after'가 하나의 숙어처럼 쓰인 것이 아니다. ③ despite: ~에도 불구하고. 그녀는 안전벨트를 하고 있었는데도 불구하고 앞으로 거세게 튕겨 나갔다. ④ once upon a time 옛날 옛적에. 옛날 옛적에 한 아름다운 공주가 있었다. ⑤ in particular: 특히. 특히 그 박물관은 인상주의 작품을 많이 소장하고 있다.

04 remind ~ of …: ~에게 …을 상기시키다. 네가 그런 말을 할 때에는 네 아버지가 생각나.

05 • for example: 예를 들어. 많은 언어들에, 예를 들어 프랑스어와 이탈리아어에도 비슷한 단어가 있다. • for this reason: 이런 이유로. 이런 이유로, 전문가들은 종종 스포츠를 전쟁에 비유한다.

06 ① frozen: 얼어붙은. 우리는 한번 한밤중에 얼어붙은 연못을 건너갔다. ② object: 물건. 그가 찾은 물건은 낡았다. ③ cancel: 취소하다. 열흘 이내에 취소하면 수수료가 청구되지 않는다. ④ bend: 굽다, 구부러지다. 다리 밑의 버팀대가 휘어지기 시작하고 있었다. ⑤ respect: 존경심. 우리는 선생님들에게 항상 존경심을 표한다.

서술형 시험대비 p.177

01 (1) appear　(2) bend　(3) dynasty　(4) remind
02 (1) fascinating　(2) disappointed
03 (1) (r)eminds　(2) (s)ymbolizes　(3) (d)espite
　　(4) (b)loom
04 (1) Is there anything in particular you'd like for dinner?

(2) For this reason, Friday was considered to be a good day for weddings.
(3) The tiger is a common subject in Korean folk paintings.
(4) The reason he came to see me is as follows.

01 (1) appear: 나타나다. 보여지기 시작하다; 생기거나 쓰이게 되다 (2) bend: 굽다, 구부러지다. 어떤 곧은 것을 구부러지거나 각이 지게 만들거나 힘을 가하다 (3) dynasty: 왕조. 일가족이 나라나 지역을 통치하는 기간 (4) remind: 상기시키다. 어떤 사람에게 어떤 것을 기억하게 만들다

02 감정동사의 '동사+-ing'나 '동사+-ed' 형태의 형용사는 감정을 유발하는 경우에는 '동사+-ing' 형태를 쓰고, 감정을 느끼는 경우에는 '동사+-ed' 형태를 쓴다. (1) 그 지역의 지역사는 아주 흥미롭다. (2) 난 나 자신에게 몹시 실망했다.

03 (1) remind A of B: A에게 B를 상기시키다 (2) symbolize: 상징하다 (3) despite: ~에도 불구하고 (4) bloom: 꽃을 피우다, 꽃이 피다

04 (1) in particular: 특히. in을 추가한다. (2) for this reason: 이런 이유로. for를 추가한다. (3) folk painting: 민화. folk를 추가한다. (4) as follows: 다음과 같이. as를 추가한다.

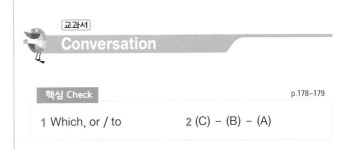

교과서 Conversation

핵심 Check p.178~179

1 Which, or / to　　　2 (C) – (B) – (A)

교과서 대화문 익히기

Check(√) True or False p.180

1 F　2 T　3 T　4 F

교과서 확인학습 p.183~185

Listen and Talk A 1

two paintings of cats / are / both, the one / prefer, seems, cuter

Which, prefer / prefer, It seems, choice / so, like, more

Which one / to choose, better / Me, too, seems, that

you're going to / nice / Which one, prefer, or / prefer, with, It seems to me

Which, prefer / prefer / prefer, prefer / Which, prefer, or / prefer / prefer, prefer, more calm / Which, or / prefer, more unique / prefer, prefer, but / Which, prefer, or / prefer, more / prefer, prefer

Which, more / prefer, that / much / so / just, also / never, before / before, sure / next to / let's watch / first

prefer, more fun to learn, prefer, like

Which, prefer / prefer / prefer, prefer

to buy / great / Which one, prefer, or / prefer

Which, prefer / prefer, the healthier choice / I heard / order

Which one, more / prefer, this / much

시험대비 기본평가　　　　　　　　　p.186

01 ③

02 It seems to me that it's more unique.　　03 ⑤

01 'I would rather(I'd rather)' 다음에는 동사가 나와야 한다. 나머지는 모두 선호를 나타내는 표현이다.

02 'It seems to me that ~'은 자신의 의견을 말할 때 쓸 수 있는 표현이다.

03 (a)와 나머지는 자신의 의견을 나타내는 것이지만, ⑤번은 상대방에 대한 기대나 희망을 나타내는 것이다.

시험대비 실력평가　　　　　　　　　p.187~188

01 ①　　　　　02 Which do you prefer　　　03 ②

04 ⑤　　　　　05 (B) - (A) - (C)　　　　06 ③

07 Which food do you prefer　　　　　　08 ④

09 ①　　　　10 ④　　　　11 ⑤　　　　12 ②, ③

---

01 I like *Batman*.은 단지 좋아한다고 말하는 것이다. 선호를 묻는 말이므로 'I prefer *Batman*.' 또는 'I like *Batman* more.'로 쓰는 것이 적절하다.

02 'Which do you prefer?'는 선호를 물을 때 쓰는 표현이다.

03 선호를 묻는 질문에 대한 답이므로 more가 적절하다.

04 'I'm very hungry.'라고 말한 것은 남자 아이이다.

05 '아름답지 않니?'라는 주어진 질문에 '그렇다'고 답하며 어떤 것이 더 좋은지를 질문하는 (B)가 이어지고, (B)의 '무엇이 더 좋은지' 묻는 질문에 '초록색 접시가 더 좋다'고 답하는 (A)가 이어진 후, (C)에서 '나도.'라고 답하며 이유를 설명하는 순서가 자연스럽다.

06 (A) 선택을 나타내는 or, (B) to me: 나에게는

07 A와 B 두 가지 중 어떤 것을 선호하는지 물을 때 prefer를 사용하여 'Which (one) do you prefer, A or B?'로 표현한다.

08 'There isn't just an exhibition.(단순히 전시회만 있는 것이 아니야.)'에 이어 'There's also a mask dance show at 4:00 and 6:00.(탈춤 공연도 4시와 6시에 있어.)'가 이어지고 여기에 Great!라고 반응하는 것이 자연스럽다.

09 (a) exhibitions와 we 사이에 관계대명사가 생략된 형태이다. go는 자동사로 목적어를 취할 수 없으므로 전치사 to가 필요하다. (b) 둘 중에서 선호를 묻고 있으므로 prefer가 적절하다. like를 쓰려면 뒤에 more나 better 등이 나와야 한다. (c) ago는 현재완료와 함께 쓰이지 않는다.

10 '공연은 어디서 해?'라는 Eric의 질문에 '전시관 옆 다솜 홀에서 해.'라고 소미가 답하고 있다.

11 자신의 의견을 말할 때 'It seems (to me) that+주어+동사 ~'로 표현할 수 있다.

12 A는 '난 스파게티를 더 좋아해.'라고 하고 있다.

서술형 시험대비　　　　　　　　　p.189

01 (D) → (C) → (A) → (B)

02 Which one do you want to see more

03 They are talking about the exhibitions.

04 such as

05 (1) It seems to the writer that science is more fun to learn.

　　(2) The writer wants to be a great inventor like Edison.

06 are

07 Because he thinks the cat in it is cuter and he also likes the bird in it.

---

01 '전에 탈춤 공연을 본 적이 없다'는 말에 이어, (D)에서 '전에 본 적이 있다며, 분명 좋아할 거'라고 언급하고, (C)에서 '공연은 어디서 하는지' 묻고, 이어서 (A)에서 '다솜 홀에서' 한다고 답하고, (B)에서 약속을 정하는 순서가 적절하다.

02 which가 의문형용사로 one을 수식해 주는 구조로 which를 쓴다.

03 그들은 전시회에 관하여 이야기하고 있다.

04 '~와 같은'의 뜻을 나타내는 like는 'such as'로 바꿔 쓸 수 있다.

05 필자는 '과학을 배우는 것이 더 즐거운 것 같아.'라고 말하며 'Edison과 같은 훌륭한 발명가가 되고 싶어서 그것을 더 좋아하기도 해.'라고 하고 있다.

06 앞에서 'Aren't they great?'이라고 물었으므로 be동사 are로 답하는 것이 적절하다.

07 '그림 속 고양이가 더 귀여운 것 같아. 새도 마음에 들어.'라고 하고 있다.

Grammar
교과서

핵심 Check
p.190~191

1 (1) of (2) for

2 (1) were you, I would hire me

(2) would not move away if he had some money

시험대비 기본평가
p.192

01 ③

02 (1) make → made (2) will → would

(3) can → could (4) will → would

03 It was not easy for Suji to ride a bike on the street.

04 ④

01 to부정사가 진주어가 되는 구문에서 to부정사의 의미상의 주어는 전치사 'for 또는 of+목적격'의 형태로 표현한다. to부정사의 '의미상의 주어'에 대해 '성격이나 태도'를 나타내는 형용사가 있을 때는 of를 쓴다.

02 문제에서 모든 문장이 가정법 문장이라고 했고, 모든 문장들의 구조는 '가정법 과거' 형태로 볼 수 있으므로, 조건절의 동사를 과거로, 주절의 조동사도 과거형으로 고치는 것이 적절하다.

03 to부정사의 의미상의 주어를 표현할 때 전치사 for를 쓴다. 일반적으로 '가주어-진주어' 구문에서 동명사 주어는 진주어로 쓰지 않으며, 문제의 조건에서 to부정사를 이용하라고 한 것에 유의한다.

04 주절에 조동사의 과거형이 나왔으므로, 가정법 문장이다. 가정법 과거에서 동사의 과거형 또는 조동사의 과거형을 사용하는 것이 적절하다.

시험대비 실력평가
p.193~195

01 ②　　　02 ③　　　03 ④　　　04 ①

05 ⑤

06 If I caught the fish, I would let my mom eat it.

07 If it had not been for Munjado, children couldn't have learned the importance of harmony.

08 It was easy for the boy to learn Chinese characters using Munjado.

09 It was impossible for the girl to catch fish without any help.

10 ①　　　11 ②　　　12 ④

13 It was careless of her to give the plants too much water

14 ③

15 If they learned Munjado, they could understand Korea more

16 ①, ③　　　17 ④

18 didn't melt → had not melted 또는
have come → come

01 wise는 사람의 성품에 관한 형용사이다. 이때 의미상의 주어는 'for+목적격'이 아니라 'of+목적격'을 쓴다. ④는 일반적인 진리이므로 과거시제로 쓰지 않아도 괜찮다.

02 가정법 과거로서 '반대' 개념의 직설법 현재 시제와 적절하게 전환된 문장은 ③번뿐이다.

03 to부정사의 의미상의 주어는 전치사 for를 사용하는데, 사람의 성격이나 태도를 나타낼 때는 of를 쓴다. ④ 'Jimmy가 선생님께 요청한 것은 무례했다'는 내용이므로 of를 써야 하며, 다른 문장들은 모두 for를 쓴다.

04 가정법 문장이라면 won't를 wouldn't로, 직설법 문장이라면 were를 is로 쓰는 것이 적절하다.

05 to부정사의 의미상의 주어를 표현할 때 알맞은 전치사를 고르는 문제이다. ⓑ, ⓕ에는 사람의 성격이나 태도에 관한 형용사가 있으므로 전치사 of를 쓰는 것이 적절하며, 나머지는 모두 for를 쓴다.

06 가정법 과거 시제의 문장이다. If절에 과거동사 caught가 오고, 주절에 조동사의 과거형 would를 쓰되, let my mom 뒤에 동사원형을 쓴다는 것에 유의하여 배열한다.

07 가정법 과거완료 표현이다. 가정법 과거시제로서 '~가 없다면'이라는 표현은 'if it were not for ~'로, 가정법 과거완료에서 '~가 없었다면'은 'if it had not been for'로 나타내는 것이 적절하고, 주절에는 '조동사 과거형+have p.p.' 형태를 사용하여, 적절하게 배열한다.

08 가주어 It과 진주어 to부정사구를 이용하고, '문자도를 사용해서 한자를 배우는 것'이므로 현재분사 using을 to부정사구의 뒤에

35

쓰는 것에 유의하여 배열한다.

09 가주어 It과 진주어 to부정사구를 이용하고, 의미상의 주어는 for를 이용해서 적절하게 배열한다.

10 ①번의 It은 비인칭 주어로서 날씨, 요일, 계절, 명암 등에 사용된다. 나머지는 모두 가주어 it으로 사용되었다.

11 ②는 시간, 요일, 날짜, 날씨, 무게, 거리, 금액, 명암 등을 표현할 때 쓰는 '비인칭 주어' it이다. 나머지는 모두 to부정사구를 진주어로 하는 '가주어-진주어' 구문으로 쓰였다.

12 가정법 과거 형태의 문장들이다. If절에는 동사의 과거형을, 주절에는 조동사의 과거형을 쓰는 것이 적절하다.

13 대화 내용상 'Jane이 식물에 물을 너무 많이 준 것이 부주의했다'라는 것이므로, of를 추가하여 알맞게 배열한다.

14 ③ 성격을 나타내는 형용사를 받을 때는 to부정사의 의미상의 주어에 of를 사용한다. '그녀가 과거에 그의 부끄러운 경험을 언급한 것은 잔인했다' ① of → for, ② for → of, ④ his → him(전치사 뒤 목적격) ⑤ of → for

15 내용상 가정법의 형태로 문장이 구성되어야 한다. have동사의 과거형과 조동사 can의 과거형을 사용하되, much의 비교급을 쓰는 것에 유의하여 영작한다.

16 '~가 없다면'이라는 가정법 표현은 'If there were no ~'로 나타내며, without[but for] 또는 'If it were not for ~'로 대체할 수 있다. 'If it were not for'는 if를 생략해서 'were it not for ~'로 표현 가능하다. 주절에는 조동사의 과거형을 쓴다.

17 옳은 문장은 ⓒ, ⓔ, ⓕ, ⓖ 4개이다. ⓐ importantly → important ⓑ for → of ⓓ using → to use

18 '얼음이 녹지 않았다면, 그 잉어들이 나오지 않았을 텐데.'라는 의미의 가정법 과거완료 문장이다. if절의 didn't melt를 hadn't melted로 고친다. 가정법 과거로 볼 경우, 종속절은 그대로 두고, 주절의 wouldn't have come을 wouldn't come으로 고치는 것도 가능하다. *carp: 잉어

서술형 시험대비
p.196~197

01 (1) ate carp, she could get well
   (2) were no letters, it would be difficult for us to deliver
   (3) necessary for his mother to recover her health
   (4) very stupid of him to try to catch fish in this cold weather

02 (1) If it were not for   (2) If there were no
   (3) Were it not for
   (4) As there are computers, we can

03 the ice had not melted, he could not have caught three carp

04 slept well enough, she could be

05 (1) dangerous for even experts to climb up the mountain covered with snow
   (2) foolish of you to attempt to kill the beast
   (3) fun for him to attend the party with his boss

06 (1) am → were[was]   (2) is → were[was]
   (3) be → have been   (4) is → were[was]
   (5) have → had

07 (1) checked → to check   (2) for → of
   (3) of → for   (4) sitting → sit   (5) let → to let

08 (1) If he were[was] rich enough, he would not go fishing in this cold weather.
   (2) If Bob were[was] in Venice, he would be happy.
   (3) If there were[was] time left, I would not cross the road at a red light.
   (4) If we had not had Munjado, it would not have been easy for children to learn Chinese characters.

01 가정법과 '가주어-진주어' 구문, to부정사의 의미상의 주어 등에 유의하여, 주어진 단어들을 적절히 배열한다.

02 '컴퓨터가 없으면, 많은 정보를 쉽게 찾을 수 없다.'는 내용으로 직설법으로 표현하면, '컴퓨터가 있어서 많은 정보를 쉽게 찾을 수 있다.'가 된다. 가정법 과거 표현, 'Without = If it were not for = Were it not for'를 기억해 두는 것이 좋다.

03 직설법으로 표현하면, '얼음이 녹았기 때문에, 그가 잉어 세 마리를 잡을 수 있었다'는 것이다. 글자 수와 어법에 맞게 가정법 과거완료시제를 활용해서 melt를 had not melted로, can을 could로 변형하고, carp는 단수와 복수가 같아 carps라고 쓰지 않는 것에 유의하여, 영작한다.

04 'Stacy가 수면을 충분히 취하지 않기 때문에 상태가 좋지 않다'라는 직설법 문장을 가정법으로 표현한 것이다. If절에 과거동사, 주절에 조동사 과거형에 유의하여 영작한다.

05 (1) '전문가들조차'를 의미상의 주어로 표현할 때는 'for even experts'로 쓴다. (2) '어리석다'는 사람의 성질을 나타내므로 전치사 of를 쓴다. (3) 의미상의 주어는 for him이다.

06 문제에서 모든 문장이 가정법이라는 전제를 주었으므로, if절의 동사를 과거시제로 고치는 것이 적절하다. 단, (3)은 yesterday로 보아 내용상 '가정법 과거완료'를 이용하는 시제이므로, 주절을 '조동사+have+p.p.'로 고치는 것이 적절하다.

07 '가주어-진주어' 구문에서 to부정사의 의미상의 주어와 그에 맞는 전치사의 활용에 유의하여, 어색한 단어를 하나만 찾아서 적절하게 고치도록 한다.

08 가정법 과거는 직설법 현재 반대, 가정법 과거완료는 직설법 과거의 반대를 나타낸다. (4)는 가정법 과거완료이다.

Reading

확인문제   p.198

1 T   2 F   3 T   4 F   5 T

확인문제   p.199

1 F   2 T   3 T   4 F

교과서 확인학습 A
p.200~201

01 into
02 on the right
03 see, character
04 see
05 is called, a type of folk painting that was popular, late
06 usually, with
07 One of, characters appears
08 represent, that were important to
09 just decorations
10 often, symbolic
11 symbolize, because of
12 goes as follows
13 Once upon a time
14 became ill, anything
15 On, would be wonderful if I could eat
16 went out to, was completely frozen
17 It, for him to catch any
18 so disappointed that, to
19 melted, out of
20 back home
21 got well
22 symbolic objects
23 in, of, in, of
24 bend
25 stays green in
26 For these reasons, came to symbolize, to
27 In the case of, but still, beautifully
28 thus, will to fight for, despite
29 much more than, to
30 reminded, of, that
31 In particular, for
32 Through it, importance, harmony in

교과서 확인학습 B
p.202~203

1 Munjado, a Window into the Joseon Dynasty
2 Look at the painting on the right.
3 Do you see the Chinese character, *hyo*(孝)?
4 Do you also see a carp, a geomungo, and a fan?
5 This kind of painting is called Munjado, and it is a type of folk painting that was popular in the late Joseon dynasty.
6 In Munjado, there is usually a Chinese character with some animals or objects.

7 One of eight Chinese characters appears in Munjado.
8 They are *hyo*(孝), *je*(悌), *chung*(忠), *sin*(信), *ye*(禮), *ui*(義), *yeom*(廉), and *chi*(恥), and they represent the values that were important to people of the Joseon dynasty.
9 The animals or objects in Munjado are not just decorations.
10 They often are symbolic.
11 For example, carp in the paintings of *hyo* symbolize respect for parents because of an old story.
12 The story goes as follows..
13 Once upon a time, a man lived with his old mother.
14 One winter, the man's mother became ill and couldn't eat anything.
15 On one very cold day, the mother said to the man, "It would be wonderful if I could eat fresh fish."
16 The man went out to the river, but it was completely frozen.
17 It was impossible for him to catch any fish.
18 The man was so disappointed that he cried out to the sky, "What should I do? Please help me."
19 Then the ice melted, and three carp suddenly came out of the water.
20 The man went back home and cooked the fish for his mother.
21 Then his mother got well.
22 There are other examples of symbolic objects in Munjado.
23 They are bamboo in the paintings of the character *chung*(忠) and lotus flowers in the paintings of *ui*(義).
24 Bamboo does not bend.
25 It stays green in all kinds of weather.
26 For these reasons, bamboo came to symbolize loyalty to the king.
27 In the case of lotus flowers, they grow in muddy ponds but still bloom beautifully.
28 They thus became a symbol of a person's will to fight for justice despite difficulties.
29 Munjado was much more than a painting to people of the Joseon dynasty.
30 It reminded them of important values that greatly influenced their behaviors and attitudes.
31 In particular, for children, Munjado was a study tool.

32 Through it, children in the Joseon dynasty could learn the importance of harmony in family and society.

01 ②

02 they represent the values that were important to people of the Joseon dynasty

03 ③   04 ④   05 ③   06 ⑤

07 ①   08 In particular   09 ④

10 ②   11 ①, ⑤

12 One of eight Chinese characters appears in Munjado.

13 ③   14 ②

15 They not only are decorations but also have symbolic meanings.

16 It stands for loyalty to the king.

17 (A) weather   (B) loyalty   (C) for

18 ①   19 ④

20 They could learn the importance of harmony in family and society.

21 Eight Chinese characters appear in Munjado.

22 (A) folk   (B) values

23 (1) some animals or objects

     (2) one of eight Chinese characters

01 ⓐ와 ②: (~의) 종류 ① (동·식물 등의) 유(類), 족(族), 종(種), ③ 성질, 본질, 특질, ④ 친절한, 상냥한, ⑤ (날씨 따위가) 쾌적한, 온화한

02 주격 관계대명사 that을 이용하고 'be important to'로 '~에게 중요하다'는 의미를 나타낸다.

03 문자도는 민화(folk painting)의 한 종류이다.

04 뒤에서 "'효' 그림 속에 있는 잉어는 옛이야기 때문에 부모님에 대한 존경심을 상징한다.'라고 하고 있으므로 '상징적'이 적절하다.

05 ⓑ와 ②, ④: 가주어, ① 비인칭 주어, ③ 인칭대명사, ⑤ 가목적어

06 out of는 '~의 안에서 밖으로, ~ 중에(서), ~에서(from)' 등의 뜻을 갖는다.

07 빈칸 ⓐ 다음에 앞 문장에 대한 결과가 이어지므로 '결과'를 이끌 수 있는 연결어구가 나오는 것이 적절하다.

08 in particular: 특히

09 '문자도에 있는 상징적인 사물의 또 다른 예가 있다.'라고 글을 시작하고 있으므로 앞에는 문자도에 있는 상징적인 사물의 예가 나왔을 것임을 추론할 수 있다.

10 주어진 문장의 also에 주목한다. 같은 것이 앞에 나왔다는 것이

므로 ②번이 적절하다.

11 빈칸 ⓐ에는 주격 관계대명사가 필요하다. 선행사가 사물이므로 that이나 which가 적절하다.

12 'one of+복수 명사'는 '~ 중 하나'라는 의미로 핵심 주어가 one이므로 동사는 one과 수의 일치를 시켜 단수 동사를 써야 한다.

13 빈칸 뒤에 앞 문장의 예가 이어지고 있으므로 For example이 적절하다.

14 ⓐ once upon a time: 옛날 옛적에, ⓑ cry out to: ~에 대고 소리치다

15 '문자도에 있는 동물이나 사물은 단순한 장식이 아니다. 그것들은 종종 상징적이다.'라고 했으므로 '장식일 뿐만 아니라 상징적인 의미를 갖고 있다.'라고 쓸 수 있다. 또한 'not only A but also B'에서 A와 B는 문법적으로 대등한 것이 와야 한다.

16 '대나무는 왕에 대한 충성을 상징하게 되었다.'라고 했다. stand for = symbolize

17 (A) '어떤 '날씨'에서도 푸르름을 유지한다.'라고 해야 하므로 weather가 적절하다. whether는 접속사로 '~인지 아니지'라는 뜻이다. (B) '이런 이유로 대나무는 왕에 대한 '충성'을 상징하게 되었다.'라고 해야 하므로 loyalty가 적절하다. royalty: 왕권, 특허권(저작권) 사용료, loyalty: 충성, 충실 (C) '정의를 위해 싸우는 사람'이라고 해야 하므로 for가 적절하다. fight against: ~에 대항하여 싸우다, fight for: ~을 위해 싸우다

18 '문자도는 조선 시대 사람들에게 그림 그 이상'이라고 했고 '자신들의 행동과 태도에 큰 영향을 미친다'고 했으므로 '가치'가 적절하다.

19 뒤에서 '그것을 통해 조선 시대의 아이들은 가족과 사회에서의 조화의 중요성을 배울 수 있었다.'라고 했으므로 '학습 도구'가 가장 적절하다.

20 '그것을 통해 조선 시대의 아이들은 가족과 사회에서의 조화의 중요성을 배울 수 있었다.'라고 했다.

21 '문자도에는 여덟 개의 한자 중 하나가 나온다.'라고 했으므로 8개의 한자가 있었음을 알 수 있다.

22 '조선 시대 후기에 인기 있었던 민화의 한 종류이다.'라고 하고, '그것들은 조선 시대 사람들에게 중요했던 가치들을 나타낸다.'라고 했다.

23 '문자도에는 보통 한자 하나가 동물이나 사물과 함께 있다.'라고 했고, '문자도에는 여덟 개의 한자 중 하나가 나온다.'라고 했으므로 (1) some animals or objects, (2) one of eight Chinese characters라고 쓸 수 있다.

01 *hyo*

02 It would be wonderful if I could eat fresh fish.

03 (A) respect for parents   (B) three carp

     (C) sick mother

04 is called   05 worthless → important

06 문자도에는 보통 조선 시대 사람들에게 중요했던 가치들을 나타내는 한자 하나가 동물이나 사물과 함께 있다.

07 even, far, a lot, still 중에서 3개 이상 쓰면 정답

08 It reminded them of important values that[which] greatly influenced their behaviors and attitudes.

09 (A) Bamboo   (B) lotus flowers

10 (1) 대나무는 구부러지지 않는다
     (2) 그것은 어떤 날씨에서도 푸르름을 유지한다.

11 got

12 It's because lotus flowers grow in muddy ponds but still bloom beautifully.

13 got well

14 It was impossible for him to catch any fish.

01 ①

02 (a)ttitude / (t)ool (1) attitude (2) tool

03 justice

04 (A) (g)et (B) (m)uch (C) (s)o

05 (1) surprised (2) disappointing (3) boring

06 Which do you like more[better]

07 ③   08 I think that it's the healthier choice.

09 ②   10 ⑤   11 prefer   12 ①

13 ④   14 ④   15 ⑤   16 ⑤

17 (1) the carp had not come out over the ice, his mother could not have eaten them
    (2) the carp came out over the ice, his mother could eat them

18 ⑤   19 symbolize

20 (A) loyalty (B) bend (C) green

21 remained → reminded   22 ①   23 ④

24 appear → appears

25 There is usually a Chinese character with some animals or objects in Munjado.

26 They symbolize peace and happiness.

27 *The Harvesters* was painted on wood in 1565.

01 '부모님에 대한 존경심을 상징한다'라고 했으므로 hyo(孝)가 적절하다.

02 가정법 과거는 'If+주어+동사의 과거형 ~, 주어+조동사의 과거형+동사원형 …'의 형태로 있을 법하지 않은 일을 가정하여 말할 때 쓴다.

03 잉어는 부모님에 대한 존경심을 상징한다. 옛이야기에서 한 남자가 얼어붙은 강에서 잉어 세 마리를 잡아서 병든 어머니를 위해 그것들을 요리했다. carp는 단수와 복수가 같은 형태임에 유의한다.

04 문자도가 무엇을 부르는 것이 아니라 '불리는' 것이므로 수동태로 써서 'is called'로 쓰는 것이 적절하다.

05 '그것들은 조선 시대 사람들에게 '중요했던' 가치들을 나타낸다.'고 하는 것이 적절하다.

06 '문자도에는 보통 한자 하나가 동물이나 사물과 함께 있다.' '문자도에는 여덟 개의 한자 중 하나가 나오고, 그것들은 조선 시대 사람들에게 중요했던 가치들을 나타낸다.'

07 ⓐ의 much는 비교급을 수식하고 있으며 even, still, a lot, far 등으로 대신할 수 있다.

08 remind A of B: A에게 B를 상기시키다. 주격 관계대명사 that[which]으로 important values를 수식하게 하는 것이 적절하다.

09 (A)와 (B)는 각각 그 앞에 나온 대나무와 연꽃을 가리킨다.

10 바로 앞에서 '대나무는 구부러지지 않는다. 그것은 어떤 날씨에서도 푸르름을 유지한다. 이런 이유로 대나무는 왕에 대한 충성을 상징하게 되었다.'라고 했다.

11 come to부정사 = get to부정사 = ~하게 되다

12 '연꽃의 경우, 그것들은 진흙투성이의 연못에서 자라지만 여전히 아름답게 꽃을 피운다. 그래서 그 꽃들은 어려움에도 불구하고 정의를 위해 싸우는 사람의 의지를 상징하게 되었다.'라고 했다.

13 '회복되었다'라는 의미의 'got well'이 적절하다.

14 가주어 'It', 의미상의 주어 'for 목적격', 진주어 'to부정사' 구문을 이용한다.

01 <보기>와 ①번은 '글자'라는 의미로 쓰였다. <보기> 나는 쓰여진 모든 글자가 균형 있고 아름답게 보이는 것을 알았어. ① 우리들만의 글자를 가지기 전에, 우리는 한자를 사용해야만 했어. ② 그 동네의 성격은 전혀 변하지 않았다. ③ Eddie는 그 쇼에서 가장 우스운 인물이다. ④ 성격은 오래 계속된 습관이다. (독일 속담) ⑤ 당신이 좋아하는 캐릭터가 활동하는 것을 보시려면 그저 버튼만 누르세요.

02 (1) attitude: 태도, 자세. 어떤 것에 대해 생각하거나 느끼는 방식. 네가 시험에 합격하려면 태도를 바꾸는 게 좋을 거야. (2) tool: 도구. 손에 쥐고 특정한 종류의 작업을 할 수 있는 어떤 기구나 간단한 장비. 소규모 회사에서도 컴퓨터는 필수 도구이다.

03 '공평하고 합리적인 특성: 사람들이 대우 받는 방식에서의 공정함'이라는 의미로 'justice(정의)'가 적절하다. 그들은 동등한 권리와 정의를 요구하고 있다.

04 (A) get well: 병이 낫다, 회복하다. 그는 어머니에게로 다가가 걱정하지 마시고 빨리 쾌유하시라고 말씀드린다. (B) much more than: ~보다 훨씬 많이. 그것들이 네가 생각하는 것 이상으로 가치가 있을지도 몰라. (C) so ~ that ...: 너무 ~해서 …하다. 네가 너무 빨리 걸어서 못 쫓아가겠다.

05 감정동사의 '동사＋-ing'나 '동사＋-ed' 형태의 형용사는 감정을 유발하는 경우에는 '동사＋-ing' 형태를 쓰고, 감정을 느끼는 경우에는 '동사＋-ed' 형태를 쓴다. (1) surprised: 놀란. 내가 그녀에게 말을 했을 때 그녀는 놀라는 것 같았다. (2) disappointing: 실망하게 만드는. 중요한 경기에서 패하는 것

은 매우 실망스러울 수 있다. (3) boring: 지루하게 만드는. 그의 연설은 너무 지루했다.

06 빈칸에는 선호를 묻는 표현이 적절하므로 'Which do you prefer' 또는 'Which do you like more[better]'라고 쓸 수 있다.

07 선호를 묻는 질문에 (B)에서 '김밥이 더 좋다'라고 답한 후, 이유를 말하며 '넌 어떠니?'라고 묻는 말에 이어 (C)에서 '떡볶이를 먹겠다'고 답하며 '여기는 떡볶이가 더 맛있다고 들었다'고 말하자, (A)에서 '그럼 주문하자'로 이어지는 것이 적절하다.

08 'It seems to me that it's the healthier choice.'는 의견을 나타내는 표현으로 'I think that it's the healthier choice.'라고 쓸 수 있다.

09 '그럼 주문하자.'라고 하면서 '난 아주 배불러.'라고 하는 것은 어색하다 'I'm very hungry.' 정도가 적절하다.

10 John과 소미가 언제 Batman을 볼지는 알 수 없다.

11 '누군가나 어떤 것을 다른 누군가나 어떤 것보다 더 좋아해서 할 수 있다면 그것을 선택하다'를 가리키는 말은 'prefer(~을 (더) 좋아하다, 선호하다)'이다.

12 옳은 문장은 ⓒ 1개이다. ⓐ going → go ⓑ possibly → possible ⓓ not be → not to be ⓔ they → them ⓕ of → for .

13 '과거시제의 직설법 문장'을 가정법으로 고치면 '가정법 과거완료'가 된다. If절에 'had+p.p', 주절에 '조동사 과거+have+p.p'를 쓰되, 직설법과 반대되도록 not을 뺀다.

14 비교급은 quite로 강조할 수 없고, 시간의 부사절에 will을 쓸 수 없다. 내용상 의미상의 주어는 for you이다.

15 가정법 과거에는 동사의 과거형이 온다. 이 경우 비인칭 주어 it과 동사 snowed를 쓸 수 있다는 것에 유의한다.

16 ⑤ this morning으로 봐서 내용상 가정법 과거완료 문장이다. If절에 'had+p.p.', 주절에는 '조동사 과거+have+p.p.' 형태가 와야 한다. 'succeeded'를 'had succeeded'로 고치는 것이 적절하다.

17 내용상 가정법 과거완료 문장이다. If절에 'had p.p' 형태, 주절에는 '조동사 과거형+have p.p' 형태를 쓰고, 직설법으로 바꿀 때는 not이 없는 과거 시제로 고치는 것이 적절하다.

18 For these reasons: 이런 이유로, fight for: ~을 위해 싸우다

19 symbolize: 상징하다, 이미지, 형태 또는 모형에 의해 간접적으로 표현하다

20 대나무는 왕에 대한 충성을 상징한다. 대나무는 구부러지지 않고 어떤 날씨에서도 푸르름을 유지한다.

21 remain은 자동사로 목적어를 받을 수 없으며 의미상으로도 '상기시켰다'라고 하는 것이 적절하므로 reminded로 고치는 것이 적절하다.

22 이 글은 '문자도는 조선 시대 사람들에게 그림 그 이상이었으며 자신들의 행동과 태도에 큰 영향을 미치는 중요한 가치를 상기시켰고, 특히 아이들에게 문자도는 학습 도구였다.'는 내용의 글

이므로, 주제로는 ①번 '조선시대에 문자도의 역할'이 적절하다.

23 '아이들에게 문자도는 학습 도구였다.'라고 했지 '아이들이 문자도를 학습 도구로 그렸다.'라는 말은 없다.

24 'one of+복수 명사'는 '~ 중 하나'라는 의미로 핵심 주어 one에 수를 일치시켜 단수 동사인 appears가 적절하다.

25 '문자도에는 보통 한자 하나가 동물이나 사물과 함께 있다.'라고 했다.

26 '이 새들은 평화와 행복을 상징한다.'라고 했다.

27 *The Harvesters*는 1565년에 목재 위에 그려졌다.

단원별 예상문제 p.216~219

01 ② **02** ④ **03** (1) (r)emind (d)espite
04 (1) (a)ttitude (2) (d)ynasty
05 What do you say to these caps here? **06** ④
07 It's because the green plate seems to be more unique to him.
08 ⑤ **09** ①
10 He is going to buy the bag with flowers for his sister.
11 ② **12** ①
13 (1) ⓒ (2) ⓑ (3) ⓐ (4) ⓓ (5) ⓑ (6) ⓐ (7) ⓓ
　　(8) ⓑ (9) ⓐ ⑩ ⓒ
14 (1) had your phone number, would call
　　(2) were[was] rich, could buy
　　(3) hadn't attended the meeting, couldn't have heard
15 ③ **16** ⑤ **17** as follows
18 ② **19** (A) ① (B) ③
20 (A) reminded (B) values (C) behaviors
　　(D) attitudes
21 they represent the values that were important to people of the Joseon dynasty
22 ⑤

01 ②번은 동의어의 관계이며 나머지는 모두 반의어의 관계이다. represent: 나타내다, 상징하다 – symbolize: 상징하다, ~을 나타내다 ① ill: 아픈 – healthy: 건강한 ③ possible: 가능한 – impossible: 불가능한 ④ respect: 존경, 경의 – disrespect: 무례, 결례 ⑤ justice: 정의, 공정 – injustice: 불평등, 부당함

02 ① 그러므로 너는 긴장하고 집중력을 유지해야 한다. ② 이런 이유로, 이 구역에 표지판이 필요하다. ③ 그녀는 검약을 매우 중요하게 여긴다. ④ loyalty: 충성, 충실. royalty: 왕족, 왕권, 저작권 사용료. Stonehenge에 묻힌 사람들은 아마도 왕족이었을 것이다. ⑤ 네 잎 클로버는 행운의 상징이다.

03 (1) remind A of B: A에게 B를 상기시키다. 이걸 보니 지난번에 네가 실수한 거 생각 안 나니? (2) despite: ~에도 불구하

고. 일반 대중의 강한 반대에도 불구하고 그 안은 추진될 것이다.

04 (1) attitude: 태도 (2) dynasty: 왕조

05 How about ~? = What do you say to ~?

06 Joe는 '삼각형이 있는 것이 더 좋아. 그것이 더 독특한 것 같아.' 라고 말하고 있다.

07 Steve는 '초록색 접시가 더 독특한 것 같아.'라고 말하고 있다.

08 'Me, too.'는 '나도 그래.'라는 뜻으로 동의를 나타낸다. 앞에서 일반동사 like가 쓰였으므로 'So do I.'로 바꿔 쓸 수 있다

09 (a) look+형용사: ~하게 보이다 (b) 선택의문문이므로 Which (c) It seems ~ = It appears ~: ~인 것 같다

10 준수는 '여동생에게 줄 선물을 살 거라고 했'고 '꽃들이 있는 것이 더 좋아. 내 여동생이 그것을 더 좋아할 것 같아.'라고 했으므로 꽃들이 있는 가방을 살 것이라고 추측할 수 있다

11 ① they → them ③ of → for ④ playing → play ⑤ for → of

12 가정법 문장들이다. ② 종속절이 가정법 과거완료이므로 'it would be ~' → 'it would have been ~' ③ will → would ④ can → could ⑤ makes → made

13 (1), (10) 인칭대명사 (2), (5), (8) It ~ that 강조구문 (3), (6), (9) 가주어 It (4), (7) 거리, 날씨 등을 나타내는 비인칭 주어

14 (1), (2)는 가정법 과거, (3)은 가정법 과거완료이다. (3)의 경우, but 뒤에 '부정 의미'의 내용이 필요하므로 종속절과 주절 모두에 not이 와야 하는 것에 유의한다.

15 뒤에서 '잉어 세 마리가 갑자기 물 밖으로 나왔다.'라고 했으므로 '얼음이 녹았다'라고 하는 것이 적절하다. ① freeze: 얼다, ④ heighten: 높게 하다, 강화시키다, ⑤ assemble: 모으다, 집합 시키다

16 주어진 문장의 the fish가 ⑤번 앞 문장의 three carp를 받고 있으므로 ⑤번이 적절하다.

17 as follows: 다음과 같이

18 앞의 내용의 결과가 나오고 있으므로 thus가 가장 적절하다.

19 (A) 대나무 그림이 있고 忠자가 있는 ①번이 적절하다. (B) 연꽃 그림이 있고 義자가 있는 ③번이 적절하다.

20 '문자도는 그들에게 자신들의 행동과 태도에 큰 영향을 미치는 중요한 가치를 상기시켰다.'라고 했다.

21 represent: 나타내다, 보여 주다 be important to: ~에게 중요하다

22 문자도에 여덟 개의 한자 중 하나가 나오는 이유는 알 수 없다. ① Yes. ② Yes. ③ Yes. ④ Yes.

서술형 실전문제 p.220~221

01 Yes, she has.

02 They will go see the exhibition.

03 very → much

04 (1) It was impossible for them to catch the tiger.
(2) It was really careless of the women to reach out to a big dog.

05 I had been in his situation, I could never have done the same thing

06 (A) the ice melted   (B) came out of

07 He went out to the river to catch fish for his sick mother.

08 Because the river was completely frozen.

09 The man was so disappointed that he cried out to the sky

10 despite

11 (A) a person's will   (B) despite difficulties (C) bloom beautifully

01 소미는 '나는 전에 본 적이 있어.'라고 하고 있다.

02 소미가 '우선 전시회부터 보자.'라고 하고 있다.

03 뒤에 나오는 비교급 more interesting을 수식하고 있으므로 very를 much나 even, far, a lot, still 등으로 고쳐야 한다. very는 비교급을 수식할 수 없다.

04 (1) possible은 impossible로, (2) women, careless, really 등의 활용에 주의한다. 의미상 주어에 알맞은 전치사 for 와 of의 구분에 유의하여 영작한다.

05 내용상 '내가 그의 상황이었다면, 나는 결코 똑같은 일을 할 수 없었을 텐데'가 빈칸에 적절하다. 가정법 과거완료 시제이므로 'If I had been'을 종속절에, 주절에는 'could have done'인데, never는 조동사 바로 뒤에 오는 것에 유의한다.

06 남자가 하늘에 대고 외쳤을 때 얼음이 녹았고, 잉어 세 마리가 갑자기 물 밖으로 나왔다.

07 '신선한 물고기를 먹을 수 있다면 좋겠구나.'라는 어머니의 말에 남자는 물고기를 잡기 위해 강으로 나갔다. to부정사를 사용하라고 했으므로 to부정사의 부사적 용법의 '목적'을 이용한다.

08 강이 완전히 얼어붙어 있었기 때문이었다.

09 so ~ that: 너무 ~해서 …하다 cry out to: ~에 대고 소리치다

10 despite+명사(구): ~에도 불구하고

11 연꽃은 어려움에도 불구하고 정의를 위해 싸우는 사람의 의지를 상징한다. 그것들은 진흙투성이의 연못에서 자라지만 여전히 아름답게 꽃을 피운다.

창의사고력 서술형 문제 p.222

|모범답안|

01 (1) A: Which plate do you prefer, the green one or the white one?
B: I prefer the green one. It seems to me that it's more unique. How about you?
A: I prefer the green one, too.

(2) A: Which painting do you prefer, the one on the left or the one on the right?

B: I prefer the one on the right. It seems to me that the cat in it is cuter. How about you?

A: I prefer the one on the right, too.

(3) A: Which food do you prefer, Tteokbokki or Gimbap?

B: I prefer Tteokbokki. It seems to me that it's more delicious. How about you?

A: I prefer Tteokbokki, too.

02 (A) *Water Lilies*: *The Clouds*

(A) *Water Lilies*: *The Clouds*

(B) Claude Monet   (C) the reflection of clouds

(D) water lilies

(E) the colors are beautiful and the scene looks peaceful

(F) as a mirror

 단원별 모의고사   p.223~226

01 (s)ociety   02 loyalty   03 object   04 ⑤

05 (1) Bend your knees when you stretch.

(2) The boy suddenly appeared from behind the tree.

(3) The dove represents peace.

06 Which one do you prefer to see

07 It seems to me that *Batman* will be much more fun.

08 They will see the Korean mask exhibition.

09 They will watch the show at 6 o'clock.

10 ⑤   11 ④   12 ④

13 (1) It is not easy for her to move the heavy table alone.

(2) It is impossible for him to take animals on an airplane.

(3) It is rude of Angelina not to show respect for other players.

14 ⑤   15 ⑤   16 ⑤

17 (A) appear   (B) the values

18 It was popular in the late Joseon dynasty.

19 ③

20 The ice melted, and three carp suddenly came out of the water.

21 the fish for   22 against → for   23 ④

01 동의어 관계이다. difficulty: 어려움, 고난 – hardship: 곤란, 고충, community: 지역사회, 공동체 – society: 사회

02 '어떤 사람이나 어떤 것에 대해 지지하는 감정'은 'loyalty(충

성, 충실)'가 적절하다. 군인들은 국가에 충성을 맹세했다.

03 '보거나 만질 수 있는 것'은 'object(물건, 물체)'가 적절하다. 하늘에 이상한 물체가 있다.

04 • represent: 나타내다, 보여 주다, 상징하다. 음표는 악음을 나타낸다. • melt: 녹다. 눈이 녹기 시작하고 있었다. • express: 표현하다, 나타내다

05 (1) bend: 굽다, 구부리다 (2) suddenly: 갑자기 appear: 나타나다 from behind: ~ 뒤에서 (3) dove: 비둘기 represent: 나타내다, 상징하다 peace: 평화

06 prefer는 'like more[better]'나 'want more' 대신 쓸 수 있다.

07 'It seems (to me) that ~'로 자신의 의견을 말할 수 있다.

08 소미가 글의 마지막 부분에서 '그래. 우선 전시회부터 보자.'라고 하고 있다.

09 Eric이 '6시 공연을 보자.'라고 하자 소미가 '그래. 우선 전시회부터 보자.'라고 하고 있다.

10 6시 공연을 볼 것이다.

11 ④의 밑줄 친 it은 인칭대명사이다. 거리를 나타내는 비인칭 주어와 혼동하는 것에 유의한다. 나머지는 모두 가주어, 진주어의 it으로 사용되었다.

12 ④의 if만이 간접의문문의 명사절을 이끄는 접속사이며, 나머지는 모두 가정법의 부사절을 이끄는 종속접속사이다.

13 to부정사 또는 동명사가 주어인 문장을 '가주어-진주어' 구조로 표현할 때, 일반적으로 'It ~ for+의미상의 주어+to V' 형태로 표현하는데, 사람의 성질이나 태도를 나타내는 형용사가 있을 때는 for 대신 of를 쓴다. (1), (2)는 'for+의미상의 주어' 형태로, (3)은 무례하다는 뜻이므로 of를 쓴다.

14 <보기>의 would는 가정법의 주절에서 쓰이는 조동사이며, 쓰임이 같은 것은 ⑤이다. "내가 당신이라면 그 쓸모없이 비싼 가방들은 사지 않을 텐데." ① 공손한 부탁 ② will의 과거시제 ③ 과거의 습관적 행위 ④ would like to = want to

15 '잉어가 없다면, 그는 어머니가 회복하도록 도울 수 없을 텐데.'라는 문장이다. '~가 없다면'은 If it were not for = Were it not for = Without = But for 등으로 표현하며, ⑤ 'Had it not been for'는 'If it had not been for'에서 if를 생략하고 도치된 표현으로서 가정법 과거완료시제에 사용한다.

16 한자 효(孝)와 잉어, 거문고, 부채가 있는 것은 ⑤번이다.

17 그것들은 문자도에 나오는 여덟 개의 한자이고, 그것들은 조선 시대 사람들에게 중요했던 가치들을 나타낸다.

18 '이런 종류의 그림은 문자도이며, 조선 시대 후기에 인기 있었던 민화의 한 종류이다.'라고 했다.

19 문맥상 disappointed가 가장 적절하다. ② 아주 기뻐하는, ④ 만족한, ⑤ 무관심한, 냉담한

20 그러자 얼음이 녹았고, 잉어 세 마리가 갑자기 물 밖으로 나왔다.

21 cook은 간접목적어를 직접목적어 다음에 쓸 때 전치사 for를 붙인다.

22 'fight against'는 '~에 대항하여 싸우다'라는 뜻이고, 'fight for'는 '~을 위해 싸우다'라는 뜻이므로 'fight for'로 쓰는 것이 적절하다.

23 '문자도는 조선 시대 사람들에게 그림 그 이상이었다.'라고 했다.

Finding the Good in Your Friends

Reading

확인문제 p.230

1 T 2 F

확인문제 p.231

1 T 2 F

교과서 확인학습 A p.232~234

01 Compliment
03 last
04 a piece of paper
05 Compliments for, last activity
06 pick
08 each other
09 whose name
10 got
11 to say
12 What about
13 looking worried
14 compliment him on
15 sits at his desk
16 have to find
18 talking with
19 except for
20 what to compliment
21 carefully
22 should be
23 he's
24 washes
25 a compliment
26 does that
27 again
28 I'm sure
30 an accident
31 is stuck
32 with arms in the air
33 Stay still
34 hurts
35 Let
36 comes back
37 put, on
39 calm
40 working
41 coming out of
43 eating dinner
44 what happened
45 a little accident
46 got stuck in
47 get, out
48 pulled it out

49 Messy, creative
50 a compliment
51 Sure
53 complimenting each other
54 what compliment
55 cheerful
56 fair
57 of you
58 hear from you
59 picked
60 hesitating
61 shyly
62 What made you think
63 pause, the other day, by using
64 creative
65 Nobody else
66 also
67 confidently
68 the best compliment ever

교과서 확인학습 B p.235~237

1 The Best Compliment Ever
2 Scene 1
3 It is the last week of school.
4 Each student has just picked a piece of paper with a name on it.
5 Ms. Kemp: "Compliments for Classmates" will be our last activity of the school year.
6 Did everyone pick a name?
7 Class: Yes, Ms. Kemp.
8 Students are talking to each other.
9 Beth: So, whose name did you pick?
10 Lucy: (smiling) I got Boyd.
11 I have a lot to say about him.
12 What about you, Beth?
13 Beth: (looking worried) Uh, I picked Peter's name.
14 Lucy: Peter? Oh, no! It won't be easy to find something to compliment him on.
15 Steve: Yeah. He doesn't talk much and just sits at his desk all day long.
16 Beth: (scratching her head) Well, I'll have to find something.
17 Scene 2
18 Beth is at home talking with her parents about the activity.
19 Beth: Everyone has long lists of compliments for other classmates, except for me.
20 I don't know what to compliment Peter on.
21 Mom: Think carefully.
22 There should be something.
23 Beth: Well, he's clean.
24 He washes his face every day.

43

25 Mom: That's not a compliment.

26 Everybody does that.

27 Dad: Try again.

28 I'm sure you can find something good to say about him.

29 Scene 3

30 The next day, there is an accident at school.

31 Boyd's foot is stuck in a bicycle stand.

32 Boyd: (with arms in the air) Help! I need help!

33 Beth: Stay still. I'm trying to pull your foot out.

34 Boyd: (screaming) Ouch! That hurts!

35 Peter: Let me help. Just a minute.

36 Peter runs to the school's kitchen and comes back with butter.

37 Peter: I'm going to put this butter on your foot.

38 Boyd: What? Butter?

39 Peter: Just stay calm.

40 Beth: (pointing to Boyd's foot) Wow! It's working!

41 Boyd's foot is coming out of the stand.

42 Scene 4

43 Beth is eating dinner with her parents.

44 She tells them about what happened to Boyd.

45 Beth: There was a little accident at school today.

46 Boyd's foot got stuck in a bicycle stand.

47 Mom: Oh, no! So how did he get his foot out?

48 Beth: Peter put butter on his foot and then pulled it out.

49 Dad: That was really creative. Messy but creative.

50 Beth: Hmm. Creative? Can that be a compliment, Dad?

51 Dad: Sure.

52 Scene 5

53 It is the last day of school, and the students are complimenting each other.

54 Ms. Kemp: Joanne, what compliment do you have for Beth?

55 Joanne: Beth, you're always cheerful.

56 You're also kind and fair to everybody.

57 Beth: Thanks, Joanne. It's so nice of you to say so.

58 Ms. Kemp: Beth, let's hear from you now.

59 You picked Peter's name.

60 Beth: (hesitating) Well, I think Peter is creative. Peter, you're … uh … creative.

61 Peter: (shyly) Really?

62 Ms. Kemp: What made you think Peter is creative?

63 Beth: (after a long pause) When Boyd's foot got stuck in the bicycle stand the other day, Peter got it out by using butter.

64 That was creative.

65 Boyd: Yeah! Nobody else thought of doing that.

66 Steve: I didn't know that. Well, then, I also think he's creative.

67 Beth: (confidently) Yeah, Peter, you ARE creative!

68 Peter: Thanks, Beth! It's the best compliment ever!

서술형 실전문제
p.238~239

01 out / out
02 accident / accident

03 (1) air   (2) confidently   (3) hesitate   (4) scratch

04 (1) compliment   (2) hurt   (3) calm

05 (w)ork
06 messy

07 (1) wonder whose name you picked

(2) what to compliment David on

(3) What made you think that

(4) about what happened to Tom

08 for → of

09 (A) last   (B) Compliments   (C) looking

10 a piece of paper

11 She picked Boyd's name.

12 stuck
13 calmly → calm

14 (A) butter   (B) worked

---

01 • come out of: ~에서 나오다. 당신이 누구든 거기서 나와. • pull out: 빠져나가다[나오다]. 그 사업은 비용이 너무 많이 들어서 우리는 손을 떼야 했다.

02 • accident: 사고. 어젯밤에 자동차 사고가 있었다. • by accident: 우연히. 우리는 공항에서 우연히 만났다.

03 (1) in the air: 공중에. 그 도시 상공에는 매연이 떠 있었다. (2) confidently: 자신 있게. 그는 모든 일을 자기가 책임지겠다고 호언했다. (3) hesitate: 망설이다, 주저하다. 나는 조금도 망설이지 않고 그 직장을 잡았다. (4) scratch: 긁다. 네가 차 긁는 거 아빠가 보셨어.

04 (1) 반의어 관계이다. deep: 깊은, shallow: 얕은, criticism: 비평, 비판, compliment: 칭찬, 찬사 (2) 반의어 관계이다. appear: 나타나다 disappear: 사라지다, heal: 고치다, 낫게 하다, hurt: 다치게 하다 (3) 동의어 관계이다. long: 긴, lengthy: 긴, 기다란, cool: 냉정한, 침착한, calm: 침착한, 차분한

05 work: 효과가 있다. 성공적이거나 효과가 있거나 만족할 만하

다. 그 약은 효험이 전혀 없었다.

06 messy: 지저분한, 엉망인

07 '의문사'가 들어가는 다양한 문장 구조이다. (1) '간접의문문'의 어순은 '의문사+주어+동사'이다. (2) '의문사+to부정사' 구조로서 'what to V'는 '무엇을 V해야 할지'라는 뜻이다. (3) '의문사 What이 주어'가 되어 'What made you think that'의 형태이다. 직역을 하면 '무엇이 당신을 그렇게 생각하게 만들었는가'라는 의미로서 '왜 그렇게 생각하게 되었는지'라는 뜻이다. (4) 간접의문문에서 '의문사가 주어'일 때는 어순이 그대로이다.

08 'to부정사'의 '의미상의 주어'는 일반적으로 전치사 for를 쓰지만, 형용사가 '사람의 성격 또는 성질'을 나타낼 때는 of를 쓴다. *thoughtful: 사려 깊은, 자상한

09 (A) '마지막' 주라고 해야 하므로 last가 적절하다. latest: 최근의, (B) 학급 친구들 '칭찬하기'라고 해야 하므로 Compliments가 적절하다. complement: 보완물, (C) look은 수동태로 쓸 수 없으므로 looking이 적절하다.

10 '종이 한 장'을 가리킨다.

11 Lucy는 'Boyd'를 뽑았다.

12 stick의 과거분사이자 형용사 형태인 stuck을 쓰는 것이 적절하다. stuck: (~에 빠져) 움직일 수 없는[꼼짝 못하는]

13 stay의 보어로 형용사를 쓰는 것이 적절하다.

14 Boyd의 발이 자전거 거치대에 끼어 더 이상 움직이지 않게 되었을 때, Peter가 Boyd의 발에 '버터'를 발랐다. 그것은 '효과가 있었고' Boyd의 발이 거치대에서 빠져나왔다.

단원별 예상문제 p.240~244

01 (1) stuck (2) creative (3) compliment
   (4) work(ed)

02 ②　　　　03 ⑤　　　　04 ③

05 (1) except for (2) all day long (3) shyly

06 ④

07 ⑤

08 (1) The bus bumps a tree and all the people scream and run away.
   (2) What made you decide on a career as a vet?
   (3) I'm awfully sorry about that problem the other day

09 will not be easy to find something to compliment her on

10 (1) how you should find something good about others
   (2) what he should put on his foot to pull it out of the bicycle stand

(3) how I should open the safe

11 ⑤

12 her finger got stuck in the bottle, Brian got it out by using butter

13 including → except for

14 I should　　15 모든 사람이 매일 세수를 한다

16 ④　　　　　　17 ③

18 putting (the) butter on Boyd's foot

19 ⑤　　　　　　20 ①

21 pulled out it → pulled it out

22 Peter put butter on his foot and then pulled it out.

23 It's so nice of you to say so.

24 Why　　25 (A) creative   (B) got stuck

01 (1) stuck: (~에 빠져) 움직일 수 없는. 우리는 교통 체증 속에 갇혀 있었다. (2) creative: 창의적인, 창조적인. 상상의 나래를 있는 대로 펼쳐서 창의력을 발휘해 보아라. (3) compliment: 칭찬, 찬사. 그녀는 그가 하는 말을 칭찬으로 받아들였다. (4) work: 효과가 있다. 내 계획이 효과가 있어서 그들이 동의하게 만들었다.

02 ②의 영영풀이는 point의 영영풀이이다. ① accident: 사고, 불운한 일; 특히 손상이나 부상을 일으키는 것 ② point: 가리키다. 누군가가 그것을 알아채도록 하기 위해 손가락을 사람이나 물건을 향해 내밀다 ③ compliment 칭찬, 찬사. 누군가에게 당신이 그의 외모를 좋아한다거나 그의 자질을 인정한다거나 그가 한 것을 지지한다는 것을 보여주기 위해 하는 공손한 언급 ④ scream: 비명을 지르다. 매우 크고 높은 음조로 소리치다 ⑤ hesitate: 망설이다, 주저하다. 불확실하거나 내키지 않아서 잠시 멈추거나 억제하다

03 compliment: 칭찬, praise: 칭찬, 찬양. ③ thrift: 검약, 검소

04 ③은 'ly', 나머지는 모두 '명사+y'로 형용사가 되는 어휘이다. ① stormy: 폭풍우의. 하늘은 폭풍이 올 것처럼 보인다. ② messy: 지저분한, 엉망인. 나는 이렇게 어질러진 책상에서는 아무것도 찾을 수 없다. ③ friendly: 친절한[우호적인]. 그 호텔 직원들은 친절하고 세심하다. ④ greedy: 욕심 많은. 그 탐욕스러운 남자는 가방에 대해 너무 비싼 값을 요구했다. ⑤ thrifty: 검소한. 지금 그들에게는 많은 돈이 있지만 늘 그렇듯이 여전히 검소하다.

05 (1) except for: ~을 제외하고 (2) all day long: 하루 종일 (3) shyly: 수줍게, 부끄러워하며

06 (A) pull out: 빠져나가다[나오다]. 우리 팀은 전반전 내내 부진을 면치 못했다. (B) stay calm: 침착함을 유지하다. 진정하고 참을성 있게 기다려야 해요.

07 <보기>의 'to부정사'는 '형용사적' 용법으로 쓰여서 앞의 a lot

을 뒤에서 수식한다. ⑤번의 'to부정사'는 부사적 용법으로 사용되었다.

08 (1) scream: 비명을 지르다 (2) What made you ~?: 왜 ~했니? (3) the other day: 일전에, 최근에

09 가주어로 it을 이용하고 진주어로 to부정사를 쓴다. '~에 관해'라는 의미로 on을 마지막에 붙이는 것에 주의한다.

10 '의문사+to부정사'는 '의문사+주어+should+동사원형'으로 바꿀 수 있다.

11 'What makes you think (that)+주어+동사?'를 직역하면, '무엇이 당신으로 하여금 ~하다고 생각하도록 만드는가?'가 되어 '왜 그런 생각을 하느냐'와 같은 의미이다. ⑤와 같이 think, believe 등이 있을 때, 의문사는 문두로 보내고, 간접의문문의 어순을 유지하는 것이 적절하다.

12 '병에 끼었다'는 'got stuck'으로, '빼냈다'는 'got it out'으로 표현하여, get을 두 번 쓰는 것과 '전치사 by+동명사'의 형태, 대명사 it의 위치 등에 유의하여, 영작한다.

13 저를 '제외한' 모두라고 해야 하므로 including을 except for로 고치는 것이 적절하다. including: ~을 포함하여, except for: ~을 제외하고

14 의문사 to부정사 = 의문사+주어+should+동사원형

15 do that은 앞에 나오는 washes his face every day를 받는다.

16 엄마는 Peter가 매일 세수를 한다고 말하는 것은 '칭찬이 아니라고' 했다.

17 ⓐ와 ③: 가만히 있는, 고요한(형용사), ①, ⑤: 아직(부사), ② (비교급을 강조하여) 훨씬(부사), ④ 그럼에도 불구하고(부사)

18 'Boyd의 발에 버터를 바른 것'을 가리킨다.

19 Boyd가 Peter에 대해 어떻게 느꼈는지는 대답할 수 없다. ① Boyd's foot got stuck in a bicycle stand. ② In a bicycle stand. ③ Peter did. ④ By putting butter on Boyd's foot.

20 ①번 앞 문장의 a little accident에 주목한다. 주어진 문장의 내용을 가리키는 것이므로 ①번이 적절하다.

21 'pull out'은 '동사+부사'로 이루어진 구동사로, 목적어가 명사일 경우에는 부사의 앞과 뒤에 모두 올 수 있지만 목적어가 인칭대명사일 경우에는 동사와 부사 사이에만 올 수 있다.

22 'Peter가 Boyd의 발에 버터를 바르고 나서 발을 당겨서 꺼낸 것'을 가리킨다.

23 사람의 성질을 나타내는 형용사 nice가 있으므로, to부정사의 의미상의 주어를 of you로 쓰는 것이 적절하다.

24 'What made you think ~?'는 '무엇 때문에 ~라는 생각을 하게 되었니?'라고 이유를 묻는 표현으로, 'Why did you think ~?'로 바꾸어 쓸 수 있다.

25 Beth는 일전에 Boyd의 발이 자전거 거치대에 '끼었을' 때,

Peter가 버터를 사용해서 그의 발을 꺼냈기 때문에, Peter가 '창의적'이라고 생각했다.

교과서 파헤치기

Lesson 5

단어 TEST Step 1 p.02

01 주된	02 고용하다	
03 (눈에) 보이지 않는, 볼 수 없는		04 운반하다
05 홍보하다	06 이미	07 팀, 조
08 추천	09 값비싼	10 완벽한
11 관리하다	12 몇몇의	13 주의, 주목
14 한계	15 보조자	16 다치다
17 선택하다	18 그러므로	19 특히
20 부족, 종족	21 등록하다	22 활동
23 방향	24 경험 있는	25 돕다, 지원하다
26 두드리는 사람	27 제안하다	28 특정한
29 숨쉬다	30 달성하다, 성취하다	
31 조화, 화합	32 숨겨진	33 허용하다
34 바람이 심한	35 간단히 말해서	36 무엇보다도
37 (낡아서) 떨어지다, 헤지다		
38 ~에 어려움을 겪다		
39 등록하다, 신청하다		40 혼자서
41 ~을 파악하다	42 여러 가지 면에서	43 ~에 따라

단어 TEST Step 2 p.03

01 achieve	02 carry	03 expensive
04 harmony	05 support	06 attention
07 breathe	08 therefore	09 assistant
10 hidden	11 cheer	12 suggest
13 experienced	14 choose	15 windy
16 main	17 invisible	18 promote
19 tribe	20 lead	21 shoot
22 already	23 limit	24 particular
25 crew	26 recommendation	
27 register	28 several	29 direction
30 especially	31 manage	32 perfect
33 allow	34 tapper	35 depending on
36 be over	37 in short	38 wear out
39 sign up for	40 get attention	41 take care of
42 have difficulty -ing		43 most of all

단어 TEST Step 3 p.04

1 hire, 고용하다   2 invisible, (눈에) 보이지 않는, 볼 수 없는
3 promote, 홍보하다   4 achieve, 달성하다, 성취하다
5 breathe, 숨쉬다   6 crew, 팀, 조
7 register, 등록하다   8 assistant, 보조자
9 wear, 입다   10 support, 돕다, 지원하다
11 tribe, 부족, 종족   12 choose, 선택하다
13 trophy, 트로피   14 suit, 정장, 옷 한 벌
15 pit, (자동차 경주의) 피트
16 wear out, (낡아서) 떨어지다, 헤지다

대화문 TEST Step 1 p.05~06

Listen and Talk A 1

often, play basketball / once, more often / suggest, three times / good, to play

Listen and Talk A 2

about, How often, swim / four times a week / That, Anyway, it, swimming / suggest, do stretching

Listen and Talk A 3

how often, take, lessons / Twice, beginner / heavy, suggest, use, lighter ball / for, one

Listen and Talk A 4

how often, to run / Every / with / suggest, wear, good for running

Listen and Talk B

how often, exercise / once a week / suggest, exercise / try

Listen and Talk C

Welcome to / to register for, class / taking swimming lessons / how to swim at all / How often, take / take, twice a week, take, on, on / that, take, on / sounds good, sign up for / a limit of / perfect

Talk and Play

how often, exercise / three times a week

Review 1

how often, swim / every day / go swimming with / suggest, bring, Without, aren't allowed

Review 2

practice over / How often, practice / twice a week

Review 3

register for, soccer class / How often, take classes / take, twice a week, take, on / suggest, take, on / good

Listen and Talk A 1

B: How often do you play basketball?

G: I play once a week, but I want to play more often.

B: I suggest you join my basketball club. We play three times a week.

G: That sounds good! It'll be fun to play with you.

Listen and Talk A 2

B: I don't swim often. How about you, Kate? How often do you swim?

G: I swim four times a week.

B: That often? Anyway, it'll be fun swimming together today.

G: Yes, but before we swim, I suggest we do stretching exercises.

B: That's a good idea.

Listen and Talk A 3

B: Suji, how often do you take bowling lessons?

G: Twice a week. I'm just a beginner. I heard you're very good.

B: Well, I love bowling. Hmm. Your bowling ball looks heavy for you. I suggest you use a lighter ball.

G: OK. I'll look for a lighter one, then.

Listen and Talk A 4

B: Mina, how often do you come here to run?

G: Every day.

B: Can I run with you today?

G: Sure, but I suggest you wear running shoes. Your shoes aren't good for running.

Listen and Talk B

A: Minsu, how often do you exercise?

B: I exercise once a week.

A: I suggest you exercise more often.

B: OK. I'll try.

Listen and Talk C

W: Hello. Welcome to Sports World. May I help you?

B: Yes, I came to register for a swimming class.

W: Is this your first time taking swimming lessons?

B: Yes, it is. I don't know how to swim at all.

W: I see. How often do you want to take classes?

B: I want to take classes twice a week. I'd like to take classes on weekdays andnot on weekends.

W: Then, I suggest that you take the Beginner 2 class. This class meets on Tuesdays and Thursdays.

B: That sounds good. I'd like to sign up for that class. How big is the class?

W: The class has a limit of 10 people.

B: That's perfect.

Talk and Play

A: Jiho, how often do you exercise?

B: I exercise three times a week.

A: That's good.

Review 1

B: Mina, how often do you swim?

G: I swim every day.

B: Can I go swimming with you this afternoon?

G: Sure, but I suggest you bring a swimming cap. Without a swimming cap, you aren't allowed in the pool.

Review 2

B: Somi, is your piano practice over?

G: Yes, it is.

B: How often do you practice?

G: I practice twice a week.

Review 3

W: Hello. May I help you?

B: Yes, I came to register for a soccer class.

W: I see. How often do you want to take classes?

B: I want to take classes twice a week. I'd like to take classes on weekends.

W: Then, I suggest that you take the Beginner 1 class. This class meets on Saturdays and Sundays.

B: That sounds good.

01 Hidden, in Sports   02 only, but, on, own

03 There, who, players   04 often hidden, get attention

05 However, as important

06 Here are, examples   07 Pacers in, Marathon

08 run with, runners, lead

09 experienced, other, manage, better

10 There can be

11 runs, speeds, finishes, times

12 Pacers, have, showing, finish

13 choose, depending on, target

14 finish, hours, follow, pacer

15 Since, track, finishing, particular

16 In short, to win   17 run for others

18 Pit Crews, Car Racing

19 during, there, behind, driver

20 is called, pit crew

21 on, of, track, several

22 main job, check, change

23 Changing, because, wear out

24 as short, seconds, crew

25 has, in perfect harmony

26 get, attention, won, pits

27 in Mountain Climbing

28 comes, tribe, which, eastern

29 climbing skills, way around

30 have little difficulty breathing

31 hire, to help, climb　　32 lead, climbers to, top

33 support, in, ways　　34 For, put up, carry

35 invisible, because, climbers, top

01 Hidden　　　　　　02 only, win on their own

03 people who help　　04 hidden, get attention

05 However, as important as

06 Here are, examples　07 Pacers

08 run with other runners, lead

09 experienced, to help, manage their race better

10 There can be

11 at different speeds, finishes, in different times

12 showing

13 can choose, depending on

14 in four hours, follow, four

15 keeps track of, can achieve, easily

16 In short, to win　　　17 for others

18 Car Racing　　　　19 during, behind the driver

20 is called

21 on the side of the race track, several times

22 main job, to check

23 Changing, is, wear out easily

24 as short as, seconds, as many as

25 Therefore, in perfect harmony

26 get all the attention, in the pits

27 Mountain Climbing

28 comes from, which, eastern part

29 good climbing skills

30 have little difficulty breathing

31 to hire, to help them climb

32 lead, to　　　　　33 in many ways

34 For, put up, carry　35 invisible, at the top of

1 스포츠 속 숨은 조력자들

3 스포츠에서 선수들만 트로피나 메달을 받지만, 그들은 혼자 힘으로 이긴 것이 아니다.

3 그 선수들을 돕는 사람들이 있다.

4 이 사람들은 종종 숨겨져 있고 주목을 받지 못한다.

5 하지만 그들은 선수들만큼 중요하다.

6 여기 몇 가지 예가 있다.

7 마라톤의 페이서들

8 페이서들은 마라톤에서 다른 선수들과 함께 달리며 그들을 이끈다.

9 페이서들은 경험이 많은 선수들이며 그들의 역할은 다른 선수들이 경기를 더 잘 운영하도록 돕는 것이다.

10 한 경기에는 여러 명의 페이서들이 있을 수 있다.

11 각각의 페이서는 다른 속도로 달리고 다른 시간대에 경기를 마친다.

12 페이서들은 주로 자신들의 완주 시간을 나타내는 깃발이나 풍선들을 가지고 있다.

13 선수들은 자신들의 목표 완주 시간에 따라 페이서를 선택할 수 있다.

14 예를 들어, 한 선수가 4시간 안에 경기를 마치고 싶다면, 그 선수는 4시간 페이서를 따라갈 것이다.

15 페이서가 시간을 계속해서 파악하기 때문에, 선수는 특정 시간에 마라톤을 완주하려는 자신의 목표를 더 쉽게 달성할 수 있다.

16 요컨대, 페이서들은 달리지만 우승을 하기 위해 달리는 것은 아니다.

17 그들은 다른 선수들을 위해 달린다.

18 자동차 경주의 피트 크루

19 여러분은 대부분의 자동차 경주에서 자동차와 레이서만 보겠지만 그 레이서 뒤에는 팀이 있다.

20 이 팀은 피트 크루라고 불린다.

21 피트는 경주 트랙의 한쪽에 있는 공간으로 레이서들은 경주 도중에 그곳에서 여러 번 정지한다.

22 피트 크루가 하는 주요 역할은 자동차를 점검하고 타이어를 교체하는 것이다.

23 빠른 속도의 경주에서는 타이어가 쉽게 마모되기 때문에 타이어를 교체하는 것이 특히 중요하다.

24 피트에서의 정지는 짧게는 2초 정도이고 한 팀에는 많게는 20명에 이르는 구성원이 있다.

25 그러므로 피트 크루는 완벽한 조화를 이루며 일해야 한다.

26 레이서만 주목을 받을지 모르지만 사람들이 말하는 것처럼, "경주의 우승은 피트에서 이루어진다."

27 등반에서의 셰르파

28 'Sherpa'라는 단어는 셰르파족에서 유래되었는데, 셰르파족은 네팔의 동쪽 지역에 산다.

29 셰르파는 훌륭한 등반 기량을 갖고 있으며 산 지리를 잘 안다.

30 그들은 또한 산의 높은 곳에서 호흡하는 데 어려움이 거의

31 그래서 등산가들은 자신들이 에베레스트산을 등반하는 것을 돕는 셰르파를 고용하기 시작했다.

32 셰르파는 등산가들을 산 정상까지 이끈다.

33 그들은 여러 방면에서 등산가들을 지원한다.

34 예를 들면, 그들은 텐트를 치고 등산가들의 가방을 운반한다.

35 셰르파는 종종 에베레스트산의 보이지 않는 사람들로 불리는데, 왜냐하면 사람들이 산 정상에서 등산가들만 찍힌 사진을 자주 보기 때문이다.

본문 TEST Step 4-Step 5 · p.15~18

1 Hidden People in Sports

2 In sports, only the players get a trophy or medal, but they don't win on their own.

3 There are people who help the players.

4 These people are often hidden and don't get attention.

5 However, they are as important as the players.

6 Here are some examples.

7 Pacers in a Marathon

8 Pacers run with other runners and lead them in a marathon.

9 Pacers are experienced runners, and their job is to help other runners manage their race better.

10 There can be several pacers in a race.

11 Each pacer runs at different speeds and finishes the race in different times.

12 Pacers usually have flags or balloons showing their finish time.

13 Runners can choose a pacer depending on their target finish time.

14 For example, if a runner wants to finish the race in four hours, the runner will follow the four-hour pacer.

15 Since the pacer keeps track of the time, the runner can achieve his or her goal of finishing the marathon in a particular time more easily.

16 In short, pacers run but they don't run to win.

17 They run for others.

18 Pit Crews in Car Racing

19 You may only see the car and the driver during most car races, but there is a team behind the driver.

20 This team is called a pit crew.

21 A pit is a place on the side of the race track, and drivers stop there several times during a race.

22 The main job of the pit crew is to check the car and change the tires.

23 Changing the tires is especially important because the tires wear out easily in a high speed race.

24 A pit stop can be as short as 2 seconds, and there are as many as 20 members on a crew.

25 Therefore, the pit crew has to work in perfect harmony.

26 The driver may get all the attention, but as people say, "Races are won in the pits."

27 Sherpas in Mountain Climbing

28 The word *Sherpa* comes from the Sherpa tribe, which lives in the eastern part of Nepal.

29 Sherpas have good climbing skills and know their way around the mountains well.

30 They also have little difficulty breathing high up in the mountains.

31 Therefore, mountain climbers started to hire Sherpas to help them climb Mount Everest.

32 Sherpas lead mountain climbers to the top of the mountain.

33 They support climbers in many ways.

34 For example, they put up tents and carry climbers' bags.

35 Sherpas are often called the invisible people of Mount Everest because people often see a picture of only the climbers at the top of the mountain.

구석구석지문 TEST Step 1 · p.19

After You Read B

1. Is there anything interesting

2. showing their finish time

3. can be as short as 2 seconds

4. has to work in perfect harmony

5. have little difficulty breathing high up

Around the World

1. to help a blind swimmer swim

2. runs with a blind runner, helps, stay on the track

3. In blind football, a shooting assistant, direction to shoot

Think and Write

1. Cheerleaders, Football Games

2. Although, usually don't think, a part of, play an important role in

3. By cheering, create team spirit

4. also encourage

5. To do their job well, need to be fit, strong

6. need to be good at jumping, dancing

7. Most of all, work as hard as players

구석구석지문 TEST Step 2   p.20

After You Read B

1. Host: Is there anything interesting about your job?

2. Pacer: Pacers have flags or balloons showing their finish time.

3. Pit Crew: A pit stop can be as short as 2 seconds.

4. So the pit crew has to work in perfect harmony.

5. Sherpa: Sherpas like me have little difficulty breathing high up in the mountains.

Around the World

1. In swimming, a tapper uses a long pole to help a blind swimmer swim.

2. In a race, a guide runner runs with a blind runner and helps him or her stay on the track.

3. In blind football, a shooting assistant tells his or her team players which direction to shoot.

Think and Write

1. Cheerleaders in Football Games

2. Although people usually don't think that cheerleaders are a part of a football team, they play an important role in a football game.

3. By cheering at a game, they create team spirit.

4. They also encourage their team and fans.

5. To do their job well, cheerleaders need to be fit and strong.

6. They also need to be good at jumping and dancing.

7. Most of all, they need to work as hard as players.

단어 TEST Step 1   p.21

01 받아들이다	02 골동품	03 붙이다, 첨부하다
04 고장 난	05 복제품	06 선출하다
07 가치; ~의 가치가 있는		08 끝없는
09 지불하다	10 정확하게	
11 값을 매길 수 없는, 대단히 귀중한		12 더하다
13 수집	14 실망한	15 발표
16 주인	17 독감	
18 끌어안다, 포옹하다		19 (금액을) 청구하다
20 다행스럽게	21 제의, 제안	22 가구
23 주문하다, 지시하다, 명령하다		24 판매상, 중개인
25 가격	26 단단하게, 꽉	27 싸게
28 불행하게도	29 호의	30 받다
31 역할, 배역	32 ~하는 동안	33 상
34 충격 받은	35 넘어지다	36 ~을 잘라내다
37 ~로 가는 길에	38 ~을 자랑스러워하다	
39 ~한 것을 기억하다		40 ~에 대하여 꿈꾸다
41 ~하지 않을 수 없다		42 ~로 유명하다
43 ~을 이용하다		

단어 TEST Step 2   p.22

01 dealer	02 pay	03 flu
04 endless	05 exactly	06 price
07 antique	08 charge	09 reproduction
10 priceless	11 accept	12 tightly
13 broken	14 unfortunately	15 furniture
16 practice	17 disappointed	18 attach
19 bored	20 favor	21 role
22 worth	23 hug	24 collection
25 yet	26 luckily	27 offer
28 elect	29 cheaply	30 owner
31 receive	32 order	33 saw
34 announcement		35 cut off
36 on one's way	37 take out	38 dream of ~
39 fall over	40 take advantage of	
41 be known for	42 cannot help -ing	
43 be proud of ~		

단어 TEST Step 3   p.23

1 priceless, 값을 매길 수 없는   2 owner, 주인

3 broken, 고장 난   4 pay, 지불하다   5 attach, 붙이다

6 reproduction, 복제품   7 price, 가격   8 order, 지시하다
9 dealer, 판매상   10 elect, 선출하다   11 flu, 독감
12 antique, 골동품   13 charge, (요금을) 청구하다
14 knock, 두드리다   15 saw, 톱
16 hug, 끌어안다, 포옹하다

대화문 TEST Step 1 p.24~25

Listen and Talk A 1
excited, up / elected as, excited / to have, chance to work

Listen and Talk A 2
on winning / must, proud of yourself / am, did, best

Listen and Talk A 3
anything wrong / lost, upset / sorry to hear, when you used it / taking, out / to look for

Listen and Talk A 4
good, the matter / the flu / bad, see / taking medicine / feel better

Listen and Talk B
up / won first prize, speech contest, excited / Congratulations / up / broken, upset / bad, sorry to hear

Listen and Talk C
get, main role, play / going to / excited / how much you wanted, happy for / about, get, role, too / Unfortunately, disappointed / sorry to hear, Anyway, practice / at, on, in, get, about

Listen and Talk D
disappeared while, Luckily, was able to / later, so happy that, tightly

Talk and Play
chosen, excited / up / broken, upset / too bad, sorry to hear that

Review 1
excited, up / going to go / how much you wanted / to get, to see

Review 2
good, the matter / disappointed / sorry to hear that, get a role / try harder

대화문 TEST Step 2 p.26~27

Listen and Talk A 1
B: Sue, you look excited. What's up?
G: I was elected as class president. I'm so excited.
B: That's wonderful. Congratulations!

G: Thanks. I'm really happy to have a chance to work for my class.

Listen and Talk A 2
G: Tim, congratulations on winning the gold medal in the school marathon.
B: Thanks, Suji. I'm very happy.
G: You must be very proud of yourself.
B: Yes, I am. I did my best.

Listen and Talk A 3
B: Mina, is anything wrong?
G: Well, I lost my smartphone. I'm upset.
B: Oh, I'm so sorry to hear that. Do you remember when you used it last?
G: Well, I remember taking it out of my bag at the snack shop.
B: Then, let's go back to the snack shop to look for it.

Listen and Talk A 4
G: You don't look so good, Inho. What's the matter?
B: I have the flu.
G: That's too bad. Did you see the doctor?
B: Yes. I'm taking medicine.
G: Well, I hope you feel better soon.
B: Thanks.

Listen and Talk B
A: What's up?
B: I won first prize in the English speech contest. I'm so excited.
A: That's wonderful. Congratulations!
A: What's up?
B: My smartphone is broken. I'm very upset.
A: That's too bad. I'm sorry to hear that.

Listen and Talk C
B: Excuse me, Ms. Carter. Can I ask you a question? Did I get the main role in the play?
W: Yes, you did. Congratulations, Jiho! You're going to be Romeo in our school play, *Romeo and Juliet*.
B: Really? I'm so excited. Thank you so much, Ms. Carter.
W: I know how much you wanted the role. I'm so happy for you.
B: Thank you. What about Sumi? Did she get the role she wanted, too?
W: Unfortunately, no. She's very disappointed.
B: Oh, I'm sorry to hear that. Anyway, when is the first practice?
W: It's at 2 p.m. on September 20th, in the acting club

room. You'll get a text message about it soon.

B: OK. I'll be there.

Listen and Talk D

Last summer, I lost my dog, Bomi. She disappeared while I was drinking water in the park. Luckily, I was able to find her two days later. I was so happy that I hugged her tightly.

Talk and Play

A: What's up?

B: I was chosen as the leader of the school band. I'm so excited.

A: That's wonderful. Congratulations!

A: What's up?

B: My bike is broken. I'm very upset.

A: That's too bad. I'm sorry to hear that.

Review 1

B: You look excited, Sally. What's up?

G: I'm going to go to the Dream Concert.

B: Congratulations! I know how much you wanted to go.

G: Thanks. I'm so happy to get a chance to see my favorite singer.

Review 2

B: You don't look good, Sumi. What's the matter?

G: Well, I didn't get a role in the school play. I'm very disappointed.

B: Oh, I'm so sorry to hear that. But I'm sure you can get a role next time.

G: Thanks. I'll try harder next time.

본문 TEST Step 1   p.28~30

01 One Lucky

02 an antique furniture dealer

03 buying, low price, high

04 had got, furniture, secret   05 secret, simple

06 went, every, knocked on

07 that, a furniture dealer

08 valuable, things, took advantage

09 able, buy things, cheaply

10 another, in, town again

11 At, house, visited, men

12 One, owner, the other   13 buy old furniture

14 have any, asked   15 don't, said

16 take a look   17 Sure, Please, in

18 went, there was nothing   19 then moved to

20 there it was

---

21 priceless piece of, furniture

22 so, that, fell over   23 wrong, asked

24 nothing, at all, lied

25 with, straight face, reproduction

26 worth only, few   27 added, may buy

28 legs, table, are broken   29 cut off, attach, mine

30 How much   31 Not, afraid

32 just a reproduction   33 So, much

34 Ten pounds   35 worth more than

36 How about   37 Make it

38 my final offer   39 yours, going, take

40 thing, go in   41 went out to bring

42 On, way, couldn't help   43 what, dealer, of

44 couldn't believe, luck   45 what if, go in

46 might not pay   47 had an idea

48 What he wants   49 cut the legs off

50 Great idea   51 took out, cut off

52 back, had been, off   53 worry, favor

54 won't charge, for

55 so shocked that, anything

본문 TEST Step 2   p.31~33

01 One Lucky

02 an antique furniture dealer

03 was known for, at a low price, at a high price

04 where he had got, secret   05 simple

06 every Sunday, knocked   07 a furniture dealer

08 how valuable their things were, took advantage of

09 able to, very cheaply   10 another Sunday

11 At a house

12 One, owner, the other   13 old furniture

14 any   15 don't

16 take a look   17 Sure

18 went to, there was nothing

19 moved to   20 there it was

21 a priceless piece of, furniture

22 so, that, fell over   23 wrong

24 nothing, at all

25 with a straight face, reproduction

26 It's worth, a few   27 added, may buy

28 are broken

29 cut off, attach them to mine

30 How much   31 afraid

32 a reproduction   33 So

34 pounds   35 It's worth more than

36 How about   37 Make it

38 thirty, final offer

39 yours, going, take

40 go in

41 went out to bring

42 On his way, couldn't help smiling

43 what, dreamed of

44 couldn't believe

45 what if

46 pay you

47 had an idea

48 What he wants

49 cut the legs off

50 Great idea

51 took out, cut off

52 came back, had been cut off

53 worry, a favor

54 charge, for

55 so, that, anything

---

1 어느 운수 좋은 일요일

2 Cyril Boggis는 런던의 골동품 가구 판매상이었다.

3 그는 좋은 물건을 낮은 가격에 사서 높은 가격에 파는 것으로 유명했다.

4 사람들은 그에게 어디서 가구를 구했는지 물어봤지만, 그는 "그건 비밀이에요."라고만 말했다.

5 Boggis 씨의 비밀은 단순했다.

6 그는 매주 일요일 작은 마을들을 방문해서 문을 두드렸다.

7 그는 사람들에게 자신이 가구 판매상이라고 말했다.

8 사람들은 자신들의 물건들이 얼마나 값진 것인지 몰랐으므로 Boggis 씨는 그들을 이용했다.

9 그는 물건들을 매우 싸게 살 수 있었다.

10 일요일이 또 찾아왔고 그날 Boggis 씨는 다시 어느 작은 마을에 있었다.

11 그는 방문한 집에서 두 남자를 만났다.

12 한 명은 주인인 Rummins였고, 다른 한 명은 그의 아들인 Bert였다.

13 "저는 고가구를 삽니다.

14 고가구가 있으신가요?" Boggis 씨가 물었다.

15 "아니요." Rummins가 말했다.

16 "한번 둘러봐도 될까요?" Boggis 씨가 물었다.

17 "그럼요. 들어오세요." Rummins가 말했다.

18 Boggis 씨는 먼저 부엌에 갔는데 아무것도 없었다.

19 그런 다음 그는 거실로 옮겼다.

20 그리고 그곳에 그것이 있었다!

21 18세기 영국 가구인 매우 귀중한 탁자가.

22 그는 몹시 흥분해서 거의 넘어질 뻔했다.

23 "무슨 일이세요?" Bert가 물었다.

24 "오, 아무것도 아니에요. 전혀 아무 일도 아닙니다." Boggis 씨는 거짓말을 했다.

25 그러고 나서 그는 정색하며 말했다 "이 탁자는 복제품입니다.

26 몇 파운드의 가치밖에 안 돼요."

27 그리고 그는 덧붙였다. "흠, 제 생각에 제가 살 수도 있을 것 같아요.

28 우리 집에 있는 탁자 다리가 부러졌거든요.

29 당신의 탁자 다리를 잘라서 제 탁자에 붙일 수 있겠어요."

30 "얼마 줄 거예요?" Rummins가 물었다.

31 "유감이지만 많이 줄 수는 없어요.

32 이것은 복제품일 뿐이니까요." Boggis 씨가 말했다.

33 "그래서 얼마 줄 수 있는데요?"

34 "10파운드요."

35 "100이요? 그것보다는 가치가 더 나가요."

36 "15는 어때요?"

37 "50으로 하지요."

38 "음, 30이요. 이게 제 마지막 제안입니다."

39 "그러죠, 이제 당신 겁니다. 그런데 이걸 어떻게 가져갈 건가요?

40 이게 차에 들어가지 않을 거예요!"

41 "한번 보죠." Boggis 씨가 말하고는 자신의 차를 가지러 밖으로 나갔다.

42 차로 가는 길에 Boggis 씨는 싱글벙글하지 않을 수 없었다.

43 그 탁자는 모든 판매상이 꿈꾸는 것이었다.

44 그는 자신의 운을 믿을 수 없었다.

45 "아버지, 만약 이게 차에 안 들어가면 어떻게 하죠?

46 그가 값을 지불하지 않을 수도 있어요." Bert가 말했다.

47 Rummins는 그때 생각이 떠올랐다.

48 "그가 원하는 건 오직 다리뿐이야.

49 그를 위해서 다리를 자르자." Rummins가 말했다.

50 "좋은 생각이에요!" Bert가 말했다.

51 그런 다음 Bert는 톱을 꺼내서 다리를 자르기 시작했다.

52 Boggis 씨가 돌아왔을 때, 다리는 잘려 있었다.

53 "걱정하지 마세요. 호의로 한 거예요.

54 이것에 대해 비용을 청구하지는 않을게요." Rummins가 말했다.

55 Boggis 씨는 너무 충격을 받아서 아무 말도 할 수 없었다.

---

1 One Lucky Sunday

2 Cyril Boggis was an antique furniture dealer in London.

3 He was known for buying good things at a low price and then selling them at a high price.

4 People asked him where he had got the furniture, but he just said, "It's a secret."

5 Mr. Boggis' secret was simple.

6 He went to small towns every Sunday and knocked on doors.

7 He told people that he was a furniture dealer.

8 People didn't know how valuable their things were, so Mr. Boggis took advantage of them.

9 He was able to buy things very cheaply

10 Now it was another Sunday, and Mr. Boggis was in a small town again.

11 At a house he visited, he met two men.

12 One was Rummins, the owner, and the other was his son Bert.

13 "I buy old furniture.

14 Do you have any?" asked Mr. Boggis.

15 "No, I don't," said Rummins.

16 "Can I just take a look?" asked Mr. Boggis.

17 "Sure. Please come in," said Rummins.

18 Mr. Boggis first went to the kitchen, and there was nothing.

19 He then moved to the living room.

20 And there it was!

21 A table which was a priceless piece of eighteenth-century English furniture.

22 He was so excited that he almost fell over.

23 "What's wrong?" Bert asked.

24 "Oh, nothing. Nothing at all," Mr. Boggis lied.

25 He then said with a straight face, "This table is a reproduction

26 It's worth only a few pounds."

27 He then added, "Hmm, I think I may buy it.

28 The legs of my table at home are broken.

29 I can cut off the legs of your table and attach them to mine."

30 "How much?" Rummins asked.

31 "Not much, I'm afraid

32 This is just a reproduction," said Mr. Boggis.

33 "So how much?"

34 "Ten pounds."

35 "Ten? It's worth more than that."

36 "How about fifteen?"

37 "Make it fifty."

38 "Well, thirty. This is my final offer."

39 "OK, it's yours, but how are you going to take it?

40 This thing will not go in a car!"

41 "We'll see," Mr. Boggis said and went out to bring his car.

42 On his way to the car, Mr. Boggis couldn't help smiling.

43 The table was what every dealer dreamed of.

44 He couldn't believe his luck.

45 "Dad, what if this thing doesn't go in his car?

46 He might not pay you," said Bert.

47 Rummins then had an idea.

48 "What he wants is only the legs.

49 Let's cut the legs off for him," said Rummins.

50 "Great idea!" said Bert.

51 Bert then took out a saw and began to cut off the legs.

52 When Mr. Boggis came back, the legs had been cut off.

53 "Don't worry, this was a favor.

54 I won't charge you for this," said Rummins.

55 Mr. Boggis was so shocked that he couldn't say anything.

After You Read A Read and Complete

1. antique furniture dealer, to buy furniture

2. priceless, eighteenth-century English furniture

3. lied, that, reproduction

4. His final offer, accepted it

5. Since what, only the legs of, cut them off

6. was very shocked to see

Around the World

1. protects, from, mean farmers

2. special powers to help

3. the best chocolate factory in the world

Think and Write

1. Review, *One Lucky*

2. was written by

3. who, antique furniture dealer

4. lied to, that, reproduction, offered, to buy

5. said, only wanted, so, cut them off

6. surprised, who, the whole table

7. because he lied to

8. What I like the most, is the surprising ending

9. I think, very interesting

After You Read A Read and Complete

1. One Sunday, Mr. Boggis, an antique furniture dealer, went to a small town to buy furniture.

2. At Rummins and Bert's house, Mr. Boggis found a table, a priceless piece of eighteenth-century English furniture.

3. Mr. Boggis lied to Rummins and Bert that the table was just a reproduction.

4. His final offer for the table was thirty pounds and Rummins accepted it.

55

5. Since what Mr. Boggis wanted was only the legs of the table, Bert cut them off.

6. Mr. Boggis was very shocked to see the table.

Around the World

1. Fantastic Mr. Fox: A fox protects his family from three mean farmers.

2. Matilda: A girl uses her special powers to help her friends.

3. Charlie and the Chocolate Factory: A boy visits the best chocolate factory in the world.

Think and Write

1. Review of the story, *One Lucky Sunday*

2. This story was written by Roald Dahl.

3. It is about Mr. Boggis, who was an antique furniture dealer.

4. In the story, he lied to Rummins that his table was a reproduction and offered 30 pounds to buy it.

5. Mr. Boggis said he only wanted the legs of the table, so Bert cut them off for him.

6. This surprised Mr. Boggis who really wanted the whole table.

7. I think Mr. Boggis was not a good man because he lied to people.

8. What I like the most about this story is the surprising ending.

9. I think this story is very interesting.

단어 TEST Step 1   p.45

01 총계, 총액	02 예측하다	03 영향을 미치다
04 주로	05 복잡한	06 전문가
07 독감	08 삽입하다	09 빌리다
10 자취, 발자국, 흔적	11 예측하다, 예보하다	
12 분석하다	13 예방	14 범죄
15 확산, 전파	16 잠금을 풀다	17 증상
18 의미 있는, 중요한	19 산업, 공업	
20 감사하다, 감상하다		21 더 이상의, 추가의
22 거대한, (크기·양·정도가) 막대한		
23 알아보다, 확인하다, 식별하다		24 구매
25 개선하다, 향상하다		
26 성장하다, 발달하다		27 다양한
28 끝없는, 무한한	29 피하다, 방지하다	30 방법
31 추천하다, 권하다	32 ~을 전송하다, 업로드하다	
33 포함하다	34 경기력, 수행, 성과	35 확실히, 분명히
36 ~에 초점을 맞추다		37 ~함으로써
38 ~할 것 같다	39 ~의 양/수량	
40 ~ 덕분에, ~ 때문에		41 결정하다
42 역할을 하다	43 ~하는 데 사용되다	

단어 TEST Step 2   p.46

01 industry	02 crime	03 expert
04 flu	05 huge	06 identify
07 various	08 develop	09 prevention
10 wisely	11 improve	12 analyze
13 include	14 amount	15 forecast
16 traffic	17 purchase	18 mainly
19 further	20 predict	21 endless
22 meaningful	23 insert	24 avoid
25 recommend	26 method	27 rent
28 spread	29 influence	30 symptom
31 trace	32 appreciate	33 upload
34 unlock	35 for sure	36 play a role
37 the amount of ~		38 be likely to ~
39 focus on	40 make a decision	
41 thanks to ~	42 more and more	
43 be used to+동사원형		

1 method, 방법   2 influence, 영향을 주다
3 analyze, 분석하다   4 rent, 빌리다   5 avoid, 피하다
6 identify, 확인하다   7 predict, 예측하다
8 recommend, 추천하다, 권하다
9 performance, 수행, 성과   10 database, 데이터베이스
11 purchase, 구매, 구매품   12 symptom, 증상, 징후
13 industry, 산업   14 develop, 발전시키다, 성정하다
15 spread, 확산, 전파   16 communication, 의사소통

Listen and Talk A 1

tell, how to add, to, transportation / First, put, in, Second, choose, amount, to add / Last, insert, into / simple

Listen and Talk A 2

know how to use / First, choose / did, next / put in, take, out / Got it

Listen and Talk A 3

rent, tell, how to use, application / log in to, touch it / what / to unlock, with / appreciate, help

Listen and Talk B

return, know how to do / simple, insert, into, put, in / Then, take, out / appreciate / add, to, know how to do / simple, First, Second, choose, amount / Then insert / appreciate, help / to buy, know how to do / simple, First, Second, put in / Then take, out / appreciate

Listen and Talk C

what's, for / that / tell, how to use / place, on, robot's screen / type, title, looking for, press / Is that all / Then, it, front desk / get / easy, isn't it / amazing

Listen and Talk D

Let, how to use, First, insert, into, Then, Last, out of

Talk and Play

know how to make / First, put / Then, pour / Last, take, out after, minutes / got it, appreciate

Review 1

how to plant / cut, into, pieces, dig, in / put, pieces in, cover, with dirt / sounds simple

Review 2

tell, how to use / put, on, copy machine, choose, the number of / what / Press, appreciate

Listen and Talk A 1

B: Excuse me. Can you tell me how to add money to my transportation card?
G: Of course. First, put your card in the machine. Second, choose the amount of money you want to add.
B: OK.
G: Last, insert your money into the machine.
B: That sounds simple. Thanks.

Listen and Talk A 2

B: I want to buy a snack. Do you know how to use this snack machine?
G: Yeah. First, choose the snack you want.
B: I already did. What's next?
G: Just put in the money. Then take the snack out.
B: Got it. Thanks.

Listen and Talk A 3

G: Excuse me. I want to rent a bike. Can you tell me how to use this application?
M: Sure. First, log in to the application. Then find the RENT button and touch it.
G: Then what?
M: Then the application will give you a number to unlock a bike with.
G: Thank you. I really appreciate your help.

Listen and Talk B

A: Excuse me. I want to return these books. Do you know how to do it?
B: Sure. It's simple. First, insert the library card into the machine. Second, put the books in this box.
A: OK.
B: Then just take your card out.
A: I really appreciate your help.

A: Excuse me. I want to add money to my transportation card. Do you know how to do it?
B: Sure. It's simple. First, put your card in the machine. Second, choose the amount of money.
A: OK.
B: Then insert the money.
A: I really appreciate your help.

A: Excuse me. I want to buy a snack. Do you know how to do it?
B: Sure. It's simple. First, choose the snack. Second, put in the money.
A: OK.
B: Then take the snack out.

A: I really appreciate your help.

Listen and Talk C

G: Excuse me, but what's this robot for?

B: Oh, it's a robot that finds books for you.

G: Really? Can you tell me how to use it?

B: Sure. First, place your library card on the robot's screen.

G: OK.

B: Second, type the title of the book you're looking for and then press ENTER.

G: Is that all?

B: Yes. Then, the robot will find the book and take it to the front desk.

G: So I can just go to the front desk and get the book?

B: Right. It's so easy, isn't it?

G: Yes, it's really amazing. Thank you.

Listen and Talk D

Let me tell you how to use a drink machine. First, insert money into the machine. Then, choose the drink you want. Last, take the drink out of the machine. It's easy.

Talk and Play

A: Do you know how to make tea?

B: Sure. First, put a tea bag in a cup.

A: OK.

B: Then, pour hot water in the cup.

A: And then?

B: Last, take the tea bag out after 3 minutes.

A: I got it. I really appreciate your help.

Review 1

G: Can you tell me how to plant a potato?

B: Sure. First, cut a potato into small pieces. Second, dig holes in the ground.

G: Then?

B: Then put the potato pieces in the holes and cover the holes with dirt.

G: That sounds simple. Thanks.

Review 2

B: Excuse me. Can you tell me how to use this machine?

G: Sure. First, put the paper on the copy machine. Then choose the paper size and the number of copies.

B: Then what?

G: Press the START button.

B: Thank you. I really appreciate your help.

본문 TEST Step 1   p.54~55

01 Living with

02 been surprised, recommended for

03 Many, looked interesting 04 So, what you liked

05 all possible because of   06 What is

07 data sets, big, complex

08 As, develops, amount, much

09 mainly, almost, leaves, trace

10 example, upload, purchases, part

11 Simply collecting, however, enough

12 has, analyzed, done, experts

13 methods, analyse, draw, results

14 results, used, decisions, predict

15 How, influencing, lives

16 influencing almost, parts, lives

17 customers' needs, sell, products

18 avoid heavy traffic

19 uses, endless, interesting examples

20 Disease Forecast

21 professionals, forecast, disease, experts

22 possible thanks to

23 comes, buy, flu medicine

24 search online, flu symptoms

25 analyzed wisely, spread, predicted

26 Improving Performance   27 sports fan

28 improving, performance, making, exciting

29 famous example, Germany's national

30 collecting, analyzing, huge amount

31 included, much, ran, long

32 With, help, improve, performance

33 Crime Prevention

34 Thanks, predict crime, happens

35 Through, analysis, hot spots

36 identifies, crime, likely, happen

37 prevent further, focusing, predicts

38 has already changed, greatly

39 industry go from here

40 sure, experts, play, role

본문 TEST Step 2   p.56~57

01 Living with

02 been surprised, recommended for

03 looked interesting   04 what you liked

05 possible because of   06 What is

07 data sets, are, complex

08 As, develops, amount of, getting much greater

09 mainly because, leaves a trace

10 upload on your blog, your purchases, all part of

11 Simply collecting data, however

12 has to be analyzed, done by

13 Using, analyze, draw meaningful results

14 can be used, to predict

15 How, influencing, lives   16 almost all parts

17 understand their customers' needs, sell more products

18 avoid heavy traffic

19 endless, interesting examples

20 Forecast   21 just as, forecast

22 thanks to

23 comes, will buy, flu medicine

24 search online about

25 is analyzed wisely, spread, be predicted

26 Improving Performance   27 sports fan

28 is improving, making, exciting

29 national soccer team

30 built, collecting, analyzing, huge amount

31 how much, how long

32 With the help of, able to improve

33 Prevention   34 Thanks to, happens

35 Through, crime hot spots

36 identifies, is most likely to happen

37 further crime by focusing, predicts

38 has already changed, greatly

39 go from here   40 play, role, lives

본문 TEST Step 3

p.58~59

1 빅데이터와 함께 살아가기

2 당신은 온라인 서점을 방문해서 그 서점이 당신을 위해 추천한 책들을 보고 놀란 적이 있는가?

3 그것들 중에 많은 것들이 당신에게 흥미로워 보였다.

4 그 서점은 당신이 무엇을 좋아하는지 어떻게 알았을까?

5 이것은 모두 빅데이터 때문에 가능하다.

6 빅데이터는 무엇인가?

7 빅데이터는 매우 크고 복잡한 데이터 집합이다.

8 정보 통신 기술이 발달함에 따라 우리가 갖고 있는 정보의 양도 이전보다 훨씬 더 많아지고 있다.

9 이것은 주로 우리가 온라인상에서 하는 거의 모든 것들이 흔적을 남기기 때문이다.

10 예를 들어, 당신이 블로그에 올린 사진들과 온라인 상점에서의 구매 기록들이 모두 빅데이터의 일부가 된다.

11 하지만 단순히 데이터를 수집하는 것만으로는 충분하지 않다.

12 빅데이터는 분석되어야 하고, 이것은 빅데이터 전문가들에 의해서 이루어진다.

13 다양한 방법들을 사용하여 전문가들은 빅데이터를 분석하고, 그것으로부터 의미 있는 결과들을 도출한다.

14 그런 다음, 이런 결과들은 결정을 하거나 또는 미래를 예측하는 데 사용될 수 있다.

15 빅데이터는 어떻게 우리 삶에 영향을 미치고 있는가?

16 빅데이터는 우리 삶의 거의 모든 부분에 영향을 미치고 있다.

17 그것은 회사들이 소비자들이 필요로 하는 것을 더 잘 이해하고 그들이 더 많은 상품을 팔도록 도와준다.

18 그것은 사람들이 교통 체증을 피하도록 도와주기도 한다.

19 그것의 활용은 끝이 없고, 여기에 몇 가지 흥미로운 예들이 있다.

20 질병 예측

21 당신은 날씨 전문가가 날씨를 예측하는 것과 같이 건강 전문가들이 현재 질병을 예측할 수 있다는 것을 알고 있는가?

22 이것은 빅데이터 덕분에 가능하다.

23 예를 들어서 독감의 계절이 오면, 사람들은 독감 약을 더 많이 구입할 것이다.

24 그들은 또한 온라인상에서 독감 증상들을 더 찾아볼 것이다.

25 만약 이런 종류의 데이터를 지혜롭게 분석한다면, 독감의 확산을 예측할 수 있다.

26 스포츠에서의 경기력 향상

27 당신은 스포츠 팬인가?

28 빅데이터는 스포츠를 더 흥미롭게 만들면서, 선수들의 경기력을 향상하고 있다.

29 유명한 사례로 독일 국가 대표 축구팀이 있다.

30 그 팀은 선수들에 관한 엄청난 양의 데이터를 모으고 분석함으로써, 데이터베이스를 구축했다.

31 예를 들어 데이터는 각각의 선수들이 얼마나 많이 달렸고, 얼마나 오랫동안 공을 소유했는지도 포함했다.

32 이 데이터베이스의 도움으로 독일 국가 대표 축구팀은 경기력을 향상할 수 있었고, 2014년 월드컵에서 우승할 수 있었다.

33 범죄 예방

34 빅데이터 덕분에 경찰은 이제 범죄가 발생하기 전에 범죄를 예측할 수 있다.

35 범죄의 유형, 시간 및 장소에 관한 빅데이터의 분석을 통해, 경찰은 범죄 다발 지역의 지도를 만들 수 있다.

36 이 지도는 범죄가 언제, 어디에서 가장 많이 발생할 것 같은지를 알려 준다.

37 경찰은 이 지도가 예측하는 장소들과 시간대에 집중함으로써, 추가 범죄를 예방할 수 있다.

38 빅데이터는 이미 세계를 크게 변화시켰다.

39 그러면 빅데이터 산업은 여기에서부터 어디로 가게 될까?

40 누구도 확실히 알지는 못하지만, 전문가들은 빅데이터가 우리 삶에서 더욱 더 중요한 역할을 할 것이라는 데에는 동의한다.

1 Living with Big Data

2 Have you ever visited an online bookstore and been surprised by the books that the store recommended for you?

3 Many of them looked interesting to you.

4 So how did the bookstore know what you liked?

5 This is all possible because of big data.

6 What is big data?

7 Big data is data sets that are very big and complex.

8 As information and communication technology develops, the amount of data we have is getting much greater than before.

9 This is mainly because almost everything that we do online leaves a trace.

10 For example, the photos you upload on your blog and the records of your purchases at online stores are all part of big data.

11 Simply collecting data, however, is not enough.

12 Big data has to be analyzed, and this is done by big data experts.

13 Using various methods, experts analyze big data and draw meaningful results from it.

14 These results then can be used to make decisions or to predict the future.

15 How is big data influencing our lives?

16 Big data is influencing almost all parts of our lives.

17 It helps companies understand their customers' needs better and helps them sell more products.

18 It helps people avoid heavy traffic.

19 Its uses are endless, and here are some interesting examples.

20 Disease Forecast

21 Did you know that health professionals can now forecast a disease just as weather experts forecast the weather?

22 This is possible thanks to big data.

23 For example, when the flu season comes, people will buy more flu medicine.

24 They will also search online about flu symptoms more.

25 If this kind of data is analyzed wisely, the spread of the flu can be predicted.

26 Improving Performance in Sports

27 Are you a sports fan?

28 Well, big data is improving the performance of players, making sports more exciting.

29 A famous example is Germany's national soccer team.

30 The team built a database by collecting and analyzing a huge amount of data on players.

31 For example, the data included information about how much each player ran and how long he had the ball.

32 With the help of this database, Germany's national soccer team was able to improve its performance and win the 2014 World Cup.

33 Crime Prevention

34 Thanks to big data, police can now predict crime before it happens.

35 Through the analysis of big data about the type, time and place of crime, police can make a map of crime hot spots.

36 This map identifies when and where crime is most likely to happen.

37 Police can prevent further crime by focusing on the areas and the times this map predicts.

38 Big data has already changed the world greatly.

39 So where will the big data industry go from here?

40 Nobody knows for sure, but experts agree that big data will play a more and more important role in our lives.

After You Read A Read and Complete

1. Health professionals, forecast the spread, by analyzing, flu symptoms

2. By collecting, analyzing a huge amount of, was able to improve

3. Through the analysis, crime hot spots, to prevent further crime

Around the World

1. late, will arrive in, minutes

2. Last time, missed, so let's review them

3. What's the weather like

4. going to rain, Take

5. is making my life, much easier

Think and Write

1. Teens' Free

2. teemagers, free time activities

3. The results, teenagers want to do the most is traveling

4. to travel in their free time

5. the free time activity, is watching TV

6. watch, in their free time

7. Looking at, a big gap, what the teenagers want to, what they actually do

After You Read A Read and Complete

1. Health professionals can now forecast the spread of the flu by analyzing the sales of flu medicine and online searches about flu symptoms.

2. By collecting and analyzing a huge amount of data on players, Germany's national soccer team was able to improve its performance and win the 2014 World Cup.

3. Through the analysis of big data, police can make a map of crime hot spots and use it to prevent further crime.

Around the World

1. Yuna: We're not late. The bus will arrive in 4 minutes.

2. Computer: Last time, you missed question numbers 3 and 5, so let's review them first.

3. Yuna: What's the weather like tomorrow?

4. AI: It's going to rain. Take your umbrella.

5. Yuna: Big data is making my life so much easier!

Think and Write

1. Teens' Free Time Activities

2. We asked 100 teemagers about their free time activities.

3. The results show that the free time activity the teenagers want to do the most is traveling.

4. 34% said that they want to travel in their free time.

5. However, the free time activity they actually do the most is watching TV.

6. 39% said that they watch TV in their free time.

7. Looking at the results, we see that there is a big gap between what the teenagers want to do and what they actually do in their free time.

01 녹다	02 갑자기	03 굴곡이 많은
04 따라서, 그러므로	05 굽다, 구부러지다	
06 나타내다, 보여 주다, 상징하다		07 ~에도 불구하고
08 취소하다	09 상징하다	10 시대, 왕조
11 효과적으로	12 민화	13 가치, 중요성
14 충성, 충실	15 행동	16 얼어붙은
17 조화	18 아픈, 병든	
19 ~하게 보이다, 나타나다		20 영향을 미치다
21 태도, 자세	22 상징적인, 상징하는	
23 정의, 공정성	24 연꽃	
25 진흙투성이의, 탁한, 흙탕물의		
26 꽃을 피우다, 꽃이 피다		27 잉어
28 의지	29 글자	30 실망한, 낙담한
31 존경, 경의	32 사회	33 장식
34 어려움, 고난	35 특히, 특별히	36 다음과 같이
37 병이 나아지다, 회복하다		38 옛날에
39 ~보다 훨씬 많이	40 ~에게 …을 상기시키다	
41 이런 이유로	42 ~ 때문에	43 ~ 직후에

01 dynasty	02 effectively	03 appear
04 influence	05 loyalty	06 justice
07 bloom	08 carp	09 represent
10 bend	11 curvy	12 decoration
13 lotus flower	14 difficulty	15 suddenly
16 folk painting	17 respect	18 society
19 value	20 character	21 behavior
22 symbolize	23 muddy	24 will
25 cancel	26 symbolic	27 harmony
28 disappointed	29 attitude	30 bamboo
31 frozen	32 melt	33 despite
34 object	35 get well	36 right after ~
37 in particular	38 as follows	39 for this reason
40 much more than		41 remind ~ of …
42 once upon a time		43 so ~ that …

1 bloom, 꽃을 피우다, 꽃이 피다   2 represent, 나타내다

3 symbol, 상징, 기호   4 object, 물건, 물체

5 attitude, 태도, 자세   6 remind, 상기시키다

7 behavior, 행동　8 symbolic, 상징적인
9 despite, ~에도 불구하고　10 frozen, 얼어붙은
11 loyalty, 충성, 충실　12 society, 사회
13 appear, 나타나다　14 bend, 굽다, 구부러지다
15 justice, 정의　16 dynasty, 왕조

Listen and Talk A 1

two paintings of cats, Aren't / are / both, the one,
about / prefer, seems to me that, cuter

Listen and Talk A 2

Which, prefer / prefer, It seems, healthier choice / so,
like, more / other

Listen and Talk A 3

old plates / Which one, prefer / to choose, better,
about / Me, too, seems, that, unique

Listen and Talk A 4

you're going to, gift, How about / look nice / Which
one, prefer, or, with / prefer, with, It seems to me

Listen and Talk B

Which, prefer / prefer, It, that, delicious / prefer,
prefer, seems to me, healthier / Which, prefer, or /
prefer / prefer, prefer, more calm / Which, or /
prefer, more unique / prefer, prefer, simple but /
Which, prefer, or, with / prefer, more / prefer, too,
prefer, cute

Listen and Talk C

exhibitions, Which, more / prefer, that / course,
much / so / just, also / never seen, before / before,
sure / next to / let's watch / Let's, first

Listen and Talk D

prefer, more fun to learn, prefer, inventor like

Talk and Play

Which, prefer / prefer, It seems to / prefer, prefer,
healthier

Review 1

to buy / great / Which one, prefer, or, with / prefer,
with triangles, more unique

Review 2

Which, prefer / prefer, the healthier choice / I heard
/ order, hungry

Review 3

Which one, more / prefer, this / much / let's go

Listen and Talk A 1

G: Minho, look at these two paintings of cats here.
Aren't they great?

B: Yes, they are.

G: They both are good, but I like the one on the left
more. How about you?

B: I prefer the one on the right. It seems to me that
the cat in it is cuter. I also like the bird in it.

Listen and Talk A 2

G: We can have Bibimbap or Galbitang. Which do
you prefer?

B: I prefer Bibimbap. It seems to me that it's the
healthier choice.

G: I think so, too. I also like Bibimbap more.

B: Let's order, then. I'm very hungry.

Listen and Talk A 3

G: Look at these two old plates, Steve. Aren't they
beautiful?

B: Yes. Which one do you prefer, the green plate or
the white plate?

G: Well, it's hard to choose, but I like the green one
better. How about you?

B: Me, too. It seems to me that the green plate is
more unique.

Listen and Talk A 4

G: Junsu, you said you're going to buy a gift for
your sister. How about the bags here?

B: They look nice.

G: Which one do you prefer, the one with flowers or
the one with animals?

B: I prefer the one with flowers. It seems to me that
my sister will like it more.

Listen and Talk B

A: Which food do you prefer, Tteokbokki or Gimbap?

B: I prefer Tteokbokki. It seems to me that it's more
delicious. How about you?

A: I prefer Tteokbokki, too. / I prefer Gimbap. It
seems to me that it's healthier.

A: Which painting do you prefer, the one on the left
or the one on the right?

B: I prefer the one on the right. It seems to me that
the cat in it is cuter. How about you?

A: I prefer the one on the right, too. / I prefer the
one on the left. It seems to me that it looks more
calm.

A: Which plate do you prefer, the green one or the

white one?

B: I prefer the green one. It seems to me that it's more unique. How about you?

A: I prefer the green one, too. / I prefer the white one. It seems to me that it's simple but beautiful.

A: Which bag do you prefer, the one with fish or the one with stars?

B: I prefer the one with stars. It seems to me that it's more my style. How about you?

A: I prefer the one with stars, too. / I prefer the one with fish. It seems to me that the fish are cute.

Listen and Talk C

G: There are two exhibitions we can go to. Which one do you want to see more, Eric?

B: I prefer the Korean mask exhibition. Is that OK, Somi?

G: Of course. And it seems to me that the mask exhibition will be much more interesting.

B: Do you think so?

G: Yes. Look at this poster. There isn't just an exhibition. There's also a mask dance show at 4:00 and 6:00.

B: Great! I've never seen a mask dance show before.

G: Well, I've seen a show before. I'm sure you'll like it.

B: So where is the show?

G: It's in Dasom Hall, next to the exhibition room.

B: It's 4:30 now, so let's watch the 6 o'clock show.

G: OK. Let's go see the exhibition first.

Listen and Talk D

I prefer science. It seems to me that it's more fun to learn. I also prefer it becausel want to be a great inventor like Edison.

Talk and Play

A: Which do you prefer, Ramyeon or spaghetti?

B: I prefer Ramyeon. It seems to me that it's more delicious. How about you?

A: I prefer Ramyeon, too. / I prefer spaghetti. It seems to me that it's healthier.

Review 1

G: Joe, didn't you say you needed to buy a cap? How about these caps here?

B: They look great.

G: Which one do you prefer, the one with triangles or the one with flowers?

B: I prefer the one with triangles. It seems to me that it's more unique.

Review 2

B: We can have Gimbap or Tteokbokki. Which do you prefer, Jenny?

G: I prefer Gimbap. It seems to me that it's the healthier choice. How about you, Minsu?

B: I'll have Tteokbokki. I heard that the Tteokbokki here is very good.

G: Let's order, then. I'm very hungry.

Review 3

John: There are two movies we can see. Which one do you want to see more, Somi?

Somi: I prefer *Batman*. I saw *Spider-Man* last week. Is this OK, John?

John: Of course. It seems to me that *Batman* will be much more fun.

Somi: Good. Then, let's go and see it.

본문 TEST Step 1   p.76~77

01 Window into, Dynasty   02 at, on the right

03 see, Chinese character   04 also see, carp, fan

05 called, type, popular, late

06 there, usually, with, objects

07 One of, characters appears

08 represent, values, important, dynasty

09 animals, objects, just decorations

10 often, symbolic

11 paintings, symbolize respect, because

12 goes as follows

13 Once upon, time, with

14 became ill, couldn't, anything

15 On, would, could, fresh

16 went out, completely frozen

17 It, for, to catch

18 so disappointed that, to

19 melted, suddenly, out of

20 went back home, cooked   21 Then, got well

22 other examples, symbolic objects

23 bamboo, paintings, character, lotus

24 Bamboo does, bend

25 stays green in, kinds

26 For, reasons, symbolize loyalty

27 case, grow, muddy, bloom

28 will, fight, despite difficulties

29 much more than, to

30 reminded, influenced, behaviors, attitudes

31 In particular, for, tool

32 Through, importance, harmony, society

01 into, Dynasty

02 Look at, on the right

03 see, Chinese character   04 see, carp

05 is called, a type of folk painting that was popular, late

06 usually, with, objects

07 One of, characters appears

08 represent, that were important to, Joseon dynasty

09 just decorations   10 often, symbolic

11 symbolize respect, because of

12 goes as follows   13 Once upon a time

14 became ill, anything

15 On, would be wonderful if I could eat fresh fish

16 went out to, was completely frozen

17 It, for him to catch any

18 so disappointed that, cried out to

19 melted, suddenly, out of

20 back home   21 got well

22 symbolic objects

23 in, of, lotus flowers in, of   24 bend

25 stays green in, kinds

26 For these reasons, came to symbolize loyalty to

27 In the case of, but still bloom beautifully

28 thus, will to fight for, despite difficulties

29 much more than, to

30 reminded, of, that, behaviors, attitudes

31 In particular, for

32 Through it, importance, harmony in, society

12 그 이야기는 다음과 같다.

13 옛날 옛적에 한 남자가 나이 드신 어머니와 살았다.

14 어느 겨울, 남자의 어머니는 병이 들어서 어떤 것도 먹을 수 없었다.

15 무척 추운 어느 날, 어머니는 남자에게 말했다. "신선한 물고기를 먹을 수 있다면 좋겠구나."

16 그 남자는 강으로 나갔지만, 강은 완전히 얼어붙어 있었다.

17 그가 그 어떤 물고기라도 잡는 것은 불가능했다.

18 남자는 몹시 낙담해서 하늘에 대고 외쳤다. "제가 어떻게 해야 하나요? 제발 저를 도와주세요."

19 그러자 얼음이 녹았고, 잉어 세 마리가 갑자기 물 밖으로 나왔다.

20 남자는 집으로 돌아가서 어머니를 위해 물고기들을 요리했다.

21 그러자 그의 어머니는 회복되었다.

22 문자도에 있는 상징적인 사물의 또 다른 예가 있다.

23 그것들은 글자 '충(忠)' 그림에 있는 대나무와 '의(義)' 그림에 있는 연꽃이다.

24 대나무는 구부러지지 않는다.

25 그것은 어떤 날씨에서도 푸르름을 유지한다.

26 이런 이유로 대나무는 왕에 대한 충성을 상징하게 되었다.

27 연꽃의 경우, 그것들은 진흙투성이의 연못에서 자라지만 여전히 아름답게 꽃을 피운다.

28 그래서 그 꽃들은 어려움에도 불구하고 정의를 위해 싸우는 사람의 의지를 상징하게 되었다.

29 문자도는 조선 시대 사람들에게 그림 그 이상이었다.

30 그것은 그들에게 자신들의 행동과 태도에 큰 영향을 미치는 중요한 가치를 상기시켰다.

31 특히 아이들에게 문자도는 학습 도구였다.

32 그것을 통해 조선 시대의 아이들은 가족과 사회에서의 조화의 중요성을 배울 수 있었다.

1 문자도, 조선 시대를 보는 창

2 오른쪽에 있는 그림을 보라.

3 한자 효(孝)가 보이는가?

4 잉어, 거문고, 그리고 부채가 보이는가?

5 이런 종류의 그림은 문자도이며, 조선 시대 후기에 인기 있었던 민화의 한 종류이다.

6 문자도에는 보통 한자 하나가 동물이나 사물과 함께 있다.

7 문자도에는 여덟 개의 한자 중 하나가 나온다.

8 그것들은 효(孝), 제(悌), 충(忠), 신(信), 예(禮), 의(義), 염(廉), 치(恥)이고, 그것들은 조선 시대 사람에게 중요했던 가치들을 나타낸다.

9 문자도에 있는 동물이나 사물은 단순한 장식이 아니다.

10 그것들은 종종 상징적이다.

11 예를 들어, '효' 그림 속에 있는 잉어는 옛이야기 때문에 부모님에 대한 존경심을 상징한다.

1 Munjado, a Window into the Joseon Dynasty

2 Look at the painting on the right.

3 Do you see the Chinese character, *hyo*(孝)?

4 Do you also see a carp, a geomungo, and a fan?

5 This kind of painting is called Munjado, and it is a type of folk painting that was popular in the late Joseon dynasty.

6 In Munjado, there is usually a Chinese character with some animals or objects.

7 One of eight Chinese characters appears in Munjado.

8 They are *hyo*(孝), *je*(悌), *chung*(忠), *sin*(信), *ye*(禮), *ui*(義), *yeom*(廉), and *chi*(恥), and they represent the values that were important to people of the Joseon dynasty.

9 The animals or objects in Munjado are not just decorations.

10 They often are symbolic.

11 For example, carp in the paintings of *hyo* symbolize respect for parents because of an old story.

12 The story goes as follows..

13 Once upon a time, a man lived with his old mother.

14 One winter, the man's mother became ill and couldn't eat anything.

15 On one very cold day, the mother said to the man, "It would be wonderful if I could eat fresh fish."

16 The man went out to the river, but it was completely frozen.

17 It was impossible for him to catch any fish.

18 The man was so disappointed that he cried out to the sky, "What should I do? Please help me."

19 Then the ice melted, and three carp suddenly came out of the water.

20 The man went back home and cooked the fish for his mother.

21 Then his mother got well.

22 There are other examples of symbolic objects in Munjado.

23 They are bamboo in the paintings of the character *chung*(忠) and lotus flowers in the paintings of *ui*(義).

24 Bamboo does not bend.

25 It stays green in all kinds of weather.

26 For these reasons, bamboo came to symbolize loyalty to the king.

27 In the case of lotus flowers, they grow in muddy ponds but still bloom beautifully.

28 They thus became a symbol of a person's will to fight for justice despite difficulties.

29 Munjado was much more than a painting to people of the Joseon dynasty.

30 It reminded them of important values that greatly influenced their behaviors and attitudes.

31 In particular, for children, Munjado was a study tool.

32 Through it, children in the Joseon dynasty could learn the importance of harmony in family and society.

구석구석지문 TEST Step 1   p.86

After You Read A Read and Complete

1. symbolize respect for parents
2. three carp in a frozen river, for his sick mother
3. symbolizes loyalty to
4. bend, stays green, all kinds of
5. person's will to fight for, despite difficulties
6. in muddy ponds, bloom beautifully

Around the World

1. shows the harvest time of a countryside
2. in the late Joseon dynasty
3. shows the marriage of, in the 19th century

Think and Write

1. Favorite
2. My favorite painting
3. was painted by
4. the reflection of clouds, as well as
5. because, scene looks peaceful
6. it, creative of the painter to draw, so that, are reflected

구석구석지문 TEST Step 2   p.87

After You Read A Read and Complete

1. Paintings of *Hyo*(孝): Carp symbolize respect for parents.
2. In an old story, a man caught three carp in a frozen river and cooked them for his sick mother.
3. Paintings of *Chung*(忠): Bamboo symbolizes loyalty to the king.
4. It does not bend and stays green in all kinds of weather.
5. Paintings of *Ui*(義): Lotus flowers symbolize a person's will to fight for justice despite difficulties.
6. They grow in muddy ponds but still bloom beautifully.

Around the World

1. This painting shows the harvest time of a countryside in Europe in the 16th century.
2. This painting shows a ssireum competition in the late Joseon dynasty.
3. This painting shows the marriage of an American farmer's daughter in the 19th century.

Think and Write

1. My Favorite Painting, *Water Lillies: The Clouds*
2. My favorite painting is *Water Lillies: The Clouds*.
3. It was painted by Claude Monet.

4. In the painting, I can see the reflection of clouds in the pond as well as water lilies.
5. I like this painting because the colors are beautiful and the scene looks peaceful.
6. I think it was very creative of the painter to draw the pond as a mirror so that the clouds in the sky are reflected in the pond.

Lesson S

단어 TEST Step 1   p.88

01 가만히 있는, 고요한	02 사고
03 뽑다, 따다, 뜯다 04 자신 있게	05 공평한, 공정한
06 칭찬, 찬사; 칭찬하다	07 목록, 명단
08 망설이다, 주저하다	
09 (~에 빠져) 움직일 수 없는	
10 난처한, 딱한, 걱정[근심]스러운	11 창의적인, 창조적인
12 효과가 있다 13 발랄한, 쾌활한	14 가리키다
15 긁다 16 지저분한, 엉망인	
17 ~을 다치게 하다, 아프다	18 (일시적인) 중단
19 비명을 지르다 20 공중, 허공	21 침착한, 차분한
22 수줍게, 부끄러워하며	23 자전거 거치대
24 ~을 제외하고 25 하루 종일	26 잠깐만.
27 빠져나가다[나오다]	28 일전에, 최근에
29 하나의 ~, 한 조각의 ~	30 ~에서 나오다
31 무엇 때문에 ~했니?	

단어 TEST Step 2   p.89

01 work	02 still	03 accident
04 compliment	05 fair	06 hesitate
07 shyly	08 worried	09 confidently
10 list	11 hurt	12 messy
13 creative	14 pause	15 stuck
16 cheerful	17 point	18 scratch
19 air	20 pick	21 calm
22 scream	23 bicycle stand	24 the other day
25 pull out	26 except for	27 all day long
28 Just a minute.	29 a piece of	30 come out of
31 What made you ~?		

단어 TEST Step 3   p.90

1 messy, 지저분한, 엉망인   2 calm, 침착한   3 air, 공중
4 scream, 비명을 지르다   5 cheerful, 발랄한, 쾌활한
6 work, 효과가 있다   7 scratch, 긁다
8 creative, 창조적인   9 accident, 사고
10 hesitate, 망설이다, 주저하다   11 pause, 중단
12 fair, 공평한, 공정한   13 point, 가리키다
14 list, 목록, 명단   15 confidently, 자신 있게
16 compliment, 칭찬, 찬사

01 Best Compliment Ever   03 the last week

04 Each, picked, piece, with

05 Compliments for, last activity

06 everyone pick, name   07 Yes, Ms.

08 talking, each other   09 whose name, pick

10 smiling, got   11 lot to say

12 What about

13 looking worried, picked

14 easy, something, compliment, on

15 sits at, all, long

16 scratching, have to find

18 at, talking with, activity

19 lists, compliments, other, except

20 what to compliment, on   21 Think carefully

22 There should, something   23 he's clean

24 washes, face every   25 not a compliment

26 does that   27 Try again

28 sure, something good, say

30 next, there, an accident

31 foot is stuck, stand   32 with arms, air, help

33 Stay still, pull, out   34 screaming, hurts

35 Let, help, minute

36 runs, comes back with

37 going, put, on, foot   38 What, Butter

39 stay calm

40 pointing, foot, working

41 coming out of, stand   43 eating dinner with

44 about what happened   45 There, little accident

46 got stuck in   47 So, get, out

48 put, on, pulled, out   49 creative, Messy but

50 Creative, be, compliment   51 Sure

53 last, complimenting, each other

54 what compliment, for   55 always cheerful

56 kind, fair, everybody   57 so, of you to

58 let's hear from   59 picked, name

60 hesitating, think, creative   61 shyly, Really

62 What made you think

63 pause, stuck, other, using   64 That, creative

65 Nobody else thought, doing

66 then, also, creative   67 confidently, creative

68 the best compliment ever

01 Best Compliment   03 last week

04 Each, a piece of paper with

05 Compliments for, last activity

06 pick   08 talking, each other

09 whose name, pick   10 smiling, got

11 a lot to say   12 What about

13 looking worried, picked

14 to find, compliment him on

15 sits at his desk all day long

16 have to find

18 talking with

19 compliments, other, except for

20 what to compliment, on   21 carefully

22 should be   23 he's clean

24 washes, every day   25 a compliment

26 does that   27 Try again

28 I'm sure, something good   30 an accident

31 is stuck, stand   32 with arms in the air

33 Stay still, pull, out   34 screaming, hurts

35 Let, minute   36 comes back

37 put, on, foot   38 What

39 calm   40 pointing to, working

41 coming out of   43 eating dinner with

44 what happened   45 a little accident

46 got stuck in   47 get, out

48 put, on, pulled it out   49 Messy, creative

50 a compliment   51 Sure

53 the last day, complimenting each other

54 what compliment   55 cheerful

56 also, fair   57 of you

58 hear from you   59 picked

60 hesitating, creative   61 shyly

62 What made you think

63 pause, got stuck, the other day, got, out by using

64 creative

65 Nobody else thought of   66 also

67 confidently, creative

68 the best compliment ever

1 최고의 칭찬

2 〈장면 1〉

3 이번 주는 학교의 마지막 주이다.

4 각 학생들은 이름 하나가 쓰인 종이 한 장씩을 막 뽑았다.

5 Ms. Kemp: '학급 친구들 칭찬하기'는 이번 학년 우리의 마지막 활동이 될 거예요.

6 모두 이름을 뽑았나요?

7 Class: 네, Kemp 선생님.

8 학생들이 서로 이야기를 나누고 있다.

9 Beth: 너는 누구 이름을 뽑았니?

10 Lucy: (웃으며) Boyd를 뽑았어.

11 그 애에 관해 할 말이 많아.

12 너는 어때, Beth?

13 Beth: (걱정스러운 표정으로) 어, Peter 이름을 뽑았어.

14 Lucy: Peter? 아, 이런! 그 애에 관해서 칭찬할 것을 찾는 게 쉽지 않을 거야.

15 Steve: 그래. 그 애는 말을 많이 하지 않고 하루 종일 그냥 책상에 앉아만 있잖아.

16 Beth: (머리를 긁적이며) 음, 무언가를 찾아야 해.

17 〈장면 2〉

18 Beth는 집에서 그 활동에 대해 자신의 부모님과 이야기를 나누고 있다.

19 Beth: 저를 제외한 모두가 다른 친구들에 대해 긴 칭찬 목록을 가지고 있어요.

20 저는 Peter에 관해 무엇을 칭찬해야 할지 모르겠어요.

21 엄마: 잘 생각해 봐.

22 뭔가 있을 거야.

23 Beth: 음, 그 애는 깔끔해요.

24 매일 세수를 해요.

25 엄마: 그건 칭찬이 아니야.

26 모든 사람들이 하는 거잖니.

27 아빠: 다시 생각해 보렴.

28 그 아이에 대해 말할 뭔가 좋은 것을 분명히 찾을 수 있을 거야.

29 〈장면 3〉

30 다음 날, 학교에서 사고가 생긴다.

31 Boyd의 발이 자전거 거치대에 끼었다.

32 Boyd: (공중에 양팔을 벌린 채) 도와줘! 도움이 필요해!

33 Beth: 가만히 있어. 네 발을 꺼내려고 노력 중이야.

34 Boyd: (비명을 지르며) 아! 아파!

35 Peter: 내가 도와줄게. 잠깐만.

36 Peter가 학교 주방으로 뛰어가 버터를 가지고 온다.

37 Peter: 네 발에 이 버터를 바를 거야.

38 Boyd: 뭐? 버터를?

39 Peter: 그냥 침착하게 있어.

40 Beth: (Boyd의 발을 가리키며) 와! 효과가 있어!

41 Boyd의 발이 거치대에서 빠져나오고 있어.

42 〈장면 4〉

43 Beth는 부모님과 저녁 식사를 하고 있다.

44 그녀는 부모님께 Boyd에게 일어난 일에 대해 이야기한다.

45 Beth: 오늘 학교에서 작은 사고가 있었어요.

46 Boyd의 발이 자전거 거치대에 끼었어요.

47 엄마: 오, 저런! 그래서 발을 어떻게 뺐니?

48 Beth: Peter가 그 애 발에 버터를 바르고 나서 발을 당겨서 꺼냈어요.

49 아빠: 정말 창의적이구나. 지저분하지만 창의적이야.

50 Beth: 흠. 창의적이라고요? 아빠, 그것이 칭찬이 될 수 있어요?

51 아빠: 물론이지.

52 〈장면 5〉

53 오늘은 학교의 마지막 날이고 학생들은 서로를 칭찬하고 있다.

54 Ms. Kemp: Joanne, Beth에게 무슨 칭찬을 해 주겠니?

55 Joanne: Beth, 너는 항상 쾌활해.

56 또한 친절하고 모두에게 공정해.

57 Beth: 고마워, Joanne. 그렇게 말해 주다니 친절하구나.

58 Ms. Kemp: Beth, 이제 네 말을 들어 보자.

59 Peter의 이름을 뽑았구나.

60 Beth: (주저하며) 음, Peter는 창의적이라고 생각해요. Peter, 너는… 어… 창의적이야.

61 Peter: (수줍어하며) 정말?

62 Ms. Kemp: Peter가 왜 창의적이라고 생각하니?

63 Beth: (한참 있다가) 일전에 Boyd의 발이 자전거 거치대에 끼었을 때, Peter는 버터를 사용해서 그의 발을 꺼냈어요.

64 그것은 창의적이었어요.

65 Boyd: 맞아! 어느 누구도 그렇게 하는 것을 생각하지 못했어.

66 Steve: 난 몰랐어. 음, 그래, 나도 그가 창의적이라고 생각해.

67 Beth: (자신 있게) 그래, Peter, 너는 창의적이야!

68 Peter: 고마워, Beth! 그건 최고의 칭찬이야!

1 The Best Compliment Ever

2 Scene 1

3 It is the last week of school.

4 Each student has just picked a piece of paper with a name on it.

5 Ms. Kemp: "Compliments for Classmates" will be our last activity of the school year.

6 Did everyone pick a name?

7 Class: Yes, Ms. Kemp.

8 Students are talking to each other.

9 Beth: So, whose name did you pick?

10 Lucy: (smiling) I got Boyd.

11 I have a lot to say about him.

12 What about you, Beth?

13 Beth: (looking worried) Uh, I picked Peter's name.

14 Lucy: Peter? Oh, no! It won't be easy to find something to compliment him on.

15 Steve: Yeah. He doesn't talk much and just sits at

his desk all day long.

16 Beth: (scratching her head) Well, I'll have to find something.

17 Scene 2

18 Beth is at home talking with her parents about the activity.

19 Beth: Everyone has long lists of compliments for other classmates, except for me.

20 I don't know what to compliment Peter on.

21 Mom: Think carefully.

22 There should be something.

23 Beth: Well, he's clean.

24 He washes his face every day.

25 Mom: That's not a compliment.

26 Everybody does that.

27 Dad: Try again.

28 I'm sure you can find something good to say about him.

29 Scene 3

30 The next day, there is an accident at school.

31 Boyd's foot is stuck in a bicycle stand.

32 Boyd: (with arms in the air) Help! I need help!

33 Beth: Stay still. I'm trying to pull your foot out.

34 Boyd: (screaming) Ouch! That hurts!

35 Peter: Let me help. Just a minute.

36 Peter runs to the school's kitchen and comes back with butter.

37 Peter: I'm going to put this butter on your foot.

38 Boyd: What? Butter?

39 Peter: Just stay calm.

40 Beth: (pointing to Boyd's foot) Wow! It's working!

41 Boyd's foot is coming out of the stand.

42 Scene 4

43 Beth is eating dinner with her parents.

44 She tells them about what happened to Boyd.

45 Beth: There was a little accident at school today.

46 Boyd's foot got stuck in a bicycle stand.

47 Mom: Oh, no! So how did he get his foot out?

48 Beth: Peter put butter on his foot and then pulled it out.

49 Dad: That was really creative. Messy but creative.

50 Beth: Hmm. Creative? Can that be a compliment, Dad?

51 Dad: Sure.

52 Scene 5

53 It is the last day of school, and the students are complimenting each other.

54 Ms. Kemp: Joanne, what compliment do you have for Beth?

55 Joanne: Beth, you're always cheerful.

56 You're also kind and fair to everybody.

57 Beth: Thanks, Joanne. It's so nice of you to say so.

58 Ms. Kemp: Beth, let's hear from you now.

59 You picked Peter's name.

60 Beth: (hesitating) Well, I think Peter is creative. Peter, you're … uh … creative.

61 Peter: (shyly) Really?

62 Ms. Kemp: What made you think Peter is creative?

63 Beth: (after a long pause) When Boyd's foot got stuck in the bicycle stand the other day, Peter got it out by using butter.

64 That was creative.

65 Boyd: Yeah! Nobody else thought of doing that.

66 Steve: I didn't know that. Well, then, I also think he's creative.

67 Beth: (confidently) Yeah, Peter, you ARE creative!

68 Peter: Thanks, Beth! It's the best compliment ever!

MEMO

MEMO

MEMO

2학기 전과정

적중100plus

영어 기출 문제집

정답 및 해설

동아 | 윤정미

적중 1○○ + 특별부록

Plan B

우리학교
최신기출

동아·윤정미 교과서를 배우는

학교 시험문제 분석·모음·해설집

전국단위 학교 시험문제 수집 및 분석
출제 빈도가 높은 문제 위주로 선별
문제 풀이에 필요한 상세한 해설

중3-2
영어

동아·윤정미

Lesson 5   The Team Behind the Team
Lesson 6   Stories for All Time
Lesson 7   Technology in Our Lives
Lesson 8   The Joseon Dynasty Through Paintings

적중 **100** + 특별부록

Plan B

우리학교 최신기출

중3-2
영어

동아 · 윤정미

Lesson 5   The Team Behind the Team

Lesson 6   Stories for All Time

Lesson 7   Technology in Our Lives

Lesson 8   The Joseon Dynasty Through Paintings

◎ 선택형 문항의 답안은 컴퓨터용 수정 싸인펜을 사용하여 OMR 답안지에 바르게 표기하시오.
◎ 서술형 문제는 답을 답안지에 반드시 검정 볼펜으로 쓰시오.
◎ 총 28문항 100점 만점입니다. 문항별 배점은 각 문항에 표시되어 있습니다.

[전북 ○○중]

01 다음 중 짝지어진 두 단어의 관계가 나머지와 <u>다른</u> 것은? (3점)

① same – different
② happy – unhappy
③ visible – invisible
④ polite – dispolite
⑤ possible – impossible

[부산 ○○중]

02 다음 문장의 빈칸에 들어갈 표현으로 알맞은 것은?   (4점)

> • My teacher always _____ my progress on the test. (선생님은 시험에서 늘 나의 진척을 파악하신다.)

① keeps track of
② takes care of
③ is known for
④ depends on
⑤ looks for

[경기 ○○중]

[3~4] 다음 대화를 읽고 물음에 답하시오.

> W: Hello. Welcome to Sports World. May I help you?
> B: Yes, I came to register (A)_____ a swimming class.
> W: Is this your first time taking swimming lessons?
> B: Yes, it is. I don't know how to swim at all.
> W: I see. How often do you want to take classes?

> B: I'd like to take classes on weekdays and not on weekends.
> W: Then, I suggest that you take the Beginner 2 class. This class meets on Tuesdays and Thursdays.
> B: That sounds good. I'd like to sign (B)_____ for that class. How big is the class?
> W: The class has a limit (C)_____ 10 people.
> B: That's perfect.

03 위 대화의 빈칸 (A), (B), (C)에 들어갈 말로 적절한 것은? (4점)

	(A)	(B)	(C)
①	for	up	of
②	on	for	of
③	for	up	with
④	on	for	with
⑤	for	with	of

04 위 대화의 B에 대한 설명으로 적절하지 <u>않은</u> 것은?   (3점)

① 수영 수업에 등록하려고 한다.
② 전에 수영 강습을 받은 적이 없다.
③ 수영하는 방법을 조금은 알고 있다.
④ 주말보다는 주중에 강습을 받는 것을 원한다.
⑤ 매주 화요일과 목요일에 수영 수업을 받게 될 것이다.

[충남 ○○중]

05 다음 대화의 빈칸에 <u>어색한</u> 표현은?   (3점)

> A: I lost my wallet.
> B: _____

① Congratulations!   ② That's too bad.
③ That's a pity.   ④ That's unfortunate.
⑤ I'm sorry to hear that.

[6~7] 다음 대화를 읽고 물음에 답하시오.

Clerk: Hello. Welcome to Sports World. May I help you?
Jinsu: Yes, I came to register for a swimming class.
Clerk: Is this your first time taking swimming lessons?
Jinsu: Yes, it is. I don't know how to swim at all.
Clerk: I see. (A)_____
Jinsu: I want to take classes twice a week. I'd like to take classes on weekdays and not on weekends.
Clerk: Then, I suggest that you take the Beginner 2 class. This class meets on Tuesdays and Thursdays.
Jinsu: That sounds good. I'd like to sign up for that class. How big is the class?
Clerk: The class has a limit of 10 people.
Jinsu: That's perfect.

06 위 대화의 빈칸 (A)에 들어갈 말로 알맞은 것은? (3점)

① How long have you learned to swim?
② How much should I pay for the classes?
③ How often do you want to take classes?
④ How many classes do you have a week?
⑤ What do you do during the swimming class?

07 위 대화에서 언급되지 <u>않은</u> 것은? (3점)

① 수강 수준   ② 수강 요일
③ 수강 종목   ④ 수업 요금
⑤ 주당 횟수

08 다음 대화의 빈칸 (A)에 들어갈 조언 내용으로 가장 적절한 것은? (3점)

B: Suji, how many times do you take bowling lessons?
G: Twice a week. I'm just a beginner. I heard you're very good.
B: Well, I love bowling. Hmm. Your bowling ball looks heavy for you. (A)_____
G: OK. I'll look for one, then.

① I suggest we study English harder.
② I suggest you wear running shoes.
③ I suggest you use a lighter ball.
④ I suggest we start to exercise.
⑤ I suggest you join my basketball club.

09 다음 대화의 흐름이 자연스럽도록 (A)~(D)를 순서대로 바르게 배열한 것은? (4점)

(A) Well. I love bowling. Hmm. Your bowling ball looks heavy for you. I suggest you use a lighter ball.
(B) Twice a week. I'm just a beginner. I heard you're very good.
(C) Suji. How often do you take bowling lessons?
(D) OK. I'll look for a lighter one, then.

① (A)-(C)-(B)-(D)   ② (B)-(A)-(C)-(D)
③ (B)-(C)-(D)-(A)   ④ (C)-(B)-(A)-(D)
⑤ (C)-(B)-(D)-(A)

10 다음 중 의도하는 바가 나머지 넷과 다른 것은? (4점)

① How about studying English?
② I study English very hard.
③ I suggest you study English.
④ Why don't you study English?
⑤ I think you should study English.

11 다음 중 짝지어진 대화가 <u>어색한</u> 것은? (3점)

① A: What is he doing?

B: He is registering for swimming classes.

② A: Minsu, how often do you exercise?

B: I exercise once a week.

③ A: How often do you play computer games?

B: I play computer games every day.

④ A: I'd like to take classes on weekdays.

B: Then, I suggest that you take the Beginner 2 class.

⑤ A: Do you know how to swim?

B: Sure, but I suggest you bring a swimming cap.

12 다음 대화의 (A), (B)의 각 빈칸에 들어갈 표현이 가장 적절한 것끼리 바르게 짝지어진 것은? (4점)

A: Hello. Welcome to Sports World. May I help you?

B: Yes, I came to register for a swimming class.

A: Is this your first time taking swimming lessons?

B: Yes, it is. I don't know how to swim at all.

A: I see. (A)_____ do you to take classes?

B: I want to take classes twice a week. I'd like to take class on weekdays and not on weekends.

A: Then, I suggest that you take the Beginner 2 class. This class meets on (B)_____.

B: That sounds good. I'd like to sign up for that class. How big is the class?

A: The class has limit of 10 people.

B: That's perfect.

	(A)	(B)
①	How often	Tuesdays and Thursdays
②	How much	Wednesdays and Fridays
③	How often	Wednesdays and Saturdays
④	How much	Tuesdays, Thursdays and Fridays
⑤	How many	Mondays, Thursdays and Sundays

13 다음 〈보기〉의 밑줄 친 단어의 쓰임과 <u>다른</u> 하나는? (3점)

> 보기
> • I saw the bands <u>playing</u> the guitar.

① The boy <u>drinking</u> water is Eric.

② The girl <u>waiting</u> there is my sister.

③ There are students <u>studying</u> in the library.

④ That is why <u>changing</u> the tires is important.

⑤ I like the girl <u>reading</u> books in the classroom.

14 다음 우리말을 영어로 옮긴 것 중 바르지 <u>않은</u> 것은? (3점)

① 캐나다는 미국만큼 면적이 넓다.

Canada is as large as the USA.

② 건강만큼 소중한 것은 없다.

Nothing is more precious than health.

③ 램프보다 테이블이 더 비싸다.

The lamp is more expensive than the table.

④ Cathy가 우리 학급에서 가장 친절한 학생이다.

Cathy is the kindest student in my class.

⑤ 내 가방이 민지의 것보다 훨씬 크다.

My bag is much bigger than Minji's.

[15~17] 다음 글을 읽고, 물음에 답하시오.

You may only see the car and the driver during most car races, but there is a team behind the driver. (A) This team is ⓐcall a pit crew. (B) A pit is a place on the side of the race track, and drivers stop there several times during a race. (C) The main job of the pit crew is to check the car and change the tires. (D)
A pit stop can be as short as 2 seconds, and there are as many as 20 members on a crew. ⓑ_____, the pit crew has to work in perfect harmony. (E) The driver may get all the attention, but as people say, "Races are won in the pits."

15 위 글의 (A)~(E) 중 다음 문장이 들어갈 위치로 알맞은 곳은? (4점)

Changing the tires is especially important because the tires wear out easily in a high speed race.

① (A)　② (B)　③ (C)　④ (D)　⑤ (E)

16 위 글의 밑줄 친 ⓐcall의 가장 알맞은 형태는? (3점)

① called　② calling
③ to call　④ have called
⑤ to have called

17 위 글의 빈칸 ⓑ에 들어갈 말로 가장 알맞은 것은? (3점)

① However　② Therefore
③ Otherwise　④ In addition
⑤ For example

[18~19] 다음 글을 읽고 물음에 답하시오.

Pacers in a Marathon
Pacers run with other runners and lead them in a marathon. Pacers are (A)[experienced / experiencing] runners, and their job is to help other runners manage their race better. There can be several pacers in a race. Each pacer runs at different speeds and (B)[finish / finishes] the race in different times. Pacers usually have flags or balloons (C)[showed / showing] their finish time. Runners can choose a pacer depending on their target finish time. (D)_____, if a runner wants to finish the race in four hours, the runner will follow the four-hour pacer. (E)_____ the pacer keeps track of the time, the runner can achieve his or her goal of finishing the marathon in a particular time more easily. In short, pacers run but they don't run to win. They run for others.

18 위 글의 괄호 (A), (B), (C) 안에 들어갈 말로 가장 적절한 것은? (4점)

	(A)	(B)	(C)
①	experiencing	finish	showed
②	experienced	finishes	showing
③	experienced	finish	showing
④	experiencing	finishes	showing
⑤	experienced	finishes	showed

19 위 글의 빈칸 (D), (E)에 들어갈 말로 가장 적절한 것은? (4점)

	(D)	(E)
①	Also	If
②	However	Since
③	In addition	Whether
④	In contrast	Although
⑤	For example	Because

20 다음 글의 빈칸 (A)~(E)에 들어갈 단어가 순서대로 바르게 배열된 것은? (5점)

You may only see the car and the driver during most car races, but there is a team behind the driver. This team is called a (A)_____. A (B)_____ is a place on the side of the race track, and drivers stop there several times during a race. The main job of the pit crew is to check the car and change the tires. Changing the tires is especially (C)_____ because the tires wear out easily in a high speed race. A (D)_____ can be as short as 2 seconds, and there are as many as 20 members on a crew. Therefore, the pit crew has to work in perfect (E)_____. The driver may get all the attention, but as people say, "Races are won in the pits."

	(A)	(B)	(C)	(D)	(E)
①	pit stop	pit crew	fantastic	pit	place
②	pit crew	pit stop	expensive	pit crew	teamwork
③	pit crew	pit	important	pit stop	harmony
④	pit stop	pit	difficult	pit	condition
⑤	pit crew	pit	not easy	pit stop	company

[21~22] 다음 글을 읽고, 물음에 답하시오.

In sports, only the players get a trophy or medal, but they don't win ⓐon their own. There ⓑare people ⓒwho helps the players. These people ⓓare often hidden and don't get attention. However, they are ⓔas important as the players. Here are some examples.

21 위 글의 밑줄 친 ⓐ~ⓔ 중 어법상 바르지 않은 것은? (3점)

① ⓐ ② ⓑ ③ ⓒ ④ ⓓ ⑤ ⓔ

22 위 글에 이어질 내용으로 가장 알맞은 것은? (4점)

① 올림픽 인기 종목
② 경기를 이기는 방법
③ 자기 힘으로 메달을 딴 운동선수
④ 스포츠 분야의 숨은 조력자들
⑤ 운동 경기에서 협력의 중요성

23 다음 중 Pacer에 대한 설명이 틀린 것은? (4점)

Pacers in a Marathon
Pacers run with other runners and lead them in a marathon. Pacers are experienced runners, and their job is to help other runners manage their race better. There can be several pacers in a race.
Each pacer runs at different speeds and finishes the race in different times. Pacers usually have flags or balloons showing their finish time.
Runners can choose a pacer depending on their target finish time. Since the pacer keeps track of the time, the runner can achieve his or her goal of finishing the marathon in a particular time more easily. In short, pacers run but they don't run to win. They run for others.

① 한 경기에는 여러 명의 Pacer가 있다.
② Pacer들은 선수들을 돕기 위해 달린다.
③ 모든 Pacer는 항상 일정한 속도로 달린다.
④ 달리기 선수가 경기를 잘 운영하도록 돕는다.
⑤ Pacer들은 자신들의 완주 시간을 나타내는 깃발이나 풍선을 가지고 있다.

24 주어진 글 다음에 이어질 글의 순서로 가장 적절한 것은? (4점)

Pit Crews in Car Racing
You may only see the car and the driver during most car races, but there is a team behind the driver.

(A) Changing the tires is especially important because the tires wear out easily in a high speed race. A pit stop can be as short as 2 seconds, and there are as many as 20 members on a crew.

(B) Therefore, the pit crew has to work in perfect harmony. The driver may get all the attention, but as people say, "Races are won in the pits."

(C) This team is called a pit crew. A pit is a place on the side of the race track, and drivers stop there several times during a race. The main job of the pit crew is to check the car and change the tires.

① (A) - (B) - (C) ② (B) - (A) - (C)
③ (B) - (C) - (A) ④ (C) - (A) - (B)
⑤ (C) - (B) - (A)

[25~26] 다음 글을 읽고 물음에 답하시오.

The word *Sherpa* comes from the Sherpa tribe, which lives in the eastern part of Nepal. ⓐSherpas have good climbing skills and know their way around the mountains well. ⓑThey also have little difficulty breathing high up in the mountains. Therefore, mountain climbers started to hire Sherpas to help ⓒthem climb Mount Everest.
Sherpas lead mountain climbers to the top of the mountain. ⓓThey support climbers in many ways. For example, they put up tents and carry climbers' bags. Sherpas are often called the ⓔinvisible people of Mount Everest because (A)_____.

25 위 글의 ⓐ~ⓔ 중 지칭하는 것이 다른 하나는? (4점)

① ⓐ ② ⓑ ③ ⓒ ④ ⓓ ⑤ ⓔ

26 위 글의 빈칸 (A)에 들어갈 말로 가장 적절한 것은? (3점)

① people like to believe what they see
② people have never met Sherpas before
③ people don't want Sherpas to help them
④ people see a picture of only the climbers, not the Sherpas
⑤ people don't know how hard Sherpas do their work for the climbers

[27~28] 다음 글을 읽고 물음에 답하시오.

Although people usually don't think that _____(A)_____ are a part of a sport team, they play an important role in a game. They create team spirit. They also (B)courage their team and fans. To do their job well, they need to fit and strong. They also need to be good at jumping and dancing. Most of all, they need to work hard like players.

27 위 글의 빈칸 (A)에 들어갈 알맞은 직업은? (3점)

① tappers ② interpreters
③ cheerleaders ④ guide runners
⑤ shooting assistants

28 위 글의 밑줄 친 (B)를 알맞은 어형으로 고치시오. (5점)

→ _____

◎ 선택형 문항의 답안은 컴퓨터용 수정 싸인펜을 사용하여 OMR 답안지에 바르게 표기하시오.

◎ 서술형 문제는 답을 답안지에 반드시 검정 볼펜으로 쓰시오.

◎ 총 31문항 100점 만점입니다. 문항별 배점은 각 문항에 표시되어 있습니다.

[대전 ○○중]

01 다음 중 반의어가 어색한 것은?　(3점)

① clear - unclear　　② visible - invisible

③ formal - informal　④ patient - impatient

⑤ correct - imcorrect

[충북 ○○중]

02 다음 주어진 영영풀이에 해당하는 단어가 들어간 문장을 고르면?　(3점)

> n. a group of people who have their own language and ways of living

① We have to pay attention to the speaker.

② Is there a particular type of book that he enjoys?

③ Ever since I was little, I've always wanted to be a pacer.

④ Some girls are walking on the road.

⑤ The tribe has hunted whales for thousands of years.

[경기 ○○중]

03 다음 대화의 빈칸에 들어갈 말로 가장 알맞은 것은?　(2점)

> A: Mina, _____
> B: I read a book twice a month.
> A: I suggest you read more books.
> B: OK, I'll try.

① how soon will you be back?

② how long have you lived here?

③ how many books do you have?

④ how often do you read books?

⑤ how far is it from here to the bookstore?

[충북 ○○중]

04 다음 대화의 내용과 일치하지 않는 것은?　(4점)

> W: Hello. Welcome to Sports World. May I help you?
> B: Yes, I came to register for a basketball class.
> W: Is this your first time taking lessons?
> B: Yes, it is. I am not good at playing basketball.
> W: I see. How often do you want to take classes?
> B: I want to take classes twice a week. I'd like to take classes on weekdays.
> W: Then, I suggest that you take the Beginner 2 class. This class meets on Tuesdays and Thursdays.
> B: That sounds good. I'd like to sign up for that class. How big is the class?
> W: The class has a limit of 3 people.
> B: That's perfect.

① The boy wants to register for a basketball class.

② The boy has never taken basketball lessons.

③ The boy will take classes twice a week.

④ The boy will take a class on Saturdays.

⑤ The boy's class has a limit of three members.

[대구 ○○중]

05 다음 대화가 자연스럽게 되도록 (A)∼(E)를 순서에 맞게 배열한 것으로 가장 적절한 것은?　(3점)

> (A) Wow, that often? Anyway, it'll be fun swimming together today.
> (B) I swim four times a week.
> (C) That's a good idea.
> (D) Yes, but before we swim, I suggest we do stretching exercises.
> (E) I don't swim often. How about you, Kate? How often do you swim?

① (B)-(D)-(E)-(C)-(A)

② (D)-(A)-(E)-(B)-(C)

③ (D)-(C)-(E)-(B)-(A)

④ (E)-(B)-(A)-(D)-(C)

⑤ (E)-(B)-(D)-(C)-(A)

07 위 대화의 내용과 일치하지 <u>않는</u> 것은? (3점)

① The boy has taken swimming lessons before.

② Less than 10 people can just take the class.

③ There is a class that the boy can sign up for.

④ The boy would like to take classes on weekdays.

⑤ The boy is registering for a swimming class at Sports World.

[경북 ○○중]

[6~7] 다음 대화를 읽고 물음에 답하시오.

W: Hello. Welcome to Sports World. May I help you?

B: Yes, I came to register for a swimming class.

W: Is this your first time taking swimming lessons?

B: Yes, it is. I don't know how to swim at all.

W: I see. (A)<u>How often do you want to take classes?</u>

B: I want to take classes twice a week. I'd like to take classes on weekdays and not on weekends.

W: Then, I suggest that you take the Beginner 2 class. This class meets on Tuesdays and Thursdays.

B: That sounds good. I'd like to sign up for that class. How big is the class?

W: The class has a limit of 10 people.

B: That's perfect.

06 위 대화의 밑줄 친 (A)의 의도로 가장 알맞은 것은? (2점)

① 축하 표현   ② 감정 표현

③ 유감 표현   ④ 조언 요청

⑤ 빈도 묻기

[경기 ○○중]

08 다음 대화의 내용과 일치하는 것은? (3점)

Sara: Joongang High School. How may I help you?

Jane: Hello. This is Jane Conner from Seonghan Middle School. I'd like to sign up for your school tour.

Sara: Hi, Jane! There's a tour every Saturday in May starting from May 5th.

Jane: Can you sign me up for May 19th?

Sara: Yes, it's possible. But if you're free on May 26th, you might want to come then.

Jane: What's going on that day?

Sara: On that day, you'll have a chance to see club activities we have.

Jane: Wonderful. I'll visit on May 26th.

Sara: Okay, see you then.

① Sara는 Seonghan 중학교 관계자이다.

② Jane은 Sara의 사인을 받고 싶어 한다.

③ Jane은 5월 19일에 Joongang 고등학교를 방문하려 했다.

④ Jane은 Joongang 고등학교의 클럽 활동에 참여하고 있다.

⑤ Jane은 Sara에게 5월 19일에 방문할 것을 권한다.

09 다음 (A)~(E) 중에서 주어진 문장이 들어가기에 가장 알맞은 곳은? (4점)

> I suggest you join my basketball club.

> B: How often do you play basketball? (A)
> G: I play once a week, (B) but I want to play more often.
> B: (C) We play three times a week.
> G: That sounds good! (D) It'll be fun to play with you. (E)
>
> *B: boy, G: girl

① (A) ② (B) ③ (C) ④ (D) ⑤ (E)

10 다음 중 어법상 올바른 문장은? (3점)

① He fixed the breaking chair.

② I jumped as high as possible.

③ It would be inpolite to leave so early.

④ I practiced until my shoes were all wear out.

⑤ The students's favorite subject was English.

11 다음 우리말과 일치하도록 주어진 단어를 바르게 배열했을 때, 6번째로 올 단어는? (3점)

> • 내 옆에 앉아 있는 소녀가 소리를 지르기 시작했다.
> (to, sitting, the, me, to, girl, scream, next, started)

① sitting ② me ③ to
④ next ⑤ started

12 다음 중 밑줄 친 곳이 알맞게 쓰인 것은? (3점)

① Betty is as cutest as Judy.

② He jumped as high as he could.

③ Your bag is two as big as mine.

④ Greece is not as larger than Canada.

⑤ This bike is more expensive as a car.

13 다음 주어진 우리말과 뜻이 같도록 영작하시오. (4점)

> • Jenny에게 말을 걸고 있는 소년은 나의 오빠야.

> **조건**
> • 8 단어로 쓸 것.
> • talk를 사용할 것.

→ _____

14 다음 중 어법상 어색한 것은? (3점)

① I like fried potatoes.

② Don't touch the boiling water.

③ A rolling stone gathers no moss.

④ I'd like to have my pictures taken

⑤ I saw the window breaking by the boys.

15 주어진 문장과 의미하는 바가 다른 것은? (3점)

> • Tom is 45 years old and Mike is 14 years old now.

① Tom is older than Mike.

② Mike is younger than Tom.

③ Mike is not as old as Tom.

④ Tom is younger than Mike.

⑤ Tom is not as young as Mike.

[16~19] 다음 글을 읽고 물음에 답하시오.

Pacers in a Marathon

Pacers run with other runners and lead them in a marathon. Pacers are ⓐ<u>experienced</u> runners, and their job is to help other runners ⓑ<u>managed</u> their race better. There can be several pacers in a race. (A) Each pacer runs at different speeds and finishes the race in different times. Pacers usually have flags or balloons ⓒ<u>showing</u> their finish time. (B) Runners can choose a pacer ⓓ<u>depending</u> on their target finish time. (C) Since the pacer keeps track of the time, the runner can achieve his or her goal of ⓔ<u>finishing</u> the marathon in a particular time more easily. (D) (가)_____, pacers run but they don't run to win. They run for (나)_____. (E)

16 위 글의 (A)~(E) 중 아래 문장이 들어갈 가장 적절한 곳은? (4점)

> For example, if a runner wants to finish the race in four hours, the runner will follow the four-hour pacer.

① (A) ② (B) ③ (C) ④ (D) ⑤ (E)

17 위 글의 (가)에 들어갈 말로 가장 적절한 것은? (3점)

① However ② In short
③ Fortunately ④ In addition
⑤ In contrast

18 위 글의 ⓐ~ⓔ 중 어법상 잘못된 것은? (3점)

① ⓐ ② ⓑ ③ ⓒ ④ ⓓ ⑤ ⓔ

19 위 글의 흐름상 (나)에 알맞은 것은? (4점)

① themselves ② first prize
③ record time ④ others
⑤ money

[20~21] 다음 글을 읽고 물음에 답하시오.

You may only see the car and the driver during most car races, but there is a team behind the driver. This team is called a pit crew. A pit is a place on the side of the race track, and drivers stop there several times during a race. The main job of the pit crew is to check the car and change the tires. Changing the tires is especially important because the tires wear out easily in a high speed race.

A pit stop can be as short as 2 seconds, and there are as many as 20 members on a crew. Therefore, the pit crew has to work in perfect (A)_____. The driver may get all the attention, but as people say, "Races are won in the pits."

20 위 글의 빈칸 (A)에 들어갈 말로 가장 알맞은 것은? (3점)

① power ② change ③ safety
④ courage ⑤ harmony

21 위 글에서 대답할 수 <u>없는</u> 질문은? (3점)

① What is a pit in car racing?
② What does a pit crew do during the race?
③ How many members are there on a pit crew?
④ What is important to be a member of the pit crew?
⑤ Why is changing tires especially important in a car race?

[22~24] 다음 글을 읽고 물음에 답하시오.

Sherpas in Mountain Climbing
The word *Sherpa* comes from the Sherpa tribe, which lives in the eastern part of Nepal. ⓐSherpas have good climbing skills and ⓑthey know their way around the mountains well. ⓒThey also have much difficulty breathing high up in the mountains. Therefore, mountain climbers started to hire Sherpas to help them climb Mount Everest. ⓓSherpas lead mountain climbers to the top of the mountain. ⓔThey support climbers in many ways. For example, they put up tents and carry climbers' bags. Sherpas are often called ⓕinvisible people of Mount Everest because people often see a picture of only the climbers at the top of the mountain.

22 위 글의 ⓐ~ⓔ 중 흐름상 어색한 것은? (3점)

① ⓐ ② ⓑ ③ ⓒ ④ ⓓ ⑤ ⓔ

23 위 글의 밑줄 친 ⓕ와 부정어 접두사가 같은 것은? (3점)

① formal ② polite
③ patient ④ possible
⑤ advantage

24 위 글을 읽고 알 수 없는 것은? (3점)

① Sherpa 단어의 유래
② Sherpa의 거주 지역
③ Sherpa들이 등반할 때 하는 일
④ 등산가들이 Sherpa를 고용하는 이유
⑤ 등산가들이 산 정상에서 사진을 찍는 순간

25 다음 글의 주제로 알맞은 것은? (3점)

In sports, only the players get a trophy or medal, but they don't win on their own. There are people who help the players. These people are often hidden and don't get attention. However, they are as important as the players. Here are some examples.

① 운동 경기에서 이기는 방법
② 가장 인기 있는 스포츠 종목
③ 스포츠 분야의 숨은 조력자들
④ 주목을 받거나 인기 있는 운동선수
⑤ 경기에서 트로피나 메달을 받는 선수들

26 다음 글의 괄호 (A), (B), (C)에 들어갈 표현으로 바르게 짝지어진 것은? (4점)

Each pacer runs at different speeds and finishes the race in different times. Pacers usually have flags or balloons (A)[showing / show] their finish time.
Runners can choose a pacer (B)[depending / depend] on their target finish time. For example, if a runner wants to finish the race in four hours, the runner will follow the four-hour pacer. Since the pacer keeps track of the time, the runner can achieve his or her goal of (C)[finishing / finish] the marathon in a particular time more easily.
In short, pacers run but they don't run to win. They run for others.

	(A)	(B)	(C)
①	showing	depending	finishing
②	showing	depending	finish
③	showing	depend	finish
④	show	depending	finish
⑤	show	depend	finishing

[27~30] 다음 글을 읽고 물음에 답하시오.

[서대문구 ○○중]

Hidden People in Sports

In sports, only the players get a trophy or medal, but ⓐthey don't win on their own. There are people who help the players. These people are often (a)hide and don't get attention. (A)_____, ⓑthey are as important as the players. Here are some examples.

Pacers in a Marathon

Pacers run with other runners and lead them in a marathon. ⓒPacers are experienced runners, and their job is to help other runners manage their race better. There can be several pacers in a race. Each pacer runs at different speeds and finishes the race in different times. Pacers usually have flags or balloons (b)which are showing their finish time. ⓓRunners can choose a pacer depending on their target finish time. (B)_____, if a runner wants to finish the race in four hours, the runner will follow the four-hour pacer. (c)Because of ⓔ the pacer keeps track of the time, the runner can achieve his or her goal of (d)finishing the marathon in a particular time more (e)easy. (C)_____, pacers run but they don't run to win. They run for others.

27 위 글의 (A)~(C)에 차례대로 알맞은 것은? (4점)

	(A)	(B)	(C)
①	Therefore	In addition	In contrast
②	However	For example	In short
③	However	For example	Furthermore
④	Besides	Similarly	Furthermore
⑤	In contrast	However	In short

28 ⓐ~ⓔ를 해석한 것이 어색한 것은? (3점)

① ⓐ - 선수들은 혼자 힘으로 승리하는 것이 아니다.

② ⓑ - 그들은 선수들만큼이나 중요하다.

③ ⓒ - 페이서들은 경험이 많은 주자들이다.

④ ⓓ - 주자들은 의지할 만한 페이서들과 함께 완주 시각을 선택한다.

⑤ ⓔ - 페이서는 시간을 파악한다.

29 위 글의 (a)~(e) 중 어법상 옳은 것을 있는 대로 고르면? (3점)

① (a), (b) 　② (a), (c) 　③ (b), (d)

④ (b), (c), (e) 　⑤ (b), (d), (e)

30 위 글의 내용과 일치하지 않는 것은? (4점)

① Every pacer has different race finish time.

② Pacers show their finish time on flags or balloons.

③ Runners manage their race better by the help of the pacers.

④ A runner who wants to finish the race in four hours will follow the four-hour pacer.

⑤ There are people who help the players in sports, so they are less important than the players.

[대구 ○○중]

31 밑줄 친 부분 중, 어법상 어색한 것은? (4점)

The word *Sherpa* comes from the Sherpa tribe, which ⓐlive in the eastern part of Nepal. Sherpas have good climbing skills and know their way around the mountains well. They also have ⓑlittle difficulty breathing high up in the mountains. Therefore, mountain climbers started to hire Sherpas ⓒto help them climb Mount Everest. Sherpas lead mountain climbers to the top of the mountain. They support climbers in many ways. For example, they put up tents and ⓓcarry climbers' bags. Sherpas are often called the invisible people of Mount Everest ⓔsince people often see a picture of only the climbers at the top of the mountain.

① ⓐ 　② ⓑ 　③ ⓒ 　④ ⓓ 　⑤ ⓔ

3학년 영어 2학기 중간고사(6과) 1회

문항수 : 선택형(25문항) 서술형(2문항) 20 . . .

◎ 선택형 문항의 답안은 컴퓨터용 수정 싸인펜을 사용
하여 OMR 답안지에 바르게 표기하시오.
◎ 서술형 문제는 답을 답안지에 반드시 검정 볼펜으
로 쓰시오.
◎ 총 27문항 100점 만점입니다. 문항별 배점은 각
문항에 표시되어 있습니다.

[부산 ○○중]

01 다음 영영풀이에 해당하는 단어로 알맞은 것은? (3점)

> a copy of something such as a picture

① saw   ② replay   ③ antique
④ furniture   ⑤ reproduction

[송파구 ○○중]

02 다음 (A)~(E) 중 밑줄 친 단어의 쓰임이 어색한 것은? (4점)

> (A) Careless drivers can cause accidents.
> (B) The Louvre has a collection of priceless art.
> (C) Don't replay the music so many times. People won't like it.
> (D) He was wearing a suit because he had to give an informal speech.
> (E) It is impossible to get a table in the restaurant because it is already full.

① (A)   ② (B)   ③ (C)   ④ (D)   ⑤ (E)

[전북 ○○중]

03 다음 대화의 빈칸에 들어갈 말로 가장 알맞은 것은? (3점)

> A: You don't look so good, Inho. What's the matter?
> B: I have the flu.
> A: _____ Did you see the doctor?
> B: Yes. I'm taking medicine.

① That's too bad.
② Don't mention it.
③ I have a sore throat.
④ Is anything important?
⑤ I was very disappointed.

[강북구 ○○중]

[4~5] 다음 대화를 읽고 물음에 답하시오.

> A: Excuse me, Ms. Carter. Can I ask you a question? Did I get the main role in the play?
> B: Yes, you did. Congratulations, Jiho! You're going to be Romeo in our school play, *Romeo and Juliet*.
> A: Really? I'm so (A)_____. Thank you so much, Ms. Carter.
> B: I know how much you wanted the role. I'm so happy for you.
> A: Thank you. What about Sumi? Did she get the role she wanted, too?
> B: Unfortunately, no. She's very (B)_____.
> A: Oh, ⒶI'm sorry to hear that. Anyway, when is the first practice?
> B: It's at 2 p.m. on September 20th, in the acting club room. You'll get a text message about it soon.
> A: OK, I'll be there.

04 위 대화의 빈칸 (A), (B)에 들어갈 말로 알맞게 짝지어진 것은? (4점)

	(A)	(B)
①	sad	nervous
②	angry	bored
③	shocked	happy
④	worried	upset
⑤	excited	disappointed

05 위 대화의 밑줄 친 Ⓐ의 의도로 가장 적절한 것은? (3점)

① 사과하기   ② 유감 표현하기
③ 도움 요청하기   ④ 설명 요청하기
⑤ 희망 표현하기

06 다음 대화의 빈칸에 들어갈 말로 가장 적절한 것은? (3점)

> A: Sue, you look excited. What's up?
> B: I was elected as class president. I'm so excited.
> A: That's wonderful. Congratulations!
> B: Thanks. _____

① I'll try harder next time.

② I'm sure I can get a role next time.

③ I hope you'll have a chance to learn.

④ You must be very proud of yourself.

⑤ I'm really happy to have a chance to work for my class.

07 다음 빈칸 ⓐ~ⓓ에 들어갈 말이 바르게 짝지어진 것은? (4점)

> W: Jiho, congratulations on getting the main role in our school play.
> M: I'm so ⓐ_____. Thank you so much.
> W: I know how much you wanted the role. I'm so ⓑ_____ for you.
> M: Did Sumi get the role she wanted, too?
> W: Unfortunately, no. She's very ⓒ_____.
> M: Oh, I'm ⓓ_____ to hear that.

	ⓐ	ⓑ	ⓒ	ⓓ
①	excited	sorry	disappointing	happy
②	excited	happy	disappointed	sorry
③	excited	happy	disappointing	sorry
④	exciting	happy	disappointed	sorry
⑤	exciting	sorry	disappointing	happy

[8~9] 다음 대화를 읽고 물음에 답하시오.

> B: Excuse me. Ms. Carter. Can I ask you a question? Did I get the main role in the play?
> W: Yes, you did. Congratulations. Jiho! You're going to be Romeo in our school play, *Romeo and Juliet*.
> B: Really? I'm so excited. Thank you so much. Ms. Carter.
> W: I know how much you wanted the role. I'm so happy for you.
> B: Thank you. What about Sumi? Did she get the role she wanted, too?
> W: Unfortunately, no. She's very _____.
> B: Oh, I'm sorry to hear that. Anyway, when is the first practice?
> W: It's at 2 p.m. on September 20th, in the acting club room. You'll get a text message about it soon.
> B: OK. I'll be there.
>
> B: Jiho, W: Ms. Carter

08 위 대화의 빈칸에 들어갈 말로 가장 적절한 것은? (4점)

① happy ② disappointed

③ excited ④ satisfied

⑤ experienced

09 위 대화의 내용과 일치하지 <u>않는</u> 것은? (4점)

① Jiho is going to be Romeo in the school play, *Romeo and Juliet*.

② Ms. Carter knows how much Jiho wanted the role in the play.

③ Sumi is going to be Juliet in the play.

④ Jiho is going to attend the practice for the play on September 20th.

⑤ Jiho will get a text message about the first practice soon.

10 다음 대화 순서를 바르게 나열한 것은? (3점)

> You don't look so good, Inho. What's the matter?
> (A) Yes. I'm taking medicine.
> (B) I have the flu.
> (C) That's too bad. Did you see the doctor?
> (D) Well, I hope you feel better soon. Thanks.

① (B)-(A)-(D)-(C) ② (B)-(C)-(A)-(D)
③ (C)-(A)-(B)-(D) ④ (C)-(B)-(D)-(A)
⑤ (B)-(C)-(D)-(A)

13 다음 보기의 단어를 이용하여 빈칸에 알맞은 말을 쓰시오. (5점)

보기
> do, want, what

조건
> • 주어진 단어를 반드시 사용할 것.
> • 한 칸에 한 단어만 쓸 것.

> A: Is there anything you want to do on your birthday?
> B: _____ _____ _____ _____ _____ on my birthday is to go on a camping trip.

→ _____ _____ _____ _____ _____

11 다음 중 어법상 옳은 문장의 개수는? (4점)

> • I'm not so faster as David.
> • A chef who baking a cake is my father.
> • Dick told me that he has never seen a parrot.
> • He felt bored because the movie was so boring.
> • I knew Seoul well because I have been there many times.

① 1개   ② 2개   ③ 3개   ④ 4개   ⑤ 5개

14 다음 빈칸에 들어갈 말이 순서대로 짝지어진 것은? (4점)

> • He _____ just taken a bath when the phone rang.
> • I had lived with my parents until I _____ 20.

① is - am   ② was - am
③ had - was   ④ has - was
⑤ had - been

12 다음 중 밑줄 친 부분의 용법이 가장 다른 것은? (3점)

① This is what he saw yesterday.
② What I know about him is only his name.
③ I asked him what he bought then.
④ What I want is not money but time.
⑤ We ate what my mom had cooked for us.

15 빈칸에 what이 들어갈 수 없는 것은? (3점)

① That's exactly _____ I expected.
② He gave me _____ I was looking for.
③ It is not _____ I want for my birthday.
④ I think _____ you want is just her understanding.
⑤ Mr. Kim was the only man _____ came to the party.

[16~17] 다음 글을 읽고 물음에 답하시오.

Mr. Boggis then added, "Hmm, I think I may buy it. The legs of my table at home are broken. I can cut off the legs of your table and attach them (A)[to / for] mine."

"How much?" Rummins asked.

"Not much, I'm afraid. This is just a reproduction," said Mr. Boggis.

"So how much?"

"Well, thirty pounds."

"OK, it's yours, but how are you going to take it? This thing will not go in a car!"

"We'll see," Mr. Boggis said and went out to bring his car.

On his way to the car, Mr. Boggis couldn't help (B)[smiling / to smile]. The table was (C)[what / which] every dealer dreamed of. He couldn't believe his luck.

"Dad, what if this thing doesn't go in his car? He might not pay you," said Bert. Rummins then had an idea. "What he wants is only the legs. Let's cut the legs off for him," said Rummins. "Great idea!" said Bert. Bert then took out a saw and began to cut off the legs. When Mr. Boggis came back, the legs had been cut off. "Don't worry, this was a favor. I won't charge you for this," said Rummins. Mr. Boggis was so shocked that he couldn't say anything.

16 위 글의 괄호 (A), (B), (C)에 들어갈 표현으로 바르게 짝지어진 것은? (4점)

	(A)	(B)	(C)
①	to	smiling	what
②	to	smiling	which
③	to	to smile	which
④	for	to smile	what
⑤	for	smiling	which

17 위 글의 내용과 일치하는 것은? (4점)

① Mr. Boggis only needed the legs of the table.

② Rummins sold the table for 13 pounds.

③ Bert suggested cutting the legs of the table.

④ Rummins cut the legs of the table.

⑤ Rummins didn't ask for money for cutting the legs of the table.

[18~19] 다음 글을 읽고, 물음에 답하시오.

Now it was another Sunday, and Mr. Boggis was in a small town again. At a house he visited, he met two men. One was Rummins, the owner, and _____ was his son Bert.

"I buy old furniture. Do you have any?" asked Mr. Boggis.

"No, I don't," said Rummins.

"Can I just take a look?" asked Mr. Boggis.

"Sure. Please come in," said Rummins.

Mr. Boggis first went to the kitchen, and there was nothing. He then moved to the living room. And there it was! A table ⓐ_____ was a priceless piece of eighteenth-century English furniture. He was ⓑ_____ excited that he almost fell over.

"What's wrong?" Bert asked.

"Oh, nothing. Nothing at all," Mr. Boggis lied. He then said with a straight face, "This table is a reproduction. It's worth only a few pounds."

18 빈칸에 들어갈 말로 알맞은 것은? (4점)

① another   ② other   ③ the other

④ the others   ⑤ others

19 빈칸 ⓐ, ⓑ에 차례대로 들어갈 알맞은 말은? (4점)

① which, so   ② which, such

③ what, so   ④ what, such

⑤ where, so

[20~21] 다음 글을 읽고 물음에 답하시오.

Now it was another Sunday, and Mr. Boggis was in a small town again. At a house he visited, he met two men. One was Rummins, the owner, and ⓐthe other was his son Bert.

"I buy old furniture. Do you have any?" asked Mr. Boggis.

"No, I don't," said Rummins.

"Can I just ⓑtake a look?" asked Mr. Boggis.

"Sure. Please come in," said Rummins.

Mr. Boggis first went to the kitchen, and there was nothing. He then moved to the living room. And there it was! A table which was a ⓒpriceless piece of eighteenth-century English furniture. He was so excited that he almost fell over.

"What's wrong?" Bert asked.

"Oh, nothing. Nothing at all," Mr. Boggis ⓓlied. He then said ⓔwith a straight face, "This table is a reproduction. It's worth only a few pounds."

20 위 글의 내용과 일치하는 것은? (4점)

① Boggis는 어떤 집에서 3명의 남자를 만났다.

② Rummins는 자기 집에 값비싼 가구가 있음을 알고 있었다.

③ Boggis는 거실부터 둘러보았다.

④ 아주 가치 있는 18세기 영국 가구가 부엌에 있었다.

⑤ Boggis는 Rummins의 집에 있는 가치 있는 가구를 알아보았다.

21 위 글의 ⓐ~ⓔ의 우리말 해석이 바르지 <u>않은</u> 것은? (3점)

① ⓐ: 다른 한 사람 ② ⓑ: 둘러보다

③ ⓒ: 귀중한 ④ ⓓ: 누웠다

⑤ ⓔ: 무표정한 얼굴로

[22~23] 다음 글을 읽고 물음에 답하시오.

On his way to the car, Mr. Boggis couldn't help (A)_____. The table was what every dealer dreamed of. He couldn't believe his luck.

"Dad, what if this thing doesn't go in his car? He might not pay you," said Bert.

Rummins then had an idea. "What he wants (B)_____ only the legs. Let's cut the legs off for him," said Rummins. "Great idea!" said Bert. Bert then took out a saw and began to cut off the legs.

When Mr. Boggis came back, the legs had been cut off. "Don't worry, this was a favor. I won't charge you for this," said Rummins. Mr. Boggis was so shocked that he couldn't say anything.

22 위 글의 빈칸 (A), (B)에 들어갈 말로 알맞게 짝지어진 것은? (4점)

	(A)	(B)
①	smile	is
②	smile	are
③	smiling	were
④	smiling	are
⑤	smiling	is

23 위 글의 내용과 일치하는 문장을 〈보기〉에서 모두 고른 것은? (4점)

> **보기**
> (A) Mr. Boggis asked Rummins and Bert to cut off the legs of the table.
> (B) Rummins and Bert were worried that the table might not go in a car.
> (C) Rummins and Bert tried to get more money by cutting off the legs of the table.

① (A) ② (B) ③ (C)

④ (A), (B) ⑤ (B), (C)

[24~26] 다음 글을 읽고 물음에 답하시오.

Mr. Boggis went to a small town again to buy antique furniture, and there met two men, Rummins, the owner of the priceless table, and his son Bert.

At Rummins' house, Mr. Boggis found a table which was a priceless piece of eighteenth-century English furniture. He was so excited that he almost fell over. Mr. Boggis said to them, "This table is a reproduction, which is ⓐ_____ only a few pounds."

He then added, "Hmm, I think I may buy it. The legs of my table at home are broken. I can cut off the legs of your table and attach them to mine."

"How much?" Rummins asked.

"Not much, I'm afraid. This is just a reproduction," said Mr. Boggis.

"So how much?"

"Ten pounds."

"Ten? It's reproduction more than that."

"How about fifteen?"

"Make it fifty."

"Well, thirty. This is my final ⓑ_____."

"OK, it's yours, but how are you going to take it? This thing will not go in car!"

"We'll see," Mr. Boggis said and went out to bring his car.

On his way to the car, Mr. Boggis couldn't ⓒ_____ smiling. The table was what every dealer dreamed of. He couldn't believe his luck.

"Dad, what if this thing doesn't go in his car? He might not pay you," said Bert.

Rummins then had an idea. "What he wants is only the legs. Let's cut the legs off for him," said Rummins. "Great idea!" said Bert. Bert then took out ⓓ_____ and began to cut off the legs.

When Mr. Boggis came back, the legs had been cut off. "Don't worry, this was a favor. I won't ⓔ_____ you for this," said Rummins. Mr. Boggis was so shocked that he couldn't say nothing.

24 위 글의 흐름상 빈칸 ⓐ~ⓔ에 알맞지 <u>않은</u> 것은? (4점)

① ⓐ worth   ② ⓑ offer   ③ ⓒ help

④ ⓓ a saw   ⑤ ⓔ pay

25 위 글을 읽고 답할 수 <u>없는</u> 것은? (4점)

① What was Mr. Boggis' final offer for the table?

② How did Mr. Boggis feel when he found a priceless table?

③ What was the false reason why Mr. Boggis bought the table?

④ When and where did Rummins get eighteenth-century English furniture?

⑤ How did Mr. Boggis feel about the legs which had been cut off when he came back?

26 다음 질문에 대한 답을 우리말로 쓰시오. (4점)

Bert was worried that the table wouldn't go in Mr. Boggis' car and that Mr. Boggis might not pay Rummins, his father. So, they decided to do something for Mr. Boggis when he went out to bring his car. <u>What did they do for Mr. Boggis?</u>

→ _____

27 다음 빈칸에 들어갈 말로 알맞은 것은? (3점)

• My teacher said that the sun _____ in the East.

① rose   ② rises   ③ raised

④ had risen   ⑤ had been raised

◎ 선택형 문항의 답안은 컴퓨터용 수정 싸인펜을 사용하여 OMR 답안지에 바르게 표기하시오.
◎ 서술형 문제는 답을 답안지에 반드시 검정 볼펜으로 쓰시오.
◎ 총 29문항 100점 만점입니다. 문항별 배점은 각 문항에 표시되어 있습니다.

[서대문구 ○○중]

01 다음 (A)~(D)의 영어 정의가 나타내는 단어를 올바르게 배열한 것은? (3점)

(A) to process something so that it can be used again
(B) to make a copy of something
(C) lasting for a very long time
(D) being worth a very large amount of money

	(A)	(B)	(C)	(D)
①	recycle	reproduce	endless	priceless
②	replay	repeat	careless	priceless
③	recycle	reproduce	endless	valueless
④	replay	reproach	careless	valueless
⑤	recycle	reduce	endless	priceless

[노원구 ○○중]

02 다음 밑줄 친 단어 중 의미상 올바른 것을 2개 고르면? (4점)

① A saw is used for attaching hard wood to the wall.
② He could manage to complete his last film within reproduction.
③ The majority of tickets of the concert are sold through the website.
④ His grandfather also promised to donate half of his money to the charity.
⑤ An allowance is an amount of money that is given back to you, especially because you are not happy with a product or service that you have bought.

[양천구 ○○중]

03 다음 대화의 빈칸에 들어갈 말로 적절한 것은? (3점)

Tim: Mina, is anything wrong?
Mina: Well, I lost my smartphone. I'm upset.
Tim: _____ Do you remember when you used it last?
Mina: Well, I remember taking it out of my bag at the snack shop.
Tim: Then, let's go back to the snack shop to look for it.

① Oh, I'm happy for you.
② I'm so sorry to hear that.
③ Well, I forgot your phone number.
④ I'm sorry to eat your snack, Mina.
⑤ Congratulations on opening a new snack shop.

[서대문구 ○○중]

04 다음 중 짝지어진 대화가 어색한 것은? (3점)

① A: I won first prize in the writing contest.
   B: That's wonderful. Congratulations!
② A: My smartphone is broken. I'm upset.
   B: That's too bad. I'm sorry to hear that.
③ A: Congratulations on winning the gold medal in the school marathon.
   B: Thanks, Suji. I'm very happy.
④ A: You don't look so good, Inho. What's the matter?
   B: I have the flu.
   A: I'm happy for you. Did you see the doctor?
⑤ A: I lost my dog in the park yesterday.
   B: That's too bad. Have you reported to the park office?
   A: Yes, but they say there's little chance of finding it.

[5~6] 다음 대화를 읽고, 물음에 답하시오.

A: Excuse me, Ms. Carter. Can I ask you a question? Did I get the main role in the play?

B: Yes, you did. Congratulations. Jiho! You're going to be Romeo in our school play, *Romeo and Juliet*.

A: Really? I'm so ⓐ_____. Thank you so much, Ms. Carter.

B: I know how much you wanted the role. I'm so happy for you.

A: Thank you. What about Sumi? Did she get the role she wanted, too?

B: Unfortunately, no. She's very ⓑ_____.

A: Oh, I'm sorry to hear that. Anyway, when is the first practice?

B: It's at 2 p.m. on September 20th, in the acting club room. You'll get a text message about it soon.

A: OK. I'll be there.

05 위 대화의 빈칸 ⓐ와 ⓑ에 들어갈 말이 순서대로 가장 바르게 짝지어진 것은? (3점)

	ⓐ	ⓑ
①	nervous	happy
②	surprised	nervous
③	excited	disappointed
④	happy	excited
⑤	disappointed	excited

06 위 대화의 내용과 일치하지 <u>않는</u> 것은? (3점)

① 지호는 '로미오와 줄리엣' 연극에서 로미오 역할을 맡게 되었다.

② 지호는 주인공 역할을 매우 하고 싶어 했다.

③ 수미는 자기가 원하는 역할을 맡지 못했다.

④ 첫 연습은 9월 20일 오후 2시에 있을 예정이다.

⑤ 첫 연습에 관한 내용은 곧 이메일로 공지될 예정이다.

07 다음 대화의 빈칸에 들어갈 말로 알맞지 <u>않은</u> 것은? (3점)

A: Jisu, I got an A⁺ on the science test.

B: _____

① That's a pity.

② Good for you.

③ That's wonderful!

④ I'm so happy for you.

⑤ Congratulations on getting an excellent grade!

08 다음 대화의 흐름으로 보아, 주어진 문장이 들어갈 곳으로 알맞은 것은? (3점)

What's up?

A: Sue, you look excited. (A)

B: (B) I was elected as class president. I'm so excited. (C)

A: (D) That's wonderful. Congratulations!

B: Thanks. (E) I'm really happy to have a chance to work for my class.

① (A) ② (B) ③ (C) ④ (D) ⑤ (E)

09 다음 대화의 밑줄 친 ⓐ~ⓔ 중 내용상 자연스럽지 <u>않은</u> 것은? (3점)

A: You don't look so good. ⓐWhat's the matter?

B: ⓑI have the flu.

A: ⓒThat's too bad, did you see the doctor?

B: ⓓYes, I'm taking medicine.

A: ⓔWell, I hope you feel disappointed soon.

B: Thanks.

① ⓐ ② ⓑ ③ ⓒ ④ ⓓ ⑤ ⓔ

10 다음 중 어법상 <u>어색한</u> 것은? (4점)

① I wished she had stayed at home.

② The teacher told us that Japan had invaded Korea in 1592.

③ I knew him at once, for I had seen him before.

④ By the time we arrived there, he had already gone.

⑤ He had been ill in bed for a week when I came back.

11 다음 중 어법상 옳은 문장의 개수는? (3점)

> • He has been cleaning the floor since 2 o'clock.
> • I asked him why to go shopping.
> • The bird singing in the tree is very big.
> • This is exactly what I want.

① 0개　② 1개　③ 2개　④ 3개　⑤ 4개

12 다음 중 어법상 바르지 <u>않은</u> 문장은? (2개) (3점)

① I ate the cookies which my friend made for me.

② What I want for dinner tonight is Bulgogi.

③ This machine is the one what I've been looking for.

④ Have you seen the book that I bought yesterday?

⑤ I like the backpack my mom bought for my birthday.

13 다음 괄호 안의 동사를 하나는 과거시제로, 또 하나는 과거완료형으로 고치시오. (6점)

(1) She (tell) me his name after he (leave).

→ _____

(2) I (be) sorry that I (hurt) him.

→ _____

14 어법상 빈칸에 들어갈 알맞은 것은? (3점)

> When I came home, everybody _____ to bed.
> (내가 집에 왔을 때, 모든 사람들은 자러 갔다.)

① goes　　　　　② going

③ has gone　　　④ had gone

⑤ have gone

15 다음 중 밑줄 친 단어의 쓰임이 나머지와 <u>다른</u> 하나는? (3점)

① I know <u>what</u> his name is.

② This is not <u>what</u> I bought.

③ <u>What</u> I have is your pencil.

④ I can't believe <u>what</u> she told me.

⑤ We ate <u>what</u> Mom had cooked for us.

16 다음 중 어법상 <u>어색한</u> 것은? (4점)

① Tom went out when I had visited him.

② I fell asleep before my mom came home.

③ I found the watch which I had lost there.

④ He had just taken a bath when the phone rang.

⑤ The TV show had already finished when I turned on TV.

[17~22] 다음 글을 읽고 물음에 답하시오.

One Lucky Sunday

Cyril Boggis was an antique furniture dealer in London. He was known (A)_____ buying good things at a low price and then selling them at a high price. People asked him where he had got the furniture, but he just said, "It's a secret."

Mr. Boggis' secret was simple. He went to small towns every Sunday and knocked on doors. He told people that he was a furniture dealer. People didn't know how valuable their things were, so Mr. Boggis took advantage of them. He was able to buy things very cheaply.

ⓐNow it was another Sunday, and Mr. Boggis was in a small town again. At a house he visited, he met two men. One was Rummins, the owner, and the other was his son Bert.

"I buy old furniture. Do you have any?" asked Mr. Boggis.

"No, I don't," said Rummins.

"Can I just take a look?" asked Mr. Boggis.

"Sure. Please come in," said Rummins.

Mr. Boggis first went to the kitchen, and there was nothing. He then moved to the living room. And ⓑthere it was! A table which was a priceless piece of eighteenth-century English furniture. (가)He was so excited that he almost fell over.

"What's wrong?" Bert asked.

"Oh, nothing. Nothing at all," Mr. Boggis lied. He then said with a straight face, "This table is a reproduction. It's ⓒworth of only a few pounds."

He then added, "Hmm, I think I may buy it. The legs of my table at home are broken. I can cut off the legs of your table and attach them to mine."

"How much?" Rummins asked.

"Not much, I'm afraid. This is just a reproduction," said Mr. Boggis.

"So how much?"

"Ten pounds."

"Ten? It's worth more than that."

"How about fifteen?"

"ⓓMake it fifty."

"Well, thirty. This is my final offer."

"OK, it's yours, but how are you going to take it? This thing will not go in a car!" "We'll see," Mr. Boggis said and went out to bring his car.

On his way to the car, Mr. Boggis couldn't help smiling. The table was what every dealer dreamed of. He couldn't believe his luck.

"Dad, ⓔwhat if this thing doesn't go in his car? He might not pay you," said Bert. Rummins then had an idea. "What he wants is only the legs. Let's cut the legs off for him," said Rummins. "Great idea!" said Bert. Bert then took out a saw and began to cut off the legs.

When Mr. Boggis came back, the legs had been cut off. "Don't worry, this was a favor. I won't charge you for this," said Rummins. Mr. Boggis was so shocked that he couldn't say anything.

17 위 글의 내용과 일치하지 <u>않는</u> 것은? (4점)

① Boggis는 골동품 가구 거래상이다.
② Boggis는 일요일마다 작은 마을에 갔다.
③ Boggis는 어느 아버지와 아들을 만났다.
④ Boggis는 먼저 부엌으로 갔다.
⑤ Boggis는 담담한 심정으로 자기 차로 갔다.

18 위 글의 (A)에 들어갈 말로 가장 적절한 것은? (3점)

① as   ② about   ③ for
④ to   ⑤ by

19 위 글의 ⓐ~ⓔ 중 어법이 잘못된 것은? (4점)

 ①ⓐ   ②ⓑ   ③ⓒ   ④ⓓ   ⑤ⓔ

20 위 글에 나타난 Boggis의 성격을 가장 잘 표현한 단어는?(4점)

① generous　　② lazy　　③ polite
④ dishonest　　⑤ thoughtful

21 밑줄 친 (가)의 이유로 알맞은 것은? (3점)

① 마을에 가는 것이 너무 즐거워서
② 부엌에서 너무 형편없는 가구를 봐서
③ 거실에 가구가 너무 많아서
④ 값을 매길 수 없을 만큼 가치 있는 가구를 봐서
⑤ 너무 돌아다녀 다리가 아파서

22 위 글에 담긴 뜻을 가장 잘 표현한 것은? (3점)

① 뛰는 놈 위에 나는 놈 있다.
② 백지장도 맞들면 낫다.
③ 고래 싸움에 새우 등 터진다.
④ 사공이 많으면 배가 산으로 간다.
⑤ 자기 꾀에 자기가 넘어간다.

[성북구 ○○중]

[23~25] 다음 글을 읽고 물음에 답하시오.

Cyril Boggis was an antique furniture dealer in London. He was known for buying good things at a low price and then selling them at a high price. People asked him where he (A)_____ the furniture, but he just said, "It's a secret."
Mr. Boggis' secret was simple. He went to small towns every Sunday and knocked on doors. He told people that he was a furniture dealer. People didn't know how valuable their things were, so Mr. Boggis took advantage of them. He was able to buy things very cheaply.
Now it was another Sunday, and Mr. Boggis was in a small town again. At a house he visited, he met two men, (B)_____ was Rummins, the owner, and (C)_____ was his son Bert.

"I buy old furniture. Do you have any?" asked Mr. Boggis.
"No, I don't," said Rummins.
"Can I just take a look?" asked Mr. Boggis.
"Sure. Please come in," said Rummins.
Mr. Boggis first went to the kitchen, and there was nothing. He then moved to the living room. And there it was! A table which was a priceless piece of eighteenth-century English furniture. He was so excited that he almost fell over.

23 위 글의 빈칸 (A)에 들어갈 단어의 형태로 알맞은 것은? (3점)

① gets　　② was got　　③ gotten
④ has got　　⑤ had got

24 위 글의 빈칸 (B), (C)에 들어갈 말로 적절히 짝지어진 것은? (3점)

	(B)	(C)
①	one	other
②	one	the other
③	some	another
④	some	other
⑤	some	the other

25 위 글을 읽고 답할 수 <u>없는</u> 것은? (4점)

① What was Mr. Boggis' job?
② What was Mr. Boggis known for?
③ Who did Mr. Boggis meet at a house he visited?
④ Why did Mr. Boggis almost fall over in Rummins' house?
⑤ How much is the table in the living room of Rummins' house?

Roald Dahl was born in 1916 in Wales. Dahl's parents were Norwegian, and Dahl was named after the Norwegian explorer Roald Amundsen. His first language was Norwegian, which he spoke at home with his parents and his sisters (Astri, Alfhild, Else, and Asta).

In 1920, when Dahl was three years old, his seven-year-old sister, Astri, died and weeks later, his father died too at the age of 57. However, Dahl's mother did not go back to Norway and stayed in Wales. It was because her husband Harald had wanted their children to be educated in British school, which he considered the world's best. Dahl went to St. Peter's, a boarding school, but his time at St. Peter's was unpleasant. He was very homesick and unhappy. Dahl later wrote about his time at St. Peter's in his autobiography *Boy: Tales of childhood*.

26 위 글을 읽고 표의 빈칸에 들어갈 내용이 잘못 짝지어진 것은?

(4점)

place of birth	ⓐ
year of birth	ⓑ
first language	ⓒ
family	parents and four sisters
school	ⓓ
title of autobiography	ⓔ

① ⓐ - Wales

② ⓑ - 1920

③ ⓒ - Norwegian

④ ⓓ - St. Peter's

⑤ ⓔ - Boy: Tales of childhood

27 위 글의 Roald Dahl에 관한 설명으로 맞는 것은? (4점)

① He didn't have a happy time at St. Peter's.

② His father died when he was seven years old.

③ His father didn't want him to attend British schools.

④ He was named after a British explorer, Roald Amundsen.

⑤ His mother went back to Norway when his father died.

Cyril Boggis was an antique furniture dealer in London. (A) He ⓐwas known for buying good things at a low price and then selling them at a high price. (B) People asked him where he had got the furniture, but he just said, "It's a secret."
(C) He went to small towns every Sunday and knocked on doors. (D) He told people that he was a furniture dealer. (E) People didn't know how valuable their things were, so Mr. Boggis took advantage of them. He was able to buy things very cheaply.

28 위 글에서 〈보기〉의 문장이 들어갈 위치로 가장 적절한 것은?

(4점)

Mr. Boggis' secret was simple.

① (A)　② (B)　③ (C)　④ (D)　⑤ (E)

29 위 글의 밑줄 친 ⓐ와 의미가 가장 유사한 것은? (3점)

① was proud of　② was ready for

③ was afraid of　④ was famous for

⑤ was different from

3학년 영어 2학기 기말고사(7과) 1회

문항수 : 선택형(26문항) 서술형(1문항)   20 . . .

◎ 선택형 문항의 답안은 컴퓨터용 수정 싸인펜을 사용하여 OMR 답안지에 바르게 표기하시오.
◎ 서술형 문제는 답을 답안지에 반드시 검정 볼펜으로 쓰시오.
◎ 총 27문항 100점 만점입니다. 문항별 배점은 각 문항에 표시되어 있습니다.

[서대문구 ㅇㅇ중]

01 다음 밑줄 친 단어의 쓰임이 <u>어색한</u> 것은?   (4점)

① You can answer this question <u>easily</u>.
② To stay healthy, you need to exercise <u>regular</u>.
③ Many people tried to help, but you're the most <u>helpful</u>.
④ Using the method <u>wisely</u>, you can solve many problems.
⑤ You can't <u>possibly</u> understand how I felt because you've never been in that situation.

[경기 ㅇㅇ중]

02 다음 빈칸에 공통으로 들어갈 말로 가장 적절한 것은?   (4점)

• He ate an unbelievable _____ of food.
• We produce a large _____ of trash every day.

① amount
② number
③ quality
④ character
⑤ discount

[양천구 ㅇㅇ중]

03 다음 빈칸 (A)에 들어갈 말로 알맞은 것은?   (3점)

Ms. Honey: (A)_____
Matilda: Of course. First, boil some water in a small pot. Second, put in dried noodles and the soup powder. Then, cover and boil 3 to 4 minutes. You can add an egg.
Ms. Honey: Thanks. It's easy.

① Can you explain how to boil eggs?
② Do you know how to cook Ramyeon?
③ Let me tell you how to cook Ramyeon.
④ Can you tell me what your favorite food is?
⑤ Do you know how to eat soup with noodles?

[충남 ㅇㅇ중]

04 다음 빈칸에 <u>어색한</u> 것은?   (3점)

A: I really appreciate your help.
B: _____

① No problem.
② My pleasure.
③ You're welcome.
④ Don't mention it.
⑤ I'm sorry to hear that.

[송파구 ㅇㅇ중]

05 다음 중 짝지어진 대화가 <u>어색한</u> 것은?   (4점)

① A: How often do you take bowling lessons?
  B: Twice a week. I'm just a beginner.
② A: I'm happy for you to win the gold medal.
  B: Thanks. You must be proud of yourself.
③ A: I suggest that you should use a lighter ball.
  B: OK. I will look for a lighter one.
④ A: How big is the swimming class on weekends?
  B: It has a limit of 10 people.
⑤ A: Do you remember where you used your phone last?
  B: Well, I took it out of my bag at the snack shop.

[6~8] 다음 대화를 읽고 물음에 답하시오.

> G: Excuse me, but what's this robot for?
> B: Oh, ⓐit's a robot that finds books for you.
> G: Really? Can you tell me how to use ⓑit?
> B: Sure. First, place your library card on the robot's screen.
> G: OK.
> B: Second, type the title of the book you're looking for and then press ENTER.
> G: Is that all?
> B: Yes. Then, the robot will find the book and take ⓒit to the front desk.
> G: So I can just go to the front desk and get the book?
> B: Right. ⓓIt's so easy, isn't it?
> G: Yes, ⓔit's really amazing. Thank you.
>
> *G: girl, B: boy

06 위 대화의 ⓐ~ⓔ 중 가리키는 것이 <u>어색한</u> 것은? (4점)

① ⓐ - the robot
② ⓑ - the robot
③ ⓒ - the book
④ ⓓ - using the robot
⑤ ⓔ - the book

07 위 대화의 내용과 일치하는 것은? (3점)

① The girl has never used the robot before.
② The robot will find the book you are looking for and bring it to you.
③ You only need to know your phone number to use the robot.
④ You say the title of the book to the robot and it will go find it.
⑤ The girl thinks that it's better to go find a book herself than using the robot.

08 위 대화를 읽고 대답할 수 <u>없는</u> 질문은? (4점)

① Where are the boy and the girl?
② What does the robot do in the library?
③ Where do you put the library card?
④ How many books can the robot carry at once?
⑤ Where will the robot take the book that it finds?

09 다음 대화를 바탕으로 감자 심는 방법을 바르게 배열한 것은? (3점)

> A: Can you tell me how to plant a potato?
> B: Sure. First, cut a potato into small pieces. Second, dig holes in the ground.
> A: Then?
> B: Then put the potato pieces in the holes and cover the holes with dirt.
> A: That sounds simple. Thanks.

(A)　　(B)　　(C)　　(D)

① (B) - (A) - (D) - (C)
② (B) - (D) - (A) - (C)
③ (C) - (B) - (A) - (D)
④ (D) - (A) - (C) - (B)
⑤ (D) - (B) - (C) - (A)

10 Which is NOT right to fill in the blanks and complete the following dialogue? (4점)

> G: Excuse me, but what's this robot for?
>
> B: Oh, it's a robot that finds books for you.
>
> G: Really? ⓐ_____ how to use it?
>
> B: Sure. First, ⓑ_____ on the robot's screen.
>
> G: OK.
>
> B: ⓒ_____, type the title of the book ⓓ_____ and then press ENTER.
>
> G: Is that all?
>
> B: Yes. Then, the robot will find the book and take it to the front desk.
>
> G: So I can just ⓔ_____ and get the book?
>
> B: Right. It's so easy, isn't it?
>
> G: Yes, it's really amazing. Thank you.

① ⓐ: Can you tell me

② ⓑ: place your library card

③ ⓒ: Second

④ ⓓ: you're reading

⑤ ⓔ: go to the front desk

11 다음 〈보기〉와 다른 용법으로 쓰인 것은? (4점)

> **보기**
> • She got onto the train, <u>waving</u> her hand.

① <u>Saying</u> goodbye, she cried.

② She looked at me, <u>eating</u> a sandwich.

③ <u>Walking</u> along the riverside, she sang a song.

④ <u>Being</u> very tired, I went to bed earlier than usual.

⑤ <u>Listening</u> to music, she studied for the final exams.

12 다음 중 어법상 어색한 것을 두 개 고르면? (4점)

① We missed the last bus. <u>Being no bus service</u>, we had to walk home.

② She ran fast to catch the bus. <u>Running for the bus</u>, she slipped on the ice and fell over.

③ I went to a basketball game, but it was boring. <u>Knowing not the rules</u>, I couldn't enjoy the game.

④ <u>Born as the youngest son in a big family</u>, he had a happy childhood. He was loved by all the family.

⑤ <u>Before coming to school</u>, students must complete the Covid-19 health self-check. If they have any problems, they should stay home.

13 다음 문장의 빈칸에 공통으로 들어갈 단어는? (대·소문자 무시) (3점)

> • _____ I told you, you should come to school tomorrow.
>
> • She got wiser _____ she got older.
>
> • _____ I was sick, I couldn't go to school.
>
> • Minsu is _____ popular _____ Jinsu.

① as   ② when   ③ because

④ that   ⑤ since

[14~16] 다음 글을 읽고 물음에 답하시오.

Living with Big Data

Have you ever visited an online bookstore and ⓐ been surprised by the books that the store recommended for you? Many of them looked interesting to you. So how did the bookstore know what you liked? This is ⓑall possibly because of big data.

What is big data?

Big data is data sets that are very big and complex. (A)As information and communication technology develops, the amount of data we have is getting ⓒmuch more greater than before. This is mainly because almost everything that we do online leaves a trace. For example, the photos you upload on your blog and the records of your purchases at online stores are all part of big data. Simply collecting data, however, is not enough. Big data ⓓhas to be analyzed, and this is done by big data experts. (B)여러 가지 방법들을 사용해서, experts analyze big data and draw meaningful results from it. These results then ⓔcan be used to make decisions or to predict the future.

14 위 글의 밑줄 친 ⓐ~ⓔ 중 바르게 쓰이지 <u>않은</u> 것을 2개 고르면? (4점)

① ⓐ ② ⓑ ③ ⓒ ④ ⓓ ⑤ ⓔ

15 위 글의 (A)As와 쓰임이 같은 것은? (4점)

① As I was reading, the phone rang.

② As I told you, we will meet at 6:00.

③ As you can see, I'm not a good cook.

④ Do in Rome as Romans do.

⑤ As time went by, she became nervous.

16 위 글의 밑줄 친 (B)의 우리말을 영어로 바르게 옮긴 것은? (3점)

① Used various methods

② If they use various methods

③ Using various methods

④ Although they use various methods

⑤ Use of various methods

[17~18] 다음 글을 읽고 물음에 답하시오.

Are you a sports fan? Well, big data is (improve) the performance of players, (make) sports more exciting. A famous example is Germany's national soccer team. The team built a database by collecting and (analyze) a huge amount of data on players. For example, the data included information about how much each player ran and how long he had the ball. With the help of this database, Germany's national soccer team was able to improve its performance and win the 2014 World Cup.

17 위 글의 괄호의 가장 올바른 형태끼리 순서대로 짝지은 것은? (4점)

① to improve – making – analyze

② improving – making – to analyze

③ improve – make – analyze

④ improving – to make – analyzing

⑤ improving – making – analyzing

18 위 글의 제목으로 가장 알맞은 것은? (4점)

① The 2014 World Cup

② How Much Is Big Data?

③ How to Win the World Cup

④ Improving Performance in Sports

⑤ Germany's National Soccer Team

[19~22] 다음 글을 읽고 물음에 답하시오.

Big data is ⓐprotecting all parts of our lives. It helps companies understand their customers' needs better and helps them sell more products. It helps people ⓑavoid heavy traffic. Its uses are endless, and here are some interesting examples.

Disease Forecast
Did you know that health professionals can now forecast a disease? This is possible thanks to big data. For example, when the flu season comes, people will buy more flu medicine. They will also search online about flu symptoms more. If this kind of data is ⓒexamined wisely, the spread of the flu can be predicted.

Crime Prevention
Thanks to big data, police can now predict crime before it happens. Through the analysis of big data about the type, time and place of crime, police can make a map of crime hot spots. This map ⓓshows when and where crime is expected to happen. Police can prevent further crime by ⓔconcentrating on the areas and the times this map predicts.

Improving Performance in Sports
Big data is improving the performance of players. A famous example is Germany's national soccer team. The team built a database by collecting and analyzing a huge (A)_____ of data on players. (B)_____, the data included information about how much each player ran and how long he had the ball. (C)_____ the help of this database, Germany's national soccer team was able to improve its performance and win the 2014 World Cup.

19 위 글의 내용과 일치하지 <u>않는</u> 것은? (4점)

① Police can prevent further crimes by monitoring hot crime spots in the map.
② Germany's soccer team improved its performance with big data and won the championship.
③ A crime spot map contains information about when and where crime can be committed.
④ Big data helps companies understand what products their customers are interested in.
⑤ Health professionals can stop the spread of the flu by uploading information about flu symptoms.

20 위 글의 밑줄 친 부분 중, 문맥상 낱말의 쓰임이 <u>어색한</u> 것은? (4점)

① ⓐ　　② ⓑ　　③ ⓒ　　④ ⓓ　　⑤ ⓔ

21 위 글의 중심 내용으로 가장 알맞은 것은? (3점)

① what we should be careful with big data
② how big data makes our lives better
③ when and where big data was used
④ where big data can be stored
⑤ how we collect big data

22 위 글의 빈칸 (A), (B), (C)에 들어갈 말이 알맞게 연결된 것은? (4점)

	(A)	(B)	(C)
①	amount	For example	With
②	number	As a result	With
③	amount	For example	Without
④	number	As a result	Without
⑤	amount	For example	Without

[23~25] 다음 글을 읽고 물음에 답하시오.

Have you ever visited an online bookstore? Were you surprised by the books ⓐ_____ the store recommended for you? Did many of them looked interesting to you? So how did the bookstore know ⓑ_____ you liked? This is all possible because of big data.

(A)_____

Big data is data sets ⓒ_____ are very big and complex. (B)As information and communication technology develops, the amount of data we have is getting much greater than before. This is mainly because almost everything ⓓ_____ we do online leaves a trace. For example, the photos ⓔ_____ you upload on your blog and the records of your purchases at online stores are all part of big data.

23 위 글의 빈칸에 들어갈 말이 나머지와 <u>다른</u> 하나는?　(3점)

① ⓐ　　② ⓑ　　③ ⓒ　　④ ⓓ　　⑤ ⓔ

24 위 글의 빈칸 (A)에 들어갈 소제목으로 가장 알맞은 것은?(4점)

① What is big data?

② How can we collect big data?

③ What is information and communication technology?

④ What do we leave online?

⑤ Where can we get big data?

25 위 글의 (B)As와 가장 비슷한 의미로 쓰인 것은?　(4점)

① He did exactly <u>as</u> his teacher had told him.

② <u>As</u> I was tired, I went to bed earlier.

③ <u>As</u> we know, it's her birthday today.

④ It gets warmer and warmer, <u>as</u> spring comes.

⑤ I missed the first train, <u>as</u> I got up late.

[26~27] 다음 글을 읽고 물음에 답하시오.

Are you a sports fan? Well, big data is improving the performance of players, (A)make sports more exciting. A famous example is Germany's national soccer team. The team built a database by collecting and analyzing a huge amount of data on players. For example, the data included information about how much each player ran and how long he had the ball. With the help of this database, Germany's national soccer team was able to improve its performance and win the 2014 World Cup.

26 위 글의 제목으로 알맞은 것은?　(4점)

① Improving Performance in Sports

② The Influence of the Exciting Sports

③ Germany's Win in the 2014 World Cup

④ An Analysis of a Huge Data on Players

⑤ The Information about 2014 World Cup

27 위 글의 (A)make를 알맞은 형으로 고치시오.　(4점)

→ _____

◎ 선택형 문항의 답안은 컴퓨터용 수정 싸인펜을 사용하여 OMR 답안지에 바르게 표기하시오.
◎ 서술형 문제는 답을 답안지에 반드시 검정 볼펜으로 쓰시오.
◎ 총 27문항 100점 만점입니다. 문항별 배점은 각 문항에 표시되어 있습니다.

[부산 ○○중]

01 다음 중 영영풀이가 옳지 <u>않은</u> 것은? (4점)

① recommend: to suggest something to someone
② rent: to pay someone for the use of something
③ flu: an illness that is like a bad cold but can be very serious
④ purchase: the action of selling something
⑤ symptom: something that shows you may have a particular illness

[서대문구 ○○중]

02 다음 단어의 의미 관계가 〈보기〉와 같은 것은? (3점)

보기
direct - indirect

① put – input   ② door – indoor
③ visible – invisible   ④ come – income
⑤ habit – inhabit

[강북구 ○○중]

03 다음 대화의 빈칸에 들어갈 말로 알맞은 것은? (4점)

A: Excuse me. I want to rent a bike. Can you tell me how to use this application?
B: Sure. First, log in to the application. Then find the RENT button and touch it.
A: Then what?
B: Then the application will give you a number to unlock a bike with.
A: _____

① That's too bad.
② I think so, too.
③ Which do you prefer?
④ What is this application for?
⑤ Thank you. I really appreciate your help.

[양천구 ○○중]

04 다음 (A)를 읽고 (B)의 안내문을 완성하려고 한다. ⓐ~ⓔ의 빈칸에 들어갈 말로 알맞지 <u>않은</u> 것은? (4점)

(A)
G: Excuse me, but what's this robot for?
B: Oh, it's a robot that finds books for you.
G: Really? Can you tell me how to use it?
B: Sure. First, place your library card on the robot's screen.
G: OK.
B: Second, type the title of the book you're looking for and then press ENTER.
G: Is that all?
B: Yes. Then, the robot will find the book and take it to the front desk.
G: So I can just go to the front desk and get the book?
B: Right. It's so easy, isn't it?
G: Yes, it's really amazing. Thank you.

(B)

	ⓐ_____ to Use The Robot	
1	ⓑ_____ your library card on the ⓒ_____.	
2	Type the ⓓ_____ of the book and then press ENTER.	
3	Go to the ⓔ_____ desk and get the book there.	

① ⓐ How   ② ⓑ Place
③ ⓒ board   ④ ⓓ title
⑤ ⓔ front

[5~6] 다음 대화를 읽고 물음에 답하시오.

> B: I want to buy a snack. (A)이 과자 자판기를 어떻게 사용하는지 아세요?
> G: Yeah. ⓐ_____.
> B: ⓑ_____
> ⓒ_____
> G: ⓓ_____.
> ⓔ_____

05 위 대화의 (A)를 다음과 같이 바꿔 쓸 때 빈칸에 들어가지 <u>않는</u> 단어는? (4점)

> • _____ _____ _____ _____
> _____ use this snack machine?

① know   ② what   ③ do
④ to   ⑤ you

06 위 문장이 가장 자연스러운 대화가 되도록 빈칸 ⓐ~ⓔ에 들어갈 문장을 순서대로 나열한 것은? (4점)

> ㉠ Just put in the money.
> ㉡ What's next?
> ㉢ First, choose the snack you want.
> ㉣ I already did.
> ㉤ Then take the snack out.

    ⓐ   ⓑ   ⓒ   ⓓ   ⓔ
① ㉠ - ㉡ - ㉢ - ㉣ - ㉤
② ㉢ - ㉡ - ㉣ - ㉤ - ㉠
③ ㉢ - ㉣ - ㉤ - ㉡ - ㉠
④ ㉠ - ㉣ - ㉡ - ㉤ - ㉢
⑤ ㉢ - ㉣ - ㉡ - ㉠ - ㉤

[7~8] 다음 대화를 읽고 물음에 답하시오.

> G: Excuse me, but what's this robot for?
> B: Oh, it's (A)a robot that (B)<u>finds</u> books for you.
> G: Really? Can you tell me how to use ⓐ<u>it</u>?
> B: Sure. First, (C)<u>place</u> your library card on the robot's screen.
> G: OK.
> B: Second, type the title of the book you ⓑ<u>look</u> <u>for</u> and then ⓒ<u>press</u> ENTER.
> G: Is that all?
> B: Yes. Then, the robot will find (D)<u>the book</u> and take ⓓ<u>it</u> to the (E)<u>front desk</u>.
> G: So I can just go and get the book ⓔ<u>there</u>?
> B: Right. It's so easy, isn't it?
> G: Yes, it's really amazing. Thank you.

07 위 대화의 주제로 알맞은 것은? (3점)

① How to fix a robot's screen
② How to make a library card
③ How to find a book by a robot
④ How to volunteer in a library
⑤ How to type a book title on a robot's screen

08 위 대화에서 짝지어진 것의 의미가 서로 가장 <u>다른</u> 것은? (4점)

① (A) ⓐ   ② (B) ⓑ   ③ (C) ⓒ
④ (D) ⓓ   ⑤ (E) ⓔ

09 다음 빈칸에 가장 적절한 말은? (3점)

> A: _____
> B: First, log in to the homepage and then click this button.

① Where is the homepage?
② How do I get to the bank?
③ Can you tell me when to log in?
④ Do you know how to sign up for the class?
⑤ Excuse me. I'm looking for the bank near here.

10 다음 대화의 밑줄 친 ⓐ~ⓔ 중 대화의 흐름상 적절하지 <u>않은</u> 것은? (3점)

> A: Excuse me, but what's this robot for?
> B: Oh, ⓐ<u>it's a robot which finds books for people</u>.
> A: Really? ⓑ<u>Do you know how to use this robot</u>?
> B: Sure. ⓒ<u>Second, place your library card on the robot's screen</u>.
> A: OK.
> B: Then, type the title of the book you're looking for and then press ENTER.
> A: Is that all?
> B: Yes. ⓓ<u>Then, the robot will find the book and take it to the front desk</u>.
> A: So I can just go to the front desk and get the book?
> B: Right. It's so easy. isn't it?
> A: Yes, it's really amazing. ⓔ<u>I really appreciate your help</u>.

① ⓐ   ② ⓑ   ③ ⓒ   ④ ⓓ   ⑤ ⓔ

11 다음 밑줄 친 As[as]의 의미가 〈보기〉와 같은 것은? (3점)

> 보기
> • I'll have to stay home <u>as</u> it's raining.

① I like him <u>as</u> a novelist.
② Leave everything <u>as</u> you found it.
③ <u>As</u> she was young, she worked for a bank.
④ <u>As</u> you can see now, I'm not a good cook.
⑤ <u>As</u> she was hungry, she ate all of the food up.

12 다음 중 어법에 맞지 <u>않게</u> 고친 것을 <u>2개</u> 고르면? (4점)

① As he came back home, he called me.
  → To come back home, he called me.
② Because he was very sick, he couldn't finish his project.
  → Being very sick, he couldn't finish his project.
③ Though Amy was only eleven years old, she went to the university.
  → Being only eleven years old, Amy went to the university.
④ Because Jin didn't finish her work, she had to stay at home.
  → Finishing not her work, Jin had to stay at home.
⑤ As Kate is interested in math, she likes her math class.
  → Interested in math, Kate likes her math class.

13 다음 〈보기〉에서 어법상 옳은 것만을 있는 대로 고른 것은? (4점)

> ⓐ Only nine years old, he went to the university.
> ⓑ Study very hard, you will pass the math exam.
> ⓒ Speaking of his appearance, he is very handsome.
> ⓓ They climbed the mountain talking to each other.
> ⓔ Not knowing what to buy, I asked Mom she wanted.

① ⓐ, ⓒ   ② ⓑ, ⓒ
③ ⓐ, ⓒ, ⓓ   ④ ⓑ, ⓓ, ⓔ
⑤ ⓒ, ⓓ, ⓔ

[14~16] 다음 글을 읽고 물음에 답하시오.

Big data is data sets that are very big and complex. (A)_____ information and communication technology develops, the amount of data we have is getting much greater than before. This is mainly because almost everything that we do online leaves a trace. For example, the photos you upload on your blog and the records of your purchases at online stores are all part of big data.

Simply collecting data, (B)_____, is not enough. Big data has to be analyzed, and this is done by big data experts. Using various methods, experts analyze big data and draw meaningful results from it. These results then can be used to make decisions or to predict the future.

14 위 글에서 알 수 있는 big data에 대한 설명이 <u>잘못된</u> 것은? (4점)

① It is very big data sets.

② It is complex data sets.

③ The amount of data is getting smaller than before.

④ The photos you upload on blogs can be big data.

⑤ The records of purchases at online stores are part of it.

15 위 글의 빈칸 (A)와 (B)에 들어갈 표현을 가장 자연스럽게 연결한 것은? (4점)

	(A)	(B)
①	As	finally
②	So	finally
③	Thus	however
④	So	however
⑤	As	however

16 위 글에서 다음 질문에 해당하는 답이 되는 문장을 찾아 쓰시오. (4점)

> What do big data experts do?

→ _____

[17~18] 다음 글을 읽고 물음에 답하시오.

Did you know that health professionals can now forecast a <u>disease</u> just as weather experts forecast the weather? This is possible thanks to big data. For example, Ⓐ<u>as</u> the flu season comes, people will buy more flu <u>medicine</u>. They will also <u>search</u> online about flu <u>symptoms</u> more. If this kind of data is analyzed wisely, the <u>spread</u> of the flu can be predicted.

17 위 글의 Ⓐ와 다음 밑줄 친 as가 같은 의미로 사용된 것은? (4점)

① It was snowing <u>as</u> I went outside.

② I have to study hard <u>as</u> my teacher said.

③ <u>As</u> you know, my English teacher is smart.

④ <u>As</u> I told you, we'll meet at the subway station.

⑤ <u>As</u> the weather forecaster predicted, it rained all day.

18 위 글의 밑줄 친 단어 중 〈보기〉의 영영풀이에 해당하는 것은? (3점)

> 보기
> something that shows you may have a particular illness

① disease ② medicine ③ search

④ symptom ⑤ spread

[19~21] 다음 글을 읽고 물음에 답하시오.

Big data is influencing almost all parts of our lives. ⓐIt helps companies understand their customers' needs better and helps ⓑthem sell more products. It helps people avoid heavy traffic. ⓒIts uses are endless, and here are some interesting examples.

Did you know that health professionals can now forecast a disease just (가)as weather experts forecast the weather? ⓓThis is possible thanks to big data. For example, when the flu season comes, people will buy more flu medicine. ⓔThey will also search online about flu symptoms more. If this kind of data is analyzed wisely, the spread of the flu can be predicted.

19 위 글의 ⓐ~ⓔ의 대명사가 가리키는 대상이 <u>어색한</u> 것은?

(4점)

① ⓐ - Big data

② ⓑ - companies

③ ⓒ - big data's

④ ⓓ - weather forecast

⑤ ⓔ - people

20 위 글의 (가)와 어법상 가장 같은 뜻으로 쓰인 것은? (3점)

① I can do it <u>as</u> well as she.

② She was dressed <u>as</u> a princess.

③ <u>As</u> I was reading, the phone rang.

④ <u>As</u> you know, this vase is very valuable.

⑤ <u>As</u> it snowed a lot, the game was cancelled.

21 위 글의 주제가 되는 질문으로 가장 적절한 것은? (4점)

① How is big data analyzed?

② What do health experts do?

③ What does 'big data' mean?

④ Why do people catch the flu?

⑤ How is big data influencing our lives?

[22~23] 다음 글을 읽고 물음에 답하시오.

Improving Performance in Sports

Are you a sports fan?

(A) For example, the data included information about how much each player ran and how long he had the ball.

(B) Well, big data is ⓐimproving the performance of players, ⓑmaking sports more exciting.

(C) With the help of this database, Germany's national soccer team was able to improve it's performance and ⓒwinning the 2014 world cup.

(D) The team built a database by ⓓcollecting and ⓔanalyzing a huge amount of data on players.

(E) A famous example is Germany's national soccer team.

22 위 글의 맥락에 맞게 순서대로 바르게 나열한 것은? (5점)

① (B) - (E) - (A) - (D) - (C)

② (B) - (E) - (C) - (A) - (D)

③ (B) - (E) - (D) - (A) - (C)

④ (C) - (B) - (D) - (E) - (A)

⑤ (C) - (A) - (D) - (E) - (B)

23 위 글의 ⓐ~ⓔ 중 어법상 쓰임이 <u>잘못된</u> 것은? (3점)

① ⓐ   ② ⓑ   ③ ⓒ   ④ ⓓ   ⑤ ⓔ

[24~25] 다음 글을 읽고 물음에 답하시오.

Disease Forecast

Did you know that health professionals can now forecast a disease just as weather experts forecast the weather? This is possible thanks (A)_____ big data. For example, when the flu season comes, people will buy more flu medicine. They will also search online (B)_____ flu symptoms more. If this kind of data is analyzed wisely, the spread of the flu can be predicted.

Crime Prevention

Thanks (A)_____ big data, police can now predict crime before it happens. Through the analysis of big data about the type, time and place of crime, police can make a map of crime hot spots. This map identifies when and where crime is most likely to happen. Police can prevent further crime by focusing (C)_____ the areas and the times this map predicts.

24 위 글의 빈칸 (A)~(C)에 들어갈 단어가 순서대로 바르게 짝지어진 것은? (3점)

① to - on - in
② on - on - at
③ to - about - on
④ on - about - of
⑤ with - of - on

25 위 글을 바르게 이해한 학생은? (4점)

① 천옥: 건강 전문가들은 날씨도 예측할 수 있어.
② 은비: 데이터의 현명한 분석을 통해, 독감의 확산을 알 수 있어.
③ 나연: 경찰은 이미 일어난 범죄에만 빅데이터를 사용해.
④ 솔라: 빅데이터를 통해 추가 범죄를 예방하기는 힘들어.
⑤ 다현: 범죄 다발 지역 지도는 범죄가 일어날 장소에 대해서만 알려주는 역할을 해.

[26~27] 다음 글을 읽고, 물음에 답하시오.

Are you a sports fan? Well, big data is improving the performance of players, making sports more exciting. A famous example is Germany's national soccer team. The team built a database by collecting and analyzing a huge amount of data on players. For example, the data included information about how much each player ran and how long he had the ball. With the help of this database, Germany's national soccer team was able to improve its performance and win the 2014 World Cup.

26 위 글을 정리한 내용으로 잘못된 것은? (4점)

Q: How did Germany's national soccer team win the 2014 World Cup?
A: ⓐGermany's national soccer team has the most sports fans in the world. ⓑIt collected and analyzed a huge amount of data on players. ⓒThis database included information about how much each player ran. ⓓIt also included information about how long each player had the ball. ⓔWith this database, the team improved its performance.

① ⓐ   ② ⓑ   ③ ⓒ   ④ ⓓ   ⑤ ⓔ

27 위 글의 밑줄 친 문장의 분사구문 형식을 참고하여, 그림 속 여자의 두 행동이 동시에 일어나는 문장을 완성하시오. (4점)

She said goodbye.

→ _____, the girl got on the train.

◎ 선택형 문항의 답안은 컴퓨터용 수정 싸인펜을 사용하여 OMR 답안지에 바르게 표기하시오.
◎ 서술형 문제는 답을 답안지에 반드시 검정 볼펜으로 쓰시오.
◎ 총 26문항 100점 만점입니다. 문항별 배점은 각 문항에 표시되어 있습니다.

[성북구 ○○중]

01 다음 중 빈칸에 들어갈 단어로 적절한 것은? (3점)

• A clover with four leaves is a _____ of luck.

① symbol   ② attitude   ③ bend

④ respect   ⑤ behavior

[부산 ○○중]

02 다음 중 영영풀이에 해당하는 것은? (4점)

to shape or force something straight into a curve or angle

① bend   ② avoid

③ bloom   ④ appear

⑤ develop

[양천구 ○○중]

03 다음 대화의 내용과 일치하는 것은? (4점)

G: There are two exhibitions, Hanbok and Korean mask. Which one do you want to see more, Eric?

B: I prefer the Korean mask exhibition. Is that OK, Somi?

G: Of course. And it seems to me that the mask exhibition will be much more interesting.

B: Do you think so?

G: Yes. Look at this poster. There isn't just an exhibition. There's also a mask dance show at 4:00 and 6:00.

B: Great! I've never seen a mask dance show before.

G: Well. I've seen it before. I'm sure you'll like it.

B: So where is the show?

G: It's in Dasom Hall, next to the exhibition room.

B: It's 4:30 now, so let's watch the 6 o'clock show.

G: OK. Let's go see the exhibition first.

① Eric은 전에도 탈춤 쇼를 본 적이 있다.

② Eric은 탈춤 쇼보다 한복 전시회를 보고 싶어 한다.

③ 탈 전시회를 4시와 6시에 다솜 홀에서 진행된다.

④ Eric과 Somi는 탈춤 쇼를 보고 전시회에 갈 것이다.

⑤ Somi는 한복 전시회보다 탈 전시회가 더 재미있을 거라고 생각한다.

[양천구 ○○중]

04 다음 대화의 문맥상 (A)에 들어갈 말로 가장 적절한 것은?(4점)

G: Junsu, you said you're going to buy a gift for your sister. How about the bags here?

B: They look nice.

G: Which one do you prefer, the one with flowers or the one with animals?

B: (A)_____

① No, I've already chosen a birthday gift for my sister.

② I like animals. Thus, I want to be an animal doctor.

③ Yes, it seems to me that my sister wants to buy flowers.

④ Of course, I will buy flowers for my sister. I'm sure she will like it.

⑤ I like the one with animals more. It seems to me that my sister will love it.

[5~6] 다음 대화를 읽고 물음에 답하시오.

> G: There are two exhibitions we can go to. Which one do you want to see more, Eric?
> B: (A)_____ Is that OK, Somi?
> G: Of course. And it seems to me that the Korean mask exhibition will be much more interesting.
> B: Do you think so?
> G: Yes. Look at this poster. There isn't just an exhibition. There's also a mask dance show at 4:00 and 6:00.
> B: Great! I've never seen a mask dance show before.
> G: Well, I've seen a show before. I'm sure you'll like it.
> B: So where is the show?
> G: It's in Dasom Hall, next to the exhibition room.
> B: It's 4:30 now, so let's watch the 6 o'clock show.
> G: OK. Let's go see the exhibition first.

05 위 대화의 빈칸 (A)에 들어갈 표현으로 옳지 <u>않은</u> 것은? (4점)

① I prefer the one with the mask.

② I prefer the other one except the Korean mask exhibition.

③ I prefer the Korean mask exhibition.

④ I like the Korean mask exhibition better.

⑤ I think the Korean mask exhibition is a good choice.

06 Which one is right to explain this dialogue? (4점)

① They don't have a choice where to go.

② Eric has seen the Korean mask dance before.

③ Somi thinks for sure Eric likes the show.

④ This show will be held in the exhibition room.

⑤ They are going to see the show first.

07 다음 중 짝지어진 대화가 <u>어색한</u> 것은? (3점)

① A: Which do you like better, chocolate or candy?
　 B: Both are delicious, but I like chocolate more.

② A: Which season do you like more, summer or winter?
　 B: I prefer summer to winter. I like cold weather.

③ A: In my opinion, Bibimbap is the healthier food than Galbitang.
　 B: I think so, too.

④ A: Which one do you prefer, the green plate or the white plate?
　 B: It's hard to choose, but I like the green one better.

⑤ A: Can you explain how to return these books?
　 B: Of course. To begin with, insert the card. Then put the books in this box.

08 다음 대화의 흐름상 <u>어색한</u> 것은? (4점)

> A: ⓐ<u>We can have Bibimbap or Galbitang.</u> ⓑ<u>Which do you prefer</u>?
> B: ⓒ<u>I prefer Galbitang to Bibimbap.</u> I think Bibimbap is the healthier choice.
> A: ⓓ<u>I think so, too.</u> I also like Bibimbap more.
> B: ⓔ<u>Let's order, then.</u> I'm very hungry.

① ⓐ　　② ⓑ　　③ ⓒ　　④ ⓓ　　⑤ ⓔ

09 다음 대화의 순서를 바르게 배열한 것은? (5점)

G: There are two exhibitions we can go to. Which one do you want to see more, Eric?

B: I prefer the Korean mask exhibition. Is that OK, Somi?

G: Of course. And it seems to me that the mask exhibition will be much more interesting.

B: Do you think so?

G: Yes. Look at this poster. There isn't just an exhibition. There's also a mask dance show at 4:00 and 6:00

B: Great! I've never seen a mask dance show before.

ⓐ Ok. Let's go see the exhibition first.

ⓑ Well, I've seen a show before. I'm sure you'll like it.

ⓒ It's 4:30 now, so let's watch the 6 o'clock show.

ⓓ So where is the show?

ⓔ It's in Dasom Hall, next to the exhibition room.

① ⓐ-ⓑ-ⓒ-ⓓ-ⓔ ② ⓑ-ⓓ-ⓐ-ⓔ-ⓒ

③ ⓑ-ⓐ-ⓔ-ⓒ-ⓓ ④ ⓑ-ⓓ-ⓔ-ⓒ-ⓐ

⑤ ⓐ-ⓓ-ⓔ-ⓒ-ⓑ

10 빈칸에 들어갈 말로 어법상 옳은 것은? (3점)

• If I made lots of money, ＿＿＿＿＿＿＿＿＿＿＿＿＿＿＿＿＿＿＿＿＿＿＿＿＿＿＿.

① I will travel around the world

② I would help the poor people

③ I would have visited Europe

④ I could bought an expensive car

⑤ I can donate a lot of money to charity

11 다음 우리말과 일치하도록 주어진 단어를 바르게 배열했을 때, 7번째로 올 단어는? (4점)

• 나는 사람들 앞에서 말하는 것이 어렵다.
(me, people, for, front, speak, it, difficult, to, is, in, of)

① me ② for ③ speak

④ to ⑤ in

12 다음 중 빈칸에 들어갈 단어가 나머지 넷과 다른 것은? (4점)

① It is natural ＿＿＿＿＿ you to get angry.

② This book is too easy ＿＿＿＿＿ Jim to read.

③ Mike pushed the door ＿＿＿＿＿ a child to enter.

④ It is hard ＿＿＿＿＿ me to get a good grade in English.

⑤ It was careful ＿＿＿＿＿ him to get to the concert early.

13 다음 문장에서 어색한 문장의 개수는? (4점)

ⓐ It is not easy for me to move this table.

ⓑ It is important for you to manage time effectively.

ⓒ It is foolish for him to make the same mistake twice.

ⓓ It's very kind of you to help my son.

ⓔ It's safer of you to wear knee pads.

ⓕ It was impossible for him to win the game.

① 1개 ② 2개 ③ 3개 ④ 4개 ⑤ 5개

[14~17] 다음 글을 읽고 물음에 답하시오.

Munjado is a type of folk painting that was popular in the late Joseon dynasty. In Munjado, there is usually a Chinese character with some animals or objects.

ⓐOne of eight Chinese characters appear in Munjado. They are *hyo*(孝), *je*(悌), *chung*(忠), *sin*(信), *ye*(禮), *ui*(義), *yeom*(廉), and *chi*(恥), and ⓑthey represent the values that were important to people of the Joseon dynasty.

The animals or objects in Munjado are not just decorations. They often are symbolic. For example, ⓒcarp in the paintings of hyo symbolize respect for parents.

ⓓThere are other examples of symbolic objects in Munjado. They are bamboo in the paintings of the character *chung*(忠) and lotus flowers in the paintings of *ui*(義). Bamboo does not bend. It stays green in all kinds of weather. For these reasons, bamboo came to symbolize loyalty to the king. In the case of lotus flowers, they grow in muddy ponds but still bloom beautifully. They thus became a symbol of a person's will to fight for justice in spite (A)_____ difficulties.

Munjado was much more than a painting to people of the Joseon dynasty. ⓔIt reminded them to important values that greatly influenced their behaviors and attitudes.

(B)_____ particular, for children, Munjado was a study tool. Through it, children in the Joseon dynasty could learn the importance of harmony in family and society.

14 위 글의 ⓐ~ⓔ 중 어법상 옳은 것을 모두 골라 묶은 것은?

(4점)

① ⓐ, ⓑ   ② ⓐ, ⓒ   ③ ⓑ, ⓒ, ⓓ
④ ⓑ, ⓓ, ⓔ   ⑤ ⓒ, ⓓ, ⓔ

15 위 글의 빈칸 (A), (B)에 들어갈 단어가 순서대로 바르게 짝지어진 것은?

(4점)

① of - In   ② to - In
③ for - With   ④ of - For
⑤ for - To

16 위 글의 문자도에 대한 설명으로 본문의 내용과 일치하는 것은?

(4점)

① 문자도는 조선 시대 전기에 유행한 일종의 민화이다.

② 문자도에 그려진 동물이나 사물은 장식물이므로 상징적 의미로 쓰이지 않는다.

③ 문자도의 대나무는 구부러지지 않기 때문에 정의를 위해 싸우는 한 사람의 의지를 나타낸다.

④ 문자도는 조선 시대 사람들에게 그 가치를 인정받지 못했다.

⑤ 조선 시대의 아이들은 문자도를 통해 가족과 사회에서 조화가 중요하다는 것을 배웠다.

17 위 글을 읽고 답할 수 있는 질문을 모두 골라 묶은 것은? (4점)

ⓐ What do the eight Chinese characters in Munjado represent?

ⓑ Why does the carp in the paintings of *hyo* symbolize respect for parents?

ⓒ Why did bamboo come to symbolize loyalty to the king?

ⓓ What do lotus flowers symbolize in Munjado?

ⓔ Why did children in the Joseon Dynasty dislike Munjado?

① ⓐ, ⓑ, ⓒ   ② ⓐ, ⓑ, ⓔ
③ ⓐ, ⓒ, ⓓ   ④ ⓑ, ⓒ, ⓔ
⑤ ⓑ, ⓓ, ⓔ

[18~20] 다음 글을 읽고 물음에 답하시오.

The animals or objects in Munjado are not just decorations. They often are symbolic. For example, carp in the paintings of *hyo* symbolize respect for parents because of an old story. The story goes as follows.

Once upon a time, a man lived with his old mother. One winter, the man's mother became ill and couldn't eat anything. On one very cold day, the mother said to the man, "(A)It would be wonderful if I could eat fresh fish."

The man went out to the river, but it was completely frozen. (B)그가 어떤 물고기라도 잡는 것은 불가능했다. The man was so disappointed that he cried out to the sky, "What should I do? Please help me." Then the ice melted, and three carp suddenly came out of the water. The man went back home and cooked the fish for his mother. Then his mother got well.

18 위 글의 내용과 일치하지 <u>않는</u> 것은? (4점)

① 문자도의 동물과 사물은 단순한 장식이 아니다.

② 효 그림에 있는 잉어는 부모님에 대한 공경을 상징한다.

③ 어느 추운 겨울날 남자는 물고기를 잡으러 강으로 갔다.

④ 남자가 하늘에 외친 후에 강의 얼음이 녹고 물고기 3마리가 물 밖으로 튀어나왔다.

⑤ 어머니는 남자가 잡아온 물고기를 먹었지만 병이 낫지 않았다.

19 위 글의 밑줄 친 (A)를 우리말로 옳게 해석한 것은? (3점)

① 내가 굉장한 물고기를 먹을 수 있을 것 같아.

② 내가 신선한 물고기를 먹었는데 참 좋았단다.

③ 내가 신선한 물고기를 먹었더라면 참 좋았을 텐데.

④ 내가 신선한 물고기를 먹을 수 있다면 참 좋겠구나.

⑤ 내가 굉장한 물고기를 먹을 수 있다면 참 신선할 텐데.

20 위 글의 밑줄 친 (B)를 영어로 옳게 바꾼 것은? (3점)

① It was possible for him to catch any fish.

② It was impossible of him to catch any fish.

③ It was impossible for him to catch any fish.

④ It was not possible to him to catch some fish.

⑤ It was not possible of him to catch some fish.

21 다음 글의 'Munjado'에 관한 글을 읽고 답할 수 <u>없는</u> 질문은? (4점)

Look at the painting on the right. Do you see the Chinese character, *hyo*(孝)? Do you also see a carp, a geomungo, and a fan? This kind of painting is called Munjado, and it is a type of folk painting that was popular in the late Joseon dynasty. In Munjado, there is usually a Chinese character with some animals or objects.

One of eight Chinese characters appears in Munjado. They are *hyo*(孝), *je*(悌), *chung*(忠), *sin*(信), *ye*(禮), *ui*(義), *yeom*(廉), and *chi*(恥), and they represent the values that were important to people of the Joseon dynasty.

① What type of painting is it?

② When was it popular?

③ What was the drawing tool used for it?

④ What are the eight Chinese characters which appear in it?

⑤ What do the eight Chinese characters in it represent?

[22~25] 다음 글을 읽고 물음에 답하시오.

Look at the painting on the bottom. (A) Do you see the Chinese character, hyo(孝)? Do you also see a carp, a geomungo, and a fan? (B) This kind of painting ⓐ_____ Munjado*, and it is a type of folk painting that was ⓑ_____ in the late Joseon dynasty. In Munjado, 보통 한자 하나가 동물들이나 사물들과 함께 나온다. (C) One of eight Chinese characters appears in Munjado. They are *hyo*(孝), *je*(悌), *chung*(忠), *sin*(信), *ye*(禮), *ui*(義), *yeom*(廉), and *chi*(恥), and they represent the values ⓒ_____ were important to people of the Joseon Dynasty. The animals or objects in Munjado are not just decorations. (D) For example, carp in the painting of hyo symbolize respect for parents ⓓ_____ an old story. The story ⓔ_____ as follows. (E)

22 위 글의 ⓐ~ⓔ에 들어갈 말로 어법상 알맞지 <u>않은</u> 것은? (4점)

① ⓐ: is called
② ⓑ: popular
③ ⓒ: what
④ ⓓ: because of
⑤ ⓔ: goes

23 위 글의 밑줄 친 우리말을 영작하시오. (5점)

→ _____

24 위 글의 (A)~(E) 중 주어진 문장이 들어갈 위치로 알맞은 것은? (4점)

> They often are symbolic.

① (A)   ② (B)   ③ (C)   ④ (D)   ⑤ (E)

25 위 글의 내용과 일치하지 <u>않는</u> 것은? (3점)

① Munjado is a type of folk painting in the Joseon dynasty.
② There are a carp, a geomungo, and a fan in the painting of hyo.
③ Munjado was popular in the late Joseon dynasty.
④ Munjado shows just plants of the Joseon dynasty.
⑤ There is an old story related to the paintings of hyo.

26 다음 글에서 전체 흐름과 관계<u>없는</u> 문장은? (4점)

> ⓐMunjado was much more than a painting to people of the Joseon dynasty. ⓑThe story goes as follows. ⓒIt reminded them of important values that greatly influenced their behaviors and attitudes. ⓓIn particular, for children, Munjado was a study tool. ⓔThrough it, children in the Joseon dynasty could learn the importance of harmony in family and society.

① ⓐ   ② ⓑ   ③ ⓒ   ④ ⓓ   ⑤ ⓔ

◎ 선택형 문항의 답안은 컴퓨터용 수정 싸인펜을 사용하여 OMR 답안지에 바르게 표기하시오.
◎ 서술형 문제는 답을 답안지에 반드시 검정 볼펜으로 쓰시오.
◎ 총 25문항 100점 만점입니다. 문항별 배점은 각 문항에 표시되어 있습니다.

[부산 ○○중]

01 빈칸에 들어갈 알맞은 단어를 고르면? (3점)

• It is difficult to _____ people by their voice.
(사람들을 목소리로 확인하기는 어렵다.)

① upload   ② identify   ③ include
④ improve   ⑤ influence

[대구 ○○중]

02 다음 단어에 대한 영영풀이가 바른 것은? (4점)

① behavior: the way a living creature acts
② symbol: a thing that you can see and touch
③ board: a sign, picture, object etc. that represents something else
④ scared: sad because something does not happen or is not as good as expected
⑤ society: a period of time during which members of the same family rule a country or region

[강북구 ○○중]

[3~4] 다음 대화를 읽고, 물음에 답하시오.

Somi: There are two exhibitions we can go to. One is the Korean mask exhibition, and the other is the Hanbok exhibition. Which one do you want to see more, Eric?
Eric: I prefer the Korean mask exhibition. Is that OK, Somi?
Somi: Of course. And _____.
Eric: Do you think so?

Somi: Yes. Look at this poster. There isn't just an exhibition. There's also a mask dance show at 4:00 and 6:00.
Eric: Great! I've never seen a mask dance show before.
Somi: Well, I've seen a show before. I'm sure you'll like it.
Eric: So where is the show?
Somi: It's in Dasom Hall, next to the exhibition room.
Eric: It's 4:30 now, so let's watch the 6 o'clock show.
Somi: OK. Let's go see the exhibition first.

03 위 대화의 내용과 일치하는 것은? (3점)

① Eric prefers the Korean mask exhibition to the Hanbok exhibition.
② A mask dance show is at 4:30 and 6:00.
③ Eric has seen a mask dance show before.
④ There is a mask dance show in the Korean mask exhibition room.
⑤ Somi and Eric will see the Korean mask exhibition after a mask dance show.

04 위 대화의 빈칸에 들어갈 말을 주어진 표현을 활용하여 바르게 배열한 것은? (4점)

that / it seems / much more interesting / to me / the mask exhibition will be

① it seems that to me much more interesting the mask exhibition will be
② it seems to me that the mask exhibition will be much more interesting
③ the mask exhibition will be that it seems to me much more interesting
④ it seems to me much more interesting the mask exhibition will be that
⑤ the mask exhibition will be much more interesting that it seems to me

05 다음 대화의 흐름상 (A)~(D)에 들어갈 문장을 〈보기〉에서 골라 순서대로 나열한 것은? (5점)

> G: There are two exhibitions we can go to.
> (A)_____
> B: I prefer the Korean mask exhibition. Is that OK, Somi?
> G: Of course. And it seems to me that the mask exhibition will be much more interesting.
> B: Do you think so?
> G: (B)_____
> There's also a mask dance show at 4:00 and 6:00.
> B: Great! I've never seen a mask dance show before.
> G: (C)_____
> B: So where is the show?
> G: (D)_____
> B: It's 4:30 now, so let's watch the 6 o'clock show.
> G: OK. Let's go see the exhibition first.

보기

> ⓐ Well, I've seen a show before. I'm sure you'll like it.
> ⓑ It's in Dasom Hall, next to the exhibition room.
> ⓒ Which one do you want to see more, Eric?
> ⓓ Yes. Look at this poster. There isn't just an exhibition.

① ⓐ-ⓒ-ⓑ-ⓓ ② ⓐ-ⓓ-ⓑ-ⓒ
③ ⓑ-ⓐ-ⓓ-ⓒ ④ ⓒ-ⓐ-ⓓ-ⓑ
⑤ ⓒ-ⓓ-ⓐ-ⓑ

06 다음 대화의 빈칸 (A)와 (B)에 들어갈 말로 가장 적절한 것은? (4점)

> G: We can have Bibimbap or Galbitang. Which do you prefer?
> B: (A)_____ (B)_____
> Bibimbap is the healthier choice.
> G: I think so, too. I also like Bibimbap more.
> B: Let's order, then. I'm very hungry.

	(A)	(B)
①	I prefer Bibimbap.	It seems to
②	I prefer Bibimbap.	It seems to me that
③	I prefer Galbitang.	It seems to me that
④	It's hard to choose.	It seems to
⑤	I don't like Bibimbap.	It seems to

07 다음 빈칸에 들어갈 말이 나머지와 <u>다른</u> 것은? (4점)

> (A) It is difficult _____ me to ride a bike.
> (B) It is safer _____ you to wear knee pads.
> (C) It is dangerous _____ my sister to ride a bike.
> (D) It is very kind _____ you to pick up the trash.
> (E) It is important _____ you to manage time effectively.

① (A) ② (B) ③ (C) ④ (D) ⑤ (E)

08 다음 우리말을 영어로 바르게 옮겨 쓰시오. (3점)

> • 내가 돈이 많다면, 나는 가난한 아이들을 도울 텐데.
> → If I _____ a lot of money, I _____ poor children. (help)

→ _____

[9～10] 다음 대화를 읽고 물음에 답하시오.

G: There are two exhibitions we can go to. _____, Eric?

B: I prefer the Korean mask exhibition. Is that OK, Somi?

G: Of course. And it seems to me that the mask exhibition will be much more interesting.

B: Do you think so?

G: Yes. Look at this poster. There isn't just an exhibition. There's also a mask dance show at 4:00 and 6:00.

B: Great! I've never seen a mask dance show before.

G: Well, I've seen a show before. I'm sure you'll like it.

B: So where is the show?

G: It's in Dasom Hall, next to the exhibition room.

B: It's 4:30 now, so let's watch the 6 o'clock show.

G: OK. Let's go see the exhibition first.

09 위 대화의 빈칸에 들어갈 말로 가장 적절한 것은? (3점)

① Why do you prefer the exhibition

② Which exhibition have you been to

③ When is the Korean mask exhibition

④ Which one do you want to see more

⑤ Do you like the Korean mask exhibition

10 위 대화의 내용과 일치하지 <u>않는</u> 것은? (4점)

① Eric and Somi are talking about the exhibition.

② Somi hasn't seen a mask dance show before.

③ Somi is sure that Eric will like the mask dance show.

④ The mask dance show is in Dasom Hall.

⑤ Eric and Somi will go see the exhibition first.

11 어법상 자연스러운 문장의 개수는? (4점)

- It was silly of him to go there alone.
- As she grows older, she became stronger.
- Lucy watched a movie, ate some cookies.
- If he follows my advice, he will not fail again.
- If you was here, you could see my beautiful dress.
- Taken off his hat, the man said, "Nice to meet you."

① 1개   ② 2개   ③ 3개   ④ 4개   ⑤ 5개

12 의미상 같게 문장을 바꾼 것 중 어법상 <u>어색한</u> 것은? (5점)

① As Mozart is not alive, we can't go to his concert.

→ If Mozart were alive, we could go to his concert.

② I didn't study, because I didn't know about the test.

→ If I had known about the test, I would have studied.

③ As Tom eats too many sweets, he has bad teeth.

→ Tom wouldn't have bad teeth if he didn't eat too many sweets.

④ As I don't have a screwdriver, I can't fix your bicycle.

→ I could fix your bicycle if I had a screwdriver.

⑤ You got into so much trouble because you didn't listen to your mom.

→ If you had listened to your mom, you hadn't have got into so much trouble.

[13~15] 다음 글을 읽고 물음에 답하시오.

There are other examples of symbolic ⓐobjects in Munjado. (A)They are bamboo in the paintings of the character *chung*(忠) and lotus flowers in the paintings of *ui*(義). ⓑBamboo does not bend. (B)It stays green in all kinds of weather. For these reasons, bamboo came to symbolize ⓒloyalty to the king. In the case of lotus flowers, they grow in muddy ponds but still ⓓbloom beautifully. (C)They thus became a ⓔsymbol of a person's will to fight for justice despite difficulties.

Munjado was much more than a painting to people of the Joseon dynasty. (D)It reminded them of important values that greatly influenced their behaviors and attitudes. In particular, for children, Munjado was a study tool. Through (E)it, children in the Joseon dynasty could learn the importance of harmony in family and society.

13 위 글의 밑줄 친 ⓐ~ⓔ의 영영풀이로 올바른 것은? (5점)

① ⓐ a sign, picture, etc. that represents something else

② ⓑ something that shows you may have a particular illness

③ ⓒ a feeling of support for someone or something

④ ⓓ to begin to be seen; come into existence or use

⑤ ⓔ the action of buying something; a thing that has been bought

14 위 글의 밑줄 친 (A)~(E)가 지칭하는 것이 잘못 연결된 것은? (4점)

① (A) They: other examples

② (B) It: bamboo

③ (C) They: lotus flowers

④ (D) It: a painting

⑤ (E) it: Munjado

15 Which is correct based on the text? (4점)

① Objects in Munjado have symbolic meanings.

② Bamboo symbolizes justice and loyalty.

③ Lotus flowers in Munjado mean the beauty and loyalty.

④ Munjado was just decoration as paintings.

⑤ Children in Joseon dynasty lived in harmony with their friends.

[16~17] 다음 글을 읽고 물음에 답하시오.

Once upon a time, a man lived with his old mother. One winter, the man's mother became ill and couldn't eat anything. On one very cold day, the mother said to the man, "It would be (가)_____ if I could eat fresh fish."
The man (A)_____ to the river, but it was completely frozen. It was (B)_____ for him to catch any fish. The man was so disappointed that he (C)_____ to the sky, "What should I do? Please help me." Then the ice melted, and three carp suddenly (D)_____ the water. The man went back home and cooked the fish for his mother. Then his mother (E)_____.

16 위 글의 빈칸 (가)에 들어가기에 가장 적절한 말은? (4점)

① sad   ② angry   ③ nervous
④ worried   ⑤ wonderful

17 위 글의 흐름상 빈칸 (A)~(E)에 들어갈 말로 알맞지 않은 것은? (4점)

① (A): went out   ② (B): possible
③ (C): cried out   ④ (D): came out of
⑤ (E): got well

[18~21] 다음 글을 읽고 물음에 답하시오.

The animals or objects in Munjado are not just decorations. They often are symbolic. For example, carp in the paintings of *hyo* symbolize respect for parents because of an old story. The story goes as follows.

Once upon a time, a man lived with his old mother. One winter, the man's mother became ill and couldn't eat anything. On one very cold day, the mother said to the man, "It would be wonderful if I ⓐ_____ fresh fish."

The man went out to the river, but it was completely frozen. It was impossible (가)_____ him to catch any fish. The man was so ⓑ_____ that he cried out to the sky, "What should I do? Please help me." Then the ice melted, and three carp suddenly came out of the water. The man went back home and cooked the fish for his mother. Then his mother ⓒ_____.

There are other examples of symbolic objects in Munjado. (A) They are bamboo in the paintings of the character *chung*(忠) and lotus flowers in the paintings of *ui*(義). (B) Bamboo does not bend. (C) It stays green in all kinds of weather. (D) In the case of lotus flowers, they grow in muddy ponds but still bloom beautifully. (E) They thus became a symbol of a person's will to fight for justice despite difficulties.

19 위 글의 제목으로 가장 알맞은 것은? (4점)

① The Origin of Munjado
② What Makes Munjado More Beautiful
③ Symbolic Animals and Objects in Munjado
④ Traditional Art Work of the Joseon Dynasty
⑤ Symbolic Meanings of the Chinese Character

20 위 글의 빈칸 (가)에 들어갈 말과 〈보기〉의 빈칸에 들어갈 말이 같은 것만을 있는 대로 고른 것은? (4점)

a. It was silly _____ her to give up her job.
b. It is interesting _____ me to learn Korean culture.
c. It is hard _____ children to read this book.
d. It is thoughtless _____ you to keep everybody waiting.
e. It is dangerous _____ you to cross the street here.
f. It was very mean _____ him to hide the truth.
g. It is good _____ you to exercise every day.

① a, d, f   ② b, c, d   ③ c, e, g
④ c, e, f, g   ⑤ b, c, e, g

18 위 글의 빈칸 ⓐ~ⓒ에 들어갈 말로 가장 적절한 것은? (5점)

	ⓐ	ⓑ	ⓒ
①	could eat	disappointed	got better
②	can eat	satisfied	got worse
③	could eat	satisfied	got worse
④	can eat	disappointed	got better
⑤	could eat	disappointed	got worse

21 위 글의 흐름으로 보아 주어진 문장이 들어가기에 가장 적절한 곳은? (4점)

For these reasons, bamboo came to symbolize loyalty to the king.

① (A)   ② (B)   ③ (C)   ④ (D)   ⑤ (E)

[22~23] 다음 글을 읽고 물음에 답하시오.

Once upon a time, a man lived with his old mother. One winter, the man's mother became ill and couldn't eat anything. On one very cold day, the mother wanted to eat fresh fish.

The man went out to the river, but it was completely frozen. It was impossible (A)[of him / for him] to catch any fish. The man was so (B)[disappointed / disappeared] that he cried out to the sky, "What should I do? Please help me." Then the ice melted, and three carp suddenly came (C)[into / out of] the water. The man went back home and cooked the fish for his mother. Then his mother got well.

22 위 글의 내용과 일치하지 <u>않는</u> 것은? (4점)

① 남자의 어머니는 아파서 아무것도 먹지 못했다.

② 남자는 신선한 물고기를 구하러 강으로 갔다.

③ 강이 얼어 붙어 물고기를 잡는 것은 불가능했다.

④ 남자는 낙담하여 강을 향해 도와달라고 소리쳤다.

⑤ 남자가 잡은 잉어를 먹고, 그의 어머니는 병이 나았다.

23 위 글의 괄호 (A), (B), (C) 안에서 어법에 맞는 표현으로 가장 적절한 것은? (5점)

	(A)	(B)	(C)
①	of him	disappointed	out of
②	of him	disappeared	into
③	for him	disappointed	into
④	for him	disappeared	into
⑤	for him	disappointed	out of

[24~25] 다음 글을 읽고 물음에 답하시오.

The animals or objects in Munjado are not just decorations. They often are symbolic. For example, carp in the paintings of hyo(孝) symbolize respect for parents because of an old story. There are other examples of symbolic objects in Munjado. They are bamboo in the paintings of the Character *chung*(忠) and lotus flowers in the paintings of *ui*(義). Bamboo does not bend. It stays green in all kinds of weather. (A)_____ bamboo came to symbolize loyalty to the king. In the case of lotus flowers, they grow in muddy ponds but still bloom beautifully. They (B)_____ became a symbol of a person's will to fight for justice despite difficulties.

24 위 글의 빈칸 (A), (B)에 들어갈 말로 가장 적절한 것은? (3점)

	(A)	(B)
①	For these reasons	thus
②	For these reasons	although
③	For example	instead
④	For instance	instead
⑤	However	really

25 위 글의 내용과 일치하는 것은? (4점)

① 문자도에서 의를 상징하는 것은 연꽃이다.

② 잉어는 어떤 옛날 이야기로 인해 왕에 대한 충성심을 상징한다.

③ 문자도에 있는 동물이나 사물은 단순히 장식품에 지나치지 않는다.

④ 연꽃은 어떤 날씨에서도 푸르름을 유지하고 아름답게 꽃을 피운다.

⑤ 대나무는 어떤 어려움에도 굽히지 않고 정의를 위해 싸우는 의지를 상징한다.

정답 및 해설

Lesson 5 (중간) 1회

01 ④	02 ①	03 ①	04 ③	05 ①	06 ③	07 ④	08 ③
09 ④	10 ②	11 ⑤	12 ①	13 ④	14 ③	15 ④	16 ①
17 ②	18 ②	19 ⑤	20 ③	21 ③	22 ④	23 ③	24 ④
25 ③	26 ④	27 ③	28 encourage				

01 모두 반의어인데 polite의 반의어는 impolite이다.

02 keep track of: (계속해서) ~을 파악하다, ~에 주의를 기울이다

03 (A) register for: ~에 등록하다 (B) sign up for: ~을 신청(가입)하다 (강좌에) 등록하다 (C) 동격의 of가 적절하다.

04 'I don't know how to swim at all.'이라고 했다.

05 '지갑'을 잃어버렸는데 '축하한다'고 하는 것은 어색하다.

06 'I want to take classes twice a week.'이라고 답하고 있으므로 '횟수'를 묻는 ③번이 적절하다.

07 '수업 요금'에 대한 언급은 없다.

08 'Your bowling ball looks heavy for you.'라고 했으므로 ③번이 적절하다.

09 (C) 볼링 수업을 얼마나 자주 받는지 묻고 (B) 두 번이라며 상대방이 볼링을 잘한다고 들었다고 하자 (A) 볼링을 좋아한다며 상대의 볼링공이 무거운 것 같다고 하자 (D) 가벼운 것을 찾아보겠다고 하는 순서가 적절하다.

10 모두 '제안'하는 표현인데 ②번은 '나는 영어를 열심히 공부한다.'라는 말로 '제안'하는 말이 아니다.

11 '수영하는 법을 아는지' 물었는데 '그렇다'면서 '수영 모자를 가져올 것을 제안한다.'는 말은 어색하다.

12 (A) 'I want to take classes twice a week.'이라고 답하고 있으므로 '횟수'를 묻는 'How often'이 적절하다. (B) 'I'd like to take class on weekdays and not on weekends.'이라고 했으므로 ①, ②, ④번이 적절하다.

13 ④번은 동명사이지만 <보기>와 나머지는 현재분사이다.

14 ③번은 '램프가 테이블보다 더 비싸다.'라는 의미이다.

15 (D) 앞에서 '피트 크루가 하는 주요 역할은 자동차를 점검하고 타이어를 교체하는 것이다.'라고 한 후 주어진 문장의 '타이어 교체의 중요성'에 대해 언급하는 것이 자연스러우므로 (D)가 적절하다.

16 팀이 '불리는' 것이므로 과거분사가 적절하다.

17 '결과'를 이끄는 Therefore가 적절하다.

18 (A) '경험이 있는'이라는 뜻의 과거분사형 형용사 (B) Each pacer가 주어이므로 단수 동사 (C) flags or balloons가 보여주는 것이므로 현재분사가 적절하다.

19 (D) 예가 이어지므로 For example (E) '이유'를 나타내는 부사절을 이끌고 있으므로 Because가 적절하다.

20 (A) 이 팀이라고 했으므로 pit crew (B) 장소이므로 pit (C) 빠른 속도의 경주에서는 타이어가 쉽게 마모된다고 했으므로 important (D) '2초 정도'라는 시간이 나왔으므로 pit stop (E) 20명에 이르는 구성원이 있으므로 harmony가 적절하다.

21 people이 선행사이므로 ⓒ는 who help가 적절하다.

22 마지막 문장에서 'Here are some examples.'라고 했으므로 ④번이 적절하다.

23 'Each pacer runs at different speeds and finishes the race in different times.'라고 했다.

24 (C)의 This team이 주어진 글의 'a team behind the driver'이므로 먼저 나오고, (C)의 'change the tires'에 (A)의 'Changing the tires'가 이어지고 (B)의 Therefore로 (A)의 결과를 언급하는 순서가 적절하다.

25 ⓒ는 climbers를 지칭하지만 나머지는 모두 Sherpas를 지칭한다.

26 '보이지 않는 사람들로 불리는' 이유에 해당하는 ④번이 적절하다.

27 'a part of a sport team'으로 생각하지 않지만 경기에서 중요한 역할을 한다고 했으므로 ③번이 적절하다.

28 courage: 용기, encourage: 용기를 북돋우다

Lesson 5 (중간) 2회

01 ⑤	02 ⑤	03 ④	04 ④	05 ④	06 ⑤	07 ①	08 ③
09 ③	10 ②	11 ②	12 ②				
13 The boy talking to Jenny is my brother.					14 ⑤	15 ④	
16 ③	17 ②	18 ②	19 ④	20 ⑤	21 ④	22 ③	23 ①
24 ⑤	25 ③	26 ①	27 ②	28 ④	29 ③	30 ⑤	31 ①

01 correct의 반의어는 incorrect이다.

02 주어진 영영풀이는 tribe이다.

03 'I read a book twice a month.'라고 답하고 있으므로 '횟수'를 묻는 ④번이 적절하다.

04 소년은 주중에 강습을 받고 싶다고 했다.

05 (E) 수영을 얼마나 자주 하는지 묻자 (B) 일주일에 네 번이라고 답하고 (A) 오늘 같이 수영하는 게 재밌겠다고 하자 (D) 그렇다며 수영하기 전에 스트레칭을 할 것을 제안하고 (C) 좋은 생각이라고 답하는 순서가 적절하다.

06 'How often ~?'으로 빈도(횟수)를 물어 볼 수 있다.

07 'Is this your first time taking swimming lessons?'라는 질

문에 'Yes, it is.'라고 했다.

08 'Can you sign me up for May 19th?'라고 했다가 Sara의 제 안에 26일로 바꿨다.

09 농구를 더 자주 하고 싶다는 말에 (C)에 주어진 문장의 농구 동아 리에 가입하라는 제안이 들어가고 이어서 일주일에 세 번 농구를 한다는 것이 적절하다.

10 ① breaking → broken ③ inpolite → impolite
④ wear → worn ⑤ students's → students'

11 주어진 단어를 바르게 배열하여 영작하면 'The girl sitting next to me started to scream.'이다.

12 ① cutest → cute ③ two → twice
④ larger than → large as ⑤ as → than

13 'talking to Jenny'가 'The boy'를 수식하도록 쓴다.

14 창문이 깨지는 것이므로 과거분사 broken이 적절하다.

15 ④번은 'Tom이 Mike보다 젊다'라는 뜻이다.

16 주어진 문장은 For example로 (C) 앞의 내용에 대한 예를 들고 있으므로 (C)가 적절하다.

17 앞에서 언급한 내용을 다시 간단하게 정리하고 있으므로 In short 가 적절하다.

18 help의 목적격보어로 동사 원형이나 to부정사가 적절하다.

19 앞에서 '페이서들은 달리지만 우승을 하기 위해 달리는 것은 아니 다.'라고 했으므로 'others'가 적절하다.

20 앞에서 '20명에 이르는 구성원이 있다'고 했으므로 harmony가 적절하다.

21 피트 크루의 구성원이 되기 위해 중요한 것이 무엇인지는 알 수 없 다.

22 문맥상 much를 little로 고치는 것이 적절하다.

23 ⓕ는 접두사 in을 붙여서 반의어가 된 어휘이다. visible이 적절하 다. 각각의 반의어는 ① informal ② impolite ③ impatient
④ impossible ⑤ disadvantage이다.

24 '등산가들이 산 정상에서 사진을 찍는 순간'에 대한 언급은 없다.

25 'There are people who help the players. These people are often hidden and don't get attention.'라고 했으므로 ③번이 적절하다.

26 (A) 'flags or balloons'가 보여주는 것으로 showing (B) 접속 사 없이 동사가 두 개 나올 수 없으므로 depending (C) of의 목적 어로 finishing이 적절하다.

27 (A) 상반되는 내용이 이어지므로 However (B) 예가 이어지므 로 For example (C) 앞에서 언급한 내용을 다시 간단하게 정리 하고 있으므로 In short가 적절하다.

28 ⓓ의 해석은 '주자들은 자신들의 목표 완주 시간에 따라 페이서를 선택할 수 있다.'이다.

29 (a) hide → hidden, (c) Because of → Because, (e) easy
→ easily

30 'they are as important as the players'라고 했다.

31 'the Sherpa tribe'가 주어이므로 lives가 적절하다.

Lesson 6 (중간)

01 ⑤	02 ④	03 ①	04 ⑤	05 ②	06 ⑤	07 ②	08 ②
09 ③	10 ②	11 ①	12 ③	13 What I want to do		14 ③
15 ⑤	16 ①	17 ⑤	18 ③	19 ①	20 ⑤	21 ④	22 ⑤
23 ②	24 ⑤	25 ④	26 탁자의 다리를 잘라버렸다.			27 ②

01 '사진 같은 어떤 것의 복사본'은 'reproduction(복제품)'이다.

02 (D)는 formal(격식을 차린)이 적절하다.

03 '독감에 걸렸다'는 말에 적절한 위로의 말인 ①번이 적절하다.

04 (A) 원했던 역할을 맡게 되었으므로 excited (B) 원했던 역할을 맡지 못하게 되었으므로 disappointed가 적절하다.

05 'I'm sorry to hear ~'는 유감을 표현하는 말이다.

06 '축하한다'는 말에 '고맙다'며 할 수 있는 말로 ⑤번이 적절하다.

07 ⓐ 감정을 느끼는 경우이므로 과거분사 excited ⓑ 원했던 역할 을 맡게 된 것을 축하하고 있으므로 happy ⓒ 감정을 느끼는 경우 이므로 과거분사 disappointed ⓓ 원했던 역할을 맡지 못하게 되 어 유감을 표현하고 있으므로 sorry가 적절하다.

08 원했던 역할을 맡지 못하게 됐으므로 disappointed가 적절하다.

09 B의 'What about Sumi? Did she get the role she wanted, too?'라는 질문에 W가 'Unfortunately, no.'라고 했다.

10 무슨 일인지 묻자 (B) 독감에 걸렸다고 답하고 (C) 안 됐다며 의사 에게 가 보았는지 묻자 (A) 그렇다며 약을 복용 중이라고 하자 (D) 곧 좋아지기를 바란다는 희망을 나타내고 고맙다고 대답하는 순서가 적절하다.

11 순서대로 • faster → fast • who → 삭제 • has → had • 맞 음 • have been → had been

12 ③번은 의문대명사이고 나머지는 모두 관계대명사이다.

13 선행사 포함되어 있는 관계대명사 what을 이용한다.

14 • 'taken'이 있으므로 완료시제가 적절한데 뒤의 when이 이끄 는 절이 과거시제이므로 과거완료가 적절하다.
• 앞에 과거완료가 나왔으므로 과거시제가 적절하다.

15 ⑤번은 앞에 'the only man'이라는 선행사가 있으므로 what을 쓸 수 없고 who[that]가 적절하다.

16 (A) attach A to B: A를 B에 붙이다 (B) can't help ~ing: ~하 지 않을 수 없다 (C) 선행사가 없으므로 선행사를 포함하는 what 이 적절하다.

17 'I won't charge you for this'라고 했다.

18 둘 중에서 나머지 하나는 the other로 쓴다.

19 ⓐ 'A table'이 선행사이므로 which ⓑ 'so ~ that' 구문으로 쓰였다.

20 'A table which was a priceless piece of eighteenth-century English furniture. He was so excited that he almost fell over.'라고 했다.

21 ⓓ의 lied는 '거짓말을 했다'라는 뜻이다.

22 (A) can't help ~ing: ~하지 않을 수 없다 (B) 관계대명사절 'What he wants'가 주어이므로 단수동사 is가 적절하다.

23 'Dad, what if this thing doesn't go in his car? He might not pay you'라고 하고 'Let's cut the legs off for him.'이라고 하자 'Great idea!'라고 했다.

24 ⓔ에는 pay가 아니라 '(요금·값을) 청구하다'라는 의미의 charge가 적절하다.

25 언제 어디서 Rummins가 18세기 영국 가구를 얻었는지는 알 수 없다.

26 'Rummins then had an idea. "What he wants is only the legs. Let's cut the legs off for him," said Rummins. "Great idea!" said Bert. Bert then took out a saw and began to cut off the legs.'라고 했으므로 'When Mr. Boggis came back, the legs had been cut off.'라고 했으므로 그들은 '탁자의 다리를 잘라버렸다'

27 과학적 사실이나 진리는 항상 현재시제로 쓴다.

Lesson 6 (중간)

```
01 ①   02 ③, ④     03 ②   04 ④   05 ③   06 ⑤   07 ①
08 ①   09 ⑤   10 ②   11 ④   12 ①, ③
13 (1) told, had left (2) was, had hurt   14 ④   15 ①   16 ①
17 ⑤   18 ③   19 ③   20 ④   21 ④   22 ⑤   23 ⑤   24 ②
25 ⑤   26 ②   27 ①   28 ③   29 ④
```

01 recycle: 재활용하다 reproduce: 복사[복제]하다, 다시 만들다 endless: 끝없는, 한없는 priceless: 값을 매길 수 없는, 대단히 귀중한

02 ① saw: 톱 ② reproduction: 복제품 ③ majority: 대부분 ④ charity: 자선[구호] 단체 ⑤ allowance: 용돈

03 스마트폰을 잃어버렸다는 말에 유감을 표현하는 ②번이 적절하다.

04 독감에 걸렸다는 말에 '기쁘다'는 말은 어색하다.

05 ⓐ 원했던 역할을 맡게 되었으므로 excited ⓑ 원했던 역할을 맡지 못하게 되었으므로 disappointed가 적절하다.

06 'You'll get a text message about it soon.'이라고 했다.

07 'A⁺를 받았다'라는 말에 '안됐다'라고 하는 것은 어색하다.

08 '너 신나 보인다.'고 한 후 무슨 일인지 묻는 것이 자연스럽다.

09 독감에 걸린 사람에게 위로하는 말로 'you feel disappointed soon'은 어색하며 'feel better soon'이 적절하다.

10 과거의 역사적 사실은 항상 과거시제로 쓴다.

11 순서대로 • 맞음 • 'why to부정사' 형태는 쓰지 않는다. • 맞음 • 맞음

12 ① made → had made ③ what → that

13 과거완료형은 had+p.p.형을 쓴다.

14 집에 온 시점보다 사람들이 잠자러 간 시점이 앞서므로 과거완료로 쓴다.

15 ①번은 의문대명사이고 나머지는 관계대명사이다.

16 방문한 시점보다 외출한 시점이 앞서므로 'Tom had gone out when I visited him.'으로 쓰는 것이 적절하다.

17 'On his way to the car, Mr. Boggis couldn't help smiling.'라고 했다.

18 be known for: ~로 유명하다

19 is의 보어로 형용사 worth가 적절하며 of는 삭제해야 한다.

20 'Mr. Boggis lied.'에서 잘 드러난다.

21 'And there it was! A table which was a priceless piece of eighteenth-century English furniture.'라고 했다.

22 거짓말로 귀한 탁자를 싸게 사려다 그 탁자의 다리가 잘려나갔으므로 ⑤번이 적절하다.

23 물어보는 시점보다 앞선 시점이므로 과거완료가 적절하다.

24 둘 중에서 처음 하나는 one, 나머지 하나는 the other로 칭한다.

25 Rummins네 집 거실에 있는 탁자의 가격은 알 수 없다.

26 'Roald Dahl was born in 1916 in Wales.'라고 했다.

27 'Dahl went to St. Peter's, a boarding school, but his time at St. Peter's was unpleasant. He was very homesick and unhappy.'라고 했다.

28 사람들의 질문에 '비밀'이라고 한 후 (C)에서 주어진 글의 '비밀은 간단하다'며 그 비밀을 밝히는 것이 적절하다.

29 be known for = be famous for: ~로 유명하다

Lesson 7 (기말) 1회

```
01 ②   02 ①   03 ②   04 ⑤   05 ②   06 ⑤   07 ①   08 ④
09 ②   10 ④   11 ④   12 ①, ③         13 ①   14 ②, ③
15 ⑤   16 ①   17 ⑤   18 ④   19 ⑤   20 ①   21 ②   22 ①
23 ②   24 ①   25 ④   26 ①   27 making
```

01 동사 exercise를 수식하는 부사 regularly가 적절하다.

02 amount: 양, 총계, 총액

03 라면 끓이는 방법을 설명하고 있으므로 ②번이 적절하다.

04 '고맙다'는 말에 '그 말을 들으니 유감이야.'라고 하는 것은 어색

05 상대방이 금메달을 따서 기쁘다고 하는데 고맙다며 너 자신을 자랑스러워하라는 말은 어색하다.

06 ⓔ는 the robot을 가리킨다.

07 'Excuse me, but what's this robot for?'라고 하고 'Can you tell me how to use it?'이라고 했으므로 ①번이 일치한다.

08 로봇이 한꺼번에 얼마나 많은 책을 가져올 수 있는지는 알 수 없다.

09 (B) 감자를 작은 조각으로 자르고 (D) 땅에 구멍을 판 후 (A) 감자 조각을 구멍에 넣고 (C) 흙으로 덮는 것이 적절하다.

10 '읽고 있는' 책이 아니라 '찾고 있는' 책의 제목을 입력해야 하므로 'you're looking for'가 적절하다.

11 ④번은 분사구문의 '이유'를 나타내고 <보기>와 나머지는 '동시동작'을 나타낸다.

12 ① 주절의 주어와 다르므로 There being no bus service가 되어야 한다. ③ 분사구문의 부정은 not을 분사 앞에 쓰므로 Not knowing the rules가 적절하다.

13 as는 • ~하는 대로 • ~함에 따라 • ~ 때문에 • ('as ~ as ...'의 형태로, 같은 정도의 비교를 나타내어) …와 같은 정도로(이때 앞의 as는 지시부사, 뒤의 as는 접속사)

14 ⓑ is의 보어로 형용사 possible ⓒ more와 greater 비교급 두 개를 겹쳐서 쓸 수 없으므로 much greater가 적절하다.

15 (A)와 ⑤: ~함에 따라 ① ~할 때 ②, ④ ~한 대로 ③ ~하다시피[듯이]

16 Using various methods는 분사구문으로 '다양한 방법들을 사용하여'라는 의미이다.

17 순서대로 진행형의 현재분사, 분사구문의 현재분사, by의 목적어로 동명사가 적절하다.

18 빅데이터를 이용한 스포츠에서의 경기력 향상에 관해 언급하고 있다.

19 건강 전문가들이 독감의 확산을 막을 수 있다고 한 것이 아니라 질병을 예측할 수 있다고 했다.

20 빅데이터가 우리 삶의 모든 부분에 영향을 미치고 있다는 것을 설명하고 있으므로 ⓐ protecting을 influencing으로 바꾸는 것이 적절하다.

21 빅데이터는 우리 삶의 거의 모든 부분에 영향을 미치고 있으며 우리의 삶을 더 낫게 만들어 준다는 글이다.

22 (A) amount: 양
(B) 예를 들고 있으므로 For example
(C) With the help of: ~의 도움으로

23 ⓑ에는 선행사를 포함하는 관계대명사 what이 들어가고 나머지는 that이 들어간다.

24 빅데이터가 어떤 것인지 설명하고 있으므로 제목으로는 ①번이 적절하다.

25 (B)와 ④: ~함에 따라서 ① ~하는 대로 ②, ⑤ ~ 때문에 ③ ~하다시피[듯이]

26 빅데이터를 이용해 스포츠의 경기력을 향상시킨다는 글이다.

27 문맥상 동시동작의 분사구문이므로 현재분사로 고친다.

Lesson 7 (기말)

> **01** ④ **02** ③ **03** ⑤ **04** ③ **05** ② **06** ⑤ **07** ③ **08** ③
> **09** ④ **10** ③ **11** ⑤ **12** ①, ④ **13** ③ **14** ③ **15** ⑤
> **16** Using various methods, they[experts] analyze big data and draw meaningful results from it.
> **17** ① **18** ④ **19** ④ **20** ④ **21** ⑤ **22** ③ **23** ③ **24** ③
> **25** ② **26** ① **27** Saying goodbye

01 purchase: 구입, 구매

02 <보기>와 ③번은 접두사 in-을 붙여 반의어로 만든 것이다. ① 넣다 - 투입, 입력 ② 문 - 실내의 ④ 오다 - 수입 ⑤ 습관 - ~에 살다

03 사용법을 알려준 사람에게 감사를 표하는 ⑤번이 적절하다.

04 'place your library card on the robot's screen'이라고 했다.

05 영작하면 'Do you know how to use this snack machine?'이다.

06 사용법을 묻는 질문에 ⓔ 먼저 원하는 과자를 고르라고 하자 ⓒ 이미 했다고 답하면서 ⓑ 다음 순서를 묻고 ㉠ 돈을 넣고 ⓜ 과자를 꺼내라는 순서가 적절하다.

07 로봇을 이용해 원하는 책을 찾는 것에 대한 대화이다.

08 (C)의 place는 '놓다, 두다'라는 의미이고 ⓒ의 press는 '누르다'라는 의미이다.

09 홈페이지에 접속해서 버튼을 누르라는 답에 어울리는 질문은 ④번이다.

10 사용법을 알려달라고 했는데 첫 번째를 건너뛰고 '두 번째'부터 말하는 것은 어색하다. Second를 First로 고쳐야 한다.

11 <보기>와 ⑤번은 '~이기 때문에'라는 뜻의 '이유'를 나타낸다. ① ~로서 (전치사) ② ~한 대로 ③ ~일 때 ④ ~하다시피[하듯이]

12 ① To come → Coming ④ Finishing not → Not finishing

13 ⓑ Study very hard, you → Study very hard, and you 또는 Studying very hard, you ⓔ asked Mom she → asked Mom what she

14 'the amount of data we have is getting much greater than before'라고 했다.

15 (A) As: ~함에 따라서 (B) 서로 상반되는 내용이 나오므로 however가 적절하다.

16 글의 마지막 부분에 빅데이터 전문가들이 하는 것이 나와 있다.

17 ⓐ와 ①: ~할 때 ②, ④, ⑤ ~한 대로 ③ ~하다시피[이듯이]

18 '특정 질병을 가졌을지도 모른다는 것을 보여주는 어떤 것'은 'symptom(증상)'이다.

19 ⓓ의 This는 앞 문장의 내용, 즉 'health professionals can now forecast a disease just as weather experts forecast the weather'를 가리킨다.

20 (가)와 ④: ~하듯이 ① (…와) 같은 정도로(부사) ② ~로서(전치사) ③ ~할 때 ⑤ ~ 때문에

21 처음에 'Big data is influencing almost all parts of our lives.'라고 하고 그것을 설명하고 있으므로 ⑤번이 적절하다.

22 (B)의 예가 (E)에 이어지고 (D)의 The team이 (E)의 Germany's national soccer team으로 (E) 다음에 (D)가 나오고 (D)의 데이터의 예가 (A)에 나오고 (C)의 this database가 (A)의 내용이므로 (A) 다음에 (C)가 나오는 것이 적절하다.

23 was able to에 improve와 병렬로 win이 적절하다. 또는 was와 병렬로 보아 won으로 쓸 수도 있다. (둘 사이에 약간의 해석 차이는 있다.)

24 (A) thanks to: ~ 덕분에 (B) about: ~에 관하여 (C) focus on: ~에 집중하다

25 'If this kind of data is analyzed wisely, the spread of the flu can be predicted.'라고 했다.

26 독일 국가 대표 축구팀이 세계에서 가장 많은 축구팬을 갖고 있다는 내용은 나오지 않는다.

27 같은 주어를 생략하고 동사를 현재분사로 바꾼다.

Lesson 8 (기말)

---

01 ① **02** ① **03** ⑤ **04** ⑤ **05** ② **06** ③ **07** ② **08** ③
09 ④ **10** ② **11** ③ **12** ⑤ **13** ② **14** ③ **15** ① **16** ⑤
17 ③ **18** ⑤ **19** ④ **20** ③ **21** ③ **22** ③
23 there is usually a Chinese character with some animals or objects.
24 ④ **25** ④ **26** ②

---

01 네잎 클로버는 행운의 '상징'이다.

02 '곧은 어떤 것을 구부러지거나 기울어지도록 모양을 잡거나 만들다'는 'bend(굽다, 구부러지다)'가 적절하다.

03 'And it seems to me that the mask exhibition will be much more interesting.'이라고 했다.

04 선택의문문으로 물었으므로 선택하여 답하는 ⑤번이 적절하다.

05 모두 한국의 탈 전시회를 더 좋아한다거나 좋은 선택이라고 말하는데 ②번은 한국의 탈 전시회 이외의 것을 더 좋아한다고 하고 있다.

06 'I'm sure you'll like it.'이라고 했다.

07 겨울보다 여름이 좋다고 한 후, 추운 날씨를 좋아한다고 하는 것은

어색하다.

08 뒤에서 '비빔밥이 더 건강에 좋은 선택'이라고 했는데 '비빔밥보다 갈비탕을 더 좋아한다'고 하는 것은 어색하다.

09 탈춤 쇼를 본 적이 없다고 하자 ⓑ 전에 봤는데 너도 좋아할 거라고 하자 ⓓ 어디서 하는지 묻고 ⓔ 다음 홀이라고 답하고 ⓒ 6시 공연을 보자고 하자 ⓐ 좋다며 전시회를 먼저 보자고 하는 순서가 적절하다.

10 가정법 과거는 'If+주어+동사의 과거형, 주어+조동사의 과거형+동사원형 …'의 형태이다.

11 주어진 단어를 바르게 배열하여 영작하면 'It is difficult for me to speak in front of people.'이다.

12 ⑤번은 사람의 성질을 나타내는 형용사 careful이 쓰여 of가 들어가야 하지만 나머지는 모두 for가 적절하다.

13 사람의 성질 또는 속성을 나타내는 형용사가 있으면 to부정사의 의미상의 주어로 'of+목적격'을 쓰는 것에 주의한다. ⓒ for → of ⓔ of → for

14 ⓐ appear → appears ⓔ to → of

15 (A) in spite of: ~에도 불구하고
(B) in particular: 특히, 특별히

16 'Through it, children in the Joseon dynasty could learn the importance of harmony in family and society.'라고 했다.

17 ⓑ '효' 그림에 있는 잉어가 왜 부모님에 대한 공경을 상징하는지는 알 수 없다.
ⓔ 왜 조선 시대 아이들이 문자도를 싫어했는지 알 수 없다.

18 'Then his mother got well.'이라고 했다.

19 가정법 과거는 현재 상황과 반대되거나 실현 가능성이 낮은 일을 가정하여 말할 때 사용한다.

20 possible이나 impossible은 사람의 성질을 나타내는 형용사가 아니므로 to부정사의 의미상의 주어로 'for+목적격'을 쓴다.

21 문자도에 사용된 그림 도구가 무엇인지는 알 수 없다.

22 'the values'라는 선행사가 있으므로 what이 아니라 관계대명사 that이나 which가 적절하다.

23 Chinese character: 한자 object: 사물

24 주어진 문장의 They가 (D) 앞의 'The animals or objects in Munjado'를 가리키므로 (D)가 적절하다.

25 'In Munjado, 보통 한자 하나가 동물들이나 사물들과 함께 나온다.'라고 했다.

26 ⓑ에서 'The story'로 말할 것이 앞에 나와 있지 않으며 ⓒ의 It이 ⓐ의 Munjado를 받고 있으므로 ⓑ를 빼고 읽으면 적절하게 연결된다.

01 identify: (본인·동일물임을) 확인하다

02 각각 ② object ③ symbol ④ disappointed ⑤ dynasty의 영영풀이이다.

03 'I prefer the Korean mask exhibition.'이라고 했다.

04 'It seems to 사람 that ~'의 형태가 적절하다.

05 (A) 전시회가 두 곳이 있다면서 어느 것을 더 보고 싶은지 묻는 ⓒ (B) 뒤에서 탈춤 쇼도 있다고 했으므로 전시회만 있는 것이 아니라는 ⓓ (C) 탈춤 쇼를 본 적이 없다고 하자 전에 봤는데 네가 좋아할 거라고 말하는 ⓐ (D) 어디서 하는지 묻자 다솜 홀이라고 답하는 ⓑ가 적절하다.

06 G가 'I also like Bibimbap more.'라고 했으므로 비빔밥을 선호하며 'It seems to 사람 that ~'의 형태인 ②번이 적절하다.

07 사람의 성질을 나타내는 형용사가 있으면 to부정사의 의미상의 주어로 'of+목적격'을 쓰는 것에 주의한다.

08 가정법 과거는 'If+주어+동사의 과거형, 주어+조동사의 과거형+동사원형 …'의 형태이다. 현재 상황과 반대되거나 실현 가능성이 낮은 일을 가정하여 말할 때 쓴다.

09 전시회가 두 개 있다고 했고 질문의 답으로 'I prefer the Korean mask exhibition.'이라고 했으므로 선호를 묻는 ④번이 적절하다.

10 'Well, I've seen a show before.'라고 했다.

11 순서대로 • 맞음 • grows → grew • ate → eating • 맞음 • was → were • Taken → Taking

12 가정법 과거완료는 'If+주어+had p.p., 주어+조동사의 과거형+have p.p. …'의 형태이다. hadn't를 wouldn't로 고친다.

13 ⓐ symbol ⓑ symptom ⓓ appear ⓔ purchase

14 (D)의 It은 Munjado를 가리킨다.

15 'There are other examples of symbolic objects in Munjado.'라고 했다.

16 문맥상 긍정적인 말이 와야 하며 ⑤번만 긍정적인 말이다.

17 강이 완전히 얼어 붙었기 때문에 impossible이 적절하다.

18 ⓐ 가정법 과거이므로 could eat ⓑ 강이 완전히 얼어 붙어 있었으므로 disappointed ⓒ 부모님에 대한 공경을 상징하므로 어머니는 병이 '나았다(got better)'고 해야 적절하다.

19 문자도에 있는 상징적인 동물들과 물건들에 관한 내용이다.

20 (가)와 b, c, e, g에는 for가 들어간다. a, d, f에는 of가 들어간다. 사람의 성질 또는 속성을 나타내는 형용사(careless, considerate, foolish, generous, kind, mean, nice, rude, silly, stupid, thoughtless, wise 등)가 있으면 to부정사의 의미상의 주어로 'of+목적격'을 쓰는 것에 주의한다.

21 주어진 문장의 'these reasons'가 (D) 앞의 내용(Bamboo does not bend. It stays green in all kinds of weather.)이므로 (D)가 적절하다.

22 'The man was so disappointed that he cried out to the sky'라고 했다.

23 (A) 부정사의 의미상의 주어로 for him, (B) 강이 얼어 붙어 실망했으므로 disappointed, (C) 물 밖으로 나왔으므로 out of가 적절하다. into: ~ 안으로 out of: ~ 밖으로

24 (A) For these reasons: 이런 이유로 (B) thus: 따라서, 그러므로

25 'lotus flowers in the paintings of ui(義)'라고 했다.